Professional
Visual Basic 6
Databases

Charles Williams

Wrox Press Ltd. ®

Professional Visual Basic 6 Databases

wrox

Published by Wrox Press Ltd
Arden House, 1102 Warwick Road, Acock's Green, Birmingham B27 6BH, UK
Printed in USA
ISBN 1-861002-2025

Trademark Acknowledgements

Wrox has endeavored to provide trademark information about all the companies and products mentioned in this book by the appropriate use of capitals. However, Wrox cannot guarantee the accuracy of this information.

Credits

Author
Charles Williams

Additional Material
Des Owen
(Chapter 3)
Dwayne Gifford
(Chapter 14)
Matthew Reynolds
(Case Study)

Editors
Kate Hall
Julian Skinner
Tony Davis

Managing Editor
Dominic Shakeshaft

Development Editor
Dominic Lowe

Project Manager
Tony Berry

Index
Catherine Alexander

Technical Reviewers
Mark Bell
Richard Bonneau
Robert Chang
Robin Dewson
Guy Fouche
Scott Haley
Garve K. Hays
Sree Nilakanta
J. Boyd Nolan
John Schenken
Marc H. Simkin
Richard Ward
Maura Wilder
Sakhr Youness

Design/Layout
Mark Burdett
Tom Bartlett
John McNulty
David Boyce
Frances Olesch
Chris Morris

Cover Photograph
Todd Gieg

About the Author

Charles Williams is the Senior Technology Consultant at MicroScript, a subsidiary of New Era of Networks (NEON). Working out of the Danvers, Massachusetts, office, he provides technical expertise in the areas of Application Integration, Data Translation, and Messaging. His experience includes System Integration in the Banking, Hospitality and Healthcare industries. Part of his role with MicroScript is working with standards groups in the Healthcare industry to promote plug-n-play interoperability.

Charles has also conducted many training courses for MicroScript and Adult Continuing Education centers in the Boston area. The courses include Microsoft Access, Visual Basic and SQL Server.

Comments may de directed to Charles at: ProVB6DB@HotMail.com

Acknowledgements

My wife laughed when I said, "I always wanted to write a book." Her reply was: "I always wanted to sail around Antigua." During the time I worked on this book, Anne has provided more help and support than I had any right to expect. Beyond her endless patience and willingness to allow me to pursue my dream, she has given me that greatest of gifts: constancy and understanding. We leave for Antigua in three weeks.

To my daughter Ava, who has taught me the joy of having a child. I have the fondest memories of Ava's critiques (raspberries) and fascination with (smashing) the keyboard.

To my parents, who taught me how to be patient and persistent. Also, thanks for buying me my first computer.

I would also like to thank everyone at Wrox for their dedication and ongoing dialog to work with me towards the creation of this book.

Suppliers

- SupplierID
- CompanyName
- ContactName
- ContactTitle
- Address
- City
- Region
- PostalCode
- Country
- Phone
- Fax
- HomePage

Products

- ProductID
- ProductName
- SupplierID
- CategoryID
- QuantityPerUnit
- UnitPrice
- UnitsInStock
- UnitsOnOrder
- ReorderLevel
- Discontinued

Categories

- CategoryID
- CategoryName
- Description
- Picture

6

Table of Contents

Introduction   1

What's Covered in This Book?   1
What You Need to Use This Book   3
Database Basics   4
   Databases   4
   Relational Databases   4
     Defining Relationships   5
      The Primary Key (PK)   5
      The Foreign Key (FK)   6
     Types of Relationship   7
     Overview of the Pubs Database   8
     Referential Integrity   9
     Indexes   10
     Queries   11
Conventions Used in This Book   11
Tell Us What You Think   12

Chapter 1: The Client-Server Model   15

Desktop Databases   16
Database Servers   18
What is Client-Server?   20
   Fat Client vs. Fat Server   20
     The Fat Server   21
     The Fat Client   21
     In Summary   22
   For Whom is the Client-Server Model?   23
   Replication   24
   2-Tier Architecture   26

3-Tier to N-Tier Architecture   27

   The Role of the Middle Tier   27

      An Aside on Components   27

   The 3-Tier Architecture   28

      The Transaction Processing Monitor   29

   Server Side Processing Functionality   30

      Triggers   30

      Stored Procedures   31

      Views   32

Other Scenarios for Client-Server Architecture   33

The Planning Process   34

   2-Tier vs. N-Tier   34

   Choosing a Transaction Processing Monitor   34

   Scheduling and Estimating Time for Development and Rollout   35

Summary   36

Chapter 2: Database Design   39

Normalization   39

   First Normal Form: No Repeating Groups   40

   Second Normal Form: Non-Key Fields Must Be Dependent on the
   Primary Key   41

   Third Normal Form: No Columns Depend on other Non-Key
   Columns   42

Database Indexes   43

   Unique and Non-Unique Indexes   43

   B-Tree Indexes   46

      Clustered Indexes   47

      Non-Clustered Indexes   48

   Creating Indexes   49

Five Steps to Building a Powerful Database   52

   Step 1: Brainstorming   52

   Step 2: Group the Fields   53

   Step 3: Build Relationships   54

   Step 4: Normalize Your Database   56

   Step 5: Test the Structure with Sample Data   57

Summary   57

Chapter 3: A Guide to Data Access

An Overview of Data Access Technologies 59
    Universal Data Access 61
    OLE DB 63
        OLE DB Providers 64
        OLE DB Consumers 65
    ADO 66
    ODBC 68
        Application Programming Interface (API) 68
        Driver Manager 69
        Driver 69
        Data Source 69
    RDO 70
    DAO 70
    ODBCDirect 70
Which Data Access Technology Should I Use? 71
    Features Supported by ADO, DAO and RDO 72
    OLE DB and ODBC 72
Where Are These Data Access Technologies? 73
Setting up an ODBC Data Source Name 74
    The ODBC Data Source Administrator 75
    Configuring a SQL Server DSN 76
        Authentication Options 76
        Connection Options 77
        Translation Options 78
        Logging Options 79
        Completing the Configuration 80
Connecting to an ODBC Data Source 80
    Connecting with VisData 80
        The Data Form Designer 81
Summary 82

Chapter 4: Working with the ADO Data Control

Application Walk-Through 85
Building the Database 86

Building the Front-End Application   94

Creating a New Project   95
The ADO Data Control   95
Building the Connection String   97
Setting the RecordSource Property   100
Setting the Other Properties   101
Building a User Interface   102
How It All Works   107
The Masked Edit Control   107
Creating Our Own Navigation Bar   109
Navigating the Recordset   111
Updating the Status Label   112
Testing the Changes   113
Further Enhancements   113
Adding New Records   115
Deleting Records   116
Updating Records   116
Refreshing Records   116
Finding Records   117
Test the Find Routine   120

Other Databound Controls   121

The Label   121
The Check Box   121
The Picture and Image Controls   122
DataGrid Control   122
The Hierarchical FlexGrid Control   122
The DataList and DataCombo Controls   123
The OLE Container Control   124
The Rich Text Box Control   124
The MS Chart Control   124
The Data Repeater Control   125

Summary   125

Chapter 5: Upsizing to SQL Server   127

How Much Data Do You Need to Store?   127
What Is the Budget of Your Project?   128

What Are the Benchmarks of Each Database?   128

TPC Benchmarks   129

Backup Benchmarks   129

What Type of Functionality Will Be Required?   129

How Many Connections to the Database Are Required?   130

Upsizing Our Address Database to SQL Server   130

Converting Our Database   131

The Upsizing Wizard   131

Converting Our Project   135

Summary   137

Chapter 6: An Overview of Structured Query Language   139

SQL Basics   140

Exactly What Is SQL?   140

Building the SQL Tester Program   141

A Note on SQL Logic   145

Null Values   145

Generating Database Queries   145

The SELECT Statement   146

SQL Clauses   148

Simple Data Manipulation   149

Creating Aliases   149

Joining Value Expressions   150

Using Arithmetic Operators   150

Concatenating Text To Fields   151

Concatenating Multiple Fields   152

Retrieving Specific Records   153

The WHERE Clause   153

Using AND, OR and NOT Operators   154

Using Predicates with the WHERE Clause   158

The IN Predicate   158

The LIKE Predicate   159

The BETWEEN Predicate   160

Working with Dates   161

The NULL Predicate   161

The ORDER BY Clause   162
The GROUP BY Clause   164
SQL Aggregate Functions   165
    SUM   165
    COUNT   166
    MIN & MAX   167
    AVG   167
Using Aggregate Functions with GROUP BY   168
Using HAVING to Apply Criteria to Groupings   169
Subqueries in SELECT Statements   169
Modifying Data   170
    Updating Records   171
    Inserting Data into Tables   172
        Inserting a Null Field into a Table   173
    Deleting Records   174
    Using Subqueries to INSERT Data from an Existing Table   175
Advanced SQL   176
Joining Tables   176
    Equi-Joins   177
    The INNER JOIN Clause   178
        Nested Inner Joins   178
        OUTER JOINS   180
        UNION Queries   181
Advanced Aggregation Queries   183
Creating Tables   184
        Default Values   187
        Check Constraints   187
    Changing Table structure with ALTER TABLE   189
Destroying Tables with DROP TABLE   190
Creating Indexes   190
Making a Backup Table   191
        The CREATE TABLE method   191
        The SELECT INTO Method   193
Finding Unmatched Records   193

Using EXISTS to Find Matched or Unmatched Records   195
Summary   196

Chapter 7: An Introduction to ADO   199

The ADO Object Model   200
   Object Hierarchy   200
      Connection, Command and Recordset Objects   201
      Property, Error, Parameter and Field Objects   201
   ADODB versus ADOR   201
   Setting a Reference to ADO   202
Connecting to a Database   203
   Creating a Connection Object   203
      Implicit Connection Objects   204
   Setting the Connection String   204
      OLE DB Provider for ODBC Drivers   205
      Examples   206
      Other OLE DB Providers   207
      Examples   207
   Opening the Connection   207
   Closing the Connection   208
Querying the Database   208
   Creating a Command Object   209
   Building the Command Text   209
      Commands that Return no Records   210
   Executing the Command   210
      The Execute Method's Optional Arguments   210
      An Example   211
      Other Command Object Functionality   211
   Executing a Command without a Command Object   212
      Using a Connection Object   212
      Using a Recordset Object   213
   Parameters   214
      Creating a Parameter Object   214
      The Name Property   215
      The Type Property   215
      The Direction Property   216
      The Size Property   216
      The Value Property   217

The Parameters Collection	217
Passing Parameters into a Stored Procedure	218
Viewing and Editing Records	**219**
Navigating through the Recordset	220
Bookmarks	221
Moving by More than One Record	221
Recordset Pages	222
Locating Records in the Recordset	223
Finding Specific Records	223
Filtering the Recordset	224
Retrieving Rows into an Array	225
Sorting the Recordset	226
Modifying the Data	226
Editing Records	226
Adding Records	227
Deleting Records	228
Refreshing the Recordset	229
Updating the Database	230
Canceling Updates	230
Cursor and Lock Types	231
Cursor Types	231
Cursor Location	232
Lock Types	232
Working with Fields	233
The Fields Collection	233
The Field Object	235
Disconnected and Persisted Recordsets	235
ADO Events	**236**
Accessing ADO Events	237
Connection Object Events	237
The WillConnect Event	237
The ConnectComplete Event	239
The Disconnect Event	240
Recordset Object Events	240
The MoveComplete Event	240
The RecordChangeComplete Event	241

Error Handling   242

    The Errors Collection   242

    The Error Object   243

Binding to VB Controls with ADO   244

Summary   246

Chapter 8: Views, Stored Procedures and Triggers   **249**

Building a Connection to SQL Server   250

Views   251

    SQL Server Views in the Pubs Database   252

    Creating a View with SQL   254

Stored Procedures   257

    Stored Procedures in the pubs Database   258

    Creating Stored Procedures Using SQL   259

        SELECT Stored Procedures   259

        UPDATE Stored Procedures   260

        INSERT Stored Procedures   260

        DELETE Stored Procedures   261

    Executing Stored Procedures from Visual Basic   261

    Output Parameters   267

    System Level Stored Procedures   268

Triggers   270

    A Note on the Mode of Operation of Triggers   271

    Existing Triggers   271

    Creating Triggers   273

    Implementing a Trigger   275

        ROLLBACK of Changes   275

Summary   277

Chapter 9: Implementing a 2-Tier Solution   **279**

Building a Sample 2-Tier Application   279

    Building the Application Shell   281

Modifying the Customers Form 287
Adding a Navigation Bar 289
Modifying the Code of the Orders Form 291
The Details Form 293
Let's Move Back to the Orders Form 294
Now Let's Move Back to the Details Form 295
The SHAPE Construct 296
Removing Fields from the Orders DataGrid Control 297
Adding an Order Total Field to the DataGrid Control 298
Modifying the DataGrid Layout on the Orders Form 298
Changing the Data Format of Fields in a DataGrid 299
Adding a Quick Customer Lookup 299
Deploying Our 2-Tier Solution 302
Summary 303

Chapter 10: Data Validation, Transactions and Error Trapping 305

Data Validation 305
Data Validation on the Server 306
Exploring Constraints in SQL Server 307
Generating SQL Scripts 308
Viewing the Script 310
Testing Constraints 311
Exploring Constraints in Microsoft Access 312
Adding Validation Constraints with SQL 313
Data Validation at the Application Level 315
What Are Transactions? 317
Handling Transactions with ADO 319
Testing the Transactions 321
Capturing ADO and OLE DB Provider Errors 324
The Form for the Error Handler 324
The Code for the Error Handler 325
Testing the Error Handler 328
Summary 329

Chapter 11: An Introduction to 3-Tier Solutions   331

The 3-Tier Architecture   332
Components   332
  Objects and Classes   332
  Designing Components   333
  Building Components   334
    Connecting to SQL Server   335
    Coding the Four Functions   336
      Add_Employee   337
      Delete_Employee   338
      Update_Employee   338
      Select_Employee   339
  Testing Our Component   340
Building a Client Application to Call the Component   340
  Configuring the ListView control   342
  Adding the References   343
  Adding the Code to Client.vbp   343
    The Form_Load Event Procedure   344
    The Select_Data Procedure   344
      The ListItem Object   345
    The cmdRefresh_Click Event Procedure   345
    The cmdDelete_Click Event Procedure   345
    The cmdInsert_Click Event Procedure   346
    The cmdUpdate_Click Event Procedure   346
    The ListView1_Click Event Procedure   346
    The cmdClear_Click Event Procedure   347
    The cmdExit_Click Event Procedure   347
Testing the 3-Tier Client-Server Solution   348
Compiling the 3-Tier Client-Server Solution   349
Transactions   350
  ACID Properties   350
    Atomicity   350
    Consistency   350
    Isolation   350
    Durability   350

Overview of Microsoft Transaction Server (MTS)   351
    Component Transaction Control   351
    Monitoring   352
    Security   352
       Roles   353
    Administration   353
    Object Brokering   355
    The Future: Object Pooling!   356
Modifying Employee.dll to Work with MTS   357
    The MTSTransactionMode Property   358
    Setting the Employee Project Properties   358
       Version Compatibility   359
          No Compatibility   360
          Project Compatibility   360
          Binary Compatibility   360
    The ObjectContext Object   360
       The Add_Employee Function   361
       The Delete_Employee Function   362
       The Update_Employee Function   362
Installing Components into MTS   364
    MTS Packages   364
       Creating a New Package   364
       Adding a Component to a Package   367
Test the Solution   368
Summary   369

Chapter 12: Passing Data in N-Tier Applications   371

How to Pass Data the Wrong Way   371
    Calling Single Properties   372
    Passing Arguments to a Method   372
Data Serialization   373
    Directly Passing User-Defined Types   373
    Variant Arrays   375
       The GetRows Method   377

Passing User-Defined Types with LSet 377
    Background 378
    The Visual Basic Implementation 379
    Memory Alignment 381
ADO(R) Recordset with Marshaling Properties 382
    Creating Recordset Objects from a Database 383
    Creating a Connectionless Recordset 384
    Passing a Recordset by Value 385
PropertyBag Objects 386
    Serializing Data into a String using the Contents 386
    Deserializing Data from a String using Contents 387
Summary 389

Chapter 13: Implementing a Practical 3-Tier Solution 391

Project Overview 392
Setting up a DSN to Connect to Northwind 394
Building the Middle Tier Component 394
    The Module-Level Variables 395
    The Class_Initialize Event 396
    The Get_Table_Recordset Function 396
    The Get_Products Function 397
    The Get_Customer_Details Function 397
    The Get_ID Function 398
    The Send_Order Function 399
Building the Client Application 403
    Building the User Interface 404
    The Module_Level Variables 408
    The Form_Load Event Procedure 409
    The cboCompany_Click Event Procedure 412
    The Create_New_Order Method 412
    The Create_New_Order_Detail Method 413
    Adding Drag-and-Drop Functionality 414
        The Hierarchical FlexGrid's MouseDown Event 414
        The DataGrid's DragOver Event 414
        The DataGrid's DragDrop Event 415

The Total_All Function 416
 The DataGrid's AfterColUpdate Event 417
The cmdNew_Click Event Procedure 417
The cmdSend_Click Event Procedure 418
Test the Solution 419
Rolling the Solution out to MTS 420
The Get_Table_Recordset Function 421
The Get_Products Function 421
The Get_Customer_Details Function 422
The Get_ID Function 423
The Send_Order Function 424
Using the ObjectControl 425
 The Activate Method 425
 The Deactivate Method 426
 The CanBePooled Method 426
Adding the DLL to MTS 426
Summary 427

Chapter 14: The Three Class Concept 429

The Customer Data Object 430
Building the Customer Object 430
Adding Code to clsCustomerSrvr 431
 The General Declarations Section 431
 The Class_Initialize Event 432
 Delete Method 432
 IsDirty Method 433
 Load Method 434
 NewCustomer Method 437
 Save Method 438
 The LoadParameters Method 441
 The UpdateCustomer Method 442
 Customers Property 443
Stored Procedures 443
 Select 443
 Insert 445
 Delete 446
 Update 446

Adding Code to colCustomers 447

Module-Level Variables 447

Add Method 447

Clear Method 448

Count Property 448

Exists Method 448

Item Property 449

NewEnum Property 449

Remove Method 450

Adding Code to clsCustomer Class 450

Key Property 451

IsLoading Property 451

IsDeleted Property 452

IsDirty Property 452

The Other Properties 453

The Tester Application 455

Building the User Interface 456

The Toolbar Control 456

The ImageList Control 457

The StatusBar 458

The Textboxes and Labels 460

The Code 460

The Module-Level Variables 460

The Form_Load Event Procedure 461

The LoadCustomerRecord Method 461

The PanelClick Event of the StatusBar Control 462

The ButtonClick of the Toolbar Control 463

The LostFocus Events of the Textboxes 464

Testing the Customer Object 465

Summary 465

Chapter 15: The Microsoft Distributed Transaction Coordinator 467

Database Transactions 467

The Architecture of Distributed Transactions 468

Two-Phase Commit with MS DTC 469

OLE Transactions and the XA Standard 470

MTS and MS DTC 470

The MS DTC in Action 471

Summary 474

Chapter 16: Securing Client-Server Applications 477

Security Models for Client-Server 477

Two-Tier Solutions 478

N-Tier Solutions 478

Security on the Middle Tier 478

Security on the Server 479

Implementing Server-Side Security 479

Managing Security in a SQL Server Database 479

Adding a New User to SQL Server 481

Assigning Server Roles 482

Assigning Access Rights 483

Permission Precedence 485

Assigning User-Level Permissions 486

The World of Roles 487

Fixed Roles 487

Creating Roles 488

Implementing Security in a Two-Tier Solution 490

The Data Form 491

The Login Form 492

The Code Behind the Forms 492

Testing the Permissions 494

Implementing Security in a Three-Tier Solution 495

Implementing Security with MTS 498

Using SQL to Implement Security 505

The GRANT command 505

The REVOKE Command 506

The DENY Command 506

Summary 507

Chapter 17: Deploying Client-Server Applications   509

Why Do We Need to Package Our Application?   509

Deploying Data Source Names   510

   Using the Registry Editor   510

   Exporting Registry Files   512

   Creating the New Registry File   514

Deploying an N-Tier Application   515

   What is DCOM?   516

   Installing DCOM   517

   Exporting the Client Configuration From MTS   517

Creating the Setup Utility   518

Testing the Setup Utility   525

Summary   528

Chapter 18: Data Warehousing   531

What is Data Warehousing?   531

What is Data Warehousing Used for?   533

   Reporting   533

   Online Analytical Processing (OLAP)   534

     Three Flavors of OLAP   535

     Taking a Closer Look at MOLAP   535

       Geographical Dimension   535

       Products Dimension   535

       Time Dimension   536

   Data Mining   537

   Executive Information Systems (EIS)   538

   Data Warehouse Models   538

     Populating the Data Warehouse   539

     Retrieving Data from the Data Warehouse   539

     Data Marts   539

     Defining the Data Structure   540

     Data Extraction   543

Implementing an OLAP Solution	544
The Mission	545
Installing Microsoft OLAP Server	545
The FoodMart Database	545
The Fact Table	546
The Dimensional Tables	547
Creating the Fact and Dimension Tables	547
Building the MultiDimensional (MD) Cube	548
Designing the Cube Storage Type	558
Setting Up Security for the New Cube	560
Browsing the Cube	562
Using OLE DB for OLAP to Build a Client Application	563
MultiDimensional Expressions (MDX)	566
The MDX Sample Application	567
Summary	568

Chapter 19: Generating Reports

571

The Data Environment Designer	572
Using the DED to create a hierarchical recordset	572
Report Generation	577
The Data Report Designer	579
Designing a Simple Products Report	579
Displaying the Report	583
Adding Splash to Your Report	585
Adding Calculations	586
Building an Invoice Report	587
Creating a SQL Command Using the Drag and Drop Method	587
Grouping Fields	590
Designing the Invoice Report	591
Adding an Extended Price Field	592
Displaying the Cost of an Order	594
Dynamic Modification of the SQL Command	596
Summary	599

Case Study: An Example 3-Tier Distributed Application using Microsoft Transaction Server 601

Building our Example 603
Building the Database 604
  The Categories Table 605
  Manufacturers Table 606
  Suppliers Table 607
  Products Table 607
  Building a Database Diagram 608
  Creating the View 611
Building the Storefront 611
  Creating an ASP Component 612
    Connecting to the Database 613
    Testing the Connection 614
    Querying the Database 615
    Testing our Page 616
    The Storefront Layout 617
Capturing the Order 619
  The Cart Class 619
  The CartItem Class 621
  Adding an Item to the Cart 621
  The Shopping Cart Page 622
    Checking for an Existing Cart 622
    Adding a Product to the Cart 623
    The Table for the Cart Items 623
Processing the Order 625
  Building the Business Object 625
    The ObjectControl Interface 626
    The ProcessOrder Method 626
    Setting Binary Compatibility 627
    Creating the MTS Package 627
    Installing the Component 628

The Checkout Page   630
    Exploring the ObjectContext Object   631
    Managing the Transaction   632
    Creating a New Customer   633
    Better Error Reporting   633
    How Does MTS Handle Database Changes?   635
        The Customers Table   635
        Viewing Tables Used by Transactions   636
Exporting Packages   637
Summary   637

Appendix A: SQL: Overview and the ANSI SQL-92 Standard   **639**
Appendix B: Transact-SQL   **655**
Appendix C: PL/SQL   **671**
Appendix D: Jet SQL   **693**
Appendix E: ADO Object Summary   **703**
Appendix F: ADO Constants   **721**
Appendix G: ADO Properties Collection   **771**
Appendix H: ADO Error Codes   **819**
Appendix I: Database Data Types   **831**
Appendix J: Installing Microsoft Transaction Server   **835**
Appendix K: Active Server Pages   **841**

Suppliers

- SupplierID
- CompanyName
- ContactName
- ContactTitle
- Address
- City
- Region
- PostalCode
- Country
- Phone
- Fax
- HomePage

Products

- ProductID
- ProductName
- SupplierID
- CategoryID
- QuantityPerUnit
- UnitPrice
- UnitsInStock
- UnitsOnOrder
- ReorderLevel
- Discontinued

6

Categories

- CategoryID
- CategoryName
- Description
- Picture

Introduction

It's an indisputable fact that most of the programmers in the world are writing applications that store and manipulate data. These applications are accessing anything from small desktop databases that track company products to large, complex company legacy databases. But it doesn't end there; today we can use Microsoft technologies to access all kinds of data stores, not just your usual databases. The data that is stored in sound files, video images, Excel spreadsheets, email archives and web pages can be accessed and presented exactly as if it had come from a database. All of this is possible through Microsoft's ActiveX Data Objects (ADO) - a central theme to this book. Right now, there's a revolution in data access!

It's relatively simple to achieve these benefits with ADO on a small desktop database. However, when you scale up your application to make it available to hundreds or maybe even thousands of users, you need to think carefully about the architecture you're going to use or your application might grind to a halt.

This book will show you the things you need to consider when creating a scalable, multi-user database application. We'll discuss the design issues that need to be considered when designing such applications and, of course, I'll show you how to implement your applications.

By the time you've finished this book, you should have a good, working knowledge of how to build database applications that can provide information to a single user or to several thousands.

What's Covered in This Book?

This book is the ideal next step if you've finished another Wrox Press book, Beginning Visual Basic 6.0 Database Programming, and are wondering what the next step is. If you didn't read that book, but have done some programming of databases with Visual Basic before, this book is also for you.

We'll begin this book by defining what the client-server model is in Chapter 1. We'll begin by discussing the difference between a desktop database and a database server. Then we'll move on to discuss different types of client-server architectures, involving two, three or even many tiers.

In Chapter 2, we'll discuss database design. I'll show you my five steps for building a powerful database. We'll discuss normalizing your database, the role of indexes and their different types.

Chapter 3 deals with data access. We'll look at what Microsoft calls Universal Data Access, which is a strategy for providing access to information across a system through OLE DB and ADO. We'll discuss the many different technologies available for accessing data from databases including ODBC, OLE DB, ADO, DAO and RDO.

In Chapter 4, we'll build a simple application that accesses a database created with the Visual Data Manager supplied with Visual Basic. This chapter is intended to provide a quick introduction to the ADO Data Control supplied with Visual Basic 6 and hence also to ADO itself.

In Chapter 5, we'll see how to upsize our database from Chapter 4 to a SQL Server 7.0 database. We'll also discuss some of the things you need to bear in mind when considering whether you want your database to be built using Access or SQL Server 7.

Chapter 6 provides an overview to Structured Query Language (SQL). We'll begin the chapter by building a simple SQL tester application in Visual Basic. Then we'll begin testing out the different SQL statements such as SELECT, UPDATE and INSERT.

In Chapter 7, we'll discuss the ADO object model. This is important information for any developer who wants to really be able to make the most of ADO. We'll discuss how to build a connection string to connect to our databases, how to query databases by using commands and manipulating data through recordsets.

In Chapter 8, we'll put our knowledge of SQL to more practical use when we deal with triggers, stored procedures and views. They are all complex SQL queries that are stored on the database server and can be called from our applications using simple, short SQL queries.

In Chapter 9, we will discuss 2-tier solutions in detail. By ensuring that we have a firm grasp of the importance and role of 2-tier solutions, we can more easily understand its flaws and determine when it might be best to use a 3-tier solution instead. We'll also briefly discuss the SHAPE construct, which allows us to create a single hierarchical recordset from two or more recordsets.

In Chapter 10, we'll discuss data validation, transactions and error trapping; three important topics that need to be considered whenever you're building a client-server solution. This chapter will provide a useful background to Chapter 11.

Chapter 11 will introduce 3-tier solutions. We'll create a component, a compiled piece of binary code that will form our middle tier. We'll also learn about the importance of Microsoft Transaction Server (MTS) in such architectures, as MTS will be used to host our middle-tier component.

In Chapter 12, we'll discuss techniques for passing data between the different tiers. We'll see that the technique that we used in the previous chapter will become inefficient when scaled up from a single machine to multiple users. We'll then discuss several more efficient ways of passing data, one of which we'll implement ourselves in Chapter 13.

Chapter 13 will provide an approach to building a 3-tier solution that is more practical in a multi-user environment. This chapter will merge the concepts and tools introduced in Chapters 11 and 12 into an application of which we can be proud.

In Chapter 14, we'll look at something called the "three class concept", which is an advanced technique for building middle-tier components. We'll build a simple "three class" component to illustrate the implementation and design of these components.

The Microsoft Distributed Transaction Coordinator is the topic of Chapter 15. This tool, which is supplied with SQL Server, allows developers to create transactions that involve more than one database, which may not even be of the same type. Using MS DTC, we can create a transaction involving a SQL Server database, an Oracle database and a DB2 database.

In Chapter 16, we'll discuss how to secure our client-server solutions. We'll discuss how to add security to the middle tier and also how to add security to our database server. We'll take a close look at SQL Server, which integrates its security closely with Windows NT. We'll finish the chapter by discussing how we can implement security using SQL.

In Chapter 17 we'll discuss how to deploy a client-server solution to the users of our applications. In this chapter, we'll take a good look at the Package and Deployment Wizard supplied with Visual Basic.

Chapter 18 deals with data warehousing and OLAP, which allows users to analyze the data stored in a database in order to make informed business decisions. We'll build a simple OLAP solution to analyze data in a database.

Chapter 19 is the final chapter in this book and deals with the topic of creating reports. We will see how to use the Data Environment Designer and the Data Report Designer to create reports of data stored in our database.

What You Need to Use This Book

To run the code discussed in this book you'll need:

- ➢ Visual Basic 6.0
- ➢ Microsoft Access (preferably 2000 although 97 will be fine)
- ➢ SQL Server 7.0
- ➢ Windows 9x with MTS and Personal Web Server installed (available for download free from Microsoft's web site http://www.microsoft.com/) or Windows NT 4.0 Service Pack 4.0 with the Windows NT Option Pack 4.0
- ➢ Internet Explorer 3 or higher

Database Basics

Before we get started on the real task at hand, let's review some of the basics of databases.

Databases

A **database** is a place where information is stored, a kind of electronic filing cabinet. There are two main types of databases, flat-files and relational databases. Flat-file databases store data in a single stream of bytes, which can grow as large as necessary. Because of the nature of flat-file databases, a single addition to the file requires updates throughout the database. They're simply not efficient in the modern era.

Relational Databases

Relational databases do not have the inefficiencies associated with flat-file databases. A relational database consists of one or more **tables** of columns and rows, arranged like a spreadsheet. The columns, such as `Customer ID` and `Order Date` are known as **fields**, and the rows, which contain the details of a particular `Customer` or `Order`, are known as **records**.

The real power of relational databases, though, is their ability to store data with minimal duplication and to link (or relate) data from different sources together. In a relational database, two or more fields can be related, hence the name. And if you can link fields, you can link entire tables. The link between the two tables is known as a **relationship**.

Let's look at an example of the sort of relationships that can exist between two tables in a database:

Customers : Table

Customer ID	Company Name	Contact Name	Contact Title
LILAS	LILA-Supermercado	Carlos González	Accounting Manager
LINOD	LINO-Delicateses	Felipe Izquierdo	Owner
LONEP	Lonesome Pine Restaurant	Fran Wilson	Sales Manager
MAGAA	Magazzini Alimentari Riuniti	Giovanni Rovelli	Marketing Manager
MAISD	Maison Dewey	Catherine Dewey	Sales Agent
MEREP			
MORGK			
NORTS			
OCEAN			
OLDWO			
OTTIK			
PARIS			
PERIC			
PICCO			
PRINI			

Record: I◄ ◄ |

Orders : Table

Order ID	Customer	Employee	Order Date	Required Dat
11039	LINO-Delicateses	Davolio, Nancy	21-May-96	18-Jun-9
10840	LINO-Delicateses	Peacock, Margaret	19-Feb-96	01-Apr-9
10919	LINO-Delicateses	Fuller, Andrew	01-Apr-96	29-Apr-9
11014	LINO-Delicateses	Fuller, Andrew	10-May-96	07-Jun-9
10811	LINO-Delicateses	Callahan, Laura	02-Feb-96	01-Mar-9
10307	Lonesome Pine Restaurant	Fuller, Andrew	18-Oct-94	15-Nov-9
10317	Lonesome Pine Restaurant	Suyama, Michael	31-Oct-94	28-Nov-9
10867	Lonesome Pine Restaurant	Suyama, Michael	05-Mar-96	16-Apr-9
10665	Lonesome Pine Restaurant	Davolio, Nancy	12-Oct-95	09-Nov-9
10544	Lonesome Pine Restaurant	Peacock, Margaret	21-Jun-95	19-Jul-9
10883	Lonesome Pine Restaurant	Callahan, Laura	14-Mar-96	11-Apr-9
11018	Lonesome Pine Restaurant	Peacock, Margaret	13-May-96	10-Jun-9
10662	Lonesome Pine Restaurant	Leverling, Janet	10-Oct-95	07-Nov-9
10754	Magazzini Alimentari Riuniti	Suyama, Michael	26-Dec-95	23-Jan-9
10939	Magazzini Alimentari Riuniti	Fuller, Andrew	09-Apr-96	07-May-9

Record: I◄ ◄ | 1 | ► | ►I | ►* | of 830

The Customers table contains relevant details of all existing customers (company name, address etc.). A particular field in this table, called Customer ID, uniquely identifies each customer. A second table - the Orders table - contains a field that is populated by the same customer ID (Customer) and thus a relationship exists between the two. Notice that in this example, each customer has placed more than one order and therefore a **one-to-many** relationship exists between the Customers and the Orders table.

This highlights one of the key advantages that multi-table databases offer over single-table databases; repetition of data is avoided. All of the customer-related information is stored in only one place (on the Customers table). This information does *not* have to be entered every time a customer places an order. Each order placed is related to a specific customer via the Customer ID field. This field can then be used to access the customer's record in the Customers table. This has two added bonuses:

> Data storage space is optimized

> The possibility of inconsistent data entry is avoided

Defining Relationships

Let's look in more detail at relationships and the idea of maintaining consistent information with an absolute minimum of duplication. Consider the following questions, with regard to the previous example:

> How, in practice, can we avoid the possibility of entering the same customer or order information twice?

> What happens if you attempt to enter order details for a customer that doesn't exist?

The answers lie in how we define the relationships between the tables in our database.

The Primary Key (PK)

When a field (or combination of fields) in a table is defined as the **primary key** then every entry in this field must be unique. The primary key is defined in the "primary" table. An example of this would be the Customer ID field in the Customers table. The PK ensures that every record in the Customers table is unique. If you attempted to enter a duplicate value in the Customer ID field it would not be permitted. The Order ID field in the Orders table performs a similar role. Since the primary key must always have a unique index, it may not be empty. Other examples of common primary keys might include:

> A Social Security Number (in some cases this may not be appropriate)

> A combination of first name, last name and date of birth (this assumes you'll never have more than one person with identical values for all of these fields)

As we established in our first example, the Customer ID (PK) field in the Customers table "points" to a field in the Orders table - the Customer field - which we define as the **foreign key.** In this manner, we can "gather up" all of the orders made by a single customer. There is no physical link between the two tables, only the logical relationship.

> As the above statement implies, the field names of linked tables do not have to be identical. It is much more usual, however, to keep the fields in sync. It makes it much easier to follow the relationship structure between two tables.

The Foreign Key (FK)

The foreign key (FK) is the field (or combination of fields) linked to the primary key (PK) of another table. A field value entered in a FK should be identical to a field value entered in the related PK table. Referring again to our first example, ideally you would not be permitted to enter order details under a `Customer ID` that did not exist in the `Customers` table. There are ways of enforcing this logic, as we'll find out a little later.

In some databases, you don't need to declare a field explicitly as a foreign key. In Access for example, the existence of a foreign key is assumed after the creation of relationships.

Let's look a second, slightly more complex, example whereby three fields (marked in bold) make up the primary key in a `Customers` table (`First_Name`, `Last_Name` and `DOB`). In the `Sent_Cards` table, these three fields act as the foreign key. When the user populates the `Sent_Cards` table, these three fields must be populated and a relating record must exist in the `Customers` table. If just one condition is not met, (e.g. the `DOB` field value in the FK does not match a `DOB` value in the PK) then the card cannot be sent:

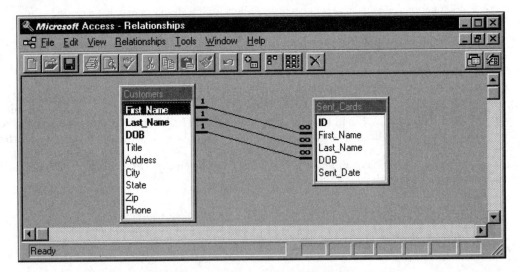

The above solution bends over backward to ensure that a card is not sent to the wrong customer - but it does have drawbacks. It's not as easy to retrieve the data you want when you have to enter multiple fields. As we'll see when we begin building queries, it is much more simple to build them when there are fewer primary and foreign keys. Overall, a better solution might have been to identify each customer with a unique ID, such as a field whose value is based on a counter. Remember that any field from these tables can be retrieved to ensure you selected the correct data.

Types of Relationship

Relationships contain very specific information regarding how the data in one table relates to the data in a second table. There are two basic types of relationships:

> ➤ **One-to-Many**. Each value in the primary key field is unique. The values in the foreign key field are not unique. There can be more than one value in the foreign key field that matches a primary key field value.

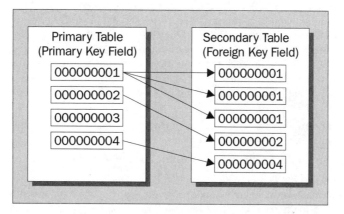

> ➤ **One-to-One**. Each value in the primary key field is unique and each field value in the foreign key field is unique. There will be zero or one value in the foreign key field that matches a primary key field value.

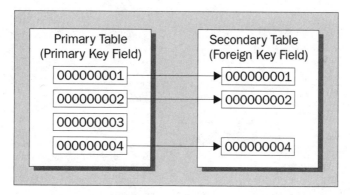

There is a further kind of relationship that can exist, the many-to-many relationship. An example of a many-to-many relationship is that between authors and titles. Each author can have multiple books and each book can have multiple authors. Many-to-many relationships are created by using a third table, which stores the relationship between the other two tables.

There are a number of tips to bear in mind when building relationships:

> ➤ Make a sentence out of the relationship. If you are dealing with customers and orders, for example, you might say, "A single customer may place several orders." It wouldn't make much sense if you reversed this to, "A single order may have several customers."

> ➤ Remember that the "One" portion of this relationship is always unique. Usually this is a supporting table, such as Customers, where each Customer ID is unique.

Now is a good time to have a look at the relationships that exist between tables in a database we have ready-made for us. It will demonstrate these key points in practice and will be a useful introduction to a database we will use several times during the course of this book.

Overview of the Pubs Database

Of the several databases that are used in this book the `pubs` database supplied with SQL Server is the most sophisticated. The `pubs` database was designed for a book distributor. It contains information about authors, publishers, customers (stores) and, of course, sales. We'll quickly discuss the function of each table, but first let's take a look at the structure of the database. The following screenshot is produced when you select to view the Database Diagram. Notice that the primary keys are marked with a small key. It doesn't show the nature of each relationship in the manner of Microsoft Access, so we'll need to do a little detective work to understand the relationships between each table. Remember that primary keys are marked with a small key. Using the following rules, you should be able to follow the logic of each relationship in the `pubs` database:

> ➢ If a primary key of one table is linked to a single field primary key of another table, a one-to-one relationship must exist between the two tables.

> ➢ If a primary key is linked to another field that is not a primary key, it must be a one-to-many relationship.

> ➢ Finally, if a primary key is linked to another primary key, and it's not the only primary key, it must be a one-to-many relationship as well.

Even if you don't plan to work with this database, spend some time analyzing it. There's a lot to learn from its design architecture:

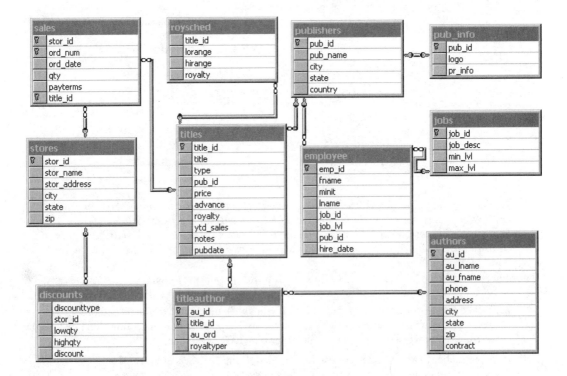

Here is a brief description of each table in the `pubs` database:

> - `jobs`: Corporate job IDs with descriptions and the salary range (min/max).
> - `publishers`: Publisher IDs with names and addresses There is a one-to-one relationship with the `pubinfo` table linked by the `pub_id` field. These tables share responsibilities for storage of the data.
> - `employee`: Employee information.
> - `pub_info`: Additional information about publishers. This allows for an image of the publisher's logo and other related text.
> - `titles`: Stores all titles on file. A one-to-many relationship exists between the `publishers` table and the `titles` table. (One publisher may publish many titles.)
> - `authors`: Contains a list of all authors and their demographic information.
> - `titleauthor`: Royalty payments may be paid to more than one individual. For example, if two authors are credited with a specific title, the payment terms may be 40% to the first author and 60% to the second. This table contains information on royalty percentages.
> - `roysched`: Contains the schedule on which titles are to produce royalties based on a range and commission level.
> - `sales`: This table contains a list of all titles ordered, by which store and the terms of the sale.
> - `discounts`: Provides a discount schedule for sales, based on bulk sales.
> - `stores`: Contains the names and locations of each store. Each store is actually a customer, since this database is for the distributor.

Referential Integrity

By defining our relationships in the manner discussed in the previous sections, we are effectively informing the database which tables are involved in the relationships and which FK relates to which PK. Once we have done this we are in a position to take advantage of **referential integrity**. With referential integrity enabled, the database will seek to ensure that data in related tables remains consistent.

First, let's consider what can happen without referential integrity. Suppose we created an order in the `Orders` table but attached it to an invalid `Customer ID`. How would we dispatch the order? Our `Customer ID` won't find a match in the `Customers` table so we won't be able to find the customer's address! In effect, the new order record is **orphaned** - it has no parent record. Even worse, say we updated a `Customer ID` in the `Customers` table and that customer had placed 100 orders. We would have to update every one of these order records with the new `Customer ID` field value - any we missed would become orphaned.

However, with referential integrity enforced, all foreign key fields must contain a record in primary key table with a matching value. In a nutshell, this means that when populating a record of a table with a foreign key, such as `Customer ID`, the primary key of the linked table must have a matching value. During data entry, this feature can be frustrating. However, when an error message such as that shown here pops up, you know your database is trying to tell you something.

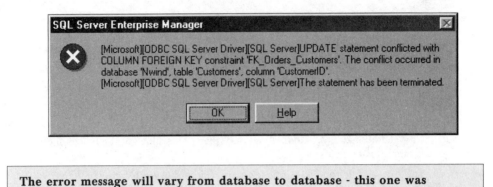

> The error message will vary from database to database - this one was generated by SQL Server.

With referential integrity enforced, you may have the option to "cascade update related fields" or to "cascade delete related fields":

> **Cascade update**: If a field value in a table's primary key is changed then the database will automatically scan all related tables and related foreign key field values will be updated accordingly. Therefore, when we update a Customer ID value (say from 100 to 101) in the Customers table, the Customer ID field values for all orders generated by that customer will change from 100 to 101 as well.

> **Cascade delete**: When you delete a record, the database will delete all related records in related tables. You should take extra care when deleting records in the primary table. For example, if we delete a customer from the Customers table, all relating orders in the Orders table will be deleted as well (whether you wanted to or not). Some databases have an on delete set null clause that handles this problem, allowing you to keep the legacy data.

The previous sections have provided a brief refresher on aspects of relational databases and, in particular, on some of the methods available to ensure the integrity of your data. However, we have only scratched the surface of this topic. Referential integrity doesn't have to be left to the database. Database developers can protect their data by writing their own procedures. These can be automatically triggered when a user attempts to manipulate data in the database (see Chapters 1 and 8).

Assuming that we have created a well-designed database that allows you access to all the data we need, the next question is: How can we optimize performance so that records can be retrieved as quickly and easily as possible? Part of the answer lies in the use of indexes.

Indexes

Indexes play a very important role in the world of relational databases. They provide us with a tool by which the database can quickly and easily retrieve specific records. An index in a database is much the same as an index in a book; it contains a list of specific values that can be found in one or more fields of a table. For example, an index is applied against the title field in the titles table of the pubs database. The database software will sort the titles into, say, ascending order and if a user requests all titles beginning with the letter 'S', the speed with which these records are retrieved will increase (you will only really notice this improved performance for larger databases). We have actually already encountered a special instance of an index - the primary key index.

Indexes are objects and they are stored on the local database, but they are not maintained by the user. We can change many available options of an index, but the database is responsible for allocating space and structuring the index.

> **Don't forget that indexes are objects so they take up storage space. If you have too many indexes in your database, your computer will run more slowly and there will be a diminishing return in terms of performance. Therefore, you should only apply indexes to fields that you query frequently.**

Queries

Once you have created your database you will want to access and manipulate the data in it. You will need to create a front-end application, probably using Visual Basic and send requests (known as **queries**) from this application to the database in order to retrieve the specific data you require.

Structured Query Language (SQL) is the standard database query language, recognized by every database. SQL is a non-procedural language that we use to tell the database exactly what data we require. The database then retrieves this data and passes it back to our application. A single SQL statement applied to a table (or tables) in our database can retrieve highly specific records quickly and easily, and can also perform operations on that data.

The industry standard version of SQL is called ANSI (American National Standards Institute) SQL. However, there are many flavors of SQL. Microsoft Access uses a somewhat different version called Jet SQL, which isn't completely ANSI compliant. All major large databases (such as SQL Server and Oracle) are completely ANSI compliant and add their own additional features (extensions) giving rise to what are called different dialects of SQL. For instance, Oracle uses PL/SQL whereas SQL Server uses a version called Transact-SQL. Appendices A to D discuss the peculiarities of these different versions of SQL.

Conventions Used in This Book

I have used a number of different styles of text and layout in this book to help differentiate between the various types of information. Here are examples of the styles I use along with explanations of what they mean:

Advice, hints or background information comes in this type of font.

> **Important pieces of information come in boxes like this.**

Bulleted lists look like this:

 ➢ **Important words** are in a bold font

> ➢ Words that appear on your monitor in menus or windows, such as in the <u>F</u>ile menu, are presented in a similar font to how they appear on the screen
>
> ➢ Keys that you press on the keyboard, such as *Enter* or *F5*, are italicized like this

Program code appears in a number of formats. Blocks of code that are to be keyed into Visual Basic or other programs appear in a gray block like this:

```
Private Sub Text1_Change()
    lblTitles.Caption = "Titles published by " & Text1
End Sub
```

Code that appears in the body of the normal text looks like this: `Adodc1.Recordset.MoveNext`.

Sometimes you'll see code in a mixture of styles, like this:

```
Private Sub Text1_Change()
    lblTitles.Caption = "Titles published by " & Text1
End Sub
```

The code with a white background is code we've already looked at and that we don't wish to examine further.

Tell Us What You Think

I've tried to make this book as accurate and enjoyable for you as possible, but what really matters is whether or not *you* find it useful. I would really appreciate your views and comments, so please contact Wrox at:

feedback@wrox.com

Suppliers

- SupplierID
- CompanyName
- ContactName
- ContactTitle
- Address
- City
- Region
- PostalCode
- Country
- Phone
- Fax
- HomePage

Products

- ProductID
- ProductName
- SupplierID
- CategoryID
- QuantityPerUnit
- UnitPrice
- UnitsInStock
- UnitsOnOrder
- ReorderLevel
- Discontinued

Categories

- CategoryID
- CategoryName
- Description
- Picture

6

1

The Client-Server Model

Everyone can take advantage of the benefits that come from using a client-server model. To create an application using the client-server model you need as little as one PC with an Access database and a front-end written in Visual Basic. In this book, we will learn how to create such an application and then go on to discover how hundreds or even thousands of computers (and hence users) can be involved in the client-server model. This chapter will cover the basic theory behind the client-server model and its many implementations. The knowledge that you gain in this chapter therefore forms the lynchpin upon which everything we cover in the rest of the book is based.

In particular, this chapter will cover:

> ➢ The difference between desktop databases and database servers
> ➢ What the client-server model is
> ➢ The 2-tier architecture
> ➢ The 3-tier architecture and beyond
> ➢ The role of the middle tier
> ➢ How to achieve server-side processing

Without further ado, let's begin by discussing the server in our client-server model, the database...

Desktop Databases

Today, desktop PCs are being used all over the world by corporations, small shops and in the home. They offer ease of use and plenty of organization power.

One of the most popular of the desktop databases is Microsoft Access. This product quickly became the de facto standard after its second release and it continues to hold strong presence in the market today. A user with average computer skills can quickly build a database to store and organize just about any type of information, then build queries to extract the data without even knowing a word of **Structured Query Language** (**SQL**). Access also provides a wizard to build reports and forms for easy data entry and organized viewing. There is one other feature that made Access irresistible - its price. Because Access was so affordable, smaller companies could afford to buy it to store client information and larger companies could place the product on many machines. Access was the first database that successfully penetrated the Home PC market. This was primarily a result of the fact that most PC's are installed with Microsoft Office and hence Access, allowing home users to organize addresses, recipes or whatever they liked.

Of course, Access isn't the only desktop database on the market. Lotus, for example, packages its own Approach desktop database with their SmartSuite. In addition, if you look for them, you can find desktop databases that are customized for just about any task, such as storing and retrieving client contacts or taking inventory in your office or home.

> *Of course, Access has evolved greatly over the years and much to the credit of Visual FoxPro. If Microsoft had not purchased Fox, Access today would be entirely different. As many would argue, the architecture behind FoxPro provides for the fastest desktop database available.*

The structure of the desktop database makes it very flexible and portable. Each database file (containing the tables, queries, forms, etc.) is stored as a file on a hard drive, in a similar manner to the way a Microsoft Word document is saved. For example, when an Access database is stored it has an extension of .mdb (for Microsoft Database). This file can be copied, moved or deleted very simply using Windows Explorer. Furthermore, if stored on a file server, multiple PCs can load the database into their own workspace, sharing the data with other colleagues.

> **Sharing a single desktop database on a network can be quite challenging, not to mention that they're vulnerable to corruption. For most, this is the time to consider using a database designed for multiple users. We'll cover this in the next section (Database Servers).**

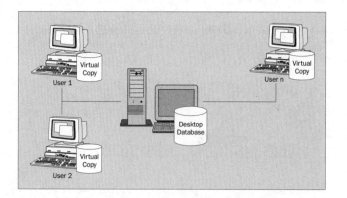

When a copy of this database file (e.g. `.mdb`) is opened using a compatible database application (Access), a virtual copy of the database is made leaving the original intact. Typically, the database application will only load the required resources into memory, however some applications will load the entire file whether it is needed or not. This is typically a problem of older released products, such as early releases of Access. As an example, you might apply a SQL statement against a table to extract some data. That table is loaded into the local PC's memory and the database engine will process the data, displaying only the requested fields.

A database engine is the software program that actually manages the information in the database. When we are trying to find all of the products associated with a particular company, it is the database engine that we make request to. It is the engine that actually retrieves the information we want from the database and performs any manipulation of data we desire.

However, if the table is quite large, you may still find yourself exhausting the available memory resources. This is primarily because the database application on your desktop must open the file and navigate through all of the records to locate the ones requested. Indexes, which we discussed in the Introduction, can play a big role in speeding up the requests by allowing your database application the ability to move directly to the locations of each record.

When the first individual opens a desktop database in their workspace, they have the option of restricting other users from opening it concurrently. The original copy still maintains control over additions, so if this first user decides to share the data, two or more instances of the database can be opened. By default, when a record is being modified, any attempt to edit that same record by the second user will result in receiving an error message indicating that the record is being edited by another user. This protects users from overwriting each other's changes. In later chapters, we'll see how databases can be modified to force updates to the records being modified. When a record is successfully updated, the other users are able to view the data when a refresh is made to the current recordset (or after the database application refreshes the recordset.

> **A recordset is a virtual table, containing a number of records in a spreadsheet style format. A recordset represents the content (or a portion of the content) of one or more tables. Updates can be made through recordsets by first populating the recordset, making changes, and then publishing the changes to the database file.**

One key point to make about desktop databases is that the actual database application does not need to be installed on the client PC or any server PC. The only requirement is that the client application understands how to open and modify the database file. Visual Basic and most other application development tools can use **ADO (ActiveX Data Objects)** to open and modify the database file. As long as the development tool of your choice supports ActiveX (those which do include Visual C++ and Visual Basic), you can use ADO to connect to and alter the database file.

> **If you're developing a self-contained application, meaning that it has its own copy of a database file (such as `.mdb` for Access), that file can be installed with the new application during the setup process (e.g. when using Visual Basic's Package & Deployment Wizard).**

One consideration to keep in mind with desktop databases is that both the number of concurrent connections and the number of transactions to be processed may vary in number. This can cause a wide range of processing requirements. As an example, you may have an Access .mdb file located on a file server, allowing over 1000 employees access to it. Initially, this sounds like it would cause an enormous overhead. Well, yes, this could cause a great deal of overhead, but what if the users are only processing requests periodically? Possibly the application is a corporate phone book. Most users may only need to look up a phone number three or four times a day. This translates to approximately 4000 requests per day. Each request would require the client to open the database, execute a request, wait for a response and then close the database. Given that the requests were not all executed simultaneously, the database should be able to handle the requests without significant wait time. We'll take a closer look at the limitations of a sample desktop database (such as Access) in Chapter 5.

Database Servers

As we have already discovered, the design of the desktop database includes loading an instance of the database file on the local PC. Database server files are stored and updated slightly differently. The user application doesn't communicate with the database files directly, but through a service running behind the scenes (see the following diagram). When the database is queried, the request is passed to the service and the service coordinates the request. The results of the request are then passed back to the requesting client. One of the major advantages with this setup is that only the requested fields are passed to the client, thus saving memory resources. With a desktop database, as you may remember, the entire table is passed to the client for processing by the local PC.

This structure offers greater speed and flexibility. Because the service is communicating with the database and is managing all requests, multiple applications attempting to apply changes don't bog down the server. The service will listen passively for requests and when a request is received, will manage the resources to complete the request.

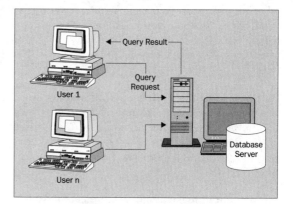

Huge sums of money have been invested in optimizing the way data is stored and retrieved from server database packages. A record can be located in a matter of milliseconds from a stack of over a million records. We'll cover some of the benchmarks of SQL Server in Chapter 5 and discuss when it might be better to use a desktop database over a server. You should note that the speed of any response depends on the processing power available.

Database server packages (known as **Relational Database Management Systems** or **RDBMS**) have come a long way with security. Desktop database packages do offer some security but the database files *are* exposed for the user to copy. A server database offers advanced security in a number of ways:

> The databases are typically stored on a network that requires a login. This allows you to restrict direct access to the server containing the database.

> Each database can require logins that impose advanced restrictions by function or by table. For example, user X may have access to a table with salary information but is restricted from updating the contents of the table. Many desktop databases are capable of imposing similar restrictions, but database servers have historically provided more advanced control mechanisms.

> Views can be created which allow the user access to the data in a specified table based on specific criteria. We'll learn more about views later in this chapter and again in Chapter 8. Views can also be found in many desktop databases. Access, for example, allows you to store and call queries that are predefined.

> Server databases can't be copied or moved without the proper authority. Most database management systems provide a utility that allows the user to backup and restore the database. Any unauthorized attempt will result in an error message.

One of the greatest advantages of these database servers is that they are capable of storing a great amount of data. They are limited only by the amount of storage space on the server. This is especially important now that corporations are storing more data for the purposes of auditing and research. This is not to say that desktop databases cannot hold a lot of data, but many restrict the amount of data to 1 or 2 Gigabytes. There are other ways to get around this limitation, but this is a point where you may want to think about using a database server.

So who are the players? Well, like the desktop database packages, there are many database server vendors from which to choose. The more common names include:

> Sybase SQL Server

> SQL Server by Microsoft (PC version of Sybase SQL Server)

> SQL Anywhere by Sybase (A scaled down PC version of Sybase SQL Server)

> ORACLE by Oracle

> DB2 by IBM

There is no clear path to choosing your RDBMS. For many, the familiar will always prevail. Others may spend large amounts of time and money carefully weighing each one's capabilities and weaknesses.

Here are a few considerations to make when choosing a RDBMS:

> Firstly, what are the requirements for data storage? How many records do you handle at present time and how much growth is expected? If you're not sure that the RDBMS can handle the job, don't use it, even if you're comfortable with the product.

> Secondly, always consider which server will be most compatible with your needs. If your project is going to be sitting in the Windows NT Server environment and you plan to build your client applications with a Microsoft tool, such as Visual Basic, then you might be inclined to choose Microsoft's SQL Server. With the emergence of ODBC and OLE DB, this has become less of an issue. However, you should keep in mind that many development tools have been designed to connect easily to specific database servers. With ADO it's even less of an issue. As already mentioned, ADO is quite flexible with respect to the programming environment and the database to which it connects.

> ➢ Thirdly, consider training and maintenance issues. If your staff are familiar with one product, you can save money and time by not choosing the unfamiliar product. Your product will be much stronger if it doesn't suffer from a training curve. In addition, experience would enable the avoidance of pitfalls throughout the development process.

What is Client-Server?

A client-server architecture consists of one or more client applications communicating requests to another application, which is designated as the server.

Bear in mind that the client and server may run on the same machine as well as on separate machines. In other words, the client application may (or may not) sit on one machine and the database server on another. Placing both on a single CPU does not exploit the benefits of the client-server model, but does allow you the flexibility to develop on a single machine or build a small and scalable client-server project.

We'll soon cover many of the various client-server architectures available, however to speak generically:

1. The client initiates a request to the server, which is standing by, waiting for requests.

2. When the server receives the request, it manages and carries out the request. It then sends a response message back to the requesting client.

3. The response may come as a group of records, an error message or a Boolean value indicating whether the statement executed successfully.

The definition of the client-server model can vary in scope. The greater mystery however, is not what constitutes a client-server architecture, but the difference between 2-tier and 3-tier models. Because database servers contain their own services, which coordinate the processing of requests, many developers mistakenly assume that they have created a 3-tier client-server application. We'll discuss the difference between 2- and 3-tier client-server models later in this chapter.

The client-server model comes in various flavors, but the concept is always the same. We'll explore these different flavors during this chapter, in order to optimize our client-server solution.

Fat Client vs. Fat Server

When speaking of fat and thin clients, we refer to the level of functionality that resides on the client. A fat client-thin server model is one in which most of the functionality and business logic resides on the client. A thin client-fat server model implies functionality and business logic resides mostly on the server.

> Business logic consists of rules that are applied to your client-server system that describes how your data is to be handled. As an example, you may have logic that specifies the following:
>
> If Field1 is populated with x, then Field2 must be populated with y or z.

The Fat Server

With the fat server-thin client model, the client contains the GUI application, which sends requests to the server. The server handles the request, executes any additional business logic and then returns a response to the client. For example, when a client requests the placement of an order, the server checks the inventory levels, reorders the stock if necessary and then sends a response to the client confirming that the order has been shipped. Much of the business logic is handled on the server by triggers and stored procedures, which we will discuss later in this chapter and expand on in Chapter 8:

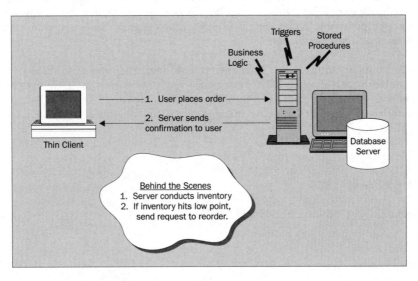

The Fat Client

With a fat client/thin server model, more network traffic is created. When the user requests an order, the server accepts the order and responds with confirmation. The client then requests an inventory status for the item ordered. If the inventory is low, the client can send a final request to have the inventory replenished:

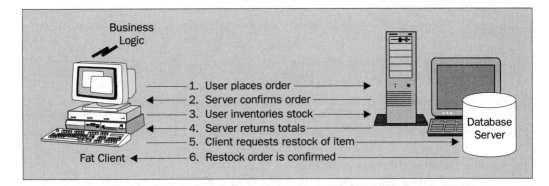

Despite this increased network traffic, fat client models are the method of choice for many client-server models. The reason for this is that fat clients are typically easier to program. This norm is changing rapidly as new technologies emerge, particularly in the area of the Internet.

As application development tools evolve, it is becoming quite easy to design a client front-end with the business logic incorporated. This requires additional programming on the client side, but programmers typically feel more comfortable applying the logic in the client as opposed to building it into a database in which s/he may not have extensive experience. This holds especially true when dealing with Visual Basic. This programming language is so simple and widespread that the application can easily be built by one individual and later updated by a second individual.

One of the major problems with fat clients is the price of upgrading each client application. The business logic exists in the client, so changes to that logic will require the application to be recompiled and redistributed. While this may not be a huge deal for smaller shops, upgrading could take days for larger corporations. When logic is stored on the client, it can become quite time-consuming to manage and update the code.

If we move this functionality to the server it can be quite difficult and time-consuming to manage – and may even require the services of a DBA. However, when the business logic changes or additional functionality is added, the programmer need only change the logic at one location. Best of all, the users of the system have no knowledge of the changes ever happening because you don't need to redistribute the client application.

In Summary

The advantages of a fat client are:

> Architecture is simple to design and build.
> Relieves server from handling business logic.

The disadvantages of a fat client are:

> Increased network traffic.
> May require a more powerful machine.
> The client machines may use a variety of operating systems. This may require more extensive testing.
> Difficult and time-consuming to upgrade multiple clients.

The advantages of a fat server are:

> Upgrade multiple machines with little effort.
> Allows for smaller executables on the client.
> Protects investments of older computers (may not need to upgrade processors, etc.).

The disadvantages of a fat server are:

> Requires the server to do more processing.
> Could require a DBA (Database Administrator) to build and maintain the business logic if it is stored in the database.
> Cannot change programming interfaces made available to the client applications without a lot of effort.
> Complex development environment.

> **There is no requirement that you specifically choose a fat client or a fat server model. You may find that your business needs include a mixture of both.**

The ultimate expression of a thin client-fat server model is the World Wide Web. Browsers have generic information on how to handle each response to a request and when a new request is received, the server processes it according to its stored logic. The only time a web browser requires a new installation is when the technology changes, bringing new browsers.

For Whom is the Client-Server Model?

The short answer to this is everyone and anyone. The client-server model can be invoked with as little as a single PC with a desktop database and a front-end application. Because of this, almost any business can take advantage of the client-server model's benefits:

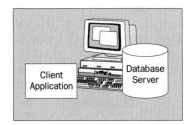

The average-sized corporation will probably have multiple clients connected to a single server. This is the more traditional model because it can accommodate anything from one to a thousand or more users, depending on the functionality involved. The power of the network and the database server are the main restrictions to the number of concurrent connections.

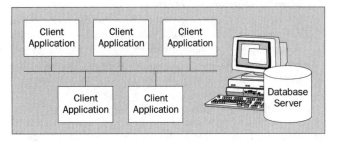

One of the greatest features of the client-server model is that it is infinitely scalable. Of course, the word *infinitely* is conditional on the amount of money you have available. At some point, the economical impact out-weighs the benefits of up scaling. Realistically, you may begin as a small shop with a few users; when new users need to be added later, the process is relatively simple. The up scale process might include adding a PC to the network, installing the client application and assigning passwords.

It seems like newer CPUs and database servers are released on a weekly basis. Just a few years ago, we were astonished with the 100MHz processor and today we see 450-500MHz processors being released. The architecture of database servers allows for easy upgrade when you purchase new equipment. Even moving to a new network server is very straightforward - simply make a backup copy of the database and restore it to the new server. All database objects, including the data tables, triggers, and stored procedures are automatically moved to the new location.

Replication

The definition of **replication** is:

> **Replication is a process by which databases or portions of databases are copied periodically. This allows the data to be accessed by a greater number of clients while balancing the work. The data is synchronized so that if changes are made to any of the replicated databases, those changes are reflected on all other databases.**

Larger corporations may have thousands of clients connecting into multiple servers. To implement this architecture, the primary database is replicated over multiple servers.

There are two reasons for doing this:

> ➤ To assign responsibilities to several servers based on functionality (such as using a dedicated server for reporting purposes)
>
> ➤ To break up the processing power between two or more servers

Many database servers are capable of accessing more than one CPU. The advantage of this is that multiple queries can be executed across a number of processors. More specifically, 'portions' of an execution plan can be divided between a number of processors. The advantage here is that larger lookup can be handled by a number of processors and completed faster. This is known as ***parallel processing****. This topic is beyond the scope of this book. For more information, consult your database's documentation to identify its capabilities with respect to parallel processing.*

In the following example, database replication is used to divide the processing power into two regions. A central database server acts as a host, which is used to update both of the regional servers on a daily basis. Sales made during the course of the day can be pushed up to the host and product modifications can be pushed down to the regional servers. When implementing this design, you must be cautious, as the regional servers don't communicate with the host on a regular basis and therefore don't have up-to-date information on stock levels:

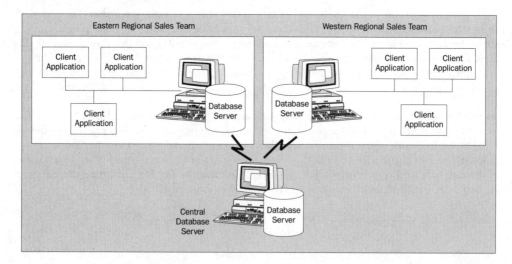

You could also use this method to divide responsibilities between multiple servers. Whichever way you decide to use your replicated databases, don't forget that the data on each server will only be as current as the frequency with which the data is replicated. The replication process may be run on a nightly, weekly or monthly basis. Many organizations even replicate their databases real time.

A second use consists of replicating data for the purpose of redirecting specific functional requirements from the primary server. For example, if you have high volume reporting that is performed on a regular basis, it's more practical to have these reports run from a copy of the original data. High volume reporting can bog down your primary database server and make for an unproductive workplace. For most companies, high reporting times are on the 1st and 15th of each month. However, you may find that there is enough reporting being conducted on a daily basis to make even the most simple database activities slow to a crawl.

There are many other reasons why you might replicate your databases. In the event of a power or network failure, you probably will not be able to access your data. This is especially true when your database is located at a different location than your client applications. For this reason, you may wish to place your replicated database at a different location than the primary database (or on a different network). If the power or network fails, you can continue to process. When the problem is resolved, the databases are replicated once again to update any changed made during the power loss.

To implement this solution, the primary database is used for your day-to-day operations such as SQL INSERTS, DELETES and UPDATES (these are covered in detail in Chapter 6). On a regular basis the primary database acts as a publisher and passes data to the other (replicated) database servers, which act as subscribers. Clients that are used for reporting purposes can then connect to the secondary databases and the primary database is unaffected by the processing:

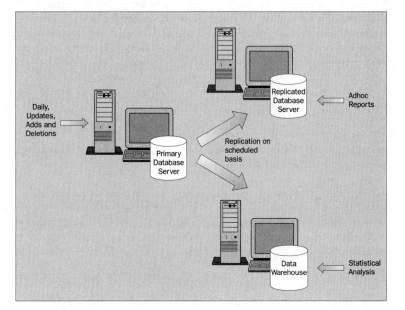

Do use replication:

> For ad-hoc reporting to relieve processing from the primary server
> For moving central data from one computer to branch PCs
> For moving or copying data to a data warehouse (we'll cover data warehouses in Chapter 18)

Don't use replication:

> As a backup database to a primary database
> When it's critical to have the most current data

Some RDBMS's, such as SQL Server 7.0, allow for partial replication of their objects. This allows for increased flexibility, providing the ability to create field replicas that reflect parts of the master publisher database. For example, these field replicas could be placed on laptops for sales representatives to work with. When a sales rep has made changes to his or her data (orders for example) s/he can sync those changes with the master database as often as desired.

While replication can be a very important tool to your organization, it's not the easiest to implement. There are many issues associated with replication and it becomes an art form very quickly. Some of the considerations made when implementing replication are:

➢ Speed of replication

➢ Amount of data to be replicated

➢ How often the replication is to be conducted

➢ What replication tools to use and their capabilities with respect to the previously listed items

2-Tier Architecture

The most common architecture implemented in corporations today involves two-tier client-server applications. This model is the same client-server model that we have been discussing up to this point in the book. The primary reason that 2-tier architecture is the most common today is that it supports a low cost of design and implementation. It's so easy that many don't even realize that they've created a client-server application. Using Visual Basic wizards, you can quickly create a client application that connects to a server database in a matter of minutes. The wizard will prompt you for connection information, the fields that you would like to include and hey presto! You have built your client application.

The 2-tier architecture, if you haven't already guessed, consists of one or more client applications connecting *directly* to a server. Sound familiar? If you've ever built an application that connects to a database then you've built a client-server application.

The following illustration demonstrates how requests are handled in a 2-tier environment. The client will send the request directly to the server. The server will handle the request and pass a response directly to the client. This architecture seems efficient, but as the number of connections increases, there needs to be some management of these connections and requests needs. Without a managing service, the database server may become overwhelmed with requests, causing a bottleneck:

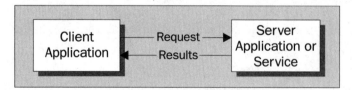

> **Don't allow the ease of design to cause you to underestimate the power of the 2-tier client-sever model. This design has been implemented in corporations all over the world with great success.**

3-Tier to N-Tier Architecture

Before we go into great detail of what a 3-tier or n-tier architecture is, let's first distinguish what they mean.

> ➤ 3-tier client-server means that a service or application resides between the client and server with the purpose of managing connections and requests.

> ➤ In a 4-tier client-server architecture, two management layers reside between the client and the server. One may be dedicated to the clients, while the other is dedicated to the server.

> ➤ N-tier client-server just means that the architecture has four or more tiers.

Of course, you can add as many tiers as you need, but the more tiers, the more complex it becomes. At some point, the benefit of adding tiers outweighs the cost of developing them.

Although the structure of 3- or 4-tier client server applications is more difficult to program, they have been proven to be the most flexible and efficient model used today, especially for larger systems with thousands of users.

The Role of the Middle Tier

The middle tier is the "glue" that holds the client and server together. There is certainly much more to it than that though. We mentioned earlier that a fat client model is a client-server model where the business logic and functionality reside on the client. Further, a thin client (or a fat server) is one where the business logic and functionality reside on the server. There's also one further possibility that we can introduce to the picture - the business logic and functionality can reside in the middle tier.

The middle tier provides the management and allocation of resources required to accomplish the job in a very efficient manner, allowing the client to handle the presentation logic and more importantly, the server to handle data access logic. When a department grows and multiple servers are needed, the middle tier can be used to bring more than one server together, coordinating resources. The job of the middle tier is to streamline requests and connections over a single server, or over multiple servers, so that the client applications act as if they were connecting to a single server.

> **To constitute a true 3-tier client-server model, the middle tier must be independent of the client and server applications. It will generally reside on the same machine as the server. However, it may run on a separate machine.**

An Aside on Components

These middle tiers are usually built from **components**. A component is just a pre-compiled, interacting piece of software that can act as a "building block" for creating applications. As Visual Basic developers, we'll want to write components in Visual Basic, but there's nothing to stop us from writing them in Visual C++, C++ or Delphi. These components are usually broken out into tasks as related to function or by the tables to which they connect. Then if any changes are necessary, for instance because a table has a new field, just one component needs to be updated and recompiled.

The type of component we will build in this book is called an **in-process server**. In-process servers run in the same memory space as the application that calls them. In Visual Basic, we create in-process servers by creating an **ActiveX DLL project** and compiling it into a .DLL file:

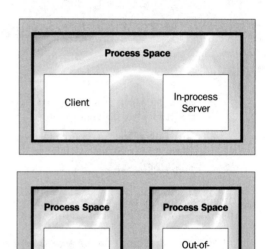

Another type of component, which we will not be using in this book, is the **out-of-process server**. An out-of-process server runs in its own memory space, not in that of the application that called it. This means that if the out-of-process server crashes for some reason, it will not take the client application down with it. However, there is a performance hit with out-of-process servers because calls have to be made across a process boundary instead of within a process. To create an out-of-process server in Visual Basic, you create an **ActiveX EXE project**, which you compile into an .EXE file.

Now, without getting too heavily involved in something known as **object-oriented programming** (**OOP**), the file that you compile (whether a DLL or EXE) is known as a component and the **instance** of that component, which exists at run-time is known as an **object**. A familiar example of an object is a Visual Basic control, such as a text box or command button. When we place a control on a form, we are actually creating an instance of a text box component, which we can alter by changing its appearance and adding code particular it.

The 3-Tier Architecture

The following illustration depicts a 3-tier system where the requests sent from the client are received by the middle tier and then passed to the server. The server handles the request and passes the response back to the middle tier, which then passes the response back to the client:

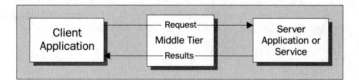

As mentioned earlier, middle tier components (and hence the object instantiated from them) are designed to accomplish specific tasks. Each of these objects is created with business rules incorporated so minimal requests are bounced between the client and server. If a client needs to insert a new record into a table, a request is passed to the appropriate middle tier object. The middle tier object then connects into the database directly and manages the request until complete. The advantages to the middle tier objects are that they can handle business logic and are capable of implementing additional security.

The downside to the above system is that it still requires each middle tier object to connect to the database. If each client instantiates its own copy of an object, you still have the same number of connections to the database as you have clients who want to pass requests. This problem can be alleviated by one or both of the following two methods:

> You can move to a 4-tier architecture. In this architecture, one tier will be responsible for maintaining connections with the clients and another tier is designed to manage connections and requests to the server.

> You can implement a Transaction Processing monitor (as described in the following section) to pool your resources.

The following image depicts an architecture where multiple clients are sharing a pool of resources, in this case database connections. An object is instantiated by a client and a connection is opened to the database. When an object releases its database connection, the connection is pooled. If another object requires an identical connection it can take one from the pool, which is much quicker than creating a new database connection. In this scenario, database connections are minimized and the architecture is much more scalable:

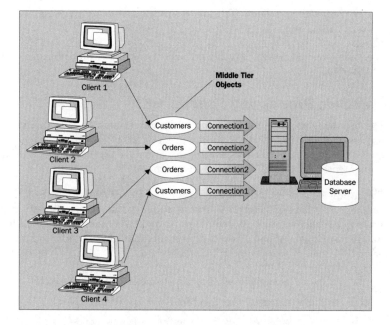

The Transaction Processing Monitor

We can achieve this pooling of resources by using a **Transaction Processing monitor** (**TP monitor**) such as **Microsoft Transaction Server** (MTS). A TP monitor acts as a host to ActiveX DLL components and manages the resources (such as processes and database connections) that they use. TP monitors allow our systems to become much more scalable, as resources can be shared between multiple clients:

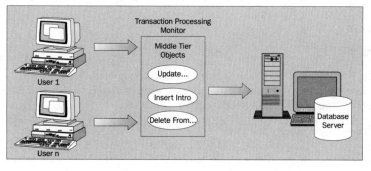

The roles of a TP monitor can include the following (depending on the product):

> **Object Request Brokering**. TP monitors can instantiate objects and destroy them if unneeded.

> **Fewer connections to the database are required**. The TP monitor handles resource pooling, allowing many clients the ability to share resources.

> **Transaction Support**. When multiple requests need to be handled as a whole, TP monitors support **rollbacks**. This allows you to gracefully handle failure of any group of SQL statements.

> **Security**. Many TP monitors allow you to configure security at the middle tier. This gives you an alternative to implementing security at the server and can actually remove the workload from the server with respect to security.

> **Monitoring Tools**. TP monitors provide a tool for tracking throughput rates, and success and failure rates.

We will cover Microsoft Transaction Server and the responsibilities of a TP monitor in more detail in Chapter 11.

Server Side Processing Functionality

The following section outlines some of the functionality available in most (if not all) of the database servers available today. We'll go into great detail of how to use each of these in later chapters. For now, just worry about understanding the concepts. Note that the amount of functionality and how it is implemented may vary from product to product.

The following section relies upon **Structured Query Language** (**SQL**). SQL is a non-procedural language that is used to retrieve, insert, update or delete data in any given database table. SQL is actually capable of much more, including database maintenance and table creation. Each SQL statement consists of one or more statements that identify how to handle your data. There are four basic SQL statements designed to handle data:

> SELECT statement - used to populate recordsets with data

> DELETE statement - used to remove records from tables

> INSERT statement - used to insert records into a table

> UPDATE statement - used to modify records in a table

Triggers

Triggers are a collection of SQL statement-like functions that automatically execute when an INSERT, DELETE or UPDATE statement is applied to a specific table. These internal triggers reside in the RDBMS and allow the server to take on responsibility for business logic. In a nutshell, triggers allow the user to enforce business rules, ensure data integrity and automate tasks without client interaction, reducing network traffic.

Triggers are usually not pure SQL statements. They use extensions to the SQL language that are specific to a particular RDBMS. For instance, Oracle triggers are written with PL/SQL and SQL Server triggers are written in Transact SQL (T-SQL). When an INSERT, DELETE or UPDATE statement is applied to a table, an event is fired (triggered), allowing you to execute that block of code.

A common use for triggers is to keep an audit log of users that have updated a specific table. For example, let's assume we have a table that contains grades for a college. If any grade changes are made we might want to keep an audit trail of these changes for reference, should a discrepancy arise.

The processing is conducted internally on the server. When a user updates a grade, a trigger event executes one or more SQL statements that write the user ID, record ID and date stamp to a specified table.

While discussing fat servers, we considered an example in which the server re-ordered products automatically when stock levels fell below a certain point. A trigger could easily handle this functionality in the following step-by-step process:

1. The order table is modified, triggering an event. (User places order)

2. The trigger calls one or more SQL statements. (Event is fired)

3. The SQL statements check product levels. (Code is used to validate levels)

4. If the product level is below standard, another SQL statement re-orders the product. (Adds a record to the Order table)

There's more to it than this, but you should now have an understanding of the concepts behind a trigger.

Stored Procedures

Stored procedures are pre-compiled SQL statements that accept arguments from clients (and just as with triggers, each RDBMS provides a language that extends the SQL that can be used in a stored procedure). If, for example, you wanted to remove all occurrences of Customers with no Orders since a specified date, you could build a stored procedure that receives a "Date" as a parameter and executes DELETE statements against the tables.

Stored procedures can be used to automate many of the routine tasks on the server. These stored procedures are kept as objects on the RDBMS and can be executed by a trigger or from the client. The list of possibilities for stored procedures is almost limitless. We'll explore a few possibilities here and then in Chapter 8 we'll build some example applications, which send parameters to the stored procedures from a Visual Basic application.

Using stored procedures has many advantages:

> You can store and execute complex operations on the server. In certain circumstances, you'll find that SQL statements may become too complex to execute from the client application, whereas a stored procedure handles them without any problems. The advanced capability comes from the inherent language provided by the server (such as T-SQL).

> Stored procedures are maintained on the server side. Therefore, they can be modified quickly and they don't require you to redistribute code to each client.

> Stored procedures can be used to automate tasks, such as purging data, archiving data or creating tables on the fly.

> Additional security can be invoked using a stored procedure. Rather than allowing the user direct access to a table, you can authorize access to a stored procedure, which selects, updates or deletes specific data from a table.

> Stored procedures run much faster than standard SQL statements. This is because they are pre-compiled at the database level.

> Stored procedures reduce network traffic by allowing the client to send smaller SQL commands and reducing the amount of "talk" between the client and server.

> Error handling can be conducted at the database level. This means that error can be raised, flagging violations of business rules or table constraints. All errors can easily be translated into friendly return codes for the calling application.

31

Of course, there are also disadvantages involved with stored procedures. The most significant problem is that they can be difficult to program, maintain and debug. For an advanced database administrator, this may seem like a routine task, but for anyone just learning, you won't find much in the way of debugging tools. Don't let this scare you though, stored procedures offer great flexibility when properly invoked.

Views

Views are SQL statements that are stored on the server. These views create a virtual table that allows clients to retrieve and work with data. For example, a view may be used to retrieve specific data from one or more tables. Later, when a client needs data from those same tables, it applies an SQL statement against the view.

There are several advantages of using views:

> Views can be used for added security. When specifying user security, you can allow users to access a view rather than allowing the client direct access to a table. The view only retrieves the records and fields that are defined in the view. If the user tries to retrieve a field that has not been defined in the view, an error is returned because the field does not exist on the virtual table.

> Users can take a large, complex SQL statement and define it as a view. The clients that require data from the view may then execute a short statement to retrieve the same data again and again.

Creating views is primarily the job of the database developers and database administrators generally maintain them. This is not to say that you can't create and maintain views yourself. They are not that complex and can add a great deal of functionality to your system. Even if you don't intend to build them, you should be aware of their existence. If you find that there are complex SQL statements that you continually call, you should work with your DBA to establish a set of standard views.

The following image depicts how a view can bring data from multiple tables into one table. The middle table (Client_Sale) is made up of two tables (Customers and Orders). Only those fields needed are pulled into the view. In this scenario, Customer ID and Company Name are pulled from the Customers table, and Order ID, Employee and Order Date are pulled from the Orders table. If other fields from either table are unnecessary, then they may be excluded. Because views are created using SQL, you can restrict the presence of any column or row of data:

Retrieving information from a view is exactly the same as retrieving information from a table. When you execute a SQL statement, you simply include the view name where the table name normally would be listed. The following is a SQL statement applied against a view named `Client_Sales`:

```
SELECT * FROM Client_Sales WHERE Client_ID = 'ALFKI'
```

Other Scenarios for Client-Server Architecture

One of the assumptions sometimes made about client-server architecture is that it's strictly for connecting to and retrieving data from databases. While this is the most common use, you should recognize that the term 'client-server' describes a relationship between two entities, which may or may not be database-related.

You can find examples of this everywhere in the marketplace. Of course, we have already mentioned the World Wide Web. Here, the client-server relationship exists at many points. Firstly, if you use an Internet Service Provider (ISP), such as America OnLine or the Microsoft Network, you probably use your telephone line to connect to a server. This server allows your computer (the client) to connect in, granting you access to the Web. Once connected in, the ISP acts as a server to you, but also acts as a client to the many the other servers on the Internet. When your PC sends a request to the ISP, the ISP will forward the request to the appropriate server and the response will filter back down to the originating client. Based on this description, you certainly could argue that an ISP is a middle tier between your browser and the Internet:

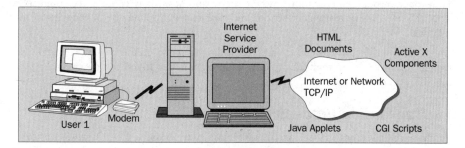

Another frequently encountered example of the client-server relationship is based on TCP/IP connections. Here, you may have an application running as a server, listening to a specific TCP/IP port. When clients connect in, they specify the IP address (e.g. 255.255.255.255) and the port to which the server is listening. Once that connection is made, clients are able to send data to the server. The server can then replicate, manage and respond to requests:

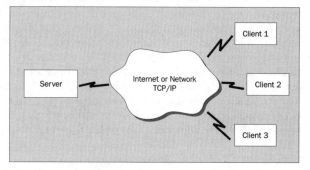

In this example, data is passed between a server and multiple clients, but a database plays no part in the client-server relationship. This is not to say that a database can't play a role, but we need to get away from the mindset that client-server architectures are solely for database connections.

The Planning Process

The implementation of client-server architecture requires very careful research and planning. This can often be a taxing and time-consuming process as there are many important questions to consider:

> Do I build a 2-tier or a 3-tier model?

> What should I use on my middle tier?

> What database server do I use?

> How do I schedule and estimate this project?

2-Tier vs. N-Tier

Choosing between 2-tier and n-tier models seems to be what's on most people's minds. There are so many variables to factor into the equation (including preference) that no single book can determine the best structure for your client-server model. Some of these variables can include:

> The flexibility and power of your chosen database server. Today's database servers are capable of handling hundreds or even thousands of concurrent connections without moving to a 3-tier architecture.

> The power and versatility of the CPU housing the server. The more powerful the CPU the faster the server will handle the requested tasks.

> How much throughput is running into the server and how many consecutive connections exist. You may have few or many connections and each connection may be passing few or many requests.

> The economical factor. How much are you willing to spend on the system? Typically, an n-tier architecture will cost more money to develop and maintain. If you can get by with a 2-tier solution, you can save a great deal of money.

Choosing a Transaction Processing Monitor

If you have chosen implement a 3-tier architecture and plan to use a TP monitor, you'll need to think about what product to use. In this book, we'll explore a few solutions using Microsoft Transaction Server as our TP monitor. This is another area to research thoroughly. Implementing a 3-tier architecture is difficult enough; don't add the complexity of TP monitor software that leaves too much mystery. This is especially true if you must learn the tool. Consider what documentation and training is available for it. If your staff has no experience in implementing a 3-tier model, consider purchasing a TP monitor product where training and documentation is readily available. If you happen to be using SQL Server with your system, Microsoft Transaction Server may prove to be the best choice simply for the reason that it has been designed around SQL Server; on the other hand, if you're using Oracle, you may choose another product. Finally, allocate plenty of extra time to plan this stage. A TP monitor can make or break your system.

Some of the TP monitor players are:

> Microsoft Transaction Server

> TUXEDO from BEA

> TOP END also from BEA

*Another aspect of client-server architectures that is gaining popularity is the notion of **queuing** the requests to and from the server. In this scenario, the client would publish a request for the server to retrieve and process. If the server were unavailable to retrieve the request, the request would be queued (stored) for the server. When the server was able to pick up the request, it would do so and process it, publishing a response to the client sending the request. Of course, Microsoft has a product available for you that can do this, Microsoft Message Queue Server (MSMQ). MSMQ is a robust messaging transport for distributed applications across your entire networked enterprise. MSMQ provides fault tolerance and is capable of encrypting the messages it sends. MSMQ is quite detailed, but easy to work with from Visual Basic. For more information on MSMQ, I suggest reading "MTS and MSMQ with VB and ASP" from Wrox Press. This provides in-depth coverage for implementing MSMQ in any application or component.*

Scheduling and Estimating Time for Development and Rollout

Scheduling and estimating is another area of difficulty. You may ask, "Is there anything I need to know about planning a client-server model?" You should be aware of a few factors. Primarily, because client-server architecture is fairly new, the experience level of your developers will determine how long you should allow for scheduling.

> **The Network**. Client-server architecture relies heavily on a well-defined network. It's important that you work closely with the network administrator to understand any issues that may exist with the setup. In the same respect, the network administrator should understand how the database server is going to treat his/her network.

> **Level of commitment by business analysts or higher management**. This is certainly not to point fingers at upper management, but you should attempt to foresee any changes that may arise during the life span of the development process. Change is constant!

> **The skill level of the developers and project managers**. It's becoming increasingly difficult to find highly skilled software engineers. When estimating timelines and man-hours for development, think about the skill level of *each* engineer involved in the project.

> **Other functions to which the developers may need to commit time**. Development may not be the only function of your engineers. If this is the case, you should plan the scheduling accordingly.

> **Learning curves for new products**. If you'll be using a product that is new to your company, allow time for the engineers to get up to speed with that product.

These may or indeed may not apply to your organization and the list is certainly not limited to these. Spend plenty of time considering the above and any other factors that may pertain to your organization.

Summary

This chapter covered the fundamentals of the client-server architecture. Hopefully, after reading this chapter you have a solid understanding of what client-server is and conceptually how it is applied. This is the only chapter of this book dedicated to the conceptual understanding of client-server. Later in the book, we'll attempt to put these concepts into practice by building both 2- and 3-tier systems. As mentioned earlier, before building a client-server system, there are a great number of considerations that come into play. Research your needs very carefully and know the limitations of the architecture and the tools you use.

To summarize, in this chapter we have discussed:

- The role of an Relational Database Management System in a client-server architecture
- The difference between the fat server-thin client model and the thin server-fat client model
- Replication
- Components
- Transaction Processing monitors
- Triggers, stored procedures and views

Suppliers

- SupplierID
- CompanyName
- ContactName
- ContactTitle
- Address
- City
- Region
- PostalCode
- Country
- Phone
- Fax
- HomePage

Products

- ProductID
- ProductName
- SupplierID
- CategoryID
- QuantityPerUnit
- UnitPrice
- UnitsInStock
- UnitsOnOrder
- ReorderLevel
- Discontinued

Categories

- CategoryID
- CategoryName
- Description
- Picture

6

Database Design

In this chapter, we will cover some basics of database design. The main purpose of this chapter is to ensure that you understand some of what it takes to design a good database. Obviously, I can't hope to turn you into a database administrator by the end of this chapter (there are whole books devoted to the subject of database administration), but I can at least teach you some of the things that need to be considered when designing a database.

Even if you are fortunate enough to work in a large team and never need to design databases yourself, you should be aware of the content of the chapter. Knowledge of the structure of databases can only help to ensure that you, as a developer, understand the databases with which you are working.

The subjects that we will consider in this chapter are:

- ➤ Normalization
- ➤ Unique and non-unique indexes
- ➤ Creating indexes
- ➤ The five steps to building a powerful database

So let's get started!

Normalization

Every database book you read will emphasize the importance of normalizing your database. Normalization consists of a set of standard rules that help prevent design flaws that cause repeated and inconsistent data. There are three basic steps in the normalization process and once you understand them, you'll be well on your way to building a powerful, fast, and efficient database.

The following table is used to organize client visits at Joe's Speedy Auto Repair Shop. When a client brings in one of their vehicles, the shop registers the car and maintains a listing of the latest service date for the applicable vehicle. This database is far from being normalized.

You'll notice that there are two groups of fields that repeat (`Vehicle_1_…` and `Vehicle_2_…`). The goal of these two groups was to allow the shop to maintain history on two vehicles for each client. This is inefficient because most client members may not have two vehicles. If the average member only has one vehicle, the database still allocates space for each one. As the size of the table grows, lookups may take longer because it could require sorting through a greater number of records. This design also restricts the shop from entering more than two vehicles for each client. If a client has three vehicles, another name will need to be created before registering the vehicle:

Clients *

- Client_ID
- Client_FirstName
- Client_LastName
- Client_Phone
- Client_Address
- Client_City
- Client_State
- Client_Zip
- Client_Discount_Code
- Client_Discount_Description
- Client_Discount_Amount
- Vehicle_1_VIN
- Vehicle_1_Make
- Vehicle_1_Model
- Vehicle_1_LastServiceDate
- Vehicle_2_VIN
- Vehicle_2_Make
- Vehicle_2_Model
- Vehicle_2_LastServiceDate

The inadvertent use of repeating groups is a mistake that is usually made by newer database developers who are used to storing information in a spreadsheet, such as Microsoft Excel. Don't worry though; this mistake can easily be resolved. In the next few steps, we'll work to make this small database efficient and effective.

First Normal Form: No Repeating Groups

The first step in the normalization process is to break the repeating groups out into a new table. Not only does it make the storage space more efficient, but it also allows for an infinite number of vehicles.

> **To achieve the first normal form, we remove any repeating groups by giving each logical group a separate table and providing a primary key in each.**

The `ClientID` is the primary key in the `Clients` table and is marked with a key symbol. The `ClientID` uniquely identifies each client, the details for which are held in the other fields of the `Clients` table. The `ClientID` is the foreign key in the `Vehicles` table; every record in the `Vehicles` table must be associated with a client. `Vehicle_VIN` is the primary key in `Vehicles` and uniquely identifies each vehicle held in the `Vehicles` table. When a new user arrives, the shop registers the client in the `Clients` table and adds a new record to the `Vehicles` table for every vehicle that the client owns. A one-to-many relationship exists between the two tables in that each client may have multiple vehicles:

Clients		Vehicles
Client_ID		Client_ID
Client_FirstName		Vehicle_VIN
Client_LastName		Vehicle_Make
Client_Phone		Vehicle_Model
Client_Address		Vehicle_LastServiceDate
Client_City		
Client_State		
Client_Zip		
Client_Discount_Code		
Client_Discount_Description		
Client_Discount_Amount		

Second Normal Form: Non-Key Fields Must Be Dependent on the Primary Key

The model has been improved by ensuring that it meets the first normal form, but notice that there are a few problems:

> ➢ For each visit, the user must either write over the existing service date, or create a new record. If you create a new record, you now have repeating information.

> ➢ This model doesn't accommodate a log of all visits made by the client or by the vehicle.

The first alteration we need to make is to change the Vehicle_LastServiceDate field to Visit_ServiceDate as we will now be keeping a log of all visits. Now we have a non-key field that is not dependent on the primary key of the Vehicles table. The Visit_ServiceDate field merely records the date of a visit by a client with a vehicle and it not dependent upon a vehicle's identification number (held in Vehicle_VIN).

> **To achieve the second normal form, non-key fields must depend on all fields in the primary key.**

We need to break out the Vehicles table into a new Vehicles table and a Visit table. We assign the Vehicle_VIN as the primary key of the Vehicles table and make it a foreign key in the Visit table. Each visit will be held as a separate record and given a unique id (Visit_ID). The shop can then query the database to track all of the previous visits of any particular auto or customer.

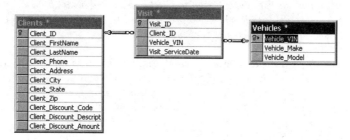

Third Normal Form: No Columns Depend on other Non-Key Columns

Look at the `Discount` codes. `Discount_Description` and `Discount_Amount` rely on the `Discount_Code`. For each new record added, the `Description` and `Amount` are added to the `Clients` table, causing extra data entry and possible errors. For example, we may have two different clients, where each has a discount code of "RPT1". However, due to an error during the data-entry process, the two clients have completely different discount descriptions and amounts. If we ensure that our database attains the third normal form, we will prevent the assignment of different values and/or descriptions to the same discount code.

> **To achieve the third normal form no fields should depend on other non-key fields.**

To resolve this, we can break the two fields dependent on the `Discount_Code` into another table. We then have a table of all the available discounts, which may apply to frequent clients. When a new customer is added, you simply need to specify the `Discount_Code`, not the description or amount.

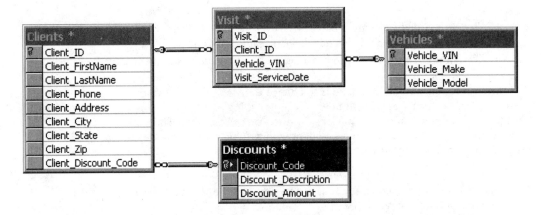

The above scheme could be broken down further. The `Vehicles` *table, for example, could be broken down so that it contains a* `Vehicle_VIN` *and a* `Vehicle_ID`, *where* `Vehicle_VIN` *still identifies a particular client's vehicle but* `Vehicle_ID` *identifies a particular make and model of vehicle. A separate table would then contain the* `Vehicle_ID`, `Vehicle_Make` *and* `Vehicle_Model` *fields. This would not only make the* `Vehicles` *table smaller and allow the data entry person to select a make and model from a drop down box, but would give Joe's Speedy Auto Repair Shop the opportunity to study what percentage of their business comes from different makes/models of cars.*

We now have a fully normalized database. Normalizing databases is really quite simple. Once you understand the basic design of relational databases, you'll find yourself normalizing them without even realizing. Although as your database scheme becomes more complex, you may consider using a tool to assist in normalizing. These tools offer a more formalized decomposition algorithm to achieve normal forms.

However, it is possible to take normalization too far by strictly following the above stated rules. As an example, you could normalize customer addresses, allowing a single customer to have multiple addresses and then normalize the zip code to contain city and state information. Finally, you could create a table of state mnemonics with their appropriate state name. The point here is that you should look at the database structure with common sense. Is it cost (or time) effective to create a table of all zip codes in the United States for the purposes of lookups? If you're a multi-million dollar outfit, the answer may be yes, but if you're a small shop then it may not.

Speed of data acquisition is another reason why you may not want to normalize some data. There is a relationship between normalization and performance. If you have your data broken out into too many tables, it could require so many joins that it actually hinders performance. Three things to consider when normalizing include:

> How large the tables will be
> How often they will be accessed
> How large the recordsets will be

Always remember to walk through these above normalization steps every time you create or modify a database. Database design is just as important as the design of the client application, which will connect into the database.

Database Indexes

Indexes play a very important role in the world of relational databases. Typically, indexes are used to improve query lookup times. An index is an object that contains a list of specific values that can be found in one or more fields of a table. These index objects are stored on the local database, but are not maintained by the user. You may change many available options of an index. The RDBMS, however, is responsible for allocating space and structuring the index.

The next few sections of this chapter will discuss what indexes are, how they work and how to create them. In larger organizations, a Database Administrator (DBA) will probably create the database for you. In smaller organizations the Application Engineer and DBA may be the same person. Regardless of whether there's a specialist DBA, it's always important to understand the structure of indexes. As the Software Engineer, you are privy to the information that dictates how the data will be retrieved and which fields are truly key to the table structure. For this reason, you should pride yourself in assisting in the creation of all indexes. Don't take indexes lightly. The larger the table, the more important the index is to the successful rollout of your project. You should also know when *not* to add an index to a field. By adding too many indexes to a table, you can actually hurt performance. In the next few sections, we'll look at when you should index a field.

Unique and Non-Unique Indexes

When creating an index, you will be prompted to select whether the data in the field will be unique or non-unique. When you specify that the data field will be unique, the index object will be checked each time a new record is added to the table. If an individual attempts to enter a value that already exists in the indexed field, the data the user is attempting to insert will be rejected and the user will

be prompted to change the value. The figure opposite identifies an error message that you might receive using Microsoft Access (note that each database will return variations of the message):

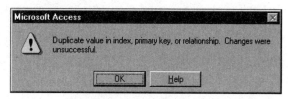

Indexes are also used to enhance the speed of lookups in tables. For example, say we have a table that contains the names and addresses of customers; we may want to locate all customers from a specific country. Because we were clever enough to create an index on the field titled `Country`, the computer will be able to quickly return the records where the `Country` field is equal to the value stated in our query.

Let's walk through an example. The following image depicts a table with customer information. This table can contain an unlimited number of customers, so it would be wise to index any fields that would be critical in returning a specified record from a query:

When an index is added to the `Country` field, a new object is created which stores a list of all countries with corresponding pointers to the records. This list is maintained by the RDBMS, so don't bother trying to find it. Here's what an index object might look like if you were able to view it:

Index Data	Row Pointer
France	7
France	9
France	23
France	45
France	79
Germany	1
Germany	6

Here you can see that there are multiple occurrences of the country France, which can be found in rows 7, 9, 23, 45 and 79 of the table. When a user executes a query, specifying all records that have a country of `France`, the RDBMS will automatically check for the existence of an index on the specified field, and use the index to return the records that meet the criterion.

> **If more than one index exists that references a given field, the database will choose to use one index over the other. While the database usually will choose the correct index, there are times that the database may choose the index that has lesser performance advantages. To avoid this problem, be cautious of creating more than one index on any single field.**

For example, if we execute a query against the `Customers` table, the following logic will be followed:

1. Check to see if any indexes exist for the fields that identify any search criteria.
2. If an index exists, open the list and locate the first occurrence of the country.
3. Using the pointer, retrieve the record identified.
4. Search for the next pointer and retrieve the associated record.
5. Continue the loop until all records have been retrieved.

The query results in the following screen:

The final result of the query will be the same as if we hadn't used an index, but the query will be executed much more quickly. On smaller tables you may not notice much of a difference. This is because smaller tables can easily be searched without the overhead of using the index. On larger tables you may be pleasantly surprised by the difference in time.

The time saved when using indexes comes from the database's ability to scan a header page (or pages) that identify where the data can be located. This is similar to the index of this book. If for example you want to locate all pages in this book that deal with SQL Server, you'll move directly to the index and find a listing of all pages which deal with the subject. You can then review each page directly until you find the record you want. As we'll discover in the next section, many databases use the B-Tree structure, which sets the index on data pages (similar to a header) and identifies the pages where the index can be found by use of pointers. The increased speed of your application is certainly worth the short amount of time it takes to build an index. Once the index is created, there's nothing else a programmer has to do. In fact, from the programmer's point of view, once the indexes are built, queries are programmed in the same way as if there were no index at all.

There are some restrictions that you must know about before building an index.

> Depending on the RDBMS, there may be a limit to the number of fields that can be indexed in a single table. Keep in mind that too many indexes can decrease the performance of table lookups and inserts.

> Indexes can only be built for tables. We'll cover views in more detail later, but for now, you should know that views are virtual tables linked to your data tables, that hide complex lookups from users while providing additional security. Indexes cannot be built for views. Plan ahead and assign indexes to the appropriate tables that the view will be calling.

> Indexes should not contain a null value. This may make a big difference to your design. Remember, if you index a field, the user will be *required* to fill in the field when entering data.

Avoid indexing fields that have large amounts of data. Don't forget the data in the indexed field will be stored in the index table as well. This can make lookups inefficient and waste valuable storage space.

B-Tree Indexes

Database servers (including SQL Server) create indexes in a **B-Tree** structure. With this structure, all tables and indexes are stored on **pages**. Each page will hold a specified number of data bytes, so the number of pages used is equal to the amount of data you store divided by how much data is stored on each page. You can manually change the amount of data stored on each page to allow for inserts after roll out to production.

> *Not all databases have the same page size. SQL Server 6.5 uses a page size of just over 2KB, while DB2 uses one of just over 4KB and SQL Server 7 uses 8KB.*

The B-Tree structure is not very different to what we have already discussed regarding indexes. There are three parts to the B-Tree structure - the root, the intermediary levels and the leaf:

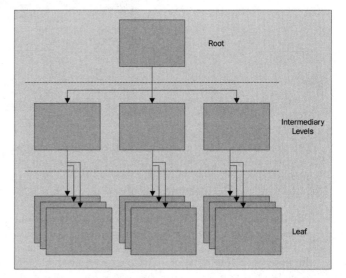

Each of the levels plays a very specific role in the structure:

> ➤ The **root** is where our SQL statements first enter the index. If we're looking for all records where the Country field is France, we can search the root for a record indicating the page of the next level where those records can be found.

> ➤ There may be zero or many **intermediary levels** created for each index. As our indexes grow in complexity, these intermediary levels are used to pinpoint our data records with the least amount of searching. As an analogy, let's look at the Zip Code system in the United States. Each of the five digits in the number zeros in on the city in which it belongs. The first character identifies a broad region in the US. The next digit identifies a central processing center within the region. We continue through the numbers until we reach the last digit, which represents the post office in a specific city. In a similar fashion relating to indexes, the root will point to an intermediary level where the results are refined until you reach the final intermediary level, which points to the leaf.

> ➤ The **leaf** is the final section of the index with which the engine deals. This section contains the page and row number of each record that you're looking for. The engine can then retrieve the record directly from the specified location.

Don't worry if this sounds confusing, we still have more to cover!

Clustered Indexes

Now that you understand the B-Tree structure, we can discuss **clustered indexes**. Clustered indexes follow the B-Tree structure. The table data is stored at the leaf level of the index and when the index is created, all data is removed from the data table and sorted on the indexed field (in the sort order specified). The structure of these indexes is fairly flat, making lookups very efficient. When we specify that we're looking for all records where the Country is equal to France, the root is scanned for the appropriate pointer. In the following example, the Country field of France points to page 7, row 5. Once the pointer tells the database engine what page and row the data begins at, it can then begin at that location, and retrieve all records until all records meeting the criterion have been located. We only need to know the location of the first record in this case because the data is sorted and stored in logical order. Very minimal scanning is done with clustered indexes because the database engine is brought directly to the first record. All other records that meet the criterion will follow the first, allowing the engine to retrieve the records from the top down.

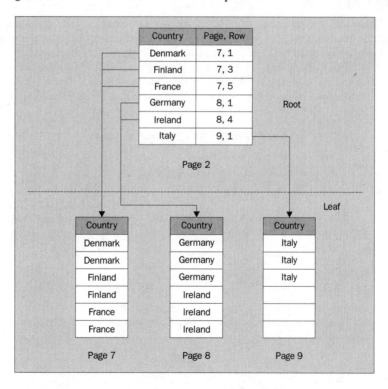

Not all databases implement clustered indexes in the same manner. This example follows SQL Server quite closely, but may not necessarily follow Microsoft Access or Oracle.

What you need to know about clustered indexes:

- ➢ You may only create one clustered index per table. Remember that the data is actually stored in the index and in the order specified (such as ascending).
- ➢ Clustered indexes require more physical space because they reorder the data in the logical order of the index and contain pointers to those fields.

As data is inserted and deleted from the database table, the clustered index may become less effective (causing a loss of speed) until the data is reorganized.

You should use a clustered index when:

- ➢ Speed is an issue and the indexed field is frequently used in lookups.
- ➢ Your SQL statements include ORDER BY, GROUP BY or table JOINs on the indexed field. We'll discuss SQL fully in Chapter 6.
- ➢ The field will be used to find ranges of data.
- ➢ You expect a large number of records to be returned in your queries.

Non-Clustered Indexes

Non-clustered indexes don't store, or even sort the table data; rather, they contain a sorted list with pointers for each indexed field. The root of the non-clustered index points to the page and row where these pointers can be located. When searching for all fields where the Country is equal to Denmark, the root would point to page 7, row 1. On page 7, the engine will find pointers to all records with a value of Denmark in the Country field, starting with the first record. The engine will retrieve the record from page 23, row 2, then continue down the list until all records meeting the criterion have been exhausted.

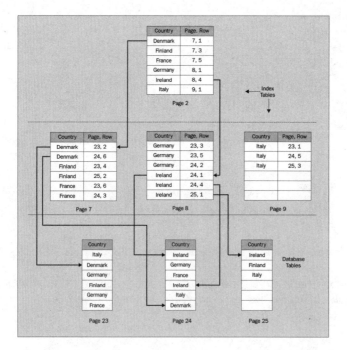

What you need to know about non-clustered indexes:

> ➢ You may have as many non-clustered indexes as the database server will allow, but performance may slip as you add more. Typically, three to four non-clustered indexes will be more than sufficient.
> ➢ Try to avoid using more than four fields in a single index. Adding more than this may cause a crunch in performance.
> ➢ Avoid indexing fields that contain more then 750-800 bytes (combined) in size. This is a judgment call, but larger fields destroy performance very quickly.
> ➢ These structures are usually much more vertical, causing reduced performance over a clustered index. A non-clustered index is still much faster than not establishing an index at all.

You should use a non-clustered index when:

> ➢ The clustered index has already been chosen.
> ➢ The field is a foreign key.
> ➢ Queries are expected to return small recordsets. For example, you might use a non-clustered index on a field such as Country, where you only want records returned with a country of France. You wouldn't want to index a field such as Gender because it consists of half the database and there is no speed advantage of using an index.

Creating Indexes

Let's now take a closer look at indexes created in Microsoft Access and SQL Server. You should first note that indexes stored in Access aren't quite as sophisticated as those in SQL Server or Oracle, but they do provide a great mechanism for speeding up your queries. The same rules that we covered earlier apply when designing an indexed field, regardless of whether it is created in Access or in any other RDBMS.

The following illustration shows all indexes for an Access table entitled Customers. To view the indexes of any Access table, first open the table in design mode, then select View from the menu and choose Indexes. Each indexed field is assigned a name, which may or may not be identical to the actual field name on which the index resides. Notice that we're given the opportunity to store the values of an index in ascending or descending order. For example, if we wanted a date field in descending order, we could speed up our query by sorting the index in descending order. Finally, notice that we're given the option of deciding if the index is a primary key, if it's unique and whether null values are acceptable:

> **Access is a bit more flexible when it comes to null values than most databases. However, as a practice, you should never allow null values on an indexed field.**

SQL Server is a bit more powerful than Access, providing greater sorting algorithms and therefore more configuration detail. Open the SQL Server's Enterprise Manager (via **Start | Programs | Microsoft SQL Server 7.0 | Enterprise Manager**), select the database that contains the table you are interested in and double-click on **Tables**. Right-click on the table for which you want to view the indexes and select **A̲ll Tasks | Manage Indexes** from the menu bar, and the **Manage Indexes** dialog will appear:

The **Manage Indexes** dialog allows us to create new indexes or modify existing ones. Notice that one of the conveniences of this tool is that it will allow us to view indexes for a selected table, in this case `Employees`. This dialog merely displays the table and database that we are currently viewing and the existing indexes in this table. We can view the name of the index, whether or not it is clustered and what fields it contains.

If we want to edit an index, we select it from the table and click on Edit:

The features of this dialog include:

> A list of all the fields in the table presented in the list box below the table name. Note that you can change the field order by clicking on the Move Up and Move Down buttons.

> The ability to select whether the index will be unique, if it will be clustered, and whether it should ignore duplicate values.

> A Fill factor check box and list box. This specifies how full SQL Server should make each index page. The amount of empty space on an index page is important because when an index page is full, the system must take time to split the page to make room for new rows. The number is represented in the form of a percentage, where a low percentage translates to more pages created and fewer records existing on each page. More pages translate to more room for new records and less time processing. Of course, the trade off here is a higher requirement for disk space. When changing the fill factor, consider how much data is to be entered or updated in the table. The greater the number of transactions, the lower the fill factor should be.

I hope that by this point, you have a pretty good idea of when you should create an index, but here are a few pointers to help you understand when you *shouldn't* create an index:

> Never index small tables. When you index smaller tables (meaning few records), the time to process a query through the index may actually take longer than without the index. A table that fits this criterion might include a 'supporting' table, with data such as state lookup codes. This is not an issue with many databases, as they have query optimizers that would identify if the index should be used or not.

> Never index a field that has a small number of possible values. If a field only has two possible values, the index becomes inefficient. A Boolean (Yes/No) field, for example, does not need to be indexed.

> Don't declare an index on a field instead of declaring a primary key. Each table should have its own primary key. If a table doesn't have a field that is unique, add an auto-number (counter), and make this field the primary key.

Five Steps to Building a Powerful Database

In the following section, we discuss the five steps that you should take each and every time you build a database from scratch. These steps will take you from the very beginning (when you must consider what sort of information should be held in the database) to the end of the process (when it becomes necessary to test the database fully with sample data). If you follow these steps, your database should not only be well-designed but it will also contain all of the information you require.

Step 1: Brainstorming

In this phase, your only mission is to generate a list of every possible field that may need to be included in your database. Don't focus too much on the tables to which these fields will belong. For your first pass, consider what you are trying to accomplish. For example, if you have a simple sales database, you may have three major groups: Customers, Products and Sales. Let's consider the Customer group. Relevant fields would include: Name, Address, City, State, Zip_Code and Phone_Number. Similarly, Products fields could include: Description, Price, Quantity_In_Stock, and ReorderPoint. When we sell a product, we will need to store the following information: All Customer Information, All Product Information, Quantity, and OrderDate.

During the following phases, you may find that there are several other fields that need to be added. It's important to recognize these fields as early as possible if you want to avoid the possibility of having to totally restructure your database, at a later date.

To avoid missing any fields, here are some tips:

> Get as many colleagues involved as possible. This may include other programmers and even the end users of the system. Keep in mind that too many users may cause disruption, especially if they don't understand the development process. One method of ensuring all fields are accounted for is to hold meetings and encourage everyone to participate in identifying fields that may be required. Initially, it is best to include every conceivable field - you can always discard the fields you don't need later. A classic problem in these types of meeting is that project functionality and screen design tend to drive the definition of the required fields. It's generally better to identify the data elements first and then move to the process of designing screens. Building pretty forms does you no good without a solid database to back it.

> ➢ Generate possible reports that will be created by the interface. If the field doesn't exist, it can't appear on a report, right? This is one of the first things to look for when building a database. In the following image, for example, several key fields have been identified on the report. After adding the fields to your list, you can be confident that you can recreate the report:

Customer Orders

Customer ID	Company Name	Contact Name	Contact Title	Address					
ALFKI									
	Alfreds Futterkiste	Maria Anders	Sales Repres	Obere Str. 57				Berlin	
	10643	Suyama, Michael	25-Sep-95	23-Oct-95	03-Oct-95	Speedy Express			£29.46
	10952	Davolio, Nancy	15-Apr-96	27-May-96	23-Apr-96	Speedy Express			£40.42
	10692	Peacock, Margaret	03-Nov-95	01-Dec-95	13-Nov-95	United Package			£61.02
	10835	Davolio, Nancy	15-Feb-96	14-Mar-96	21-Feb-96	Federal Shipping			£69.53
	11011	Leverling, Janet	09-May-96	06-Jun-96	13-May-96	Speedy Express			£1.21
	10702	Peacock, Margaret	13-Nov-95	25-Dec-95	21-Nov-95	Speedy Express			£23.94
ANATR									
	Ana Trujillo Empareda	Ana Trujillo	Owner	Avda. de la Constitució			México		
	10759	Leverling, Janet	29-Dec-95	26-Jan-96	12-Jan-96	Federal Shipping			£11.99
	10926	Peacock, Margaret	03-Apr-96	01-May-96	10-Apr-96	Federal Shipping			£39.92
	10308	King, Robert	19-Oct-94	16-Nov-94	25-Oct-94	Federal Shipping			£1.61
	10625	Leverling, Janet	08-Sep-95	06-Oct-95	14-Sep-95	Speedy Express			£43.90

This phase may also include selecting the data types of each field. Selecting data types isn't always as easy as you might expect. When I came to SQL Server after using Access, I was surprised to see how many different data types were available. I have included a listing of the data types in Appendix I to help you make your choice. The best advice I can provide you with is: choose the data type that allows for the smallest storage space (taking into consideration growth potential of the field). Lastly, always test the fields with plenty of sample data. You can learn a great deal about your data by doing this. You'll know immediately when you attempt to populate data into a field that is too small, or one that does not allow for a numeric field that is out of the acceptable range.

Step 2: Group the Fields

Once you have a list of fields, you'll next need to group them logically. In smaller databases, this is very simple. However, in more complex databases, you may feel overwhelmed by the number of fields you're working with. Start with the familiar. If you can group the Employee fields together for example, you have just dealt with a chunk of the fields. These groups should evolve into tables as you follow this step. These tables will be connected by relationships, so we need to think about which fields will play the role of a primary key and where the foreign key will exist on the connecting tables:

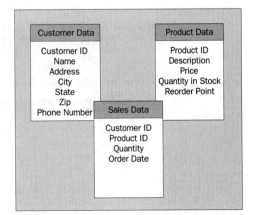

The product and customer groups each have a field that is suitable for a primary key (`ProductID` and `CustomerID`), however, the Sale Data grouping will need a primary key. We could have used a combination of `CustomerID` and `OrderDate`, but it is possible that a single customer could place more than one order each day. For this reason, we should add a new field called `SaleID`. This will be the primary key for the Sale Data table.

Step 3: Build Relationships

In this phase, we'll want to build the relationships that will exist between our tables. We did some pre-planning in the previous step and this phase should establish a fairly concrete data model for our database. At this point, it matters very little whether you complete this phase on paper, or in the actual database. The important point is that you need a visual model to keep track of the relationships. If your database server doesn't have a graphical interface for viewing the tables and relationships, I would suggest that you first design the model on paper, or on an appropriate software package, such as ERWin or my personal favorite, VISIO.

Once you have created a database, you may find that you want to document the definitions of the database tables. Documentation comes in very handy for meetings, and saves a lot of time when the time comes to write your specifications. There are a lot of tools available to assist in documenting the table definitions, but I have found that one of the easiest to use is Database Documenter, which is supplied with Microsoft Access. To use the Database Documenter, open a database in Access, then select Tools | Analyze | Documenter from the menu bar.

> While the Documenter is available with all releases of Microsoft Access, it may not install by default.

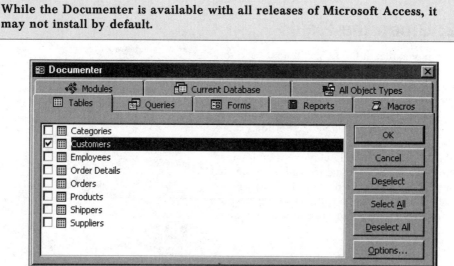

You will be prompted to decide what pieces of information you want to include in the document. You're given the option to add just about everything in the definition of the tables. However, you may find that your document grows large very quickly when you select all of them. To open the Print Table Definition dialog click on the Options button:

Once you finish selecting your options, the document will be created. You can print the document, or export it to Word:

Step 4: Normalize Your Database

Step 4 can be a simple process, or a time-consuming process. If you don't have experience building relational databases, make sure the normalization rules are fresh in your mind before you begin building the tables. This way you'll find that your design technique is much stronger, and less time will be spent attempting to normalize a database that has already been created.

> **Always take the time to review your database for normalization, ensuring that no fields are being unnecessarily duplicated. As you'll discover when we discuss Data Warehouses, there are some instances when you may not want your database completely normalized.**

When normalizing tables, it's common practice to create code tables. These can be used to reduce the amount of storage space required by tables that contain a huge number of records. A simple table may include as little as two fields, with two records:

Code	Value
0	Male
1	Female

If we have an `Employees` table, we can have a field where the data type has been declared as a `bit` (to contain the code), versus a `char` field that contains the actual word (Male or Female). For each employee added, we may save several bytes. For a large number of employees this equates to a significant saving in storage space.

The `Employees` table will have a field containing the data that will relate to the gender code table. When we want to generate reports, the RDBMS will replace the code (0 or 1) with the value (Male or Female).

Step 5: Test the Structure with Sample Data

OK, so you've made it to Step 5 but don't get lazy here. You're well on your way to building a powerful database but testing your database structure with sample data is a critical final step. Before you begin to build your client application, add as much data as you can to the tables to test the structure. If time permits, try building a few queries to see if the data that you expected to retrieve is being returned. Not only will this test your relationships and the structure in general, you'll also get some practice building SQL statements. It's highly likely that you will need this test data later when testing the finished client application. So a little extra work now will save you considerable time further down the road.

> **Another benefit of adding data to your tables is that the field definitions such as length, data type and null/not null will also be tested.**

Summary

This chapter has provided a brief glimpse of the world of the database administrator responsible for the creation of databases. I have only been able to scratch the surface of this topic, but you should find that the detail provided here is sufficient for your needs. If you ever need to take a much closer look at database design, then browse through one of the multitude of computer science books that cover this topic.

In particular, we looked at:

> ➢ How to achieve the first, second and third normal form
> ➢ What a B-Tree index is
> ➢ The difference between clustered and non-clustered indexes and when to use them
> ➢ The five steps in building a well-designed, powerful database

Suppliers

- SupplierID
- CompanyName
- ContactName
- ContactTitle
- Address
- City
- Region
- PostalCode
- Country
- Phone
- Fax
- HomePage

Products

- ProductID
- ProductName
- SupplierID
- CategoryID
- QuantityPerUnit
- UnitPrice
- UnitsInStock
- UnitsOnOrder
- ReorderLevel
- Discontinued

Categories

- CategoryID
- CategoryName
- Description
- Picture

6

A Guide to Data Access

As new acronyms arrive on what seems like a daily basis, it's easy to get bogged down in new terminology and the technology they describe. This seems particularly true in the world of database programming and data access technology, where such acronyms as ODBC, OLE DB, ADO, RDO, DAO and UDA abound.

First, let's just expand these acronyms to see what it is we're talking about:

- ➤ **ODBC**. Open DataBase Connectivity
- ➤ **OLE DB**. Object Linking and Embedding for Databases
- ➤ **ADO**. ActiveX Data Objects
- ➤ **DAO**. Data Access Objects
- ➤ **RDO**. Remote Data Objects
- ➤ **UDA**. Universal Data Access

That's all very nice, but what exactly are these technologies? Are they related in any way? Where can they be found? How do we use them? Which is the best to use?

These are the questions we're going to try to answer in this chapter.

An Overview of Data Access Technologies

Before we consider data access technologies, we need to understand fully what 'data' itself is. The dictionary definition of data is:

- ➤ A series of observations, measurements or facts; information.
- ➤ Also called information. Computers: the information operated on by a computer program.

And for a 'database', the dictionary provides this definition:

> ➤ A store of a large amount of information especially in a form that can be handled by a computer.

The dictionary definition sees data as needing a "form" that can be handled by a computer. What if that "form" is not quite so structured and rigid as we might expect. What if the data is simply not visible or viewable and the actual structure of the data is unknown to us?

Consider the following examples:

> ➤ Raw data taken directly from a text file.
> ➤ Data formatted for direct access by a proprietary programming language or desktop database such as Microsoft Access, Microsoft Visual Basic or Microsoft Visual FoxPro.
> ➤ Data residing in a proprietary back-end database such as Oracle or Microsoft SQL Server.
> ➤ Data formatted for access by applications such as Microsoft Excel, Microsoft Outlook and a vast host of others.

Most of us, at some point, need to access data from one source using the access technology of another. For instance, you may have just spent hours producing a Microsoft Visual Basic application that calculates time sheet data to monitor hours worked by groups of people in your organization. This works fine, but then your boss tells you that someone else already collects the data and enters the data into a spreadsheet such as Microsoft Excel.

There are several possible ways of converting that Excel data into a format which your application can use. You could, for example:

> ➤ Export the Excel data into a raw ASCII file and then import it as ASCII into your application.
> ➤ Write code to access the Excel data file directly. You could achieve this in a variety of ways, including using Visual Basic or Visual Basic for Applications (VBA) and OLE (Object Linking and Embedding) Automation to manipulate the Excel data directly from within the application.
> ➤ Use a data access technology that is common to both the application and the Excel data.

One disadvantage with the first option is that you will constantly need to run the Excel application and run the menu options to export the comma-delimited data. Another is that you may not have access to the application itself.

OLE Automation is powerful and widely used, but perhaps suits the manipulation and retrieval of small amounts of flat-file data better than it would the retrieval of large volumes of relational data. For example, OLE would be great for getting an application to open up an Office application such as Excel and making it automatically load the contents of an ASCII file produced in a Visual Basic application. OLE could then get Excel to display a floating toolbar giving the user a simple button that returns them to the application.

For more information on using OLE Automation with Visual Basic, see VB COM: A Visual Basic Programmer's Introduction to COM from Wrox Press, ISBN 1-1861002-13-0.

Option three, however, offers a bewildering choice. Which data access technology do we use? Where can we find these technologies? To try to answer these questions, we'll look at these technologies in turn, working our way back in time from the very latest thinking, Universal Data Access (UDA), right along the timeline to ADO, DAO, RDO, ODBC and ODBCDirect. So let's start with Universal Data Access and we'll see the relationship between the better-known technologies.

Universal Data Access

Let's start from first principles. In the complex world of working with data we deal with the following types of data sources (amongst others):

> Traditional database applications.

> Workflow type applications making use of message stores in Microsoft Exchange or Lotus Notes.

> A program that manipulates the file system by looking at directory and file structures.

> A desktop application that uses one of the Office object models to manipulate data in an Excel spreadsheet or perhaps a Word document.

> A communications program that identifies all users currently logged onto a network.

These applications will all need data that can be represented in tabular format but notice that each one provides a different interface for manipulating that data.

Wouldn't it be great if we had a generalized or universal recordset structure that allowed us to use the same code to work with each of the above structures? Imagine little or no loss of performance when compared to native access and the ability to join data from any or all of the above data sources with a simple SQL statement.

Microsoft would like us to start thinking in terms of this Universal Data Access (UDA).

> **Universal Data Access is the Microsoft Strategy for providing access to information across the enterprise. Through OLE DB and ADO, Universal Data Access provides high performance access to a variety of relational and non-relational data sources. It does this using an easy to use programming interface. This interface is independent of the programming language.**

There are other reasons why we need a model of data access that is common to many applications. It's particularly important for corporate and distributed software development. Most enterprises store their data in different media and on different platforms. This data could also be of different types: spreadsheet data, email or text files, as well as data in relational database tables.

In good software design you'll need at least two layers of code to access this data. There are a number of reasons for this:

> Single-tiered applications access the base tables on a server and in many cases treat the intelligent server as if it were a common file-based database server. This means that data is fetched directly, using hard-coded queries and references to the underlying database structure. Also, single-tiered applications rely on the use of updatable recordsets to update back-end database tables which prohibit the use of stored procedures.

> ➤ Single-tiered applications can generate tremendous network traffic unless queries explicitly limit the amount of data that can be returned by the database. Such an application may work well with a few users but can in fact degrade the stability of the network and the application when the number of users increases.

> ➤ Single-tiered applications are usually coded using intimate knowledge of the underlying data structure. When this structure changes it usually requires the re-coding and rebuilding of the entire application.

The following figure shows the architecture of an application which uses a common data access layer. The client application communicates with this layer, which in turn communicates with the appropriate data store through a driver designed specifically for that store:

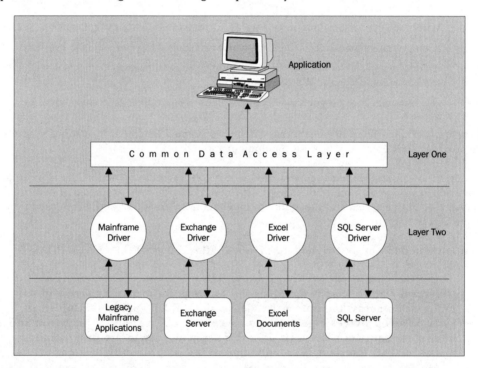

Why is this structure so important to Microsoft? It's because UDA is tightly integrated with Microsoft Windows Distributed interNet Applications or DNA.

> **DNA is a software roadmap. It's designed to help developers, technology planners and Information Systems managers avoid getting lost in the jungle of new technologies, tools, operating systems and applications. DNA is a conceptual model, an architecture, which is aimed at simplifying Microsoft's message to developers.**

There are many benefits to be gained by using a common access layer as in the figure above:

> ➤ A greatly reduced number of technologies that you, as the programmer, will need expertise in.

> ➤ It's part of a standard architecture for distributed applications and this means scalability. When you need to scale up or upsize it becomes much less of an issue.
> ➤ It's free, and it's already been written and tested.
> ➤ Because of the push for UDA from Microsoft, it will have good third party support.
> ➤ UDA works particularly well with **multidimensional data**, which is used in data warehousing applications. This helps us build decision-support functionality into our applications.

> **A multidimensional data structure is a database paradigm that treats data not as relational tables and columns, but as information cubes that contain dimension and summary data in cells, each addressed by a set of coordinates that specify a position in the structure's dimensions. For example, a cell at coordinates** {SALES, 1997, WASHINGTON, SOFTWARE} **would contain the summary of sales of software in Washington in 1997.**

But what is our common access layer? It represents the essence of UDA. UDA uses OLE DB to provide unified data access and manipulation.

OLE DB

OLE DB is the universal glue that UDA relies on. OLE DB is a set of COM-based programming interfaces that allow transparent data access, but in such a way that the client applications don't know or need to know what kind of data they are connected to. So Universal Data Access is the goal that Microsoft hopes OLE DB will help them reach.

In some respects OLE DB is similar to the earlier ODBC technology (we will be looking at this later in the chapter), in that the remote data is opened up to the calling client application, but there is a very important difference: the great advantage of OLE DB is that it exposes the remote data through the Component Object Model (COM). This means that there is little restriction on how the data can be fetched and manipulated, because OLE DB providers can expose interfaces that offer as much or as little functionality as the provider sees fit for the purpose. For instance, it may be felt inappropriate to offer advanced SQL functionality for Exchange Server email data.

> **The Component Object Model (COM) is Microsoft's standard for object interaction. It provides a standard mechanism by which objects can communicate regardless of what language is used to create the components. There are two major Windows technologies that rely on COM to function. These are Object Linking and Embedding (OLE) and ActiveX. Both technologies use COM to facilitate the interaction between objects. OLE uses COM to communicate between applications, allowing users to link or embed parts of one application's data and display it in another. ActiveX has a wider brief. ActiveX uses COM to communicate between controls (i.e. ActiveX controls such as Microsoft's calendar control) and components.**

The OLE DB architecture is composed of two entities: **providers** and **consumers**. Let's look at these in more detail.

Chapter 3

OLE DB Providers

OLE DB providers form the underlying structure of OLE DB. These are COM components which are built upon a native data format (that is, the format used for data by the data store itself) and their purpose is to abstract the data from the data store. They break down or reduce the native data into a stream, which can be accessed using standard interfaces.

There are currently providers available for a number of data sources, such as SQL Server, Microsoft Exchange and legacy mainframe data. Relational data is also accessible using an OLE DB provider for data sources available through ODBC; this could be considered a kind of hybrid. Microsoft has helped itself here in that it has encouraged the implementation of OLE DB via the ODBC provider (this is in fact the default provider). Since many applications already have ODBC access to remote data, switching to an OLE DB implementation (using the ODBC provider) is a relatively straightforward affair.

So OLE DB is a COM server (that is, compiled code consisting of COM components which are used by a client object) which implements a specific set of interfaces to disparate data sources. Let's just see how providers fit into the general picture of UDA and COM.

There are three objects that each OLE DB provider (an existing provider or any provider you may write) must implement. In addition, there are a number of other objects that an OLE DB provider may expose. The following figure represents the most important of the objects exposed by OLE DB.

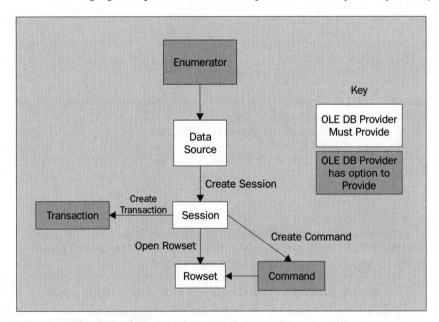

Let's have a look at these objects in a bit more detail.

> ➤ **Enumerator (Optional).** This is an object that lists the `DataSource` objects available to your machine. OLE DB provides a component (named the **Data Links Component**) to manage connections between consumers and providers, and normally OLE DB consumers would use this component to select a data source and set initialization properties. If enumerators are used instead of the Data Links component (which references the Windows registry) then OLE DB consumers will continue to work even if the registry information changes.

> ➤ **DataSource (Required)**. `DataSource` objects contain the machinery to connect to a data source, such as a file or a DBMS. They act as factories for sessions.

> ➤ **Session (Required)**. `Session` objects are used to create transactions, commands, and rowsets. Every `DataSource` object can have more than one `Session` object. Sessions also provide support for transactions (a way of grouping together several operations against a database into a single operation) .

> ➤ **Transaction (Optional)**. `Transaction` objects are used for any nested transactions above the lowest level; that is, for transactions which are included within other transactions. Transactions at the lowest level are managed by the `Session` object.

> ➤ **Command (Optional)**. `Command` objects are used to execute a text query, such as a SQL statement. If the command specifies a rowset, such as a SQL `SELECT` statement, the command is a factory for the rowset. A single `Session` object can have multiple dependent `Command` objects.

> ➤ **Rowset (Required)**. The `Rowset` object exposes data from the data source as a table; rowsets can be created from the `Session` or `Command` objects.

> ➤ **Error (Optional)**. `Error` objects can be created by any interface on any OLE DB object. They provide information about any errors which occur.

The minimum requirement for all OLE DB providers is that they must expose `DataSource`, `Session` and `Rowset` objects; providers have the option to expose the other objects, but are not required to do so.

The following figure illustrates the relationship between the main OLE DB objects:

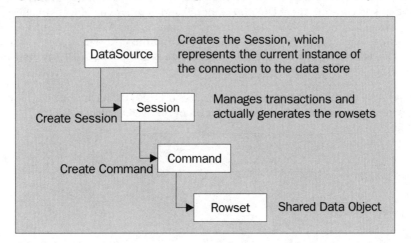

OLE DB Consumers

An OLE DB data consumer is any piece of system or application code that needs access to a wide range of data. This includes tools, languages and personal productivity tools.

Consumers, then, are components that provide or expose a common interface for accessing your data. This interface is independent of the OLE DB provider. You can think of an interface as a set of functions.

Remember the `Rowset` object that the provider *must* implement? The consumer obtains data in a tabular format from this rowset object. You can also think of the rowset as a resultset if you like: a set of data returned as the result of a query against the database. It can execute any command which is supported by the provider. (Not all SQL commands are supported by all providers; for instance, you may want to execute an elaborate SQL self-join on a single table and the provider may not have implemented that functionality in their interface.)

In terms of UDA, the specification identifies three basic programming interfaces which OLE DB-compliant data sources must expose to consumers.

- ➢ Basic COM interfaces which map to the provider objects such as our `Rowset`, `Session` and `Command` objects.
- ➢ An object library. A good example of this is the object library provided by ActiveX Data Objects (ADO), which we will be looking at in the next section and in Chapter 7.
- ➢ Remote Data Services (RDS), which are based on ADO and oriented towards a web client interface (browser).

Microsoft has no hesitation in recommending ADO as a preference for the object library to be used with OLE DB, but see the section titled 'Which data access technology should I use?' later in this chapter.

ADO

ActiveX Data Objects (ADO) is a code layer built over the specification for OLE DB. You can see this clearly when you consider the ADO object model and compare its object structures with those of OLE DB. For example, the OLE DB `Session` object maps to the ADO `Connection` object, the OLE DB `Command` object to the ADO `Command` object and the OLE DB `Rowset` to the ADO `Recordset`. This is the reason why Microsoft recommends and pushes ADO as their preferred data access technology.

Architecturally, ADO is the application-level interface to OLE DB; ADO's actual implementation of OLE DB is shown here in a simplified representation of the ADO object model:

Let's look at each object in more detail and see the relationship between the OLE DB and ADO object models.

The ADO Connection object represents a connection to the underlying data source (that is, the OLE DB provider). The Connection object exposes an Execute method allowing the execution of commands to the data source. The executed command may generate rows of returned data, and if so, an ADO Recordset object will be returned with default settings. You may also specify explicitly how this returned data is to behave. You can create a new Recordset object, bind it to the connection and access the data.

The Command object in ADO is the equivalent to the Command object in OLE DB. This, believe it or not, is optional within the OLE DB specification and providers need not actually provide a way to execute commands on the data. If the provider does support Command objects, so does ADO. With the Command object you may execute queries, provider-specific statements and stored procedures. The Command object supports the Execute method, but it can also be associated with a Recordset object when opening a recordset. The Command object supports the use of a Parameters object collection which typically holds variable parameters to SQL statements or input or output parameters for a stored procedure call.

The Parameters object is a collection of a number of individual Parameter objects. These objects each represent a parameter which is passed into the command. Using these Parameter objects is heavier on the coding requirement but much lighter on the execution overhead. If Parameter objects bound to the Command object are used, ADO does not need to refer to the system catalogue to populate the parameter binding information for each and every command execution. ADO validates the structure, size and type of parameter earlier on in the execution chain and is thus much more efficient.

All information about the data that is returned by the command and the way it is to be manipulated is contained in the Recordset object. This makes the Recordset the most complex by far of these objects. This object is similar to the recordset used by DAO and the resultset used by RDO.

The Fields object is a collection of Field objects, each of which represents a column in the recordset that you use to modify or return values.

The Error object represents an error which is returned from the data source. This is yet another optional interface that OLE DB providers are not required to provide.

Because ADO is built on top of OLE DB, it benefits from the rich data access infrastructure that OLE DB provides, but shields the application developer from the necessity of programming COM interfaces.

You can read more about Microsoft UDA from a range of sources including the Microsoft Web site at http://www.microsoft.com/data/download.htm and the Microsoft Developers Network (MSDN). Also check out *ADO 2.1 Programmer's Reference* from Wrox Press, ISBN 1-861002-68-8. On the Web and when using MSDN, just search for UDA and all will be revealed in much more detail than this chapter can hope to cover.

The diagram below depicts the role of OLE DB and ADO in Microsoft's vision of Universal Data Access. OLE DB is used as the common data access layer which communicates with the data store(s), but ADO is added as a thin layer between OLE DB and the client application or internet server which uses the data:

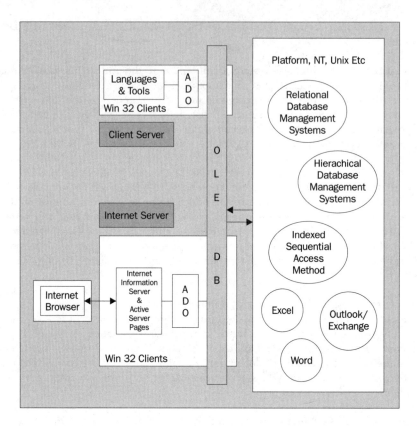

ODBC

Open DataBase Connectivity (ODBC) has been around for a long time now, and has become a standard for data access between a multitude of applications and back-end data sources.

ODBC employs the SQL database language to fetch data from the data source. However, the SQL implementation provided by different ODBC drivers ranges from basic to nearly full implementation of the ANSI SQL specification. This imposes obvious restrictions on your applications. For instance, some single-tier ODBC drivers do not allow transaction-based rollbacks and buffered data updates. These levels of support or conformance (termed **compliance levels**) are defined by the ISO standards for ODBC. There are three of these compliance levels: Core (ISO), Level 1 (X/Open) and Level 2; these inform the application what features are available to it from the driver.

The ODBC architecture (or, more accurately, the architecture of ODBC-based applications) consists of four main components:

Application Programming Interface (API)

An API is basically just the set of functions which are exposed to programmers. The ODBC API calls the ODBC functions that connect and disconnect from the data source and the functions that fetch the data and manipulate it.

Driver Manager

The Driver Manager provides a list of the data sources available and the ability to create new drivers. It dynamically loads the drivers for these data sources and checks the arguments passed in to API functions (for example, the number of arguments and their data type). Finally, it also checks for changes to the state of various objects for which the Driver Manager is responsible.

Driver

The driver itself processes all function calls and manages the exchanges between the application and the connected relational data source. The driver will need to translate standard SQL syntax into the native SQL syntax of the data store.

Data Source

The data source comprises not only the data store itself but also its database engine. A good example of this is SQL Server. The data itself simply resides in files, but the SQL Server engine does not allow direct access to the database. ODBC drivers, for instance, 'go through' the database engine to validate access and SQL integrity.

The figure below provides a graphic representation of the ODBC architecture. As you can see, the application communicates with the Driver Manager through the ODBC API. This manages the drivers which connect to specific data stores:

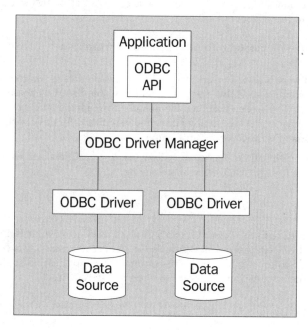

RDO

Remote Data Objects (RDO) was introduced in the 32-bit version of VB4 Enterprise Edition. RDO provides an object model for accessing ODBC data. It's similar to DAO except that it's aimed at relational SQL databases such as SQL Server or Oracle, rather than at ISAM data.

> **ISAM stands for Indexed Sequential Access Method; this is a way of accessing data which involves almost all the data handling being conducted on the client, with the server used merely as a storage place for records. ISAM data sources include Microsoft Access, Microsoft FoxPro, dBase, Paradox and others.**

RDO was designed to give Visual Basic developers the ability to access ODBC data sources without the need to code the ODBC API directly. RDO is a thin layer over the ODBC API and accesses all the functionality of ODBC, but with an easy-to-use object model.

DAO

Data Access Objects (DAO) was introduced with Visual Basic 3. DAO enables the developer to access and manipulate data in local or remote databases. DAO also allows the programmer to manage database structures and their objects.

DAO supports two different database environments or workspaces:

> ➤ **Microsoft Jet workspaces.** Jet workspaces allow access to data in Microsoft Jet databases, Microsoft Jet-connected ODBC databases and installable ISAM databases such as Access, dBase, Paradox etc. DAO has been traditionally operated through the Jet data engine. DAO could be thought of as a data access technology designed specifically for desktop applications, whereas RDO is designed for client-server applications.

> ➤ **ODBCDirect.** ODBCDirect workspaces allow you to access database servers though ODBC without loading the Microsoft Jet database engine.

ODBCDirect

ODBCDirect was introduced with Visual Basic 5 and is based on RDO. ODBCDirect provides a simple way to switch from Jet-based to RDO-based data access. In fact, this switch is very easy to make: simply insert the following line at the beginning of the application (before any DAO objects are referenced), and the application will be converted to ODBCDirect:

```
DBEngine.DefaultType = dbUseODBC
```

In order to access a data source, ODBCDirect-based applications must first create a workspace. This defines the connection in terms of a user session, user name, password and database type. The connection to the data source can then be opened; the information needed to make the connection is passed in as a **connection string** - a semicolon-delimited string which contains information such as the data source name for the database to connect to. We can then run a SQL query against the database; this will open and populate a recordset. This allows us to browse or change data within the recordset rows depending on the type of recordset requested and the permissions granted on the connection. Finally, the recordset and database must be closed, and the connection released.

If you wish to upsize an application which uses DAO to ODBCDirect, there are a number of differences between the technologies to consider:

> We must create a workspace object in ODBCDirect for each different recordset on a connection.

> Any transactions are handled at the workspace level and not at the connection or database level.

> With ODBCDirect, we must programatically check whether operations such as updates and queries have been completed. There are no events to inform us when an operation has been completed! Instead, we must poll for completion with the StillExecuting function.

> Unlike DAO, you can't use ODBCDirect to perform DDL (Data Definition Language, the name given to the SQL commands used for basic administration) operations, such as updating the database structure and granting user access to the database, although you can do the same thing with SQL statements albeit in a more longwinded way.

> DAO can perform heterogeneous joins across tables in different data sources where ODBCDirect cannot. It's possible, for example, to join a table in a Microsoft Access database with another table in a FoxPro database. Such a join between tables created in different DBMSs is called a heterogeneous join.

> ODBCDirect can perform batch optimistic updating; this means that your application can cache data locally and refresh the server in batch mode, which is faster. The term 'optimistic' means that there is an assumption that the records have not been updated by more that one user.

> ODBCDirect is limited to ODBC data sources. However, there are ODBC suppliers for most data sources, and even if you can't find one, it is possible to write your own driver using software development kits (SDKs).

Which Data Access Technology Should I Use?

We've discussed the major options available to today's developer, but we haven't really considered yet which one should you use for any given task. One point to remember is that ODBC has now matured to a point where it is a good technology for accessing SQL databases. As a result, Microsoft has produced an OLE DB provider for ODBC data sources, allowing OLE DB consumers to access ODBC drivers. Of course, the most appropriate technology will depend on many factors, such as the task you wish to accomplish, the environment in which you are programming and the data sources you need to access. It is impossible to give a blanket recommendation. However, here are a number of points to consider:

> If you're accessing standard relational databases but from a non-OLE environment then ODBC is still your best choice technology.

> Obviously, if you are programming in an OLE environment then OLE DB is your best bet.

> For building interoperable database components, OLE DB is the only choice you can make.

> You should use DAO if you need to access Microsoft Jet features such as compacting and repairing databases or use DDL though objects.

> You should use RDO if you need to use binding controls in Visual Basic 5.

> If you are designing a new application now then ADO is the technology of choice. Bearing in mind that ADO will become a superset of DAO and RDO anyway, and unless you need features which are available in RDO or DAO now but not in ADO, then stick with ADO.

Features Supported by ADO, DAO and RDO

At this point, it will be useful to present a comparison of the most important data access technologies used by VB programmers: ADO, DAO and RDO. This table lists some of the major features found in the most widespread versions of these technologies. The individual features may not mean much to you at this stage (most of them will be covered in later chapters), but the table does show how much more functionality is provided by ADO in comparison to DAO and RDO:

Feature	ADO 2.0	DAO 3.5	RDO 2.0
Asynchronous connections	X		X
Queries can run asynchronously	X		X
Inward, outward and return value parameters	X	X	X
Multiple recordsets returned	X	X	X
Batch updates	X	X	X
Error handling	X	X	X
Events	X		X
Integration with data binding in Visual Basic 6	X		
Persistent recordsets	X		
Distributed Transactions	X		X
Threadsafe	X	X	X
Disconnected recordsets	X		X
Queries as methods	X		X

OLE DB and ODBC

At this point, it's worth taking a quick look at some of the technical differences between ODBC and OLE DB, the technologies which lie underneath these. Remember that, even if you decide to use ADO, you still have the option to connect to a data source through the OLE DB provider for ODBC.

ODBC	OLE DB
Data access API	Database component APIs
Data is SQL-based	Can access all tabular formatted data
Standard is SQL-based	Standard is COM-based
API is C-based	API is COM-based

It's important to note that the current versions of Internet Information Server, Internet Explorer, Visual Basic, Visual InterDev, Visual C++ and J++ all have ADO set as their primary data access technology. Microsoft Office 2000 does the same, providing a standard across the Visual Basic for Applications (VBA) language of Microsoft Office.

Where Are These Data Access Technologies?

In this section we'll see how to find some of the data access technologies we've discussed in the previous section. This section will give you an idea how to find or install them on your computer and where to find them within your software.

Microsoft realizes that the bewildering array of technology and acronyms is growing and users need help in keeping up with them. Their answer to this is to coin yet another acronym! MDAC stands for Microsoft Data Access Components, and brings together all these technologies into one complete kit.

MDAC 2.1 is the current version whilst MDAC 2.5 is just starting its beta programme (June 1999).

The following address is a very useful web page relating to MDAC. This address is correct at the time of writing, but if you fail to connect, simply go to the Microsoft home page and search for MDAC then follow the links. Remember to look for the latest version of MDAC.

Http://www.microsoft.com/data/download.htm or Http://www.microsoft.com/data/download2.htm

This is a great page from Microsoft. Here you can:

> Download the latest version of MDAC components in one hit.
> View release documentation.
> Download service packs for MDAC.
> Link to documents on Universal Data Access, OLE DB, ADO and ODBC.
> Link to other technical material.

Remember that if you have problems with the links, just search for the text from the home page and they will be there somewhere.

Before installing MDAC 2.0 or 2.1 on a machine with Windows 95 or Windows 98, you will need first to install DCOM (a version of COM for use over a network). To download DCOM95 from the Web, either use the following address or search for DCOM95 from the Microsoft home page:

http://www.microsoft.com/com/dcom.asp

You can also download the MDAC 2.1 Software Development Kit (SDK) from the same site.

So what do you get with MDAC 2.1? Let's have a look...

> ActiveX Data Objects (ADO) 2.1
> Remote Data Service (RDS) 2.1
> OLE DB Providers for ODBC data sources, SQL Server, Oracle, Microsoft Jet databases

> ➤ The OLE DB Simple Provider (OSP) Toolkit (for building custom OLE DB providers)
> ➤ OLE DB for OLAP (On-Line Analytical Processing) (for use with multidimensional data)
> ➤ ODBC Driver Manager
> ➤ ODBC Drivers for Microsoft SQL Server, Oracle, Microsoft Jet databases, Microsoft Visual FoxPro
> ➤ Microsoft Jet Engine

With MDAC 2.1 you also get ActiveX Data Objects with Extensions (ADOX). This provides support for Data Definition Language (DDL) and security with certain OLE providers.

What's rather cool is that this download is free, is just one executable and about six megabytes in size.

So MDAC is all you need. It's well worth downloading straight away if you haven't already got it. Once you have downloaded it, just run the executable and the set-up takes care of itself. Documentation is included and well worth reading.

Once this has been set-up (and you have rebooted your machine) you have access to all the above mentioned technology for free. Not bad, eh?

Setting up an ODBC Data Source Name

We can connect to an ODBC data source through ADO and OLE DB by providing all the required connection details in a connection string. However, there is a much easier way of doing this: we can set up an ODBC **Data Source Name** (DSN). A DSN is simply a name which is assigned to a particular set of connection details for an ODBC connection to a given database. After setting up a DSN, whenever we want to connect to this database in future, all we need to do is provide the name given to the data source, a user name and a password. There may be some slight loss of performance in making the connection (because the connection information must be sought on the hard disk), but this may be outweighed by ease of programming.

To set up a DSN, have a look at your control panel. If you're using Windows 95 or 98, you should see an icon like this:

ODBC (32bit)

The ODBC Data Source Administrator

In Windows NT and Windows 2000 it may be described differently, as ODBC Data Sources. Clicking on this icon launches the ODBC Data Source Administrator dialog, which gives us access to the ODBC Driver Manager:

This screen makes several tabs available to us. The first three of these tabs display and allow us to create DSNs. There are three types of DSNs; these differ in the extent that they are made available to other users. The first tab allows us to specify a User data source name (User DSN). These DSNs are local to a computer and only available to the current user. The System DSN tab shows all data sources which are visible to all users on the current machine and includes NT services. The third tab (File DSN) shows all DSNs which can be shared by any users who have the same drivers installed.

Selecting the Drivers tab shows all ODBC drivers available on the current machine. Drivers can also be added on this page.

The Tracing tab allows you to specify log files to contain ODBC connection and usage information which may be useful to support staff. Tracing should only be switched on when a problem needs resolving.

The sixth tab, Connection Pooling, allows applications to re-use connections to data sources which saves on connection speed within the application.

Configuring a SQL Server DSN

Selecting a data source takes you to the set-up screen for that data source; this can differ, depending on the driver selected. Here is the set-up screen for a SQL Server driver.

The Name option specifies the name for the DSN; this is the name which will be used to make the connection when the DSN has been set up. The Description is an arbitrary text field, used to describe the DSN. The Server in this example is SPOCK. This means that SQL Server is registered on an NT Server machine called SPOCK.

Clicking Next > allows us to set up the connection characteristics for the ODBC SQL Server driver.

Authentication Options

Integrated security

ame (Login ID) for the systems administrator (sa) is shown here with no
lefault for a new installation of SQL Server. On your own existing systems you
ystem administrator has assigned himself or herself a password. You must use a
o you through Windows NT authentication or through SQL Server directly.

ittle tricky. If you select Windows NT authentication, SQL Server will validate
n based on your NT user name and password. Selecting SQL Server
SQL Server handle all user access levels, login ids and passwords.

ices between these two important choices in more detail:

curity enables Windows NT user accounts to access SQL Server. Windows NT is
ing user accounts and passwords. It manages password aging and minimum
th.

andard security is not as robust as Windows NT in how it handles user accounts.
nly provides users, roles and passwords. Therefore many of the important features
that Windows NT can provide are not available to you when SQL Server provides the
authentication without integrated security.

- Another point worth noting is that having gone to the trouble of setting up your work group configurations within Windows NT, it seems a shame not to make use of those within SQL Server. Moreover, with integrated security the user simply identifies the server when logging on – SQL Server will validate the user based on the user name and password supplied by Windows NT.
- There are some network transport issues that can affect the security authentication choices, but this is beyond the scope of this chapter. SQL Server setup also allows for a mixture of security modes.

Here is a summary of the differences:

- **Standard**. SQL Server user accounts are maintained separately from existing Windows NT domain accounts. This is the default mode.
- **Integrated**. SQL Server dynamically maps SQL Server user names to NT domain accounts. This mode is useful when the enterprise wishes to minimize SQL Server account administration.
- **Mixed**. Mixed security mode is a combination of standard and integrated modes. It is used in environments where some client workstations are able to take advantage of NT Security and some are not.

Connection Options

If you then select the option to Connect to SQL Server to obtain default settings for the additional configuration options, the driver manager will attempt a connection to SQL Server to pick up information such as the default database to use and the language settings, etc. The following screen will appear:

In the figure above, the default database in the option to Change the default database is actually blank when the DSN is first set up. We show that we want pubs as our default in this example, just for compatibility with other examples in this chapter.

The ODBC driver manager may not always get a connection through to SQL Server, depending on how SQL Server has been set up. If the default system administrator password has been left blank (which is the default, but not at all to be recommended), you can log on with sa as the user name and a blank password.

Translation Options

If we now select Next >, we'll see the screen depicted below:

This gives us the option to select the appropriate language for SQL Server; this should have defaulted to the default language for the operating system.

On most installations, you will probably want to leave the default for character translations. Finally, it's your choice as to how currency, numbers, dates and times are output, but following your Windows regional settings is a good idea.

Logging Options

Pressing Next > here gives the following screen:

This page allows you to set options for information about database operations to be saved to log files. The option to log long-running queries is useful for finding out why that query you set off two days ago is still running! You can set the number of milliseconds after which logging will start on a long-running query.

Recording ODBC statistics may prove useful when you encounter connection problems. Only use these logging options when absolutely necessary because some resource overhead is required.

Completing the Configuration

Clicking Finish completes the configuration of the DSN and displays a dialog showing a summary of the connection details. You should see a screen similar to this one:

```
ODBC Microsoft SQL Server Setup                                    [X]

         A new ODBC data source will be created with the following
                              configuration:

  Microsoft SQL Server ODBC Driver Version 03.60.0319

  Data Source Name: SQL Server
  Data Source Description: sfsd
  Server: SPOCK
  Database: (Default)
  Language: (Default)
  Translation Option: Automatic
  Log Long Running Queries: No
  Log Driver Statistics: No
  Use Integrated Security: Yes
  Use Regional Settings: Yes
  Prepared Statements Option: Drop temporary procedures on
  disconnect
  Use Failover Server: No
  Use ANSI Quoted Identifiers: Yes
  Use ANSI Null, Paddings and Warnings: Yes

     [ Test Data Source... ]              [ OK ]    [ Cancel ]
```

Clicking on the Test Data Source button causes the ODBC Data Source Administrator to attempt to make a connection to SQL Server based on the information you have just supplied. The connection will either succeed or fail and the message from SQL Server must be read in order to determine the problem. If you have got this far, any problem will probably be related to an invalid user name or password.

Connecting to an ODBC Data Source

So, we now have our ODBC connection to SQL Server. How would you use this connection in a VB application?

Connecting with VisData

Remember that this is an ODBC data source. So we can use tools within Visual Basic to connect to that ODBC data source. One fast and pretty efficient tool is **VisData**. We'll look at this tool in more detail in Chapter 4, but for now we'll just see how to use it to build a data form for SQL Server data using an ODBC data source. Our ODBC data source is assumed to be available and set up.

Start a new Standard EXE project in Visual Basic and select Add-Ins | Visual Data Manager from the menu. Then select File | Open Database | ODBC from the VisData menu. You will be presented with a dialog box prompting you for information needed to log on to the data source:

Select or enter your SQL Server DSN. If you have not set up your own user ID, enter the user name for the administrator (sa) and the appropriate password (leave this blank if the default has not been changed). Enter pubs as the database and hit OK. If you have an existing SQL Server set up, you will probably have your own user name and password, or your Windows NT user name and password will be used by SQL Server using integrated security (as we discussed above).

The Data Form Designer

We now have a connection to our data source! In order to build a quick form to access the data, we'll use a handy wizard supplied with VisData: the **Data Form Designer**. To open this, select Utility | Data Form Designer from the menu. Enter the name SQLForm in the Form Name field and select dbo.authors as the RecordSource.

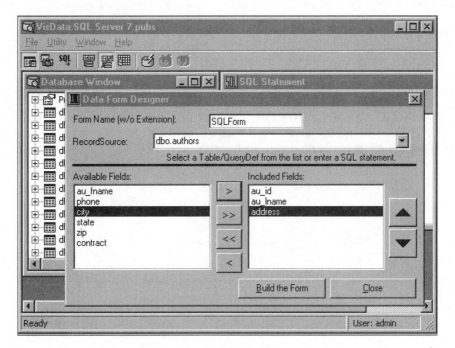

For this quick demo, we'll just add the three fields shown: au_id, au_lname and address. Add the fields to the form by selecting them and clicking on the <u>B</u>uild the Form button for a very quick and neat way to build a data form using ODBC.

The form is now added to your project. Remove the default form that the new project created and set the new form as the start-up form in the project's **Properties** panel. Run the form and you should see this:

Well, producing a data entry form accessing SQL Server data doesn't get much easier than that, does it?

Summary

In this chapter we've looked at a range of data access technologies. We've seen what all the acronyms mean, how the technologies compare, where to find them and which to use.

In the rest of this book you'll find references to and examples of some of these technologies in more detail than we've covered here. The purpose of this chapter is to bring them all together into one place and look at them, not in immense detail, but in an overview with reference to each other.

It's important to remember what Microsoft and others are hoping to bring about: a universal method to access all data source types such as email, Office documents, text files, and HTML pages, as well as the more usual relational data held in a variety of proprietary formats on a diverse range of hardware and platforms. Based on this fine ideal, it's probably better to get into the Universal Data Access way of doing things sooner rather than later.

Suppliers

- SupplierID
- CompanyName
- ContactName
- ContactTitle
- Address
- City
- Region
- PostalCode
- Country
- Phone
- Fax
- HomePage

Products

- ProductID
- ProductName
- SupplierID
- CategoryID
- QuantityPerUnit
- UnitPrice
- UnitsInStock
- UnitsOnOrder
- ReorderLevel
- Discontinued

Categories

- CategoryID
- CategoryName
- Description
- Picture

Working with the ADO Data Control

Before jumping into building a multi-tier client-server application, we first need to understand fully how to connect to a database, then input and retrieve the data. The objective of this chapter is to provide a solid understanding of the ADO Data Control. This control will enable us to use ADO as a method of connection to databases, without having to worry too much about its object model.

In this chapter:

> We'll begin by using the Visual Data Manager to build a database, which will contain addresses and phone numbers.
> Then we'll build an application that allows us to view the data present in our database. We'll extend our application to include a navigation bar that allows us to add, delete, modify and search for data.
> Finally, we'll take a look at some of the other controls that we didn't use in the example, but are readily available for you to use in your projects.

Application Walk-Through

The application that we will build in this chapter consists of a form that houses the ADO Data Control. This control connects to a database containing addresses. The database doesn't exist yet, so we'll build it using Visual Basic's Visual Data Manager (VisData) program. This database will have one table, which holds address information such as name, phone number and address. The functionality that we'll design into this application includes:

> Ability to navigate and locate records
> Ability to update records
> A status label indicating the current record and the record count
> Ability to add and delete records
> Ability to locate a record, given a search string

When complete, the user interface will have a professional look and feel to it, allowing the user to enter or edit data quickly. Notice that the phone number field is masked with hyphens and parentheses to guide the user in the input process. In the screenshot, the user is half way through entering a phone number and any places not entered are being held by hyphens. Finally, the Comments box is configured to accept multiple lines of text so that the user can add many lines of comments.

Building the Database

As already mentioned, we are using our own database, rather than a ready-made one, so the first thing we need to do is build this database. We'll build the database as a Jet database using Microsoft's VisData. A Jet database is any database that uses Jet as its database engine. Access is a Jet database, but we can create Jet databases without having Access installed, by using VisData instead.

VisData provides functionality that allows us to:

> Build and maintain databases and tables
> Create indexes on tables
> Enter/edit data in tables
> Create queries
> Repair or compact any Jet database
> Create and test SQL statements

Our database will be fairly simple in design and will have just one table, called Address. In this table, we'll have the following fields: AddressID, Last_Name, First_Name, Street, City, State, Zip, Phone and Comments. The AddressID will be created as a long number, with an auto counter activated. This field will also be our primary key. The Last_Name and First_Name fields will be created with indexes attached. Although we won't be using SQL in this chapter, it's always better to plan for future sorting and data selection.

To open VisData, open a new Standard Executable project in Visual Basic. Select Add-Ins from the menu bar and Visual Data Manager... from the drop down list. The VisData program should now open. From the VisData menu, select File | New | Microsoft Access | Version 7.0 MDB...

If you have an older version of Access (such as Access 2.0) installed on your computer, you can build your databases using **Version 2.0 MDB**. This isn't necessary for our application, but if you want to view the database directly from Access, you'll need a compatible version. Building a database in Version 7.0 is the same thing as Access 95. Whether you have Access 95 or 97, you should choose Version 7.0. If VisData will be your primary means of data entry, you may want to avoid creating an Access 2.0 database.

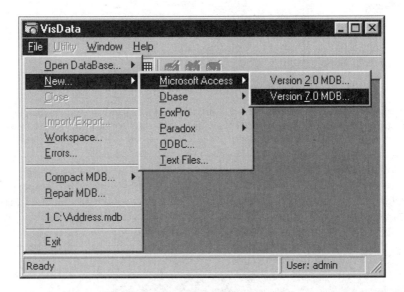

We are now prompted to choose a location and name for our database. Create a folder, which will sit on the C: drive and call it ProVB6DB (the third button from the right on this dialog allows us to create a new folder). Save the database in this new folder as Address. The extension .mdb will automatically be appended.

VisData will create a
generic Access database
without any tables. The
workspace includes a
Database Window pane
and a SQL Statement
test pane. The SQL
Statement pane can be
used to build and test
SQL statements:

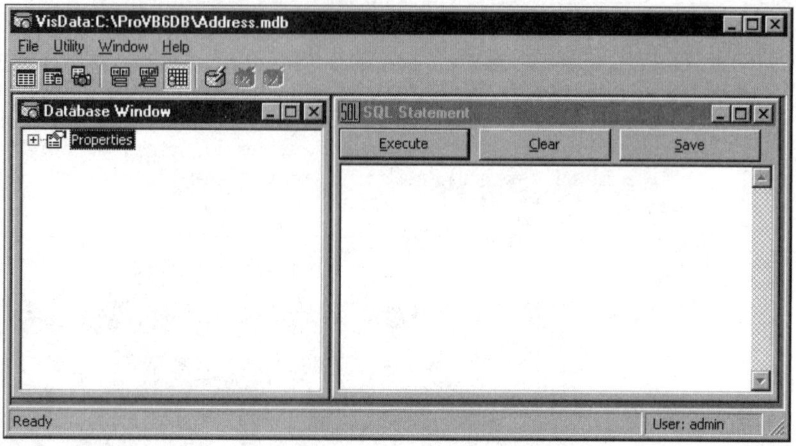

A database isn't much good without at least one table, so let's jump right into designing one. To create a new table, right-click on the word Properties in the Database Window and select New Table from the pop-up menu.

The **Properties** item of the **Database Window** pane allows you to view any associated properties of the database that is currently opened. Examples of these properties include database location, the version that the database was created in and time-out parameters for queries. Properties exist on databases, tables and even fields. They are an intricate part of the schema of the database as a whole.

This opens the Table Structure dialog, which allows us to create a new table. Enter Address in the Table Name box:

As I have already outlined, this table has several fields. To add new fields, click on the Add Field button. The Add Field dialog will open, allowing us to create new fields. Our first field will be called AddressID, so type this name in the Name box. This field will store a long number and will automatically increment when a new record is added. To set this, select Long from the drop-down box labeled Type and check the AutoIncrField box. We have just specified the data type for the AddressID field and indicated that the field should automatically increment by one each time a new record is added. Lastly, click on the Required check box. Although the database assigns a value automatically, we need to ensure that the user does not remove the value later. The other field options available are:

> Size: Allows you to limit the number of characters the user can enter. Primarily for text-based data types.
> FixedField/VariableField (Text fields only): Specifies if the data will always be a fixed length or variable.
> AllowZeroLength: Indicates if a zero length value is acceptable, such as spacebars or nulls.
> OrdinalPosition: The order of the fields in the database. This is zero-based, so the first field is zero, the second is one and so on. This is significant because you may reference the field based on its ordinal position (although it's not a common practice) rather than its field name. Additionally, when you use form wizards, this is the order that your fields will be added to the form and the order that tab stops will be added (as a default).
> ValidationText: An error message that will be shown if the user breaks the validation rule.
> ValidationRule: A rule that limits the acceptable values for the field. For example, a rule ">10" would cause an error to be generated if a number less than 11 is entered.
> DefaultValue: A default value that is entered if the user leaves the field blank.

For this example, we won't add any validation text or descriptions, so just click on <u>O</u>K and the field will be added. The dialog remains open until you click on <u>C</u>lose, so that we can add numerous fields without too much repetition:

There are still eight more fields to add, so using the following table, repeat the above steps to add the remaining fields.

Name	Type	Size	Required	FixedField/VariableField
Last_Name	Text	35	No*	Variable
First_Name	Text	25	No*	Variable
Street	Text	50	No	Variable
City	Text	20	No	Variable
State	Text	2	No	Variable
Zip	Text	10	No	Variable
Phone	Text	10	No	Variable
Comments	Memo	N/A	No	Variable

Although this would be the best place to require the Last_Name and First_Name fields to be populated, we'll leave this unchecked for now so that later we can demonstrate how to implement business rules in code.

Notice that text fields such as Last_Name are automatically selected as a **VariableField** because we can't predict the exact length of the field.

Once you have finished adding the fields, click on the Close button, the Table Structure dialog should appear as in the following screenshot. This dialog presents the properties of each field as you click on them. The final step before we build the table is to specify the indexes that will exist. To add an index, click on the Add Index button.

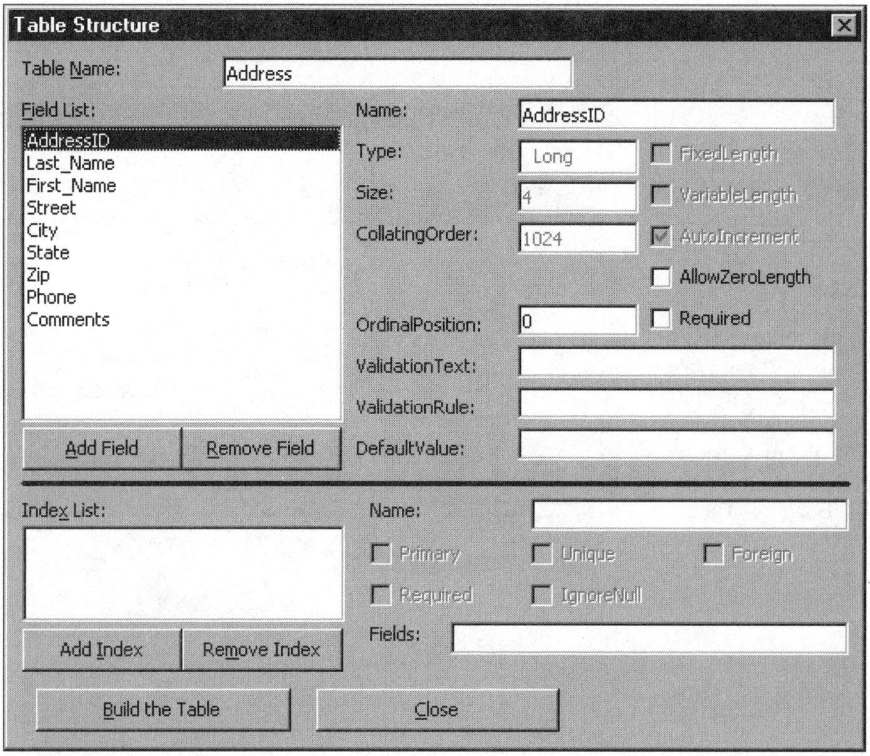

When the Add Index to Address dialog appears, specify AddressID as the name for the index. Click on the AddressID field to add it to the Indexed Fields list box. Then copy and then paste it into the Name box as the name for the index. This way, you won't accidentally misspell it (and you can rationalize being lazy!). In this table, the AddressID field will be classified as a primary key and will always be unique, so leave both boxes checked:

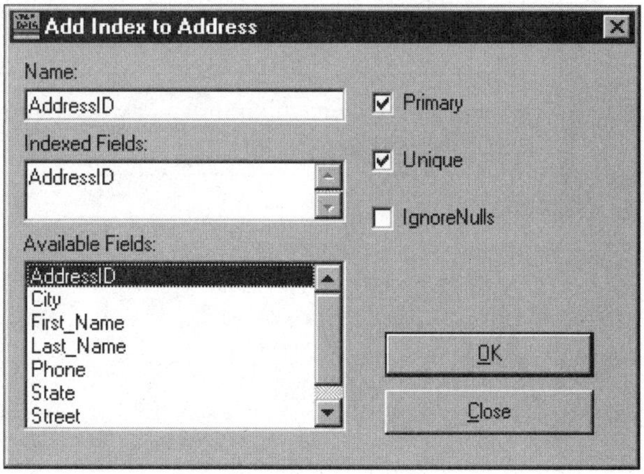

Build two more indexes as follows:

Index Name	Fields Added	Primary Key	Unique	Ignore Nulls
First_Name	First_Name	Unchecked	Unchecked	Unchecked
Last_Name	Last_Name	Unchecked	Unchecked	Unchecked

After adding these indexes, our **Table Structure** dialog should look like this one. We're now ready for the final step: building the table. Review the properties of each field and then click on the **B**uild the Table button:

Once the table has been built, you'll be able to review the properties of the table, fields and indexes. The **Database Window** works in a very similar way to Windows Explorer. Click on the + sign to expand an item and click on the - sign to collapse an item.

> **Although some items might not show the + sign, clicking on the item name itself may expand that item.**

The following image depicts how the properties of the First_Name field can been exposed by expanding the tree in the Database Window pane:

The properties of the various fields can be modified by double-clicking on them in the Database Window. A dialog then appears where you can modify the property; when finished, click on the OK button. For example, to alter the OrdinalPosition property, double-click on the property's name and the following dialog will appear:

VisData has a few quirks to it. The first of which is that it is temperamental about allowing you to enter the first record into your table through its graphical user interface. To get around this, you have two options. Firstly, you can enter the first record through a database application that fully supports its capabilities, such as Access. Of course, if you're using VisData, then you simply may not have Access. The second option is to enter your first record using a SQL statement.

If you wish to enter the record using a SQL statement, type the following statement into the SQL Statement pane and click on the Execute button:

```
INSERT INTO ADDRESS (Last_Name, First_Name, Street, City, State, Zip)
VALUES('Smith', 'John', '123 Main Street', 'Boston', 'MA', '02202')
```

If you are not very knowledgeable about SQL, don't worry. We'll cover it in detail when we get to Chapter 6.

Once you click on the Execute button, the following message box will appear:

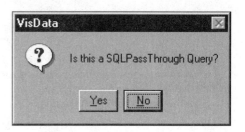

A SQLPassThrough Query allows you to work directly with the table on the database. If, for example, the database has its own dialect of SQL, the SQL statement can be passed directly to the database without being optimized by the client application. Just click on the No button and the record will be added to the table.

Now that we've built the table and added a record, let's add some more data. In VisData, click once on the Table type Recordset button (the furthest left button on the toolbar). This allows you to view the data in the table. Now click on the toolbar button with the yellow database sitting on the grid (the tool tip should indicate Use DBGrid Control on New Form). This button will allow you to view multiple records simultaneously in a database grid. Finally, double-click on the Address table name in the Database Window. It may take a few seconds to open the database, while it does so you should see a message similar to, Opening Full Table, please wait… in the status line at the bottom of VisData.

The table grid should appear, allowing you to enter data. Remember that the AddressID field is auto-incremented and required. Add three or four records as a minimum. We'll use this data later when testing our interface. When complete, your VisData window should look similar to the following image. Keep in mind that your data is likely to be very different from mine:

Table:Address

AddressID	Last Name	First Name	Street	City
1	Smith	John	123 Main Street	Boston
2	Williams	Charles	55 Data Lane	Nowhere
3	Williams	Jose	320 South Street	New York
* 4				

Data Grid

You can now close VisData and return to Visual Basic.

Building the Front-End Application

In this section, we'll build an application that connects to our database, and allows us to navigate through the records, modify them and enter new ones.

Creating a New Project

Now that we have built our database, we can build the interface that will connect to it. Return to Visual Basic. You should already have a new Standard EXE project opened. Follow the steps below:

1. Change the `Name` property of the project to `prjAddress`.

2. Change the `Name` property of the form to `frmAddress`.

3. Change the `Caption` property of `frmAddress` to `Address Database`.

4. Create a folder off the `C:\ProVB6DB` directory and call it `Chapter4`.

5. Save the form and project as `Address.vbp` and `Address.frm` in the new folder.

As your project grows in size, it is ideal to save each of the objects associated with your project in different folders. You might have a folder for each of the project files, forms, databases and classes. This will avoid a cluttered directory.

The ADO Data Control

The ADO Data Control is not included in the Toolbox for Standard Executable projects by default. To add it, select Project from Visual Basic's menu bar and then select Components. The Components dialog will open, allowing you to choose which components you want to add to the project. Locate the Microsoft ADO Data Control 6.0 (OLEDB) in the list and click on it so that a check mark appears in the box to the left of the item. This control should have installed automatically with Visual Basic. If you are unable to locate the control, re-install Visual Basic and ensure that the Database options are selected (if using a custom install).

To open the Components dialog, you can also right click on the toolbox and select Components.

After selecting this, click on the OK button and the ADO Data Control will be added to the Toolbox. It looks like a horizontal scrollbar with a yellow database symbol attached.

Add the ADO Data Control to your form and set its `Align` property to `vbAlignBottom`:

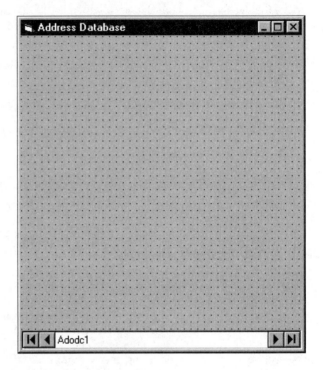

If you are familiar with the DAO or RDO Data Controls from previous releases of Visual Basic, the transition to the ADO Data Control will be very simple. The primary difference is the method that the control uses to connect to the database. With the DAO Data Control, for example, you could simply specify the database name and location. This method has its advantages, ease of use being one of them.

The ADO Data Control requires a connection string, which allows the control to connect to virtually any database server. The main difference between the DAO and RDO Data Controls, and the ADO Data Control, is that the ADO Data Control allows you to access data sources other than databases. For example, you can access LDAP data sources, email data sources, text data sources, etc.

> **Connection strings contain information such as the drivers, security access and location of the database server.**

Building the Connection String

To build a connection string, open the Properties window for the ADO Data Control and locate the `ConnectionString` property. When you click your mouse pointer in the property box, a button with three dots will appear. This button opens a wizard, which walks you through the process of building the string:

This dialog prompts you to choose one of three mechanisms for connecting to the database:

> ➤ Use Data Link File: Allows you to specify a file that contains the connection information. These files can be created in Windows Explorer by choosing Microsoft Data Link from the list of New items. When saved, the file will have an extension of UDL.

> ➤ Use ODBC Data Source Name: Allows you to specify an ODBC Data Source Name (DSN). DSNs are created from the ODBC Data Source Administrator located in the Control Panel. We covered this in more detail, including how to create a DSN, in Chapters 3.

> ➤ Use Connection String: Allows you to build a connection string that specifies drivers, database location and password information.

Ensure the Use Connection String option button is selected and click on the Build button. The next dialog prompts you to select the database provider:

This dialog lists all the OLE DB providers detected on your hard drive. These providers are added to the dialog after installation of each database, so you may have a different number of providers listed in your dialog. If you have Access 2000 installed on your machine, select **Microsoft Jet 4.0 OLE DB Provider**; otherwise select **Microsoft Jet 3.51 OLE DB Provider**. Then click on **Next**. The **Connection** tab is then displayed:

The **Connection** tab allows you to select the location of the database, and any username and password that will be used to connect to it. Click on the button with the three dots and locate the `Address.mdb` database. You can leave the username and password as they appear.

Once you have found our database, click on the **Test Connection** button. The wizard will then attempt to connect to the database. If you have configured the options correctly, the following message box should appear:

Click on the **OK** button to close the message box.

Now click on the **Advanced** tab. This tab allows you to implement security access for the database and specify time-out parameters for the connection attempt. A time-out setting of 30 for example would indicate that if a connection attempt does not complete after 30 seconds, Visual Basic should stop trying and return an error. The **Network settings** frame allows you to set protection levels for database servers using the network. Finally, the **Access permissions** box allows you to specify permission for reading, writing to and sharing data with other users. This pertains to the database as whole, not just the table:

Finally, click on the **All** tab. The **All** tab provides a list of properties relevant to your database. Depending on which database you are connecting to, these properties will vary. To modify any of the properties, select it and click on the **Edit Value** button:

Click on the **OK** button at the bottom of the dialog and your connection string will appear in the text box below the **Use Connection String** option button:

Notice that the connection string contains information about the provider, security and data source. This connection string could have been manually typed in, but even developers who understand the connection strings inside out find it easier to use the wizard:

```
Provider=Microsoft.Jet.OLEDB.4.0;Data Source=C:\ProVB6DB\Address.mdb;
Persist Security Info=False
```

If you're working with an earlier version of Access that requires the Jet 3.51 OLE DB Provider, the connection string will look like the following:

```
Provider=Microsoft.Jet.OLEDB.3.51;Data Source=C:\ProVB6DB\Address.mdb;
Persist Security Info=False
```

Setting the RecordSource Property

The `RecordSource` property allows you to specify from where in the database the data will come. The `RecordSource` property is very flexible. You can specify a single table, or use a SQL statement to join several tables, select criteria and even sort the data. As we work through examples in the book, we'll see how we can apply SQL to this property to extract the data we want.

Click on the `RecordSource` property and on the button with three dots that appears. A **Property Pages** dialog will open, allowing you to customize the `RecordSource`:

Select **adCmdTable** from the drop down box. The **Table or Stored Procedure Name** list box now becomes enabled. Click on the down arrow and select **Address**. This indicates that your control will connect directly to a specific table (`Address`).

The other available recordset connection types include:

- ➤ `adCmdUnknown`: Used when you're unsure what the `RecordSource` type will be.
- ➤ `adCmdText`: Used when you expect to issue a SQL statement against the database.
- ➤ `adCmdTable`: Used when a table will be used as the `RecordSource`.
- ➤ `adCmdStoredProc`: Used when you expect to call a stored procedure located inside the database.

If we had chosen `adCmdText` instead, we could have entered a SQL statement in the **Command Text (SQL)** text box.

Click on the **OK** button. Your `RecordSource` property has been selected and the ADO Data Control is now configured to connect to the `Address` table of the `Address` database on startup.

Setting the Other Properties

Change the `EOFAction` property of the ADO Data Control to `adDoAddNew`. This identifies that if the 'End of File' (end of recordset) is reached, a new record should be created for entry.

Finally, change the `BOFAction` property to `adDoMoveFirst`. This will keep you from passing the beginning of the recordset, thus avoiding errors.

Building a User Interface

We now need to add more controls that will bind to the ADO Data Control. Each of these will represent a field for a specific record in the recordset. Follow these steps:

1. Add a label and a text box to the form.

2. Rename the label as `lblField`.

3. Change the `BorderStyle` property of the label to `Fixed Single`, the `Alignment` property to `Center` and the `BackColor` property to pale yellow.

4. Rename the text box as `txtField`.

5. Clear the `Text` property of `txtField` so that it's blank.

6. Move the label control immediately above the text box.

7. Locate the `DataSource` property of `txtField` and change its value to `Adodc1`. All text boxes will be bound to this data source, and later we'll assign a specific field in the `DataField` property of each text box.

Your form should now look as shown opposite:

We'll need nine text boxes to contain the nine fields of each record. To achieve this, we can copy the label and text boxes we already have and paste eight more instances of them, creating a control array. A control array is simply an array of controls. All nine textboxes will have the same name, but they will have different index values. Copying them after changing their properties prevents us from having to change the properties of each individual control. To create a control array follow these steps:

1. Click on the label control to select it, then while holding down the *Shift* button, click on the text box. Both controls should now be selected.

2. From Visual Basic's menu, select <u>E</u>dit I <u>C</u>opy (or use the shortcut keys *Ctrl + C*).

3. From Visual Basic's menu, select <u>E</u>dit I <u>P</u>aste (or use the shortcut keys *Ctrl + V*).

4. When prompted to create a control array, select <u>Y</u>es. This prompt will appear twice, because we have two controls that we are duplicating.

5. Paste seven more instances of the controls and arrange them as shown below:

The nine label controls will all have the name of lblField and the nine text boxes will all have the name txtField. Each of the controls will have an index value ranging from 0 to 8, allowing us to manipulate these controls within a loop of our code. The alternative to this approach is to give each control its own unique name. There is no wrong way but, depending on the functional requirements, you may find yourself writing more code without an array. For example, if we wanted to change the BackColor property of all nine labels during runtime, we could easily loop through all of the controls without directly referencing each one of them with a unique name.

An alternative to creating a control array is to loop through each of the controls using a For...Each loop. In this scenario, you can identify if each of the controls is of the type 'Text Box' and change its properties accordingly. If only a few of the text boxes need to be changed, you may use the Tag property to 'mark' those controls and evaluate the value as you loop through them.

Now change the Caption properties of the labels according to their Index properties:

Index Property	Caption Property
0	Last Name:
1	First Name:
2	Street Address:
3	City:
4	State:
5	Zip Code:
6	Phone:
7	Address ID:
8	Comments:

After changing the Caption property of each label, resize each control to allow for various length names and addresses, etc. The Comments text box will accommodate multiple lines of text, so stretch it vertically to allow three or four lines of text. The form should now look like this:

Now review the Name and Index property of each text box. Check that the Index properties range from 0 to 8 as you move from left to right, and top to bottom. This will ensure your application remains in sync with the chapter.

The Comments text box will need to accommodate multiple lines of text so change the MultiLine property of this text box to True. When this property is set to True it will move all text following a carriage return/linefeed to the next line in the box. Then set its ScrollBars property to Vertical.

Now change the following properties of the AddressID text box, txtField(7):

Property	Value
Enabled	False
TabStop	False
Locked	True

As you recall, this field is to be automatically entered by the database, so there is no need to allow the user to change its value.

The last step is to specify which field each text box will be bound to. Let's begin with the first text box, txtField(0). Locate the DataField property of txtField(0) and select the Last_Name field. The text box will now be populated with the Last_Name field from the Address table.

> *With many of the data fields, you may want to alter the format of the data presented. The DataFormat property exposes a dialog, which allows you to do this. Select the **Format Type** and the available formats will appear for your customizing. This property is primarily used for formatting numbers and dates.*

We don't need to format any of the fields for this project, so if you have made any changes to the DataFormat property, click on the **Cancel** button now.

Using the following table, change the DataField properties of the remaining text boxes:

Index Property	DataField Property
1	First_Name
2	Street
3	City
4	State
5	Zip
6	Phone
7	AddressID
8	Comments

The last step is to set the TabIndex property of all text boxes. This will give your application a more professional feel to it, as the user can enter data and tab to the next field without jumping around too much. Set the TabIndex properties so that the user moves from left to right, and down the page as the TabIndex increases.

Once you've completed modifying the properties, you're ready to test the application. Save your work and run the project. You'll notice that the application opens with the first record displayed in the text boxes. Navigate through the records using the data control and modify some of the fields. Test out our **Comments** field by adding multiple lines of text.

You may notice hard drive activity as you edit and move through the records. This is because each record is saved as you move off an edited record. You may recognize that this is a feature of the Microsoft Jet database engine, which is Access' database engine.

Without writing a single line of code, we have successfully built an application that connects to a database, allows us to navigate through the records and update the fields of each record. We're still missing a lot of functionality, such as the ability to add and delete records, but we'll be adding this functionality to the project later in the chapter.

How It All Works

Thankfully, this is all programmed for us, so we can simply set the properties and the control handles the rest. In a later chapter, we'll get into the nuts and bolts of populating data inside controls manually. For now, let's look at this at a high level.

The first thing we added was the ADO Data Control. This control was configured to manage a connection to our database. Once the connection is made, the control is capable of navigating through the records. The records are stored in memory on a recordset. The recordset is a sub collection of records from a table (or group of joined tables) based on a very specific criterion. The size of any given recordset will depend on the number of records that meet the criteria of the query, the cache size limit and the MaxRecords property within ADO. When a change is made to a record in the recordset, that change is made in the database after the user has navigated off the current record or if there is a call to the Update method of the ADO Data Control's Recordset object. Any changes made to the tables in the database will only be viewed in the recordset after calling the Refresh method of the ADO Data Control. This is because the ADO Data Control uses a CursorType of adOpenStatic as the default when connecting and retrieving data from the database.

Once connected to the database, the ADO Data Control takes on the responsibility of passing data back and forth between the database and all the bound controls. Let's consider the project we're building. We have a text box, named txtField(0), which is bound to the Last_Name field of the Address table. When we open a recordset, the current record's Last_Name field appears in the text box because the ADO Data Control recognized that the text box was bound to that specific field. When the user navigates to another record, the ADO Data Control passes the new information to the text box. If any changes were made to the data in the text box, the ADO Data Control will receive a copy of the new value and update the database with that respective value.

The Masked Edit Control

To enhance our project, we need to mask specific fields that fit a fixed format. For example, phone numbers and zip codes are always a specific length with hyphens or parentheses between the text, e.g. (555) 555-5555. The Masked Edit Control will allow you to accomplish this, presenting placeholders to the user until all of the text has been entered.

The Masked Edit Control can be added by opening the **Components** dialog box and placing a check mark next to **Microsoft Masked Edit Control 6.0**. The Masked Edit Control now appears in the Toolbox after the ADO Data Control as a button with the following text - ##|.

We want to create a mask for the phone number field, so delete txtField(6) and add the Masked Edit Control in its place. Name the new control mskPhone.

The new control needs to be bound to the ADO Data Control, so set the DataSource property to Adodc1 and DataField property to Phone.

Open the property pages of the Masked Edit Control by right-clicking on it and selecting Properties. The Property Pages dialog will appear:

Property Pages

General | Color | Font | Picture

☐ AutoTab   ☑ HideSelection   ☐ AllowPrompt
☐ PromptInclude   ☑ Enabled

Mask: (###) ###-####   MaxLength: 14

Format: (###) ###-####   PromptChar: _

MousePointer: 0 - mskDefault

BorderStyle: 1 - mskFixedSingle

ClipMode: 0 - mskIncludeLiterals

OLEDragMode: 0 - mskOLEDragManual

OLEDropMode: 0 - mskOLEDropNone

OK   Cancel   Apply   Help

This control can be tricky to configure and if you incorrectly change one of the properties, the control will not bind to the data source properly when you run your project. Let's walk through configuring the control.

Uncheck the PromptInclude check box. This value indicates whether the literals and prompt values, such as an underscore, should be included as part of the text to be passed to the database when the value is not populated.

The Mask property creates a structure for entering your text. For example, it will display hyphens and brackets to separate the values, providing placeholders for values not yet entered. Change the Mask to (###) ###-####. This tells the control to accept numbers only between the fixed positional hyphens, parentheses and spaces. If a ? is used instead, only letters can be entered into the placeholder value. The following placeholders are valid:

> # = Numbers only
> ? = Letter placeholder
> & = All characters placeholder

The Format property identifies how the data should be displayed when the value is not being edited. In this case, the Format property describes how the phone number will be displayed after the number is entered. Enter the same value in the Format text box as you entered for the Mask property.

These two fields are distinguished differently because you may want to display them differently during and after the data is entered.

The PromptChar property allows us to specify a character that will take the place of our values before we enter text, we'll just keep the underscore.

Click on the OK button.

Change the `TabIndex` of the Masked Edit Control so that it replaces the removed text box in the *Tab* order.

Run the application and test the results. You'll now notice that your phone number appears within a mask of characters. The Masked Edit Control is important to understand, as it gives your application a professional look and feel:

Creating Our Own Navigation Bar

The next step will be to build our own navigation bar. It's not always vital to build a navigation bar, but there are several advantages:

> ➢ Allows you to build a navigation bar that reflects your GUI style. Use of command buttons with images, or use of any caption on the command button that fits your needs.
> ➢ Allows you to enable/disable portions of the navigation bar, based on criteria of your data.
> ➢ Provides more flexibility for custom error trapping.
> ➢ Allows you to apply business rules against your data before moving to the next record, such as ensuring values meet criteria.

Add a single command button and name it `cmdNegotiate`. Copy the command button and paste it on the form three times, creating a control array. Again, we use a control array to reduce the amount of code we write.

Add one label to your form. Move and resize the command buttons and the label below the Comments text box as shown opposite:

Change the properties of each of the new controls according to the following table:

Object	Property	Value
Label	Name	lblRecord
	Caption	{Blank}
	BorderStyle	Fixed Single
	BackColor	Pale Yellow
Command Button	Name	cmdNegotiate
	Index	0
	Caption	l<<
	Font	System, 10, Bold
Command Button	Name	cmdNegotiate
	Index	1
	Caption	<
	Font	System, 10, Bold

Object	Property	Value
Command Button	Name	cmdNegotiate
	Index	2
	Caption	>
	Font	System, 10, Bold
Command Button	Name	cmdNegotiate
	Index	3
	Caption	>>|
	Font	System, 10, Bold

Because we no longer need the ADO Data Control to navigate through the record, change its `Visible` property to `False`. This will hide the control during runtime. We still need the control to do our work for us, but it's not necessary to show it.

Navigating the Recordset

Recordset navigation has been rolled into a single sub procedure attached to the `Click` event of the `cmdNegotiate` command buttons. When any of the command buttons are clicked, the value of the `Index` property is passed so that we can query it and execute the proper code.

In locating the next, previous, first or last record, only one line of code needs to be executed. However, good coding technique says that we should attempt to trap any errors that arise during our navigation. For this reason, we have added some simple error handling. In the following example, the `MoveFirst`, `MoveLast`, `MoveNext` and `MovePrevious` methods of the ADO `Recordset` object are called. When this method is called, the data control locates and retrieves the specific record, and then refreshes the bound controls. If an error occurs during the navigation, a message box will display an error message.

When locating the next record or the previous record, we need to be cautious of hitting the End of File marker (`EOF`). To avoid this, we check to see if the `EOF` has been reached after we have called the `MoveNext` method. If we have reached the `EOF`, we move to the last record (back stepping one position). The same principle applies after we have called the `MovePrevious` method; we check that we have not passed the `BOF`, if we have then we call the `MoveFirst` method. The importance of not passing the `EOF` marker is that when you do pass it, the system no longer has a current record to work with and an error is returned. We could handle this with our error handler, but when you have the opportunity to avoid an error situation, you should always do so.

```
Private Sub cmdNegotiate_Click(Index As Integer)

    On Error GoTo goNegotiateErr

    With Adodc1.Recordset
```

Continued on Following Page

```
Select Case Index
        Case 0  'First Record
          .MoveFirst
        Case 1  'Previous Record
          .MovePrevious
          If .BOF Then .MoveFirst
        Case 2  'Next Record
          .MoveNext
          If .EOF Then .MoveLast
        Case 3  'Last Record
          .MoveLast
    End Select

  End With

Exit Sub


goNegotiateErr:

  MsgBox Err.Description

End Sub
```

Updating the Status Label

After the ADO Data Control has completed navigating to a specific record, an event is fired. This event is called `MoveComplete`. We'll use this event to execute code that checks our current position in the recordset and the total number of records in that recordset. Open the form's code window for your form and select **Adodc1** from the **Object** drop-down. Then from the **Procedure** drop-down box, select **MoveComplete**.

Add the following code to the event:

```
Private Sub Adodc1_MoveComplete(ByVal adReason As ADODB.EventReasonEnum, _
                                ByVal pError As ADODB.Error, _
                                adStatus As ADODB.EventStatusEnum, _
                                ByVal pRecordset As ADODB.Recordset)

    lblRecord.Caption = "Record: " & _
                        CStr(Adodc1.Recordset.AbsolutePosition) & _
                        " of " & Str(Adodc1.Recordset.RecordCount)

End Sub
```

The code that you have added updates your label with information about the absolute position of the current record in the recordset and the total number of records in your recordset. The results are concatenated into a string and then moved to the `Caption` property of the label control. This code uses two properties of the ADO `Recordset` object:

> ➢ `AbsolutePosition` - returns the current record position within a recordset.
> ➢ `RecordCount` - returns the number of records within a recordset.

If we were still using the ADO Data Control to navigate through our recordset, we could have assigned the same concatenated string to its `Caption` property.

Testing the Changes

Run your program and test it. Your new command buttons navigate through the recordset just as the ADO Data Control buttons did. Keep in mind that the code used in this example need not be attached to a command button. These methods (MoveFirst, MoveNext, etc.) can be called from any event. This makes for a very flexible and powerful development environment.

Further Enhancements

We're almost done with our first example application. To further enhance our application, we will add the following functionality:

> ➢ Ability to add new records
> ➢ Ability to delete records
> ➢ Ability to locate records with a find function
> ➢ Ability to update any changes made to the fields
> ➢ Ability to refresh the data field, aborting any changes made

To begin, add a single command button to the form and name it cmdAction. As you might have guessed, we'll create a control array to handle our logic. Copy the command button and paste it four more times. Arrange the new command buttons as shown below. Note that you can place these controls over the ADO Data Control because it will be invisible during run time:

Change the `Index` and `Caption` properties of the command buttons to reflect the following table:

Object	Caption
cmdAction(0)	&Add
cmdAction(1)	&Delete
cmdAction(2)	&Find
cmdAction(3)	&Update
cmdAction(4)	&Refresh

Now enter the following code into your `cmdAction_Click` event:

```
Private Sub cmdAction_Click(Index As Integer)

   On Error GoTo goActionErr

   With Adodc1

      Select Case Index

         Case 0   'Add
            If cmdAction(0).Caption = "&Add" Then
               varBookMark = .Recordset.Bookmark
               .Recordset.AddNew
               txtField(0).SetFocus
               cmdAction(0).Caption = "&Cancel"
               SetVisible False
            Else
               .Recordset.CancelUpdate
               If varBookMark > 0 Then
                 .Recordset.Bookmark = varBookMark
               Else
                 .Recordset.MoveFirst
               End If
                  cmdAction(Index).Caption = "&Add"
                  SetVisible True
            End If

         Case 1   'Delete
            If .Recordset.EditMode = False Then
               .Recordset.Delete
               .Recordset.MoveNext
               If .Recordset.EOF Then .Recordset.MoveLast
            Else
               MsgBox "Must update or refresh record before deleting!"
            End If

         Case 2   'Find
            frmFind.Show

         Case 3   'Update
            .Recordset.Update
            varBookMark = .Recordset.Bookmark
            .Recordset.Requery
            If varBookMark > 0 Then
               .Recordset.Bookmark = varBookMark
```

```
            Else
                .Recordset.MoveLast
            End If
            cmdAction(0).Caption = "&Add"
            SetVisible True

         Case 4   'Refresh
            varBookMark = .Recordset.Bookmark
            .Refresh
            If varBookMark > 0 Then
                .Recordset.Bookmark = varBookMark
            Else
                .Recordset.MoveLast
            End If

      End Select

   End With

Exit Sub


goActionErr:

   MsgBox Err.Description

End Sub
```

Adding New Records

When you add a record, the ADO Data Control handles the task of creating the new record. However, you, as the programmer, need to protect the record until it is either updated or cancelled. The best method of protecting the new record is to disable the other options. To ease this process, we'll build a simple procedure to toggle the Enabled property of each command button.

With the form's code window open, select Tools I Add Procedure... from Visual Basic's menu. The Add Procedure dialog will open. Enter SetVisible into the Name box and click on OK. Modify the procedure to receive one Boolean argument (blnstatus). Now enter the following code to change the Enabled properties of each command button:

```
Public Sub SetVisible(blnStatus As Boolean)

   Dim intIndex As Integer

   For intIndex = 0 To 3
      cmdNegotiate(intIndex).Enabled = blnStatus
   Next intIndex

   cmdAction(1).Enabled = blnStatus ' Delete
   cmdAction(2).Enabled = blnStatus ' Find
   cmdAction(4).Enabled = blnStatus ' Refresh

End Sub
```

We'll call this procedure to disable command buttons when we call the Add method, then re-enable the command buttons when we call the Update or Cancel method. The status (True or False) will be passed into this procedure and projected to the Enabled property of each command button.

In the General Declarations section, add a new variable called `varBookMark`. This variable will be used by a few of our command buttons to revert back to the record that we were working with prior to the Add method being called:

```
Option Explicit
Dim varBookMark As Variant
```

In this application, the `cmdAction(0)` (Add) command button will be used as a toggle to add or cancel a new record. When we click on the command button, the `Caption` of the command button is first checked. If it's equal to `"&Add"`, then we set `varBookMark` to the current record position and call the `AddNew` method. We then set the focus to the Last Name text box (`txtField(0)`), so that the user is ready to enter data. The `Caption` of the command button is changed to `"&Cancel"` and all command buttons except `cmdAction(0)` (Add) and `cmdAction(3)` (Update) are disabled. At this point, the user must either finish entering the data of the record and update, or undo the change.

If the `Caption` of the command button isn't equal to `"&Add"` then it must be `"&Cancel"`. When this is `True`, we call the `CancelUpdate` method to cancel the addition of the record. We then revert back to the original record that we were on before we called the Add method by setting the `Bookmark` property to be equal to the value stored in `varBookMark`. Finally, all command buttons are re-enabled.

Deleting Records

When the user clicks on `cmdAction(1)`, which is the Delete button, we check to see if the user has modified any of the data fields. We can check this status using the `EditMode` property associated with the `Recordset`. The `EditMode` property will flag `True` any time the user changes a bound control's data value. If the user attempts to delete a record to which he or she has made changes, the `Update` or `Refresh` methods must be used against the record first. Once we've checked the `Recordset`'s `EditMode` property, we can delete the record. Finally, we can then move to the next record.

Updating Records

The `Update` method is designed to move any changes made in a bound control to the database table. In this example, we follow the `Update` method with the `Requery` method. Normally, this would not be required. However, because we have an `AutoNumber` field, we may want to display the value of this after submitting a new record to the database. The `Update` method in itself will not do this. If we call the `Requery` method after the record has been updated, the number will populate the `Address_ID` field in the appropriate text box. Again, we set a bookmark after calling the `Update` method to ensure that we remain on the current record. The last step is to ensure the `cmdAction(0)` command button's `Caption` is set to `"&Add"` in case it was set to `"&Cancel"` and reset all command buttons to `Enabled` by calling the `SetVisible` procedure.

Refreshing Records

At various points during the editing of a record, the user may decide to abandon the changes and refresh the fields with the current data in the database table. The `Refresh` method is called against the ADO Data Control directly, not against the `Recordset` object. When called, it will abandon all changes made and reload the data as it exists in the database table. The `Refresh` method moves the user to the first record, just as when the first connection was made to the database. For this reason, we set the bookmark equal to the current record, call the `Refresh` method and then move to the bookmarked record. If we didn't move back to the record that was set in the bookmark, the user would be stranded and would have to re-locate the record that was being modified.

> Note that if another user has deleted the record, it will not be possible to move back to the bookmark. Therefore, an error will be returned.

The Refresh method can also come in handy when more than one user may be modifying the same record. When one user makes updates to a record, a second can call the Refresh method to view the changes.

Finding Records

If the user clicks on cmdAction(3) we open a new form called frmFind. This additional form will provide a mechanism for entering the text that the user wants to find. We could use Visual Basic's InputBox command, but we'll implement the solution using a second form, which gives us greater flexibility. This form will have several command buttons, allowing us to locate the first occurrence of the string, the next occurrence of the string, or cancel the operation.

To add another form, select Project I Add Form from Visual Basic's menu. When the Add Form dialog appears, select Form and click on Open. Save this new form as Find.frm in the same directory as Address.frm. Add three command buttons and a text box to the form as shown:

Modify the properties of the form to reflect the following table:

Object	Property	Value
Form	Name	frmFind
	Caption	Find
Text Box	Name	txtSearch
	Text	{Blank}
Command Button	Name	cmdFind
	Caption	&Find
Command Button	Name	cmdFindNext
	Caption	Find &Next
Command Button	Name	cmdCancel
	Caption	&Cancel

We now need a procedure to scan through the records, searching for a match. Add a new procedure to the frmFind form and name it FindString. Add the following code to the new procedure:

```
Public Sub FindString()

    Dim strFind As String
    Dim intFields As Integer

    On Error Goto FindError

    If Trim(txtSearch) <> "" Then
        strFind = Trim(txtSearch)
        With frmAddress.Adodc1.Recordset
            Do Until .EOF
                For intFields = 0 To 1
                    If InStr(1, frmAddress.txtField(intFields), strFind, _
                            vbTextCompare) > 0 Then
                        frmAddress.txtField(intFields).SelStart = _
                                InStr(1, frmAddress.txtField(intFields), _
                                    strFind, vbTextCompare) - 1
                        frmAddress.txtField(intFields).SelLength = Len(strFind)
                        frmAddress.txtField(intFields).SetFocus
                        Exit Sub
                    End If
                Next
                .MoveNext
                DoEvents
            Loop
            MsgBox "Record not found"
            .MoveFirst
        End With
    End If

Exit Sub


FindError:

    MsgBox Err.Description
    Err.Clear

End Sub
```

The FindString code first ensures that the text box is not empty, then initiates a loop that searches for the text requested until it reaches the EOF of the ADO Data Control Recordset. There's a lot of code here, so let's break it down a bit.

The procedure currently searches only the text boxes for the first and last names, txtField(0) and txtField(1):

```
For intFields = 0 To 1
```

This could be easily modified to search all of the text boxes by changing the For loop to:

```
For intFields = 0 to 8
```

Don't forget that we deleted the text box for the phone number! This would require us to either re-index the control array, or manually skip over the phone number Index, which was number 6. Two alternative solutions include:

➢ Conduct a For - Each loop, running through all text boxes looking for a match.
➢ Check all fields directly in the recordset. The field count can be attained from Adodc1.Recordset.Fields.Count.

We use the InStr function to look for the string in any part of the field. This returns an integer indicating the beginning position of the substring to be found. If it returns a 0, we know the substring does not occur in the field. If it is greater than 0, we can highlight the text and exit the search routine. In the following code, the search type is set to vbTextCompare. This will provide a stronger search mechanism, avoiding misses due to case sensitivity and other anomalies:

```
If InStr(1, frmAddress.txtField(intFields), strFind, _
         vbTextCompare) > 0 Then
```

To highlight the string we're searching for we use the SelStart and SelLength properties of the text box. First, we establish where the highlighted text begins by finding the start position and subtracting 1 from it. To find the start position, we use the InStr function in exactly the same way as above. We must subtract one because InStr will return the text position and the SelStart property needs to be set equal to the value just before the character we want to highlight:

```
frmAddress.txtField(intFields).SelStart = _
        InStr(1, frmAddress.txtField(intFields), _
              strFind, vbTextCompare) - 1
```

The Len keyword is used to determine the length of the string we're looking for. Once we have this, we highlight the string by setting the SelLength property of the text box equal to the length of the string that was searched for:

```
frmAddress.txtField(intFields).SelLength = Len(strFind)
frmAddress.txtField(intFields).SetFocus
```

When we have set these SelStart and SelLength properties, followed by the SetFocus method, the selected text will be highlighted, so that the user can quickly recognize it.

The cmdFind button is used to locate the first instance of the string. If the RecordCount property of the Recordset is less than one, there is no need to continue. To ensure that the data is searched from the beginning, we need to move to the first record before calling the FindString procedure:

```
Private Sub cmdFind_Click()

  If frmAddress.Adodc1.Recordset.RecordCount > 0 Then
    frmAddress.Adodc1.Recordset.MoveFirst
    Call FindString
  Else
    MsgBox "Recordset is Empty"
  End If

End Sub
```

When searching for the next instance of the string, we don't need to move to the first record. However, we should move to the next record so that the FindString procedure doesn't find the same record again. Of course, if we call the MoveNext method, we need to check for the EOF marker. In this scenario, if we reached the end of the file, there's no need to continue searching:

```
Private Sub cmdFindNext_Click()

    With frmAddress.Adodc1.Recordset
      .MoveNext
      If .EOF Then
        .MoveLast
        MsgBox "End of File Reached!"
      Else
        Call FindString
      End If
    End With

End Sub
```

Finally, if a user clicks on the Cancel button, we can close the form by calling its Unload method. The keyword Me refers to the object that the code resides on, so in this case the code unloads frmFind. You could have said Unload frmFind instead. Many programmers may choose to use the Hide method (frmFind.Hide). However, to save resources, it's better practice to unload the form out of memory:

```
Private Sub cmdCancel_Click()

    Unload Me
    Set frmFind = Nothing

End Sub
```

Test the Find Routine

To test your new code, run the application and click on the Find button. The Find dialog will appear. Type in a name, or a portion of a name and click on Find:

The application will search through the records until a match is made or the EOF is reached. When a match is made, the search string is highlighted.

Moving through the records looking for a match works well in this example because the table size is small, however with larger tables, a better solution is to apply a SQL statement to the Recordset, or to use the Filter property of the Recordset object. We'll learn more about the ADO Control methods, properties and events that allow this functionality in the following chapters.

Other Databound Controls

Not all of the following controls will automatically be added to the Toolbox. Many will need to be added with the **Components** dialog just as you did with the ADO Data Control.

The Label

The label control works in a similar way to the text box control. The advantage of the label control is that it restricts the user from entering, selecting, or copying any values. You could therefore add a label, bind it to your data source and the user would only be able to view the field. In a nutshell, the label provides a different look and feel over a text box.

The Check Box

The check box allows the user an alternative to typing when a field contains Yes/No, True/False values. The check box has three possible values:

➢ Unchecked = 0
➢ Checked = 1
➢ Grayed (i.e. undetermined) = 2

The Picture and Image Controls

Both the picture and image controls work in very similar fashion. They both can be bound to an image field in a database. There are advantages to each control. An image control, for example, has the ability to stretch to the size of the image. A picture box requires pre-knowledge of the image size. This is simply one example of differences between the image and picture controls. Each has its own advantages and disadvantages.

DataGrid Control

The DataGrid control has been around for some time, and allows the user to view and edit multiple records at once. It works and looks like the table view of Access, so many people are comfortable with its design:

Country	City	CompanyName	ContactName
Argentina	Buenos Aires	Rancho grande	Sergio Gutiérrez
Argentina	Buenos Aires	Océano Atlántico Ltda.	Yvonne Moncac
Argentina	Buenos Aires	Cactus Comidas para lle	Patricio Simpson
Austria	Salzburg	Piccolo und mehr	Georg Pipps
Austria	Graz	Ernst Handel	Roland Mendel
Belgium	Bruxelles	Maison Dewey	Catherine Dewe
Belgium	Charleroi	Suprêmes délices	Pascale Cartrair
Brazil	São Paulo	Queen Cozinha	Lúcia Carvalho
Brazil	Rio de Janeiro	Hanari Carnes	Mario Pontes
Brazil	Campinas	Gourmet Lanchonetes	André Fonseca
Brazil	Rio de Janeiro	Que Delícia	Bernardo Batista
Brazil	Resende	Wellington Importadora	Paula Parente
Brazil	Rio de Janeiro	Ricardo Adocicados	Janete Limeira
Brazil	São Paulo	Comércio Mineiro	Pedro Afonso

The Hierarchical FlexGrid Control

This control supercedes the DataGrid control. It's powerful in the sense that it has many layout options to allow the user the best viewing capability. As seen below, the control allows you to group records that have repeating fields. In this case, the Customers table has been grouped by country and then by city. This is just the beginning of the Hierarchical FlexGrid's capabilities though. This control also allows many display formats, with shading and font styles. When working with the Hierarchical FlexGrid control, it is probably easier to use the Data Form Wizard to build the form, rather than modifying the control and form properties once it has been created. The Data Form Wizard can be found in the Add-Ins menu.

The DataList and DataCombo Controls

The DataList and DataCombo box controls both offer the user a mechanism for selecting an item from a list of choices. Each of the controls pulls data from one record source, then when an item is selected it populates a field in another record source. It's not always practical to use them when there are thousands of possibilities, as it may slow down your application. For this reason, I would recommend that you use them for populating a field where the number of records to choose from is limited. This rule is especially true when you have several boxes on a single form.

These two controls have four data-binding properties, which you must know how to use. As mentioned above, the data is fed from one database table to another:

> ➢ `RowSource`: The Data Control from which the DataCombo or DataList box will be filled (could be ADO, DAO, RDO or other).
> ➢ `ListField`: The field from which the DataCombo or DataList box will be filled.
> ➢ `DataSource`: The ADO Data Control that specifies where the selected data will be stored.
> ➢ `DataField`: The field that will be populated with the selected data.

Each of these controls has its own look and feel to it. It's likely that you have seen these two controls used in applications. The DataCombo box allows you to do a lookup in a table with minimal wasted space. The user can click on the down arrow, choose the selection, then the results are stored in the retracted control. The DataList box doesn't retract; it allows the user to see all of the choices without expanding the box:

The OLE Container Control

This control allows you to view any embedded OLE object inside your database table. This object may be a bitmap image, Excel worksheet or even a Word document. Once embedded, you can double-click on the object, bringing it to edit mode and then change the data. Any changes made to the object are made to the original document that it is linked to.

The Rich Text Box Control

This control works in a similar way to the text box. However, it allows for more precise custom editing. You can link this control to a memo field, which allows underlining, specific font types, bold, and much more.

The MS Chart Control

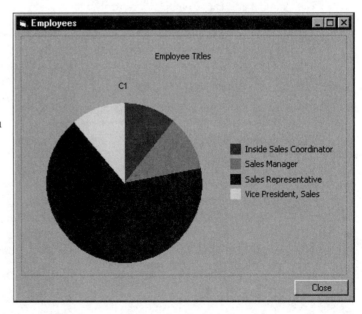

With the MS Chart Control, you can build a wide range of charts that feed off the data of the ADO Data Control. Just a few of the possible chart types include: pie, line, area, step, scatter and bar. There's a wizard to assist you in creating your chart, which is the best place to begin if you're not familiar with this control. The property pages of this control allow you to define color types, titles, footers and much more.

The Data Repeater Control

This is one of the newest additions to the family of data-bound controls. It's very flexible in the sense that you can design a data form (as an ActiveX control) then, using the Data Repeater control, display the form multiple times, showing multiple records at once.

These are just a few of the most common controls that can be bound to your ADO Data Control. Don't forget, that if you don't find a control that suits your needs, you can always build it using Visual Basic. In addition, you can find a great number of vendor controls available. These controls can vary greatly in price, however. But if the control fits your needs and is cheaper than building it yourself, it's worth the investment.

Summary

In this chapter, we reviewed the basics of the ADO Data Control, and some of the controls that can be bound to it. We also demonstrated that even if you don't have a database program on your computer, you can still create a database using VisData. In particular we looked at:

> - The Visual Data Manager (VisData)
> - The `ConnectionString` property
> - The `RecordSource` property
> - The Masked Edit Control
> - Creating our own navigation bar
> - Other data bound controls, including the DataGrid, Hierarchical FlexGrid, DataList, DataCombo, OLE Container, Rich Text Box, MS Chart and Data Repeater

In future chapters, we will explore the properties, methods and events of the ADO Data Control in more depth. The more you know about them, the more likely you are to succeed in your project implementation.

Now that we've seen how we can connect to an Access database using ADO, we will see how (and why) we might want to move to using SQL Server, in the next chapter.

Suppliers

- SupplierID
- CompanyName
- ContactName
- ContactTitle
- Address
- City
- Region
- PostalCode
- Country
- Phone
- Fax
- HomePage

Products

- ProductID
- ProductName
- SupplierID
- CategoryID
- QuantityPerUnit
- UnitPrice
- UnitsInStock
- UnitsOnOrder
- ReorderLevel
- Discontinued

Categories

- CategoryID
- CategoryName
- Description
- Picture

6

Upsizing to SQL Server

One question that never seems clear is when to upgrade to a more powerful, enterprise-level database. In this section, we'll take a closer look at some of the considerations to weigh when considering this decision. Once you have decided that you need to move an enterprise-level, high-performance database, consider if there are tools available to assist you in your migration. Access 2000, for example, provides a multitude of wizards, some of which are designed for upsizing your database to SQL Server.

So, what should you consider when deciding on a database? Well, since we have dedicated much of this book to Microsoft products, let's weigh the differences of Microsoft Access and SQL Server.

How Much Data Do You Need to Store?

This is probably the first question you should ask yourself. The most important point here is, "Don't overlook long term requirements". Currently, your storage space may be minimal, but in the long term your needs may double, triple or even become tenfold the current amount. Access will allow you to store two gigabytes of information on each database, SQL Server allows you to store up to a terabyte of information, potentially even more. While these are represented as limitations, multiple databases can be linked together, giving the appearance of a single database. This extends the limitations of each.

To prove that a terabyte of information could be stored on a single database, Microsoft sponsored a web page where you can look up satellite images of the world. This site can be viewed at www.terraserver.com:

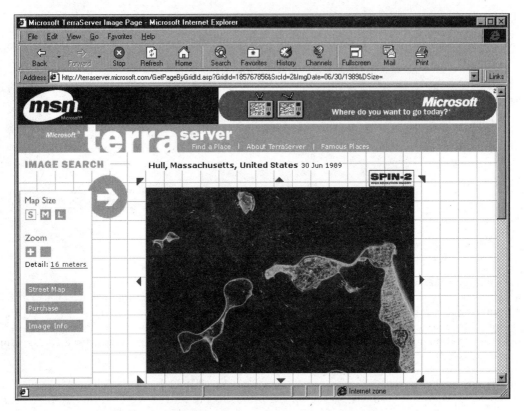

What Is the Budget of Your Project?

Of course, the database is only one factor in the equation of cost, but with a tight budget it can make a major difference in whether you use Access, which may be readily available to your users, or if you buy SQL Server. Decisions are not made solely on this criterion, but it is a factor that is always weighed into the equation. This is especially true for those who control the budget. Training and maintenance should also be factored in. Getting staff up to speed on a new database can be costly in more than one way.

What Are the Benchmarks of Each Database?

A benchmark is a test that is used to compare hardware and/or software. Whenever you are comparing performance in benchmark tests it is vital that you know exactly what the test was designed to show, the specification of the system it was run on (CPU, memory etc) and how the benchmark will relate to your needs.

Although it's difficult to find much in the way of benchmarks for Access, Microsoft has no problem bragging about SQL Server's benchmarks. In fact, they even claim to outperform Oracle on the Windows NT Server. Let's look at two of the benchmarks you might want to consider.

TPC Benchmarks

A non-profit corporation (Transaction Processing Performance Council) was formed specifically to define benchmark standards. Many standards came to light from this corporation, but the standard that you should be most concerned with is TPC-C, which is a standard of performance and scalability. This standard is believed to be the most representative of real-world transactions; measuring transactions per minute (tpmC) and Price per tpmC. The Price per tpmC equals the total system cost divided by the tpmC. Therefore, if the total system cost is $900,000 and the tpmC is 1500, the result equals $900,000/1500 or $600 per tpmC. The calculations of system cost must include all aspects of the costs including terminals, software, database software, transaction monitors, computer systems, backup storage and 3 years of maintenance. Microsoft has identified SQL Server to be the first database server to break the $20 mark.

To find out more about benchmarks, locate the Transaction Processing Performance Council on the web at www.tpc.org.

Backup Benchmarks

These benchmarks gauge the speed that a large database can be backed up and restored. This can become very important when you have small windows of opportunity to execute such tasks. Keep in mind that Backup Benchmarks are likely to be a reflection of a database's ability to replicate too.

Microsoft's SQL Server allows you to backup your database whilst it's in use. There is no need for all your users to leave the database before you can back it up. As a consequence, your database can run 24 hours a day, 7 days a week.

What Type of Functionality Will Be Required?

SQL Server is clearly more function-rich than Access. Let's take a look at some of the extra functionality of SQL Server.

Although we will discuss more about security later, many programmers (myself included) have more confidence in SQL Server's ability to secure a database over Access. For example, SQL Server integrates with the Windows NT security, allowing you to use a single log on for both the network and the database. This is especially beneficial if you have a complex security system where there is restricted access to parts of the database for some users and complete access for others.

SQL Server has an automatic recovery mechanism that recovers a database to its last state of consistency in the event of an operating system crash or power outage. This mechanism can recover the database in a matter of minutes without the need for a DBA to intervene.

Furthermore, we'll discover that SQL Server allows us to process a batch of requests and actions as a single atomic unit. With the benefit that if one of these requests fails, the whole group of requests will fail together. This is vital for systems in banking or online order entry.

Ease of function implementation will inherently play a role here too.

How Many Connections to the Database Are Required?

This is another one of those considerations that must be made with the future in mind. You may need 100 concurrent connections today, but where do you expect to be in five or ten years? Access limits the number of connections to 255, so if you expect growth to expand past this value, you may want to consider another option. The number of connections into SQL Server depends greatly on how you configure the system, including any connection pooling that may be done, but this number can reach 5000, 10,000 or even greater.

Additionally, SQL Server was designed to be used in a client-server architecture from the outset. SQL Server can process database queries on the server machine before sending data across the network to the clients. Access on the other hand, was designed for use on the desktop. It expects the client to do most of the processing. By moving to SQL Server and processing data queries on the server, we can reduce network traffic, which also enables our system to handle large numbers of clients.

Upsizing Our Address Database to SQL Server

When building our Address book example, we chose to use an Access database created with VisData. Suppose we decide that Access is no longer sufficient to meet our needs. Perhaps we intend to make the Address application available to 500 users as a company-wide store of contacts' names and addresses. We need to convert the application to use SQL Server. This means that we need to make two major changes:

> Convert the database to SQL Server
> Convert any existing applications to connect to the new database

Well, the truth is that neither of these is too difficult. In fact, if your applications are built using ADO, the latter requirement may only take a few minutes to change.

When converting databases from Access to SQL Server, you have a few options available. Here's an outline:

> If you are converting an Access 2000 database to SQL Server 6.5 or 7.0 you can use the Upsizing Wizard supplied with Access 2000.

If you are converting Access 97 to SQL Server 6.5 or 7.0 you can download the **Microsoft Access 97 Upsizing Tools** (which includes the Upsizing Wizard) for free from Microsoft's web site. For more information on these tools, locate the following web address:

```
http://www.microsoft.com/accessdev/prodinfo/AUT97dat.htm
```

> Regardless of what Access version you use, you can export tables from Access into *any* ODBC-compliant database. This is a quick and dirty way of moving your tables where no relationships or indexes will be moved with the tables.

As a demonstration of how easy it is to port an application to another database, we'll take our Address project, and move it to a SQL Server 7.0 database.

Converting Our Database

Before we upsize our `Address` database to SQL Server we should ensure that we have a made a backup copy of it. The Upsizing Wizard does not remove anything from the Access database, but it's always a good idea to have a backup copy of the original database before you begin any upsizing.

With our `Address` database we can just copy and paste `Address.mdb` into a folder called `Backup` (or something similar).

The next precaution we should take is to ensure that the machine that will take the upsized database has enough disk space. Our `Address` database will only need a few Mega bytes, but if you are upsizing a very large Access database you will need to leave plenty of space for the extra system files that are added in the upsizing process and to allow the database to grow.

> *In the event that the Upsizing Wizard runs out of space, it will stop, causing there to be a partial database. If this does ever happen to you, you can simply delete tables or the database in the Enterprise Manager.*

Next, make sure that your machine has a default printer. The Upsizing Wizard will automatically create a printout of an Upsizing report at the end.

Finally, make sure that you have permissions on both the Access and SQL Server databases to create a new database - system administer will be sufficient.

The Upsizing Wizard

Begin by opening up the `Address` database in Access. From the main menu select Tools | Database Utilities | Upsizing Wizard.

> *Depending on the options you selected when you installed Access, you may not have the Upsizing Wizard installed. If so, simply instead your Office CD when prompted.*

When the Upsizing Wizard appears select Create new database from the first page and the click on Next:

In the next screen that appears, enter the name of your server, a login ID and password, and give the name of the SQL Server database, which in this case will be Address. Then click on Next:

Now we must specify the tables that we want to upsize. We just want to export our Address table to SQL Server, so click the > button and then Next:

The next table allows us to export table attributes in addition to their data. By default, all table attributes are checked for upsizing. The four attributes that can be upsized are:

> **Indexes**: If the Indexes check box is selected, the Upsizing Wizard will upsize all of the indexes. The primary keys in the Access database will be converted to SQL Server non-clustered, unique indexes, marked as SQL Server primary keys. All other indexes will also be converted, unique Access indexes will be converted to unique SQL Server indexes; non-unique Access indexes will be converted to non-unique SQL Server indexes. The new SQL Server indexes will have the same name as their Access counterparts, except that characters that are illegal in SQL Server (e.g. spaces) will be replaced by underscores.

> **Validation Rules**: If the Validation rules check box is selected, the Upsizing Wizard will upsize all validation rules and Required properties. For example, we could have specified that First_Name and Last_Name would be Required and we could have applied a validation rule against the City field to prevent numbers from being added. The validation rules will be upsized to triggers (we'll learn a lot about these in Chapter 8) and the Required fields will be upsized to fields that don't allow null values (or empty fields).

➤ **Defaults**: If your Access database has default values for any fields, checking the <u>D</u>efaults check box will ensure that they are upsized. For instance, we could have had an extra field for someone's country of residence called `Country`, which had a default value that would be USA. When upsized these defaults are ANSI (American National Standards Institute) defaults and are not bound to any particular field or table - you can use them against any number of different fields.

➤ **Table Relationships**: The Table <u>r</u>elationships check box allows you to specify how you would like the table relationships to be upsized. You have two options for how your relationships should be upsized, the default being Use DRI. If you select Use DRI then your relationships will use Declared Referential Integrity (DRI), which works the same way as Access referential integrity. However, DRI does not support the cascading update or delete that you can specify with Access. Therefore, if you specified that the table relationships in your Access database have cascading updates or deletes, and you want these features to be in the upsized SQL Server database you should select Use triggers. This option will ensure that triggers (discussed in Chapter 8) in the SQL Server database will achieve the same result.

The next selection, Add <u>t</u>imestamp to tables?, may not be quite as obvious as the previous ones were. SQL Server uses **timestamp fields** to indicate that a record has been changed by creating a unique value field, which it updates whenever a record has been updated. If there is no timestamp field present, SQL Server has to check all the fields in a record to determine if the record has changed, hindering performance. There are two different Yes options:

➤ Yes, let wizard decide - means that the wizard will create timestamp fields where appropriate.

➤ Yes, always - means that the wizard will add a timestamp field to all tables, regardless of the field types they contain. This improves performance of upsized Access tables that have field types other than Memo, OLE Object or floating point (i.e. Single or Double).

For our `Address` database just say Yes, always to Add <u>t</u>imestamp fields to tables? and keep all the other default options. Click on <u>N</u>ext:

The next screen allows you to specify how you would like your Access database application (i.e. the queries, forms and reports you have created in Microsoft Access) to be upsized. We don't have any of these in our `Address` database so just select **No application changes** and click **Next**:

In the final screen, just select **Finish** and the Upsizing Wizard will create a new SQL Server database. Notice that it creates a report of the upsizing:

If you read through the Upsizing Wizard Report, you'll see that the wizard has converted all of our Access fields to SQL Server fields, keeping all our original names and changing `text` field types to `varchar`, `memo` to `text`, and `long` to `int`. It has also converted all of our indexes, retaining both their names and their ability to contain duplicates. We've also gained the additional timestamp field that we requested.

If you now open SQL Server's Enterprise manager, via Start | Programs | Microsoft SQL Server 7.0 | Enterprise Manager, you'll find the `Address` database with an `Address` table and a large number of system tables that have been added during the upsizing process:

Converting Our Project

The last step in converting our system is to change the connection string of the ADO Data Control in the project. To do that, follow these steps:

1. Open the `Address` project located in the `C:\ProVB6DB\Chapter4` folder.

2. Right-click on the ADO Data Control (of the `frmAddress` form) and select **ADODC Properties**. The property pages should open with the connection information.

3. A connection string should already exist, but we want to change this to connect to our new database, so click on the B**u**ild button.

4. In the Provider tab, select Microsoft OLE DB Provider for SQL Server and click on the Next button:

5. Select the server where your database exists, any security information, and type in the database name (**Address**) in the Select the database on the server text box:

6. Click on the <u>T</u>est Connection button, then the OK button.

7. Click on the OK buttons in both the Data Link Properties dialog and the Property Pages dialog.

8. Save your project.

You can now test your changes by running the project. The system should run just as it did prior to the change. It just connects to a SQL Server database instead of an Access database.

See, I told you it was easy!

Summary

In this chapter, we've considered some of the reasons why we might want to upsize an Access database to SQL Server. Whether or not to upsize is a complex decision with many factors to consider. In some cases upsizing will be the right thing to do, in others it will not. My aim in this chapter, was to give you some food for thought, there are rarely easy answers to the question of whether or not it is time to upsize.

We saw how to upsize a database to SQL Server and connect our application from the previous chapter to our new SQL Server 7.0 database.

In particular, we considered:

➢ SQL Server 7.0's size of up to one terabyte

➢ The TPC and Backup benchmarks

➢ SQL Server integrates its functionality with NT security - a feature unavailable in Access

➢ Using Access' Upsizing Wizard

➢ Converting our Address project so that it uses the Address database in SQL Server rather than Address.mdb

Suppliers

- SupplierID
- CompanyName
- ContactName
- ContactTitle
- Address
- City
- Region
- PostalCode
- Country
- Phone
- Fax
- HomePage

Products

- ProductID
- ProductName
- SupplierID
- CategoryID
- QuantityPerUnit
- UnitPrice
- UnitsInStock
- UnitsOnOrder
- ReorderLevel
- Discontinued

Categories

- CategoryID
- CategoryName
- Description
- Picture

6

An Overview of Structured Query Language

In this chapter, we'll discuss how to retrieve, manipulate and analyze the data in a database using **Structured Query Language (SQL)**. An understanding of SQL is essential to building a powerful, function-rich, multi-tier client-server application.

In Chapter 4, we called specific methods of the `Recordset` object, using the ADO Data Control (ADODC), in order to add, modify, update and delete data from a table. These methods included `Delete`, `MoveNext` and `AddNew`. The ADODC works well and for simple applications it would probably suit our needs more than adequately. However, more advanced applications require a more versatile method of retrieving and manipulating our data. For example, we may need to home in on very specific data, often pulled together from a number of tables. To handle such tasks, SQL is the perfect solution.

In the context of data manipulation, we can think of SQL as an extension of ADO. Rather than programming our application to parse through the data one record at a time, SQL statements can be used to let our database engine do the work for us. Without SQL, certain tasks would be very arduous (and would become more so the bigger the database). For example, suppose we wanted to delete all the records from a table that satisfied specific criteria. We would have to navigate through every record, checking the values of each one and deleting the ones we didn't need anymore. *A SQL statement can accomplish this with just one line of code.*

The chapter has been broken down into two sections: **SQL Basics** and **Advanced SQL**. In the **SQL Basics** section we'll discuss exactly what SQL is and what it can do for us. We'll build a simple SQL Tester program (using the ADODC and a few data bound controls), which we'll use to apply a range of basic SQL data manipulation statements to individual tables on the `Northwind` database on SQL Server. We will use the `SELECT` statement to send queries to the database and retrieve data. We'll then cover use of `DELETE`, `INSERT` and `UPDATE` commands to modify the data in database tables. In the **Advanced SQL** section, we'll take all of this knowledge a step further and review some more advanced features of SQL. Due to the inherent design of a relational database, we will commonly need to bring the data from many tables together and display the data in a single result table. We'll explore some of the SQL commands that will allow us to do this. Finally we'll cover the basics of how to create, alter and drop tables and indexes in a database.

SQL Basics

The majority of this section is concerned with how to query our databases using the SELECT statement. The data we retrieve will be displayed in a "spreadsheet-style" recordset. We'll look at how to attach clauses and predicates to this basic statement in order to home in on specific data and we'll see how to manipulate this data using various functions. Toward the end of the section we'll insert, remove and modify data in a database using the INSERT, DELETE and UPDATE statements respectively. Firstly, though, let's find out more about the SQL language.

Exactly What Is SQL?

In short, SQL is an industry-standard language used to create, maintain and query databases. The first thing to note about it is that, unlike common programming languages such as C, Basic, Pascal etc., SQL is a **non-procedural** language. This means that instead of specifying *how* to perform a particular task, we simply tell SQL *what* we want to achieve and let the DBMS decide the best way to go about it. SQL is referred to as a set-oriented language. It gives us access to all the tables in the database in one go and returns data in a spreadsheet-style recordset - basically a table with a set of rows (analogous to records) made up of various columns (analogous to fields).

SQL comes in the form of a single statement that is applied to a database. In generic terms, this statement may specify, for example, which table in the database to work with and will indicate specific fields to be retrieved or modified.

> **Several SQL statements may be grouped together and passed to the database as a single transaction. This promotes faster execution time. However, if one statement fails, all the statements fail as a batch. This will be discussed in much more detail later in the book when we cover the implementation of transactions, in Chapter 10.**

As I briefly mentioned in the introduction to this book, there are many variations on the industry standard (ANSI-92) version of SQL. Large database servers provide procedural extensions to ANSI-92 SQL. The syntax of the keywords is typically the same, but additional built-in functions are added to make our data manipulation tasks easier. **Transact-SQL** is the "extended" language supported by MS SQL Server. Another example is **PL/SQL**, supported by Oracle database servers. The singularities of Transact-SQL and PL/SQL are discussed in Appendices B and C.

This chapter follows the ANSI-92 standard but will occasionally use syntax that is specifically Transact-SQL. I'll make a point of identifying keywords that are extensions specific to this provider. Additional functions, such as these, provide convenience to the programmer and it's well worth taking the time to investigate those that are provided by your database engine (your database user manual should provide a complete listing of available functions and the context in which they are used). However, if we want our databases to be "portable" from server to server then we should try to avoid their use. ANSI SQL is quite robust, and in most circumstances we can get by without them.

Don't worry unduly if you do find yourself using them. Most database engines have comparable functions and the syntax is usually quite similar.

Building the SQL Tester Program

Throughout this chapter, we'll be working with tables located in the Northwind database, installed with SQL Server. We'll need to modify this database so I recommend that you make a backup copy of it called NWind.

> *In order to make a back up copy of a database on SQL Server: 1. Click on the appropriate database to load up the database information. 2. Select* **backup database** *from the* **Backup** *section. 3. Click on the* **Add** *button and enter the filename string (e.g.* C:\MSSQL7\BACKUP\Nwind*). 4. Select* **restore database** *from the* **Backup** *section 5. In the* **Restore as database** *drop-down box, enter the name* NWind*.*

There are a number of ways that we can build and test SQL statements. In this chapter, we use Visual Basic to create a simple program with which to test our SQL statements. The program is fine for our purposes but if we were handling very complex SQL statements we would need to employ a user-friendlier program that assisted with debugging. Many SQL editors will identify the locations of any errors in our statements by line number. Some of the alternative programs include:

> ➤ VisData: This program has many inherent weaknesses. However, for general building and testing purposes, it's great. I tend to use this tool only for simple SQL statements.

> ➤ MS Access: This tool is readily available and capable of handling the most complex SQL statements. Access also allows the user to create queries with a drag-and-drop interface. The queries can then be viewed as text and copied. When first learning the SQL language, this is the best way to go. The GUI-based drag-and-drop environment makes SQL very easy for anyone to use and learn. Even if you're working with a SQL Server database, this is an ideal tool. Access has the capability of linking to SQL Server tables, so you can still create statements in Access.

> ➤ MS Query: This tool is available with a number of products. For example, it comes installed with SQL Server and allows you to connect to, and build SQL statements for, any ODBC-compliant database. This tool also provides a drag-and-drop environment.

There are also many third party tools available. These tools can greatly reduce the amount of time that is spent writing and testing SQL so consider all options, even the ones that are not free.

Our program will accept a SQL statement as a string, execute the query using the ADO Data Control and then display the results in a DataGrid control. To begin building this program, open Visual Basic and create a new Standard EXE project.

1. Change the Name property of the project to SQLTest.

2. Change the Name property of the form to frmSQLTest.

3. Change the Caption property of frmSQLTest to SQL Tester.

4. Create a folder off the C:\ProVB6DB directory called Chapter6.

5. Save the form and project as SQLTest.vbp and SQLTest.frm in the new folder.

6. Now that we have our project saved, we'll need to add the ADO Data Control, a DataGrid, a text box and a command button to the form. Both the ADO Data Control and the Data Grid control need to be added to the toolbox before we can use them in our project. Right-click on the toolbox and select Components. The DataGrid control can be found as Microsoft DataGrid Control 6.0 (OLEDB). Arrange the controls to resemble the following layout:

7. When building the connection string, select the Microsoft OLE DB Provider for SQL Server provider. In the Connection tab, enter a server name, a user name and password, and the name of the database (NWind). If you've forgotten how to build a connection string to SQL Server, refer back to Chapter 5. Feel free to connect to the Northwind database on Access if you prefer (see Chapter 4).

8. Instead of simply binding our ADO Data Control to a specific table, as we did in Chapter 4, we'll allow it to receive text commands in the form of SQL statements. After opening the RecordSource property pages for the ADODC, select adcmdText as the Command Type. We need to input the Command Text (SQL). If we leave this field blank, Visual Basic may throw us an error during run-time, so enter the following simple SQL statement (we'll discuss exactly what this statement does later in the chapter):

```
SELECT * FROM Customers
```

9. We'll want to modify the DataGrid control to allow us to enter new records or delete existing records. This is not the default, so open the property pages and make the change. To open the property pages, right click on the DataGrid control and select **Properties**:

10. Check the AllowAddNew and AllowDelete option buttons to enable the functionality.

11. Using the following table, modify the remaining properties of each object:

Object	Property	Value
Form	`Name`	`frmSQLTest`
	`Caption`	**SQL Tester**
ADO Data Control	`Name`	`Adodc1`
	Database `(ConnectionString)`	`Provider=SQLOLEDB.1;Persist Security Info=False; User ID = sa;Initial Catalog=NWind;Data Source=[Your Server Name]`
	`RecordSource`	`adCmdText`
		`SELECT * FROM Customers`
DataGrid Control	`Name`	`DataGrid1`
	`DataSource`	`Adodc1`
Command Button	`Name`	`cmdSQL`

Table Continued on Following Page

Object	Property	Value
	Caption	Apply SQL
	Font	MS Sans Serif, Bold, 12
Text Box	Name	txtSQL
	Text	blank
	MultiLine	True

OK - we're now ready to begin coding our project.

The first section of code utilizes the `MoveComplete` event of the ADO Data Control. This event is fired each time we navigate through the recordset and every time the data is retrieved. The added code simply evaluates the number of records in our recordset and assigns that value to the `Caption` property of the ADO Data Control. Thus, we will know the total number of records returned to the DataGrid each time a new SQL statement is applied. This code should look rather familiar, as we encountered a similar version in Chapter 4:

```
Private Sub Adodc1_MoveComplete(ByVal adReason As ADODB.EventReasonEnum, _
                         ByVal pError As ADODB.Error, _
                         adStatus As ADODB.EventStatusEnum, _
                         ByVal pRecordset As ADODB.Recordset)

    Adodc1.Caption = Adodc1.Recordset.RecordCount & " Records Returned!"

End Sub
```

Next, we code the `Click` event of our command button:

```
Private Sub cmdSQL_Click()

    On Error Resume Next
    Adodc1.RecordSource = txtSQL.Text
    Adodc1.Refresh

End Sub
```

The second line of code assigns the SQL statement in the text box to the `RecordSource` property of the ADO Data Control. In effect, we are specifying the source of the required data through a simple SQL statement. However, before this SQL statement will execute, we must call the `Refresh` method. The `Refresh` method will re-query the database using the new properties assigned to the ADO Data Control. In this case, the only property changed was the `RecordSource` property.

> **Applying the text to the `RecordSource` property has no immediate effect. We must also call the `Refresh` method.**

If an error is generated, it is likely it will happen during this `Refresh` method, which is when the ADO Data Control will attempt to retrieve our records for us. In this instance, our "error trap" simply invokes the `Resume Next` statement. This specifies that, if an error occurs, Visual Basic should continue without stopping the program! This is acceptable while we are only testing our statements but otherwise we should trap the error, write it to an error log and then notify the user in easy-to-understand text.

We've now dealt with the Visual Basic code, so we're ready to explore the various SQL data manipulation statements. Before we move on, run your program and have a look at the records that appear. Notice that the DataGrid control is automatically populated with the data from the `Customers` table of the `NWind` database.

A Note on SQL Logic

SQL allows us to search and manipulate data in databases using logical expressions, called **search conditions**. Almost every programming language uses Boolean logic - based on the two values, `TRUE` and `FALSE`, and on the three basic operators `AND`, `OR` and `NOT`.

SQL, however, uses a three-valued logic based on the values `TRUE`, `FALSE` and `UNKNOWN`. So how, when database field values are compared, does the `UNKNOWN` logical value arise? The answer lies in the presence of **null** field values.

Null Values

SQL handles "missing" data using a null value. A null value indicates that a field's value is undefined or simply not known (no data has been entered into the field).

> A null value in a numeric field is not the same as a value of zero. In a character field, a null value is not the same as a blank. Both of these are definite values.

While working with database tables, we may often need to work with fields that have null values. For example, a field may have a null value if the field value is not yet known, doesn't yet exist or is outside the accepted range of values for that particular field.

If a null value is compared to a definite value (or even another null) the resulting logical value is `UNKNOWN`. Since it is not possible to say what the null stands for, it is not possible to say if the comparison is `TRUE` or `FALSE`.

We will encounter null values, in various contexts, as we progress through the chapter.

Generating Database Queries

SQL is sometimes broken down into three sub-languages:

> ➢ **Data Definition Language** (DDL): used to create, alter or drop objects in a database
> ➢ **Data Manipulation Language** (DML): used to retrieve, and operate on, the data in a database
> ➢ **Data Control Language** (DCL): used to provide security to a database

The remainder of this section deals with the generation of database queries using DML. This sub-language allows us to query the database, as well as insert, delete and update data in the database.

Various aspects of DDL are covered towards the end of the 'Advanced SQL' section. DCL is touched upon in Chapter 16.

At the heart of DML is the SELECT statement. This is the command that is responsible for querying the database and returning the requested information to the application.

The SELECT Statement

As was stated above, the SELECT statement is used to retrieve data from our database tables. The simplest SELECT statement identifies firstly the fields we want to return, and secondly from which table we wish to retrieve them, as follows:

```
SELECT FieldName FROM TableName
```

When we built our SQL Tester program, we applied the following SQL statement against the RecordSource property of the ADO Data Control:

```
SELECT * FROM Customers
```

The asterisk in our SELECT statement specifies that our recordset should be populated with *all* of the fields located in the Customers table:

CustomerID	CompanyName	ContactName	ContactTitle	Address
ALFKI	Alfreds Futterkiste	Maria Anders	Sales Representative	Obere Str. 57
ANATR	Ana Trujillo Emparedadc	Ana Trujillo	Owner	Avda. de la Constitución
ANTON	Antonio Moreno Taqueri	Antonio Moreno	Owner	Mataderos 2312
AROUT	Around the Horn	Thomas Hardy	Sales Representative	120 Hanover Sq.
BERGS	Berglunds snabbköp	Christina Berglund	Order Administrator	Berguvsvägen 8
BLAUS	Blauer See Delikatesser	Hanna Moos	Sales Representative	Forsterstr. 57
BLONP	Blondesddsl père et fils	Frédérique Citeaux	Marketing Manager	24, place Kléber
BOLID	Bólido Comidas prepara	Martín Sommer	Owner	C/ Araquil, 67
BONAP	Bon app'	Laurence Lebihan	Owner	12, rue des Bouchers
BOTTM	Bottom-Dollar Markets	Elizabeth Lincoln	Accounting Manager	23 Tsawassen Blvd.
BSBEV	B's Beverages	Victoria Ashworth	Sales Representative	Fauntleroy Circus

SQL Tester

91 Records Returned!

Apply SQL

However, in many cases we will want to refine or restrict our SELECT command in order to retrieve only the specific fields we need to view, manipulate or analyze. In order to do this we simply specify those fields in the statement (in place of the asterisk). With your SQL Tester program still running, type in the following SQL statement and click on the **Apply SQL** button (since the RecordSource property can be modified during runtime, we have the flexibility of being able to change the contents of the DataGrid control without stopping and restarting the program):

```
SELECT CustomerID, ContactName
FROM Customers
```

The DataGrid control should now be populated only with the `CustomerID` and `ContactName` fields of the `Customers` table. Pretty straightforward, I'm sure you'll agree!

If you use the asterisk in conjunction with specified field names, you will receive duplicates of those field names specified. This can be a waste of processing time and to accomplish this without error, you may need to assign an alias name to the repeating fields (we cover aliases later in the chapter).

You may be wondering why we would want to restrict the number of fields returned from a query. The more information we have at our fingertips the better, right? Well, there are two things to bear in mind. Firstly, the greater the number of fields returned, the more memory that must be allocated to store the data and the slower our application will run. If we're retrieving a very large number of records, even a single field can push the memory envelope, especially if that field is storing a large image or memo. Secondly, in client-server systems, transferring large recordsets from your database to our application is time-consuming and can result in excessive, and often unnecessary, network traffic.

> **Always try to restrict queries to the data that is actually required.**

You might like to practice creating these simple SQL statements in order to retrieve information from one of the numerous other tables in the database. For example, try executing the following statements:

```
SELECT *
FROM Categories
```

```
SELECT LastName, FirstName, BirthDate
FROM Employees
```

You may have noticed that the correct fields are retrieved whether or not you follow the exact upper/lower case scheme that I've demonstrated. The main reason for keeping SQL keywords in uppercase is to distinguish field and table names from the SQL keywords. It's also good practice to name fields using the same case scheme as is used in the database. Apart from anything else, it makes them easier to locate in the SQL statement.

147

SQL Clauses

SQL statements such as those above are very simple to construct. However, in order to return records that meet highly detailed criteria, they can become extremely complex - expanding to include various clauses, expressions and subqueries. The following table summarizes some of the SQL clauses that we can attach to our SELECT statement in order to retrieve data based on more specific criteria (say, for example, we only wanted to view specific fields and only for those customers based in a certain country). They are listed in the order that they should appear in the SELECT query:

SELECT	Required	Identifies the fields to be returned
DISTINCT	Optional	Specifies that each record displayed in the recordset should be unique
FROM	Required	Identifies the table(s) where the fields are found
WHERE	Optional	Identifies criteria that records returned must satisfy
GROUP BY	Optional	Gathers rows into groups, based on the values in the grouping column
HAVING	Optional	Allows filtering out of groups that don't satisfy a search condition
ORDER BY	Optional	Identifies the order of sorting of field values for a particular field

We'll encounter all of these clauses, and more, as we work through this chapter. Of course, we have already used one of them - the FROM clause - to specify the tables from which we want to retrieve our data. This is the only mandatory clause in the SELECT statement.

> A SQL statement may run on a single line, or broken out onto multiple lines. For more complex statements, multiple line code is much easier to read and understand.

Since the DISTINCT clause appears right after SELECT, let's have a quick look at it now. As stated in the above table, the DISTINCT clause ensures that each particular field value is displayed only once.

Suppose we were examining our customer base and wanted to see a list of all the countries where we had customers. A standard SQL statement, such as: SELECT Country FROM Customers, would not be much good to us. If we had 20 customers in Mexico, then Mexico would be listed twenty times!

In the following statement the DISTINCT clause rejects any duplicate fields or null values in the Country field value before returning the data set:

```
SELECT DISTINCT Country FROM Customers
```

Simple Data Manipulation

Before we move on to consider some of the other modifying clauses, let's have a look at some of the simple operations we can perform using the basic SELECT statement alongside various operators.

Creating Aliases

The AS keyword allows us to create a field that exists only in the recordset. The aliased field can be populated with data drawn from one or more fields, or with the results of arithmetic operations. The following simple example demonstrates how a field can temporarily (for the lifetime of the query) be renamed to produce a customized output:

```
SELECT CompanyName AS Corporation_Name
FROM Customers
```

The alias name cannot duplicate a field name that already exists in the table. The new field name may contain numbers, letters and spaces, but must still be a valid field name/identifier. In other words, it must follow the same naming conventions used when creating the database fields.

Joining Value Expressions

This section deals with joining value expressions and will cover the following:

> **Arithmetic Operators**: Bring fields and/or hard-coded values together in an expression.
> **Concatenating Text**: Joins hard-coded text to a field, to represent a single field.
> **Concatenating Fields**: Brings multiple fields together as a single field.

Using Arithmetic Operators

We can perform simple calculations, bringing together two or more **numeric** field values, using the four basic arithmetic operations: addition (+), subtraction (-), division (/) and multiplication(*). In the following example we combine the `UnitPrice` (data type=money) and `UnitsInStock` (data type=smallint) fields, using the multiplication operator, in order to calculate the value of each product in existing stock. We create a new recordset field (`InventoryValue`) in which to store this information:

```
SELECT ProductName, UnitPrice * UnitsInStock AS InventoryValue
FROM Products
```

We may also use hard-coded values in the equation, as demonstrated in the following example:

```
SELECT ProductName, UnitPrice * 1.07 FROM Products
```

Notice that an alias was not included in the above statement. When the AS keyword is missing, either a generic name will be created for the new field (when Access is used as the database) or the new field will not be assigned a name (when SQL Server is used).

Concatenating Text To Fields

At times, it may be necessary to concatenate a string to one of the table fields. To do this, we enclose our string in single quotation marks and use the addition operator to concatenate it to the desired field. However, we can only concatenate fields of similar data type.

You may have come across this practice before, when using variables in Visual Basic. If you intend to compare a string with an integer, you first must change the integer to a string, or vice versa.

In the following example we wish to concatenate the text 'NW' to the EmployeeID field (numeric data type). Therefore, we must use the CONVERT function to transform the EmployeeID field to the varchar data type (a character string data type of variable character length):

```
SELECT LastName, FirstName, 'NW' + CONVERT(varchar(10), EmployeeID)
AS Employee_ID
FROM Employees
```

The CONVERT function is specific to SQL Server. MS Access databases permit the concatenation of fields of non-similar data types using the ampersand (&) character.

> **Remember, numeric fields must be converted to a non-numeric format prior to concatenation. Otherwise the addition operator will simply add the fields together.**

Concatenating Multiple Fields

Not only can we concatenate text to a field, we can also concatenate multiple fields. The following example concatenates the LastName field with a hard-coded comma and space, then the FirstName field. This new field (Name) reduces the number of separate fields that must be displayed, creating a more professional look:

```
SELECT LastName + ', ' + FirstName AS Name
FROM Employees
```

Retrieving Specific Records

We will now look in more detail at how to refine SELECT statements in order to retrieve exactly the data we want.

The WHERE Clause

One of the most powerful aspects of SQL is its ability to retrieve records based on highly specific criteria. The WHERE clause is the most common method used to restrict (or 'filter') the data returned by a SQL query. For example, if we wanted to view records for only those customers located in the United States, we could execute the following SQL statement:

```
SELECT *
FROM Customers
WHERE Country = 'USA'
```

The WHERE clause applies a search condition to the records gathered by the SELECT statement. In the above example, the WHERE clause navigates through all the records in the Customers table and applies the search condition Country='USA' to them. Only those records that test TRUE are displayed in the recordset. If the search condition returns a FALSE or UNKNOWN value for a record then that record will not be displayed.

Notice that character field values must be enclosed in single quotes (double quotes for a few select databases). If we fail to do this, an error will be returned so it's important that we know our database tables when specifying search conditions. For example, in order to specify a condition relying on the EmployeeID field we would need to know whether the field contained numeric or character values.

We can use the WHERE clause with comparison predicates other than "equal to", such as those listed in the following table:

Operator	Description
<	Is less than
<=	Is less than or equal to
>	Is greater than
>=	Is greater than or equal to
=	Is equal to
<>	Is not equal to

In the following example, we refine our query to include only those employees whose EmployeeID is greater than 5. Notice that numeric values do not have to be enclosed in single quotation marks:

```
SELECT *
FROM Employees
WHERE EmployeeID > 5
```

Using AND, OR and NOT Operators

We can refine and modify our query still further using basic AND, OR and NOT operators. We can use the AND operator to specify multiple criteria within the WHERE clause. The following query requires both search conditions in the WHERE clause to be evaluated as TRUE before a record is displayed in the recordset:

```
SELECT * FROM Customers
WHERE Country = 'Mexico' AND
ContactTitle = 'Owner'
```

Only those records from the `Customers` table where the `Country` is `Mexico` and the `ContactTitle` is `Owner` are displayed. Any record that evaluates to `FALSE` or `UNKNOWN` for either search condition is excluded. Applying multiple search conditions is very common way of pinpointing specific records in our database tables:

The `OR` operator is deployed in a similar fashion. This time, if either of the search conditions evaluates to `TRUE`, then the record is included in the recordset:

```
SELECT *
FROM Customers
WHERE Country = 'Mexico' OR
  Country = 'Spain'
```

The situation becomes a little more tricky when we want to use both AND and OR operators to specify search conditions in our WHERE clause. Say, for example, we wanted to locate all records for customers based in Mexico or Spain, for whom the ContactTitle was Owner. Try the following query and have a good look at the resulting recordset:

```
SELECT * FROM Customers
WHERE Country = 'Mexico' OR
Country = 'Spain' AND
ContactTitle = 'Owner'
```

It didn't work, did it? In this situation the processing order is critical in determining the result of the query. What happened was that the AND operator took precedence over the OR operator in the processing order. So records were displayed for those customers who satisfied the search condition: "located in Spain with Owner as ContactTitle" alongside *all* customers located in Mexico (regardless of their ContactTitle field value).

Fortunately, we can influence the processing order using parentheses. The search condition within the parentheses will be evaluated first and then search conditions outside the parentheses are evaluated from left to right. Thus the correct manner in which to express our request is as follows:

```
SELECT * FROM Customers
WHERE (Country = 'Mexico' OR
Country = 'Spain') AND
ContactTitle = 'Owner'
```

All records for customers located in Spain or Mexico are gathered up and then subjected to the second search condition that `ContactTitle=Owner`. Only those records that evaluate to `TRUE` for this search condition are displayed:

We can use the `NOT` operator to, essentially, reverse the outcome of a search condition. Thus, the following query gathers specific fields for all records for which the parenthesized search condition evaluates to `FALSE`, before applying the second criterion:

```
SELECT CompanyName,ContactTitle,Country FROM Customers
WHERE NOT (Country = 'Mexico' OR
Country = 'Spain')
AND ContactTitle='Owner'
```

157

Using Predicates with the WHERE Clause

We now know how to use comparison predicates (such as equals, greater than etc.) and the basic AND, OR and NOT operators within the WHERE clause. In this section we will consider other predicates that can be used in a similar fashion.

The IN Predicate

The IN predicate provides a useful alternative to the OR operator when we're looking for multiple values in a single field. It essentially asks if a field value is in a set of other field values. The following query searches for Mexico and Spain values in the set of values presented by the Country field. Note how values specified in the IN predicate are listed within parentheses, separated by commas:

```
SELECT *
FROM Customers
WHERE Country IN ('Mexico', 'Spain')
```

Use of the IN predicate can make our SQL statement much shorter and less intimidating (especially when we have multiple values to locate)

Again, we can retrieve every record *except* those for which the search condition is satisfied by using the NOT operator:

```
SELECT *
FROM Customers
WHERE Country NOT IN ('Mexico', 'Spain')
```

The LIKE Predicate

The LIKE predicate allows us to specify a pattern to search for when implementing a SQL statement. It provides a more flexible alternative to the 'equals' comparison predicate. If, for example, we wanted to return all records for which the ContactName begins with an 'A', we could implement the following statement:

```
SELECT * FROM Customers
WHERE ContactName LIKE 'A%'
```

The percent sign (%) acts as a wildcard, specifying that there are a number of characters missing and that all records should be returned that match the general pattern. The result should look like this:

A single missing character in a string may be represented by an underscore(_).

If the portion of the text we want to locate is potentially at the beginning, middle or end of the field, we can use two wildcards. The following statement locates any instance of the word 'Fran' in the ContactName of the Customers table (note that the syntax is case-insensitive so '%fran%' or '%FRAN%' etc. will achieve the same result):

```
SELECT * FROM Customers
WHERE ContactName LIKE '%Fran%'
```

The BETWEEN Predicate

The `BETWEEN` predicate allows us to specify a range of possible values to return. These values can come in a variety of forms including dates, letters or numeric values. The `BETWEEN` predicate usually goes hand in hand with the `AND` operator.

The following example returns all values between `'AA'` and `'BO'`:

```
SELECT * FROM Customers
WHERE CustomerID BETWEEN 'AA' AND 'BO'
```

Again, the `BETWEEN` predicate provides a useful and often less cumbersome alternative to the use of comparison operators. The alternative to this statement, using comparison operators, is as follows (again, the syntax is case insensitive):

```
SELECT * FROM Customers
WHERE CustomerID >= 'AA' AND
CustomerID <= 'BO'
```

Note that when using the BETWEEN predicate with numeric values, the records returned will not include the values specified. For example, if we wanted to retrieve all values from 50 to 100, we would have to specify a range of: BETWEEN 49 AND 101.

Working with Dates

Each Database Management System has specific rules for working with dates. Typically, dates will be enclosed either by pound signs (#) (as for the Jet engine) or single quotes (e.g. SQL Server). Once enclosed in these single quotes, we can work with the data just as if it were a string. The following statement uses the BETWEEN clause to return all employees with hire dates that are between 1/1/92 and 1/1/93:

```
SELECT * FROM Employees
WHERE HireDate BETWEEN '1/1/92' AND '1/1/93'
```

The NULL Predicate

The NULL predicate can be used to find all records where the value in a selected field is null. The NULL predicate works in conjunction with the IS keyword. The following statement will search the Customers table for all records where the Region field value is null:

```
SELECT * FROM Customers
WHERE Region IS NULL
```

161

Remember, a null value occurs when a field has not yet been assigned. It is not the same as, for example, a space character. When a space character is assigned to field, it's no longer null.

Once again, we can "invert" or search condition using the NOT operator:

```
SELECT * FROM Customers
WHERE Region IS NOT NULL
```

The ORDER BY Clause

You will almost certainly have noticed that most of the queries we have implemented so far seem to return records in no particular order - in fact, they are returned in the order they were entered into the database. The ORDER BY clause is applied to a specific field (or fields) and allows us to sort the records that are returned into ascending or descending order, with respect to that field. Anyone who has programmed bubble sorts will certainly appreciate this clause, for its ease of use and flexibility.

Bubble sorts are algorithms that parse through all records in order to retrieve (or "bring to the top") one specific record. In a single parse a specific value pertaining to the required record can be compared to the records both sides of it and subsequently moved ("bubbled up") by one space. So, in theory, if we had 200 records and the one we wanted was at the bottom, we would have to parse through the records 199 times in order to bring it to the top.

The ORDER BY clause appears last in a SQL statement. Following the ORDER BY clause are listed all the fields that we wish to sort on, in the order of preference that they are to be ordered. The following statement will return all fields in the Customers table with a Country of France. In addition, the data will be sorted into ascending alphabetical order, with regard to the ContactTitle field:

```
SELECT * FROM Customers
WHERE Country = 'France'
ORDER BY ContactTitle
```

In order to sort data by more than one column, we list the fields back to back, delimited by commas:

```
SELECT * FROM Customers
WHERE Country = 'France'
ORDER BY ContactTitle, ContactName
```

The records are first sorted by ContactTitle and then, when there is more than one record with the same ContactTitle (such as Owner), the records are sorted by ContactName:

It should be obvious from these examples that, by default, the records will be returned in ascending order (unless an index specifies otherwise). In order to return a column in descending order, we must tack the DESC keyword onto the ORDER BY clause. Note that each field can have its own sort order. The following statement sorts the records returned in descending order from the ContactName field:

```
SELECT * FROM Customers
WHERE Country = 'Mexico'
ORDER BY ContactName DESC
```

The GROUP BY Clause

The GROUP BY clause allows us to group our records based on a field. Once we specify a field (or fields) as a grouping field then our recordset will group together all records that have the same value for that particular field. Basically, this clause takes the records of a table and sorts them into separate "piles".

The GROUP BY cause is at its most powerful when used in conjunction with other functions. For now, though, let's look at this clause in its most simple form:

```
SELECT Country FROM Customers
GROUP BY Country
```

You may be thinking that we achieved the same result using the DISTINCT clause, at the beginning of this chapter. Well yes, we did, but it's important to realize that the GROUP BY clause operates in a very different manner. Every record with, say, a value of Mexico for its Country field has been grouped into one pile. Try executing the following code:

```
SELECT Country, City FROM Customers
GROUP BY Country
```

You will probably receive an error message similar to the following:

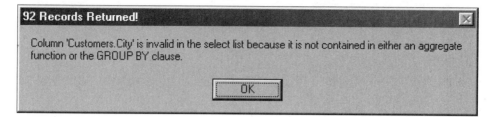

> **92 Records Returned!**   ☒
>
> Column 'Customers.City' is invalid in the select list because it is not contained in either an aggregate function or the GROUP BY clause.
>
>   OK

The reason for this error is fairly clear if you understand how the GROUP BY clause works. In the above example the first thing that happens is that the DBMS groups records according to their value in the Country field. These results are held in a temporary table, separate from the original. The SELECT statement then specifies which *groups* to display in our recordset. The City field hasn't been grouped so the above query is rendered meaningless. There are probably customers in several cities in, say, Mexico. Which city should be displayed against the Mexico pile?

If you examined the error message closely you will have realized that we could have overcome the error by containing our City field in the GROUP BY clause or in an **aggregate function**. The GROUP BY clause is most often used in conjunction with such functions.

SQL Aggregate Functions

Aggregate functions are applied to sets of records rather than a single record. The information in the multiple records is processed in a particular manner and then is displayed in a single record answer. This answer is an "aggregation" of the information contained in each record. The next few sections will introduce the following ANSI standard aggregate functions:

- ➤ SUM: Returns the sum of all field values in a given recordset.
- ➤ COUNT: Returns the count of records that meet a criterion.
- ➤ MIN: Returns the minimum value of a field in a recordset.
- ➤ MAX: Returns the maximum value of a field in a recordset.
- ➤ AVG: Returns the mean average of the field in a recordset.

SUM

The SUM keyword allows us to add the values of a specific numeric field, for a particular set of records, and return the total as a single field. It returns the numeric total for all known values (i.e. it doesn't include null values). Consider the following statement:

```
SELECT SUM(UnitsInStock * UnitPrice) AS InventoryValue
FROM Products
```

The processing order works like this: Firstly, the values of the UnitsInStock and UnitPrice fields are multiplied together, for every record in the Products table. Secondly, the SUM function adds the values of all results together to produce a single result. This result is displayed as a single aliased field (InventoryValue):

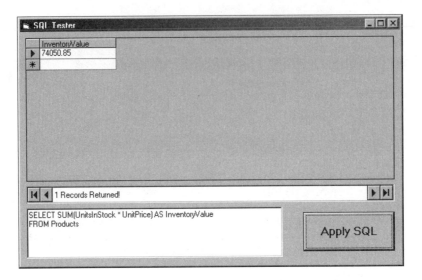

COUNT

The COUNT function is used to count the number of records that meet a specific criterion. It is the only aggregate function that can operate on any data type. If, say, we wanted to return a count of the total number of orders placed, we could execute the following SQL statement:

```
SELECT COUNT (CustomerID) AS Order_Count
FROM Orders
```

In this instance we could achieve the same result using an asterisk in place of CustomerID. COUNT(*) counts the number of rows in a table and includes in the count even those records where every field contains a null value. When we specify a specific field in the COUNT function, null values are not included in the count.

Again, the result is returned as a single field with a single record:

MIN & MAX

The MIN and MAX functions locate the lowest or highest known values of a given field. They can be used with numeric, date and character fields. The uses for these functions are almost limitless, especially when dealing with dates. If we wanted to know when both the newest and longest-serving employees began work, we could apply the following statement:

```
SELECT MIN (HireDate) AS MinHire,
MAX (HireDate) AS MaxHire
FROM Employees
```

AVG

The AVG function retrieves the mean average of a specific field. It can only operate on numeric data types. The following statement allows us to evaluate the average number of units in stock over all products:

```
SELECT AVG (UnitsInStock) AS AverageStock FROM Products
```

Using Aggregate Functions with GROUP BY

Used together, the GROUP BY clause and an aggregate function provide powerful functionality for the analysis of data in our database. We'll put the two into action in a practical situation when we begin reporting in Chapter 19. For now, we're just going to look at a fairly basic example:

```
SELECT Country, COUNT(Country) AS Total
FROM Customers
GROUP BY Country
```

Each record with the same value entered in the Country field is grouped together into a "pile". The COUNT function performs an aggregate calculation *for each group* (in other words, it counts the number of occurrences of each country in each "pile". This result is displayed in an aliased Total field, alongside the grouped Country field:

> Remember, if the Select statement has more than two selected columns, then the GROUP BY clause would need to have additional fields too. The following SELECT statement would fail because three fields are returned, but only one has been identified for grouping:
>
> ```
> SELECT City, Country, COUNT(Country) AS Total
> FROM Customers GROUP BY Country
> ```
>
> To correct this problem, we add another field (City) to the grouping and our SELECT statement returns the proper records:
>
> ```
> SELECT City, Country, COUNT(Country) AS Total
> FROM Customers GROUP BY Country, City
> ```

Using HAVING to Apply Criteria to Groupings

The HAVING clause can be used as a restriction on the GROUP BY clause (in fact, can only be used in conjunction with the GROUP BY clause). The HAVING clause allows us to apply a search condition to the grouped field:

```
SELECT Country, COUNT(Country) AS Total
FROM Customers
GROUP BY Country
HAVING COUNT(Country) > 10
```

From our previous example, we already know that the first three lines of the SQL statement return a list of countries with the number of records where the country was found. The HAVING clause specifies that we only want the list to include those countries where we have more than 10 customers:

Subqueries in SELECT Statements

Subqueries are SQL statements embedded inside other SQL statements. These subqueries can appear inside UPDATE, INSERT, or DELETE statements, as well as another SELECT statement. The easiest way to introduce one is within the WHERE clause of the SELECT statement. The following statement allows us to retrieve those orders dealt with by a specific employee, even if we don't know their EmployeeID. The subquery retrieves the EmployeeID field from the Employees table and passes the value to the outer query, which then retrieves the relevant orders from the Orders table: :

```
SELECT * FROM Orders
WHERE EmployeeID =
(SELECT EmployeeID FROM Employees
WHERE LastName = 'King' AND FirstName = 'Robert')
```

Bear in mind the following:

> ➤ Since the subquery is connected to the outer query using a comparison operator, the subquery must return only a single field value.

> ➤ A subquery within a WHERE clause must appear in parentheses.

The results of the previous SQL statement are as follows:

Modifying Data

The remainder of this chapter will focus on modifying the data in our database tables. We use three SQL commands to accomplish this - UPDATE, DELETE and INSERT. In previous sections we used the SELECT statement, in conjunction with various functions and operators, to perform simple data manipulation tasks. However, we were not actually modifying the data in the base database tables. The three commands we use in this section will allow us to do just that. The syntax of these commands is fairly simple but great care should be taken in their use. It is important to be very clear about exactly which fields need to be modified, and for which records.

If you ever develop your own database you will quickly realize the importance of having measures in place to prevent a user from entering invalid field values into the tables or from performing any modification that may degrade the integrity of your data. We discussed this to some extent in the introduction to this book, when we considered the role of primary and foreign key constraints, and we will hear about other types of constraint in the **Advanced SQL** section. In business, the integrity of the data in the database is of paramount importance. Important business decisions are based on the data and any modifications that threaten the validity of that data could have dire consequences. Database modification will be subject to strict security clearance and a database administrator (DBA) may insist that all such changes are made via highly complex SQL statements such as **stored procedures** (we'll discuss these in Chapter 8). These statements contain the basic UPDATE, INSERT or DELETE statements along with a wealth of subsidiary code that checks that every aspect of the modification is correct before allowing permanent changes to be made to the base tables.

OK, I think you're all now aware of the possible consequences of the careless use of these sometimes innocuous-looking statements, so let's see exactly what they can do.

Updating Records

The UPDATE statement, in conjunction with the SET clause, can be used to amend specific fields in database tables. The syntax is very simple:

```
UPDATE [Table Name]
SET [Field Name] = '[Value]'
WHERE [Criteria]
```

The table we wish to modify is appended to the UPDATE statement. The next section contains the SET clause followed by the specific field on that table that we would like to modify and the new value we wish to apply to the field. The new values may be hard-coded or drawn from another field or a formula (including the original field being modified). Finally, the WHERE clause restricts the modification to specific records - a very important clause in this context! It is surprisingly easy to inadvertently modify the wrong records. In order to implement an UPDATE command, most SQL implementations will make several passes through the table. The first pass gathers up all records which satisfy the WHERE clause and makes a duplicate copy of each. A second pass uses the SET clause to make the appropriate changes to the copied data. In a final pass, the original data is replaced with the new data.

The following SQL statement modifies a specific record in the Employees table, updating the LastName field where the EmployeeID is equal to 9:

```
UPDATE Employees
SET LastName = 'Williams'
WHERE EmployeeID = 9
```

Type the above statement into your SQL tester and click on the Apply SQL button:

After clicking on the Apply SQL button, we receive an error message telling us that "The operation requested by the application is not allowed if the object is closed". This error message is caused by the manner in which the ADO Data Control attempts to modify data in the table. This message will pop up whenever we attempt to INSERT, DELETE or UPDATE table records and when we attempt to create a new database object. When working with these types of SQL statements it is better to connect to the database using ADO (without the use of a control), then apply the statement to the Connection object. In the next chapter, we will discuss how to establish and maintain a Connection object. For the time being, click on OK and ignore the message - the SQL statement *will* be applied to the table

In order to confirm that the command was executed:

```
SELECT * FROM Employees
```

Inserting Data into Tables

When inserting new records into a table via SQL, we use the INSERT INTO statement and the VALUES keyword. The statement begins with INSERT INTO, followed by the table name and the field names (in parentheses) that we wish to insert. It's important to ensure that we pass *all* required fields, although optional fields may be left out. The second section begins with the VALUES keyword followed by the values for the new fields (in parentheses), delimited by commas. The field data must appear in the exact order that the field names appear in the first section. Any deviation from this will cause incorrect data placement or errors.

```
INSERT INTO [Table Name]([Field Name 1],[Field Name 2],[Field Name n])
VALUES([Field Data 1],[Field Data 2],[Field Data n])
```

> **Identifying the field names is optional - by default, SQL will populate fields in accordance with their ordinal position in the database table. However, it's a very good practice to follow. It guarantees that data populates the intended field.**

The following statement inserts two fields into the Shippers table:

```
INSERT INTO Shippers(CompanyName, Phone)
VALUES'Airborne Express', '(503) 555-5555')
```

Note it is not possible to explicitly assign a value to the ShipperID field unless the appropriate security permission has been assigned. When we execute the above command, the RDBMS will *automatically* assign a value for ShipperID. After executing the SQL statement, execute a SELECT statement to review the addition:

Inserting a Null Field into a Table

It is often necessary to update or enter fields with a null value. When doing this, we can simply replace the data field with the word NULL. The following statement inserts a new record into the Shippers table, leaving the Phone field NULL:

```
INSERT INTO Shippers(CompanyName, Phone)
VALUES('Airborne Express', NULL)
```

> If the field in the database has a default value defined as **NULL**, then we don't need to populate the field.

Create a SELECT statement to review the contents of the Shippers table and review the results.

Deleting Records

The DELETE statement allows us to remove unwanted or archived data quickly and easily. The syntax of the DELETE statement is basically the same as a SELECT statement with the exception that SQL Server does not allow an asterisk after the DELETE command. It is capable of removing one or all records from a table. Before we jump in, let's find some data to remove. Using your SQL Tester, execute the following statement:

```
SELECT * FROM Orders
```

Review the OrderDate field of the records. Notice that there were well over 100 orders made in 1996:

Let's assume that we want to remove all records from our table that have an OrderDate pre-dating 11th July 1996. The following statement will handle our request:

```
DELETE FROM Orders
WHERE OrderDate < '7/11/96'
```

> It is a very good idea to formulate your DELETE statement then replace DELETE with SELECT *. This will allow you to view the records you are about to delete, before actually doing so!

After clicking on the OK button to pass the error message, confirm that the records have been deleted by reapplying the initial SELECT statement to display all records from the Orders table.

Using Subqueries to INSERT Data from an Existing Table

Earlier in this section, we used a subquery embedded inside a SELECT statement. We noted at the time that subqueries can also be used inside a DELETE, INSERT, or UPDATE statement. It's especially common to use a subquery inside an INSERT statement in order to:

- ➢ Create sample data
- ➢ Archive data to a backup table

We can embed a SELECT statement within an INSERT statement and use it in a similar fashion to any other INSERT statement (the subquery replaces the VALUES section). The key thing to remember is that the number of columns returned must match the number of fields in the INSERT portion of the SQL statement and that the fields should be declared in the same order in each section.

If we execute the following SQL statement, nine records are returned:

```
SELECT * FROM Employees
```

Execute the following command:

```
INSERT INTO Employees (LastName, FirstName, Title,
TitleOfCourtesy, BirthDate, HireDate, Address, City, Region)
SELECT LastName, FirstName, Title, TitleOfCourtesy, BirthDate,
HireDate, Address, City,Region FROM Employees
```

Now, if we execute our initial SELECT statement again, double the number of original records will be returned:

This example demonstrates a good method of generating sample data. If we ran this INSERT statement another time, we would have 36 records and so on. It doesn't take too long to generate thousands, or even millions of records.

Advanced SQL

In the previous sections we covered a great deal of ground with regard to database queries and how to modify (update, delete etc.) data in our databases. We'll now expand on this knowledge as we take a look at some more complex aspects of SQL. Up to now we've drawn all our data from a single table. In the following sections we'll see how to draw together information from multiple tables in the database. Furthermore we'll delve into the basics of creating, indexing and altering our own tables. We'll continue to use the `NWind` database on SQL Server (if you have been using Visual Data Manager in Visual Basic and/or Access, feel free to continue doing so). The SQL statements we'll discuss in this chapter are fairly complex and will require a good understanding of the relationships between the database tables. Have a good look at the following diagram and refer back to it as required:

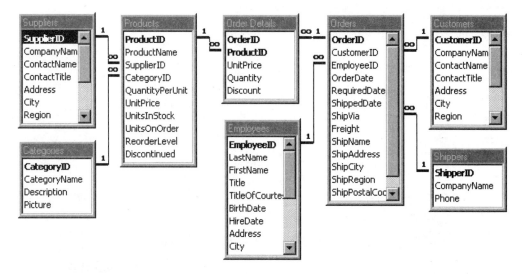

Joining Tables

There are a number of SQL commands that allow us to bring together multiple tables in a `SELECT` statement. In the following section we'll cover some of these commands (equi-joins, inner joins, outer joins and union queries) and explain when to use each of them.

In Chapter 2, we went to great lengths to normalize our data tables. The advantages of a well-normalized database include optimized space allocation, minimal data repetition, and of course the avoidance of mistakes associated with entering the same data fields repeatedly (such as customer information). Later, in the data warehousing chapter (Chapter 18) we'll cover specific methods of analyzing our data. Much of this analysis begins with **denormalizing** our database tables. Inner joins are a very important part of this process, as they are specifically designed to bring the data of multiple tables together into one spreadsheet-style recordset.

Of course, we don't bring tables together solely for data warehousing. Table joins provide an easy mechanism for the manipulation of highly specific data. Once we have constructed a SQL statement to "pull together" the information we require, we can define it as a **view** (see Chapter 8). This is a great time-saver when frequent access to this data is required .Of course; report generation also drives the requirement for joined tables (Chapter 19).

Equi-Joins

The equi-join is a generic name for a type of join that requires common field values to exist in each table in order for a record to be returned. In general syntax, a record is only returned when:

```
TableName1.FieldName = TableName2.FieldName
```

If, for example, we wanted to view a list of company names and the dates on which they had placed orders, then we could execute the following statement:

```
SELECT Customers.CompanyName, Orders.OrderDate
FROM Customers,Orders
WHERE Orders.CustomerID = Customers.CustomerID
```

This SQL statement is similar to the ones we encountered in the **SQL Basics** section, except now we're dealing with two tables. Note that the SELECT portion of the statement clearly identifies the tables from which the fields are to be drawn (the same field name can appear in more than one table!). The tables from which the fields are to be collected are listed in the FROM clause. Finally, the WHERE clause refines the query such that a record only appears in the resulting recordset if a common CustomerID field value exists in both tables. If a customer existed but had not yet placed an order, then that customer would *not* appear in the recordset.

The result of the above query should look like this:

> Equi-joins are really a special example of an INNER JOIN (discussed in the next section). It is worth noting that it is possible to have a non-equi join, where the relationship between fields in different tables can be expressed by any of the following comparison operators: >, <, <>, >= or <=.

The INNER JOIN Clause

SQL-92 syntax supports the INNER JOIN clause. As intimated in the previous section, if we use this clause then a record will only appear in the recordset if a common field value exists in each of the tables involved in the join. The following statement will produce exactly the same recordset as the previous SELCET...WHERE statement:

```
SELECT Customers.CompanyName,
       Orders.OrderDate
FROM Customers
INNER JOIN Orders
ON Orders.CustomerID = Customers.CustomerID
```

Firstly we identify specific fields on specific tables using the SELECT statement. Secondly, we specify the primary table from which the data will be extracted followed by the second table that is to be joined (following the INNER JOIN clause). Lastly, in the ON clause we specify the fields that will link the two tables and their relationship (such as being equal).

Nested Inner Joins

The INNER JOIN syntax really shows its value when many tables are to be joined. The syntax is self-documenting and it provides much greater control over data updates. When we use nested inner joins we are effectively creating a hierarchy of subqueries. We use parentheses to nest these queries inside each other and thus we can control the order of their execution. The innermost subquery is the first to be executed and the results from this are joined to the next level out. This process is repeated until all query operations are complete.

> *A close analogy is the execution of embedded functions in Visual Basic. The innermost functions are executed first, and the remaining ones are executed from the inside to the outside, continuously modifying the inner data.*

In the following example, the LastName and Title fields from the Employees table are "pooled" with the OrderDate field from the Orders table (but only if, for example, the employee has actually registered an order). Next, these "pooled fields" are joined with the CompanyName field from the customers table (the CompanyName field is only joined if, for example, the customer has actually placed an order):

```
SELECT Employees.LastName, Employees.Title,
       Orders.OrderDate,
       Customers.CompanyName
FROM Customers
INNER JOIN (Employees
       INNER JOIN Orders
       ON Employees.EmployeeID = Orders.EmployeeID)
ON Customers.CustomerID = Orders.CustomerID
```

Notice how the use of indents helps elucidate the command hierarchy. The statement should produce the following result:

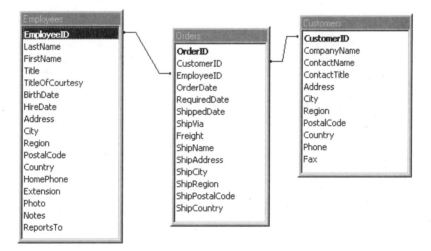

The join criteria can be depicted as follows:

Of course this image includes *all* fields, while we only selected a few in our query. Let's refine our query still further to include shipping information:

```
SELECT Employees.LastName, Employees.Title,
       Orders.OrderDate,
       Customers.CompanyName,
       Shippers.CompanyName AS Shipper
FROM Shippers
INNER JOIN (Customers
      INNER JOIN (Employees
            INNER JOIN Orders
          ON Employees.EmployeeID = Orders.EmployeeID)
      ON Customers.CustomerID = Orders.CustomerID)
ON Shippers.ShipperID = Orders.ShipVia
```

All we had to do, effectively, was place the multiple INNER JOINS from the previous example within yet another INNER JOIN. Notice that since we were including two CompanyName fields in the recordset, we gave one of them an alias (Shipper):

OUTER JOINS

An OUTER JOIN allows us to specify that the records returned should include *all* of the records from one table, even if a correlating record in the second table does not exist. There are two types of OUTER JOIN statements:

> ➢ LEFT OUTER JOIN. Returns all records from the table specified first in the FROM clause.

> ➢ RIGHT OUTER JOIN. Returns all records from table listed in the joined clause.

Let's say, for example, that we want a list of customers and their respective orders but, as part of that list, we also want to include customers who have not placed any orders. To accomplish this, we can use an OUTER JOIN to bring the two tables together.

First of all, however, we'll need to create a customer that hasn't made any orders - because none exist in the Northwind database on SQL Server! Using knowledge gained in the "Inserting Data into Tables" section, create a new customer in the Customers table. Insert values for as many fields as you like, but make sure you enter values into the CustomerID and CompanyName fields. Review the new Customers table to make sure that your new data has been added then execute the following SQL statement:

```
SELECT Customers.CustomerID, Customers.CompanyName,
       Orders.*
FROM Customers
LEFT OUTER JOIN Orders
ON Customers.CustomerID = Orders.CustomerID
```

As you can see, the syntax is nearly identical to that of an INNER JOIN. However, this statement selects the CustomerID and CompanyName fields for *every* record in the Customers table (since it is specified in the FROM clause), regardless of whether there is a record with a matching CustomerID in the Orders table. If a customer doesn't have an order, one line item will represent the customer, but no order details will be attached. The output should look something like this:

UNION Queries

Whereas JOINS allowed us to merge related tables of dissimilar structure, UNION queries allow us to merge two unrelated tables based on similar field structures. As an example, let's assume we have two contact lists (Customers and Suppliers). Say we wanted to send holiday cards to all of these contacts. The UNION query will allow us to build a single recordset with data from both tables (without this option, we would have to create two separate queries).

The rules of a UNION query are quite simple: all UNION queries must request the same number of fields from each table and the fields must be of compatible data types. The fields don't, however, have to be the same size. If the data types don't match, we can use the SQL Server CONVERT function to change the underlying data type of one of the fields.

Have a look at the following code and then we'll discuss how it works:

```
SELECT CustomerID AS ID,City, CompanyName,
       ContactName, 'Customers' AS Relationship
FROM Customers
UNION
SELECT convert(varchar,SupplierID), City, CompanyName,
       ContactName, 'Suppliers'
FROM Suppliers
ORDER BY City, CompanyName
```

The first SELECT statement sets up the format of the data to be populated in the recordset. The field names of the recordset, including any aliases, are based on the field names used in this statement.

181

We use an alias (`ID`) to represent the first field because it will contain both `CustomerID` and `SupplierID` field values. The fifth field selected also uses an alias (`Relationship`). For all records returned from the `Customers` table, the default value for this field will be 'Customers'.

The `UNION SELECT` statement is used to append a second `SELECT` statement to the first. Notice that the order in which we list the fields matches the order we used in the original `SELECT` statement. Thus `SupplierID` field values will populate the `ID` column of the recordset and all records from the `Suppliers` table will be designated as 'Suppliers' in the `Relationship` column of the recordset.

The only difficulty we have is that `CustomerID` and `SupplierID` are incompatible data types. `CustomerID` is a string data type (`Text`) and `SupplierID` is a numeric data type (`Long`). The obvious solution is to convert numeric to string, rather than vice-versa. Thus we will make `SupplierID` a **character varying** data type using the `CONVERT` function:

```
CONVERT(varchar,SupplierID)
```

The `CONVERT` function accepts three arguments: the new data type, the field to convert, and a third, optional argument indicating any special formatting to be done.

The results of the query should look something like this:

ID	City	CompanyName	ContactName	Relationship
DRACD	Aachen	Drachenblut Delikatess	Sven Ottlieb	Customers
RATTC	Albuquerque	Rattlesnake Canyon Gr	Paula Wilson	Customers
OLDWO	Anchorage	Old World Delicatessen	Rene Phillips	Customers
3	Ann Arbor	Grandma Kelly's Homes	Regina Murphy	Suppliers
28	Annecy	Gai pâturage	Eliane Noz	Suppliers
VAFFE	Århus	Vaffeljernet	Palle Ibsen	Customers
GALED	Barcelona	Galería del gastrónomo	Eduardo Saavedra	Customers
LILAS	Barquisimeto	LILA-Supermercado	Carlos González	Customers
16	Bend	Bigfoot Breweries	Cheryl Saylor	Suppliers

122 Records Returned!

```
FROM Customers
UNION
SELECT   convert(varchar,SupplierID), City, CompanyName,
         ContactName, 'Suppliers'
FROM Suppliers
ORDER BY City, CompanyName
```

Apply SQL

By default, no duplicate records are returned when `UNION` queries are used. The following simple modification to our original statement incorporates the `ALL` keyword to ensure all records are returned, regardless of duplication.

```
SELECT CustomerID AS ID,City, CompanyName,
       ContactName, 'Customers' AS Relationship
FROM Customers
UNION ALL
SELECT  convert(varchar,SupplierID), City, CompanyName,
        ContactName, 'Suppliers'
FROM Suppliers
ORDER BY City, CompanyName
```

Advanced Aggregation Queries

Now that we've covered the process of pulling together information from multiple tables, we can create some fairly advanced statements with which to analyze our data. As I mentioned earlier, much of the advanced data analysis in commerce is carried out on data stored in data warehouses (Chapter 18), often in the form of aggregated "fact tables". These fact tables present data from a variety of tables in a single spreadsheet-style recordset. In the following example we create a summary table, showing the total sales revenue accrued from each product for the years 1996 to 1998. It puts into practice many of the skills we've covered in this chapter. We pull information from three tables using nested INNER JOINS; use an aggregate function, in conjunction with a GROUP BY clause, to perform the aggregation calculation and, in addition, use CONVERT and Date functions:

```
SELECT Products.ProductName AS Product,
YEAR(OrderDate) AS Year,
('$' + CONVERT(varchar(10), SUM([Order Details].Quantity*[Order
Details].UnitPrice*(1-[Order Details].Discount)))) AS "Total Sales"
FROM Products
    INNER JOIN(Orders
        INNER JOIN [Order Details]
        ON [Order Details].OrderID = Orders.OrderID)
    ON Products.ProductID = [Order Details].ProductID
WHERE YEAR(yy, OrderDate) BETWEEN 1996 AND 1998
GROUP BY Products.ProductName, YEAR(OrderDate)
ORDER BY ProductName
```

The YEAR function extracts a year value (e.g. "1996") from the date. Notice that the fields are grouped by ProductName, and then by the year value of the OrderDate field. Thus the ProductName grouping gathers together every occurrence of a certain ProductName into a single pile then, effectively, each pile is separated into three according to the year value. We use the SUM aggregate function to calculate the total sales revenue for each group of rows. We convert this numeric data type to a string data type (varchar) and concatenate it to a dollar sign. The result should be as follows:

183

Creating Tables

Sometimes, when we need to create a new table, we may have the luxury of simply copying the structure from an existing table. However, this may not always be possible and, fortunately, there is a statement in SQL that allows us to create a table on the fly. The syntax of this statement may vary from provider to provider, depending on whether the ANSI standard is followed. For this reason, I would suggest reviewing the CREATE TABLE documentation for the specific database provider you wish to use. There are several reasons why the syntax tends to vary so much. Firstly, each provider accepts different data types and secondly, the provider may have a unique mechanism for creating constraints and keys. The basic syntax is as follows:

```
CREATE TABLE table (field1 type [(size)] [NOT NULL] [index1]
  [, field2 type [(size)] [NOT NULL] [index2] [, ...]]
  [, CONSTRAINT multifieldindex [, ...]])
```

When executing CREATE SQL statements from our sample project, you may receive the standard 'Object Closed' error. Just click on OK, and the table will be created.

This may look a bit overwhelming; so let's break it out a bit:

```
CREATE TABLE table      ' The name of the table that we want to create
(field1 type            ' The first field name, followed by the data type
[(size)]                ' The size of the field (optional)
[DEFAULT Expression]    ' Identifies a default value for the field
[NOT NULL]              ' Specify whether or not the field may be NULL
                        ' (optional - default is NULL)
[index1]                ' If the field is indexed or not(optional)
[, field2 type [(size)] [NOT NULL] [index2] [, ...]]
                        ' Repeat the above for each field
[, CONSTRAINT multifieldindex [, ...]])
                        ' Any constraints or keys that consist of
                        ' more than one field.
```

Easier said than done, right! Let's take a simple example. The following statement builds a table called myTable1 with two fields (FirstName and LastName). Both fields are of the TEXT data type and some of the optional arguments have been excluded. Run this statement and then run a SELECT statement against the new table:

```
CREATE TABLE myTable1
(FirstName varchar(30) NOT NULL,
 LastName varchar(35) NOT NULL)
```

If you are using Visual Data Manager (VisData) to execute these commands, you may experience errors due to the limitations of the VisData product.

Note that if a table called `myTable1` already exists in your database, you will receive a message telling you so:

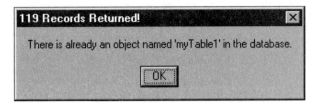

Let's expand on the previous example and introduce a third field, the Date of Birth (`DOB`) field:

```
CREATE TABLE myTable2
   (FirstName varchar(30) NOT NULL,
    LastName varchar(35) NOT NULL,
    DOB DateTime NOT NULL,
CONSTRAINT MyTable2Constraint UNIQUE
      (FirstName, LastName) )
```

The `DOB` field is a `DateTime` field, and may not be `NULL`. We've also added a constraint to this table (called `MyTable2Constraint`). This `UNIQUE` constraint is applied to the `FirstName` and `LastName` fields. It doesn't mean that `FirstName` must be unique, or that the `LastName` must be unique, rather that these two fields collectively must be unique in each record. We can apply any number of `UNIQUE` constraints to any one table (whereas there can only be one primary key)

Another way of creating a constraint is to do so immediately after the declaration of the field. In the following example, we add a field titled `SSN` (Social Security Number) of the data type integer. We then append a `CONSTRAINT` clause to the field (called `MyTable3Constraint`) and specify the constraint type as `PRIMARY KEY`. This statement creates the table with the `SSN` field as a `PRIMARY KEY`:

```
CREATE TABLE myTable3
   (FirstName varchar(30) NOT NULL,
    LastName varchar(35) NOT NULL,
    DOB DateTime NOT NULL,
    SSN INTEGER NOT NULL CONSTRAINT MyTable3Constraint PRIMARY KEY)
```

This is the required syntax for MS Access. It also works for RDBMSs such as SQL Server and Oracle but, in fact, we do not actually need to use the `CONSTRAINT` keyword with the `PRIMARY KEY` constraint, in these cases. The last line of the above code could simply read:

```
SSN INTEGER NOT NULL PRIMARY KEY
```

The RDBMS automatically names the constraint. Remember; primary keys may not contain `NULL` fields, so all fields in the list should be identified as `NOT NULL`.

We can also create a constraint containing more than one field. We simply specify the fields that make up the constraint after we declare the constraint type:

```
CREATE TABLE myTable4
   (FirstName varchar(30) NOT NULL,
    LastName varchar(35) NOT NULL,
    DOB DateTime NOT NULL,
    SSN INTEGER,
    CONSTRAINT MyTable4Constraint_pk Primary key (SSN,DOB) )
```

Again, for SQL Server, the last line of this code could read simply: `Primary key (SSN, DOB))`.

We can review the structure of our table by simply executing a SELECT statement. We can also view our table in the `NWind` database in SQL Server (if you can't see it, right click on the **Tables** icon and select **Refresh**). We can view the properties of each table and of our constraints under **Properties** and **All Tasks | Manage Indexes**, respectively. For example:

We can implement a FOREIGN KEY constraint in a very similar fashion, with the exception that we must identify the table to which the FK relates.

```
CREATE TABLE myTable5
   (FirstName varchar(30) NOT NULL,
    LastName varchar(35) NOT NULL,
    DOB DateTime NOT NULL,
    SSN INTEGER NOT NULL CONSTRAINT SSN_fk Foreign key (SSN) REFERENCES myTable3 )
```

In the above example, `myTable5` has a foreign key (`SSN`) that relates to the primary key in `myTable3`. To check that this is the case, highlight `myTable5` in the database, right-click and navigate to **All Tasks | Display Dependencies**:

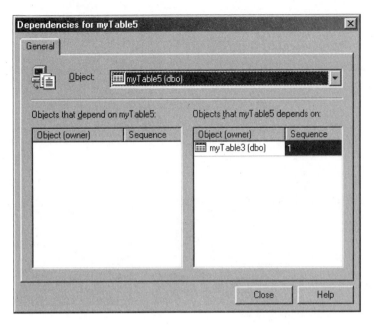

Default Values

When creating tables, we may also specify a default value for any given field. This is especially useful when we want to have a field that must not contain a null value, or a field that will have a common value. To implement a default value, simply insert the `DEFAULT` keyword followed by the text to be used, in this case the default 'U' (for unknown) is applied to the `Gender` field:

```
CREATE TABLE myTable6
   (FirstName varchar(30) NOT NULL,
   LastName varchar(35) NOT NULL,
   Gender char(1) DEFAULT 'U' NOT NULL,
   DOB DateTime NOT NULL,
   SSN INTEGER NOT NULL,
   CONSTRAINT MyTable6Constraint Primary key (SSN,DOB)
```

Check Constraints

We can a use a `CHECK` constraint in order to implement data validation. It tests a field value against a search condition and rejects those that do not conform to the validation rule. The search condition can consist of a range, or list, of possible values.

In the following example, we implement a `CHECK` constraint that requires the `Gender` field to be populated with 'F', 'M', or 'U'. Any other value results in an error. Here, we use the `IN` keyword to provide a list of possible values:

```
CREATE TABLE myTable7
  (FirstName varchar(30) NOT NULL,
   LastName varchar(35) NOT NULL,
   Gender char(1) DEFAULT 'U' CHECK(Gender IN ('F','M','U')) NOT NULL,
   DOB DateTime NOT NULL,
   SSN INTEGER NOT NULL,
   CONSTRAINT MyTable7Constraint Primary key (SSN,DOB) )
```

After executing the above SQL statement, we can validate that the rule works by attempting to execute the following INSERT statement. Notice that the Gender field will be assigned the letter 'D', which should violate the rule:

```
INSERT INTO myTable7 (FirstName, LastName, Gender, DOB, SSN)
VALUES ('John','Smith', 'D', '01/01/79', 0010100001)
```

The following error message should appear:

Now, change the Gender field value to 'M', and ensure that it's accepted:

Other types of validation can include:

➢ Minimum or Maximum Values:

```
Check (Cost >= 30.00)
```

> ➢ Validating Ranges:

```
CHECK (Price >= 12.00 AND <=45.00)
                 or
CHECK (Price BETWEEN 12.00 AND 45.00)
```

> ➢ Lookups from another table using sub-queries:

```
CHECK (Sale_Price <= (SELECT MIN(Min_Price) FROM
tblCompetitor WHERE Product = Sale_Item)
```

> ➢ A search condition that disallows a NULL value

```
CHECK (LastName IS NOT NULL)
```

> ➢ A search condition that ensures that a value doesn't exist in another table:

```
CHECK (Product <> ANY (SELECT Product FROM tblProducts)
```

Changing Table Structure with ALTER TABLE

The ALTER TABLE statement allows us to add a new field, destroy a field, or alter an existing field. The structure is fairly simple:

```
ALTER TABLE myTable7
ADD Contact_Address varchar(40) NULL
```

In the first line we identify the SQL statement as an ALTER TABLE command and follow it with the name of the table that we want to modify. Next, we identify whether we want to add a new field, drop a field, or alter an existing field. The above code adds a new field called Contact_Address:

`ALTER TABLE` only allows us to add columns that will accept null values or for which we have defined a default value

To remove a field:

```
ALTER TABLE myTable7
DROP column Contact_Address
```

To alter field characteristics, specify the field name, then re-declare the details of the field:

```
ALTER TABLE myTable7
Alter column Contact_Address varchar(50) NULL
```

We can also modify constraints and default values using `ALTER TABLE`. The syntax, in this case, is the same as that used for the `CREATE TABLE` command.

Destroying Tables with DROP TABLE

The `DROP TABLE` command is pretty self-explanatory - it allows us to destroy any of our tables. The syntax is quite simple: specify the table name after the `DROP TABLE` command. This command can be our best friend or worst enemy, as it returns no message asking for confirmation of our intentions:

```
DROP TABLE myTable7
```

Creating Indexes

Once we have built a table, we can add indexes to it. As you'll recall from Chapter 2, indexes can greatly increase performance of lookups for larger databases. The syntax of creating indexes can be quite complex. As with the `CREATE TABLE` statement, the `CREATE INDEX` statement can vary greatly from RDBMS to RDBMS. When working with indexes, I would suggest that you consult your provider documentation for optional arguments. For now, let's look at a simple example.

The following statement creates an index called `myIndex`. This index will be placed on the `myTable4` table and it will include the fields `LastName` and `FirstName`:

```
CREATE INDEX myIndex ON myTable4
(LastName, FirstName)
```

To remove an index, use the `DROP INDEX` statement. The `DROP INDEX` statement is similar in syntax to the `DROP TABLE` statement:

```
DROP INDEX myTable4.myIndex
```

Making a Backup Table

You may find that you want to duplicate the layout and/or data of a table. One practical reason for doing this would be to track any records that are changed during the process of any given day. Here's a simple scenario:

A backup copy of the `Customers` table is created. As changes are made to the backup table, the original table remains untouched. At some later point, a query can be executed that compares the contents of the two tables and returns all records that are different. The changes made can be reviewed and any that are not authorized can be rejected.

Let's begin by reviewing the contents of the `Customers` table:

```
SELECT * FROM Customers
```

There are two ways of creating a backup table. We can use the `CREATE TABLE` command or the `SELECT INTO` statement.

The CREATE TABLE Method

We'll create a copy of the *structure* of the `Customers` table with one command, then move the data in with a second.

First, execute the following command to create a new table (`Customer_2`) with fields of the same data types and sizes as the `Customers` table:

```
CREATE TABLE Customers_2
(CustomerID      varchar(5)   NULL,
CompanyName      varchar(40)  NULL,
ContactName      varchar(30)  NULL,
ContactTitle     varchar(30)  NULL,
Address          varchar(60)  NULL,
City             varchar(15)  NULL,
Region           varchar(15)  NULL,
PostalCode       varchar(10)  NULL,
Country          varchar(15)  NULL,
Phone            varchar(24)  NULL,
Fax              varchar(24)  NULL)
```

The result should look as follows:

Now let's populate this table with the records that exist in the Customers table. To do this, we'll use some of our knowledge from the **SQL Basics** section. We want to apply an INSERT statement against the Customers_2 table that pulls the values from the Customers table.

The syntax was as follows:

```
INSERT INTO Customers_2 (Field1, Field2, ...)
SELECT (Field1, Field2, …) FROM Customers
```

However, because the structure of each table is identical, we can exclude the field names, and simply apply the following statement:

```
INSERT INTO Customers_2
SELECT * FROM Customers
```

To confirm that the new Customers_2 table has all of the Customers data:

```
SELECT *
FROM Customers_2
```

The SELECT INTO Method

The second method is much simpler but is only valid for certain RDBMSs (such as SQL Server). The following code duplicates the structure of the `Customers` table and populates the fields with all of the data from the `Customers` table (Note: if you want to run this code you will need to `DROP` the `Customers_2` table we created in the previous section):

```
SELECT *
INTO Customers_2
FROM Customers
```

In order to create a copy of the table structure without data, we can simply tack on a `WHERE` clause that can never be satisfied:

```
SELECT *
INTO Customers_3
FROM Customers
WHERE 1=2
```

Clearly one will never equal two so the recordset populated to the new table will be empty. We could also use the `WHERE` clause to populate our backup table with a *sample* of the records from the original table.

> *Once you have experimented with both of these methods, and before you move on to the next section, make sure you end up with a* `Customers_2` *table that is identical to the original* `Customers` *table.*

Finding Unmatched Records

Let's make some changes to the `Customers_2` table and find out how we can keep track of the alterations made. Execute a `SELECT` statement against the `Customers_2` table and modify a few of the records using the `UPDATE` command. In the following screenshot, I have changed each of the `ContactTitle` fields for the records corresponding to `BERGS` (`'Order Administrator'`) and `BLONP` (`'Marketing Manager'`) to `'Sales Representative'`:

Keeping track of these changes is a relatively straightforward process:.

```
SELECT Customers.ContactTitle AS OLD_Title, Customers_2.*
FROM Customers
INNER JOIN Customers_2
ON Customers.CustomerID = Customers_2.CustomerID
WHERE Customers.ContactTitle <> Customers_2.ContactTitle
```

We select all fields from the `Customer_2` backup table along with the `ContactTitle` field from the original `Customers` table, which we give an alias (`OLD_Title`). We instigate a join using the `CustomerID` field. This field is unique in each of the tables, a one-to-one relationship occurs during the comparison. Finally, the query is restricted to only those records where `ContactTitle` is different in each table. The results look like this:

However, the above code will not allow us to keep track of new records added to the `Customers_2` table. Add a new record now, for example:

```
INSERT INTO Customers_2 (CustomerID,CompanyName,ContactName,ContactTitle,Address)
VALUES('TESTA','Test Company','Joe Test','Owner','123 Main St.')
```

Now re-run our "tracking" code and you will see that the new record is not logged. Try the following code instead:

```
SELECT Customers.ContactTitle AS [OLD Title], Customers_2.*
FROM Customers
RIGHT OUTER JOIN Customers_2
ON Customers_2.CustomerID = Customers.CustomerID
WHERE (Customers.ContactTitle <> Customers_2.ContactTitle)
OR (Customers.ContactTitle IS NULL)
```

```
SQL Tester                                                    _ □ ✕

  | OLD Title          | CustomerID | CompanyName           | ContactName       | ContactTitle        | Addr |
▶ | Order Administrator | BERGS     | Berglunds snabbköp    | Christina Berglund | Sales Representative | Berg |
  | Marketing Manager   | BLONP     | Blondesddsl père et fils | Frédérique Citeaux | Sales Representative | 24, p |
  |                     | TESTA     | Test Company          | Joe Test          | Owner               | 123  |



◀                                                                    ▶

|◀ ◀ | 3 Records Returned!                                          | ▶ ▶|

FROM Customers
RIGHT OUTER JOIN Customers_2                                   ┌─────────────┐
ON Customers_2.CustomerID = Customers.CustomerID               │             │
WHERE (Customers.ContactTitle <> Customers_2.ContactTitle)     │  Apply  SQL │
OR (Customers.ContactTitle IS NULL)                            │             │
                                                               └─────────────┘
```

Earlier in the chapter you encountered a left outer join - now here's your example of a right outer join! In this case it ensures that our new record is not rejected on the grounds that no matching `CustomerID` exists in the `Customers` table.

Using EXISTS to Find Matched or Unmatched Records

We can also use the `EXISTS` predicate in order to find unmatched (or matched) records in two or more tables. This predicate is easy to implement if we choose a primary key upon which to base our comparison. In the following example the sub-query selects every record from the `Customers` table that has a matching `CustomerID` in the `Customers_2` table. The `NOT EXISTS` predicate essentially reverses this so that the outer query only retrieves those records from `Customers_2` that *don't* have a matching `CustomerID` in `Customers`:

```
SELECT * FROM Customers_2
WHERE NOT EXISTS
(SELECT * FROM Customers
   WHERE Customers.CustomerID = Customers_2.CustomerID)
```

The result set will contain the one record we added.

Summary

In terms of retrieving, manipulating and modifying data in relational databases, SQL is ubiquitous. It is *the* universally recognized language of the RDBMS. Having reached the end of this chapter, you should have a solid understanding of much of SQL's core functionality.

In particular, you should feel comfortable with:

> Use of the SELECT statement to construct database queries. You should know how to restrict your queries to the specific records using the WHERE clause.
> Performing simple arithmetic and concatenation operations on your data.
> Use of the GROUP BY clause and aggregate functions for data analysis.
> The INSERT, UPDATE and DELETE statements for database modification.
> Pulling information together from multiple tables using JOIN and UNION clauses.
> Creating, indexing, updating and dropping simple database tables of your own.

SQL comes in many flavors, and extensions to the languages can be found in most database providers. It's well worth taking some time to investigate the functions that each database provides.

When developing your own SQL commands, it makes life much easier if you have sample statements to work from. Hopefully, you now have a good understanding of the syntax of each command and the uses to which you can put them. You'll be deploying your SQL knowledge in the majority of the following chapters. Refer back to the examples of this chapter as often as you need to, in order to consolidate your knowledge and understanding of the language.

SQL is a user-friendly language, but it's only with practice that you become fluent in its use. There are a lot of tools available for designing SQL statements and these tools can save you time and money to form more complex queries. The more you learn about the subject, the more you'll appreciate that you can become quite creative when it comes to building SQL statements. In many cases, you're only limited by your own creativity.

Suppliers

- SupplierID
- CompanyName
- ContactName
- ContactTitle
- Address
- City
- Region
- PostalCode
- Country
- Phone
- Fax
- HomePage

Products

- ProductID
- ProductName
- SupplierID
- CategoryID
- QuantityPerUnit
- UnitPrice
- UnitsInStock
- UnitsOnOrder
- ReorderLevel
- Discontinued

Categories

- CategoryID
- CategoryName
- Description
- Picture

An Introduction to ADO

This chapter gives a whirlwind introduction to Microsoft's data access technology of choice – ActiveX Data Objects (ADO). We'll focus on the objects exposed by ADO, and on properties, methods and events of those objects.

There are three main objects to ADO, plus four subsidiary objects and four associated collections. ADO is perceived to be rather difficult to use, but as you'll see in this chapter, it's really rather easy to get started. Here's what we'll cover in this chapter:

> The ADO object model

> How to open a connection to the database (and how to close it when you've finished!)

> Using a command to query the database

> Using a recordset to manipulate data

> Cursor types and lock types

> Using VB Controls with ADO

There is a lot to learn about ADO, but this chapter should give you enough to get you under way. You can use the complete ADO object model description (in Appendix E) to get a better idea of the full set of keywords and functionality offered by ADO – and as you get to use it more, you'll become familiar with the syntax. Before long, you should be well placed to use ADO quite effectively.

One more thing: if you haven't yet learned to use the Visual Basic help files, you should spend some time having a look around them. In addition to giving you the exact syntax, they also provide plenty of examples.

The ADO Object Model

There's a good chance that you've already seen the ADO Object Model in one form or another. Lots of developers have copies of the ADO Object Model poster hanging up in their offices and cubicles. And yet, folks seem not to understand how it works or how they can use it to their advantage. If you have one of those posters, don't tear it down yet. By the end of this chapter, that poster will make sense to you, and you will be able to use it as a reference.

There are three main objects in ADO:

> ➤ The Connection object, which is designed to handle the connection to the database
> ➤ The Command object, which is designed to help us handle SQL commands
> ➤ The Recordset object, which we use to hold data and to manipulate it

In addition to these three main objects, ADO makes use of four subsidiary objects – Property, Error, Parameter and Field – and four associated collections, which are used to access these subsidiary objects.

The following diagram should give you an idea of how all these objects and collections relate to one another. We'll take a closer look at each of the objects in turn later in the chapter:

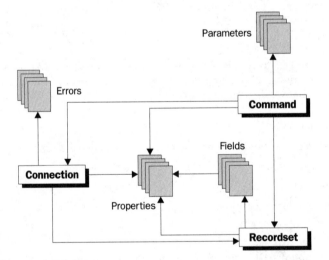

Object Hierarchy

One of the reasons for the confusion is that people don't understand the structure of the ADO object hierarchy. This is actually quite simple, but there is very little documentation explaining it.

It's probably most effective to think of ADO as having a 2-level hierarchy, with the three main ADO objects in the top layer and the four subsidiary objects in the bottom layer.

Connection, Command and Recordset Objects

Essentially, in order to talk to the database, you need to establish a connection to it. Therefore, the Connection object is sometimes perceived to be alone at the very 'root' of the hierarchy, with the Command and Recordset objects coming after it.

In practice, however, you can connect to the database without creating an explicit Connection object in your code. For example, you can use a Recordset object to fetch some data from a database. In this case, instead of using an explicit Connection object in your code, you can simply tell the Recordset what the connection details are – and the Recordset will go away and create an implicit connection behind the scenes.

And later, you can make that implicit connection into an explicit Connection object in your code (by using the Recordset object's ActiveConnection property). So, in terms of using the three main ADO objects in your code, the hierarchy is essentially flat. It's designed so that your code doesn't need to contain any more objects than you need.

Property, Error, Parameter and Field Objects

So what about the remaining four objects? It doesn't really make sense for them to exist independently, because the information that they contain relates directly to the other ADO objects. So, for example, when you create a Connection object you'll also get an Errors collection. The Errors collection gives you access to all of the Error objects that relate to that Connection, and indeed, you can only access this collection through the Connection object.

Similarly, the Command object gives you a Parameters collection, which in turn gives you access to the Parameter objects pertaining to that command. And the Recordset object gives you a Fields collection, by which you can access the individual Field objects.

Finally, the Properties collection contains a number of Property objects, each of which represents an OLE DB property. There are many of these properties, and they're not all supported by all OLE DB providers. There's a complete list of these properties in Appendix G.

> *The OLE DB properties are sometimes known as dynamic properties. Be careful of the ambiguous terminology – the OLE DB properties are not the same as the properties of an ADO object!*

ADODB versus ADOR

It's worth noting that ADO comes in two 'flavors'. In this introduction, we've been discussing the full implementation of ADO, also referred to as **ADODB**. This provides full access to the complete ADO object model, with support for events. However, there is also a lightweight version, known as the ADO Recordset Library or **ADOR**, which supports just the Recordset object (and its dependent Fields and Properties collections), and does not support events.

ADOR is designed for client applications that require the minimum of overhead, and is particularly suited to web-based applications. However, because of the much greater functionality provided by the full implementation, we will concentrate our discussion on ADODB throughout the remainder of the book.

Setting a Reference to ADO

Before attempting to connect to any database using ADO, you will need to add a reference to ADO in your project. Visual Basic 6 was released with version 2.0 of ADO. The reference gives your project the functionality that you need to connect to a database and work with its data.

ADO now exists in version 2.1, which was released with Internet Explorer 5, but for our purposes the differences are fairly minor. The most significant difference is that ADO 2.1 includes a provider for SQL Server 7. A further new version, ADO 2.5, is due to be released with Windows 2000. If you wish, you can download the Microsoft Data Access Components (MDAC) – of which ADO is a part – from http://www.microsoft.com/data/ download.htm.

To add the ADO reference to your project, open your Visual Basic project and select Project | References... from the main menu bar. The References dialog will open, allowing you to view all registered references. Scroll down and click the checkbox labeled Microsoft ActiveX Data Objects 2.0 Library. (If you're using the reduced-functionality version, ADOR, the reference will be Microsoft ActiveX Data Objects Recordset 2.0 Library.) When you select the reference, you'll notice that the location, file name and language are displayed at the bottom of the dialog box. The name of the ADO 2.0 DLL happens to be `msado15.dll` (don't let this name confuse you – it really is version 2.0!).

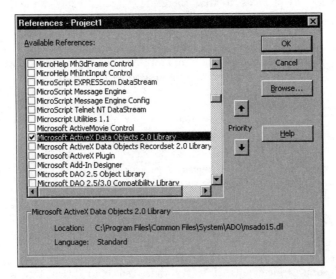

With the new ADO reference checked off, click on the OK button. You have successfully added the reference to your project. Your project will look just the same as it did prior to adding the reference. Remember, the reference doesn't include any viewable components. If you compile your project into a setup process, the reference will automatically be added to your project by the wizard.

This highlights a significant difference between using the ADO Data Control and the ADO reference – namely that the former is an `.ocx` file with a viewable component, while the latter is a `.dll` file, which does not have a viewable component. When you set the reference to this DLL, your project will act as if the code in the DLL were part of the project. Your project code can call functions from the DLL, and it's just as though it were running local to the project. If you fail to add this reference to your project, your code will fail because it won't be able to locate the functions.

> In short, setting this reference exposes your project to the ADO object model.
>
> You'll need to add this reference to every new project that connects to a database using ADO. Forgetting to add the reference is one of the most common errors in ADO VB programming.

In the following sections we'll look at the ADO objects. We've already covered some of the properties and methods of the ADO Data Control (such as `AddNew`, `MoveNext`, and `Delete`), and so these will already be familiar to you. Remember that the methods and properties you see here (and in Appendix E) are not only applicable when you use ADO in your VB code – you can also use them in the ADO Data Control (and indeed in any COM-compliant programming language).

Connecting to a Database

In order to access a database, we need to establish a connection to it. In ADO, the connection is represented by a `Connection` object.

Because the connection is fundamental to database access, the `Connection` object is sometimes considered to be the most important item you use while working with your database. With previous data connection mechanisms, such as DAO, establishing the database connection was the real challenge – particularly when dealing with remote databases and databases such as Oracle. However, ADO really has taken much of the work out of establishing the connection.

Creating a Connection Object

The first task is to declare and create the `Connection` object. The following code declares and creates a `Connection` object called `objConn`:

```
Dim objConn As ADODB.Connection
Set objConn = New ADODB.Connection
```

These two lines of code will be fairly standard from one project to another. Keep in mind that if you're connecting to more than one database, you may have more than one `Connection` object.

Note that we could have declared the connection with this line:

```
Dim objConn as Connection
```

This is a little dangerous, because previous data access technologies (like DAO) also used a `Connection` object. Therefore, it's safer to explicitly state that you want an **ADO** `Connection` object, by specifying `ADODB.Connection`.

Implicit Connection Objects

As we mentioned in the introduction, we can choose not to create a `Connection` object explicitly. Instead, we can supply the necessary connection details direct to a `Recordset` or `Command` object – in this case, when we open the recordset (or run the command) a nameless `Connection` object will be created under the covers.

If we subsequently need to refer to this `Connection` object, we can get a reference to it through the `ActiveConnection` property exposed by the `Command` and `Recordset` objects. For example:

```
Dim objRec As ADODB.Recordset
objRec.Open "OrderDetails", "Provider=Microsoft.Jet.OLEDB.3.51;" & _
    "Data Source=C:\Program Files\Microsoft Visual Studio\VB98\Nwind.mdb"
...
...
Dim objConn As ADODB.Connection
Set objConn = objRec.ActiveConnection
```

In fact, we can also use the `ActiveConnection` property in the opposite direction – assigning an existing `Connection` object to the `ActiveConnection` property of a `Command` or `Recordset` object.

Setting the Connection String

Now that we have created a `Connection` object, we need to prepare the object for a connection to the database. Amongst other information, we must provide the location and name of the database. This information is provided in a semicolon-delimited string known as the **connection string**. We saw in Chapter 4 how to build a connection string with the wizard provided by the ADO Data Control. When connecting to a database programmatically through ADO, we'll build the connection string ourselves.

The connection string is constructed from a number of arguments. The most important of these arguments is `Provider` – this dictates the OLE DB data provider that will be used for the connection. The following OLE DB providers are supplied with the data access components:

Provider	Description
MSDASQL	Connects to ODBC data sources
Microsoft.Jet.SQLOLEDB.3.51	Connects to MS Access databases
SQLOLEDB	Connects to SQL Server databases
MSDAORA	Connects to Oracle databases
MSIDXS	Connects to MS Index Server
ADSDSOObject	Connects to Active Directory Services
MSDataShape	Connects to hierarchical recordsets
MSPersist	Connects to locally saved recordsets
MSDAOSP	For creating custom providers for simple text data

The form of the connection string depends upon which data provider we choose, because different providers need different information in order to connect you to the database. We'll have a look at some different connection strings in a moment.

The most direct way to assign a connection string to the Connection object is to assign it directly to the Connection object's ConnectionString property, like this:

```
objConn.ConnectionString = "Provider=SQLOLEDB; Data Source=bigsmile;" & _
                           "Initial Catalog=Nwind; User Id=sa; Password="
```

Alternatively, you could build up a character string (like strConn in the next example), and then assign that string to the ConnectionString property:

```
Dim strConn
strConn = "Provider=SQLOLEDB; Data Source=bigsmile;"
strConn = strConn & "Initial Catalog=Nwind; User Id=sa; Password="

objConn.ConnectionString = strConn
```

Now, let's look at how connection strings are constructed.

OLE DB Provider for ODBC Drivers

The OLE DB Provider for ODBC is the default provider, so if you don't specify a Provider argument, this is what you'll get. Of course, you should specify the provider, and to specify the OLE DB Provider for ODBC you'll need to give the rather obscure name MSDASQL.

Having specified this provider, connecting through ODBC requires that we give the desired Driver (we enclose this in curly brackets). If we're connecting to a desktop database, we also need to specify the path and filename of the database:

```
Provider=MSDASQL;Driver={Driver_Name};DBQ=Database_Filename
```

If we're connecting to a database that's hosted on a database server, we must provide the server name (using server), the database name (database), a user ID (uid) and a password (pwd):

```
Provider=MSDASQL;Driver={Driver_Name};server=Server_Name;
                database=Database_Name;uid=User_ID;pwd=Password
```

The Driver Name might be one of those which are usefully displayed in the **Drivers** tab of the ODBC Control Panel applet:

To connect to a desktop database through a previously created ODBC Data Source Name, we need only supply the DSN itself:

```
Provider=MSDASQL;DSN=Data_Source_Name
```

To connect to a database server through a DSN, we also need to supply a user name and password:

```
Provider=MSDASQL;DSN=Data_Source_Name;uid=User_ID;pwd=Password
```

Examples

Let's look at some examples. A simple connection string might specify just the OLE DB provider and the data source. For an Access database, this might be as simple as follows:

```
objConn.ConnectionString = "Provider=MSDASQL;" & _
                           "Driver={Microsoft Access Driver (*.mdb)}" & _
                           "DBQ=C:\Databases\MyDataBase.mdb"
```

In the next few examples, we connect to a SQL Server Nwind database, hosted on a server called bigsmile, through the ODBC driver:

```
objConn.ConnectionString = "Driver={SQL Server};server=bigsmile;" & _
                           "Database=Nwind;uid=sa;pwd="
```

This format can be abridged slightly if we have set up an ODBC Data Source Name for the database. The following example connects to the Nwind database using an ODBC DSN with ODBC tags:

```
objConn.ConnectionString = "DSN=Nwind;UID=sa;PWD=;"
```

Other OLE DB Providers

Among the other data providers, it's usually (though not always) necessary to specify the `Provider` and the `Data Source`. For a desktop database, the `Data Source` is the path and filename to the database to which the connection will be made:

```
Provider=Provider_Name;Data Source=Database_Filename
```

If we're connecting to a database server, the `Data Source` is the name of the server; we can also supply the name of the database to connect to (this is the `Initial Catalog`), and a user ID and password if necessary (alternatively, these can be supplied later when the connection is open):

```
Provider=Provider_Name;Data Source=Server_Name;Initial Catalog=Database_Name;
User ID=User_ID;Password=Password
```

Examples

A couple more examples will make this a bit clearer. Here's an example that will use the Microsoft Jet provider to connect to an Access database:

```
objConn.ConnectionString = "Provider=Microsoft.Jet.OLEDB.3.51;" & _
    "Data Source=C:\Databases\MyDataBase.mdb"
```

To connect to a SQL Server database through OLE DB, we must specify the OLE DB provider, the name of the server, the name of the database, and the name and password of the user who is logging on to the database:

```
objConn.ConnectionString = "Provider=SQLOLEDB; Data Source=bigsmile;" & _
    "Initial Catalog=Nwind; User Id=sa; Password="
```

> *If you need to check that you're creating your connection string correctly, you can to add the ADO Data Control to your project and use the wizard to create your connection string. Then copy it over to your code and remove the ADO Data Control.*

Opening the Connection

So the database and provider have been specified and the database is in place (and the DSN has been set up, if we're using one). Now we're in a position to make the connection. The most straightforward way to do this is to call the `Connection` object's `Open` method:

```
objConn.Open
```

When this method is called, the `Connection` object attempts to connect to the database that you specified in the `ConnectionString` property. If it fails, an error message will be returned. If it's successful, you have your connection and are ready to work with your database.

Note that the line above doesn't specify any connection details – so the `Connection` object assumes that you want to use the connection details that you specified in the `ConnectionString` property. It is also possible to call the `Open` method without having specified the connection string in advance – we simply pass the connection string as a parameter to the method:

```
objConn.Open ConnectionString, UserID, Password, OpenOptions
```

As you can see, we can also specify a user ID and password (if they're not included in the *ConnectionString* parameter or specified in the `Connection` object's `ConnectionString` property), as well as additional options for the connection.

OpenOptions may be one of the `ConnectOptionEnum` constants. The only permissible value in ADO 2.0 is `adAsyncConnect` (numerically equal to -1), which specifies that the connection be opened asynchronously. This means that, instead of waiting for the connection to open before proceeding to the next line of code, the application will continue to run while the connection is being made.

Closing the Connection

For completeness, we should really also know how to close a connection – so let's quickly look at that now. When we've finished using our open connection, we can close it by using the `Connection` object's `Close` method:

```
objConn.Close
```

Note that this does not uninstantiate the object. If you want to destroy the `Connection` object completely, and release its memory, we must also set the object to `Nothing`:

```
objConn.Open strConn1
...     ' do some data manipulation
objConn.Close
Set objConn = Nothing
```

Alternatively, you can re-open a closed `Connection` object with different settings:

```
objConn.Open strConn1
...     ' do some data manipulation on database #1
objConn.Close
objConn.Open strConn2
...     ' do some data manipulation on database #2
objConn.Close
Set objConn = Nothing
```

Later in this chapter we'll look at events – special routines that are fired when certain things happen in your code. We'll also look at the `Error` object and the `Errors` collection, and how we can use these in harness with events to do some basic error-handling. Before that, let's get at the data in those databases!

Querying the Database

So we know how to create a `Connection` object, and how to use it to open and close database connections – but we still don't have any records to view or edit. ADO works by capturing a recordset from the database and caching it locally. We query the database by asking it to return all the data that matches our desired criteria – the data that we get back is placed into a recordset.

The query itself may be a SQL statement or a stored procedure, and is represented in the ADO object model by the `Command` object. In addition, the `Command` object allows you to execute batch operations, and even modify the structure of your database.

Creating a Command Object

When creating a `Command` object, we must first declare an instance of the object, just as we did with the `Connection` object. It's generally best to declare this in the `General Declarations` section of your form or module. Here, we'll declare a `Command` object with the name `objComm`:

```
Dim objComm As ADODB.Command
```

Once the `Command` object has been declared, we can create the object by setting it to a new instance of the `ADODB.Command` object:

```
Set objComm = New ADODB.Command
```

The `Command` object's methods and properties can then be invoked. Note that parameters can be used in conjunction with `Command` objects to execute stored procedures with parameters, or parameterized queries.

There are other ways to assign a reference to a `Command` object. For example, we can use a `Recordset` object's `ActiveCommand` property to get a reference to the `Command` object that was used to create that recordset:

```
Dim objRec As ADODB.Recordset
'... use the recordset object to query the database
Dim objComm As ADODB.Command
Set objComm = objRec.ActiveCommand
```

Building the Command Text

The actual command that is to be executed against the database is held in the `CommandText` property of the `Command` object. This property is where we place our SQL statement, stored procedure, table name, or file name before executing the command. For example:

```
objComm.CommandText = "SELECT * FROM Employee"
```

We need to be sure that our data provider is able to interpret the text of our command efficiently. Therefore, we also use the `CommandType` property, which specifies the type of command in question. The `CommandType` property tells the provider whether the `CommandText` contains a text command (such as a SQL statement), or the name of a table or of a stored procedure, or the path and filename of a persisted recordset. The value of this property may be any of the following `CommandTypeEnum` constants:

- ➤ `adCmdFile`. The command text is to be evaluated as the path and filename of a recordset persisted on the local hard drive.
- ➤ `adCmdStoredProc`. The command text is to be evaluated as a stored procedure.
- ➤ `adCmdTable`. The command text is to be evaluated as a SQL statement which will return all rows from the named table.
- ➤ `adCmdTableDirect`. The command text is to be interpreted as a table name.
- ➤ `adCmdText`. The command text is to be interpreted as a text command, such as a SQL statement.
- ➤ `adCmdUnknown`. The type of command is unknown.

For example, if we want to retrieve the entire `Authors` table as a recordset, we would need to set the `CommandText` and `CommandType` properties as follows:

```
objComm.CommandText = "Authors"
objComm.CommandType = adCmdTable
```

When this command is executed, the query `"SELECT * FROM Authors"` will be sent to the provider, and the table will be returned as a recordset.

Commands that Return no Records

Sometimes, we'll want to execute commands that don't return any records – for example, if we intend only to add records, but not to view or edit existing ones. In this case, we can also specify the command type `adExecuteNorecords` in conjunction with `adCmdText` or `adCmdStoredProc`:

```
objComm.CommandType = adCmdStoredProc + adExecuteNoRecords
```

Executing the Command

Before we can execute the command defined in the `CommandText`, we must specify the connection to be used. This involved setting the `Command` object's `ActiveConnection` property, either to a valid connection string, or to an existing `Connection` object. For example:

```
objComm.ActiveConnection = "Provider=SQLOLEDB;Data Source=bigsmile;" & _
                           "Initial Catalog=pubs;User ID=sa;Password="
```

Alternatively:

```
objConn.ConnectionString = "Provider=SQLOLEDB;Data Source=bigsmile;" & _
                           "Initial Catalog=pubs;User ID=sa;Password="
objComm.ActiveConnection = objConn
```

There is a subtle difference in the way these two code fragments work. The first creates a new connection (with an implicit `Connection` object, running under the surface of your code). The second re-uses an existing connection, and is therefore a more efficient use of resources.

Now we're ready to execute the query. The `Command` object has an `Execute` method, which applies the command text to the database, and returns any resulting data to the assigned `Recordset` object:

```
Set objRec = objComm.Execute(RecordsAffected, Parameters, Options)
```

If we know that the command will not return any data (that is, if `CommandType` was set to `adExecuteNoRecords`), or if we don't wish to capture the rows returned by the command, then we can simply miss out the part that assigns the results to a recordset – like this:

```
objComm.Execute RecordsAffected, Parameters, Options
```

The Execute Method's Optional Arguments

You'll see that there are three arguments that can be used with the `Execute` method. They're all optional, and are described as follows:

> ➤ *RecordsAffected*: You can specify a variable name here. If specified, the provider returns the number of affected records to that variable.

> ➤ *Parameters*: This is an array of any `Parameter` objects, which represent parameters that are to be passed to the command.

> ➤ *Options*: Specifies how the provider should evaluate the `CommandText` property of the `Command` object. This parameter can contain one of the `CommandTypeEnum` constants identical to that in the `CommandType` property seen above. In addition, to this can be added `adAsyncExecute` to specify that the command is to be executed asynchronously, and `adAsyncFetch` or `adAsyncFetchNonBlocking` to specify that the recordset is to be returned asynchronously.

An Example

The following snippet of code illustrates the usage of the `RecordsAffected` parameter. A `Long` variable is passed into the `Execute` statement as a parameter. The value of this variable is set to the number of records affected by the operation after the command has been executed.

```
Set objConn = New ADODB.Connection
objConn.Open "Provider=SQLOLEDB;Initial Catalog=pubs;User ID=sa"

Set objComm = New ADODB.Command
objComm.ActiveConnection = objConn
objComm.CommandText = "UPDATE titles SET royalty=royalty * 1.10"
objComm.CommandType = adCmdText

objComm.Execute lngRecs
MsgBox lngRecs & " records have been updated."
```

Note that recordsets with a firehose (read-only, forward-only) cursor do not support the `RecordsAffected` argument. The firehose cursor is the default cursor type for a recordset. We'll look at cursor types and lock types later in this chapter.

Other Command Object Functionality

In this section we'll briefly mention a couple of other useful things that the `Command` object can do.

Sometimes, the execution of a command can take longer than you expect – for example, if the application has a problem communicating with the database server. In situations like this, it's useful to be able to limit to the length of time to wait before terminating the operation and generating an error. This functionality is provided by the `Command` object's `CommandTimeout` property. This is set to a `Long` value, specifying the number of seconds after which the command will be timed out:

```
objComm.CommandTimeout = 20
```

Setting it to zero causes ADO to wait indefinitely (or until the command has been executed). The default value is 30 seconds.

We can programmatically cancel an asynchronous command at any point during its execution, up to the point when it has completed executing. This is achieved through the Cancel method. This method only works if the command was executed asynchronously (that is, with adAsyncExecute added to the Options parameter of the Execute method), and it must be called before the execution of the command has been completed.

Executing a Command without a Command Object

So far we have only seen how to execute a query against a database using a Command object. But, just as we can open a connection without explicitly creating a Connection object, we can also execute a command without creating a Command object. In fact, there are two ways to do this. First, we can execute the command directly through the Connection object; second, we can open a pre-created Recordset object by querying it directly against the database.

Using a Connection Object

To execute a command directly from the Connection object, we use that object's Execute method. This is similar to the Command object's Execute method, but we must also pass in the command text as a parameter. Here's the syntax:

```
Set Recordset = Connection.Execute(CommandText, [RecordsAffected], [Options])
```

The optional RecordsAffected and Options arguments are identical to those for the Command object's Execute method. The CommandText argument is a string value, equivalent to the Command object's CommandText property – so it might be a text command (such as a SQL statement), or a stored procedure or table name.

For example, to open the Authors table from the SQL Server pubs database asynchronously:

```
Dim objConn As ADODB.Connection
Dim objRec As ADODB.Recordset

Set objConn = New ADODB.Connection
objConn.ConnectionString = "Provider=SQLOLEDB;Data Source=bigsmile;" & _
                           "Initial Catalog=pubs;User ID=sa;Password="
objConn.Open
Set objRec = objConn.Execute("authors", , adCmdTable + adAsyncExecute)
```

As with a query executed through the Command object, we have the ability to cancel the operation and to set a limit to the length of time the application will wait for the command to be executed. To cancel a command executed through a Connection object, we use the same Cancel method that is used to cancel the opening of a connection. Again, only an asynchronously executed command (with the argument adAsyncExecute added to the Options parameter of the Execute method) can be canceled.

To set a timeout limit for a command executed through the Connection object's Execute method, we can use Connection object's CommandTimeout property. This property performs the same task as the Command object's CommandTimeout property. However, the two properties are entirely independent – and neither property inherits its value from the other.

Using a Recordset Object

We can use the Recordset object's Open method with or without a Command object. In the former case, the Command object is passed as a parameter to the Open method; in the second, the command text is passed in instead. The syntax for the Open method is:

```
Recordset.Open([Source], [ActiveConnection], [CursorType], [LockType], [Options])
```

The *Source* argument can be either a valid command text or a Command object; *ActiveConnection* may be a connection string or an existing Connection object. Thus, if we choose, we can open a recordset and query a database without explicitly creating a Command object or a Connection object.

In fact, the *Source* and *ActiveConnection* arguments are both optional – because we can set them prior to calling the Open method with the Recordset object's Source and ActiveConnection properties.

The *CursorType* and *LockType* arguments define what type of recordset will be returned; lock and cursor types will be discussed later in this chapter. Note that this is the only way of specifying lock and cursor types: recordsets opened with a Connection or Command object are limited to the defaults. Finally, *Options* specifies the type of the command in the Source parameter, and is identical to the *Options* argument of the Command object's Execute method.

For example, to retrieve the Authors table from the SQL Server pubs database with existing Connection and Command objects:

```
Dim objConn As ADODB.Connection
Dim objComm As ADODB.Command
Dim objRec As ADODB.Recordset

'Create and open the Connection object
Set objConn = New ADODB.Connection
objConn.ConnectionString = "Provider=SQLOLEDB;Data Source=bigsmile;" & _
                           "Initial Catalog=pubs;User ID=sa;Password="
objConn.Open

'Create and set the Command object
Set objComm = New ADODB.Command
objComm.CommandText = "authors"
objComm.CommandType = adCmdTable

'Create and set the Recordset object
Set objRec = New ADODB.Recordset
objRec.ActiveConnection = objConn
Set objRec.Source = objComm

'Open the Recordset object, thus executing the command
objRec.Open
```

The following code retrieves the same table, but without explicitly creating `Connection` or `Command` objects:

```
Dim objRec As ADODB.Recordset

Set objRec = New ADODB.Recordset
objRec.Open "authors", "Provider=SQLOLEDB;Data Source=bigsmile;" & _
            "Initial Catalog=pubs;User ID=sa;Password=", , , adCmdTable
```

While the second sample is clearly more concise, it can be more efficient to create the objects explicitly. This allows us to re-use connections, rather than creating a new `Connection` object each time we want to connect to the database, and to pass parameters into the command.

Like the `Command` and `Connection` objects, the `Recordset` object provides a `Cancel` method to halt the execution of an asynchronous command. Unlike the other objects, however, the `Recordset` object does not provide a `CommandTimeout` property.

Parameters

One important point to note is that neither the `Connection.Execute` nor `Recordset.Open` methods provides a means of passing return or output parameters back from a stored procedure. In order to do that, we must explicitly create a `Command` object. Then, each parameter of the stored procedure can be represented in the form of a `Parameter` object: these parameter details are passed with the other command details to the provider when the command is executed.

The `Parameter` objects reside in the `Parameters` collection of the `Command` object, which can be accessed via the `Parameters` property of the `Command` object:

```
Set colParam = objComm.Parameters
```

We'll take a closer look a the `Parameters` collection in a moment. First, let's find out about the individual `Parameter` objects.

Creating a Parameter Object

To create a new `Parameter` object, we must use the `CreateParameter` method of the `Command` object. The following demonstrates the syntax of the `CreateParameter` method:

```
Set Parameter = Command.CreateParameter([Name],[Type],[Direction],[Size], _
                                         [Value])
```

The `CreateParameter` method has five optional arguments:

> *Name*: The name of the `Parameter` object.
> *Type*: The data type of the `Parameter` object. The constants for these are listed below.
> *Direction*: The type of `Parameter` object: input, output, both, or the return value of a stored procedure. The constants for these are listed below.
> *Size*: The maximum length for the value of the parameter in characters or bytes.
> *Value*: The value of the parameter.

Here's an example, in which we declare an `ADODB.Parameter` object, then create an input parameter of type integer with the name `Parameter1`:

```
Dim objParam As ADODB.Parameter
Set objParam = objComm.CreateParameter("percentage", adInteger, adParamInput)
```

The arguments are all optional, because they can be supplied by setting properties of the `Parameter` object. For example:

```
Dim objParam As ADODB.Parameter
Set objParam = objComm.CreateParameter
objParam.Name = "percentage"
objParam.Type = adInteger
objParam.Direction = adParamInput
```

The Name Property

Note that the `Name` property or *Name* argument (which is used to identify the parameter) does not have to be the same as the name given in the stored procedure or query, although it does make sense to keep them the same.

The Type Property

The data type for the parameter can be set through the `Type` property. This is set to one of the `DataTypeEnum` values. The following table shows some of the data types available, and the data types of the SQL Server and Access providers that they map to:

Constant	SQL Server type	Access type
adBoolean	bit	Yes/No
adCurrency	money, smallmoney	Currency
adDate		Date/Time
adDBTimeStamp	datetime, smalldatetime	
adDouble		Double
adEmpty		Value
adGUID		Replication ID
adInteger	int	Long Integer
adSingle	float, real	Single
adSmallInt	smallint	Integer
adUnsignedTinyInt	tinyint	Byte
adVarBinary	binary, varbinary, timestamp, image	Binary, OLE Object
adVarChar	char, varchar, text	Text, Memo

The Direction Property

The `Direction` property specifies whether the parameter is an input parameter, an output parameter, an input/output parameter or a return value. It may be set to any of the `ParameterDirectionEnum` constants:

> - **adParamUnknown**. Indicates that the parameter direction is unknown.
> - **adParamInput**. Default. Indicates an input parameter.
> - **adParamOutput**. Indicates an output parameter.
> - **adParamInputOutput**. Indicates both an input and output parameter.
> - **adParamReturnValue**. Indicates a return value.

The distinction between `adParamOutput` and `adParamReturnValue` is quite subtle. A return value is returned from the SQL stored procedure in a much the same way that a Visual Basic function returns a value. By contrast, output parameters are populated during the execution of the procedure. In many cases, there will be little practical difference between the two.

> **MS Access does not support output parameters or return values.**

The Size Property

In addition to specifying the data type of the parameter, we can specify its size – either its maximum possible length in characters (for a text parameter) or the maximum number of bytes it can hold (for a numeric parameter). The `Size` property indicates the maximum size allowable in the `Value` property of a `Parameter` object. This is a required property if the specified data type is of variable length, such as `VarChar`.

If this property is not set when it is required, an error will be generated when the parameter is appended to the `Parameters` collection. For example, consider the following code, which defines the `Type` as adVarChar, but does not specify the `Size`:

```
Set objParam = objComm.CreateParameter("strDescription", adVarChar, _
                                       adParamInput, , "Quite Tasty")
objComm.Parameters.Append objParam
```

Here, note that the fourth parameter has deliberately been left blank. If we try to execute this, we generate the following error:

Microsoft Visual Basic

Run-time error '3708':

The application has improperly defined a Parameter object.

| Continue | End | Debug | Help |

The Value Property

The final property we can set when we create a parameter is its value – that is, the value that will be passed into the stored procedure when the command is executed. The `Parameter` object's `Value` property can be used to set or return the data in a `Parameter` object. Note that the data populated in the `Value` property must have the same data type as declared in the `Type` property.

The Parameters Collection

The `Parameters` collection exposes a number of methods and properties that allow us to manage the parameters for a given command. We can add an existing `Parameter` object to the collection using the `Append` method (we will see a little later how to create a `Parameter` object):

```
objComm.Parameters.Append objParam
```

The `Parameters` collection also exposes a `Delete` method, which removes a specified `Parameter` object from the collection. The `Delete` method has one parameter – the index value of the object you want to remove. This zero-based value indicates the position of the `Parameter` object within the collection. For example, to delete the second parameter in the collection, we would write:

```
objComm.Parameters.Delete 1
```

We can also retrieve a specific parameter from the collection. In this case, we use the `Parameters` collection's `Item` method – employing the index value once again. For example, to set a reference to the first `Parameter` object in the collection:

```
Set objParam = objComm.Parameters.Item(0)
```

> *Note that, when retrieving or deleting parameters, an error will be returned if you give an index value of an object that does not exist.*

We can also retrieve parameters by using the the `Item` method in conjunction with the `Parameter` object's `Name` property. To do this, we simply specify the name of the parameter that we want to retrieve. For example:

```
Set objParam = objComm.Parameters.Item("MyParam")
```

There's one more `Parameters` method, `Refresh`, which updates the `Parameter` objects in the collection, retrieving information from the provider:

```
colParam.Refresh
```

In addition to these methods, the `Parameters` collection also has one property – the `Count` property – which returns a `Long` value indicating the number of `Parameter` objects in the collection. If the value is 0, there are no objects in the collection. The following example displays the number of `Parameter` objects in a message box:

```
MsgBox "There are " & objComm.Parameters.Count & _
       "parameters in the collection.", vbInformation
```

Passing Parameters into a Stored Procedure

Now let's see all this in action. The SQL Server pubs database is supplied with a stored procedure named byroyalty, which selects (from the titleauthor table) the au_id field for every author with a specified royalty percentage. The SQL for this stored procedure is:

```
CREATE PROCEDURE byroyalty @percentage int
AS
SELECT au_id FROM titleauthor
WHERE titleauthor.royaltyper = @percentage
```

The royalty percentage to be matched is passed into the stored procedure as the parameter @percentage. So, we must supply a value for the @percentage parameter when we execute this procedure – otherwise an error will be generated. We will execute this stored procedure by creating a Command object with its CommandType set to the procedure name (byroyalty). In order to pass in the parameter information, we'll create a new Parameter object and add this to the Parameters collection of our Command object.

First we must dimension our Connection, Command, Recordset and Parameter objects, and open the connection:

```
Dim objConn As ADODB.Connection
Dim objRec As ADODB.Recordset
Dim objComm As ADODB.Command
Dim objParam As ADODB.Parameter

Set objConn = New ADODB.Connection
objConn.Open "Provider=SQLOLEDB;Data Source=bigsmile;" & _
             "Initial Catalog=pubs;User ID=sa;Password="
```

Now we instantiate the Command object and set its CommandText and CommandType properties. CommandText will be the name of the stored procedure, "byroyalty", and CommandType will be set to adCmdStoredProc, to indicate that the command is a stored procedure. We also set the Command object's ActiveConnection property to our existing Connection object, objConn:

```
Set objComm = New ADODB.Command
objComm.CommandText = "byroyalty"
objComm.CommandType = adCmdStoredProc   ' the command is a stored procedure
objComm.ActiveConnection = objConn      ' use the existing connection
```

We can now create our Parameter object. We'll call it percentage (for convenience, since that's the name of the parameter used in the stored procedure), and indicate that it's an integer input parameter with a value of 40. Once we've created the parameter, we can add it to the Parameters collection:

```
Set objParam = objComm.CreateParameter("percentage", adInteger, _
                                        adParamInput, , 40)
objComm.Parameters.Append objParam
```

Finally, we instantiate and open the recordset. The only parameter we need to pass into the Open method is our Command object, objComm, since this contains references to the Connection and Parameter objects:

```
Set objRec = New ADODB.Recordset
objRec.Open objComm
```

This last line will open the recordset based on the stored procedure with the parameter which we passed into it.

Now, the requested data is contained in the recordset and ready for use to analyze and manipulate. This is the subject of the next section.

Viewing and Editing Records

Once we have retrieved a recordset from the database, we can start to view and manipulate that data. We can retrieve the value of a named field of the current record using the exclamation mark syntax, which may well be familiar to you from DAO. To access the value, we simply place an exclamation mark and the field name after the name of the Recordset object. For example, to display a message box containing the first and last names of the current author from the Authors table of the pubs database, we would write:

```
MsgBox "Current author is: " & objRec!au_fname & " " & objRec!au_lname, _
       vbInformation
```

The fields that we want to access in this case are named au_fname (the author's first name) and au_lname (the author's last name). We can also use a slightly longer notation with the Recordset's Fields property, specifying the field either through an index value or through its name (note that the index is zero-based, so the first field returned into the recordset has an index value of 0):

```
MsgBox objRec.Fields(0).Value
MsgBox objRec.Fields("au_fname").Value
```

Each of these lines uses a reference to an object representing the field, and generates a message box, containing the value of that object. The Field object has a Value property, which we use to extract the value of the field for the current record.

In fact, Value is the default property for an ADO Field object, so it can be omitted from the code. Thus, the following two lines of code therefore have exactly the same effect:

```
MsgBox objRec.Fields(0)
MsgBox objRec.Fields(0).Value
```

> **We will look more closely at the Field object later in this chapter.**

We can now retrieve the value of a record's fields, but to access specific records we will need to know how to find our way around the recordset.

Navigating through the Recordset

We have already met some of the most important methods for navigating through the recordset and moving from one record to another. The simplest way of doing this is with the `MoveFirst`, `MoveLast`, `MoveNext` and `MovePrevious` methods. These methods take no arguments and simply move the record pointer to the appropriate record. For example, to move the record pointer to the beginning of the recordset and make the first record the current one, we simply write:

```
objRec.MoveFirst
```

Similarly, `MoveLast` moves the record pointer to the end of the recordset.

The `MoveNext` and `MovePrevious` methods work in a similar way, but (as we saw when using the ADO Data Control) we must be careful not to go beyond the beginning or end of the file. We can do this by checking the `BOF` or `EOF` properties of the `Recordset` object.

The best way to think of this is to imagine a BOF 'pseudo-record' that sits before the first record of the recordset, and an EOF pseudo-record that sits just after the last record. While the record pointer is placed before the first record of the recordset, on the BOF pseudo-record, the `BOF` property will be `True`. While the record pointer is placed past the last record, on the EOF pseudo-record, `EOF` is set to `True`.

The record pointer can reside at these BOF and EOF pseudo-records without generating an error, but any attempt to move beyond them will generate an error. An error will also be raised if we attempt to access the current record while the record pointer is set to `BOF` or `EOF`. Therefore, it's a good idea to check the `BOF` property after every `MovePrevious` method call and `EOF` after every `MoveNext`. If the property returns `True`, we can then move the record pointer back to a valid record. For example:

```
objRec.MoveNext
If objRec.EOF Then
    objRec.MoveLast
End If
```

> **Not all cursor types support all types of movement within the recordset. We shall look at the implications of different cursor types later in this chapter.**

We can also move directly to a specific record by specifying its position in the recordset with the `AbsolutePosition` property. Note that this property is one-based (not zero-based), so, for example, to move to the fifth record, we would write:

```
objRec.AbsolutePosition = 5
```

We can also use this property to return the current position of the record pointer in the recordset. We used this property to update the status label in the application developed in Chapter 4. This label gave the number of the current record and the total number of records in the recordset (for example, "Record 1 out of 4"). The other property used here is `RecordCount`, which returns the total number of records in the recordset.

The `RecordCount` property only works with static and keyset cursors (see later in this chapter).

Bookmarks

Of course, we sometimes want to move straight to a record without knowing its position in the recordset – particularly since its position may change as records are added or deleted. We can do this by assigning a **bookmark** to the record. A bookmark will uniquely identify the record, and we can use it to jump to the record whenever we want.

To assign a bookmark to a record, we first move the record point to that record; then we set a variant to the `Bookmark` property of the `Recordset` object. For example, this code sets a bookmark named `varBkmrk` to point to the first record of the recordset:

```
Dim varBkmrk As Variant

objRec.MoveFirst
varBkmrk = objRec.Bookmark
```

That's it. We can move around the recordset, visiting other records, and when we want to move the record pointer to this record, we simply have to set the `Bookmark` property of the `Recordset` to our bookmark variant:

```
objRec.Bookmark = varBkmrk
```

> **Bookmarks are generally only supported on keyset and static cursors, although some providers also support bookmarks on dynamic cursors.**

We saw in Chapter 4 how we can use this property temporarily to store the current position in the recordset, so we can return to that record if any operation is canceled or is unsuccessful.

Moving by More than One Record

We've seen that we can move backwards and or forwards through the recordset by one record at a time (as long as the cursor type allows!). In addition, we can move by a specified number of records using the `Recordset` object's `Move` method. We must supply as a parameter the number of records we wish to move from the current record; a positive value indicates forward movement, a negative value backward movement. So, for example, to move to a record five records before the current one:

```
objRec.Move -5
```

In addition, we can also specify the starting point from which we want to move by the given number of records, by supplying a bookmark as a second argument. So, to move forwards three records from our `varBkmrk` bookmark, we would use:

```
objRec.Move 3, varBkmrk
```

As well as using our own bookmarks as a starting point, we can use any of the `BookmarkEnum` constants in the second argument:

- ➢ adBookmarkCurrent. Move from the first record by the specified number of records.
- ➢ adBookmarkFirst. Move from the last record by the specified number of records.
- ➢ adBookmarkLast. Move from the first record by the specified number of records.

For example, to move to the antepenultimate record in the recordset:

```
objRec.Move -2, adBookmarkLast
```

Recordset Pages

Because a recordset will frequently contain a large number of records (often an entire table), ADO gives us the ability to subdivide the recordset into a number of **pages**. This makes record-handling more manageable, and allows for faster navigation within the recordset.

We can specify or determine the number of records contained on each page by using the PageSize property. For example, to limit each page to five records, we would use:

```
objRec.PageSize = 5
```

We can determine the number of pages in the recordset using the PageCount property. For example, the following line displays a message box indicating the number of pages of data returned by a query and the number of records on each page:

```
MsgBox objRec.PageCount & " pages of " & _
       objRec.PageSize & " records were returned."
```

Finally, the Recordset object also exposes an AbsolutePage property. This allows us to determine the current page in the recordset for the current record, or to move to a specific page within the recordset. We could use these properties to navigate quickly through the recordset, jumping *x* records at a time (where *x* can be chosen by setting the value of the PageSize property). For example, the following two snippets of code could be used for command buttons to move backwards and forwards through a recordset by one page at a time:

```
Private Sub cmdPrevPage_Click()
   Dim intPage As Integer
   intPage = objRec.AbsolutePage
   intPage = intPage - 1
   If intPage > 0 Then objRec.AbsolutePage = intPage
End Sub
```

```
Private Sub cmdNextPage_Click()
   Dim intPage As Integer
   intPage = objRec.AbsolutePage
   intPage = intPage + 1
   If intPage <= objRec.PageCount Then objRec.AbsolutePage = intPage
End Sub
```

We set a variable to equal the current value of AbsolutePage and increase or decrease by one – then we check that we won't move be moving before the first page or after the last page when we set AbsolutePage to its new value. When moving forwards, we check the new page value against PageCount to ensure that we don't move beyond the end of the recordset.

Locating Records in the Recordset

Even though the recordset is returned from a query against a database – and as such is a subset of the full set of database data – it can still be very large, and could contain many thousands of records. For this reason, ADO provides methods to search, filter and sort the recordset.

Finding Specific Records

The `Recordset` object's `Find` method will search for the next record that matches the given SQL criterion. The syntax for this method is:

```
Recordset.Find(Criteria, [SkipRecords], [SearchDirection], [Start])
```

The `Criteria` argument is a string containing an expression against which the records will be matched. This expression takes the form of a SQL `WHERE` clause, without the `WHERE` keyword. For example, to find the next author whose last name begins with R, in the `Authors` table of the SQL Server `pubs` database, we could use the following line:

```
objRec.Find "au_lname LIKE 'r*'"
```

This expression will usually consist of the name of a field, a comparison operator and a value against which the field is to be compared. It is not permitted to combine multiple expressions with `AND` or `OR` operators. For more information on building SQL `WHERE` clauses, see Chapter 6.

By default, the search begins at the current record. However, this can be modified by specifying a value for the `SkipRecords` argument. This argument specifies an offset value from which the search will start. For example, a value of 0 (the default) indicates that the search will commence at the current record; a value of 1 causes the search to begin at the next record in the recordset, and a value of -1 at the previous record.

The `SearchDirection` parameter specifies whether the search is to run forwards or backwards from the current record. This parameter must be one of the `SearchDirectionEnum` constants: `adSearchBackward` (or -1) for a backwards search, or `adSearchForward` (or 1) for a forward search. The default is `adSearchForward`.

It is also possible to specify a bookmark from which the search is to commence. This is useful if we wish to search from a specific record, but we don't know the offset of that record from the current record. This is indicated in the `Start` argument, which may hold a valid bookmark or one of the three `BookmarkEnum` constants:

> ➤ `adBookmarkCurrent`. The search will start from the current record.

> ➤ `adBookmarkFirst`. The search will start from the first record.

> ➤ `adBookmarkLast`. The search will start from the last record.

For example, to search backwards from the last record through a recordset based on the `sales` table of the `pubs` database for sales orders with a quantity greater than or equal to 30, we would use:

```
objRec.Find "qty >= 30", 0, adSearchBackward, adBookmarkLast
```

Note that the Find method simply moves the record pointer to the **first** record that matches the specified criterion, and thus returns only a single record. If we want to execute a search that returns more than one record, we should apply a filter to the recordset using the Recordset object's Filter property.

Filtering the Recordset

This property temporarily filters the recordset. While a filter is active, only the records that meet the given criteria are visible to the user of the recordset. The filter may be a valid filter string, an array of bookmarks or one of the FilterGroupEnum constants:

> ➤ adFilterNone. The filter is reset, and the full recordset restored.

> ➤ adFilterPendingRecords. The recordset is filtered to show only the records that have been modified but not yet sent to the server (batch update mode only).

> ➤ adFilterAffectedRecords. The recordset is filtered only to show only records affected by the last Delete, Resync, UpdateBatch or CancelBatch method call.

> ➤ adFilterFetchedRecords. The recordset is filtered to show the records in the current cache only.

> ➤ adFilterPredicate. The recordset is filtered to show only deleted records.

> ➤ adFilterConflictingRecords. The recordset is filtered to show only records which caused a conflict in the last batch update attempt.

The filter is applied simply by setting the Filter property to the desired value. For example, to view the records that caused a problem during an attempt to update the database, we would use the adFilterConflictingRecords constant:

```
objRec.Filter = adFilterConflictingRecords
```

A filter string is similar to the criteria used by the Find method. However, unlike the Find method, Filter does allow you to string together multiple criteria, using the AND and OR keywords, and you may use parentheses to group them. For example:

```
objRec.Filter = "qty > 30 AND ord_date >= 1/1/94"
```

We can filter our recordset to show only selected records which need not match a specific criterion. The best way to do this is by setting the Filter property to an array of bookmarks. The bookmarks in the array are defined individually, and the filter is then set to the entire array. For example, to filter the recordset to contain only the first and last records:

```
Dim arrBkmark(1)

objRec.MoveFirst
arrBkmark(0) = objRec.Bookmark
objRec.MoveLast
arrBkmark(1) = objRec.Bookmark
objRec.Filter = arrBkmark
```

To reset the filter and restore the full recordset, set Filter to an empty string or to adFilterNone:

```
objRec.Filter = ""
```

or:

```
objRec.Filter = adFilterNone
```

Retrieving Rows into an Array

We can retrieve records into an array using the GetRows method of the Recordset object. The first dimension of the returned array corresponds to the columns of the recordset, the second to the rows (although this is not particularly intuitive, this system is preserved for compatability with DAO and RDO). The syntax for this property is:

```
Variant = Recordset.GetRows([Rows], [Start], [Fields])
```

The *Rows* argument specifies how many records are to be retrieved. The default is adGetRowsRest, which specifies that all the remaining records are to be retrieved into the array.

By default, rows are retrieved from the current record, but it is possible to move the start point by setting the *Start* parameter to any valid bookmark in the recordset, or to one of the BookmarkEnum constants:

➤ adBookmarkCurrent. The operation will start at the current record.

➤ adBookmarkFirst. The operation will start at the first record.

➤ adBookmarkLast. The operation will start at the last record.

We can also specify which fields are to be retrieved, by using the *Fields* parameter. This can be set to a single field name or an array of field names, or to the index position of a field in the Recordset's Fields collection or an array of index values. For example, to retrieve the au_lname field from the first 10 records of the recordset, we would use:

```
Dim varRows As Variant
varRows = objRec.GetRows(10, adBookmarkFirst, "au_lname")
```

To retrieve both the au_fname and the au_lname fields, these values must be held in a variant array, which is passed in as the final parameter to the GetRows method:

```
Dim varRows As Variant
Dim varFlds(1) As Variant

varFlds(0) = "au_fname"
varFlds(1) = "au_lname"
varRows = objRec.GetRows(10, adBookmarkFirst, varFlds)
```

Alternatively, we can pass the index number for the field into the method:

```
Dim varRows As Variant
varRows = objRec.GetRows(10, adBookmarkFirst, 1)
```

Or, to retrieve more than one field:

```
Dim varRows As Variant
Dim varFlds(1) As Variant

varFlds(0) = 2
varFlds(1) = 1
varRows = objRec.GetRows(10, adBookmarkFirst, varFlds)
```

Because the first dimension in the array represents the columns in the recordset, to display the full name in a message box, we would use:

```
MsgBox varRows(0, 0) & " " & varRows(1, 0)
```

Note that the fields are placed in the array in the order that they are passed into the method, not in the order in which they occur in the recordset.

Sorting the Recordset

In addition to filtering the recordset, it's often useful to sort the records into a specific order. This can be achieved with the Recordset object's Sort property. This works in a similar way to the Filter property: the property is set to a string, which indicates the fields on which the sort is to take place, and the order for the sort for each field:

```
objRec.Sort = "ord_date ASC, qty DESC"
```

If we choose to sort by multiple fields, we can separate the fields using commas. The sort order is indicated by the keywords ASC for ascending order (the default) and DESC for descending order.

The Sort property is not supported by the providers for SQL Server or MS Access.

Modifying the Data

We can retrieve data from a database into our recordset, and we can manipulate the recordset in order to find the records that we're interested in. Now, we need to know how to modify the data in the recordset – by editing the values of individual fields, and by adding and deleting records.

The first thing to note is that, if the recordset's lock type is set to adLockReadOnly, then the recordset is a read-only recordset. This means that the data in the recordset can only be viewed; it cannot be modified.

> **Recall that the Recordset object's lock type is set when the Recordset is created. We'll discuss lock types in greater detail later in this chapter.**

Editing Records

Editing records through ADO does not require a special method. We simply modify the value of the appropriate field. We can access the field value for editing using much the same ways that we could retrieve it for viewing. So, to change the value of the au_fname field for the current record, we might use any of the following lines:

```
objRec!au_fname = "Archibald"
```

```
objRec.Fields("au_fname") = "Roderick"
```

```
objRec.Fields(2) = "Herbert"
```

In all of the above lines, we've left out the `.Value` part of the syntax because `Value` is the default property of a `Field` object. But we can make it explicit if we want to:

```
objRec!au_fname.Value = "Friedrich"
```

Of course, it's not often that the new value will be hard-coded into the application. More commonly, it will be generated dynamically or inputted by the user into a text box or input box:

```
Dim strName As String

strName = InputBox("Please enter new name:", "Edit record")
objRec!au_fname = strName
```

It is also possible to modify the data in a database using the SQL UPDATE statement. However, this causes the database itself to be updated, not just the cached recordset. In this case, we place the SQL statement in the `CommandText` property of a `Command` object and then execute the command, as we did when opening a recordset:

```
Dim objComm As ADODB.Command

Set objComm = New ADODB.Command
objComm.ActiveConnection = objConn
objComm.CommandText = "UPDATE authors SET au_fname='Archie' " & _
                      "WHERE au_fname='Archibald'"
objComm.CommandType = adCmdText
objComm.Execute
```

Adding Records

To add a new record to the recordset, we call the `Recordset` object's `AddNew` method. This creates a new record, which we can populate with data in two ways. The first technique is to pass the field names and values for the new record, as arguments to the `AddNew` method:

```
objRec.AddNew "au_lname", "Schmidt"
```

The example above creates a new record, and assigns the string `Schmidt` to the new record's `au_lname` field.

In fact, this technique also allows us to assign values to more than one field: to do this, we must pass in two arrays containing the field names and the values:

```
objRec.AddNew Array("au_id", "au_lname", "au_fname", "contract"), _
    Array("123-45-6789", "Schmidt", "Johannes", True)
```

The second technique to populate the new record is to assign values to the fields individually:

```
objRec.AddNew
objRec!au_id = "123-45-6789"
objRec!au_fname = "Johannes"
objRec!au_lname = "Schmidt"
objRec!contract = True
```

This works because the AddNew call leaves the record pointer pointing to our new record – which allows us to populate the fields immediately without having to move around the recordset.

> **Remember that you must assign values to all required fields before updating the database. We'll look at how to update the database from a recordset shortly.**

We can, of course, also add a new record using a Command object and a SQL INSERT statement:

```
Dim objComm As ADODB.Command

Set objComm = New ADODB.Command
objComm.ActiveConnection = objConn
objComm.CommandText = "INSERT INTO authors(au_id,au_lname," & _
                                          "au_fname,contract) " & _
                      "VALUES('245-43-5432','Schmidt','Johannes',1)"
objComm.CommandType = adCmdText
objComm.Execute
```

Deleting Records

The Recordset object's Delete method allows us to delete a single record or a group of records. This method takes a single parameter, which can have any of the following AffectEnum values:

> ➢ adAffectAllChapters. All child recordsets of the current record or group of records will be deleted.

> ➢ adAffectCurrent. Only the current record will be deleted.

> ➢ adAffectGroup. All records in the current filter will be deleted.

> ➢ adAffectAll. All records in the recordset will be deleted.

If none of these values is given, the default adAffectCurrent will be assumed. Therefore, to delete only the current record we simply need the line:

```
objRec.Delete
```

To delete a selected group of records, we must first set the Recordset's Filter property to the criterion by which we want to delete records. For example, to delete all records for which the ord_date field has a value earlier than 1st January 1993, we would use:

```
objRec.Filter = "ord_date < 1/1/93"
objRec.Delete adAffectGroup
```

Not all recordsets support this option.

Refreshing the Recordset

If we want to cancel any changes we have made to the recordset, or if we want to re-check the data in the database (in case it has been updated by another user), we must refresh the recordset from the underlying database. ADO provides two ways to do this: the `Requery` method and the `Resync` method.

The `Requery` method re-executes the query on which the recordset is based, and is thus equivalent to closing and re-opening the recordset using the original command. It's syntax is quite simple:

```
Recordset.Requery Options
```

This method takes a single optional argument, `Options`. Because the original command cannot be changed, this will only have any effect if it is used to specify that the recordset is to be cached asynchronously, using either `adAsyncFetch` or `adAsyncFetchNonBlocking`. An error will be generated if `Requery` is called while a record is being edited or added.

The `Resync` method does not re-execute the query, and allows specific records to be updated, whereas `Requery` always updates all records. The syntax for `Resync` is:

```
Recordset.Resync [AffectRecords], [ResyncValues]
```

The *AffectRecords* argument allows us to specify which records will be refreshed. It can be set to one of the following `AffectEnum` constants:

> ➤ `adAffectCurrent`. Only the current record will be refreshed.

> ➤ `adAffectGroup`. All records in the current filter will be refreshed.

> ➤ `adAffectAll`. All records in the recordset will be refreshed (the default).

ResyncValues may be one of the `ResyncEnum` constants:

> ➤ `adResyncAllValues`. All of the value properties will be refreshed.

> ➤ `adResyncUnderlyingValues`. Only the `UnderlyingValue` property will be changed.

We have seen already that each `Field` object has a `Value` property, which contains the value of the field for the current record in the recordset. In fact, there are also two closely related properties, called `UnderlyingValue` and `OriginalValue`. The `UnderlyingValue` property holds the current value of the field in the database, while `OriginalValue` contains the original value of the field at the time before any changes were made to the recordset. When changes are made to the `Value` of a field, the `UnderlyingValue` and `OriginalValue` remain unchanged until the database is updated or the recordset is refreshed.

When we call `Resync` with `adResyncAllValues`, the `Value`, `OriginalValue` and `UnderlyingValue` properties are all updated to the current value in the database. This means that any pending updates to the value of the field will be lost. However, when we use `adResyncUnderlyingValues`, only the `UnderlyingValue` property is changed, leaving the `Value` and `OriginalValue` intact. This means that any pending updates are retained.

Updating the Database

Once changes have been made to the cached recordset, we need to save these changes to the database itself. ADO provides two methods to do this, depending on whether the recordset is in update or batch update mode.

> **Batch update mode is set by opening the recordset with a lock type of `adLockBatchOptimistic`. We will be discussing lock types shortly.**

The difference between these two modes is this:

> ➤ In update mode, the database will automatically be updated to reflect changes to a record as soon as the user moves off that record or calls `Update`

> ➤ In batch update mode, the database will only be updated when an explicit method call is made

Note that, even in update mode, we may need to call the `Update` method after changing a record, in order to update the `UnderlyingValue` and `OriginalValue` properties, or update the database without moving to another record.

We can also use the `Update` method to assign new values to given fields. For example, to change the value of the `au_fname` field to `"Vitezslav"`, we could write:

```
objRec.Update "au_fname", "Vitezslav"
```

If we wish to update more than one field, we can pass both the field names and the new values in arrays (as we did when we added a new record with the `AddNew` method):

```
objRec.Update Array("au_fname", "au_lname"), Array ("Vitezslav", "Novak")
```

The corresponding method for batch update mode is `UpdateBatch`. This takes one optional parameter, to specify which records will be updated. This may be one of the `AffectEnum` constants:

> ➤ `adAffectAll`. All records in the recordset will be updated.

> ➤ `adAffectCurrent`. Only the current record will be updated.

> ➤ `adAffectGroup`. All records in the current filter will be updated.

Canceling Updates

A pending update can be canceled using the `CancelUpdate` method, or, for a batch update, the `CancelBatch` method. The `CancelUpdate` method can only affect the current record, and therefore takes no parameters:

```
objRec.CancelUpdate
```

`CancelUpdate` cancels any changes made to the current record since the last `Update` method call.

In batch update mode, we must instead use the `CancelBatch` method, which cancels any changes made to records since the last `UpdateBatch` method call. This method has the single parameter `AffectRecords`, which specifies which records are to be affected by the operation:

> `Recordset.CancelBatch AffectRecords`

This parameter may be one of the `AffectEnum` constants:

> ➢ `adAffectAll`. Updates to all records in the recordset (even those not in the current filter) will be canceled; this is the default.

> ➢ `adAffectAllChapters`. All child recordsets of the current record or group of records will be affected.

> ➢ `adAffectCurrent`. Only updates to the current record will be canceled.

> ➢ `adAffectGroup`. Updates to all records in the current filter will be canceled.

Cursor and Lock Types

When we open a recordset with the `Recordset` object's `Open` method, we have the option of specifying a cursor type and a lock type. We have up to now treated the recordset as an ordered sequence of records; in fact, the records are ordered not by the recordset, but by a **cursor**. Cursors expose the entire recordset, but present the records as though they were sequentially ordered, and allow us to iterate through the records one at a time.

Cursor Types

There are a number of different types of cursor available, and the cursor we choose impacts dramatically on the features available to us and the performance of the application. ADO provides four types of cursor:

> ➢ **Forward-only** (`adOpenForwardOnly`). This cursor only allows forward movement through the recordset, one record at a time.

> ➢ **Keyset** (`adOpenKeyset`). This cursor supports both forward and backward movement through the recordset. The records are up-to-date with the underlying data, but added records are not visible.

> ➢ **Static** (`adOpenStatic`). Both forward and backward movement is permitted. The data in the recordset is fixed at the time the cursor is created; no changes, additions or deletions by other users will be visible.

> ➢ **Dynamic** (`adOpenDynamic`). Both forward and backward movement is permitted. Changes, additions and deletions by other users are visible. This cursor type is not supported by the MS Access provider.

Because a forward-only cursor only supports movement forwards through the recordset by one record at a time, we can only use `MoveNext` or `Move` with a value of one with this cursor. `RecordCount` is also not supported. It should be noted that the forward-only cursor is the default, so this is the cursor that will be returned if no cursor type is specified in the `Recordset`'s `Open` method, or if the recordset is opened with the `Execute` method of the `Connection` object or the `Command` object.

As well as being specified when the recordset is opened, the cursor type may be defined in the `Recordset` object's `CursorType` property. For example, to set the cursor type as keyset:

```
objRec.CursorType = adOpenKeyset
```

However, this can only be done before the recordset is opened: once the recordset has been opened, the cursor cannot be changed. We can, however, use this property to verify the type of cursor in use. This is useful because, if a we request a cursor type that is not supported by the provider being used, another cursor type will automatically be substituted.

Cursor Location

As well as specifying the type of cursor to use, we may also specify the location of the cursor – that is, whether the cursor is to be situated on the client or on the server. To do this, we use the `Connection` object's `CursorLocation` property. To specify a client-side cursor, we use:

```
objConn.CursorLocation = adUseClient
```

And for a server-side cursor:

```
objConn.CursorLocation = adUseServer
```

There is also an option `adUseNone`, to specify that no cursor services are required, but this is obsolete and appears solely for the sake of backward compatibility. The default is `adUseServer`.

Server-side cursors are supplied by the data provider or driver. These cursors are sometimes very flexible and allow for additional sensitivity to changes others make to the data source. However, some features of the Microsoft Client Cursor Provider (such as disconnected recordsets) cannot be simulated with server-side cursors and these features will be unavailable with this setting.

Client-side cursors are supplied by a local cursor library. Local cursor engines often allow many features that driver-supplied cursors may not, so using this setting may provide an advantage with respect to features that will be enabled. However, only the static cursor-type is supported.

> The `CursorLocation` **property can only be set while the connection object is closed. It should therefore be set before the** `Open` **method is called.**

Lock Types

The `LockType` property indicates the type of locking that applies to records while they are being edited: for example, how the provider will attempt to prevent multiple users editing the same record simultaneously, and thus avoid data integrity conflicts. This can be an important part of your client-server environment. It's important to specify the limits to prevent one application being able to edit a record while another is editing the same record. The available lock types are:

data cannot be modified. This is the default.

➤ ~~adLockOptimistic. Pessimistic~~ locking. This shifts control to the provider, which will attempt to lock edited records.

➤ adLockOptimistic. Optimistic locking. The provider only locks records as they are being updated.

➤ adLockBatchOptimistic. Optimistic batch updates. Used to specify batch update mode.

For example, to specify pessimistic locking:

```
objRec.LockType = adLockPessimistic
```

Specifying pessimistic locking is a safe way of avoiding data conflicts, since the record is locked as soon as one user starts to edit it: no other user can edit the record until the first user's edit has been completed. With optimistic locking, the locking occurs only when the user attempts to update the database. This means that another user may already have edited the record by this time, and a conflict can arise. This is clearly less satisfactory if avoiding conflicts is the main priority, but it is more efficient in its use of resources, since pessimistic locking implies a permanent connection to the database.

Batch optimistic locking is typically used with client-side cursors and disconnected recordset. In batch update mode, updates are cached locally until the UpdateBatch method is called.

Working with Fields

We have already seen that every field in the recordset is represented by a Field object. These Field objects are contained in the Recordset object's Fields collection.

The Fields Collection

If we want to obtain a reference to this collection, we use the Fields property of the Recordset object:

```
Set colFields = objRec.Fields
```

The Fields collection has three methods and two properties used for managing the fields of the recordset. The Item property is used to return a specific Field object from the collection and can be used in conjunction with either the index position of the Field object in the collection or the name of the field:

```
Set objField = objRec.Fields.Item(1)
```

or:

```
Set objField = objRec.Fields.Item("au_lname")
```

Since `Item` is the default property we can also use either of the following:

```
Set objField = objRec.Fields(1)
```

```
Set objField = objRec.Fields("au_lname")
```

But `Fields` is also the default property for the `Recordset` object, so in fact, either of the following will do the same job:

```
Set objField = objRec(1)
```

```
Set objField = objRec("au_lname")
```

This is, of course, equivalent to the familiar exclamation mark syntax:

```
Set objField = objRec!au_lname
```

The other property exposed by the `Fields` collection is `Count`, which returns the number of `Field` objects in the collection. This can be used as an alternative to the `For...Each` construction to iterate through the collection:

```
For intCount = 0 To objRec.Fields.Count - 1
    Set objField = objRec.Fields.Item(intCount)
    ' Do something with the field...
Next
```

Like other ADO collections, the `Fields` collection is zero-based, so the first field has an index value of zero, and the last of `Fields.Count - 1`.

The `Fields` collection also provides methods to refresh the collection, add fields to and delete fields from the collection. However, the `Refresh` method has no visible effect: the `Recordset` object's `Requery` method should be used instead. And note that fields can only be added to or deleted from recordsets that you have created yourself.

The `Append` method adds a `Field` object to the collection. We must supply as parameters the name of the field and its data type (one of the `DataTypeEnum` constants); we can also supply a defined size (in characters or bytes) for the field, and attributes for the new field (such as whether the field can contain Null values). This can be any of the `FieldAttributeEnum` constants. This method can be used to create recordsets programmatically:

```
Dim objRec As New ADODB.Recordset

objRec.Fields.Append "Name", adVarChar, 25, adFldMayBeNull
objRec.Fields.Append "Age", adInteger, 8, adFldFixed
```

This method cannot be used on an open recordset (even a disconnected one), or one for which an `ActiveConnection` has been set. In addition, the `CursorLocation` must be set to `adUseClient`.

The final method, `Delete`, allows us to remove fields from a programmatically created recordset. The field to be deleted can be specified by its index value or by its name:

```
objRec.Fields.Delete(1)
```

```
objRec.Fields.Delete("Age")
```

The Field Object

The `Field` object exposes a number of properties that define what kind of data can be held in that particular field. Some of these are identical to the parameters passed into the `Fields` collection's `Append` method. The `Name` property simply specifies the field's name, and can be used, as we have seen, to retrieve a specific field object. For example, this line makes use of a `Field` object whose `Name` property is `au_lname`:

```
Set objField = objRec("au_lname")
```

The `Type` property indicates the data type for values in the field, and may be one of the `DataTypeEnum` constants. A list of these constants and the corresponding data types in SQL Server and Access can be found in the section on 'Creating a Parameter Object'.

The `Attributes` property contains one or more of the `FieldAttributeEnum` values (these are listed in Appendix F). For example, to specify that a field may be updated and also that it can contain Null values:

```
objField.Attributes = adFldUpdatable + adFldIsNullable
```

The `Attributes` property can contain more than one of these values – they are compounded by bitwise addition. Thus, when reading this property, we can use the logical AND to check the `Attributes` property for the attribute that we seek:

```
If (objField.Attributes AND adFldUpdatable) = adFldUpdatable Then
    ' Field can be updated
End If
```

The other parameter passed into the `Append` method, indicating the maximum size in bytes or characters for values in the field corresponds to the `Field` object's `DefinedSize` property. Related to this is the `ActualSize` property, which returns the actual size of a specific entry in the field. For fixed length fields, `ActualSize` and `DefinedSize` will have the same value.

> **Remember that these properties of the `Field` object can only be set when creating a recordset. For an open recordset, they will be read-only.**

Disconnected and Persisted Recordsets

While it is possible to keep open the connection to the database for the whole time that the application is running, this is clearly inefficient in its use of resources: it requires the connection to be open even when no data is being passed between the client and the server, and more network traffic is used when the database is updated every time a record changes than is needed for batch updates.

The solution to this is to use **disconnected recordsets**. These are recordsets which are not actively connected to the database server. They can be manipulated on the client, and batch updates can be sent in one go when required. To disconnect a recordset, we must:

> ➤ Set the CursorLocation to adUseClient
> ➤ Set the Recordset's ActiveConnection to Nothing
> ➤ Set the LockType to adLockBatchOptimistic

To update the recordset, we must call the UpdateBatch method. We can specify whether all records are to be marshaled back to the server, or only those that have been modified, by setting the Recordset object's MarshalOptions property. If this is set to adMarshalAll (the default), all rows will be returned to the server; if it is set to adMarshalModifiedOnly, only those records which have been altered will be returned. This can greatly improve performance.

As well as disconnecting a recordset temporarily from the server, we can create a more permanent local copy of the recordset on the hard drive. In order to create a persisted recordset, we use the Save method of the Recordset object. This takes two parameters: the path and filename under which the recordset is to be saved, and the format in which the recordset is to be saved. In ADO 2.0, the only possible value for this second parameter is adPersistADTG. So, to save a recordset with the filename Recordset.adtg in the My Documents folder, we would use:

```
objRec.Save "C:/My Documents/Recordset.adtg", adPersistADTG
```

When we wish to open this persisted recordset, we pass the path and filename into the Recordset's Open method, and use a command type of adCmdFile:

```
objRec.Open "C:/My Documents/Recordset.adtg", , adOpenStatic, _
             adLockOptimistic, adCmdFile
```

ADO 2.1 also permits files to be saved in XML format. To do this, we specify a persist format of adPersistXML:

```
objRec.Save "C:/My Documents/Recordset.xml", adPersistXML
```

This will cause the recordset to be saved as an XML file, in which each recordset is represented by an XML element and each field as an attribute of that element. For example, the first record in the SQL Server pubs database will appear as:

```
<z:row au_id="409-56-7008" au_lname="Bennet" au_fname="Abraham" phone="415 658-
9932" address="6223 Bateman St." city="Berkeley" state="CA" zip="94705"
contract="True" />
```

ADO Events

In Chapter 4, we wrote some code which changed the caption of a label whenever the user moved to a different record. In order to be able to react to this change, we placed the code in an event handler for the Recordset object's MoveComplete event. ADO supports a number of such events. These events are raised when an operation is executed against an object or when one of its properties changes, and they allow us to react to changes as they occur, rather than having to check whether something has happened before we execute code that is dependent on the change.

ADO events fall into two classes - events which are fired immediately before an action occurs, and events which are fired after the operation has taken place. The former always have names beginning `Will...`, the latter frequently (but by no means always) end in `...Complete`. Although many of these events fall into pairs, such as `WillConnect` and `ConnectComplete`, the first occurring just before the action and the second just after it, many of the events fired after an action have no corresponding `Will...` event. In this chapter, we will only look at a few of the more important events, but complete coverage of the ADO events can be found in Appendix E.

Accessing ADO Events

Two of the ADO objects support events: the `Connection` object and the `Recordset` object. To access the events of one or other of these objects, we must first dimension the `Connection` or `Recordset` object `WithEvents` in the `General Declarations` section of a class module or form:

```
Dim WithEvents objConn As ADODB.Connection
```

The events now become available and appear in the Procedure drop-down box of the code window:

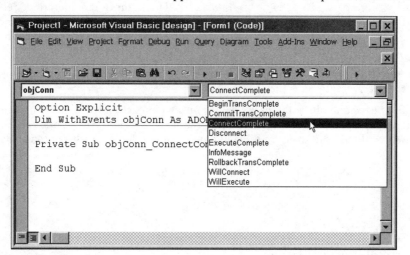

Connection Object Events

The events exposed by the `Connection` object relate to changes in the state of the connection, such as when a connection is opened or closed. There are also events which are fired whenever a command is executed against the connection, and events which relate to transactions performed against the connection.

The WillConnect Event

The first event to be fired in an ADO session is the `WillConnect` event, which is raised immediately before a connection is made to the database. The event handler supports six arguments, which expose connection details to the code in the event handler:

Name	Data type	Description
ConnectionString	String	The connection string for the current connection.
UserID	String	The user ID for the current connection. This will be empty if the user ID was passed in as part of the connection string, rather than as a separate parameter.
Password	String	The password for the current connection. Again, this will be empty if the password was entered as part of the connection string.
Options	Long	The options specified in the method call for opening the connection.
adStatus	EventStatusEnum constant	The status of the operation. Setting this to adStatusCancel or 4 cancels the operation, and causes the connection not to be opened.
pConnection	Connection object	The Connection object for the event.

This event could be used to check the user's details or the connection string before making the connection. If any of these details are invalid, they can be corrected or the operation can be halted. For example, we could use this event to prevent any attempt to log on as the systems administrator:

```
Private Sub objConn_WillConnect(ConnectionString As String, _
        UserID As String, Password As String, Options As Long, _
        adStatus As ADODB.EventStatusEnum, _
        ByVal pConnection As ADODB.Connection)
    If UserID = "sa" Then
        MsgBox "Sorry. It is not permitted to log on as the " & _
            "Systems Administrator.", vbExclamation
        adStatus = adStatusCancel
    End If
End Sub
```

This code checks the UserID argument to see if it is equal to "sa", the default user name for the Systems Administrator in SQL Server. If it is, we display a message box informing the user that it is not permitted to log on as the SA and cancel the operation by setting adStatus to adStatusCancel. This code assumes that the user ID and password were passed in separately as parameters to the Open method; if they were included in the connection string, we need to parse the ConnectionString argument instead:

```
If InStr(UCase(ConnectionString), "USER ID=SA") <> 0 Then
```

We use the UCase function to capitalize the connection string to ensure that the comparison does not fail due to case sensitivity. Of course, if we did not know how the user details were passed in, we would have to check both these methods:

```
If UserID = "sa" Or InStr(UCase(ConnectionString), _
          "USER ID=SA") <> 0 Then
```

The ConnectComplete Event

The ConnectComplete event is fired when the connection has been made, or when the attempt to connect fails. It allows us to halt the application until the connection is complete and to check that the connection was successful, or to handle any errors that occurred. The event has three arguments:

Name	Data type	Description
pError	Error object	An object representing any error which occurred.
adStatus	EventStatusEnum	The status of the operation.
pConnection	Connection object	The Connection object for the event.

Since the user could be waiting a few seconds for the connection to be made, it is a good idea to use this event to inform the user either that the connection was successful, or that an error occurred. If the mouse pointer was set to vbHourglass before making the connection, we could reset it here. For example, the following code sets the mouse pointer to the hourglass and opens the SQL Server Northwind database when a command button called cmdOpen is clicked, and informs the user of the result when the ConnectComplete event fires:

```
Option Explicit
Dim WithEvents objConn As ADODB.Connection


Private Sub cmdOpen_Click()
    Me.MousePointer = vbHourglass
    Set objConn = New ADODB.Connection
    objConn.Open "Provider=SQLOLEDB;Data Source=bigsmile;" & _
              "Initial Catalog=Northwind;User ID=sa"
End Sub


Private Sub objConn_ConnectComplete(ByVal pError As ADODB.Error, _
          adStatus As ADODB.EventStatusEnum, ByVal pConnection As _
          ADODB.Connection)
    Me.MousePointer = vbArrow
    Select Case adStatus
       Case adStatusOK
          MsgBox "Connection successful."
       Case adStatusErrorsOccurred
          MsgBox "Error occurred: " & pError.Description
       Case Else
          MsgBox "Connection status unknown."
    End Select
End Sub
```

This ensures that the user is aware of what's happening until the connection is made, and will be less likely to assume that the system has hung.

The Disconnect Event

When a connection is closed, either because the Connection object's Close method was called, or because of a network problem, the Disconnect event is fired. This event takes only two arguments:

Name	Data type	Description
adStatus	EventStatusEnum	The status of the operation.
pConnection	Connection object	The Connection object for the event.

This event could be used to inform the user and perform error handling when a connection drops unexpectedly, or to track users as they log into and out of the database. The following code shows how we might achieve the latter. When the Disconnect event is fired, an entry is added to a log file (called Pubs.log) in a directory named Database Log, indicating that the current user has logged out at the current time. The user ID for the current user is returned by the User ID property in the Connection object's Properties collection.

```
Private Sub objConn_Disconnect(adStatus As ADODB.EventStatusEnum, _
                        ByVal pConnection As ADODB.Connection)
Dim intFileHandle As Integer
intFileHandle = FreeFile
Open "c:/Database Log/Pubs.log" For Append As intFileHandle
Print #intFileHandle, "User '" & objConn.Properties("User ID") & _
                    "' logged out at " & Now() & "."
Close #intFileHandle
End Sub
```

Recordset Object Events

The events exposed by the Recordset object are raised when a property of the Recordset object is altered or when one of the Recordset's methods is called. For example, events are fired when changes are made to the recordset, when the user navigates to a different record and when the recordset is refreshed.

The MoveComplete Event

We have already met (in Chapter 4) the MoveComplete event, which is fired after the record pointer has been moved from one record to another. This event has four arguments:

Name	Data type	Description
adReason	Long	The reason why the event was fired. This is one of the EventReasonEnum constants, and indicates whether the event was fired because of a Move, MoveFirst, MoveLast, MoveNext, MovePrevious or Requery method call. This will also be adRsnMove if the event was fired due to the Bookmark or AbsolutePosition properties being set.

Name	Data type	Description
adStatus	Long	The status of the operation.
pError	Error object	An object representing any error which occurred.
pRecordset	Recordset object	The Recordset object for the event.

We saw in Chapter 4 how this event can be used to update the caption of a label indicating the position of the current record in the recordset:

```
Private Sub objRec_MoveComplete(ByVal adReason As ADODB.EventReasonEnum, _
        ByVal pError As ADODB.Error, adStatus As _
        ADODB.EventStatusEnum, ByVal pRecordset As ADODB.Recordset)
lblStatus.Caption = "Record " & objRec.AbsolutePosition & " out of " & _
            objRec.RecordCount
End Sub
```

The RecordChangeComplete Event

The last event we'll look at in this chapter is RecordChangeComplete. This is fired, as its name suggests, whenever the value of a record has been changed. Its arguments are:

Name	Data type	Description
adReason	EventReasonEnum	The reason the event was fired.
cRecords	Long	The number of records which changed.
pError	Error object	An object representing any error which occurred.
adStatus	EventStatusEnum	The status of the operation.
pRecordset	Recordset object	The Recordset object for the event.

We could use this event for auditing. For example, to record the ID of the user who made the changes, the number of records affected and the time the changes were made to a log file named Pubs.log in the Database Log folder, we could use the following code:

```
Private Sub objRec_RecordChangeComplete(ByVal adReason As _
        ADODB.EventReasonEnum, ByVal cRecords As Long, ByVal pError _
        As ADODB.Error, adStatus As ADODB.EventStatusEnum, ByVal _
        pRecordset As ADODB.Recordset)

Dim intFileHandle As Integer
intFileHandle = FreeFile

Open "c:/Database Log/Pubs.log" For Append As intFileHandle
Print #intFileHandle, "User '" & objRec.ActiveConnection.Properties _
     ("User ID") & "' changed " & cRecords & " records at " & Now() & "."
Close #intFileHandle

End Sub
```

Error Handling

We can use the `Connection` object's events to perform error handling when errors occur, such as whenever a connection fails or is broken. ADO provides an `Error` object to facilitate this. Each `Connection` object contains an `Errors` collection with information on any errors that occurred. Each error is represented by an `Error` object, which is used to hold a description and other information for the error. Note that an `Error` object represents an error from the OLE DB provider, and not an ADO error. ADO raises runtime errors, which must be handled using the normal `On Error GoTo` or `On Error Resume Next` line. In contrast, provider errors do not necessarily halt the execution of the program.

The Errors Collection

In order to access a specific `Error` object, we must first get a reference to the `Errors` collection, using the `Errors` property of the `Connection` object:

```
Dim colErrors As ADODB.Errors

Set colErrors = objConn.Errors
```

The `Errors` collection provides methods and properties for accessing the individual `Error` objects exposed by the connection. To retrieve a specific `Error` object, we can use the `Item` property with the index value specifying the position of the object in the collection. This index value is zero-based, so, for example, to retrieve the first `Error` object, we need to write:

```
Dim objError As ADODB.Error

Set objError = objConn.Errors.Item(0)
```

We can determine the number of `Error` objects in the collection (that is, the number of errors returned from the provider for a given connection) using the `Count` property of the `Errors` collection:

```
MsgBox objConn.Errors.Count & " errors occurred."
```

We can use these two properties in conjunction to iterate through the `Errors` collection:

```
For intCount = 0 To objConn.Errors.Count - 1

    Set objError = objConn.Errors.Item(intCount)

    '
    ' Error handling goes here.
    '

Next
```

Because the `Errors` collection is zero-based, its first member has an index value of zero, and its last member an index of `objConn.Errors.Count - 1`, not `objConn.Errors.Count`. Alternatively, we can of course use the `For...Each` construction:

```
Dim colErrors As ADODB.Errors
Dim objError As ADODB.Error

For Each objError In colErrors

    '
    ' Error handling goes here.
    '

Next
```

The `Errors` collection is automatically cleared every time a new error occurs, so any information about previous errors is lost when a new error occurs. This does not mean that the `Errors` collection can only ever contain one object, since providers can return multiple errors. In addition, providers sometimes return warning information, and these warnings are represented by `Error` objects in the `Errors` collection. For this reason, ADO provides a method to clear the `Errors` collection programmatically:

```
objConn.Errors.Clear
```

This allows us to reset the `Errors` collection when desired, so that we know the collection is empty at that point. We consequently know that any errors or warnings in the collection occurred subsequent to that line. Finally, the `Errors` collection also has a `Refresh` method. This method can be called before working with an `Error` object, to ensure that we have access to the latest information from the provider.

The Error Object

The `Error` object has a number of properties which provide specific information about the error which the object represents. Perhaps the most useful of these is `Description`, which returns a string describing the error. This can be returned directly to the user when an error occurs:

```
On Error GoTo Err_handler

...

Err_handler:
Dim objError As ADODB.Error

For Each objError In objConn.Errors
    MsgBox objError.Description, vbExclamation, "ADO Error"
Next
```

Alternatively, we can provide our own, more user-friendly error messages. To do this, we can use the `Error` object's `Number` property to identify the error which occurred, and match that with our custom description:

```
On Error GoTo Err_handler


Err_handler:
Dim objError As ADODB.Error

For Each objError In objConn.Errors
```

```
      Select Case objError.Number
          Case -2147217843
MsgBox "SQL Server could not authenticate you. Please check" & _
              vbCrLf & "that your user name and password were " & _
              "correctly entered.", vbExclamation, "ADO Error"

          ' etc. ...

      Case Else
          MsgBox "An unknown error has occurred:" & vbCrLf & _
              objError.Description, vbExclamation, "ADO Error"
      End Select
Next
```

Here we use Visual Basic's `Select Case` construction to enumerate through the codes for any errors we want to trap for, including a final `Case Else` clause, in case any errors occur which we were unable to foresee.

The other properties provide further information about the cause of the error. Perhaps the most important is the `NativeError` property, which returns a provider-specific error code: that is, an error code returned by the OLEDB provider in use, and defined by that provider. These error codes are therefore not generic to ADO or OLEDB, but vary according to the provider in question. For this reason they may be more specific than the generic errors. For information on these error codes, consult the provider's documentation.

We will be looking at the subject of error handling in more detail in Chapter 10.

Binding to VB Controls with ADO

When we used the ADO Data Control in Chapter 4, we bound the other controls in our form via that control to the data provider, and so avoided populating them with data programmatically. We can do the same with ADO, binding controls directly to the recordset or to a middle-tier data component. This is done by setting the control's `DataSource` and `DataField` properties. We can illustrate this with a very simple, minimalistic database application. Design a form with two text boxes, named `txtFirst` and `txtLast`, and two command buttons, `cmdFirst` and `cmdLast`:

When the form loads, we will connect to the SQL Server `pubs` database, selecting the `au_fname` and `au_lname` fields from the `authors` table. We set the `DataSource` property for the two text boxes to our recordset (named `objRec`), and the `DataField` property to the fields that they will represent, `au_fname` and `au_lname`:

```
Private Sub Form_Load()

    Set objConn = New ADODB.Connection
    objConn.Open "Provider=SQLOLEDB;Data Source=julians;" & _
                "Initial Catalog=pubs;User ID=sa;Password="
```

```
        Set objRec = New ADODB.Recordset
        objRec.Open "SELECT au_fname,au_lname FROM authors", objConn, _
                    adOpenStatic, adLockOptimistic, adCmdText

        Set txtFirst.DataSource = objRec
        txtFirst.DataField = "au_fname"
        Set txtLast.DataSource = objRec
        txtLast.DataField = "au_lname"

        objRec.MoveFirst

    End Sub
```

And that's all there is to it! When the user navigates through the recordset, the text boxes will automatically be updated, just as they were when we used the ADO Data Control. Two command buttons provide the basic functionality for this navigation through the recordset (for simplicity's sake, we have only included Previous and Next buttons):

```
    Private Sub cmdNext_Click()
        objRec.MoveNext
        If objRec.EOF Then objRec.MoveLast
    End Sub
```

```
    Private Sub cmdPrev_Click()
        objRec.MovePrevious
        If objRec.BOF Then objRec.MoveFirst
    End Sub
```

Notice that we check the EOF and BOF properties after MoveNext and MovePrevious calls, to avoid generating an error if the record pointer goes beyond these markers.

Finally, when the form is closed, we update the database with the new values, and uninstantiate our Recordset and Connection objects:

```
    Private Sub Form_Unload(Cancel As Integer)
        objRec.Update
        objRec.Close
        Set objRec = Nothing
        objConn.Close
        Set objConn = Nothing
    End Sub
```

Summary

In this chapter, we took a tour of all the objects – and many of the methods, properties and events – of the ADO object model. As I mentioned at the beginning of the chapter, it's through using these that you will learn them.

We have deliberately avoided trying to cover every little detail about ADO here – that would be impossible in a chapter of this size, and indeed, there are probably some methods, properties and events you will never use. However, now that you have a good knowledge of the most important of them, you will be able quickly to find the methods and properties you need to accomplish any given task in Appendix E.

In the following chapters, we will use much of what we covered here, so get out your trusty bookmark for future reference.

Suppliers
- SupplierID
- CompanyName
- ContactName
- ContactTitle
- Address
- City
- Region
- PostalCode
- Country
- Phone
- Fax
- HomePage

Products
- ProductID
- ProductName
- SupplierID
- CategoryID
- QuantityPerUnit
- UnitPrice
- UnitsInStock
- UnitsOnOrder
- ReorderLevel
- Discontinued

Categories
- CategoryID
- CategoryName
- Description
- Picture

Views, Stored Procedures and Triggers

We've covered a lot of ground in the previous chapters. We have discussed client-server architecture and touched on some of the considerations involved in designing a successful client-server application. We've covered database design, the latest in data access technology and we've looked in some detail at SQL - the language we use to query, modify and manipulate data in our database. We now need to look at some of the functionality that is of vital importance in creating an efficient, secure, high-performance client-server application.

We have already discussed one of the central ideas of client-server architecture - that the client acts as a user interface to an *intelligent* server (database engine).

> *Of course, one cannot over-stress the importance of an efficient, well-designed GUI that provides all of the functionality needed to access our data in a clear, easily understandable manner. We cover this aspect of client-server architecture, in some detail, in the next chapter.*

The key point here is that the client should not perform low-level data manipulation - this processing is taken care of by the server. The client sends requests for data, through a network, to the server and the server does not merely send back data for the client to work with, but is capable of processing complex SQL commands and returning highly specific sets of data. In this chapter we take this further and discuss some key issues in multi-user client-server systems:

> ➤ How can we make retrieval of specifically focused data as easy and efficient as possible?

> ➤ How can we minimize network traffic and improve performance?

> ➤ With potentially hundreds of people wanting access to the database, what steps can we take to ensure that the data does not become corrupted?

The topics of views, stored procedures and triggers should not be entirely new to you - we covered them briefly in Chapter 1. They are all complex SQL queries that are stored as objects *on the server* and can be called from the client with simple, short SQL queries. With just this one statement, you can perhaps begin to see how this functionality reduces network traffic and speeds up data retrieval.

We are going to have a fairly in-depth look at each of these topics in turn. We'll start with views - SQL queries that can allow users easy access to highly specific information in the database and can be used in a security context. We'll then move on to stored procedures and triggers - precompiled SQL statements that provide vital functionality relating to data integrity and performance issues.

Typically, a Database Administrator would be the one to create these views, stored procedures and triggers for us. However, times are changing quickly for programmers and these are just some of the many tasks that you may find yourself required to do.

Building a Connection to SQL Server

Throughout this chapter, we'll pass several SQL statements to the pubs database located on SQL Server (up to this point we have worked with the Northwind Database). You should recall that in Chapter 6 we developed a Visual Basic SQL Tester application to connect to this database, via the ADO Data Control. ADO is easily modified to switch to a different database, so it should be a snap to modify the connection information. We want to keep the original SQL Tester program intact, so we'll make a copy of the entire project and modify that. Let's get started:

> ➤ Create a new folder titled C:\ProVB6DB\Chapter10

> ➤ Copy the contents of C:\ProVB6DB\Chapter6 to your newly created folder

> ➤ Open the copied project, C:\ProVB6DB\Chapter10\SQLTest.vbp

This chapter will modify some of the data in the pubs *database so now is an ideal time to create a backup of the database, in case you need to restore the data to its original state.*

To set up the program to connect to the pubs database, we simply need to change the name of the database in the ConnectionString property of the ADO Data Control (which establishes the database to which your program will connect along with any security information). In addition, we need to modify the SQL command in the ADO Data Control's RecordSource property. The pubs database has no table entitled Customers so change the code to select data from the employee table and run the program:

Views

Back in Chapter 1, under the heading "Server-side Processing Functionality", we briefly discussed the role of views in our client-server applications. We are now going to discuss them in rather more detail, covering exactly what they are, what their function is and how they are created.

A view is a SQL query that is stored on the database server. When a view is executed, an object is created - a *virtual* table - that allows us to retrieve and work with data in the underlying base tables.

> It is important to understand that data in the base database tables is *not* duplicated and stored in the virtual table. When the query is terminated the virtual table is destroyed. However the view remains on the server and can be called the next time a client wishes to view the data.

Some of the main benefits derived from the use of views are as follows:

> ➤ *They can be used for security purposes.* A view extracts and displays in a virtual table *only* the records and fields that are defined in the view. A user can be assigned permission to a view in the same way they can be assigned permission to a normal table. Thus, a user may be granted access only to a certain view and, in effect, denied access to other confidential data stored elsewhere in the database.

> ➤ *They can be used to extract only the information that is relevant to the user's needs.* Different groups of people within an organization require frequent access to different data from the database. Furthermore, large and complex SQL statements are often required in order to provide access to highly specific data, often drawn from multiple tables. This complex SQL statement can be defined as a view and a 'special purpose' view can be created to suit each requirement. The clients that require data from the view may then execute a simple SQL statement to retrieve the same data, over and over.

> *Views confer the ability to modify field names and aliases on the server rather than on the client.* If, for example, a field is re-named in a table, the view can then allow the clients to call the field name by its old name. In addition to this, there are many other changes that can be handled by a view in order to avoid having to modify all of the client applications.

Before we start thinking about creating some views of our own, using the SQL Tester program, it's well worthwhile having a look around the SQL Server enterprise manager. There are many existing views for us to have a look at and, in addition, it provides an environment for the quick and easy creation of views.

SQL Server Views in the Pubs Database

First, let's take a look at an existing view. This will help provide a solid understanding of the SQL code required to build a view.

We'll need to use the SQL Server Enterprise Manager, so from the Start menu select Programs | Microsoft SQL Server 7.0 | Enterprise Manager. Once the Enterprise Manager opens, navigate to Databases | pubs | Views. Amongst the views listed you should see one called titleview.

To see the definition of this view, double click on it. The View Properties dialog will appear with the SQL statement, which generated the view. This dialog allows you to design new views or modify existing ones:

You may notice that this looks very similar to SQL statements we've seen previously. The only difference is that this SQL statement has a header that specifies that a view is to be created from the SELECT statement that follows. To do this, the AS keyword is used. We previously used the AS keyword to define fields as aliases. We're now using it to define a view as an alias to the SQL statement. The view below pulls fields from several tables to create one single virtual table (titleview) that clients can call. The au_id and title_id fields provide the link between the three tables:

```
CREATE VIEW titleview
AS
SELECT title, au_ord, au_lname, price, ytd_sales, pub_id
FROM authors, titles, titleauthor
WHERE authors.au_id = titleauthor.au_id
  AND titles.title_id = titleauthor.title_id
```

Creating views on SQL Server couldn't be much easier. Simply right-click on the Views icon and select New view. A "four-level" data view window will appear. Click on Add table and Add any tables from which you want to draw data for your view (the tables will appear in the top tier of the window, along with the relationships between the tables). In order to include specific fields in the view, click on the box to the left of each field name - a tick will appear and the field will pop up in a column cell in the second level. As you select tables and fields, a SELECT statement - which defines the records and fields to be included in the view - is gradually built up, in the third level. Finally, click on Run and the resulting virtual table (often actually referred to as a view) is created and displayed in the fourth level:

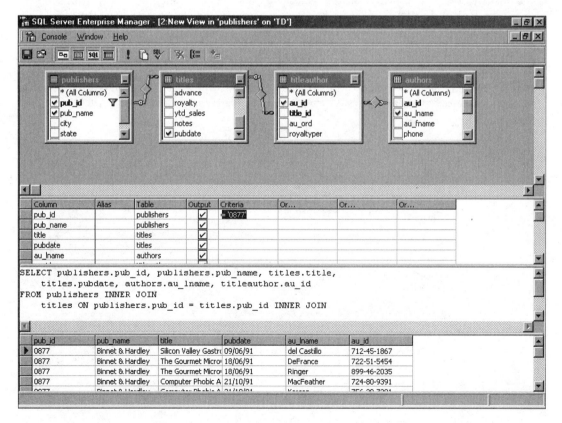

Creating a View with SQL

As you will have gathered from the previous section, a view is really just a complex SELECT statement which we define as a view using the CREATE VIEW command and the AS keyword. So, if you understand the SELECT SQL statement, creating views should come quite easily.

Let's create a simple view using the SQL Tester program. You may want to refer back to the diagram displaying the tables in the pubs database, and the relationships between them, in the introduction to this book. The following section of code creates a view called Emp_List that restricts the number of fields that can be accessed from the Employee table and, also, for which records they can be viewed:

```
CREATE VIEW Emp_List AS
SELECT emp_id, fname,minit,lname, hire_date
FROM Employee
WHERE job_id = 5
```

> *You may receive the following error: "The operation requested by the application is not allowed if the object it closed". This is the same error message we encountered when creating, modifying or deleting tables in Chapter 6. Click on the OK button. The view will be created.*

Congratulations, you have just created a new view in the pubs database! It may not be as exotic as the ones we saw in the previous section, but at least it's a view to call your own. To confirm its existence, look at the Views folder of the pubs database. If the view does not appear immediately, right-click on the Views folder and select Refresh.

To actually see the view (in other words, to create the virtual table), we need to call it from our SQL Tester program. Remember, a view is just a special instance of a normal table, so there is nothing extraordinary about the way you call it. Treat it just like any other table and remember; the data of a virtual table does not get stored in its own location. If you change the data in a virtual table you are altering the base tables:

```
SELECT * FROM Emp_List
```

emp_id	fname	minit	lname	hire_date
PTC11962M	Philip	T	Cramer	11/11/89
PXH22250M	Paul	X	Henriot	19/08/93
CFH28514M	Carlos	F	Hernadez	21/04/89
JYL26161F	Janine	Y	Labrune	26/05/91
LAL21447M	Laurence	A	Lebihan	03/06/90
RBM23061F	Rita	B	Muller	09/10/93
SKO22412M	Sven	K	Ottlieb	05/04/91
MJP25939M	Maria	J	Pontes	01/03/89

8 Records Returned!

SELECT * FROM emp_list

Apply SQL

The previous single line of code can be executed each time we want to view this data. What good would the `Emp_List` view be in practice? Well, data is only made available for records where `job_id` =5, and then only for certain fields from the `employee` table. It may be that a particular user simply has no interest in records for other `job_id` values. On the other hand, these records may have restricted access - in which case this is a first step to the implementation of field-level security! Of course, for this to be effective, we would have to restrict users from viewing the `jobs` table altogether, but for now it's a good start.

A point to bear in mind is that we cannot implement an `ORDER BY` clause when creating a view, but we can apply one once a virtual table has been created from the view. The following statement refines the virtual table to display the records in ascending order of `hire_date`:

```
SELECT * FROM Emp_List
ORDER BY hire_date
```

Now that we've covered the basics of view design, we're ready to take it a step further. In the introduction to this section, we mentioned that we could use views to hide complex SQL statements - so let's give it a try! Say we wanted to pull together fields from three separate tables (`titles`, `titleauthor` and `authors`). You might write the following SQL statement (we constructed a similar statement in Chapter 6):

```
SELECT titles.title, titles.type,
   authors.au_lname, authors.au_fname
FROM titles
INNER JOIN titleauthor
   INNER JOIN authors
   ON authors.au_id = titleauthor.au_id
ON titles.title_id = titleauthor.title_id
```

Execute this statement in your SQL Tester program and review the results:

As it stands, you would have to input this rather lengthy statement each time you wanted access to this information. The good news is that you can create a view called, say, vw_Titles_Author and define the characteristics of this view using the previous statement:

```
CREATE VIEW vw_Titles_Author AS
(SELECT titles.title, titles.type,
  authors.au_lname, authors.au_fname
FROM titles
INNER JOIN titleauthor
  INNER JOIN authors
  ON authors.au_id = titleauthor.au_id
ON titles.title_id = titleauthor.title_id)
```

Note the use of parentheses – they help distinguish the entire SELECT statement as part of the view. Now that you have created this view, all you need do each time you want to access your data is to enter the following simple SELECT statement:

```
SELECT * FROM vw_Titles_Author
```

Try it out - the result should be identical to that obtained using our first SELECT statement.

When working with the data of a view, we can use the UPDATE and INSERT commands to modify data in the base tables, via the view. Remember though, that all constraints and keys of each view are enforced just as though we were editing the base table directly. There are a few other things to remember:

> We can only update and insert data into fields that are included in the SELECT statement of our view. So, the emp_list view would not allow us to update, for example, the job_id field.

> If we decided to insert a new record via our view, all fields that were not included in our view would be assigned a null value. If a null value were forbidden in one of those fields then the update would not be permitted.

> We can only update fields from one table at a time. So, in the vw_Titles_Author view, we would have to be careful that we didn't try to update, say, the au_lname and the title field at the same time.

The main point is that, once a view is created, we don't have to look at the code again: we simply call the view with a single line SELECT statement. This makes it easier to forget exactly what was specified in this code and, therefore, easier to make mistakes. Say we *had* included the job_id field when we created our emp_list view? We would then be perfectly free to call the view at a later date and update the job_id field - we could change its value to, say, two. However, the next time we called the view we would receive an empty table (in creating the view we specified WHERE job_id=5, remember!). In order to prevent this sort of occurrence, we can include the WITH CHECK OPTION parameter in our view creation code:

```
CREATE VIEW Emp_List AS
SELECT emp_id, fname,minit,lname, hire_date
FROM Employee
WHERE job_id = 5
WITH CHECK OPTION
```

Once WITH CHECK OPTION is implemented, the DBMS will check the WHERE clause (and any other conditions) and ensure that the only modifications permitted will be those that can be seen in the virtual table. Thus we would not be allowed, at a later date, to change the job_id value.

Stored Procedures

As you may recall from Chapter 1, stored procedures are precompiled SQL statements that accept arguments (parameters) from clients and are designed to automate a wide range of tasks. They also provide return values that can inform the client of the success or failure of the execution process. The SQL statements are compiled into an object that is stored on the RDBMS and can be called by a trigger, or by the client. SQL-92 doesn't supply standard syntax for stored procedures so they are created and employed using server-specific dialect (SQL Server stored procedures are written with Transact-SQL etc.).

Stored procedures bring many benefits to our client-server system, mainly relating to performance enhancement and the protection of data integrity. Let's review in more detail, a few of the many advantages of using stored procedures:

> Complex operations can be stored and executed on the server. In certain circumstances, SQL statements may become too complex to execute from the client application, whereas a stored procedure handles them without any problems. The advanced capability comes from the inherent language provided by the server (such as Transact-SQL).

> Stored procedures are maintained on the server side; therefore, they can be modified quickly and they don't require you to redistribute code to each client.

> One of the key points about stored procedures is that they can automate a wide variety of tasks (purging data, archiving data, or creating tables on the fly...) and this drastically reduces network traffic. Instead of sending complex SQL queries over the network (which may often contain hundreds of lines of code), an application sends a small command calling a stored procedure on the RDBMS. This also means that there is much less "talk" between the client and server.

> With stored procedures came a vast improvement in the level of database security. Complex business logic (rules that govern how data can be stored in the database, value ranges for certain fields etc.) and other constraints can be encapsulated in a stored procedure. These procedures can be put in place (either on the server or in the middle tier - see Chapter 10) to protect the database from queries and modifications that may threaten the integrity of the data, or from modifications for which the user does not have appropriate security clearance. The basic INSERT, UPDATE and DELETE commands are embedded in highly complex SQL code that often, in turn, calls numerous other stored procedures. The purpose of all this code is to validate every aspect of the proposed modification before permanent changes are made to the data. In some cases, the DBA may provide stored procedures as the *only* interface to the data. Additional security can be invoked by granting user access only to the stored procedure object rather than to the database table(s). Thus the user can only select, update or delete specific data from a table.

> ➤ Error handling can be conducted at database level. If the server detects any error in, for example, the validation process described above then the error will be flagged and a unique error message sent to the calling application, describing precisely why the procedure failed. Database servers also offer numerous variables that can return useful information to the calling application. For example, `@@rowcount` returns the number of rows affected by the execution of a stored procedure.

> ➤ Stored procedures run much faster than standard SQL queries. Once a stored procedure has been designed the SQL code will reside on the RDBMS until the stored procedure is first called. On this occasion the RDBMS parses through the code (validating the syntax) and compiles the code for future use. Thus, the first execution may take some time, but subsequent runs will be much faster (many of the newer RDBMSs will allow you to pre-compile the stored procedure *before* using it). An additional point concerning improved performance is that once the procedure has been executed the procedure plan is stored in RAM for the duration of that particular session. This allows even greater speed.

OK, I think you're now fully aware of the benefits that stored procedures bring in terms of database performance and reliability, so let's have a look at some.

Stored Procedures in the pubs Database

Before we create our own stored procedure, let's get an idea of what they look like. Open the SQL Server Enterprise Manager and locate the Stored Procedures folder of the pubs database:

Double click on the **byroyalty** stored procedure. The **Stored Procedure Properties** dialog opens and displays the SQL code used to create (or re-create) a stored procedure called `byroyalty`:

```
CREATE PROCEDURE byroyalty @percentage int
AS
select au_id from titleauthor
where titleauthor.royaltyper = @percentage
```

After specifying the name of the stored procedure, any arguments that are to be received should be listed along with their data types. In this example, the procedure expects to receive an integer that will populate the `@percentage` argument. Next, using an alias, we assign a `SELECT` statement to the new stored procedure, dynamically returning the records where the royalty percentage is equal to the value passed. Before we move on to the details of how to execute these stored procedures from our application, let's create a couple of our own.

Creating Stored Procedures Using SQL

Creating elementary stored procedures is a relatively straightforward process. However, there are various quirks you need to know about and we will explore some of these while demonstrating how stored procedures can be used to `SELECT`, `INSERT`, `UPDATE` and `DELETE` data in your tables.

SELECT Stored Procedures

In the following example, the procedure receives one argument, `@title`, of the character data type. The `SELECT` statement uses the `LIKE` keyword to locate records that contain the argument passed to the procedure in the description field. It's important to pay close attention to spacing when working with stored procedures. In this case, there are no spaces in the code after the space following the `LIKE` keyword. If you add spaces in this statement, the results could be very different. To create the stored procedure, run this statement through your SQL Tester program:

```
CREATE PROCEDURE select_jobs @title varchar (50)
AS
SELECT job_id,job_desc
FROM jobs
WHERE job_desc LIKE '%'+@title+'%'
```

We can test our stored procedures, before calling them from our application, using the SQL Server Query analyser. Simply open up the analyser, log on to the server and select the appropriate database in the drop-down box. Follow the `exec` SQL Server command with the name of the stored procedure and a valid value for the argument that the procedure expects to receive (in this case a search string for `job_desc`). Then click on the **Execute Query** button:

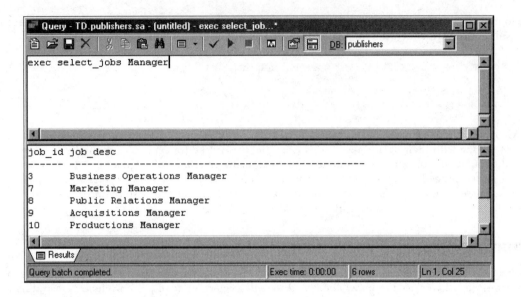

UPDATE Stored Procedures

UPDATE stored procedures are no more difficult to code than SELECT stored procedures. However, we do increase the complexity level in the following example, because we now receive two arguments, @job_desc and @new_desc, both of the varchar data type. This procedure will modify a given job description to the new job description passed:

```
CREATE PROCEDURE update_jobs @job_desc varchar(50),
     @new_desc varchar(50)
AS
UPDATE jobs
SET jobs.job_desc = @new_desc
WHERE jobs.job_desc = @job_desc
```

> **If you are unclear what data type to use for a particular field, you can look it up in the Table Properties dialog on SQL Server. For example, in the Properties dialog for the jobs table, job_desc is declared as a varchar data type of length 50.**

INSERT Stored Procedures

Next, we create a simple INSERT stored procedure. This one receives three arguments and enters them into the jobs table as a new record:

```
CREATE PROCEDURE insert_jobs @job_desc varchar(50), @min_lvl tinyint,
     @max_lvl tinyint
AS
INSERT INTO jobs
     (job_desc, min_lvl,max_lvl)
VALUES(@job_desc,@min_lvl,@max_lvl)
```

DELETE Stored Procedures

Finally, here's a DELETE stored procedure that receives a job_id, and deletes all records with a job_id equal to the argument passed:

```
CREATE PROCEDURE delete_jobs @job_id int
AS
DELETE FROM jobs
WHERE jobs.job_id = @job_id
```

As you can see, building simple stored procedures quickly becomes routine. The basic syntax is similar in each case, although you may find yourself toying with the spacing and parentheses. When your stored procedure doesn't do what you expect it to, don't give up on it too quickly.

Ensure that you execute all of the above statements. In the next section, we'll create a Visual Basic project that will call them. To confirm that you have created four new stored procedures, check that you can see them in the **Stored Procedures** folder of the pubs database.

Executing Stored Procedures from Visual Basic

It is relatively easy to execute stored procedures from within a Visual Basic project, using ADO code. Let's walk through the code we need to call a stored procedure. Don't enter any of it yet, just follow along.

When executing stored procedures, the first step is to declare a new Command object. The Command object will be used to execute our stored procedure:

```
Dim objSPCommand As ADODB.Command
```

If we want to pass more than one parameter to our stored procedure, we'll need to declare an array to hold the values. However, our array *must* be declared as a variant and *must* be designed to hold exactly the number of parameters that our stored procedure requires. Remember, Visual Basic arrays are zero-based, so the following code will hold three parameters, not two:

```
Dim pr_insert(2) As Variant
```

Next, we'll create the Command object and set its ActiveConnection n
Connection object. Ideally, we should create a Command object
procedure call. This is because new parameters tend to app
causing an imbalance in the number of parameters p
we let ADO know that the command to be executed
CommandType property to adCmdStoredProc:

```
Set objSPCommand = New ADODB.Command
objSPCommand.ActiveConnection = objActiveConn
objSPCommand.CommandType = adCmdStoredProc
```

The `CommandText` property should be set to the name of the stored procedure. Then the array is populated with the parameters to be passed. The array must be populated in the *exact* order in which the arguments are received in the procedure. Any deviation from this will cause an error or corrupt data. Once we've done this, we're ready to execute the stored procedure against the `Command` object. The comma immediately after the `Execute` method acts as a placeholder for the `RecordsAffected` argument of the `Execute` method. This is followed by the `Parameters` argument, which specifies the input parameters that we will pass to our stored procedure. These arguments are discussed in Chapter 7.

```
objSPCommand.CommandText = "insert_jobs"
pr_insert(0) = "President"
pr_insert(1) = 50
pr_insert(2) = 250
objSPCommand.Execute , pr_insert
```

The last step is to destroy the `Command` object, which we do by simply setting the object equal to `Nothing`:

```
Set objSPCommand = Nothing
```

Simple, right? Let's create a project!

Our project will use both ADO standalone code and the ADO Data Control. The ADO code will create a connection object and a command object then execute the specified stored procedure. The ADODC will display the contents of the `jobs` table, showing the changes effected by the stored procedure.

To begin, create a new **Standard EXE** project and add a command button to it. Name the command button `cmdExecute`, then copy the new button and paste it three times (creating a control array). Add a list box, an ADO Data Control and a DataGrid control. Don't forget to add the Microsoft DataGrid Control 6.0 (OLEDB) and the Microsoft ADO Data Control 6.0 (OLEDB) components from Project I Components. Then arrange the controls as follows:

Change the properties to reflect the following table. The ADO Data Control should be setup to connect to the `pubs` database just as we did with the SQL Tester program:

Object	Property	Value
Form	Name	frmStProc
	Caption	**Calling Stored Procedures**
ADO Data Control	Name	Adodc1
	Database (ConnectionString)	pubs
	RecordSource	adCmdText
		SELECT * FROM jobs
Grid Control	Name	DataGrid1
	DataSource	Adodc1
Command Button	Name	cmdExecute
	Caption	**&SELECT**
	Index	0
Command Button	Name	cmdExecute
	Caption	**&INSERT**
	Index	1
Command Button	Name	cmdExecute
	Caption	**&UPDATE**
	Index	2
Command Button	Name	cmdExecute
	Caption	**&DELETE**
	Index	3
List Box	Name	List1

In the General Declarations section, declare a `Connection` object, a `Command` object and a `Recordset` object. In addition, we'll need to declare an array for each stored procedure to be called. The `SELECT` and `DELETE` stored procedures only require one parameter each, so we could have put them in the same array. However, for the sake of clarity and organization it is better to keep them separate:

```
Option Explicit
Dim objActiveConnection As ADODB.Connection
Dim objSPCommand As ADODB.Command
Dim objSPRecordset As ADODB.Recordset

' Declare an array of variants for parameters
Dim pr_Select(0) As Variant
Dim pr_Insert(2) As Variant
Dim pr_Delete(0) As Variant
Dim pr_Update(1) As Variant
```

In the `Form_Load` event, we'll establish our connection to the `pubs` database:

```
Private Sub Form_Load()

    Set objActiveConnection = New ADODB.Connection
    objActiveConnection.ConnectionString = "Provider=SQLOLEDB.1;" & _
        "Persist Security Info=False;User ID=sa;Initial Catalog=pubs"
    objActiveConnection.Open

End Sub
```

Next, in the `Click` event of the command button array, we set up our connection and specify the `CommandType` property. Now, we're ready to execute each of our four stored procedures. Our command button array allows us to place all of this code in one procedure since we can use the `SELECT CASE` statement to query the index value and find out which button was clicked:

```
Private Sub cmdExecute_Click(Index As Integer)

    ' Create a new Command object and set the active
    ' connection and CommandType
    Set objSPCommand = New ADODB.Command
    objSPCommand.ActiveConnection = objActiveConnection
    objSPCommand.CommandType = adCmdStoredProc

Select Case Index
    Case 0 ' SELECT statement called
        List1.Clear

        ' Create a new recordset object
        Set objSPRecordset = New ADODB.Recordset

        ' Get the parameters and specify the SP name
        pr_Select(0) = InputBox("Search Criteria", "Search", "Manager")
        objSPCommand.CommandText = "select_jobs"

        ' Call the stored procedure
        Set objSPRecordset = objSPCommand.Execute(, pr_Select)

        ' Pull the results from the RS
        Do Until objSPRecordset.EOF
            List1.AddItem objSPRecordset("job_id") & " - " & _
                        objSPRecordset("job_desc")
            objSPRecordset.MoveNext
        Loop
```

```
               ' Destroy the recordset object
               Set objSPRecordset = Nothing

           Case 1 ' INSERT statement called
               ' Get the parameters and specify the SP name
               objSPCommand.CommandText = "insert_jobs"
               pr_Insert(0) = "President"
               pr_Insert(1) = 50
               pr_Insert(2) = 250

               ' Execute the SP
               objSPCommand.Execute , pr_Insert

               ' Refresh the ADO Data Control with the results
               Adodc1.Refresh

           Case 2 ' UPDATE statement called
               ' Get the parameters and specify the SP name
               objSPCommand.CommandText = "update_jobs"
               pr_Update(0) = InputBox _
                           ("Which Job_Desc do you want to Change?", "Modify")
               pr_Update(1) = InputBox("What is the new title?", "Modify")

               ' Execute the SP
               objSPCommand.Execute , pr_Update

               ' Refresh the ADO Data Control with the results
               Adodc1.Refresh

           Case 3 ' DELETE statement called
               ' Get the parameters and specify the SP name
               objSPCommand.CommandText = "delete_jobs"
               pr_Delete(0) = Int(InputBox _
                           ("Which Job_Id do you want to delete?", "Delete"))

               ' Execute the SP
               objSPCommand.Execute , pr_Delete

               ' Refresh the ADO Data Control with the results
               Adodc1.Refresh

               'Destroy the Command object
               Set objSPCommand = Nothing

           End Select

       End Sub
```

In order to keep the code simple, I've not included any error handling. I'll leave that to you - I'm sure you can find plenty of bugs!

When you have completed building your code, run the project and test the buttons. If you click on the buttons from left to right, your project should:

➢ Populate the list box with values specific to your request

➢ Insert a new record

➢ Update a record of your choosing

➢ Delete a record of your choosing

265

Let's have a look at the objective of each section of code in a bit more detail:

➤ SELECT: Since this stored procedure may generate several records we need a recordset in which to store them. Thus, when a user clicks the SELECT button a recordset object is created. An input box then pops up in which the user must enter an appropriate @title search string (a portion of, or the whole, job description). This input parameter is passed to the stored procedure and, upon execution, the recordset is populated. We then navigate through this recordset, populating the list box with the job_id and job_desc for those jobs that match the supplied search string:

➤ INSERT: This code is designed to insert new data into the jobs table. For the sake of simplicity, we have hard-coded this data. However, you may elect to modify this routine in order to grab values from a text box or file. Once we execute the stored procedure, the Refresh method is called against the ADO Data Control. When this occurs, the data grid should display the new entry.

➤ UPDATE: The UPDATE code is designed to allow the user to change any job description. We use two input boxes to indicate the job_desc to be changed followed by the new description. Unless you're working on a backup copy of the pubs database, I would suggest that you only modify the job description of President, which can be added using the INSERT button.

➤ DELETE: The DELETE code is very similar to the INSERT and UPDATE code. The user supplies the appropriate parameter to be passed to the stored procedure (in this case, the job_id to be deleted). The query is executed and the ADO Data Control refreshed. If the job_id field of any record matches that supplied by the user, then that record will be deleted.

Output Parameters

A stored procedure can generate a return value or several output parameters as a result of its execution. This output is not necessarily data from the database; it could be, for example, an error message or a server variable (such as @@rowcount). Such output can be stored in a parameter object, as you may recall from Chapter 7.

In the previous section, the data set generated by our SELECT stored procedure was stored in a recordset object then the data displayed in a list box. Sometimes, however, a user may wish to supply an input parameter (e.g. an author ID) to a stored procedure and expect to receive only one or two specific values from the database (such as the author's first and last names). Here, too, is a situation where the Recordset object can be dispensed with, in favour of the Parameter object. The following stored procedure expects to receive a single input parameter (@au_id) and, subsequently, returns two output parameters (variables that contain fname and lname field values from the authors table):

```
CREATE PROCEDURE auth_proc @au_id id,
@lname varchar(40) output, @fname varchar(20) output
AS
SELECT @fname=au_fname, @lname=au_lname
FROM authors
WHERE au_id = @au_id
RETURN
```

Now we need to create an application that will pass the input parameter to the stored procedure and, in turn, store and display the output parameters. Create a new **Standard EXE** project, add a command button and a list box to the form then enter the following code:

```
Private Sub Command1_Click()
Dim objConn As ADODB.Connection
Dim objComm As ADODB.Command
Dim objParam1 As ADODB.Parameter
Dim objParam2 As ADODB.Parameter
Dim objParam3 As ADODB.Parameter
Dim strID As String

Set objConn = New ADODB.Connection
objConn.Open "Provider=SQLOLEDB;Data Source=TD;Initial Catalog=publishers;" & _
            "User ID=sa"

Set objComm = New ADODB.Command
Set objComm.ActiveConnection = objConn
objComm.CommandText = "auth_proc"
objComm.CommandType = adCmdStoredProc

strID = InputBox("Enter ID of author to find:")
Set objParam1 = objComm.CreateParameter("au_id", adVarChar, adParamInput, 11, _
                                strID)
objComm.Parameters.Append objParam1

Set objParam2 = objComm.CreateParameter("lname", adVarChar, adParamOutput, 40)
objComm.Parameters.Append objParam2

Set objParam3 = objComm.CreateParameter("fname", adVarChar, adParamOutput, 20)
objComm.Parameters.Append objParam3
```

Continued on Following Page

```
objComm.Execute
List1.Clear
List1.AddItem objParam3 & " " & objParam2

Set objParam1 = Nothing
Set objParam2 = Nothing
Set objParam3 = Nothing
Set objComm = Nothing
Set objConn = Nothing
End Sub
```

Most of the code is fairly straightforward, and will be familiar to you from previous examples. The user supplies the input parameter (as a `String`) via an input box. We then create a parameter object to store this value and pass it to the stored procedure. The `CreateParameter` method accepts five arguments, as described in Chapter 7 (notice that the third argument specifies the direction of the parameter). We then create two more parameter objects to store the output parameters, which we then display in a list box.

System Level Stored Procedures

SQL Server has many built-in system level stored procedures designed to assist in your database maintenance and administration needs. These procedures provide the ability to, for example, add and remove users and grant/revoke user access. They are executed in the same manner as the user-defined stored procedures and are identified by a prefix 'sp_'. With this in mind, you should avoid using this character scheme when naming your own stored procedures.

The first **system stored procedure** we'll explore is the `sp_addlogin` procedure, which allows a new login ID and password to be added to SQL Server. The procedure receives five arguments, the only mandatory one being `login_id`.

sp_addlogin adds a new login to SQL Server
`login_id`
`password` (optional)
`default_db` (optional)
`default_language` (optional)
`login_suid` (optional)

Create a new standard EXE project, add a command button to the form and enter the following code (if you add the command button to your `StProc` project, then you only need to add the code for the command button):

```
Option Explicit
Dim objActiveConnection As ADODB.Connection
Dim objSPCommand As ADODB.Command

Private Sub Form_Load()
   Set objActiveConnection = New ADODB.Connection
   objActiveConnection.ConnectionString = "Provider=SQLOLEDB.1;" & _
         "Persist Security Info=False;User ID=sa;Initial Catalog=pubs"
   objActiveConnection.Open
End Sub

Private Sub cmdLogin_Click()
   Dim pr_Login(1) As Variant
```

```
      Set objSPCommand = New ADODB.Command
      objSPCommand.ActiveConnection = objActiveConnection
      objSPCommand.CommandType = adCmdStoredProc
          objSPCommand.CommandText = "sp_addlogin"
          pr_Login(0) = "CharlieB"    ' new login ID
          pr_Login(1) = "Snoopy"      ' new password

          objSPCommand.Execute , pr_Login
      Set objSPCommand = Nothing
    End Sub
```

Run the code and `CharlieB` should be added as a new login on SQL Server (check that this is the case under **Security I logins**). Let's have a look at a second system level stored procedure: `sp_password`. This procedure allows the password for a specified user to be updated. The procedure receives three arguments, the last of which is optional:

sp_password - changes the password of a specified `login_id`.
`old_password`
`new_password`
`login_id` (optional)

The default value for `login_id` is your Server ID. Therefore, if the `login_id` is not passed, the Server ID will be used in its place. You must also ensure that you are logged in with proper access to change the specified login ID password. If you are not authorized, the request will be rejected.

Add a new command button to your opened project, and then add the following code:

```
    Private Sub cmdPassword_Click()

    Dim pr_password(2) As Variant

    Set objSPCommand = New ADODB.Command
    objSPCommand.ActiveConnection = objActiveConnection
    objSPCommand.CommandType = adCmdStoredProc

        objSPCommand.CommandText = "sp_password"
        pr_password(0) = "Snoopy"         ' old password
        pr_password(1) = "Woodstock"      ' new password
        pr_password(2) = "CharlieB"       ' login id

        objSPCommand.Execute , pr_password

    Set objSPCommand = Nothing

    End Sub
```

The password for the user "CharlieB" will be changed from "Snoopy" to "Woodstock".

Other commonly used system level stored procedures include:

> **sp_addgroup** - adds a new group to the current database
  `group_name` - group name to be added

- > **sp_addUser** - adds a new user to the current database
  `login_id`
  `user_name` (optional)
  `group_name` (optional)
- > **sp_droplogin** - removes a login from SQL Server
  `login_id`
- > **sp_dropuser** - removes a user from the current database
  `user_name`
- > **sp_help** - Returns information about a specific database object.
  `object_name`
- > **sp_helptext** - Displays information about Triggers, Stored Procedures, and Views.
  `object_name`
- > **sp_helpuser** - Displays information about a specified users security.
  `user_name`

The above list simply summarizes the system stored procedures that I have found most useful, but there are many more available. If you have further interest in System Stored Procedures, you should consult the documentation for your specific provider.

Triggers

A trigger is a special type of stored procedure that responds to specific events. It is a compilation of SQL commands that is stored as an object on the RDBMS. Unlike normal stored procedures, triggers *cannot* be called directly from within Visual Basic. A trigger is associated with a database table and is automatically invoked whenever a user attempts to modify (UPDATE, DELETE, INSERT) data on the table that is "protected" by the trigger. It cannot be circumvented.

A trigger is executed only once, even if the modification statement that caused it to execute involves the alteration of hundreds of records. As you can imagine, the code encompassed by a trigger can be extremely complex.

The real key issue with a trigger is its ability to maintain the integrity of your data, preventing unauthorized or inconsistent changes from being made. Triggers are executed immediately before the data is changed, so the data can be validated and the changes can be "rolled back" if they threaten data integrity.

> **As an aside, it is worth noting that triggers cannot be invoked against views.**

Triggers are commonly used to:

> Enforce business rules. They can be used to enforce complex business logic, validate data and ensure proper security clearance for alterations made to a database table. This might include capturing an UPDATE, INSERT or DELETE trigger on a specific table, then validating the changes made and even comparing the values to those found in another table. A trigger forms part of a **transaction** and can be programmed to accept or roll back the changes attempted by the user. Transactions are covered in detail in Chapter 10. We'll look at an example of ROLLBACK later in this chapter.

> Log transactions. Every time certain data in the database is altered, a trigger can query the user's login ID and write the changes to another table for later reference. We will implement a transaction log later in the chapter.

> Maintain data integrity. A trigger can ensure that a field value conforms to value or format restrictions and that the value is in accordance with related values in other tables. A trigger can cascade changes made in one table down to other tables in the database.

> To call user-defined and other stored procedures. This allows repeated use of ready tested stored procedures.

You will have noticed that the functionality provided by a trigger overlaps that available through the server's inherent referential integrity constraints. Triggers should not be used to perform tasks that can easily be handled using normal constraints (e.g. setting simple default values). However, triggers do provide a much more flexible environment in which to handle business rules. For example, if a rule relating to data integrity is transgressed, a check constraint will simply return an error message. A trigger can check the rule, and execute further logic based on the value passed. A trigger can handle much more complex business logic due to the procedural extensions to SQL provided by the database server.

A Note on the Mode of Operation of Triggers

In the previous section we discussed how triggers could be used to enforce restrictions on data modification processes. You may have asked yourself: How does the trigger know exactly what rows were affected by the modification? The answer is through virtual tables - the inserted table and the deleted table. When an INSERT command is executed, the new rows are added to the table on which the trigger acts and, simultaneously, are copied to the inserted table. When a DELETE command is executed, records are deleted from the base table and copied to the deleted table. An UPDATE command is treated like a DELETE command followed by an INSERT command so the records containing the old values are copied to the deleted table and the new records are copied to the inserted table. The trigger refers to records in these table in order to perform its data validation functions.

Existing Triggers

Triggers provide complex functionality but can be difficult to program. There's a lot to learn about them and in this chapter we'll just be covering the basics. It's only through practice and examination of existing triggers you can perfect the art of creating and executing them.

First, let's take a look at an existing trigger in the pubs database. Highlight the **employee** table, right click then navigate as follows: **All Tasks | Manage Triggers**. Select **employee_insupd (dbo)** in the drop-down **Name** box. The trigger should appear in the box provided, allowing you to copy or modify the code:

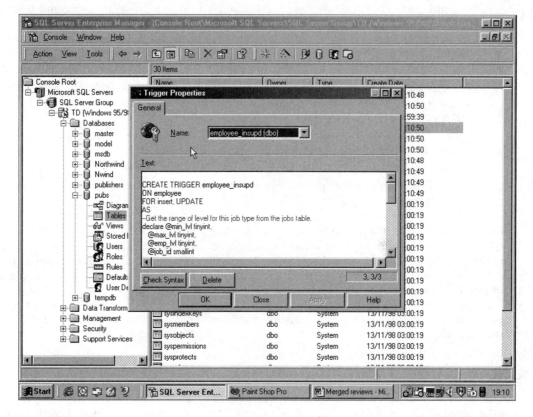

The first portion of the code creates the trigger and names it `employee_insupd`. The `ON` keyword specifies the table on which the trigger is to execute. The `FOR` keyword specifies the conditions under which the trigger should execute. If, for example, `INSERT` is specified, the code in the trigger will execute when a record is inserted into the `employee` table:

```
CREATE TRIGGER employee_insupd
ON employee
FOR INSERT, UPDATE
AS
```

The next section of code establishes the values that were entered into the record. It first declares a number of variables. These variables are then populated with values from the tables of the pubs database. The letters e, j and i are identified as aliases for the table names listed. In addition, when retrieving the values, a `SELECT` statement is executed against the *virtual* `inserted` table. The `inserted` table contains all of the fields of the record that has been modified. The fields from the `inserted` table have identical names to those fields that have been modified or inserted into the database, making it easy for you to retrieve them:

```
declare @min_lvl tinyint,
    @max_lvl tinyint,
    @emp_lvl tinyint,
    @job_id smallint
select @min_lvl = min_lvl,  @max_lvl = max_lvl,
    @emp_lvl = i.job_lvl,
    @job_id = i.job_id
from employee e, jobs j, inserted i
where e.emp_id = i.emp_id AND i.job_id = j.job_id
```

Once we have all of the data we need, we can apply some business rules. There are two validation rules in this section. The first rule ensures that any job_id with a value of 1 has an emp_lvl value of 10. If this is incorrect, we raise an error, which is sent back to the user. The transaction is rolled back and no changes are saved to the database. The second validation rule ensures that the min and max employment levels have not been violated, given the job_id specified. Again, if the rule is broken, an error is raised and the transaction is rolled back:

```
IF (@job_id = 1) and (@emp_lvl <> 10)
begin
    raiserror ('Job id 1 expects the default level of 10.',16,1)
    ROLLBACK TRANSACTION
end
ELSE
IF NOT (@emp_lvl BETWEEN @min_lvl AND @max_lvl)
begin
    raiserror ('The level for job_id:%d should be between %d and %d.',
    16, 1, @job_id, @min_lvl, @max_lvl)
    ROLLBACK TRANSACTION
end
```

Creating Triggers

Now that we have reviewed a sample trigger, let's build one of our own. We will design our trigger to monitor the transactions that are applied to the employee table in the pubs database. If a user updates data in this table or creates a new record, these values will be stored in a new table. In this way, we can monitor what changes were made, when they were made and who made them.

Triggers can cause headaches during programming and especially testing, so great care and planning should be taken. Most of all, stored procedures should be very well documented and all members of the team should be aware of the current and up-to-date state.

We're pushing any changes made into a new table, which needs to be created. The following SQL statement creates a table entitled changed_employee, with fields relevant to an audit process, including the user ID identifying the person who modified the employee table. Run this statement through your SQL Tester program:

```
CREATE TABLE changed_employee (
    emp_id char (9) NOT NULL ,
    new_job_lvl tinyint NOT NULL ,
    modify_date datetime NOT NULL ,
    modify_user char (10) NOT NULL
)
```

Right-click on the Tables folder under pubs to see the new table listed.

We're now ready to build our trigger. We'll break this process into three sections. The first section is pretty straightforward. It specifies the trigger name, the table on which the trigger exists and for what type of statements the trigger should execute:

```
CREATE TRIGGER trigger_employee_changed ON employee
FOR INSERT,UPDATE
AS
```

Next, we declare two variables (@emp_id and @new_job_lvl), which will be populated with the values of the modified job level and the corresponding emp_id, from the virtual inserted table:

```
DECLARE @emp_id char(9),
    @new_job_lvl tinyint
SELECT @emp_id = inserted.emp_id,
    @new_job_lvl = inserted.job_lvl
FROM inserted
```

Finally, we populate the fields in our changed_employee. The @emp_id and @new_job_lvl (supplied by the user) provide two of these values. The others are provided by two built-in SQL Server functions. GETDATE() is designed to return the current date and time, and USER_NAME() will return the user's ID who modified the employee table:

```
INSERT INTO changed_employee
    (emp_id, new_job_lvl, modify_date, modify_user)
VALUES
    (@emp_id,@new_job_lvl,GETDATE(),USER_NAME())
```

The final statement looks like this:

```
CREATE TRIGGER trigger_employee_changed ON employee
FOR INSERT,UPDATE
AS
DECLARE @emp_id char(9),
    @new_job_lvl tinyint
SELECT @emp_id = inserted.emp_id,
    @new_job_lvl = inserted.job_lvl
FROM inserted

INSERT INTO changed_employee
    (emp_id, new_job_lvl, modify_date, modify_user)
VALUES
    (@emp_id,@new_job_lvl,GETDATE(),USER_NAME())
```

Execute this SQL Statement using your SQL Tester program and the trigger will be created.

Implementing a Trigger

Now we have our trigger in place, any modification of the values in the `employee` table should be logged in the `changed_employee` table. Run the following SQL statement:

```
UPDATE employee
SET job_lvl = 55
WHERE emp_id = 'PMA42628M'
```

When the command is sent, the trigger executes and the modified row is copied to the virtual `inserted` table. The trigger then proceeds as described above. To confirm that the trigger worked properly, execute a `SELECT` statement against the `changed_employee` table:

```
SELECT * FROM changed_employee
```

Remember that you can test your trigger using the SQL Server Query Analyser. Select **Tools | SQL Query Tool**. *Make sure the* `pubs` *database is selected in the database drop-down list and enter your SQL statement in the* **Query** *tab. Click on the green arrow on the right side of the dialog box and you'll see the result in the* **Results** *tab.*

ROLLBACK of Changes

As I have mentioned, when we invoke a trigger we can evaluate the data modification and execute logic around it. One of the great advantages here is the ability to rollback the changes, and send the user an informative error message. The following code extends the functionality of the previous trigger, allowing the database server to validate the data. If the `new_job_lvl` field is greater than 100 then an error is returned to the user and the transaction is rolled back:

```
CREATE TRIGGER trigger_employee_changed ON employee
FOR INSERT,UPDATE
AS

DECLARE @emp_id char(9),
        @new_job_lvl tinyint
SELECT @emp_id = inserted.emp_id,
       @new_job_lvl = inserted.job_lvl
FROM inserted
IF (@new_job_lvl > 100)

begin
  raiserror ('Job Level must be less than 100',16,1)
  ROLLBACK TRANSACTION
end
ELSE
begin
INSERT INTO changed_employee
      (emp_id, new_job_lvl, modify_date, modify_user)
VALUES
      (@emp_id,@new_job_lvl,GETDATE(),USER_NAME())
end
```

Now, execute the following code:

```
UPDATE employee
SET job_lvl = 155
WHERE emp_id = 'PMA42628M'
```

You should receive an error message indicating that the Job Level is out of range. Click on the **OK** button. If you change the SQL command's `job_lvl` to 50, the command will execute without a hitch, and an audit trail will be written to the `changed_employee` table.

Triggers are another mechanism for implementing referential integrity where tables are not explicitly joined. After a record is added, updated, or deleted in a table, a trigger can execute a SELECT statement against related tables in order to validate the existence of related records. These changes are then forwarded throughout the database and an error is returned to the user if the data change is invalid.

Summary

Views, stored procedures and triggers are not, strictly speaking, *necessary* for the successful implementation of all client server systems. Each of these is capable of greatly enhancing the reliability, efficiency, performance and security of your system. The range and scope of each of these methods may vary, depending on the RDBMS. This chapter demonstrated how to create views, stored procedures and triggers in SQL Server, and then call them from a Visual Basic application. Just a few of the benefits gained from using these methods include maintaining data integrity, implementing security with views, enforcing business logic and automating tasks.

Suppliers

- SupplierID
- CompanyName
- ContactName
- ContactTitle
- Address
- City
- Region
- PostalCode
- Country
- Phone
- Fax
- HomePage

Products

- ProductID
- ProductName
- SupplierID
- CategoryID
- QuantityPerUnit
- UnitPrice
- UnitsInStock
- UnitsOnOrder
- ReorderLevel
- Discontinued

Categories

- CategoryID
- CategoryName
- Description
- Picture

6

Implementing a 2-Tier Solution

Having read the previous chapters, there's no doubt that you can easily whip together a 2-tier client-server application. In this chapter, we'll build an application that accesses the `Northwind` database and displays customer information and order details. The main focus of this chapter will be on form design and the key concepts for providing useful functionality.

One of the most challenging aspects of building a client-server application is screen design: to produce a functional and user-friendly interface in a relatively limited workspace. You should aim to provide as much functionality and data as possible on a *single* form, but without cluttering the workspace. When the workspace becomes cluttered, users easily become lost or confused. Conversely, users may become frustrated if forced to navigate through a large number of forms.

Building a Sample 2-Tier Application

In this chapter, we'll build an application that displays customer information along with order details. The application will be designed with a **MDI** (**Multiple Document Interface**) form and two data access forms, which we will use to connect to our `Northwind` database.

> **MDI forms are parent forms that have child forms, which are viewed within the parent form's workspace. There can only be one MDI form per project. When child forms are minimized, their icons are viewed inside the parent (MDI) form. An example of a MDI application that everyone is familiar with is Microsoft Word. Previous to Word 2000, when you opened multiple documents in Word, each document was a child of the Word parent form.**

Our first child form will be used to enter or update customer information. The ADO Data Control will therefore connect to the `Customer` table of the `Northwind` database. The user will be able to add, delete or edit the `Customer` table. In addition, users will be able to view multiple instances of the form, giving them the flexibility to work simultaneously with data for more than one customer. In the following example, the user has opened two instances of the Customers form:

The next child form displays the orders placed by various companies. When this form opens, the user will be able to select a company name from a drop-down box. The application will then display contact information in text boxes as well as a grid control with all orders placed by the company and with a total for each order:

Finally, a third form will display all line items associated with any given form. To view the line items, the user will highlight an order on the DataGrid, then right-click on it. The following form will display each line item of the form:

OrderID	ProductID	UnitPrice	Quantity	Discount
10436	46	9.6	5	0
10436	56	30.4	40	0.1
10436	64	26.6	30	0.1
10436	75	6.2	24	0.1

Now that we understand our mission, let's get started.

Building the Application Shell

The first step is to build an application shell. Visual Basic comes with many wizards that can help reduce your development time by as much as 90%. When you have a wizard to work with, it's always wise to use it. The code generated is of high quality, and is usually well documented. Wizards can also provide a great learning tool. If you're a beginner, and want to learn something new, generate some code with a wizard, then read the code.

Before beginning, you should create a Data Source Name for the Northwind database located on SQL Server. If you don't have SQL Server, you may use the Nwind database located in Access instead, but there may be some minor changes in the code. If you need to review how to create a DSN name, refer to Chapter 3.

We'll be using a wizard to design our interface, so start up Visual Basic and open the VB Application Wizard by selecting its icon from the New Project dialog. You will now be asked a series of questions regarding the application structure:

1. The first dialog is the Introduction. We don't yet have a profile to select, so click on the Next button.

2. At the Interface Type dialog, select the Multiple Document Interface (MDI) type, and name the application Orders. Once done, click on the Next button.

3. We won't need a menu in our project, so disable all of the available menu items and click on the Next button.

4. We won't need a toolbar in our application either, so click on the double arrows pointing to the left, <<, to remove the toolbar items from the project, then click on the Next button.

5. Although most projects could benefit from a resource file, we don't need one in this project, so ensure the N<u>o</u> option button is selected and then click on the <u>N</u>ext button.

6. At the Internet Connectivity dialog click on the <u>N</u>ext button.

7. Again, we'll keep this project as simple as possible, so we won't use any of the standard forms in our project. Ensure all options are unchecked and click on the <u>N</u>ext button.

8. The next dialog (Data Access Forms) is the reason we came to the wizard for help. As I mentioned in the introduction, we'll need to build two primary data forms. To begin creating them, click on the <u>C</u>reate New Form... button.

9. Bypass the Introduction dialog by clicking on the <u>N</u>ext button. (If we had saved a previous template, we could have called it from here).

10. The next dialog presented is the Database Type dialog. This allows us to select the type of database with which we wish to connect. We want to connect to an ODBC database, so select Remote ODBC and then click on the <u>N</u>ext button.

11. The Connect Information dialog allows us to specify the database and its location. We'll connect to the `Northwind` Data Source Name, so locate `Northwind` from the DSN Combo Box. You must also specify the name of the database, so enter `Northwind` in the database text box. Then provide the user ID and password required to access the database. Once your database has been selected, click on the <u>N</u>ext button. An attempt to connect to the database will occur, and if any errors are encountered, you'll receive an error dialog.

12. The next dialog allows us to specify the form name, layout and binding type. This form will be the Customers form, displayed as a Single Record and will be built using the ADO <u>D</u>ata Control. Once you have set these three parameters, click on the <u>N</u>ext button. We could use the AD<u>O</u> Code option, but the wizard will then go and produce navigation bars and error handling code, and I want us to do that instead.

13. The <u>R</u>ecord Source will be populated from the Customers table, and we'll use all of the fields, so select all fields available by clicking on the >> arrows. Sort your data by the `CompanyName` field. When complete, click on the <u>N</u>ext button.

14. The next dialog allows us to add buttons to our form. We will want to add all of them to our form, so click on the Select A<u>l</u>l button, then click on the <u>N</u>ext button.

15. We're now finished building the first data form. Don't forget that we're not done yet. We still need to build one more data form and then finish building the MDI form. Click on the <u>F</u>inish button.

16. After clicking on the <u>F</u>inish button, you will be asked if you want to Create another Data Form? Click on the <u>Y</u>es button.

17. The process of adding our second form will be very similar to the first, except the next form will have a Master/Detail form layout. Also name the form, Orders, and specify that it should be built using the ADO <u>D</u>ata Control. Click on the <u>N</u>ext button.

> **A Master/Detail form allows us to view groups of associated records from more than one table on one form. In our example, we'll display the customer information (from the `Customers` table) in text boxes and group all orders (from the `Orders` table) for the respective customer in a grid control.**

18. Next, select the <u>R</u>ecord Source for the Master section of your form. This is will be the Customers table. Add all fields and sort the records by CompanyName and then click on the <u>N</u>ext button.

19. The next dialog specifies information pertaining to the Detail section of the data form. Select the Orders table as the <u>R</u>ecord Source, and add all fields from the list. Finally, choose OrderDate as the column to sort by and click on the <u>N</u>ext button.

20. We now need to link these two tables by a common field (the `CustomerID` field). This is the primary key field of the master record source and the foreign key field of the detail record source. Select CustomerID in each list box and then click on the <u>N</u>ext button.

21. To keep this form simple, we won't add any controls. This does limit the ability to update, add and delete records, but we've covered the methods behind each of these in previous chapters and will explore them more in later chapters. Uncheck each of the check boxes and click on the <u>N</u>ext button.

22. We've finished building the second data form. We're almost done, but we need to finish creating the MDI interface. Click on the <u>F</u>inish button.

23. Again, you will be prompted to Create another Data Form? This time click on the <u>N</u>o button. If you want to add more data forms later, you can build them from scratch or use the Data Form Wizard, which is available in the <u>A</u>dd-Ins section of Visual Basic.

24. The Data Access Forms dialog should appear, now with two forms added. This is your last chance to abandon the forms that you built. Click on the <u>N</u>ext button.

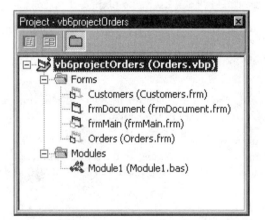

25. You have completed building the shell of our application. The Finished! dialog appears for the third time. Click on the <u>F</u>inish button.

26. After some processing, a message box will appear, indicating that the application has been created. Click on the <u>O</u>K button.

Your Project Explorer window should now present four forms and one module. Explore the layout and code of these four forms. Note that the parent form (MDI form) is titled `frmMain`. The module (`Module1`) is used to allow an initialization to occur before the form is loaded. In this example, no initialization takes place. However, the module is used to open the MDI form. This structure allows for future modifications, such as adding a login dialog or splash screen.

The Toolbox now contains many additional ActiveX controls. The two controls that we'll focus on during this chapter are the ADO Data Control and the Microsoft DataGrid Control 6.0 (OLEDB). These controls are represented by the last two icons in the following image:

Two of the event procedures of the ADO Data Controls in our forms (`datPrimaryRS_WillChangeRecord` and `datPrimaryRS_MoveComplete`) reference an ADODB recordset. To use this recordset, we must first declare its existence. Because of this, a reference to ADO should be added to the project (if it's not already there). To confirm that the reference is added, select **References** from the **P**roject menu. Ensure that the **Microsoft ActiveX Data Objects 2.x Library** is selected and click on the OK button:

This is an appropriate time to save your project. Create a new folder off the ProVB6DB folder called Chapter9, and save all of the objects with their default names. From this point forward, you should save your work frequently.

You can now run your project, notice that the project produces a **Document 1** form when it runs. This **Document 1** form is a default form produced from the wizard while creating an MDI form:

We don't need this form, unless we want to incorporate a text editor in our project, so let's get rid of it.

To remove the form from the project, stop the project and click on frmDocument from the Project Explorer to highlight it. From the menu bar, select Project | Remove frmDocument.frm.

The form has now been removed from the project. However, there is still code that references the form. We'll need to remove any reference to the form in modules and forms of the project, or an error may be produced during run-time or compilation. To do this, open the code for frmMain and locate the MDIForm_Load event procedure. Remove the call to the LoadNewDoc sub procedure. We can also do a global 'replace' by selecting the Replace from the Edit menu. If we select Current Project as our search criteria, we can locate all instances with no mistakes.

Next locate the LoadNewDoc sub procedure and delete the entire procedure. This is the code that actually loads an instance of the form we removed.

The Orders and Customers forms are currently designed to allow the user to load multiple instances of each. We would like to keep this functionality for the Customers form. However, let's remove this from the Orders form. Locate the mnuDataOrders_Click event procedure in frmMain. The code should look like this:

```
Private Sub mnuDataOrders_Click()

    Dim f As New Orders
    f.Show

End Sub
```

Each call to this sub procedure declares a new instance of the form and shows the new instance. We can remove this code and replace it with one line of code to eliminate the loading of multiple instances. This code will load the form and give it focus if it's not already loaded. If the form is loaded, it will simply give the form focus:

```
Private Sub mnuDataOrders_Click()

    Orders.Show

End Sub
```

Have a look at the code of the `Main` sub procedure in the module. This uses the same concept, but there will only ever be one instance of the `fMainForm` loaded. The `Main` sub procedure is a great place to initialize any variables before the form loads, so this is the ideal location to control the opening and shutdown of your forms:

```
Sub Main()
    Set fMainForm = New frmMain
    fMainForm.Show
End Sub
```

Modifying the Customers Form

The next task will be to arrange the `Customers` form. This should be somewhat trivial considering we have already done this in previous chapters. When modifying the layout of your form, your personal tastes will certainly play a role in the final output of the form. Remember who your users are though; exotic colors and layouts may be offensive to the user who may be spending a good portion of their day in front of your application.

Re-arrange the controls of `Customers` form. All of the functionality we need has been included by the wizard, so there is no need to modify the code of each button. Again, the key is to use your form space wisely. Don't waste space by allowing a text box to be too large when only a small text box is needed. This is how I laid out my form:

Run your project and select **Customers** from the **Data** menu. Open a few more instances of the `Customers` form.

Notice that each of the forms added has the same window caption. For a user, this can result in unnecessary searching if multiple windows are open. Ideally, each window should have a unique caption. We could easily implement a solution utilizing the current `CustomerID` or `CompanyName` as part of the caption. For now, let's just create a counter.

To implement a counter on your form, change the `mnuDataCustomers_Click` event procedure as follows:

```
Private Sub mnuDataCustomers_Click()

    Static intCountCustomers As Integer
    intCountCustomers = intCountCustomers + 1
    Dim frmCustomer As New Customers
    frmCustomer.Caption = "Customers: " & intCountCustomers
    frmCustomer.Show

End Sub
```

The `Static` keyword is used to keep the scope of our variable to a minimum. If we had used the `Dim` keyword instead, the variable would have reinitialized to zero each time the procedure was called. The next two added lines increment the counter and include the count as part of the form's caption. Notice also that we have replaced `f` with the more descriptive `frmCustomer`.

Save your project and test your changes.

To implement the contact name as part of the solution, change the `datPrimaryRS_MoveComplete` event procedure of `Customers` as follows to pull the name from the recordset:

```
Private Sub datPrimaryRS_MoveComplete(ByVal adReason As _
                    ADODB.EventReasonEnum, _
                    ByVal pError As ADODB.Error, _
                    adStatus As ADODB.EventStatusEnum, _
                    ByVal pRecordset As ADODB.Recordset)

    'This will display the current record position for this recordset
    datPrimaryRS.Caption = "Record: " & _
                    CStr(datPrimaryRS.Recordset.AbsolutePosition)
    Me.Caption = "Customer: " & datPrimaryRS.Recordset.Fields("ContactName")

End Sub
```

Adding a Navigation Bar

Run the project again and select Customers from the Data menu. Now try to navigate off the recordset by pressing the < and > arrows when on the first and last records respectively. Visual Basic will send an error message stating: Run-time error '3021'.

To prevent this error from occurring we need to add some code to our `Customers` form to prevent the user from navigating off the recordset. This code is identical to that which we used in Chapter 4 and will be contained within a navigation bar.

As in Chapter 4, add a control array of four command buttons called `cmdNegotiate` with a label called `lblRecord` between them. Arrange the command buttons in increasing `Index` value from left to right as shown here:

Give the ADO Data Control an `Align` property of `vbAlignNone` and set its `Visible` property to `False`.

Now add the following code to the cmdNegotiate_Click event procedure:

```
Private Sub cmdNegotiate_Click(Index As Integer)

    On Error GoTo goNegotiateErr

    With datPrimaryRS.Recordset

        Select Case Index
          Case 0  'First Record
            .MoveFirst
          Case 1  'Previous Record
            .MovePrevious
            If .BOF Then .MoveFirst
          Case 2  'Next Record
            .MoveNext
            If .EOF Then .MoveLast
          Case 3  'Last Record
            .MoveLast
        End Select

    End With

Exit Sub


goNegotiateErr:

    MsgBox Err.Description

End Sub
```

Finally, we need to add a line of code to our datPrimaryRS_MoveComplete event procedure. This is called whenever we call the MoveFirst, MovePrevious, MoveNext or MoveLast methods and displays the current record position in the recordset.

Say we are at the first record and press cmdNegotiate(1). The MoveComplete event will be fired when the MoveFirst method has finished and Visual Basic will attempt to find the AbsolutePosition of the current record. However, we are at the first record, so there is no current record, only the BOF, which we will be dealt with in the next line of cmdNegotiate_Click.

As we know that under certain circumstances an error will be raised in the datPrimaryRS_MoveComplete event procedure, we add the following line, which informs Visual Basic to continue with the next line if any errors are raised:

```
Private Sub datPrimaryRS_MoveComplete(ByVal adReason As _
          ADODB.EventReasonEnum, ByVal pError As ADODB.Error, _
          adStatus As ADODB.EventStatusEnum, _
          ByVal pRecordset As ADODB.Recordset)

    'This will display the current record position for this recordset

    On Error Resume Next
        datPrimaryRS.Caption = "Record: " & _
    CStr(datPrimaryRS.Recordset.AbsolutePosition)

    Me.Caption = "Customer: " & datPrimaryRS.Recordset.Fields("ContactName")

End Sub
```

Modifying the Code of the Orders Form

I have saved the most challenging changes for last. We'll want to modify the code in the `Orders` form to provide more functionality and a much needed professional presentation. Run your project and open the `Orders` form. To view the entire detail you may need to maximize the form. As you can see, the data uses most of the form's workspace. We'll want to re-arrange this form to allocate space more efficiently:

Based on the current configuration of this form, here are a few thoughts for improvements:

1. Rearrange the order of the master fields. By reducing the size of each field (to accommodate only the required field size) and then sorting the fields, we can reduce the wasted space.

2. Give the users the ability to view all line items in any given order. Each order placed contains multiple line items, which make up the order. We'll need a mechanism for displaying this data.

3. Show the total cost of each order in the grid control and remove any unnecessary fields from the same grid control. This option could be implemented in multiple locations. For instance, we could apply the value to each line item. In our example, we'll display the total cost for each order. This will provide a bit more of a challenge.

4. Provide a drop-down box with a listing of all the customer IDs. When the user selects a customer from the list, the master and detail sections should update accordingly.

You may also want to change the Caption property of each form to correctly identify its function. The Orders form, for example, should have a caption of **Customer Orders** or something similar.

The first logical step here is to modify the layout of the master fields. You can re-arrange this in any order you want. Again, the goal is to reduce the amount of wasted space. I've added a shape control to group the customer's address information, the FillColor property is set to a dark gray and FillStyle is set to Solid. When adding the shape control, you may need to send its position behind the other controls by right-clicking on it and selecting <u>S</u>end to Back. Additionally, you may elect to drop any of the fields that you don't need. The purpose of this form is to display the status of an order, so there may be fields that have no relevance to this task; I have not included the PostalCode and Region fields in my form. Finally, I changed the BorderStyle property of each label to Fixed Single, with a BackColor of light yellow. This is where your preference will come into play. You may choose to place the labels on top of the text boxes, or to the left. Whatever you decide, choose a color scheme which reflects the entire project.

If you want to remove fields at this point, remove the text boxes that are bound to the fields (and the associated label), then open the RecordSource property of datPrimaryRS to view the SQL statement used. Remove any reference to those fields you don't need to display. I removed the PostalCode and Region fields.

After reorganizing the form, it may look similar to this:

The Details Form

The next item on our list is to provide a mechanism for viewing the line items of each order. To accomplish this, we'll create a form which will display the records in a grid.

Add a new form to your project. This new form will be designed as a child of the MDI parent, so locate the `MDIChild` property and change its value to `True`.

On your new form, add an ADO Data Control and a DataGrid control (these controls should already be in your toolbox) so that it looks similar to the following:

Name the form `frmDetails` and change its `Caption` to **Order Details**. You may also want to change the `BorderStyle` property to `3 - Fixed Dialog`. This will prevent the user from re-sizing the form, but will still provide the user with a close control button.

Configure the ADO Data Control's `ConnectionString` property to connect to the `Northwind` database using the `Northwind` DSN, by clicking on the **Use ODBC** **D**ata Source Name option button and selecting **Northwind** from the drop-down box. In the Other **A**ttributes text box, enter the user ID and password for your SQL Server database:

Next, specify the `CommandType` to be `adCmdText` and add the following SQL statement to the `RecordSource` property. This will prevent the data source from being populated before the `OrderID` is specified. Because '1 = 2' can never be true, no records will be returned.

```
SELECT * FROM [Order Details] WHERE 1=2
```

Locate the `DataSource` property of the DataGrid control and change it to `Adoc1`. This will bind the grid control to the new ADO Data Control.

When we open the recordset of the ADO Data Control, we will want to create a SQL statement that searches for a specific `OrderID` and returns all details of the order. To pass this between forms, add a declaration to the module's **General Declarations** section. For a declaration to be shared between multiple forms, it must be declared as `Public` and inside a standard module, not a form module:

```
Public lngOrderID As Long
```

We'll want to display the `RecordCount` in the ADO Data Control's `Caption` property, so add the following code to the `MoveComplete` event procedure of the ADO Data Control:

```
Private Sub Adodc1_MoveComplete(ByVal adReason As ADODB.EventReasonEnum, _
                        ByVal pError As ADODB.Error, _
                        adStatus As ADODB.EventStatusEnum, _
                        ByVal pRecordset As ADODB.Recordset)

    Adodc1.Caption = Adodc1.Recordset.RecordCount & " line items"

End Sub
```

When the form loads, we ensure that a `lngOrderID` value was selected. Then we select all order line items with an `OrderID` field equal to that value:

```
Private Sub Form_Load()

    If lngOrderID <> 0 Then
      Adodc1.RecordSource = "SELECT * FROM [Order Details] " & _
                        "WHERE OrderID = " & lngOrderID
      Adodc1.Refresh
    End If

End Sub
```

Let's Move Back to the Orders Form

Next, we need to ensure that the `frmDetails` form opens when the user right-clicks on the DataGrid control of the `Orders` form. To do this, locate the `MouseDown` event procedure of the DataGrid control of the `Orders` form. This event will pass an integer, `Button`, which identifies which button was clicked. The right button is assigned the value 2, so we'll query for that number. Next, we set `lngOrderID` equal to the current record's `OrderID` field. Lastly, display the form:

```
Private Sub grdDataGrid_MouseDown(Button As Integer, Shift As Integer, _
                                  X As Single, Y As Single)

   If Button = 2 Then
      lngOrderID = grdDataGrid.Columns("OrderID")
      frmDetails.Show
   End If

End Sub
```

It would also be nice to add a tool tip so that when a user places the mouse over the DataGrid control, a message informed him/her of this capability. To do this, change the `ToolTipText` property of `grdDataGrid` to **Right-click on grid for Order details**.

Now Let's Move Back to the Details Form

If `frmDetails` is deactivated, we need to unload it. This will prevent the form from remaining open while other forms of the project, such as the `Orders` form, are selected. Without this code, the form will remain open, behind any other form selected. This not only produces an unprofessional appearance, but if multiple unrequired forms are running, you may experience a performance hit.

```
Private Sub Form_Deactivate ()

   Unload Me
   Set frmDetails = Nothing

End Sub
```

The previous code controls the `frmDetails` form when another form in the project is selected, but not if a form of another project is selected or if the parent form is moved, resized, or minimized. Notice that we have set `frmDetails` equal to `Nothing`, this removes the instance of `frmDetails` from memory. Simply calling `Unload Me` will allow `frmDetails` to continue running, although it will be hidden from view.

The following code, which should be added to `frmMain`, keeps `frmDetails` in line with the actions of the parent form;

```
Private Sub MDIForm_Resize()

   Unload frmDetails
   Set frmDetails = Nothing

End Sub
```

If the MDI form is unloaded, the children forms will automatically close. Should you have additional forms that are not children of the `frmMain` form, you should pass control to the `Module1` module and allow it to close down the remaining forms, if they are open.

If this was the case, you might call an `End_Program` procedure in the module in the following way:

```
Private Sub MDIForm_Unload(Cancel As Integer)

    If Me.WindowState <> vbMinimized Then
        SaveSetting App.Title, "Settings", "MainLeft", Me.Left
        SaveSetting App.Title, "Settings", "MainTop", Me.Top
        SaveSetting App.Title, "Settings", "MainWidth", Me.Width
        SaveSetting App.Title, "Settings", "MainHeight", Me.Height
    End If

    Call End_Program

End Sub
```

The `End_Program` procedure in the module would then be called, closing each form individually. We don't have any additional forms, so don't enter the above code. It's not necessary.

The SHAPE Construct

The `SHAPE` construct is a feature of ADO 2.x that allows us to create a single hierarchical recordset from two or more recordsets. To do this, one recordset is treated as a parent and the other a child. The parent recordset will contain aggregate information, and the child recordset the repeating detail relating to the parent records. This construct is highly scalable, allowing you to nest `SHAPE`s to any depth you require (a parent may have a child that is a parent to another).

The recordset that populates our `Orders` form with the customer information and the order details is the `SHAPE` construct. This construct is applied against the `RecordSource` property of the ADO Data Control. To view its syntax, view the `RecordSource` property of the ADO Data Control on the `Orders` form:

To get a better view of the SHAPE construct, copy the **Command Text** and paste it in Notepad. I've rearranged the statement and capitalized all SQL keywords for greater readability:

```
SHAPE {SELECT CustomerID,CompanyName,ContactName,ContactTitle,Address,
       City,Country,Phone,Fax FROM Customers ORDER BY CompanyName}
       AS ParentCMD

APPEND ({SELECT OrderID,CustomerID,EmployeeID,OrderDate,RequiredDate,
         ShippedDate,ShipVia,Freight,ShipName,ShipAddress,ShipCity,
         ShipRegion,ShipPostalCode,ShipCountry FROM Orders ORDER BY
         OrderDate } AS ChildCMD

RELATE CustomerID TO CustomerID) AS ChildCMD
```

The SHAPE construct contains three parts:

➤   SHAPE: A SQL statement used as a base (or parent) recordset. The SHAPE keyword identifies that the SQL statement to follow is a parent recordset with a child recordset definition to follow. An alias will follow the first SQL statement, identifying the entire recordset by name. In the above example, ParentCMD is the alias.

➤   APPEND: Following the APPEND keyword a SQL statement identifies the recordset which is to contain the detail (or child). Again, an alias is used to identify the recordset by name. Here, the name is ChildCMD.

➤   RELATE: This keyword is used to identify which fields within each of the recordsets are to be used to join the parent and child recordsets. The parent column is listed first, then the child column.

To apply this SHAPE construct to a DataGrid control, you set the DataGrid control's DataSource property equal to the alias name of the child recordset's UnderlyingValue. This is typically done in the Form_Load, or whenever a change is made to your SQL statements. Here, the ChildCMD command is applied to the DataGrid control of the Orders form:

```
Private Sub Form_Load()
    Set grdDataGrid.DataSource = _
        datPrimaryRS.Recordset("ChildCMD").UnderlyingValue
End Sub
```

Removing Fields from the Orders DataGrid Control

The third item on our list of enhancements was to remove any unnecessary fields and include a new field that displays the total cost of all line items combined. Because the DataGrid control is assigned to the ChildCMD command, it will automatically be populated with the fields listed in the APPEND SQL statement. Any fields that we want to drop from the DataGrid control can simply be removed from the APPEND section.

Remove the following fields from the SQL statement in the APPEND section:

RequiredDate	ShipAddress	ShipCity
ShipCountry	ShipName	ShippedDate
ShipPostalCode	ShipRegion	ShipVia

Adding an Order Total Field to the DataGrid Control

To summarize the line totals of each order, we'll need to refer back to our SQL chapter. Specifically, we'll need a subquery to summarize (UnitPrice * Quantity * (1-Discount)) only for those records where the OrderID field of the Order Details table is equal to that of the current OrderID field of the Orders table. Our SQL statement might look something like this:

```
(SELECT SUM(UnitPrice * Quantity * (1-Discount)) FROM
  [Order Details] WHERE OrderID = Orders.OrderID) AS SubTotal
```

This code is returning a field (just like the other fields of the Orders table) so bury the subquery statement in with the selection of the other fields in the SHAPE construct.

We'll next want to replace the EmployeeID field with the actual last name of the employee. To accomplish this, we'll build a subquery that does a lookup in the Employees table. The code looks like this:

```
(SELECT LastName FROM Employees WHERE EmployeeID = Orders.EmployeeID)
  AS EmployeeID
```

This statement can replace the field identifier for EmployeeID in the Orders table section of the SHAPE construct.

After all three changes have been applied, the final result should look like this:

```
SHAPE {SELECT CustomerID,CompanyName,ContactName,ContactTitle,Address,
       City,Country,Phone,Fax FROM Customers ORDER BY CompanyName}
    AS ParentCMD

APPEND ({SELECT OrderID,CustomerID,
          (SELECT LastName FROM Employees WHERE EmployeeID = Orders.EmployeeID)
          AS EmployeeID,
          OrderDate,Freight,
          (SELECT SUM(UnitPrice * Quantity * (1-Discount)) FROM
           [Order Details] WHERE OrderID = Orders.OrderID) AS SubTotal
         FROM Orders ORDER BY OrderDate } AS ChildCMD

RELATE CustomerID TO CustomerID) AS ChildCMD
```

Modifying the DataGrid Layout on the Orders Form

The DataGrid control allows a great amount of flexibility when it comes to layout. Some of the modifiable properties include column width (Width), Caption and Alignment. The following code, when added to the Form_Load event, demonstrates these properties. Note that when calling a specific column, you can select it by its index number or by the column's name:

```
Private Sub Form_Load()

    Set grdDataGrid.DataSource = _
        datPrimaryRS.Recordset("ChildCMD").UnderlyingValue
    grdDataGrid.Columns(5).Caption = "Line Totals"
    grdDataGrid.Columns(5).Alignment = dbgRight
    grdDataGrid.Columns("OrderDate").Width = 1100
    grdDataGrid.Columns(0).Visible = False
    grdDataGrid.Columns(4).Alignment = dbgRight

    End Sub
```

Changing the Data Format of Fields in a DataGrid

When attempting to create a professional look and feel for your application, one thing is a must. Currency fields *must* be displayed in a format that is easy to read. This means, add a dollar sign to the beginning and require two decimal places. Visual Basic comes with a reference to data type conversion. To use this reference, you must first add it to your project. To do this, select Project | References and locate: Microsoft Data Formatting Object Library. Select it and click on OK.

Add the following code to the `Form_Load` event procedure of the `Orders` form:

```
Dim fmtCurr As New StdDataFormat
fmtCurr.Format = "Currency"
Set grdDataGrid.Columns(4).DataFormat = fmtCurr
Set grdDataGrid.Columns(5).DataFormat = fmtCurr
```

The first line declares `fmtCurr` as a new Standard Data Format. Once it has been declared, `fmtCurr` is assigned the `Format` of `Currency`. From this point forward, `fmtCurr` can be used to change the format of any control that can be bound to a text-based field in a database, including DataGrid control columns, text boxes and labels. In this example, we use it to change the format of the Freight and Line Totals columns.

> *The appearance of the* `"Currency"` *format is dependent upon the* Regional Settings *in the* Control Panel *of your machine. For instance, if you set the* Regional Settings *to* English (United Kingdom) *you'll get a £ instead of a $. Selecting* French (Standard) *will result in the decimal symbol being a comma rather than period and the monetary symbol, F, will appear after the value instead of before.*

Adding a Quick Customer Lookup

The fourth and last item on our list was to provide a DataCombo box that allows the user to quickly select the customer for which he or she wants to view orders. Currently, when our `Orders` form opens, the customer listed happens to be the first alphabetically listed customer from our `Customers` table. To locate a customer, we must use the navigation buttons, to run through the records one at a time. Because there could potentially be hundreds or even thousands of customers, we need a better way of locating the desired customer.

Return to the design mode of the `Orders` form. We have a great deal of flexibility when it comes to the search criteria. We could give the user the ability to search by virtually any of the fields. In this case, however, let's assume we want to search for a specific company ID.

Add a new ADO Data Control and a DataCombo box (from Microsoft DataList Controls 6.0 (OLEDB)) to your form. The DataCombo box will replace the text box, which is bound to the `CompanyID` field. Delete the text box and move the DataCombo box directly over the position where it was:

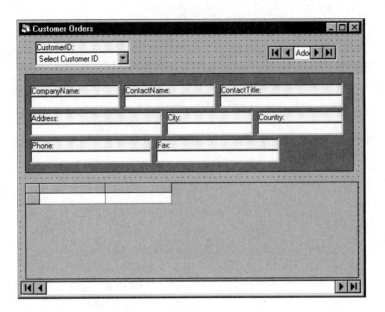

Set up the new ADO Data Control so that it connects to the `Northwind` DSN and set its `RecordSource` to the `Customers` table. The `Customers` table will be used to populate the DataCombo box with a list of all `CustomerID`s.

Set the following properties of the DataCombo box:

Property	Value
RowSource	Adodc1
ListField	CustomerID
Text	Select Customer ID

Note that we did not bind the `DataSource` property of this box to any fields. This is because the box is not used to update any fields. If it were bound to the `CustomerID` field, the `CustomerID` value in the `Customers` table would be changed every time the DataCombo box value changed.

The following code should be added to the DataCombo box's `Change` event procedure. This code applies a filter to the recordset, filtering out all records where the `CompanyID` field is not equal to the value of the DataCombo box. For increased flexibility, you could also use the `LIKE` keyword, which would return all `CustomerID`s with a similar name:

```
Private Sub DataCombo1_Change()

    datPrimaryRS.Recordset.Filter = "CustomerID = '" & DataCombo1.Text & "'"

End Sub
```

Add the following code to the `Form_Load` event procedure. This code will ensure that the form is empty when it loads.

> **You must add this code after the code that assigns the `DataSource` equal to the `ChildCMD` recordset. If this code is applied before assigning the recordset, an error will occur.**

```
Private Sub Form_Load()

    Set grdDataGrid.DataSource = datPrimaryRS.Recordset("ChildCMD").UnderlyingValue
    grdDataGrid.Columns(5).Caption = "Line Totals"
    grdDataGrid.Columns(5).Alignment = dbgRight
    grdDataGrid.Columns(5).Width = 1000
    grdDataGrid.Columns("OrderDate").Width = 1100
    grdDataGrid.Columns(0).Visible = False

    Dim fmtCurr As New StdDataFormat
    fmtCurr.Format = "Currency"
    Set grdDataGrid.Columns(4).DataFormat = fmtCurr
    Set grdDataGrid.Columns(5).DataFormat = fmtCurr

    datPrimaryRS.Recordset.Filter = "CustomerID = ' '"

End Sub
```

Note that there is a space between the single quotes, which is then followed by a double quote.

The final step is to hide both of the ADO Data Controls - the one that populates the DataCombo box and the one which drives the order detail. We won't need either because the DataCombo box provides the navigation mechanism. Change the `Visible` property of `datPrimaryRS` and `Adodc1` to `False`.

> *If you decide to use the LIKE keyword, you'll need to keep the main ADO Data Control (datPrimaryRS). This is because using the LIKE keyword will allow multiple records. If there are multiple records, you'll need a method for navigating through them.*

In the `Form_Resize` event procedure of the `Orders` form, the following code should exist:

```
Private Sub Form_Resize()

    On Error Resume Next
    'This will resize the grid when the form is resized
    grdDataGrid.Width = Me.ScaleWidth
    grdDataGrid.Height = Me.ScaleHeight - grdDataGrid.Top - _
                     datPrimaryRS.Height - 30

End Sub
```

When the form is resized, we want to dynamically change the size of the grid control (grdDataGrid). Because we no longer can see datPrimaryRS, it should be removed from any equation in the Resize event procedure. Therefore, the last line of code should be changed to the following:

```
grdDataGrid.Height = Me.ScaleHeight - grdDataGrid.Top - 30
```

Run your application and view the results. Select various CustomerIDs from the list:

Deploying Our 2-Tier Solution

Now that we have created our 2-tier client-server application, we need to deploy it to the users. Although this may seem like a difficult process, it's quite simple. In this example, we designed the ADO Data Control to connect to the SQL Server database using a configured Data Source Name. The DSN is responsible for locating the server database. As you recall, when you create a DSN, you indicate the server that the database resides on and the database name. When you test your connection, you know you have set up the connection properties of the DSN correctly, and all that remains is to program the client application to talk through the DSN (which we already did).

What this means is that for you to deploy your application to any other computer, a DSN called Northwind needs to be created on the new computer. You should then be able to drop your compiled client application on the new computer and run it normally.

Of course, we still have not dealt with the issue of security, that's coming in Chapter 15. You should find it easy enough to include security into this example after you have read that chapter.

In Chapter 16 (Deployment), we'll cover some techniques for deploying DSNs over a number of computers using registry files.

Summary

This chapter was a compilation of much of what you have already learned. We did cover new material including the SHAPE construct, which allowed us to create a single hierarchical recordset from two other recordsets, and using a DSN. We also focused on using the VB Application Wizard to build the shell of our project. We certainly gained considerable time advantages by using the wizard. These wizards not only provide a mechanism for speeding up application development, they also can be used as a learning tool.

The application works well as a tool for displaying the customers and their orders from the Northwind database, the executable is small in size and the load on the network does not cause the application to grind to a halt. However, what happens if we need to add more processing so that our application becomes more sophisticated than the viewer it is presently? Do we continue to add the processing to the client? The answer is no. The more processing we move to the client, the more load we tend to put on the network. The solution to this problem is to add another (middle) tier. Our user interfaces on the client machines communicate with the middle tier and the middle tier communicates with the database server. By spreading the load out over three tiers, we reduce the network traffic. In the next two chapters, we'll discover how to create a 3-tier solution.

Suppliers

- SupplierID
- CompanyName
- ContactName
- ContactTitle
- Address
- City
- Region
- PostalCode
- Country
- Phone
- Fax
- HomePage

Products

- ProductID
- ProductName
- SupplierID
- CategoryID
- QuantityPerUnit
- UnitPrice
- UnitsInStock
- UnitsOnOrder
- ReorderLevel
- Discontinued

Categories

- CategoryID
- CategoryName
- Description
- Picture

Data Validation, Transactions and Error Trapping

This chapter brings together a number of further topics, which you will need to consider when designing your client-server system. These will help you ensure that your data conforms to the specifications required for your business, and does so with minimal network traffic. The topics covered here are:

➤ **Data Validation**: This is the process of ensuring that data entered into your tables conforms to your business rules. For example, you wouldn't want to allow a user to enter a date of birth value after today's date into a database holding people's details. If such a value were provided, you would want to alert the user of the error.

➤ **Transactions**: Transactions give the user the ability to execute a number of SQL statements as a single entity. If any one of the statements fails, the entire transaction fails. This can be critical to ensuring that data is not lost, especially for accounting systems where money is transferred from one account to another.

➤ **Error trapping**: While error trapping is usually fairly easy to incorporate into your project, it takes time and plenty of thought. Just forecasting all of the conditions that could occur is half the battle. Once you know what conditions to expect, you need to have a plan of action to handle the errors. This may include ignoring the error, writing the error to an error log or notifying the user.

Data Validation

As we have already discussed, data validation is performed to ensure that the data entered into your database conforms to your business specification. The list of possible rules is nearly endless. Some of the common validation criteria include:

➤ Values must be greater or less than a specific number
➤ Text must be a specific length or no more then x characters long

> ➤ Values cannot be null
> ➤ Text must be in upper or lower case
> ➤ Values must exist in another table
> ➤ Values must be one of several specific possibilities, such as M, F or U to record a person's gender
> ➤ Dates must be in a specific range or format
> ➤ If one field is populated, another must be as well
> ➤ If one field is populated, another field must not

The impact of trapping data that doesn't conform to your rules can be essential to a successful implementation. Remember, the data that goes into the database will eventually come back out. This may be in the form of a report, or displayed on a form. There's nothing more frustrating than seeing invalid data in a field (such as a value of 'L' in the gender code field).

Data validation can occur at one or more of the following three places:

> ➤ On the client
> ➤ On the server
> ➤ In the middle-tier objects

There's no absolute rule stipulating where to put this business logic. You may find that it's practical to place the logic on both the client and the server. There are benefits to each.

Placing the business logic on the client reduces network traffic because the data is validated before it is sent to the server. The down side of this is that updating your logic rules can be quite cumbersome. This should come as no surprise; recall the discussion on the benefits of a fat server vs. fat clients in Chapter 1.

Data Validation on the Server

When the business logic resides on the database server, the client sends a request to insert a new record or update or delete an existing record. The server receives this request and validates the data according to all validation criteria or **constraints** that have been placed on the table. If a constraint rule has been broken, the server will send an error notification back to the client. The client should then interpret the error message and display a useful message to the user. The user can then make changes to the data and attempt to re-send the request:

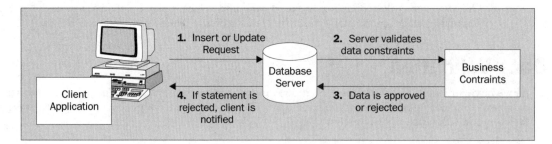

As the figure shows, this causes more network traffic and the server has to spend more time validating the data received. For this reason, you may choose to place the business logic on the client. Just remember that the greater the number of clients, the greater the number of upgrades that must be made each time your logic changes.

> Business logic does not necessarily equate to data validation. Validation such as ensuring all zip codes are entered as numbers and have no letters does not constitute a business rule. This type of validation should be placed on the client to minimize network traffic.

Exploring Constraints in SQL Server

Now that you understand how data is validated on the server, let's examine the types of constraints available in SQL Server and then we'll look at an existing constraint on the pubs database in SQL Server.

SQL Server supports five different types of constraint. These types restrict in different ways the possible values that the columns on which they are placed can take:

> **Primary Key**. Designates the constraint as a primary key. This causes the column(s) on which the constraint is placed to be the primary key for the table and creates a unique index for the column(s). There may be only one PRIMARY KEY per table and the value of the column(s) must be unique in the table.

> **Foreign Key**. Designates the constraint as a foreign key. Each entry in the column must have a corresponding entry in the column of the table to which the FK refers.

> **Unique**. Similar to a PRIMARY KEY, in that each entry in this column must have a unique value. However, there may be more than one UNIQUE constraint per table.

> **Check**. This is the usual type of constraint for data validation; it stipulates specific limits for the values of the entries in the column.

> **Default**. This constraint specifies the value that is to be inserted into the column if no other value is supplied.

We looked in detail at the primary keys, foreign keys, unique and default types of constraint in Chapter 6; in this chapter, we will be concentrating solely on the CHECK constraint - the others are concerned more with referential integrity than with data validation.

Constraints are typically created during the creation of a table; however, they can also be created with an ALTER TABLE SQL command and, in some RDBMSs such as Oracle, with a CREATE CONSTRAINT command. There are a number of methods for creating SQL Server tables and constraints. One of the most practical methods is to use scripts. A script is simply a text file containing one or more sets of SQL commands to be executed by SQL Server; scripts can be saved and then re-used at a later time. When minor changes need to be made to a table, or a new constraint needs to be added, the script can be modified and re-executed. SQL Server provides a wizard to generate scripts automatically, without writing any SQL statements ourselves.

Generating SQL Scripts

To see this in action, let's look at a script that recreates the `jobs` table on the `pubs` database, including any constraints. Open the SQL Server Enterprise Manager and navigate to the `jobs` table in the `pubs` database as shown. Right-click on the jobs table name and select **All Tasks | Generate SQL Scripts...** from the pop-up menu:

The **Generate SQL Scripts** dialog will appear. This dialog allows you to create a script to recreate the table specified. In this case, we'll use it to generate a script capable of recreating the `jobs` table:

The script builder is capable of creating scripts that include everything from the basic table definition to indexes, keys and dependencies. For now, we just want to generate the commands to drop the table if it already exists, to recreate the table and to recreate any constraints. To do this, ensure that the following check boxes are selected: Generate the CREATE <object> command for each object and Generate the DROP <object> command for each object on the Formatting tab, and Script PRIMARY Keys, FOREIGN Keys, Defaults and Check Constraints on the Options tab (in SQL Server 6.5, this option appears as Table Keys/DRI):

You may select more than these three options, but they are unnecessary at this point. We're more interested in seeing the script stripped down with just table constraints and the table definition. Once you have made your choices, click on the OK button:

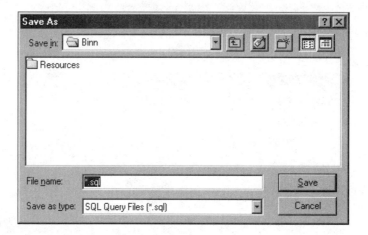

You will be prompted to save your script. You may place it in the default directory or another directory if you prefer. Remember the location for later use. When the script has been created, it may be viewed and modified in any text editor such as Word or Notepad. Specify the filename `jobs.sql` and click on the Save button. After some processing you should receive a message indicating that the script was successfully created:

Viewing the Script

Now that we have our script generated, let's take a look at its contents. From the main menu, select Tools I SQL Server Query Analyzer. The following window opens:

This tool is designed to assist the creation and testing of SQL queries. This is an ideal tool to view your script because the script that you built is a SQL statement, but you may use Notepad to view the script if you prefer. Click on the **Load SQL Script** icon and select the `jobs` script from the **Open Query** dialog. The script will load into the **Query** window:

In the above image, there are four constraints: the `PRIMARY KEY` constraint on the `job_id` column, a `DEFAULT` constraint on the `job_desc` column, and `CHECK` constraints on the `max_lvl` and `min_lvl` columns. However, here we are interested only in the `CHECK` constraints; they are as follows:

> The `max_lvl` field must be less than or equal to 250
> The `min_lvl` field must be equal to or greater than 10

In SQL Server, each constraint must have a unique name. For this reason, it's preferable to use a naming convention which includes the type of constraint (such as `CK` for `CHECK`), the name of the table and the name of the field. We'll explore creating constraints in more detail a bit later.

> **Later in the chapter we'll explore how constraints are added to a table using the `CREATE TABLE` SQL command. But first, let's see how an application reacts to a constraint.**

Testing Constraints

Now that we know of these constraints, we can build an application to test their validity. Open Visual Basic and create a new standard executable project. Add a reference to the Microsoft ActiveX Data Objects 2.x Library and enter the following code in a command button or the `Form_Load` event:

311

```
Dim objConn As ADODB.Connection
Set objConn = New ADODB.Connection
objConn.ConnectionString = "Provider=SQLOLEDB.1;" & _
                           "Persist Security Info=False;" & _
                           "User ID=sa;Initial Catalog=pubs"
objConn.Open
objConn.Execute "INSERT INTO jobs (job_desc,min_lvl, max_lvl)" & _
                "VALUES ('Programmer',0,210)"
```

Your connection string may differ from the above code, depending on the configuration of your database server and the version of SQL Server or other database you are using. If you have trouble connecting, use the Connection Wizard as outlined in Chapter 4 to create the connection string.

This code is no different to any other you have seen to this point. The first section establishes a connection to the pubs database and the second section executes a SQL INSERT statement. This INSERT statement has been designed with the intention of breaking the CK_jobs_min_lvl constraint. Notice that the value that corresponds to min_lvl is 0. This is an invalid value because the value passed must be greater than or equal to 10.

When you run the project, the following error dialog appears:

Microsoft Visual Basic

Run-time error '-2147217900 (80040e14)':

INSERT statement conflicted with COLUMN CHECK constraint
'CK__jobs__min_lvl__24927208'. The conflict occurred in database
'pubs', table 'jobs', column 'min_lvl'.

Continue   End   Debug   Help

This error has a number and description, just like any other error. This allows you to trap any anticipated constraint errors such as this one.

Depending on the database server, you may have the capability of returning specific text to the user (such as an error description) when a constraint is violated.

Exploring Constraints in Microsoft Access

Microsoft Access also allows you to set up constraints. To view the constraints in an Access database, open the table in Design View:

The following properties concern the constraints applicable to a given field:

> Validation Rule - the actual constraint

> Validation Text - the descriptive text passed to a user when a constraint is violated

In the image above (showing the Order Details table of the Nwind database), notice that the Quantity field has a constraint specifying that the value must be greater than zero. If this rule is broken, the user will receive the message in the validation text: Quantity must be greater than 0. These properties can also be changed in this screen.

Adding Validation Constraints with SQL

As we have seen, validation constraints are also known as CHECK constraints. A CHECK constraint allows us to compare the values that are about to be saved to a specific field in the table with rules applied to the table. The syntax for a CHECK constraint is similar to that for a primary key. As you recall, when we learned how to create primary keys in tables, we used the CONSTRAINT clause. We'll now use that same keyword to create a CHECK constraint. The syntax is:

```
CONSTRAINT Constraint_Name CHECK (Expression)
```

Constraint_Name is the name of the constraint and Expression is the formula which will be used to validate the data. Usually this will consist of the name of a field, an operator and a value against which the column's data is to be matched. This clause can be added to a CREATE TABLE or ALTER TABLE statement.

The following SQL statement is designed specifically for a SQL Server database. It creates a table titled Employer with three fields:

> emp_id - a small integer acting as a unique identifier

> emp_name - a varchar (max 50 characters long) used to store a name

> ➢ emp_commission - a tinyint used to store commission percentages on sales

The last line of the SQL statement creates a constraint titled CK_Commission. The word CHECK identifies the constraint as a CHECK constraint. The validation criterion is then placed inside parentheses. In this example, we ensure that all commission payoffs are less than or equal to 25 percent:

```
CREATE TABLE Employer(
    emp_id smallint IDENTITY (1, 1) NOT NULL,
    emp_name varchar (50) NOT NULL,
    emp_commission tinyint NOT NULL,
CONSTRAINT CK_Commission CHECK (emp_commission <= 25))
```

The following code is another example of a CHECK constraint. As you can see, many of the operators you learned when we first covered SQL are valid. This example applies a CHECK constraint to the emp_name field. Its purpose is to ensure that all names entered begin with the letters se. While this has little practical application, it nicely illustrates the use of the keyword LIKE and % as a wildcard:

```
CREATE TABLE employer1(
    emp_id smallint IDENTITY (1, 1) NOT NULL,
    emp_name varchar (50) NOT NULL,
    emp_commission tinyint NOT NULL,
CONSTRAINT CK_Name CHECK (emp_name LIKE 'se%'))
```

Try running these SQL statements, then enter data that breaks the rules. You should receive an error message with details about which constraint was violated:

When a field has been identified as an automatically generated field (such as using IDENTITY), you should NOT attempt to populate it. The RDBMS is responsible for ensuring that a unique value is stored in the field, and you may disrupt the integrity of the field's unique values.

Data Validation at the Application Level

Data validation can take place at the client level in a number of ways. As I'm sure you have discovered with Visual Basic, there is usually more than one way to accomplish any given task. Data validation is no exception. However, there are two basic methods for performing client-side data validation. The first is to validate data whenever the user attempts to update the database; the second is to perform the validation as the user types the data. To demonstrate these two methods, we will revert back to our sample Address application from Chapter 4. As you recall, the application connected to a table that stored names and addresses:

We'll implement field validation in the following ways:

➤ Ensure the last and first name fields are not blank

➤ Ensure the zip code does not include any letters (A-Z)

Let's begin with the name fields. To implement this restriction, we need to ensure that the first and last name text boxes are both populated with data. The question is when we should test this condition. In this case, we cannot validate the data as it is typed, because we only want to check that there is *something* in the fields. We must therefore perform the validation when the user attempts to update the database. There are two possible points at which this might happen: when the Update button is pressed, and after the fields have been modified and the user attempts to move to a new record.

To begin, create a new function called `ValidateFields`. This function will return a Boolean value indicating whether either of the two name fields breaks the validation rule. Inside this procedure, we check the contents of the two text boxes. If either is blank, we return a message box to the user and then return `False` to the calling procedure:

```
Public Function ValidateFields() As Boolean

    If Trim(txtField(0).Text) = "" Then
        MsgBox "Last Name field cannot be empty"
        Exit Function
    End If

    If Trim(txtField(1).Text) = "" Then
        MsgBox "First Name field cannot be empty"
        Exit Function
    End If

    ValidateFields = True

End Function
```

We'll first call the new procedure from the <u>Update</u> command button. The code that updates the database table is embedded inside an `If` statement that evaluates the result of `ValidateFields`. This causes the record to update only if the function returns true; otherwise, the remaining code is ignored. Apply the following changes to the `cmdUpdate_Click` event procedure:

```
Private Sub cmdUpdate_Click()
    On Error GoTo UpdateErr
    If ValidateFields = True Then
        With Adodc1
            myBookMark = .Recordset.Bookmark
            .Recordset.Update
            .Refresh
            If myBookMark > 0 Then
                .Recordset.Bookmark = myBookMark
            Else
                .Recordset.MoveLast
            End If
        End With
        cmdAdd.Caption = "&Add"
        SetVisible True
    End If
    Exit Sub

UpdateErr:
        MsgBox Err.Description
End Sub
```

The other point in our code where we want to call our `ValidateFields` procedure is when the user is attempting to navigate from the current record. The goal is to prevent the record from being saved if the fields are empty. For this, we need to trigger an event that indicates we're about to change the record. The appropriate event we need is `Adodc1_WillChangeRecord`. This event only fires when a change has been made to the current record and it is about to be saved due to navigation. In the code for this event, we call the `ValidateFields` function again. If the function returns false, then we set the `adStatus` property to `adStatusCancel`, which cancels the record change:

```
Private Sub Adodc1_WillChangeRecord(ByVal adReason As _
                ADODB.EventReasonEnum, ByVal cRecords As Long, _
                adStatus As ADODB.EventStatusEnum, _
                ByVal pRecordset As ADODB.Recordset)

    If ValidateFields = False Then
        adStatus = adStatusCancel
    End If

End Sub
```

The second validation task is to prevent letters from being entered in the zip code text box (although in some countries, letters are used in zip codes, so this validation rule is geographically specific). Since we know which specific characters can be entered into this field, we can perform validation as the keys are pressed, and ignore any 'illegal' characters (such as letters) the user attempts to enter. To restrict letters from being entered, we can capture the KeyPress event of the zip code text box and reject any letters passed. Because we have several boxes with the same name, we need to ensure this logic only applies to the zip code box (the text bound to the "ZIP" field). To implement this, we simply check the DataField property of the text box. If this is not set to "ZIP", no validation is required. The KeyPress event takes an argument KeyAscii which returns the ASCII value corresponding to the key pressed. The character value is pulled from this ASCII value with the Chr$ function; this is then evaluated to check whether it is a number or not. If the value is not numeric, the KeyAscii value is set to 0, which prevents any text from being entered.

```
Private Sub txtField_KeyPress(Index As Integer, KeyAscii As Integer)
    If UCase(txtField.Item(Index).DataField) = "ZIP" Then
        If Not IsNumeric(Chr$(KeyAscii)) Then
            KeyAscii = 0
        End If
    End If
End Sub
```

> **Another method to achieve the same result is to compare the** KeyAscii
> **value with the ASCII values of the numeric characters (48-57).**

Test the new code. As you can see, client-side validation is essentially quite easy. You simply need to know where to place your code; the rest is simple Visual Basic coding logic.

What Are Transactions?

One of the important concepts you must understand as a client-server developer is that of **transactions**. Transactions consist of one or more SQL statements that are processed together as a single unit of work. If any one of those SQL statements fails, the entire batch of statements fails. When you understand this, you might wonder why you would want to do this.

The primary reason for using transactions is to avoid the loss of data integrity; that is, to ensure that no discrepancies occur in our data (for example, due to a systems failure). To illustrate this more clearly, let's walk through a scenario. Let's assume that we have two accounts in XYZ Bank, called Checking and Savings. If we wanted to move $500 from one account to the other, it would involve four steps:

1. Request a deduction from the Checking account.

2. Wait for a response that the action completed successfully.

3. Request that our Savings account be credited.

4. Wait for a response indicating that the action completed successfully.

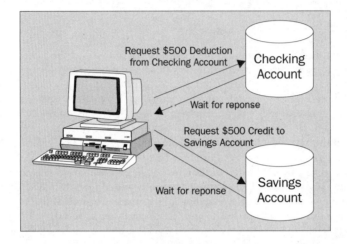

Now, let's assume that when we requested that the Savings account be credited, an error was returned. We're now left in a situation where $500 has been deducted from the Checking account, but not placed in the Savings account. This discrepancy needs to be accounted for. There are a number of ways to handle this. If you don't know about transactions, one solution might include re-deposit of $500 to the Savings account and alerting the user that an error occurred. The problem with this is that it causes confusion as to where the initial $500 went to and where the second $500 came from, not to mention the additional network and server traffic.

The optimal solution is to use a transaction. Transactions allow you to mark the beginning of a transaction. Then the transaction is either **committed** (that is, all the operations within the transaction are confirmed and actually performed) upon the successful completion of the final SQL statement or it is **rolled back** (that is, the transaction and all operations within it are aborted), which will cancel any SQL statements executed prior to the error. Let's walk through this same problem using transactions:

1. Mark the beginning of the transaction.

2. Request a deduction from the Checking account.

3. Wait for a response that the action has completed successfully.

4. Request that our Savings account is credited.

5. Wait for a response indicating that the action has completed successfully.

6. If all SQL statements succeed, commit the transaction and save changes. Otherwise, rollback the transaction and abort any changes made.

If the transaction does fail, the error will need to be logged with the transaction information. This will allow the user to track down the cause of the error and correct the situation. No data is lost and because the transaction is rolled back, no trace of the changes exists in the database.

Handling Transactions with ADO

ADO has three methods which are used to handle transactions:

> BeginTrans

> CommitTrans

> RollBackTrans

These three methods are applied to the `Connection` object at their appropriate times. We'll now build a sample application that uses these methods.

Create a new **Standard EXE** project, and add three command buttons to the form. Arrange the command buttons and change their captions to resemble the following image:

The three command buttons should be named as follows:

> `cmdConnect` - connects to the appropriate database

> `cmdUpdate` - creates a new table, populates it with data, updates the data, then commits the transaction

> `cmdCommit` - manually pushes changes through a table, then allows the user the ability to cancel all changes

We'll first build the code to connect to the `pubs` database. Begin by adding a reference to the Microsoft ActiveX Data Objects 2.x Library. To do this, select **Project | References** from Visual Basic's main menu. When the dialog opens locate the **Microsoft ActiveX Data Objects 2.0 Library**. If you have a newer version of ADO, the reference version may change. The following image illustrates version 2.0:

Then add the following code to the `General Declarations` section of your form. We will call our `Connection` object `objConn`, and our recordset object `objRec`, allowing us to return recordsets from the database:

```
Option Explicit
Dim objConn As ADODB.Connection
Dim objRec As ADODB.Recordset
```

Next, add the code to your `cmdConnect` button. This will connect to the `pubs` database located in Microsoft SQL Server (you might of course need to alter the connection string to suit your own database setup):

```
Private Sub cmdConnect_Click()

    On Error GoTo Connection_Error

    Set objConn = New ADODB.Connection
    objConn.ConnectionString = "Provider=SQLOLEDB.1;" & _
                               "Persist Security Info=False;" & _
                               "User ID=sa;Initial Catalog=pubs"
    objConn.Open
    MsgBox "Connection successful!", , "Connect"

    Exit Sub

Connection_Error:
    MsgBox "Unable to connect:" & vbCrLf & Err.Description, , "Connect"

End Sub
```

The code for the `cmdUpdate` button is broken out into a number of functions. Initially, we DROP the `Employee_BK` table if it already exists. The reason for this is that if the table already exists, an error will be generated when we attempt to build it, unless we have first used the DROP TABLE statement. The line `On Error Resume Next` is added at the top of the DROP TABLE code. This is to handle the possibility that the table may not exist, generating an error when we attempt to DROP it.

After ensuring that we don't already have a table called `Employee_BK`, we create a table of that name. When we're sure we have our new table `Employee_BK`, we call the `BeginTrans` method of our newly established connection. This will mark the beginning point of our transaction. After this, we pass any errors to an error handler located at the bottom of the procedure. Any SQL statements after this point will be rolled back if an error should occur. Inside the error handler, we pass the user a message box with the reason for the error and rollback the transaction using `RollbackTrans`. Inside the transaction, we pass two SQL statements, which add all records from the `Employee` table and then modify any records with a `job_id` of 5. If all three statements succeed, we commit these three transactions using `CommitTrans`:

```
Private Sub cmdUpdate_Click()

    Dim strSQL As String

    objConn.CommandTimeout = 15

    ' DROP the table if it exists. We'll ignore any errors
    ' that might occur if the table doesn't exist
    On Error Resume Next
    strSQL = "DROP TABLE Employee_BK"
    objConn.Execute strSQL
```

```
        ' Create a backup table to work with
        strSQL = "CREATE TABLE Employee_BK " & _
                "(emp_id    empid          NOT NULL ," & _
                "fname      varchar (20)   NOT NULL , " & _
                "minit      char (1)       NULL ," & _
                "lname      varchar (30)   NOT NULL ," & _
                "job_id     smallint       NOT NULL ," & _
                "job_lvl    tinyint        NOT NULL ," & _
                "pub_id     char (4)       NOT NULL ," & _
                "hire_date  DateTime       NOT NULL)"
        objConn.Execute strSQL

        objConn.BeginTrans
        On Error GoTo Update_Error

        ' Populate it with backup data
        strSQL = "INSERT INTO Employee_BK " & _
                "SELECT * FROM Employee"
        objConn.Execute strSQL

        ' Update the new salary information
        strSQL = "UPDATE Employee_BK " & _
                "SET job_lvl = job_lvl + 3 " & _
                "WHERE job_id = 5"
        objConn.Execute strSQL

        MsgBox "Completed Successfully!" & vbCrLf & _
                "Committing Changes.", ,"Update"

        objConn.CommitTrans

        Exit Sub

Update_Error:

        MsgBox "Error occured - " & Err.Description & vbCrLf & _
                "Rolling Back the last transactions.", , "Update"

        objConn.RollbackTrans

    End Sub
```

Testing the Transactions

Run the application and click on the <u>C</u>onnect button. Once you have connected, click on the <u>U</u>pdate button. If you have made no errors with your code, the following message should appear:

To confirm the successful execution further, apply a SELECT SQL statement to the Employee_BK table. You can use the SQL Server Query Analyzer from SQL Server's Enterprise Manager to view the results, making sure that you select pubs from the DB drop down.

Now, let's try to break the code. In the section that populates the table with data, create an error in your SQL statement by changing the table name from Employee_BK to Employee_B. This will generate an error, rolling back all SQL statements:

```
' Populate it with backup data
strSQL = "INSERT INTO Employee_B " & _
         "SELECT * FROM Employee"
objConn.Execute strSQL
```

When you re-run the project, the following error is returned:

```
Update                                    [X]

Error occured - Invalid object name 'Employee_B'.
Rolling Back the last transactions.

              [ OK ]
```

The last command button is designed to demonstrate how transactions can be used whilst you are manually stepping through your recordset. In this example, we set the objRec recordset's Locktype property to adLockOptimistic, which allows us to prevent other users from modifying the records to be updated after the Update method has been called. We call the BeginTrans method just as in the Update command button. Once the table is open, we call the MoveFirst method to set the current record to the first record in the recordset. The loop allows us to navigate through the records until we reach the end of the recordset. As we navigate through these records, we check the value of the job_id field for each record. If the job_id is 5, we reassign its value to 3 and increment intCounter. The final stage is to ask the user if s/he would like to commit or rollback the changes:

```
Private Sub cmdCommit_Click()
    Dim strSQL As String
    Dim intRetval As Integer
    Set objRec = New ADODB.Recordset
    Dim intCounter As Integer

    objRec.LockType = adLockOptimistic

    objConn.CommandTimeout = 15
    objConn.BeginTrans

    On Error GoTo Update_Error

    ' Navigate through all Employees and count affected records

    objRec.Open "Employee_BK", objConn, , , adCmdTable
    objRec.MoveFirst

Do Until objRec.EOF
    ' Get the Job code & update
    If objRec("job_id") = "5" Then
        objRec("job_id") = "3"
        intCounter = intCounter + 1
    End If
```

```
        'Move to the next record
        objRec.MoveNext
    Loop

    ' Ask the user if the information is correct
    intRetval = MsgBox(intCounter & " records are about to be modified." & _
              " Commit Changes? ", vbQuestion + vbYesNo, "Commit Changes?")

    If intRetval = vbYes Then
        ' If so, commit the changes
        objConn.CommitTrans
    Else
        ' Otherwise, rollback the changes
        objConn.RollbackTrans
    End If

    Exit Sub

Update_Error:

    MsgBox "Error occured - " & Err.Description & vbCrLf & _
          "Rolling back the last transactions."

    objConn.RollbackTrans

End Sub
```

Run the project and click on the <u>C</u>onnect button followed by the C<u>o</u>mmit button. The following message should appear:

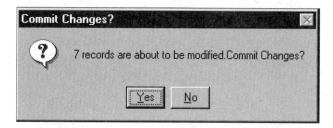

Click on <u>Y</u>es. You can confirm that the changes worked by running the code again. This time there should be 0 records in the count. This is because all records with a `job_id` of 5 have already been changed to a 3 the first time you ran the project:

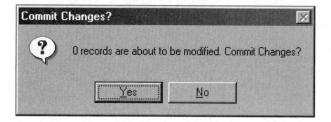

If you want to continue with more testing, re-run the project and click on the <u>U</u>pdate button. This creates a fresh copy of the table.

Capturing ADO and OLE DB Provider Errors

Capturing errors will be one of the most important chores of developing your application. As I mentioned at the beginning of this chapter, it's a long and time-consuming task to consider all of the possible errors that can be encountered. For this reason, you should attempt to log these as you think of them, right from the beginning stages of your project. Many of the errors you encounter will become apparent during your testing phase. However, a number of them may not be apparent until your product is released and live data is filtered through it.

The next project we build will work specifically with errors. We'll attempt to apply a number of invalid commands to a database, and handle the error messages that are returned.

Create a new project and add one new command button to the form. Name the button cmdError. We want to create an array of command buttons, so copy the command button and paste it five more times. Set the properties of the form and the command buttons as described in the following table:

The Form for the Error Handler

Object	Property	Value
Form	Name	frmError
	Caption	Errors
Command Button	Name	cmdError
	Index	0
	Caption	Invalid Table
Command Button	Name	cmdError
	Index	1
	Caption	Invalid Field
Command Button	Name	cmdError
	Index	2
	Caption	Locked Record
Command Button	Name	cmdError
	Index	3
	Caption	Deleted Record
Command Button	Name	cmdError
	Index	4
	Caption	No Current Record
Command Button	Name	cmdError
	Index	5
	Caption	Wrong Data Type

When finished, your form should look like this:

Add a reference to the Microsoft ActiveX Data Objects 2.x Library. Then declare a Connection and Recordset object in the General Declarations section. We'll also declare some constants to refer to error codes. This will make our code more readable than if we had used the actual values:

```
Option Explicit

Dim objConn As ADODB.Connection
Dim objRec As ADODB.Recordset

Const INVALID_TABLE = -2147217865
Const INVALID_FIELD = 3265
Const TABLE_LOCKED = 3251
Const DELETED_RECORD = -2147217885
Const NO_CURRENT_RECORD = 3219
Const WRONG_DATA_TYPE = -2147352571
```

For simplicity, we'll connect to the database when the form loads:

```
Private Sub Form_Load()

    Set objConn = New ADODB.Connection
    objConn.ConnectionString = "Provider=SQLOLEDB.1;" & _
                               "Persist Security Info=False;" & _
                               "User ID=sa;Initial Catalog=pubs"
    objConn.Open

End Sub
```

The Code for the Error Handler

When each of the command buttons is clicked, the Index value is passed with it. Each command button has a specific task associated with it. We have purposely created errors for each. Some have invalid table and field names, while others have errors such as the record being locked. Regardless of the case, the error is passed to an error handler at the bottom of the procedure. The error handler queries the error for its number (using the constants we defined earlier in place of the actual values of the error codes) and handles it by calling another procedure called ErrorLog. This procedure presents a message to the user and writes an entry describing the error to a log file. It is designed to receive one argument, a customized (user-friendly) error message:

```
Private Sub cmdError_Click(Index As Integer)

    Set objRec = New ADODB.Recordset

    On Error GoTo errHandler

    Select Case Index

        Case 0
            ' Error caused by invalid Table Name
            objRec.Open "FakeTableName", objConn, , , adCmdTable
            MsgBox "This line of code is called after calling 'Resume Next'"

        Case 1
            ' Error caused by invalid Field Name
            objRec.Open "Employee", objConn, , , adCmdTable
            MsgBox objRec("InvalidField")

        Case 2
            ' Error caused by failing to unlock the table
            objRec.Open "Employee", objConn, , , adCmdTable
            objRec.Delete adAffectCurrent

        Case 3
            ' Error caused by calling a field of a deleted record
            objRec.LockType = adLockOptimistic
            objRec.Open "Employee_BK", objConn, , , adCmdTable
            objRec.Delete adAffectCurrent
            MsgBox rs("emp_id")

        Case 4
            ' Error caused by navigating beyond the BOF marker
            objRec.Open "Employee", objConn, , , adCmdTable
            objRec.MoveFirst
            objRec.MovePrevious

        Case 5
            ' Error caused by entering data of the wrong type
            objRec.LockType = adLockOptimistic
            objRec.Open "Employee_BK", objConn, , , adCmdTable
            objRec("job_id") = "EM"

    End Select
    Exit Sub


NextLine:
    MsgBox "This line is only called after calling 'Resume NextLine'"
    Exit Sub

errHandler:

    Select Case Err.Number

        Case INVALID_TABLE        ' Table not found
            ErrorLog "Table not found in database! "
            Resume Next

        Case INVALID_FIELD        ' Field not found
            ErrorLog "Field not found in table! "
            Resume NextLine
```

```
        Case TABLE_LOCKED         ' Table Locked
            ErrorLog Err.Description & " Use Optimistic Locking!"

        Case DELETED_RECORD        ' Deleted Record
            ErrorLog "The requested field of the current record" & _
                    " has been deleted!"

        Case NO_CURRENT_RECORD     ' No Current Record
            ErrorLog "There is no current record!"

        Case WRONG_DATA_TYPE        ' Wrong data type
            ErrorLog "You are attempting to enter a value that" & _
                    " is a different data type than declared in the DB."

        Case Else
            ErrorLog Err.Number & Err.Description

    End Select

End Sub
```

The code in the error handler above illustrates how we continue running the application after an error has been raised, using the Resume statement. The code uses the Resume statement in two different places, and with slightly different syntax. In the first case, we use the statement Resume Next, which tells the procedure to continue with the line of code immediately after the line of code that caused the error. The second occurrence is in the format Resume NextLine, which tells the program to continue the procedure at the marker specified - in this case NextLine.

Create a new procedure, and call it ErrorLog. It should be configured to receive one parameter, msg, which is a string. In this procedure, we'll open a file, and write the contents of msg to it. In addition, we throw a message box to the user with the same message.

> It's a good idea to place any error and audit log procedures in a module (or, better, in a class module). This allows any procedures in the project to use them. However, for simplicity's sake, we have kept the procedure in the form's code window.

```
Public Sub ErrorLog(strMsg As String)

    ' Retrieve a reference id for the file
    Dim intErrorLog As Integer
    intErrorLog = FreeFile

    ' Open the log for append
    Open App.Path & "\error.log" For Append As intErrorLog

    ' Print to the error log
    Print #intErrorLog, Now() & " : " & strMsg

    'Close the error log
    Close intErrorLog

    ' Let the user know about the error
    MsgBox "Error: " & strMsg

End Sub
```

This procedure opens a file called `error.log` in the same directory as the application, creating the file if it does not already exist. We are going to add data onto the end of this file, so we use the `For Append` keyword when we open it. We also assign a file handle to the file - a unique integer label that Windows uses to identify the file, and by which we can subsequently refer to it. This is held in the variable `intErrorLog`. These file handles are frequently preceded by the pound sign (#). We can assign a specific integer to our file handle, but a better solution is to use the `FreeFile` function. This returns the first integer value not currently in use as a file handle.

Having opened the file, we write to it the current date and time, which are returned by the `Now()` function, and the error message, which was passed into the procedure as the parameter `strMsg`. We then close the log file, and finally display the error message to the user in a message box.

To test the program, create a directory on the `C:\ProVB6DB` directory called `Chapter10` (if you have not already done so), and save your project here.

Run the project. Click on each of the buttons in turn to cause the appropriate error and view the message box with the respective error message:

Testing the Error Handler

Each of the errors is logged in the application's path with the name `error.log`. Open this file in Notepad to see how the project saved each error. Error logs can be a critical part of ensuring all data is processed correctly. However, remember that error logs are only useful if checked frequently and if the cause of each error is investigated.

As well as a failure in the middle of a transaction caused by a system error, other data errors are made possible by conflicts when multiple users are accessing the data concurrently. It's important to identify any possible scenarios where multiple users will be accessing your database and test accordingly. You'll save yourself a great deal of unnecessary re-compiles after the system has been distributed.

Summary

In this chapter, we covered data validation, transactions and error trapping. While some applications can survive without consideration of any of these, a professional application should utilize all three. The question is when to implement each of the three. It should come as no surprise that error trapping ought to be part of all applications. With regard to transactions, consider what data will be lost if your application should crash before completion. Finally, consider how great the possibility is that invalid data will reach your database tables. For a field that is drawn directly from a list box, little to no validation will be required. Fields that allow freeform entry will require more validation.

Suppliers

- SupplierID
- CompanyName
- ContactName
- ContactTitle
- Address
- City
- Region
- PostalCode
- Country
- Phone
- Fax
- HomePage

Products

- ProductID
- ProductName
- SupplierID
- CategoryID
- QuantityPerUnit
- UnitPrice
- UnitsInStock
- UnitsOnOrder
- ReorderLevel
- Discontinued

Categories

- CategoryID
- CategoryName
- Description
- Picture

6

An Introduction to 3-Tier Solutions

In Chapter 9, we created a 2-tier solution comprised of a client tier and a server tier. Our example worked well and we experienced no problems with it. But what happens when we add more functionality to our application and distribute it to 100 or even 1000 users? The network traffic would become very high, as every client machine would maintain a dialog with the database. The database itself would probably become a bottleneck as many users tried to access the same resources at the same time. And what happens if we need to update some business processing under the surface? Even though the interface that the users see might not change at all, every client application would have to be replaced by the upgraded one. Replacing ten or fifteen client applications wouldn't take long, but imagine if you had thousands to replace.

The solution to this problem is to take any business processing that does not directly produce what the users see on their screens and move it into a middle tier that sits between the client application and the database. The middle tier is then responsible for managing the network traffic and the load on the database. Furthermore, we can decide to have a separate, dedicated machine for our middle tier, which serves our several hundred users. Any updates that need to be made to our business processing can be done quickly and easily - on the middle tier machine only and not on the many client machines.

The next two chapters will cover examples of how to implement a 3-tier solution and roll it out effectively using **Microsoft Transaction Server** (**MTS**). This will encompass the basics of passing arguments or even recordset objects through the middle tier, which returns results to the client. To gain a better understanding of 3-tier solutions, we'll first build a simple project that calls four basic functions. The four basic functions that we will cover include retrieving a recordset, inserting a record, deleting a record and updating a record. In Chapter 13, we'll expand on this chapter to develop a client-server solution that encompasses real-world application needs.

The 3-Tier Architecture

In Chapter 1, we outlined the structure of a 3-tier system. Here, a layer called the middle tier plays a key role in communicating requests and results between the client application and the database server. The following image depicts the process of passing these requests and results:

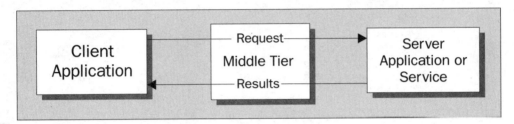

In this model, the middle tier can handle a great deal of business logic, relieving both the client and the server of that responsibility. Keeping the client as thin as possible means that even if you make radical changes to your application on the middle tier, the client tier probably won't need to be updated too, hence you'll need to provide fewer releases of the client application. An excellent example of a thin client is a web browser - you can view millions of completely different web pages without needing to replace your web browser (usually!). There are also benefits of keeping the logic off the database server. As your user base increases in size, the server will undoubtedly become more and more stressed. As it becomes stressed, it may become sluggish. You should therefore try to eliminate any additional work on the server.

Another benefit of using the 3-tier architecture is that we can pool connections. Literally, hundreds of clients can be filtered through a handful of connections on the server. This of course leads into the scalability factor. The larger the user base, the more connection pooling becomes a necessity. The 3-tier client-server model is capable of handling just a few connections, or hundreds of connections with minimal to no modifications to the code that supports it.

Components

The middle tier is comprised of **components**. A component, as we discussed in Chapter 1, is a *precompiled* piece of binary code. As Visual Basic programmers, we can create components from ActiveX EXE or ActiveX DLL projects, which we then compile into a DLL or EXE.

In this book, we will create components using the ActiveX DLL project type. The reason for this is that they can be created dynamically as needed and destroyed (or removed from memory) after their task has completed.

Objects and Classes

A component may consist of one or more **objects**, where an object is a code-based abstraction of a real-world entity or relationship. Every object has a **class** that defines it. A class is a blueprint or template from which the object is created. We can create many objects based on a single class. Every object created from that class would be an **instance** of the class.

That's a lot of jargon, let's look at an example.

For example, we might have a *Customer* class. We could use this class to create instances of the *Customer* class called *Jane Smith*, *Andrew Jones* and *James Green*. These instances are all objects. Every actual customer, such as Jane Smith, is represented by an object, but all of the objects are created from the same template, the *Customer* class.

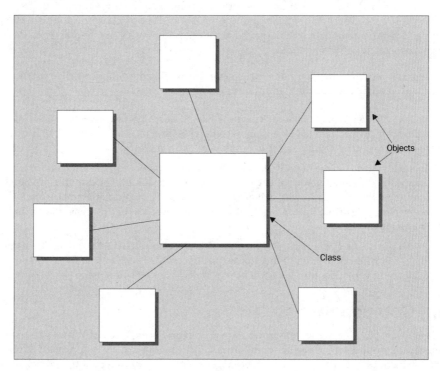

In Visual Basic, we use **class modules** to define classes. We can then create objects based on the class module, each object being an instance of the class.

Designing Components

Each class module can have many functions and procedures, just as any other module or form. The code that connects directly to the database will be maintained in the class module, and any client requesting data from the database will do so through the object created. The process might look like this:

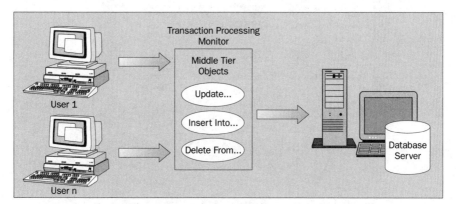

The above image should look familiar, as it was discussed in Chapter 1. As you recall, in a 3-tier solution, the clients typically execute function and procedure calls against objects in the middle tier. When called, a copy of the object is loaded into memory. The object establishes a connection to the database server, requesting the appropriate transaction, and returns the results to the requesting client. Once the transaction is complete, the object is removed from memory. One benefit associated with this model is the ability to centrally maintain a library of objects without updating numerous clients for minor enhancements or changes in business rules. Refer to Chapter 1 for the many other advantages associated with this model.

When designing components, you have the option of distributing functions over a number of objects. Here are a few thoughts to consider while designing your objects:

> Avoid placing too many functions inside a class. It's common to break out your classes by function type. For example, you may place all business rules and functions that deal with customers into one class and everything relating to employees into another.

> If one function is to make multiple calls against a database, keep the functions in a single object. This will reduce the number of database connections required. For example, if a single function is to validate that stock levels are adequate before entering an order, then place the order, and remove the stock from inventory; all of the respective pieces of this transaction should be included in a single object.

> Avoid building a single class per function. This can cause difficulty in maintaining components and it can be more difficult to monitor the productivity of each object. Don't forget that for each component you build, the client will need to reference that component.

Building Components

Visual Basic provides a very easy environment for creating components. When you open Visual Basic, the dialog appears for creating a new project or opening an existing project. Up to this point in the book, we have only built Standard Executable projects, so we selected the Standard EXE icon from the New tab. We're now interested in creating an ActiveX DLL, so select the icon as shown and click on the Open button:

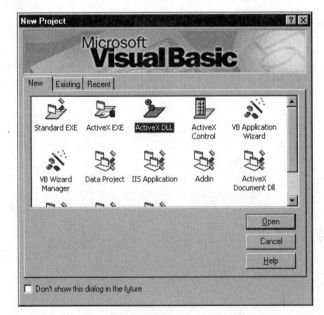

When the project opens, you'll notice that it contains a class module (Class1), rather than a form. As we discussed earlier, a class is a template that is used to create objects. The template defines the attributes (properties) and behavior (methods) of the instantiated objects:

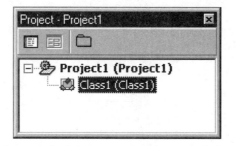

First of all, change the name of the project to Employee and the class to clsEmployee.

Next, create a new folder in the ProVB6DB directory called Chapter11. This project will be completed in two stages. We'll first create a 3-tier solution, and then we'll port it to Microsoft Transaction Server. To keep these two stages separate, create two more folders from the Chapter11 folder. Name the two folders Lab1 and Lab2. Finally, save both the class and the project in the Lab1 folder with their default names and extensions.

We'll be using ADO to connect to our database so we'll need to add a reference to ADO. As you have done in the past, select **References** from the **Project** menu, and locate the **Microsoft ActiveX Data Objects 2.x Library** reference. Select it and click on the **OK** button.

Connecting to SQL Server

The first thing that we will want to code is the connection to the database when the object is created and disconnection from the database before the object is destroyed. To assist in this task, open your code window for the clsEmployee class and notice the events associated with the class. To view these events, select **Class** from the left drop-down box and then click on the right drop down box:

```
Option Explicit

Private Sub Class_Initialize()

End Sub

Private Sub Class_Terminate()

End Sub
```

You should see two events, Initialize and Terminate. You can think of these two events as being equivalent to the events Load and Unload of a form. Initialize is executed after the object is instantiated and Terminate is executed before the object is destroyed. We'll add code to both of these event procedures.

First, declare a Connection object to be used for any functions added later. This will go in the General Declarations section of your code:

```
Option Explicit
Dim cnEmployee As ADODB.Connection
```

Now add code to the Class_Initialize event procedure. This code connects to the pubs database. We first create a new connection object (cnEmployee), then we set the connection string and finally we open the connection. Modify the connection string to accommodate your specific security information. Remember that if you are not yet comfortable editing a connection string, you can copy the code from a previous project, or use the ADO Data Control to build the connection string for you.

```
Private Sub Class_Initialize()

    Set cnEmployee = New ADODB.Connection
    cnEmployee.ConnectionString = "Provider=SQLOLEDB.1;" & _
                "Integrated Security=SSPI;Persist Security Info=False;" & _
                "Initial Catalog=PUBS"
    cnEmployee.Open

End Sub
```

In the Class_Terminate event, add the following code to close your database connection and destroy the connection object:

```
Private Sub Class_Terminate()

    cnEmployee.Close
    Set cnEmployee = Nothing

End Sub
```

It is not generally a good idea to keep a connection to the database open for the duration of an object's lifetime. To allow for scalability and multiple user access we should open the connection only when needed and close it immediately when no longer required. When we create our improved 3-tier solution in Chapter 13, we will look at how we can do this.

Coding the Four Functions

We're now ready to build the functions that will directly call the database. We'll build four functions:

> Add_Employee inserts a new employee into the employee table. This function will receive all required fields from the client, create an INSERT statement, and apply it to the connection object. A Boolean value will be returned to the client indicating if it was successful or not.

> Delete_Employee deletes a specific employee from the employee table. This function will receive a specific employee ID, and delete any record with an equivalent emp_id value. A Boolean value will be returned to the client indicating if it was successful or not.

> ➢ Update_Employee updates the fields of an employee in the employee table. This function will receive all relevant fields from the client that may be updated, create an UPDATE statement and then apply it against the connection string. A Boolean value will be returned to the client indicating if it was successful or not.

> ➢ Select_Employee selects employees from the employee table. This function will receive an optional value (emp_id), retrieve all employees from the employee table given the criteria selected in the optional parameter. This function returns a recordset with the results of the SELECT statement.

Add_Employee

Let's begin by creating a new function to support the employee insert. Enter the following code into the class' code window:

```
Public Function Add_Employee(emp_id As String, fname As String, _
                             minit As String, lname As String, _
                             job_id As Integer, job_lvl As Integer, _
                             pub_id As String) As Boolean

    Dim strSQL As String

    On Error GoTo BadInsert

    strSQL = "INSERT INTO employee (emp_id, fname, minit, lname, " & _
             "job_id, job_lvl, pub_id)"
    strSQL = strSQL & " VALUES"
    strSQL = strSQL & "('" & emp_id & "',"
    strSQL = strSQL & "'" & fname & "',"
    strSQL = strSQL & "'" & minit & "',"
    strSQL = strSQL & "'" & lname & "',"
    strSQL = strSQL & job_id & ","
    strSQL = strSQL & job_lvl & ","
    strSQL = strSQL & "'" & pub_id & "')"

    cnEmployee.Execute strSQL

    Add_Employee = True
    Exit Function

BadInsert:

    Debug.Print Err.Number & Err.Description
    Add_Employee = False
    Err.Clear
End Function
```

In the previous code, a SQL statement is created in strSQL by concatenating strings containing parts of the statement together. This means that we can create one long SQL statement, but keep the code readable within our development environment. This SQL INSERT statement is similar to the ones covered in Chapter 6. Here, we're inserting a record consisting of the fields in the employee table. Once the statement is built it is executed against the connection object. We have also included an error trap. Any errors that are a result of building or applying the SQL statement will be passed to BadInsert, where we return a False value to the calling client to indicate that an error has occurred. If no errors are detected, a True value is returned. We use Debug.Print to display any error codes to us during debugging.

You may want to return an integer value or a string to the client, indicating a specific error or success code. This would be in the place of our Boolean value.

Delete_Employee

We'll now create another function, called `Delete_Employee`. This function will receive one argument (`emp_id`) and return a Boolean value indicating whether the function call was successful. Add the following code:

```
Public Function Delete_Employee(emp_id As String) As Boolean

    Dim strSQL As String

    On Error GoTo BadDelete

    strSQL = "DELETE FROM employee"
    strSQL = strSQL & " WHERE emp_id = '"
    strSQL = strSQL & emp_id & "'"

    cnEmployee.Execute strSQL

    Delete_Employee = True
    Exit Function

BadDelete:

    Debug.Print Err.Number & Err.Description
    Delete_Employee = False
    Err.Clear

End Function
```

The logic behind the function is similar to the `Add_Employee` function. We create the SQL statement, apply it to the connection object, trap any errors and return a Boolean indicator to the client.

Update_Employee

Now add the following code to create the `Update_Employee` function:

```
Public Function Update_Employee(emp_id As String, fname As String, _
                                minit As String, lname As String, _
                                job_id As Integer, job_lvl As Integer, _
                                pub_id As String, hire_date As Date) _
                                As Boolean

    Dim strSQL As String

    On Error GoTo BadUpdate

    strSQL = "UPDATE employee SET "
    strSQL = strSQL & "fname = '" & fname & "',"
    strSQL = strSQL & "minit = '" & minit & "',"
    strSQL = strSQL & "lname = '" & lname & "',"
    strSQL = strSQL & "job_id = " & job_id & ","
    strSQL = strSQL & "job_lvl = " & job_lvl & ","
    strSQL = strSQL & "pub_id = '" & pub_id & "',"
```

```
    strSQL = strSQL & "hire_date = '" & hire_date & "' "
    strSQL = strSQL & "WHERE emp_id = '" & emp_id & "'"

    cnEmployee.Execute strSQL

    Update_Employee = True
    Exit Function

BadUpdate:

    Debug.Print Err.Number & Err.Description
    Update_Employee = False
    Err.Clear

End Function
```

When building the above SQL statement, you may choose to validate fields before concatenating them to the statement. You may even go as far as marking the fields that changed as 'dirty' when the Changed *event is triggered. This will help you identify any fields that need to be updated.*

Select_Employee

The final function will return a recordset to the calling client. The rules are the same, but you may choose to be creative when dealing with recordsets. Add the following code for the Select_Employee function:

```
Public Function Select_Employee(Optional emp_id As String) As Object

    Dim strSQL As String

    On Error GoTo BadSelect

    strSQL = "SELECT * FROM employee"

    If Trim("" & emp_id) <> "" Then
      strSQL = strSQL & " WHERE emp_id = '" & emp_id & "'"
    End If

    Set Select_Employee = cnEmployee.Execute(strSQL)

    Exit Function

BadSelect:

    Debug.Print Err.Number & Err.Description
    Select_Employee = Err
    Err.Clear

End Function
```

Select_Employee receives one optional argument (emp_id), and returns an object. The reason for returning an object, rather than a recordset is that an object is more flexible when it comes to allowing the client the ability to view and parse. Notice also that, if an error occurs, the error object can be returned to the client. We could have used this approach in all of our functions. Another possibility is to simply extract the error code and pass that as a string. In most of our functions, we simply return a True/False indicator.

Note that if `emp_id` is not present, all records in the table are returned. Otherwise, we narrow the result set to a specific record (the record with an employee ID equal to the argument passed). In our `If` statement, we concatenate a zero-length string (`" "`) to our argument. If `emp_id` is null, the concatenation converts it to a zero-length string, and you avoid getting an error.

We then execute the SQL statement and set the result directly to the object. Finally, we exit the function. There's no need to declare an intermediary recordset.

Testing Our Component

Before you test the component, ensure that the `Instancing` property of the class is set to `5 - MultiUse`. This allows multiple instances of the object to be instantiated by our client; an essential piece to scalability. For the most part, we'll keep the remaining properties of the class as they are defaulted. We'll explain many of these properties as we move through the remainder of the chapter.

To do some preliminary debugging, select Run | Start With Full Compile from the menu bar. This will run our ActiveX DLL project and check the code. Another dialog will appear that asks if you want to Wait for components to be created. Choose this option because we need our client project to instantiate the new component. Debug any errors that appear and save your code.

We're now done writing the code for our component. This component will be no good to us without a client to call it, so let's jump into the next step.

Building a Client Application to Call the Component

The next step in our solution will be to develop the client. The client will instantiate an object from the class that we just built and pass requests to it. Because we have not yet debugged the class properly, it's best to run both the ActiveX DLL project and the client project through Visual Basic simultaneously. Any errors that arise from either application will be identified immediately for you to fix, as Visual Basic's programming environment allows for this.

To create a new project with our existing DLL project open, select File | Add Project... from the main menu to open the Add Project dialog. Select Standard EXE and click on the Open button.

This will add the new project to our programming environment. Next, change the project's `Name` property to `Client` and the form's `Name` to `frmClient` to reflect the image below:

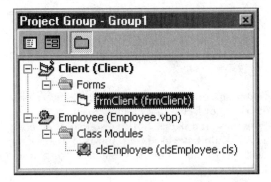

The following image depicts how our form will look after we have added all the necessary controls for the Graphical User Interface (GUI) of our client application:

Using the screenshot as a guide, place the following controls onto your form and set their properties according to this table:

> To use the ListView control, you'll first need to add it to the toolbox. To do this, add the *Microsoft Windows Common Controls 6.0 from the Components dialog.*

Object	Property	Value
Form	Caption	Simple 3-Tier Client-Server Example
ListView	Name	ListView1
	View	3 - lvwReport
	FullRowSelect	True
Command Button	Name	cmdExit
	Caption	E&xit
Command Button	Name	cmdInsert
	Caption	**INSERT New Item in Database**
Command Button	Name	cmdDelete
	Caption	**DELETE Item from Database**
Command Button	Name	cmdUpdate

Table Continued on Following Page

Object	Property	Value
	Caption	UPDATE Item in Database
Command Button	Name	cmdRefresh
	Caption	REFRESH List from Database
Command Button	Name	cmdClear
	Caption	&Clear
Text Box	Name	txtEmpID
	Text	{blank}
Text Box	Name	txtFName
	Text	{blank}
Text Box	Name	txtMI
	Text	{blank}
Text Box	Name	txtLName
	Text	{blank}
Text Box	Name	txtJobID
	Text	{blank}
Text Box	Name	txtJobLvl
	Text	{blank}
Text Box	Name	txtHireDate
	Text	{blank}
Text Box	Name	txtPubID
	Text	{blank}

Also, add labels to describe each of the fields displayed in the text boxes.

Configuring the ListView control

The ListView control will display the employee recordset in a grid format. We'll need to configure the ListView columns with headers and width definitions. This is partially for professional appearance, but it is also necessary so that we can populate the respective values when necessary.

To view the properties of the ListView, right-click on it and select Properties from the pop-up menu. The Property Pages dialog will appear. Click on the Column Headers tab and add the columns according to the following table. To add a new column, click on the Insert Column button, and enter the respective information:

Index	Text	Width
1	Employee ID	1100
2	Employee Name	1900
3	Job ID	650
4	Job Lvl	700
5	Hire Date	1000
6	Pub ID	1000

Adding the References

Now that our form is built, we'll need to add two programming references. The first reference will be to ADO. We'll need this reference to receive the object and populate a recordset. The second reference will be used to call the functions of the Employee.vbp project we created earlier.

As usual, select Project | References, and locate Employee and Microsoft ActiveX Data Objects 2.x Library as shown below. Note that Employee has automatically been added to the list of possible references because it is in the same project group as the Client project.

Adding the Code to Client.vbp

We're now ready to code our client project!

In the General Declarations section of frmClient, add the following code. These two lines of code declare objEmployee as an Employee.clsEmployee object, and rsEmployee as a Recordset object:

```
Option Explicit
Dim objEmployee As Employee.clsEmployee
Dim rsEmployee As ADODB.Recordset
```

The Form_Load Event Procedure

When the form loads, the first thing that we will want to do is instantiate the `objEmployee` object and populate the ListView control with the records that exist in the `employee` table. To do this we call a procedure (`Select_Data`), which will handle this task:

```
Private Sub Form_Load()

    Set objEmployee = New Employee.clsEmployee
    Select_Data

End Sub
```

The Select_Data Procedure

Now let's create the `Select_Data` procedure. `Select_Data` won't be accessed from anywhere outside the form, so we must set its scope as `Private`. Type in the following code:

```
Private Sub Select_Data()

    Dim itmNew As ListItem

    Set rsEmployee = New ADODB.Recordset
    Set rsEmployee = objEmployee.Select_Employee

    ListView1.ListItems.Clear

    If rsEmployee.EOF And rsEmployee.BOF Then
      Set rsEmployee = Nothing
      Exit Sub
    End If

    Do Until rsEmployee.EOF
      Set itmNew = ListView1.ListItems.Add _
                  (, rsEmployee("emp_id"), rsEmployee("emp_id"))
      itmNew.SubItems(1) = rsEmployee("lname") & ", " & rsEmployee("fname") _
                        & " " & rsEmployee("minit")
      itmNew.SubItems(2) = rsEmployee("job_id")
      itmNew.SubItems(3) = rsEmployee("job_lvl")
      itmNew.SubItems(4) = rsEmployee("hire_date")
      itmNew.SubItems(5) = rsEmployee("pub_id")

      rsEmployee.MoveNext

    Loop

    Set rsEmployee = Nothing

End Sub
```

This procedure creates a new `Recordset` object, `rsEmployee`, and then calls the `Select_Employee` function of the `objEmployee` object. Remember that this is one of the functions we created in the `Employee` project. The ListView control is then cleared and populated with the results of the recordset. To do this, we loop through the records until we reach the end of the file, adding new items to the ListView control.

Once the recordset has been extracted, we set the `rsEmployee` object to `Nothing`. This will remove it from memory.

The ListItem Object

Each `ListItem` object is part of a collection of objects called `ListItems`. By calling the `Add` method of the `ListItems` collection, we can add a new `ListItem` to the collection. The syntax of the `Add` method of the `ListItems` collection is as follows:

```
ListItems.Add(index, key, text, icon, smallIcon)
```

All the parameters within the parentheses are optional.

> *index* is an integer and specifies the position of the `ListItem`. We are expecting the `ListItem`'s index value to change, as we will be adding and removing `ListItems`. Therefore, we leave this blank. The `ListItem` will just be added onto the end of the `ListItems` collection.

> *key* is a string and it must be unique. In our code, we just used the primary key of our recordset, `emp_id`.

> *text* is the string we want used in the first column of the ListView. In this case, we want to display `emp_id`.

> *icon* and *smallIcon* are both integers. These two parameters set the icon and small icon that is to be displayed if the ListView control's view is set to `lvwIcon` and `lvwSmallIcon` respectively. We set our ListView's `View` property to `lvwReport`, so we have left these parameters empty.

The cmdRefresh_Click Event Procedure

The `cmdRefresh` button refreshes the results at any requested time. Because we have already built the `Select_Data` procedure, we simply need to call it from the `cmdRefresh_Click` event procedure:

```
Private Sub cmdRefresh_Click()

    Select_Data

End Sub
```

The cmdDelete_Click Event Procedure

The `cmdDelete` button's job is to identify the employee ID from the `txtEmpID` text box and pass it to the `Delete_Employee` function. The Boolean result is returned to `blnRetval`. If `blnRetval` is false, a message box is returned to the user. Finally, the ListView control is updated by calling the `Select_Data` procedure:

```
Private Sub cmdDelete_Click()

    Dim blnRetval As Boolean
    blnRetval = objEmployee.Delete_Employee(txtEmpId)

    If blnRetval = False Then MsgBox "Error deleting selected record!"

    Select_Data

End Sub
```

The cmdInsert_Click Event Procedure

The cmdInsert button works in a similar fashion to the cmdDelete button. When the button is clicked, the values located in the text boxes are passed to their respective fields in the Add Employee function. Again, the ListView is updated by calling the Select_Data procedure:

```
Private Sub cmdInsert_Click()

    Dim blnRetval As Boolean
    blnRetval = objEmployee.Add_Employee(txtEmpId, txtFname, txtMI, _
            txtLName, txtJobID, txtJobLvl, txtPubId)

    If blnRetval = False Then MsgBox "Error entering record!"

    Select_Data

End Sub
```

The cmdUpdate_Click Event Procedure

The cmdUpdate button calls the Update_Employee function. Update_Employee is similar to Add_Employee with the exception that it requires a value for the hire_date field. By default, the hire_date field is populated with the system date and time. Here, you can modify it to any valid date:

```
Private Sub cmdUpdate_Click()

    Dim blnRetval As Boolean
    blnRetval = objEmployee.Update_Employee(txtEmpId, txtFname, txtMI, _
            txtLName, txtJobID, txtJobLvl, txtPubId, txtHireDate)

    If blnRetval = False Then MsgBox "Error updating record!"

    Select_Data

End Sub
```

The ListView1_Click Event Procedure

When the user clicks on the ListView control, our job is to populate the fields of the recordset into their appropriate text boxes. Add the following code to the ListView1_Click event procedure. This code is similar to the Select_Data procedure. In this event procedure, we will pass the emp_id of the selected item to the Select_Employee procedure. This is a benefit of the ListView control. It maintains and exposes the Key of any item in its list. In this example, we want the Key of the item that has been clicked, so we call for ListView1.SelectedItem.Key. The Key is passed to the Select_Employee. We don't need to loop through the recordset, because the Key will be a unique key in the table; the first record should be the one we want:

```
Private Sub ListView1_Click()

    On Error GoTo SelectError:

    Set rsEmployee = New ADODB.Recordset
    Set rsEmployee = objEmployee.Select_Employee(ListView1.SelectedItem.Key)

    If rsEmployee.EOF And rsEmployee.BOF Then
        Set rsEmployee = Nothing
        Exit Sub
    End If

    txtEmpId = rsEmployee("emp_id")
    txtFname = rsEmployee("fname")
    txtMI = rsEmployee("minit")
    txtLName = rsEmployee("lname")
    txtJobID = rsEmployee("job_id")
    txtJobLvl = rsEmployee("job_lvl")
    txtPubId = rsEmployee("pub_id")
    txtHireDate = rsEmployee("hire_date")

    Set rsEmployee = Nothing

    Exit Sub

SelectError:

    MsgBox Err.Number & Err.Description
    Err.Clear

End Sub
```

The cmdClear_Click Event Procedure

Next, add code to the cmdClear_Click event procedure. This will clear the contents of each of the text boxes:

```
Private Sub cmdClear_Click()

    txtEmpID = ""
    txtFName = ""
    txtMI = ""
    txtLName = ""
    txtJobID = ""
    txtJobLvl = ""
    txtPubID = ""
    txtHireDate = ""

End Sub
```

The cmdExit_Click Event Procedure

Finally, add the following code to the cmdExit_Click event procedure to close the project:

```
Private Sub cmdExit_Click()

    Set objEmployee = Nothing
    Unload Me

End Sub
```

Testing the 3-Tier Client-Server Solution

We have now completed building the `Client` project, so save it.

In the Project Explorer, right-click on **Client.vbp** and select **Set as Start Up**. This tells Visual Basic that you want to use the `Client.vbp` as your startup project. `Client.vbp` will be the first project to run and it will instantiate the object in `Employee.vbp`.

Now run the project group. The `Client` project will run and display `frmClient`. The `Employee` project will also automatically run, so you can debug both at once. When you run your project, the form should open with a list of all employees in the `employee` table.

Click on one of the employees to populate the text boxes with the appropriate data:

Click on the **Clear** button to clear all of the text boxes, then enter the following values into the text boxes and click on the INSERT New Item in Database button:

Text Box	Value
Emp ID	JLS23245M
First Name	John
MI	L
Last Name	Smith
Job ID	10
Job Level	80
Hire Date	{blank}
Pub ID	0877

Study the ListView control to ensure the item was added.

Select the new record from the ListView control. This should populate the text boxes with all relevant data, including the `hire_date`.

Change the last name to Stone and click on the UPDATE button. View the results in the ListView control.

> *Note that this only works if your Regional Settings are set to English (United States). If you are working with dates in a format other than the American mm/dd/yy you should change the type declaration of `hire_date` in `Update_Employee` from `Date` to `String` and convert the data type of `hire_date` in `pubs` from `datetime` to `vchar`. To convert a data type in a SQL Server database, right-click on the table and select Design Table.*

Select the new record once more, and click on the DELETE button. This will remove the item from the `employee` table. The record should now be removed from the ListView box.

Compiling the 3-Tier Client-Server Solution

If the above testing worked properly, you're now ready to compile the two projects. First, compile the `Employee` project. Select the Employee project from the Project Explorer by selecting it, then select File | Make Employee.dll from the menu. `Employee.dll` will be registered automatically. Next, compile the `Client` project.

> **Should you ever need to register a DLL, select Run from the Start menu, and enter `regsvr32` followed by the path and name of the DLL. Click on OK and you should receive a message indicating success or failure. This is primarily done when distributing the DLL to other machines without using an install utility. Install utilities will typically register them for you.**

Once you have compiled both projects, close Visual Basic and run `Client.exe`. Ensure that the application runs exactly the same as it did when run from Visual Basic.

Congratulations, you have completed your first 3-tier client-server solution. The next section will explain how to include a Transaction Processing monitor in the solution, then in Chapter 17 we'll discuss the specifics of deploying our applications to multiple machines.

Transactions

Before installing and implementing Microsoft Transaction Server, we should fully understand the reasons for using transactions. In earlier chapters, we briefly discussed how transactions maintain the integrity of our data. We illustrated the point with a banking example where money is transferred between two accounts. The process of this transaction might include removing $3000 from the first account, then adding the $3000 to the second account. If any error occurs during this process, the entire transaction should be rolled back, protecting from unbalanced accounts.

It's not only system errors that your processes must be protected against; you must also protect your data from multi-user anomalies. A database that you are working with may be shared by hundreds of concurrent users. This being the case, the odds are that eventually one user will step on another.

Let's look at an example that demonstrates this point:

Suppose we have a catalog sales company with twenty sales people. If two of those sales people each have a customer who wants to buy a widget, but only one is available in stock, only one customer will be able to order the widget. Both computers will show that one widget exists in stock, but even if both sales people click on the 'Send Order' button simultaneously, one order will be submitted first. The second order that makes it to the system will need to be rolled back. Rolling back the order involves returning the order status back to its previous state. In this case, it might involve removing the order from the order table and removing any stock items placed in the order.

ACID Properties

The above examples identify one anomaly that a transaction is designed to protect against, but there are others we should also mention. The properties that protect against such anomalies are identified as the ACID properties:

Atomicity

The updates should complete under a specific transaction and be committed and made durable, or the transaction should be aborted and changes should be rolled back to their previous state (as identified in the previous example).

Consistency

The transaction should be an accurate transformation of the system state. What this means is that the transaction must not break any business rules. In the catalog sales company example, the two customers cannot both have the last widget.

Isolation

Concurrent transactions should be restricted from seeing other transaction's state. This prevents inconsistencies in the application. In a nutshell, one client's transaction should refrain from interfering with another client's transaction.

Durability

The client should only be notified that a transaction has occurred, when an update has occurred to a resource. Additionally, if the system fails for some reason, after the notification has been sent, the changes should still be reflected when the system restarts.

Overview of Microsoft Transaction Server (MTS)

MTS is a component-based run-time environment that makes it easy for us as developers to develop and deploy scalable n-tier solutions. MTS hosts components contained in ActiveX DLLs, relieving the developer of complex tasks such as managing the creation and destruction of objects, transaction processing, and creating pools of resources (such as database connections). As we saw in Chapter 1, the efficient operation of these tasks becomes vital as we move to a 3-tier solution with large numbers of users.

Microsoft Transaction Server is capable of much more than just transaction processing, despite its name. Let's look now at a few of the benefits it provides.

Component Transaction Control

When a component is declared as an MTS component, MTS encapsulates it. This means that MTS will associate the components with a transaction until the transaction is committed or aborted. Further, while the component is encapsulated by MTS, the transaction will maintain the ACID properties listed above.

This capability is extremely useful when we are working with multiple databases. We can apply SQL in a transaction to multiple databases and not have to worry about what we should do if the transaction fails, because MTS takes on the responsibility of rolling back the transactions for us.

The concept remains the same; the goal is to ensure that no data is compromised during normal processing. The following diagram demonstrates this concept:

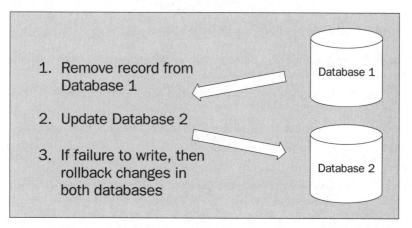

Here, a record is removed from a table in the database and written to file. If at any point the transaction should fail, such as while writing to file, the transaction is rolled back and logged. No data is lost and data integrity is maintained.

Monitoring

Microsoft Transaction Server provides an excellent tool for monitoring the current status of any transaction and statistics on transactions. To view the statistics, open the Microsoft Management Console, select My Compute from the tree view and click on Transaction Statistics. The right-hand pane should look as follows:

Some of the information available includes:

> **Current**: The total number of current connections to components and the maximum number of connections recorded at any one point.

> **Aggregate**: Tracks the number of transactions that have been Committed or Aborted (rolled back).

> **Response Times**: The number of milliseconds taken to return a query response.

> **MS DTC**: If MS DTC is started and when.

MS DTC is Microsoft Distributed Transaction Coordinator. This service allows for a highly scalable, distributed transaction model. MTS uses this service to monitor transactions executing against your databases. Not all databases support this service, so if you are using MTS with a database that doesn't, you may not be able to monitor the transactions that occur. The MS DT will be covered in Chapter 15.

Security

MTS also has built-in security functionality, although MTS security only works when MTS is running on a Windows NT machine instead of Windows 9x. This is because MTS works very closely with NT security.

Roles

Roles are simply lists of NT users and groups that have access to components. Only users that can be authenticated as one of the users in the list, or as a member of one of the groups, will be allowed permission to use the component. For example, we could have NT security groups called Administrators, Standard and Clerks, each of which contains lists of users who are part of that group. We could then assign the Clerks and Administrators groups, and a few individual users, to a role called "Customer Order Users".

Once users have been established, permissions can be assigned to components as a whole or to specific methods of the component. MTS will then validate each attempt to execute the methods called by any particular computer. In addition, roles can be validated programmatically to further enhance your security functionality.

It is quick and easy to add new users based on the network's configured pool of users, because MTS works so closely with Windows NT security. We don't need to worry about adding new users with passwords, and such.

As you can see in the following illustration, the CHARLESW user is a user in the Administrator group:

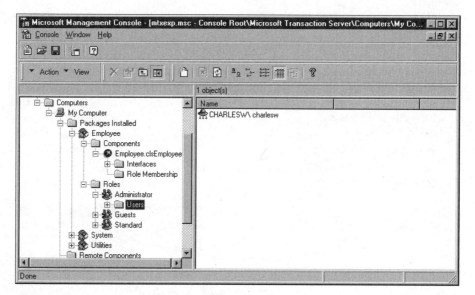

Administration

MTS provides an easy drag-and-drop interface to quickly configure and maintain your components. This includes wizards for adding new components, and incorporating security functions.

We can modify the properties of each component by right-clicking on it and selecting Properties. This brings up the components Properties dialog. The first tab, General, provides useful information about the component and allows us to enter a description for it:

The Transaction tab, allows us to indicate if the component is to be used in conjunction with a transaction, or not.

> ➤ **Requires a transaction** means that the component's objects will execute within a transaction. If an object is created from a client that does not have a transaction, one will be created automatically.
> ➤ **Requires a new transaction** means that the component's objects will execute within their own transactions. When an object is created, it will automatically have its own transaction, regardless of whether its client had one.
> ➤ **Supports transactions** means that the component's objects will execute within their client's transactions. If the client has no transaction, the object will also have no transaction.
> ➤ **Does not support transactions** means that the component's objects will not execute within a transaction.

I usually set this value to Supports transactions. This allows me the flexibility to change my component on the fly.

The Security tab allows us to check <u>E</u>nable authorization checking:

Object Brokering

MTS is also capable of acting as an **Object Request Broker** (**ORB**). This means that when a request is passed, MTS will check to see if a new instance of the component is required. If a new component is required, MTS will create the environment, instantiate the new object and return a reference to the client application. While the component is active, MTS maintains the state between the client and the component. MTS will then destroy the component object when the client no longer needs it.

MTS is capable of being configured to destroy objects after they have been idle for a period of time, such as three minutes. If the client then needs the object, MTS will re-instantiate a component, and handle the new request. This reduces the amount of memory required by the server. However, it requires the component to be re-instantiated, which could be a performance disadvantage.

One major advantage of using MTS as an ORB is that MTS handles the task of locating the object. The client therefore does not need to reference the component directly. When a request is passed, MTS will locate the object and instantiate it. If you want to physically re-locate your DLL, you can simply re-install the component. Remember that the major advantage of storing your business logic in a single location is that it's easy to maintain, and redistribute.

The Future: Object Pooling!

Future releases of MTS are to include the capability for object pooling. Object pooling is the ability for any number clients to share a finite number of component instances. You could for example, have twenty clients sharing five component objects, as shown below.

The following depicts the architecture without object pooling. Each client requires a connection to a business object, which in turn connects to the database:

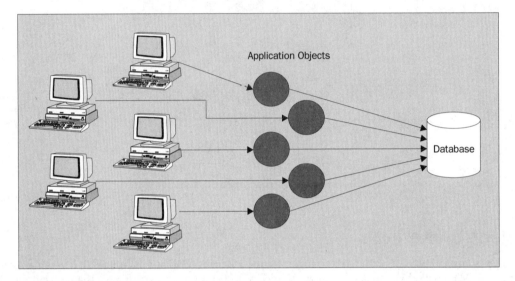

Using object pooling (as depicted in the image below), multiple clients can connect to a few business objects that work slightly harder. The result is increased performance with fewer objects loaded into memory, and fewer connections to the database:

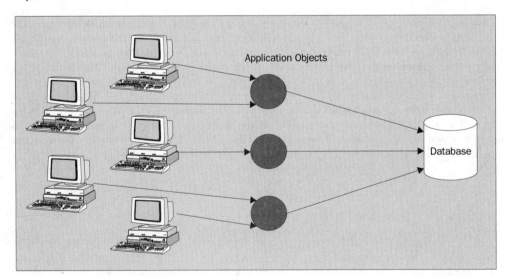

Modifying Employee.dll to Work with MTS

When migrating a solution to MTS, we don't need to modify the client application in the least bit. The client application cares very little whether it speaks to a component directly, or through MTS. The component on the other hand, will require some modification. The object (or server) must relinquish some control over to MTS, so that MTS can evaluate how many instances of the object already exist, and monitor the progress of each request.

To begin with, copy everything except `Employee.dll`, `Employee.exp` and `Employee.lib` from `C:\ProVB6DB\Lab1` folder, and paste it into the `Lab2` folder that you created at the beginning of this chapter. I have found it to be a good practice to create a backup of your work before moving on to the phase where you migrate your applications to MTS. From this point forward, we will work with the applications in the `Lab2` folder.

Open the `Employee.vbp` project. As you recall, this is the project that we compiled into the DLL.

Before we can write code to talk to MTS, we must reference it. To do this, select Project | References from the menu. Locate the Microsoft Transaction Server Type Library reference, select it and click on OK:

The MTSTransactionMode Property

Now view the properties of `clsEmployee` and change the `MTSTransactionMode` property to `2 - RequiresTransaction`.

The default is `0 - NotAnMTSObject`. `RequiresTransaction` indicates that the object should execute within the scope of a transaction. The options are:

Property Value	Description
NotAnMTSObject (0)	The component does not support MTS.
NoTransactions (1)	The component doe not run within a transaction.
RequiresTransaction (2)	The object creates a transaction if it does not already exist.
UsesTransaction (3)	This indicates that an object can support a transaction, if one exists. If a transaction does not already exist, a new transaction will not be created.
RequiresNewTransaction (4)	When a new object is created, a new transaction is automatically created.

Note that the possible values for the `MTSTransactionMode` property correspond to the options on the Transaction tab of the component's Properties dialog that we looked at earlier.

Setting the Employee Project Properties

From the menu, select Project | Employee Properties... This will expose the properties relating to the project as a whole. From the General tab, change the following properties:

> Check Unattended Execution. This will disable a number of error dialogs that may be presented during execution. These error dialogs could prevent your solution from continuous processing.

> ➤ Check Retained In Memory. This will turn off what's known as **Pessimistic Tear-Down**, which is a memory management method used by Visual Basic. Pessimistic Tear-Down identifies a set of rules defining when an object should be removed from memory. The benefit of specifying Retained In Memory is that your component does not have to take time to load itself into memory, improving performance. On the negative side, you can have an object that won't destroy itself when references are set to 0, this can generate errors in some applications. Always be careful when using Retained In Memory.

With the Properties dialog still open, click on the Component tab.

Version Compatibility

When you compile a component, Visual Basic creates unique identifiers called **GUIDs** (which stands for **Globally Unique Identifier**) for your classes. GUIDs are used as a key to retrieve information from the system registry; similar to the way that we use a primary key to access information in a database.

The three Version Compatibility options are:

No Compatibility

Setting No Compatibility means that every time you compile your component, a new set of GUIDs will be created. What this means is that every time you recompile the component you must also recompile the client that calls the component, otherwise it will try to call the old version. No Compatibility is best reserved for times when you want to make a clean break in your application.

Project Compatibility

Project Compatibility means that Visual Basic will generate GUIDs on the first compile and attempt to use those same GUIDs in any subsequent compiles. This setting is best when you are debugging. As the component's GUIDs will remain largely constant, the client programs won't lose their reference to the component.

Binary Compatibility

Once you've compiled your component, you should switch its compatibility to Binary Compatibility. If you make any changes that will break compatibility (for instance if you remove a method or property from an object) you will be warned.

Let's select the Binary Compatibility option Notice that Visual Basic automatically identifies the component with which any new versions of Employee.dll should be compatible.

The ObjectContext Object

When MTS provides a reference to object it is hosting, it also creates another object behind the scenes called the ObjectContext. It is sometimes known as the shadow object, because every object hosted by MTS has an ObjectContext. The ObjectContext allows MTS to provide transaction support and security features to our objects - without the ObjectContext object, MTS would not be able to provide the resource management that makes it so attractive as a host for our components.

To do this, we first need to instantiate an instance of an ObjectContext object and then call the GetObjectContext function.

The following code should be added to the beginning of each function that has direct control over the database:

```
Dim objContext As ObjectContext
Set objContext = GetObjectContext()
```

While processing each request, you may, or may not, encounter errors. Before destroying the object, you should notify MTS whether to accept or reject any changes. To do this, use one of the two lines of code:

> ➤ To accept the changes:

```
objContext.SetComplete
```

> ➤ To reject the changes:

```
objContext.SetAbort
```

> `SetComplete` is the equivalent of the `COMMIT` command in the database world, while `SetAbort` is equivalent to the `ROLLBACK` command.

Using `SetComplete` or `SetAbort` will generate an error should MTS be disabled. To avoid this, you can query the status of the `ObjectContext`, and avoid attempting to set the transaction as 'complete' or 'abort' if the MTS is disabled. To do this, use the following code:

```
If Not objContext Is Nothing Then
    ' Program is running under MTS control
    objContext.SetComplete
End If
```

After these modifications have been made, the four functions of the `Employee` object should look as follows:

The Add_Employee Function

```
Public Function Add_Employee(emp_id As String, fname As String, _
                             minit As String, lname As String, _
                             job_id As Integer, job_lvl As Integer, _
                             pub_id As String) As Boolean

    Dim strSQL As String

    Dim objContext As ObjectContext
    Set objContext = GetObjectContext()

    On Error GoTo BadInsert

strSQL = "INSERT INTO employee (emp_id, fname, minit, lname, " & _
            "job_id, job_lvl, pub_id)"
    strSQL = strSQL & " VALUES"
    strSQL = strSQL & "('" & emp_id & "',"
    strSQL = strSQL & "'" & fname & "',"
    strSQL = strSQL & "'" & minit & "',"
    strSQL = strSQL & "'" & lname & "',"
    strSQL = strSQL & job_id & ","
    strSQL = strSQL & job_lvl & ","
    strSQL = strSQL & "'" & pub_id & "')"

    cnEmployee.Execute strSQL

    Add_Employee = True

    If Not objContext Is Nothing Then
      objContext.SetComplete
    End If

    Exit Function

BadInsert:

    Debug.Print Err.Number & Err.Description

    Add_Employee = False
    Err.Clear
    If Not objContext Is Nothing Then
      objContext.SetAbort
    End If

End Function
```

The Delete_Employee Function

```
Public Function Delete_Employee(emp_id As String) As Boolean

    Dim strSQL As String

    Dim objContext As ObjectContext
    Set objContext = GetObjectContext()

    On Error GoTo BadDelete

    strSQL = "DELETE FROM employee"
    strSQL = strSQL & " WHERE emp_id = '"
    strSQL = strSQL & emp_id & "'"

    cnEmployee.Execute strSQL

    Delete_Employee = True

    If Not objContext Is Nothing Then
        objContext.SetComplete
    End If

    Exit Function

BadDelete:

    Debug.Print Err.Number & Err.Description
    Delete_Employee = False
    Err.Clear
    If Not objContext Is Nothing Then
        objContext.SetAbort
    End If

End Function
```

The Update_Employee Function

```
Public Function Update_Employee(emp_id As String, fname As String, _
                                minit As String, lname As String, _
                                job_id As Integer, job_lvl As Integer, _
                                pub_id As String, hire_date As Date) _
                                As Boolean

    Dim strSQL As String

    Dim objContext As ObjectContext
    Set objContext = GetObjectContext()

    On Error GoTo BadUpdate

    strSQL = "UPDATE employee SET "
    strSQL = strSQL & "fname = '" & fname & "',"
    strSQL = strSQL & "minit = '" & minit & "',"
    strSQL = strSQL & "lname = '" & lname & "',"
    strSQL = strSQL & "job_id = " & job_id & ","
    strSQL = strSQL & "job_lvl = " & job_lvl & ","
    strSQL = strSQL & "pub_id = '" & pub_id & "',"
    strSQL = strSQL & "hire_date = '" & hire_date & "' "
    strSQL = strSQL & "WHERE emp_id = '" & emp_id & "'"
```

```
    cnEmployee.Execute strSQL

    Update_Employee = True

    If Not objContext Is Nothing Then
        objContext.SetComplete
    End If

    Exit Function

BadUpdate:

    Debug.Print Err.Number & Err.Description
    Update_Employee = False
    Err.Clear

    If Not objContext Is Nothing Then
        objContext.SetAbort
    End If

End Function
```

> **You normally would not use a transaction with a SELECT statement, so the Select_Employee code will remain unchanged.**

In addition to `SetComplete` and `SetAbort` there are a handful of other methods that apply to `ObjectContext`:

Method	Description
CreateInstance	Instantiates another MTS object.
DisableCommit	Prevents committing of the transaction until the `EnableCommit` or `SetComplete` method is called.
EnableCommit	Allows the transaction to be committed.
IsCallerInRole	Indicates if the caller is in a specified security role.
IsInTransaction	Indicates whether an object is executing within a transaction.
IsSecurityEnabled	Indicates whether security is enabled or disabled.

Now recompile our DLL by selecting File | Make Employee.dll from the menu.

We now have an MTS enabled object! The next step is to install our component into MTS.

Installing Components into MTS

Now that we have modified our code to work with MTS, we need to install the object in MTS. This involves configuration of the Microsoft Management Console. Open the Management Console and navigate through the left-hand directory structure to locate My Computer. Expand it and the Packages Installed folder. You should see at least two packages installed at this point:

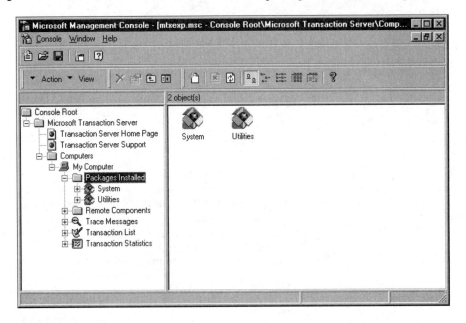

MTS Packages

Packages are containers for our components and their respective security roles. Each package contains a series of components based on functionality. You might place components that update the employee table in one package and components that update the authors table in another. This makes it much easier to distribute, administer and use multiple components.

Furthermore, each package runs in its own separate **process**. The advantage of this is that you can avoid sudden terminations of your entire system if one package fails. If, for example, we have an Employee package that fails, the Author package continues to run without interruption.

We can also avoid any unnecessary component loading or unloading, with components being very quickly created and destroyed. We can configure a package to stay loaded for a set period, even if there are no clients using it. The default period of time is three minutes.

Creating a New Package

To create a new package, right-click on the Packages Installed folder and select New | Package. The following dialog will appear. If you have saved a previous package, you can re-install it by selecting the first button (Install pre-built packages). Packages are highly portable, so if we wanted to move a package from one server to another, we could export it from the first PC and then install it to the new computer. As we have not built a package for our Employee component before, we must build a new package. Click on the Create an empty package button:

This dialog allows us to select a name for the new package. Enter Employee and click on the Next button:

This last dialog allows us to specify user information pertaining to the package (if you're using Windows 9x, you will not see this dialog, as this is not an available option). Had we set up security access for MTS in the NT User Manager, we might indicate this default user information here. We'll use the default, so leave the setting as it is and click on the Finish button. Our package is now installed.

Notice that two folders have been created under the Employee package, Components and Roles:

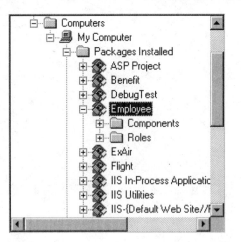

These two folders contain the following:

> The Components folder holds a listing of the classes contained in the DLL, shown as components in this package. *Note that this is a different usage of the term "component" to what we have been using, where component meant the compiled DLL, and not the classes inside the DLL.*

> The Roles folder contains the users or groups that are allowed to use this package.

Adding a Component to a Package

To add a new component to our new package, right-click on the Components folder and select New |
Component. The following dialog should appear:

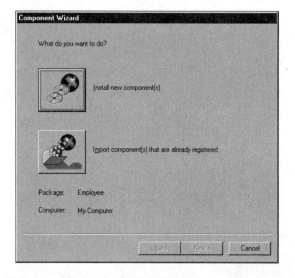

Again, we have two choices. We can choose to Install new component(s) or Import component(s)
that are already registered. Which option should we use? The answer is easy:

> ➢   If the component is already registered, we want to import the component. MTS doesn't need to
>   register the component, it simply needs to import it into a package.

> ➢   If the component has not been registered (maybe it was moved to the machine as a file), you need
>   to install it. The reason for this is that MTS will register the component for you, and then import it
>   into the package.

Our component should already be registered because we compiled it, so let's select Import
component(s) that are already registered.

You may have to wait several seconds while a list is built. When the list appears, locate Employee.clsEmployee. Select it and click on the Finish button.

Our component will now be installed and can be viewed in the right-hand pane:

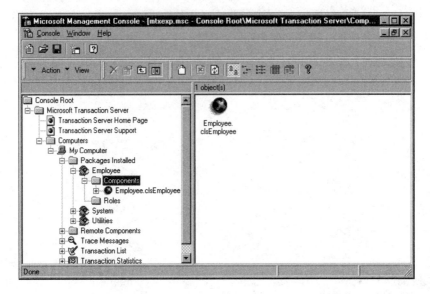

Next, we need to indicate that the component will always require a transaction. To do this, right-click on Employee.clsEmployee and select Properties. Click on the Transaction tab and select Requires a transaction.

Test the Solution

We're now ready to test our solution. Because the client application was not modified, we can still run the executable that we built earlier in this chapter. Review the steps for testing our application as we did earlier in this chapter. Notice that the component ball will turn as the component is being used. As you complete the testing process, try opening multiple instances of the client. This can be done from the same PC that you developed on, by running the Client.exe several times. View the statistics through MTS. Did any of the transactions fail? If so, do you know why?

Summary

In this chapter, we built a 3-tier solution using Visual Basic, ADO and MTS. By using 3-tier architecture, we gained scalability, processing speed and ease of maintenance. As we saw, implementing a 3-tier solution is not much different than implementing a 2-tier solution. Most of the code required is identical; such as establishing a connection, passing requests, then returning results.

Our 3-tier solution consisted of a client application, a component and SQL Server. Our component was designed to access a SQL Server database directly. The client application instantiated the component and passed requests through it.

After our 3-tier solution was tested, we added code to access `ObjectContext`, which is vital for all components hosted within MTS. Then, with little effort on our part, we installed our component into MTS. MTS offers us a tool for monitoring the status of objects and providing statistics on success rates.

In the next chapter, we will look at the various methods of passing data between objects and tiers, and see that some techniques are more efficient than others. This will enable us to create a practical 3-tier solution and continue to expand on our MTS skills in Chapter 13. Finally, in Chapter 17, we'll discuss how to deploy our 3-tier solution.

Suppliers
- SupplierID
- CompanyName
- ContactName
- ContactTitle
- Address
- City
- Region
- PostalCode
- Country
- Phone
- Fax
- HomePage

Products
- ProductID
- ProductName
- SupplierID
- CategoryID
- QuantityPerUnit
- UnitPrice
- UnitsInStock
- UnitsOnOrder
- ReorderLevel
- Discontinued

Categories
- CategoryID
- CategoryName
- Description
- Picture

6

Passing Data in N-Tier Applications

In Chapter 11, we passed data from our client to our server by passing multiple arguments to a method. This method was fine for a simple application with only one user, but it is not scalable to a larger system with more users. Every time our client application calls a method or property of the middle-tier object there is a speed hit. Multiply this speed hit over multiple calls to an object by many users and this becomes significant.

In this chapter, we're going to learn about five different methods of passing large amounts of data. We'll begin, however, by discussing two simple methods of passing data and why we should not use them in an n-tier solution.

How to Pass Data the Wrong Way

Passing data between objects in an n-tier solution is not quite as simple as passing data within a single object or 1-tier application. This reason for this is that our compiled components communicate with the client application and database via something called COM (Component Object Model).

> **COM is a standard mechanism by which objects and components communicate, independent of the language in which the components were created.**

All components created with Visual Basic are ActiveX components; this means that they use COM to communicate. COM's language independence is a great benefit; we can take the Employee.dll component we created in the last chapter and reference it from a Visual C++ client and it will work in exactly the same way.

An in-depth discussion of COM is beyond the scope of this book, but there are some important implications that effect the way that we should pass data between our objects and components, as we'll see in this chapter.

Calling Single Properties

From a high-level view, every time we access a property or call a method, COM needs to find the object that we want to talk to; and then it needs to find the property or method. Once COM has done all that work, it moves any parameter data over to the other process and calls the property or method. Once the call is done, COM has to move the results back over to our process and return the values.

Take the following code, for example:

```
Set objEmployee - New Employee.clsEmployee

With objEmployee
    .Emp_ID = "B-F26748M
    .FName = "Benton"
    .MInit = "-"
    .LName = "Fraser"
    .Job_ID = 12
    .Job_Lvl = 100
    .Pub_ID = "42"
End With
```

This code has four cross-process or cross-network calls (depending on whether Employee is on the same machine or across the network). The New call is remote and has overhead. Each of the seven property calls is also remote and has similar overhead. For seven properties, this might not be too bad; but suppose our object had fifty properties, or suppose that our program was calling these properties repeatedly in a loop. We'd soon find this performance unacceptable.

Passing Arguments to a Method

Passing multiple arguments to a method, rather than setting individual properties, is significantly faster and is the method we used in Chapter 11. For example:

```
Set objEmployee = New Employee.clsEmployee

Dim retval As Boolean
retval = oEmployee.Add_Employee(txtEmpId, txtFname, txtMI, txtLName, _
                                txtJobID, txtJobLvl, txtPubId)
```

Where Add_Employee is a method of the Employee object and expects the parameters:

- ➢ emp_id As String
- ➢ fname As String
- ➢ minit As String
- ➢ lname As String
- ➢ job_id As Integer
- ➢ job_lvl As Integer
- ➢ pub_id As String

However, because of the way that COM processes the arguments on this type of call, there is still far too much overhead with this method. We have to find another way.

Data Serialization

Many programmers have tried the techniques we've just seen and given up, saying that COM is too slow to be useful. This is completely untrue. As long as we design our applications using an architecture designed to work with it, COM provides perfectly acceptable performance.

When we're designing applications that will communicate across processes or across the network, we need to make every effort to minimize the number of calls between objects, because of COM's overhead. If possible, we should bring the number of calls down to one or two, with very few parameters on each call.

> **Instead of setting a series of parameters or making a method call with a list of parameters, we should try to design our communication to call a method with a single parameter, which contains all the data we need to send.**

There are five main approaches that we can take to move large amounts of data in a single method call:

- ➢ Directly passing user-defined types
- ➢ `Variant` arrays
- ➢ User-defined types with the `LSet` command
- ➢ ADO(R) `Recordset` with marshaling properties
- ➢ PropertyBag objects

All of these techniques rely on the **serializing** of the data in our objects. This means that we're collecting the data into a single unit that can be efficiently passed to another object and then pulled out for use by that object.

Directly Passing User-Defined Types

Visual Basic 6.0 provides us with the ability to pass **user-defined types** (UDTs) as parameters. This means we can easily pass structured data from one object to another object, whether the objects are in different Visual Basic projects, running in different processes or even running on different computers.

For instance, suppose we create a class named `clsPublishers` in an ActiveX DLL server:

```
Option Explicit

Public Type PublishersProps
    Pub_ID As String
    Pub_Name As String
    City As String
    State As String
    Country As String
End Type
```

373

```
Private mudtPubProps As PublishersProps

Public Property Let Pub_ID(ByVal Value As String)

    mudtPubProps.Pub_ID = Value

End Property

Public Property Get Pub_ID() As String

    Pub_ID = mudtPubProps.Pub_ID

End Property

Public Property Let Pub_Name(ByVal Value As String)

    mudtPubProps.Pub_Name - Value

End Property

Public Property Get Pub_Name() As String

    Pub_Name = mudtPubProps.Pub_Name

End Property

Public Property Let City(ByVal Value As String)

    mudtPubProps.City = Value

End Property

Public Property Get City() As String

    City = mudtPubProps.City

End Property

Public Property Let State(ByVal Value As String)

    mudtPubProps.State = Value

End Property

Public Property Get State() As String

    State = mudtPubProps.State

End Property

Public Property Let Country(ByVal Value As String)

    mudtPubProps.Country = Value

End Property

Public Property Get Country() As String

    Country = mudtPubProps.Country

End Property
```

```
Public Function GetData() As PublishersProps

    GetData = mudtPubProps

End Function
```

This class is very straightforward, it simply allows a client to set or retrieve a couple of property values. Notice that the UDT, `PublishersProps`, is declared as `Public`. This is important. Declaring it as `Public` makes the UDT available for use in declaring variables outside the object. The other interesting bit of code is the `GetData` function:

```
Public Function GetData() As PublishersProps

    GetData = mudtPubProps

End Function
```

Since the object's property data is stored in a variable based on a UDT, `mudtPubProps`, we can provide the entire group of property values to another object simply by allowing it to retrieve the UDT variable. All that the `GetData` function does is return the entire UDT variable and hence provide that functionality.

Now we can create another class named `clsClient`:

```
Option Explicit

Private mudtPubProps As PublishersProps

Public Sub PrintData(ByVal Publisher As clsPublishers)

    mudtPubProps = Publisher.GetData
    Debug.Print mudtPubProps.Pub_ID
    Debug.Print mudtPubProps.Pub_Name

End Sub
```

This class simply declares a variable based on the same UDT from our `clsPublishers`. Then we can retrieve the data in the `clsPublishers` object by using its `GetData` function. Once we've retrieved the data and stored it in a variable within our new class, we can use it as we wish. In this case, we've simply printed the values to the **Immediate** window, but we could do whatever is appropriate for our application.

This mechanism allows us to pass an object's data to any other code as a single entity. By serializing our object's data this way, we can efficiently pass the data between processes or even across the network.

Variant Arrays

The `Variant` data-type is the ultimate in flexibility. A `Variant` variable can contain virtually any value of any data-type - numeric, string, or even an object reference. As you can imagine, an *array* of `Variants` extends that flexibility so that a single array can contain a collection of values, each of a different data-type.

For instance, consider this code:

```
Dim vntSales(3) As Variant

vntSales(0) = "Hall Computer Books"
vntSales(1) = 39.99
vntSales(2) = "10/6/99"
vntSales(3) = 100
vntSales(4) = "Professional Visual Basic 6 Database Programming"
```

Inside the single array variable `vntSales` we've stored five different values, using four data types. We can then pass this entire array as a parameter to a procedure:

```
ShowValues vntSales
```

In a single call, we've passed the entire set of disparate values to a procedure. We could also pass this array to a method, because the methods of objects are actually procedures:

```
objMySales.ShowValues vntSales
```

The `ShowValues` procedure might look like this:

```
Public Sub ShowValues(Values() As Variant)

    Dim intCount As Integer

    For intCount = LBound(Values) To UBound(Values)
        Debug.Print Values(intCount)
    Next intCount

End Sub
```

This code just loops through the array from its lower bound to its upper bound, printing the values in the array to the Immediate window. This example illustrates how simple it is to get at the array data from within an object's method.

Despite the ease of use of `Variant` arrays, we must be very careful about how and when we use them to pass data. The `Variant` data type is highly inefficient compared to the basic data types, such as `String` or `Long` and using a `Variant` variable can be many times slower than a comparable variable with a basic data type.

Every time we go to use a `Variant` variable, Visual Basic needs to check and find out what kind of data it contains. If the data isn't of the right type then Visual Basic will try to convert it. All this adds up to a lot of overhead and our performance can suffer.

If our object's data is stored in a `Variant` array, we will incur this overhead every time we use any of our object's data from that array. As the code in most objects works with data a great deal, we risk creating objects with poor performance if we use `Variant` arrays.

The GetRows Method

In this book, our objects need data from a database. If we want to use a `Variant` array to send this data across the network, we need some way to get the data from the database into the array.

`Recordset` objects provide us with an easy way to copy the database data into a `Variant` array. This is done using the `GetRows` method of the `Recordset` object. The `GetRows` method simply copies the data from the `Recordset` object into a two-dimensional `Variant` array.

For example, the following code copies the entire result of a SQL query into a `Variant` array named `vntRecordset` and passes it to the `PrintData` method of the `objDisplay` object:

```
Dim rsRecordset As ADODB.Recordset
Dim cnConnection As ADODB.Connection
Dim strSQL As String
Dim intCount As Integer

Dim vntRecordset As Variant

Set cnConnection = New ADODB.Connection
cnConnection.ConnectionString = "Provider=SQLOLEDB.1;" & _
            "Persist Security Info=False;User ID=sa;" & _
            "Initial Catalog=pubs;Data Source=CELERY"
cnConnection.Open

Set rsRecordset = cnConnection.Execute _
                ("SELECT * FROM employee WHERE fname = 'Maria'")
rsRecordset.MoveFirst

vntRecordset = rsRecordset.GetRows(rsRecordset.RecordCount)

objDisplay.PrintData vntRecordset
```

`vntRecordset` now contains the contents of the recordset as a two-dimensional array. The first dimension indicates the field in the recordset and the second dimension indicates the record. Therefore, to retrieve values from the `Variant` array you need to specify both the field and the record. The `PrintData` method might look something like:

```
Public Sub PrintData(Values() As Variant)

    Debug.Print Values(1, 0), Values(2, 0), Values(3, 0)
    Debug.Print Values(1, 1), Values(2, 1), Values(3, 1)

End Sub
```

The order of columns is entirely dependent upon the field order returned in the recordset. This means that if we add a field to our SQL `SELECT` statement, in the middle of other fields that we're retrieving, we'll have to change all of our programs that rely on `Variant` arrays to pass data.

Passing User-Defined Types with LSet

Many people store their object's data in a variable based on a UDT, because it's a concise and convenient way to handle the values. While Visual Basic allows us to pass UDT variables as parameters, this approach has some serious drawbacks.

In particular, we need to make the UDT `Public` in order to pass it as a parameter. This feature can't be used if our objects are not part of an ActiveX server – for instance from a Standard EXE project. Additionally, this approach makes it very easy for someone to write a client program that retrieves our object's data, manipulates it without our business logic and places it back in the object. Finally, VB passes UDT variables in a way that is not supported by other tools or languages. Using this technique prevents us from passing the data to routines written in other languages or through other tools such as Microsoft Message Queue Server.

The ideal solution would be to use a UDT to store our object's data, but also be able to retrieve that data as a single stream of data – say in a `String` variable.

Luckily, a very nice solution enables us to convert efficiently a UDT variable into a `String` variable, so that we can pass its data to another ActiveX component. We'll take a good look at this solution, but first let's put it in perspective.

Background

Consider the following user-defined type:

```
Private Type DetailType
   Name As String * 30
   Age As Integer
End Type
```

Provided we're working in a Win32 environment such as Windows 9x or Windows NT, all strings are Unicode. What this means is that each character in a string will actually consume 2 bytes of memory. This allows Windows to support more complex character sets, such as those required by Arabic or languages in the Far East. Therefore, `DetailType` is a total of 62 bytes in length: 60 for the `Name` field and 2 for the `Age` field.

If we want to create a `SummaryType` UDT, which is exactly the same length as `DetailType`, we must make it 62 bytes in length. As a 62 byte `String` is actually half that many characters, we find that `SummaryType` needs to be 31 characters long:

```
Private Type SummaryType
   Buffer As String * 31
End Type
```

> It's worth noting that if `DetailType` were 61 bytes in length (say `Age` was a `Byte`) then `SummaryType` would still need to be 31 characters long, since we must round up. If we didn't round up, then `SummaryType` would be just 30 characters long and could only hold 60 of the 61 characters: we'd lose one byte at the end.

Some languages (but not Visual Basic) would allow a single variable to be referenced as `DetailType` or `SummaryType`. In other words, they would let us get at the same set of bytes in memory in more than one way. This means that we could set the `Name` and `Age` values with `DetailType`, and also treat the memory as a simple `String` without having to copy any values in memory.

Since Visual Basic doesn't allow us to pass a UDT variable as a parameter to an object, we need some way to convert our UDT variables to a data-type that can be passed. The ideal situation would be one in which we could simply define the same chunk of memory as both a UDT and a simple `String` variable.

Although Visual Basic doesn't allow us to do this, it does provide us with a very efficient technique that we can use to provide an excellent workaround.

The Visual Basic Implementation

Visual Basic's approach does require a memory copy, but it's performed with the `LSet` command, which is very fast and efficient. Let's take a look at how `LSet` works.

Open a **Standard EXE** project and type in the `DetailType` and `SummaryType` UDT's that we just looked at. They need to be entered in the **General Declarations** section of our form. Then add the following code to the `Form_Click` event:

```
Private Sub Form_Click()

    Dim udtDetail As DetailType
    Dim udtSummary As SummaryType

    With udtDetail
      .Name = "Ray Vecchio"
      .Age = 33
    End With

End Sub
```

This code simply defines a variable, using each UDT, and then loads some data into the `udtDetail` variable, which is based on the `DetailType` type. So far, this is pretty simple - so here comes the trick. We'll add a line using the `LSet` command:

```
Private Sub Form_Click()

    Dim udtDetail As DetailType
    Dim udtSummary As SummaryType

    With udtDetail
      .Name = "Ray Vecchio"
      .Age = 33
    End With

    LSet udtSummary = udtDetail

End Sub
```

This new line uses the `LSet` command to do a direct memory copy of the contents of `udtDetail` into `udtSummary`. Visual Basic doesn't perform any type checking here. In fact, it doesn't even look at the content of the variables; it just performs a memory copy. This is very fast and very efficient, substantially faster than trying to copy individual elements of data, for instance.

The result of this code is that the `Name` and `Age` values are stored in the `udtSummary` variable and can be accessed as a string using `udtSummary.Buffer`. Of course, the values stored aren't all printable text, so if we try to print this value we'll get garbage. That's OK though. The objective here is to get the data into a single variable.

Now we can pass that string to another procedure using the following code:

```
Private Sub Form_Click()

    Dim udtDetail As DetailType
    Dim udtSummary As SummaryType

    With udtDetail
       .Name = "Ray Vecchio"
       .Age = 33
    End With

    LSet udtSummary = udtDetail
    PrintValues udtSummary.Buffer

End Sub
```

The `PrintValues` subroutine just accepts a `String` as a parameter. Of course, we're really passing a more complex set of data, but it's packaged into a simple `String` at this point so it's easy to deal with.

Now let's look at the `PrintValues` routine:

```
Private Sub PrintValues(Buffer As String)

    Dim udtDetail As DetailType
    Dim udtSummary As SummaryType

    udtSummary.Buffer = Buffer
    LSet udtDetail = udtSummary

    With udtDetail
       Debug.Print .Name
       Debug.Print .Age
    End With

End Sub
```

Again, we declare variables using `DetailType` and `SummaryType` for use within the routine. Then we copy the parameter value into `udtSummary.Buffer`. Both values are simple `Strings`, so this isn't a problem. Next, to get at the details of `Name` and `Age`, we use the `LSet` command to perform a memory copy and get the data into the `udtDetail` variable:

```
    LSet udtDetail = udtSummary
```

Once that's done, we can simply use `udtDetail` as normal. In this case, we just print the values to the Immediate window.

If you run this program, and click on the form, the appropriate output will appear in the Immediate window accordingly.

Memory Alignment

There is a factor we must take into account when defining the length of our string buffer UDT. In Visual Basic, certain user-defined data types are aligned in memory so that they fall on **longword** boundaries. What this means is that filler space will be inserted if an element doesn't start on a 4-byte boundary.

Consider the following user-defined type:

```
Private Type TestType
    B1 As Byte
    L1 As Long
End Type
```

A variable defined as `Byte` is 1 byte long and a variable defined as `Long` is 4 bytes long. Therefore, we might assume that the length of `TestType` is 5 bytes. In fact, `TestType` is actually 8 bytes long, 3 bytes have been added as filler space.

Let's assume that the type starts on a memory boundary, so `B1` will be at the start of a 4-byte boundary. However, `B1` is only a single byte long and it's required that `L1` starts on a longword boundary. What this means is that there is 3 bytes of space between `B1` and `L1` that needs to be taken up. This is where filler space will be inserted.

To check the actual length (in bytes) of a UDT, we can declare a variable based on it and use the `LenB` function. The `LenB` function will return the length, in bytes, of any variable - including one based on a UDT. For instance, we could write the following code:

```
Private Sub Form_Click()

    Dim udtTest As TestType

    MsgBox LenB(udtTest)

End Sub
```

Open a new **Standard EXE** project. Type in the `Form_Click` event procedure above and add the `TestType` UDT into the **General Declarations** section of the form. Now run the project and click on the form, you'll get a message box showing that the total number of bytes in the `TestType` UDT is 8.

Don't forget that not all data-types are longword-aligned. We've already seen that the `String` data type consumes 2 bytes for every character and an `Integer` is also 2 bytes long. Data types that fall on 2-byte boundaries instead of 4-byte boundaries are **word-aligned**.

The following data-types are always aligned to a word (2-byte) boundary:

```
Byte
Integer
Boolean
String
```

The following data-types are aligned to a longword (4-byte) boundary:

Long	Single
Double	Date
Currency	Decimal
Object	Variant

Visual Basic will add space as needed in front of any of these data-types, so they always start on a longword boundary.

The addition of filler space becomes important when we use UDTs to pass our data across our system. If we're going to create another UDT to copy our data into, we need to know exactly how long to make that UDT so that it can fit all the data. If we don't include filler space into our calculation of the required length for our buffer UDT, we will create a UDT that is too short to hold all the information and the last few bytes of data will be lost during the copy.

The following UDT holds 6 bytes of data:

```
Private Type StringType
    Buffer As String * 3
End Type
```

At first glance, we might expect `StringType` UDT to be able to contain the `TestType` elements shown above, since a `Byte` and `Long` combined are only 5 bytes in length. However, because L1 (the `Long`) needs to be longword-aligned, the compiler inserts 3 filler bytes before L1. This means that the total length of `TestType` is actually 8 bytes. Hence, we need the following UDT to hold all the data from `TestType`:

```
Private Type StringType
    Buffer As String * 4
End Type
```

While the issue of longword-alignment makes it more complicated to determine the length of the buffer UDT, it is a predictable behavior and it really isn't very hard to ensure that we get the length correct.

ADO(R) Recordset with Marshaling Properties

ADO 2.x provides us with some powerful capabilities that we can use to help us serialize an object's data and transfer it. The core of this capability lies with ADO's support for **batch mode updating** of a `Recordset` object. What this means is that ADO is not only able to provide a reference to a `Recordset` object, but it can actually copy the object's data from one process to another or from one machine to another – essentially allowing us to pass ADO `Recordset` objects by value rather than by reference.

Couple the ability to move `Recordset` objects across the network with ADO's support for `Recordset` objects that are disconnected from any database connection and we can create a `Recordset` object out of thin air – no database required. We can define the columns of data we want to provide and then add or manipulate rows of data at will.

We can use ADO to create an arbitrary `Recordset` object to store any data we'd like and then pass that `Recordset` from process to process or machine to machine as we choose. ADO takes care of all the details of serializing the `Recordset` itself, allowing us to simply interact with a `Recordset` object to view, update or add our data.

Before we can pass a `Recordset` around our network, we need to create it. There are two ways to create a `Recordset` object for serializing our object's data:

> ➢ Creating the `Recordset` from a database
> ➢ Creating a connectionless `Recordset` through code

Creating Recordset Objects from a Database

The most common way to create a `Recordset` object is to select some data from a database to be loaded into the object. However, if we're going to pass that `Recordset` around the network we do need to take some extra steps as we open it.

In particular, we need to ensure that the `CursorLocation` property of our `Connection` or `Recordset` object is set to `adUseClient`. This causes ADO to use a cursor engine located on the client machine rather than one within the database server itself. Since the cursor engine is local to the client, we can send the `Recordset`'s data to any machine where ADO or ADOR (the lightweight client version of ADO, which is suitable for Internet applications) is installed.

We also need to specify the `LockType` property of our `Recordset` as `adLockBatchOptimistic`. This causes ADO to build our `Recordset` object in a batch update mode, allowing us to manipulate the `Recordset` and its data even if it is not currently connected to the data source.

By setting these two properties as we initialize our `Recordset` object, we will cause ADO to automatically support batch processing of our data, and to automatically pass the `Recordset` object's data to any process that interacts with the object.

There is one caveat to this approach. Our `CursorType` property can only be `adOpenKeyset` or `adOpenStatic` when we are using a batch mode `Recordset`. If we are passing the `Recordset` to a machine that only has ADOR installed (such as a thin client workstation), then we can only use the `adOpenStatic` setting for the `CursorType` property.

Let's take a look at some code that opens a `Recordset` and returns the object upon request:

```
Public Function GetData() As Recordset

   Dim rsRecordset As Recordset
   Dim strConnect As String

   Set rsRecordset = New Recordset

   strConnect = "Provider=SQLOLEDB.1;Persist Security Info=False;" & _
                "User ID=sa;Initial Catalog=Northwind;Data Source=CELERY"

   With rsRecordset
     .CursorLocation = adUseClient
     .Open "SELECT * FROM Employees", strConnect, adOpenStatic, _
     adLockBatchOptimistic
   End With
```

```
    Set GetData = rsRecordset
    Set rsRecordset = Nothing

End Function
```

This code doesn't look much different than what we'd expect to see any time we open a Recordset based on some data in a database. However, there are two interesting things to note. First off, before calling the Open method we set the CursorLocation property of the object:

```
.CursorLocation = adUseClient
```

Then, in the call to the Open method we set the LockType to adLockBatchOptimistic. We also set the CursorType to adOpenStatic. We could have set it to adOpenKeyset if we'd chosen, but by selecting adOpenStatic we know we can pass the Recordset to a client that might only have ADOR installed without having ADO convert our cursor type during that process

Creating a Connectionless Recordset

This section is something of an aside. Connectionless recordsets are used to pass data in a Recordset object, where the data has not originated from a database. In this book, we shall access data only from a database, but I have included this discussion of connectionless recordsets for completeness.

It is actually quite common for an object's state to include information that isn't necessarily stored in a database. For instance, we may wish to pass a flag indicating whether our object is new or other types of information between our client workstation and the application server. If our Recordset object is generated directly from a database query, we are restricted to only passing information that comes from that database.

Fortunately, ADO provides a very elegant solution to this problem by allowing us to create a Recordset object that is totally unrelated to any data source. The steps involved in this process are quite straightforward:

1. Create the Recordset object

2. Add columns to the Recordset using the Fields object's Append method

3. Open the Recordset

4. Add or manipulate data in the Recordset

As an example, the following code creates a connectionless recordset with two columns of data: Name and BirthDate. We then add a couple rows of information to the Recordset object and return it as the result of the method:

```
Public Function MakeData() As Recordset

    Dim rsRecordset As Recordset

    Set rsRecordset = New Recordset

    With rsRecordset
      .Fields.Append "Name", adBSTR
      .Fields.Append "BirthDate", adDate
```

```
          .Open

          .AddNew
          .Fields("Name") = "Samantha"
          .Fields("BirthDate") = "1/6/70"
          .Update

          .AddNew
          .Fields("Name") = "Bernard"
          .Fields("BirthDate") = "8/3/68"
          .Update
      End With

      Set MakeData = rsRecordset

      Set rsRecordset = Nothing

   End Function
```

The first couple of lines simply declare and create an instance of a Recordset object. Once that's done, we can move on to adding columns to the empty Recordset by calling the Append method of the Fields object:

```
      .Fields.Append "Name", adBSTR
      .Fields.Append "BirthDate", adDate
```

After we have defined the columns, all that remains is to load our object with some data. This is as simple as calling the AddNew method, loading some data and calling Update to store the data into the Recordset. Of course, the data isn't stored into any database, since this Recordset exists only in our computers' memory.

Passing a Recordset by Value

We've now looked at two different ways to create a Recordset object that we can pass to another process or across the network. Both of the routines shown above are written as Function methods, returning the Recordset object as a result.

ADO itself handles all the details of moving the Recordset object's data to the client process or computer, so we really don't need to do any extra work at all beyond setting the properties as we did to create the Recordset. Our client code can be quite simple as shown by the following fragment:

```
   Public Sub Form_Click()

      Dim objServer As Object
      Dim rsRecordset As Recordset

      Set objServer = New MyDataServer.DataMaker

      Set rsRecordset = objServer.GetData

      Set MSHFlexGrid1.Recordset = rsRecordset

      Set objServer = Nothing

   End Sub
```

Once this code fragment is complete, we have a `Recordset` object to work with. This code assumes that the code to create the `Recordset` is in an ActiveX server (DLL or EXE) named `MyDataServer` and in a class named `DataMaker`. This ActiveX server could be running in another process or on another machine on the network.

Regardless, once we've got the `Recordset` through this code, the `MyDataServer` ActiveX server can be totally shut down – the machine it is running on could even be shut off – and our code can still continue to work with the `Recordset` and its data. In this case, we're simply displaying the recordset created in the `GetData` procedure, in a Microsoft Hierarchical FlexGrid control that has been placed on a form.

The Standard EXE program running this code fragment does require a reference to either the ADO or ADOR library in order to function. In many cases (this one included) the lighter-weight ADOR library is sufficient, as it provides basic support for interacting with `Recordset` objects that are created and updated by another process or machine.

PropertyBag Objects

A **property bag** is an object that supports the concept of a key-value pair. The idea is that the property bag can store a value associated with a key (or name) for that value. For instance, we might store the value 5 along with the key `Height`. At any point, we can also retrieve the `Height` value from the property bag.

Visual Basic 5.0 introduced the `PropertyBag` object as part of the ability to create ActiveX controls. While the `PropertyBag` object was useful when storing properties of our control that the developer set at design time, we couldn't take advantage of the `PropertyBag` object outside of control creation.

Visual Basic 6.0 extends the `PropertyBag` object such that we can use it anywhere we choose within our applications. We can make use of the `PropertyBag` object anywhere that we need to manage key-value pairs.

Better still, the `PropertyBag` object implements a `Contents` property that allows us to access the entire contents of the object as a single `Byte` array – essentially it provides built-in support for streaming its own data. We can retrieve the data, send the `Byte` array as a parameter to another process or across the network, and then place it into a `PropertyBag` object, giving us an exact duplicate of the object with which we started.

Of course, `Byte` arrays aren't nearly as easy to manipulate or work with as a `String` variable would be. Fortunately, this isn't a serious problem, as Visual Basic makes it very easy for us to convert a `Byte` array to a `String` and then back to a `Byte` array.

Serializing Data into a String using the Contents

Let's look at some simple code that illustrates how we can use a `PropertyBag` to serialize the data in an object.

Suppose we have an object with two pieces of data: `Name` and `BirthDate`. We can store this data in a `PropertyBag` object with code similar to this:

```
Public Function GetObjectData() As String

    Dim pbData As PropertyBag

    Set pbData = New PropertyBag

    With pbData
      .WriteProperty "Name", mstrName
      .WriteProperty "BirthDate", mdtBirthDate
    End With

End Function
```

Once we've created the `PropertyBag` object, we can simply use its `WriteProperty` method to store the values from our object into the property bag. In this case, we're assuming that the name and birth date data are stored in the variables `mstrName` and `mdtBirthDate`.

After our property bag has our object's data, we can place all of the data into a single `Byte` array using the `PropertyBag` object's `Contents` property. The `Byte` array is then set as the return value of the `GetObjectData` function:

```
Public Function GetObjectData() As String

    Dim pbData As PropertyBag

    Set pbData = New PropertyBag

    With pbData
      .WriteProperty "Name", mstrName
      .WriteProperty "BirthDate", mdtBirthdate
    End With

    GetObjectData = pbData.Contents

End Function
```

With this simple code, we've converted our object's data into a single `String` variable that we can easily pass as a parameter to another object, even across the network.

Deserializing Data from a String using Contents

Now that we've seen how we can take data from an object and use a `PropertyBag` object to serialize that data into a simple `String` variable, let's look at how we can use that `String` variable to load another object with the data.

Since we know we'll be receiving a `String` value, the first step is to convert that `String` into a `Byte` array so that we can place it into the `PropertyBag` object's `Contents` property. While we're doing this, we'll also need to create a `PropertyBag` object to work with:

```
Public Sub LoadObject(StringBuffer As String)

    Dim arData() As Byte
    Dim pbData As PropertyBag

    Set pbData = New PropertyBag

    arData = StringBuffer

    pbData.Contents = arData

End Sub
```

Once we've converted the String to a Byte array, we simply set the Contents property of our PropertyBag using that value. This causes the PropertyBag object to contain the exact data that was contained in the other PropertyBag object that we used to create the String variable.

Now that the PropertyBag object has been populated, we can use the ReadProperty method to retrieve the individual data values for use by our object:

```
Public Sub LoadObject(StringBuffer As String)

    Dim arData() As Byte
    Dim pbData As PropertyBag

    Set pbData = New PropertyBag

    arData = StringBuffer

    pbData.Contents = arData

    With pbData
      mstrName = .ReadProperty("Name")
      mdtName = .ReadProperty("BirthDate")
    End With

End Sub
```

In many ways, the use of a PropertyBag object for serializing our object's data is comparable to how we used the LSet command to convert a UDT to a String. Either approach results in our object's data being converted into a single String value that we can pass as a parameter, store in a database or send as the body of an email or Microsoft Message Queue (MSMQ) message. Once the data reaches the other end of its journey, we can easily reconstitute our object by converting the String value back into its original form.

Summary

In this chapter, we've looked at seven different methods of passing data between objects in our system. The first two methods we considered, calling single properties of an object and passing arguments to a method (the method we used in Chapter 11), were shown to be poor from a performance perspective.

We then discussed serialization of data, meaning that the data was collected into a single unit that could be passed more efficiently to another object. We considered passing user-defined types directly and with the LSet command, passing variant arrays, passing ADO Recordset objects and finally using the PropertyBag object.

Specifically, we've looked at:

> User-defined types (UDT)

> The GetData function

> The GetRows method of the Recordset object

> The LSet command

> The LenB function

> Passing Recordset objects by value

> The PropertyBag object and its Contents property

In Chapter 13, we will practise one of these techniques as we build another 3-tier application with a disconnected recordset that we will pass by value.

Suppliers

- SupplierID
- CompanyName
- ContactName
- ContactTitle
- Address
- City
- Region
- PostalCode
- Country
- Phone
- Fax
- HomePage

Products

- ProductID
- ProductName
- SupplierID
- CategoryID
- QuantityPerUnit
- UnitPrice
- UnitsInStock
- UnitsOnOrder
- ReorderLevel
- Discontinued

Categories

- CategoryID
- CategoryName
- Description
- Picture

Implementing a Practical 3-Tier Solution

A few chapters back, we built a 2-tier client-server solution that was designed specifically to view the details of an order previously placed in the Northwind database. In this chapter, we'll build a 3-tier client-server solution that takes that project a step further. We'll also see a practical implementation of our discussion on passing data in Chapter 12. In Chapter 11, we passed data between tiers by passing arguments to methods. However, this creates a performance hit when the system is scaled up to cope with passing larger amounts of data to a large number of client machines. This chapter will demonstrate another method of passing data, that of creating disconnected recordsets.

One of the challenges of a 3-tier solution is to pass a group of new records back to the database server to be added to database. In this scenario, we want to create a new order, populate the details (line items) of the order, and then pass them to the middle tier. The middle tier will then populate the database.

In a 2-tier solution, this may seem trivial because the client always has direct access to the database, but in a 3-tier environment, the client has no direct access to the database. The application that we will build in this chapter deals with this problem, extending what you have already learned up to this chapter.

Project Overview

Following is a snapshot of the completed application we'll build in this chapter. As you can see, the form is broken down into a number of parts:

> The Customer section allows the user to select the customer who is to receive the order and display any relevant information pertaining to where the order should be shipped.

> The Available Products section allows the user to quickly locate the products that the customer has an interest in ordering. The user is able to view stock on hand levels, and the amount of product on order.

> The Order Detail section allows the user to specify which products the customer is ordering, how many and any relevant discounts.

> The Order section allows the user to specify when the order was placed, when the customer needs the order by, and the delivery information. In addition, the subtotal, freight charge and total are provided to the user.

Let's break down the functionality so that we know what we need to program.

When the form loads, we first need to retrieve a number of recordsets, which will populate the combo boxes and grid controls. They are as follows:

> **Customer Combo Box**: This Combo Box will be populated with the company names of all customers listed in the `Customers` table.

> **Ship Method Combo Box**: This Combo Box should be populated with the names of all shipping companies that are available to the customer. The names of these shippers can be acquired from the `Shippers` table.

> **Employee Combo Box**: The Employee Combo Box provides a list of all employees who might be creating an order. Keep in mind that when security is implemented, a better solution might be to retain this information from the login.

> **Products Hierarchical FlexGrid**: The Products Hierarchical FlexGrid is to be populated with all products available for sale. For ease of use when locating the product, they are to be displayed by category in alphabetical order.

We want to provide an environment that allows the user the ability to create orders with the least amount of effort. To do this, the following functionality will need to be created:

> When the user chooses a company's name from the Customer Combo Box, the address will be pulled from the `Customers` table. This provides the user with a default shipping address. The address can then be modified if needed, and will identify where the product is to be shipped.

> When the user locates a product that the customer wishes to purchase, the user should be able to "drag" the product from the Products Hierarchical FlexGrid and "drop" it into the Order Detail Grid. This will allow the user the ability to quickly add products to the order without typing the product ID. Once the product is added, the quantity and discount percentages can be entered.

> As each product is added, and the price and discount is modified, each line item should be tallied, and a subtotal should be produced for the user. Finally, the freight should be added to the subtotal to produce a total order price.

> Once the order details are complete, the user may click on the Send Order button to pass the order to the database. The application will receive the order confirmation number or, if an error is generated during the process, the error should be passed to the user for rectification. From here, the order can be abandoned for a new order to be entered or, if the user chooses, changes can be made to the existing order and re-sent to the object in middle tier.

The following illustration depicts the order of events for updating the production database with a new order:

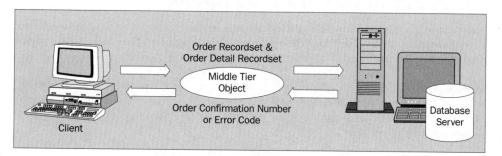

1. The user establishes the order criteria. This identifies the customer, what products were purchased and the shipping details.

2. When the user clicks on the Send Order button, two recordsets are populated. These are disconnected, programmatically created recordsets; meaning they are created as empty recordsets, populated, then passed to the middle tier to populate the database. The recordset's table structure is modeled after the tables that they will eventually be populating. The two recordsets are the *Order* recordset, which contains the relevant data to populate the Orders table, and the *Order Details* recordset, which contains all product and quantity information pertaining to the order. This data will populate the Order Details table of the production database.

3. Both recordsets are passed to a middle tier object. The middle tier object passes the information from the *Order* recordset to another *Order* recordset, which is linked to the production database. The recordset is then populated with the new order record and the OrderID is retrieved after the recordset is updated.

4. Once the order has been created, the order details are added in the same method. The OrderID is used as a foreign key in the Order Details table to identify each line item as it relates to the order.

5. If no errors are generated, the OrderID is returned to the user as a confirmation number. If errors are encountered, the error code is returned and the client handles it.

Setting up a DSN to Connect to Northwind

For this project, we'll need a Data Source Name (DSN), which will be used to connect to the Northwind database. As you will see when we build our connection string for the middle tier object, this pushes a lot of the connection responsibility to ODBC. In a nutshell, this allows our ADO connection string to be much more generic and flexible.

If you have not yet created a DSN for the Northwind database on SQL Server, do this now. For a review of creating a DSN, refer to Chapter 3.

Building the Middle Tier Component

We will approach this project just as we did the one in the Chapter 11. We'll first build our middle tier component, then the client application. Once each of these has been adequately tested, we'll port the solution to Microsoft Transaction Server.

Before we start, let's create a folder on our hard drive to save the projects that we'll build. Create a new folder in the ProVB6DB directory called Chapter13. We need to save our two project stages separately so create two more folders from the Chapter13 folder. Name the two folders Lab1 and Lab2. We're now ready to begin.

Open Visual Basic and select the ActiveX DLL icon from the New tab of the New Project dialog. As a reminder, our components are built as DLLs for ease of re-use and extensibility. Once you have the shell of your new project open, change the Name property of the class to clsServer and the Name property of the project to ServerApp. Now, save the class and project in the Lab1 folder you created, using the default given names.

For this project, we'll only need to add one reference to the project, so select References... from the Project menu. The reference we'll need is the standard ADO reference that we have been working with throughout this book. Locate Microsoft ActiveX Data Objects 2.x Library, select it and click on the OK button.

The Module-Level Variables

In this project, we'll need to declare six module-level variables:

> strSQL: Used as a buffer to build SQL statements which will be executed against a database connection. This will be used in several functions.

> cnNorthwind: This variable will act as our active connection to the Northwind database.

> rsGeneric: The variable is declared as a recordset. It will be used as a generic recordset to retrieve results and pass them back to the requesting function caller.

> rsOrder: This recordset will maintain our connection to the table as we add a new order to it and update the results.

> rsOrderDetails: This recordset serves the same purpose as rsOrder, except it is specific to the details of the order, and connects to the Order Details table.

> rsStock: This recordset will serve the purpose of connecting to the Products table, allowing us to remove stock from inventory as each item is placed on order.

Locate the General Declarations section of your class code window and enter the following declarations:

```
Option Explicit

Dim strSQL As String
Dim cnNorthwind As ADODB.Connection          ' Connection object to Northwind
Dim rsGeneric As New ADODB.Recordset         ' Generic recordset for looking up IDs

Dim rsOrder As New ADODB.Recordset           ' Recordset for Orders
Dim rsOrderDetails As New ADODB.Recordset    ' Recordset for Order Details

Dim rsStock As New ADODB.Recordset           ' For updating inventory stock levels
```

The Class_Initialize Event

In the `Class_Initialize` event procedure, we'll add the connection string for a connection to the `Northwind` database. For this project, we'll use a DSN as our connection string. You can see that it's very easy to code. The only drawback of using a DSN is that any computer using the objects *must* have the DSN configured. The established connection is assigned to `cnNorthwind`. The actual `Open` method of the `Connection` object will be called at the beginning of each function and the connection will be closed upon completion of the function's task. Keeping the connection open for the entire duration of the program run, as we did in Chapter 11 is not the best solution. As more and more users simultaneously access the database, the vast amount of network traffic created slows retrieval times dramatically. In other words, the solution is not scalable.

> Don't forget to specify your user ID and password in the `ConnectionString` property of `cnNorthwind`.

```
Private Sub Class_Initialize()

    Set cnNorthwind = New ADODB.Connection
    cnNorthwind.ConnectionString = "DSN=NorthWind;uid=sa;pwd="

End Sub
```

The Get_Table_Recordset Function

We're now ready to write some functions to retrieve recordsets from the various tables, and populate the Combo Boxes and DataGrids. We have three Combo Boxes to populate: the Customer Combo Box, the Employee Combo Box and the Ship Method Combo Box. We could write three separate functions for each of these, but it would be better to create one function that we can use to retrieve recordsets for all three Combo Boxes.

Create a new function in your class and title it `Get_Table_Recordset`. The function will receive a single table name and return a recordset. While the 'ideal' function would have some error handling, there are only two lines of code that are essential to this function. The first line will dynamically build a SQL statement to retrieve all records, and all fields of the specified table.

> *If we knew that one of these tables was fairly large, we might want to restrict the SQL statement to only include the fields we needed. In this case, none of the tables are too large, so we'll pass the entire recordset back to the client. However, if the tables were larger (or a larger user base existed), this might create heavy network traffic and CPU processing.*

The second line of code executes the SQL statement, and assigns the recordset to `Get_Table_Recordset`, which was declared as a recordset.

In addition to our `Open` method, we also must indicate that the `CursorLocation` is to be run on the client. The reason for this is that we need to pass the recordset object to the client, severing the relationship with the `Connection` object. If this property is not set, the recordset that is opened is dependent upon the connection. Also, notice that we physically sever the recordset's connection by setting it to `Nothing` before closing the connection:

```
Public Function Get_Table_Recordset(strTable As String) As ADODB.Recordset

    cnNorthwind.Open
    cnNorthwind.CursorLocation = adUseClient

    strSQL = "SELECT * FROM " & strTable

    Set Get_Table_Recordset = cnNorthwind.Execute(strSQL)

    Get_Table_Recordset.ActiveConnection = Nothing
    cnNorthwind.Close

End Function
```

The Get_Products Function

The next function will be designed to return specific product-related fields to the client. We will pull this information from two tables: `Products` and `Categories`. In the `Products` table, there is a field that identifies what category the product belongs in: `CategoryID`. `CategoryID` relates to a primary key field in the `Categories` table. From the `Categories` table, the field that we are interested in is `CategoryName`. This will make our client application much more user-friendly because the user will see a category by its name, rather than an identification number. As with the previous function, this function only requires two lines of code. The first line builds your SQL statement, the second executes it and returns the recordset.

```
Public Function Get_Products() As ADODB.Recordset

    cnNorthwind.Open
    cnNorthwind.CursorLocation = adUseClient

    strSQL = "SELECT Categories.CategoryName, Products.ProductID, " & _
             "Products.ProductName,Products.QuantityPerUnit," & _
             "Products.UnitPrice,Products.UnitsInStock, " & _
             "Products.UnitsOnOrder FROM Categories " & _
             "INNER JOIN Products ON Categories.CategoryID " & _
             "= Products.CategoryID " & _
             "ORDER BY Categories.CategoryName"

    Set Get_Products = cnNorthwind.Execute(strSQL)

    Get_Products.ActiveConnection = Nothing
    cnNorthwind.Close

End Function
```

The Get_Customer_Details Function

The next task is to return the details of any customer, when requested by the client. When a user clicks on the Customer Combo Box, selecting a specific customer, we want to retrieve the details of that specific customer. In this function, we'll receive the `CompanyName` field and return the appropriate recordset. Keep in mind that the recordset should only contain a single record.

You'll notice that the first line of code calls another function that we have yet to create. The `Replace` function here is used to take any field, and search for the existence of single quotes. As you know, single quotes are used in SQL statements when passing character-based values. If a single quote exists in our data when we pass it in a SQL statement, it will generate an error. Specifically, in the `Customers` table, there is a customer with the name Bon App'. If we attempt to pass this as an argument in our SQL statement, an error message will be returned. To handle this, we need to add an additional single quote next to the existing single quote. This identifies the quote as being a literal and no error is generated. Bon app' now becomes Bon app''.

The following two lines of code are similar to the previous two functions we built. We build our SQL statement, then return the recordset after executing it against the connection:

```
Public Function Get_Customer_Details(CompanyName As String) As ADODB.Recordset

    cnNorthwind.Open
    cnNorthwind.CursorLocation = adUseClient

    CompanyName = Replace(CompanyName, "'", "''")

    strSQL = "SELECT * FROM Customers WHERE CompanyName = '" & CompanyName & "'"

    Set Get_Customer_Details = cnNorthwind.Execute(strSQL)

    Get_Customer_Details.ActiveConnection = Nothing
    cnNorthwind.Close

End Function
```

The Get_ID Function

In the client application, we will make considerable efforts to present usable information to the user. As an example, we'll display the `CompanyName` to the user, rather than the `CustomerID`. This will allow the user to quickly locate the customer from the Combo Box. The `CompanyName` field does very little good for us when creating an order though. This is because the `Orders` table requires the population of the `CustomerID`.

For the above reason, the following fields will need to be converted:

Table Name	Original Field/s	Destination Field
Customers	CompanyName	CustomerID
Employees	LastName & FirstName	EmployeeID
Shippers	CompanyName	ShipperID

To accomplish this, we'll create a single function (`Get_ID`), which will receive two arguments (the table name and the original field name). The result will be returned as a string.

This function first identifies which table we're dealing with. Each table will have a slightly different SQL statement. Let's first look at the `Customers` table. Our SQL statement will be executed against the `Customers` table and will only retrieve the records that have a `CompanyName` equal to the value passed. This should return only one record! The `CustomerID` field is then extracted from the recordset and returned to the client.

> If the `CompanyName` field is not unique, you must use a different algorithm than the one described above. This example assumes that the `CompanyName` is unique.

The `Employees` table is a bit more complex. Our Employee Combo Box will contain the last name and first name of the employee. Because of this, we need to parse each of these out into our SQL statement. Our SQL statement will therefore have two conditions (`LastName` and `FirstName`). We parse these fields out using the `Left`, `Right` and `InStr` keywords in Visual Basic.

> Again, if there is more than one employee with the same name, you'll run into problems. To reduce this probability, you may want to include middle initial, or use a unique identifier to represent the employee.

The `Shippers` table uses the same concept as the `Customers` table.

```
Public Function Get_ID(strTable As String, strValue) As String

    cnNorthwind.Open
    cnNorthwind.CursorLocation = adUseClient

    Select Case strTable

       Case "Customers"
          strSQL = "SELECT * FROM Customers WHERE CompanyName = '" & strValue & "'"
          Set rsGeneric = cnNorthwind.Execute(strSQL)
          Get_ID = rsGeneric("CustomerID")

       Case "Employees"
          strSQL = "SELECT * FROM Employees WHERE " _
                 & "LastName = '" & Left(strValue, InStr(strValue, ",") - 1) _
                 & "' AND FirstName = '" & _
                 Right(strValue, Len(strValue) - InStr(strValue, ",") - 1) & "'"
          Set rsGeneric = cnNorthwind.Execute(strSQL)
          Get_ID = rsGeneric("EmployeeID")

       Case "Shippers"
          strSQL = "SELECT * FROM Shippers WHERE CompanyName = '" & strValue & "'"
          Set rsGeneric = cnNorthwind.Execute(strSQL)
          Get_ID = rsGeneric("ShipperID")

    End Select

    rsGeneric.ActiveConnection = Nothing
    cnNorthwind.Close

End Function
```

The Send_Order Function

The final and most difficult function to code is the `Send_Order` function. This is the function that receives the order and details from the client and must pass the request on to the database, then return the results to the client in the form of an order confirmation number or an error code.

Create the function shell so that it receives two arguments (both as recordsets). These arguments are rsNewOrder and rsNewOrderDetail. The results will be returned as a string:

```
Public Function Send_Order(rsNewOrder As ADODB.Recordset, rsNewOrderDetail As _
                           ADODB.Recordset) As String

End Function
```

In the General Declarations section of this class, we declared two recordsets (rsOrder and rsOrderDetails). The goal now will be to open these recordsets with our connection to the database, then add a new record from the recordsets passed to us:

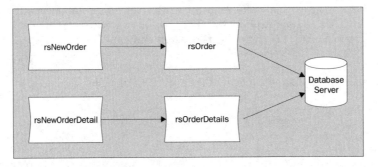

The first step is to open each of the recordsets with a connection to the database. When we construct the SQL statements, we create a WHERE clause of WHERE 1 = 2. This returns an empty recordset with the structure of the table in the FROM clause. The reason for this is that we don't need any of the existing records in the recordset. We only need to retrieve the structure of the table. This will allow us to populate a new record and update the results.

We also set the LockType to adLockOptimistic and the CursorType to adOpenKeyset. Setting the CursorType to adOpenKeyset is important because it handles a number of inherent problems for us. This allows us to view fields of the record immediately after updating by opening a dynamic recordset. In this case, the OrderID is assigned as an automatic counter. When an order is created, we need to extract the OrderID immediately so that we can enter the details of the order in another table. The adOpenKeyset allows us to do this:

```
cnNorthwind.Open
cnNorthwind.CursorLocation = adUseServer

strSQL = "SELECT * FROM Orders WHERE 1=2"
rsOrder.LockType = adLockOptimistic
rsOrder.CursorType = adOpenKeyset                  ' allows us to see the
                                                   ' OrderID after update
rsOrder.Open strSQL, cnNorthwind, , , adCmdText

strSQL = "SELECT * FROM Order_Details WHERE 1 =2"
rsOrderDetails.LockType = adLockOptimistic
rsOrderDetails.CursorType = adOpenKeyset           ' allows us to open simple
                                                   ' table name (OrderDetails)
rsOrderDetails.Open strSQL, cnNorthwind, , , adCmdText

rsStock.LockType = adLockOptimistic
rsStock.CursorType = adOpenKeyset
```

The next step is to transfer the contents of the rsNewOrder recordset to the rsOrder recordset. We do this by calling the AddNew method of the rsOrder recordset, and populating each of the fields from the rsNewOrder recordset. Note that we evaluate the ShipRegion field to ensure it's not null. If the field is null, an error will be returned. It's often best to check the other fields as well, but in this database, the ShipRegion field is the only one that is commonly null. Once we have filled each of the fields of the record, we call the Update method of the recordset object, and instantly retrieve the OrderID of the new record. This will be used when we enter the details of the record.

```
With rsOrder
    .AddNew
    !CustomerID = rsNewOrder!CustomerID
    !EmployeeID = rsNewOrder!EmployeeID
    !OrderDate = rsNewOrder!OrderDate
    !RequiredDate = rsNewOrder!RequiredDate
    !ShipVia = rsNewOrder!ShipVia
    !Freight = rsNewOrder!Freight
    !ShipName = rsNewOrder!ShipName
    !ShipAddress = rsNewOrder!ShipAddress
    !ShipCity = rsNewOrder!ShipCity
    If Trim(rsNewOrder!ShipRegion) <> "" Then
        !ShipRegion = rsNewOrder!ShipRegion
    End If
    !ShipCountry = rsNewOrder!ShipCountry
    !ShipPostalCode = rsNewOrder!ShipPostalCode
    .Update
    Send_Order = !OrderID
End With
```

When entering the order details, we move to the first record of the recordset and create a loop that navigates through the records from beginning to finish. For each line item, we add a new record to the rsOrderDetails recordset using the AddNew method and then populate each of the fields. Notice that the OrderID field is used when populating the Order Details table so that it can be linked back to the specific order in the Orders table. After the line item is added to the order, the product's stock level needs to be reduced by the quantity purchased. To do this we open a recordset specific to the product, then set the UnitsInStock value equal to itself minus the quantity purchased. Finally, the rsStock recordset is updated and closed. We close the recordset because if it were open, an error would be returned when resetting the LockType and CursorType.

```
If rsNewOrderDetail.RecordCount > 0 Then
    rsNewOrderDetail.MoveFirst
    Do Until rsNewOrderDetail.EOF
        With rsOrderDetails
            .AddNew
            !OrderID = rsOrder!OrderID
            !ProductID = rsNewOrderDetail!ProductID
            !UnitPrice = rsNewOrderDetail!UnitPrice
            !Quantity = rsNewOrderDetail!Quantity
            !Discount = rsNewOrderDetail!Discount
            .Update

        rsNewOrderDetail.MoveNext
```

```
        strSQL = "SELECT * FROM Products WHERE ProductID = " & !ProductID
        rsStock.Open strSQL, cnNorthwind, , , adCmdText
        rsStock!UnitsInStock = rsStock!UnitsInStock - !Quantity
        rsStock.Update
        rsStock.Close
      End With
    Loop
  End If


cnNorthwind.Close
```

One business rule that was not entered here is the process of ensuring that the quantity doesn't drop below a specified threshold. This logic could be placed on the server, or in the middle tier. The function might handle this in the following manner:

1. Do a lookup to find out what the threshold is for that product.

2. If the count is below the threshold, check to see if an order has already been placed.

3. If no order has been placed, then place a new order to replenish the stock.

The function (with some generic error handling added) should be structured as follows:

```
Public Function Send_Order(rsNewOrder As ADODB.Recordset, rsNewOrderDetail As _
                     ADODB.Recordset) As String

On Error GoTo BadSend

    cnNorthwind.Open
    cnNorthwind.CursorLocation = adUseServer

    strSQL = "SELECT * FROM Orders WHERE 1=2"
    rsOrder.LockType = adLockOptimistic
    rsOrder.CursorType = adOpenKeyset
    rsOrder.Open strSQL, cnNorthwind, , , adCmdText

    strSQL = "SELECT * FROM [Order Details] WHERE 1 =2"
    rsOrderDetails.LockType = adLockOptimistic
    rsOrderDetails.CursorType = adOpenKeyset
    rsOrderDetails.Open strSQL, cnNorthwind, , , adCmdText

    rsStock.LockType = adLockOptimistic
    rsStock.CursorType = adOpenKeyset

    With rsOrder
      .AddNew
      !CustomerID = rsNewOrder!CustomerID
      !EmployeeID = rsNewOrder!EmployeeID
      !OrderDate = rsNewOrder!OrderDate
      !RequiredDate = rsNewOrder!RequiredDate
      !ShipVia = rsNewOrder!ShipVia
      !Freight = rsNewOrder!Freight
      !ShipName = rsNewOrder!ShipName
      !ShipAddress = rsNewOrder!ShipAddress
      !ShipCity = rsNewOrder!ShipCity
```

```
            If Trim(rsNewOrder!ShipRegion) <> "" Then
              !ShipRegion = rsNewOrder!ShipRegion
            End If
            !ShipCountry = rsNewOrder!ShipCountry
            !ShipPostalCode = rsNewOrder!ShipPostalCode
            .Update
            Send_Order = !OrderID
         End With

         If rsNewOrderDetail.RecordCount > 0 Then
            rsNewOrderDetail.MoveFirst
            Do Until rsNewOrderDetail.EOF
              With rsOrderDetails
                .AddNew
                !OrderID = rsOrder!OrderID
                !ProductID = rsNewOrderDetail!ProductID
                !UnitPrice = rsNewOrderDetail!UnitPrice
                !Quantity = rsNewOrderDetail!Quantity
                !Discount = rsNewOrderDetail!Discount
                .Update

                rsNewOrderDetail.MoveNext

                strSQL = "SELECT * FROM Products WHERE ProductID = " & !ProductID
                rsStock.Open strSQL, cnNorthwind, , , adCmdText
                rsStock!UnitsInStock = rsStock!UnitsInStock - !Quantity
                rsStock.Update
                rsStock.Close
              End With
            Loop
         End If

         cnNorthwind.Close

      Exit Function

      BadSend:

         Debug.Print Err.Number & Err.Description
         Err.Clear
         cnNorthwind.Close
         Send_Order = "Error Entering Order"

      End Function
```

Our middle tier component is now ready for testing. First, let's build the client application, and then
we can test the two together.

Building the Client Application

To build the client application, keep the ActiveX DLL project open and select File | Add Project
from the menu. When the Open dialog appears, select the Standard EXE icon to create a new
project. Next, change the Name property of the form to frmClientApp and the Name property of
the project to ClientApp.

Now, save the form and project in the `Lab1` folder we created earlier. Use the default names given.

This project will use several ActiveX controls, so select Project | Components... from the menu bar. This will allow us to add the required components. Locate the following components and select them:

> **Microsoft DataGrid Control 6.0 (OLEDB)**: This control will be used to store the order details as each product is chosen.

> **Microsoft Hierarchical FlexGrid Control 6.0 (OLEDB)**: This control will hold a list of the products offered by `Northwind`.

> **Microsoft Windows Common Controls-2 6.0**: This is a group of ActiveX controls. The one we will use from this group is the Date Picker, which allows us to pick a date from a drop-down box that displays a miniature calendar.

The DataGrid and Hierarchical FlexGrid controls are described in Chapter 4.

Once you have located and selected all three of these, click on the OK button.

Next, we'll add the appropriate references to our project. Select Project | References... from the menu and locate the following references:

> **Microsoft ActiveX Data Objects 2.x Library**

> **ServerApp** – this is the reference to our middle tier component

Building the User Interface

We're now ready to build the Graphical User Interface for our project. Below is the form in design mode. Use this as a reference when building your form:

Using the following table, add the appropriate objects and change their properties as specified. Use the above image in adding objects and labels. You may name each of the labels as you want.

Object	Property	Value
Form	Name	frmClientApp
	Caption	Client Order Application
Frame Control	Name	fraCustomer
	Caption	Customer Detail
Combo Box	Name	cboCompany
	Text	{blank}
Text Box	Name	txtAddress
	Text	{blank}
Text Box	Name	txtCity
	Text	{blank}

Table Continued on Following Page

Object	Property	Value
Text Box	Name	txtRegion
	Text	{blank}
Text Box	Name	txtCountry
	Text	{blank}
Text Box	Name	txtPostal
	Text	{blank}
Text Box	Name	txtPhone
	Text	{blank}
MSHFlexGrid	Name	hfgProducts
Data Grid	Name	dgrOrderDetails
Combo Box	Name	cboShipVia
	Text	{blank}
Date Picker	Name	dtpOrder
Date Picker	Name	dtpRequired
Combo Box	Name	cboEmployee
	Text	{blank}
Text Box	Name	txtSubTotal
	Text	$ 0.00
	Alignment	1- Right Justify
Text Box	Name	txtFreight
	Text	$ 8.00
	Alignment	1- Right Justify
Text Box	Name	txtTotal
	Text	$ 0.00
	Alignment	1- Right Justify
Text Box	Name	txtOrderID
	Text	{blank}

Object	Property	Value
Command Button	Name	cmdNew
	Caption	New Order
Command Button	Name	cmdSend
	Caption	Send Order

Some properties of the Hierarchical FlexGrid Control can be viewed by right-clicking on it and selecting Properties. The following dialog will appear:

Change the Fixed Cols property to 0. This will eliminate the advance column on the left side of the control. Note that you can restrict the user's activity during runtime by altering many of these properties. Also set the FillStyle property to 1 - Repeat and the SelectionMode property to 1 - By Row.

Right-click on the DataGrid and select **Properties** to view its properties. The important property to change here is **AllowDelete**. Ensure that it is selected by checking it. This will allow the user the ability to delete a product from the `dgrOrderDetails` DataGrid control (should the customer change his/her mind):

We're now ready to write some code!

The Module_Level Variables

The first item on our list is to add our module-level variables. Open the form's code window and locate the **General Declarations** section. Declare an instance of `clsServer` with the name `objServer`:

```
Option Explicit
Dim objServer As clsServer
```

Next, declare all required recordsets that are to be returned (or passed). They are as follows:

➢ `rsGeneric` – This will be used as a generic recordset when we retrieve a recordset to populate the Combo Boxes or the `hfgProducts` Hierarchical FlexGrid.

➢ `rsOrder` – This recordset will be populated with a single record which will contain the fields required for an order to be processed. It will then be passed to the middle tier object.

➢ `rsOrderDetails` – This recordset serves a similar purpose to the `rsOrder` recordset. The difference being that this will contain the order detail information, which can consist of numerous records.

```
Dim rsGeneric As New ADODB.Recordset          ' Generic Recordset
Dim rsOrder As ADODB.Recordset                ' Order Recordset
Dim rsOrderDetails As ADODB.Recordset         ' Order Details
```

Finally, because we're providing a drag and drop interface for the user to drag a product to the `dgrOrderDetails` DataGrid, we will need to temporarily store some critical information while it's being dragged. These fields are `ProductID`, `ProductName` and `UnitPrice`, and will all be declared as strings:

```
Dim Drag_ProductID As String
Dim Drag_ProductName As String
Dim Drag_UnitPrice As String
```

The Form_Load Event Procedure

Logically, the first piece of code that will execute is the `Form_Load` event procedure. For this reason, we'll begin here. The `Form_Load` procedure executes a great deal of functionality. For a clear understanding of the code, let's step through it.

The first line of code instantiates a new instance of the `clsServer` middle tier object:

```
Set objServer = New clsServer
```

Next, we'll call the functions in the middle tier component, which populate the Combo Boxes. The code that accomplishes this will be repeated for each Combo Box that we want to populate. The first Combo Box is the `cboCompany` Combo Box. The `Customers` table populates this box, so we pass the parameter `Customers` to the `Get_Table_Recordset` function. This will return the entire table as a recordset. We can then navigate through the table and add each record's `CompanyName` field to the Combo Box.

The following two Combo Boxes are populated in a similar fashion with the exception that the `cboShipVia` and `cboEmployee` Combo Boxes set the default value equal to the field of the first record. In addition, the `cboEmployee` Combo Box is populated with two fields (`LastName` and `FirstName`):

```
Set rsGeneric = objServer.Get_Table_Recordset("Customers")
Do Until rsGeneric.EOF
  cboCompany.AddItem rsGeneric("CompanyName")
  rsGeneric.MoveNext
Loop

Set rsGeneric = objServer.Get_Table_Recordset("Shippers")
cboShipVia = rsGeneric("CompanyName")
Do Until rsGeneric.EOF
  cboShipVia.AddItem rsGeneric("CompanyName")
  rsGeneric.MoveNext
Loop

Set rsGeneric = objServer.Get_Table_Recordset("Employees")
cboEmployee = rsGeneric("LastName") & ", " & rsGeneric("FirstName")
Do Until rsGeneric.EOF
  cboEmployee.AddItem rsGeneric("LastName") & ", " & rsGeneric("FirstName")
  rsGeneric.MoveNext
Loop
```

Next, we populate the `hfgProducts` Hierarchical FlexGrid control. After calling the `Get_Products` function, populating the `rsGeneric` recordset, we need to set up the Hierarchical FlexGrid control to group common product categories. We have already established that the product category will be the first field, and have sorted the recordset by this field, but to present the data so that the common product categories blend together we need to set a few properties. The first is the `MergeCol` property. This identifies that the first column (index value 0) is to be grouped. The second property (`MergeCells`) identifies what type of grouping will take place. The possible values for this property are:

> `flexMergeNever` - 0: The cells containing identical content are not grouped. This is the default.

> `flexMergeFree` - 1: Cells with identical content always merge.

> `flexMergeRestrictRows` - 2: Only adjacent cells (to the left of the current cell) within the row containing identical content merge.

> `flexMergeRestrictColumns` - 3: Only adjacent cells (to the top of the current cell) within the column containing identical content merge.

> `flexMergeRestrictBoth` - 4: Only adjacent cells within the row (to the left) or column (to the top) containing identical content merge.

After the above properties are set, you can assign the `rsGeneric` recordset to the Hierarchical FlexGrid's `Recordset` property and the data will be populated in the respective field, grouped as directed:

```
Set rsGeneric = objServer.Get_Products()

hfgProducts.MergeCol(0) = True
hfgProducts.MergeCells = flexMergeRestrictColumns
Set hfgProducts.Recordset = rsGeneric
' Format Grid Width's
hfgProducts.ColWidth(0) = 1200
hfgProducts.ColWidth(1) = 800
hfgProducts.ColWidth(2) = 2000
hfgProducts.ColWidth(3) = 1500
hfgProducts.ColWidth(4) = 800
```

We'll need to create two empty recordsets for the order. We have already declared two recordsets for this purpose (`rsOrder` and `rsOrderDetails`). Before we can populate a recordset, we need to specify its structure. To do this, we'll call two procedures to assign each of the recordsets a structure that is in alignment with the structure of the database tables that the data will eventually populate. The two functions are named as follows. (We'll investigate each of these in detail later).

```
Create_New_Order
Create_New_Order_Detail
```

The last section of code in the event destroys the `rsGeneric` recordset object and sets the two Date Pickers (`dtpOrder` and `dtpRequired`) to a default value. In this scenario, I have chosen the system date as the order date's default value and the required date equal to the system date plus 7 days:

```
    Set rsGeneric = Nothing

    dtpOrder = Date
    dtpRequired = Date + 7
```

When complete, our `Form_Load` code looks as follows:

```
Private Sub Form_Load()

    Set objServer = New clsServer

    Set rsGeneric = objServer.Get_Table_Recordset("Customers")
    Do Until rsGeneric.EOF
      cboCompany.AddItem rsGeneric("CompanyName")
      rsGeneric.MoveNext
    Loop

    Set rsGeneric = objServer.Get_Table_Recordset("Shippers")
    cboShipVia = rsGeneric("CompanyName")
    Do Until rsGeneric.EOF
      cboShipVia.AddItem rsGeneric("CompanyName")
      rsGeneric.MoveNext
    Loop

    Set rsGeneric = objServer.Get_Table_Recordset("Employees")
    cboEmployee = rsGeneric("LastName") & ", " & rsGeneric("FirstName")
    Do Until rsGeneric.EOF
      cboEmployee.AddItem rsGeneric("LastName") & ", " & rsGeneric("FirstName")
      rsGeneric.MoveNext
    Loop
    Set rsGeneric = objServer.Get_Products()

    hfgProducts.MergeCol(0) = True
    hfgProducts.MergeCells = flexMergeRestrictColumns

    Set hfgProducts.Recordset = rsGeneric

    ' Format Grid Width's
    hfgProducts.ColWidth(0) = 1200
    hfgProducts.ColWidth(1) = 800
    hfgProducts.ColWidth(2) = 2000
    hfgProducts.ColWidth(3) = 1500
    hfgProducts.ColWidth(4) = 800

    Create_New_Order
    Create_New_Order_Detail

    Set rsGeneric = Nothing

    dtpOrder = Date
    dtpRequired = Date + 7

End Sub
```

The cboCompany_Click Event Procedure

When the user selects a customer from the Combo Box, we need to fetch the appropriate company details. To do this we can call on the cboCompany_Click event. This is fired after each click of the mouse on the combo box, which would identify a customer as being selected. When a customer is selected, we pass the value of the Combo Box to the Get_Customer_Details function of objServer. The objServer object will then select the data from the database and return a recordset to the caller. The company name should be unique so the recordset should only contain one record. For this reason, we don't need to implement a loop; we can simply pull the values from the recordset and populate the text boxes.

You may notice that we need to handle the possibility that the Region field may be null. The reason for this is that text boxes don't handle null values very well. If there are any fields that you suspect might be null, you should implement logic that appends a zero length string to it. We also call the cmdNew button to clear out any order details that may exist:

```
Private Sub cboCompany_Click()

    Set rsGeneric = objServer.Get_Customer_Details(cboCompany)

    txtAddress = rsGeneric("Address")
    txtCity = rsGeneric("City")
    txtPhone = rsGeneric("Phone")
    txtCountry = rsGeneric("Country")
    txtPostal = rsGeneric("PostalCode")
    txtRegion = "" & rsGeneric("Region")


    cmdNew.Value = True

    Set rsGeneric = Nothing

End Sub
```

The Create_New_Order Method

We'll create two procedures to create empty recordsets. When creating an empty recordset, we will declare the recordset and then append all fields required. Each new field should be declared as a compatible data type to the relating field in the database. The goal is to populate the recordset with data that will ultimately be pushed to the database. Once the recordset has been created, we open it and create a new record. In this manner, we're ready to add the record when we want to create a new order:

```
Public Sub Create_New_Order()

    ' Create the Order recordset
    Set rsOrder = New ADODB.Recordset
    With rsOrder.Fields
        .Append "CustomerID", adVarChar, 8
        .Append "EmployeeID", adBigInt
        .Append "OrderDate", adDate
        .Append "RequiredDate", adDate
        .Append "ShipVia", adBigInt
        .Append "Freight", adCurrency
        .Append "ShipName", adVarChar, 40
        .Append "ShipAddress", adVarChar, 60
        .Append "ShipCity", adVarChar, 15
        .Append "ShipRegion", adVarChar, 15
        .Append "ShipCountry", adVarChar, 15
        .Append "ShipPostalCode", adVarChar, 10
    End With

    With rsOrder
        .Open
        .AddNew
    End With

End Sub
```

The Create_New_Order_Detail Method

The procedure to create a new order detail recordset uses code similar to the previous method. In this example, we wait to execute the AddNew method because this will be called inside a loop. Don't forget that we may have a number of line items (detail records) in our order:

```
Public Sub Create_New_Order_Detail()

    ' Create the recordset for the OrderDetails grid.
    Set rsOrderDetails = New Recordset

    With rsOrderDetails.Fields
        .Append "ProductID", adInteger
        .Append "ProductName", adVarChar, 255
        .Append "UnitPrice", adCurrency
        .Append "Quantity", adDouble
        .Append "Discount", adDouble
        .Append "ExtendedPrice", adCurrency
    End With
    rsOrderDetails.Open

End Sub
```

Adding Drag-and-Drop Functionality

Next, we'll implement the drag-and-drop functionality of our interface. The first step will be to identify two icons that will serve as visual cues to the user:

> ➤ Drag icon: Identifies that the user has successfully selected the record and the record is being dragged with the movement of the mouse.

> ➤ Drop icon: Identifies that the record being dragged may be dropped on the specific ActiveX control.

You'll find these icons in the Visual Basic Samples folders. If you can't find suitable icons, don't worry too much at this point. The drag-and-drop functionality will still work without icons. If you did find icons you would like to use, move them to your application path and rename them to `Drag.ico` and `Drop.ico`. This will keep you in sync with the remaining code.

The Hierarchical FlexGrid's MouseDown Event

We'll use the `MouseDown` event to identify that a user is about to drag a record. When a user does click on a specific record (to drag it), that row becomes the active row for data retrieval. All that we need to do is set the column that we want to retrieve data from, and assign our variable to the text property of the Hierarchical FlexGrid control. In this example, we retrieve data from columns 1, 2 and 4. If you did not arrange your columns as specified earlier, you'll have your data scrambled. The three fields we want to drag to the DataGrid are `ProductID`, `ProductName` and `UnitPrice`. Note that we could have retrieved `ProductName` and `UnitPrice` from a SQL lookup, but if we already have the data available, there's no sense in causing additional network traffic.

The last step is to call the `Drag` method, passing the `vbBeginDrag` argument. This identifies that the record is being dragged. Lastly, we assign our `drag.ico` icon:

```
Private Sub hfgProducts_MouseDown(Button As Integer, Shift As Integer, _
                                  X As Single, Y As Single)

    hfgProducts.Col = 1
    Drag_ProductID = hfgProducts.Text
    hfgProducts.Col = 2
    Drag_ProductName = hfgProducts.Text
    hfgProducts.Col = 4
    Drag_UnitPrice = hfgProducts.Text

    hfgProducts.Drag vbBeginDrag
    hfgProducts.DragIcon = LoadPicture(App.Path & "\drag.ico")

End Sub
```

The DataGrid's DragOver Event

When the user drags the record over the `dgrOrderDetails` DataGrid, we need to identify that this is an acceptable location to drop the record. To do this, we call the `DragOver` event of the `dgrOrderDetails` DataGrid. This trigger is fired each time *any* control is dragged over it.

We then check the state of the drag. We're interested in two states. A 0 identifies that the control is being moved over the DataGrid and a 1 identifies that the control is being moved off the DataGrid control. We change the icon of our drag for each of the two instances:

```
Private Sub dgrOrderDetails_DragOver(Source As Control, X As Single, _
                                     Y As Single, State As Integer)
   Select Case State
     Case 0
       hfgProducts.DragIcon = LoadPicture(App.Path & "\drop.ico")
     Case 1
       hfgProducts.DragIcon = LoadPicture(App.Path & "\drag.ico")
   End Select

End Sub
```

The DataGrid's DragDrop Event

Finally, the drop! The `DragDrop` event identifies that the user has dropped the record on to the
DataGrid control. In a nutshell, the user let go of the control by letting the mouse button up. The goal
here is to identify if the dragged record already exists in the DataGrid control. If the product has
already been added, we want to alert the user. Otherwise, we'll add the information to the DataGrid
Control.

When looking for duplicates, we first check to see if the record count is greater than zero. If it's not,
the record cannot exist yet, so we can move on. Otherwise, we move to the first record, then navigate
through each of the records. As we navigate through them, we compare the `ProductID` of the
dragged record with each of the records in the `rsOrderDetails` recordset. The `rsOrderDetails`
recordset will be maintained as we add new records, so it's an excellent source to check for
duplicates. If we have a duplicate, we'll alert the user with a message box and exit the sub procedure,
abandoning the drop.

If the product does not already exist in the DataGrid, we need to add it. To do this, we'll call the
`AddNew` method against the `rsOrderDetails` recordset and then populate each of the fields.
Initially, the `Quantity` field will be set to 1 and the discount to 0. Once the record is complete, we'll
reassign the recordset to the `DataSource` property of the DataGrid control. This will refresh our
grid. When we reassign the `DataSource` of the Datagrid, we may lose the formatting or width of
each column. To overcome this, we reassign the column width properties of each column. Lastly,
we'll need to provide a *total* cost of the products ordered, so we'll call a procedure titled `Total_All`
to calculate this for us:

```
Private Sub dgrOrderDetails_DragDrop(Source As Control, X As Single, _
                                     Y As Single)

   ' Look for dups
   If rsOrderDetails.RecordCount > 0 Then
     rsOrderDetails.MoveFirst
     Do Until rsOrderDetails.EOF
       If rsOrderDetails("ProductID") = Drag_ProductID Then
         Beep
         MsgBox "Item already exists!"
         Exit Sub
       End If
       rsOrderDetails.MoveNext
     Loop
   End If

   rsOrderDetails.AddNew
```

```
    With rsOrderDetails
      !ProductID = Drag_ProductID
      !Quantity = 1
      !Discount = 0
      !ProductName = Drag_ProductName
      !UnitPrice = Drag_UnitPrice
    End With
    Set dgrOrderDetails.DataSource = rsOrderDetails

    dgrOrderDetails.Columns(1).Width = 2200
    dgrOrderDetails.Columns(2).Width = 1000
    dgrOrderDetails.Columns(3).Width = 1000
    dgrOrderDetails.Columns(4).Width = 1000

    Total_All

End Sub
```

The Total_All Function

The `Total_All` function is fairly simple but, however, a great deal of formatting takes place here to present the data in an easy to read manner. This formatting causes some confusion when reading and building the code. This procedure assigns the value of the fifth index field of the DataGrid control to the product of the columns 2, 3 and 4. With the discount field, we multiply the product of `UnitPrice` and `UnitsinStock` by 1 minus the discount value. If a customer receives a 30 percent discount on a product, the discount would be 0.30. The amount to be paid is 1-0.30 = 0.70 or 70 percent of the product cost.

The next step is to loop through the DataGrid and pull the sum of all extended prices. This is a fairly easy task, but the value is modified so that it's presented in the `txtSubTotal` text box in a standard currency format. After this takes place, the freight must be calculated in to produce the total.

> **When calculating values, it's best to transform all values by removing any dollar signs, etc.**

```
Public Sub Total_All()

    Dim curAmount As Currency
    If rsOrderDetails.RecordCount > 0 Then

      dgrOrderDetails.Columns(5) = dgrOrderDetails.Columns(2) * _
                                   dgrOrderDetails.Columns(3) * _
                                   (1 - dgrOrderDetails.Columns(4))

      rsOrderDetails.MoveFirst

      Do While Not rsOrderDetails.EOF
        curAmount = curAmount + rsOrderDetails!ExtendedPrice
        rsOrderDetails.MoveNext
      Loop
      txtSubTotal = Format(curAmount, "$ ##0.00")
```

```
          txtTotal = Format(Right$(txtFreight, Len(txtFreight) - 2) + _
                         curAmount, "$ ##0.00")

       Else
         txtSubTotal = "$ 0.00"
         txtTotal = "$ 0.00"
       End If

   End Sub
```

The DataGrid's AfterColUpdate Event

To ensure that the application keeps a strict running total of all products purchased, you should call the `Total_All` procedure in the `AfterColUpdate` event of the DataGrid control. This will ensure that the total is re-calculated after the user modifies the quantity or discount.

```
   Private Sub dgrOrderDetails_AfterColUpdate(ByVal ColIndex As Integer)

       Total_All

   End Sub
```

The cmdNew_Click Event Procedure

At any time, the user may want to clear the slate, and build a new order. This may occur after an order has been placed and confirmed, or if the customer changes his/her mind during the construction of the order. Clearing the order is easy because we structured the application to be re-usable.

As you will see later, when an order is sent to the database, some of the form's functionality will disable. The reason for this is that if an order is placed, the user should not have the ability to add more items. When handling this, we will disable the **Send Order** button, the DataGrid and the Hierarchical FlexGrid controls. When the slate is cleared, we want to enable these controls so that the user can add the next order. In addition, a confirmation number may exist in the `txtOrderID` textbox, so this should be cleared. To clear the `rsOrderDetails` recordset, we can simply call the `Create_New_Order_Detail` procedure. This will destroy the existing `rsOrderDetails` recordset and create a fresh one for us. The final step is to re-assign the *empty* recordset we just created to the DataGrid. This will create the appearance that the slate has been cleared. You may also elect to clear the Company Combo Box:

```
   Private Sub cmdNew_Click()

       cmdSend.Enabled = True
       dgrOrderDetails.Enabled = True
       hfgProducts.Enabled = True

       txtOrderID = ""

       Create_New_Order_Detail

       Set dgrOrderDetails.DataSource = rsOrderDetails

       Total_All

   End Sub
```

The cmdSend_Click Event Procedure

Saving the best procedure for last, we need to build code to send the order to the component on the middle tier. As a reminder, the goal here will be to build the order record, and pass it, along with the rsOrderDetails recordset to the server. First, declare strOrderConfirm as a string. This will contain the confirmation/error code that is returned from the middle tier.

Some generic business rules should be applied at this point. These rules will validate that the company has been chosen, and actual products have been added to the list. It's often a more practical solution to apply simple logic such as this at the client than at the server. Remember that one of our primary objectives should be to minimize the amount of network traffic. In this scenario, the odds that this logic will be modified after it has moved to production are fairly slim.

The next step is to populate all elements of the rsOrder recordset. This is fairly straightforward database programming; the only hitch here is that we need to populate the elements with the appropriate values. What is meant by this is that CustomerID should be populated with CustomerID and not CompanyName. As you recall, we built a function to handle this, so we can pass the CompanyName and retrieve the CustomerID. We call this function again when dealing with the EmployeeID Field.

Once the rsOrder recordset is populated, we pass both recordsets (rsOrder and rsOrderDetails) to the middle tier component. The component will then process the recordsets and add the new records to the database. If no errors are detected, the confirmation number is returned (which is assigned to the Confirmation text box) and the key controls are disabled (as discussed above). If an error is returned, the error message is displayed in a text box. This is where more time should be spent translating the error message into a string to which the user can relate. This might entail describing the error in 'laymen's terms' or even prompting the user to enter more information by setting the focus to the field that was in error.

The last step is to refresh the product Hierarchical FlexGrid control. We need to do this because the product was removed from inventory. Because many users may be removing stock from inventory, you may want to take this a step farther, and have the client periodically re-populate the products grid. This will reduce the possibility of selling stock you don't have.

```
Private Sub cmdSend_Click()

    Dim strOrderConfirm As String

    ' Validate some business Rules

    If cboCompany = "" Then
      MsgBox "Company Name must be valid!"
      Exit Sub
    End If

    If rsOrderDetails.RecordCount < 1 Then
      MsgBox "No items listed in the order detail section!"
      Exit Sub
    End If

    Me.MousePointer = vbHourglass
```

```
    With rsOrder
      !CustomerID = objServer.Get_ID("Customers", cboCompany)
      !EmployeeID = objServer.Get_ID("Employees", cboEmployee)
      !OrderDate = dtpOrder
      !RequiredDate = dtpRequired
      !Freight = Val(txtFreight)
      !ShipVia = objServer.Get_ID("Shippers", cboShipVia)
      !ShipName = cboCompany
      !ShipAddress = txtAddress
      !ShipCity = txtCity
      !ShipRegion = txtRegion
      !ShipCountry = txtCountry
      !ShipPostalCode = txtPostal

    End With

    'Send order to Server
    strOrderConfirm = objServer.Send_Order(rsOrder, rsOrderDetails)

    Me.MousePointer = vbArrow

    If IsNumeric(strOrderConfirm) Then
      txtOrderId = strOrderConfirm

      MsgBox "Your order has been placed. The " _
            & vbCrLf & "confirmation number is: " & strOrderConfirm

      cmdSend.Enabled = False
      dgrOrderDetails.Enabled = False
      hfgProducts.Enabled = False

    Else
      MsgBox strOrderConfirm
    End If

    Set rsGeneric = objServer.Get_Products()
    Set hfgProducts.Recordset = rsGeneric

End Sub
```

Test the Solution

We're now ready to test our solution. Our ServerApp project should be open along side this application, so set the ClientApp project as the StartUp project by right-clicking on it and selecting Set As Start Up. Finally, click on the Start button. Follow the following step to test your solution:

1. Select a customer from the Company Combo Box. Do the customer's details populate correctly? Try choosing a customer with a single quote embedding in the name, such as BonApp'

2. Try dragging a product from the Products Hierarchical FlexGrid to the Order Details DataGrid. The product should be added with all fields properly filled in.

3. Add the same product again. Does it warn you that the product is already added to the list?

4. Add a few more products and try changing the quantity of each. Ensure that the ExtendedPrice updates, as well as the Sub Total and Total text boxes.

5. Select one of the products from the Order Details DataGrid control and hit the *Delete* keyboard button. The product should be removed from the list.

6. Choose the Ship Method and Employee and make any changes you need, then click on the Send Order button. If no errors are encountered, the confirmation number should be returned.

7. To confirm that our order made it to the database, open the Orders and Order Details tables.

Now compile both the client and the server applications. Close down Visual Basic and run ClientApp.exe. Everything should work in exactly the same way.

Rolling the Solution out to MTS

Now that our client and middle tier applications have been tested, we'll roll this solution out to MTS. We'll do this just as we did in the Chapter 11. In a later chapter we'll explore how to use MTS to implement security. Finally, in Chapter 17, we will see how to roll out a 3-tier solution to many computers.

Copy the entire ServerApp project and move it to the Lab2 folder (C:\ProVB6DB\Chapter13\Lab2).

Open the ServerApp project and set a reference to the Microsoft Transaction Server Type Library.

Then open the Properties window for clsServer and change its MTSTransactionMode property to 2 - Requires Transaction.

Now select Project | ServerApp Properties... from the menu. In the General tab, change the following properties:

➤ Check the Unattended Execution check box.
➤ Check the Retained In Memory check box.

Then click on the Component tab and select the Binary Compatibility option.

> **If the DLL name does not appear in the text box, click on the button to the right of it and locate the compiled ServerApp.dll.**

We're now ready to make our code modifications. As you recall, earlier in the chapter we did not implement much in the way of error handling in our ServerApp functions. As we roll this out to MTS, we'll implement some loose error handling.

As I mentioned before, functions where data is being retrieved, but not updated, do not need a transaction wrapper. Only the `Send_Order` function really requires a transaction. However, by implementing transactions on all components, valuable statistics are provided.

Start by adding the declaration for the `ObjectContext` object in the General Declarations section of `clsServer`:

```
Dim objContext As ObjectContext
```

The Get_Table_Recordset Function

```
Public Function Get_Table_Recordset(strTable As String) As ADODB.Recordset

    Set objContext = GetObjectContext()

    On Error GoTo errHandle

    cnNorthwind.Open
    cnNorthwind.CursorLocation = adUseClient

    strSQL = "SELECT * FROM " & strTable

    Set Get_Table_Recordset = cnNorthwind.Execute(strSQL)

    Get_Table_Recordset.ActiveConnection = Nothing
    cnNorthwind.Close

    If Not objContext Is Nothing Then
       objContext.SetComplete
       Set objContext = Nothing
    End If

Exit Function

errHandle:
    If Not objContext Is Nothing Then
       objContext.SetAbort
       Set objContext = Nothing
    End If
    Err.Clear

End Function
```

The Get_Products Function

```
Public Function Get_Products() As ADODB.Recordset

    Set objContext = GetObjectContext()

    On Error GoTo errHandle

    cnNorthwind.Open
    cnNorthwind.CursorLocation = adUseClient
```

```
        strSQL = "SELECT Categories.CategoryName, Products.ProductID, " & _
                 "Products.ProductName,Products.QuantityPerUnit," & _
                 "Products.UnitPrice,Products.UnitsInStock, " & _
                 "Products.UnitsOnOrder FROM Categories " & _
                 "INNER JOIN Products ON Categories.CategoryID " & _
                 "= Products.CategoryID " & _
                 "ORDER BY Categories.CategoryName"

        Set Get_Products = cnNorthwind.Execute(strSQL)

        Get_Products.ActiveConnection = Nothing
        cnNorthwind.Close

        If Not objContext Is Nothing Then
            objContext.SetComplete
            Set objContext = Nothing
        End If

    Exit Function

    errHandle:

        If Not objContext Is Nothing Then
            objContext.SetAbort
            Set objContext = Nothing
        End If
        Err.Clear

End Function
```

The Get_Customer_Details Function

```
    Public Function Get_Customer_Details(CompanyName As String) As ADODB.Recordset

        Set objContext = GetObjectContext()

        On Error GoTo errHandle

        cnNorthwind.Open
        cnNorthwind.CursorLocation = adUseClient

        CompanyName = Replace(CompanyName, "'", "''")

        strSQL = "SELECT * FROM Customers WHERE CompanyName = '" & CompanyName & "'"

        Set Get_Customer_Details = cnNorthwind.Execute(strSQL)

        Get_Customer_Details.ActiveConnection = Nothing
        cnNorthwind.Close

        If Not objContext Is Nothing Then
            objContext.SetComplete
            Set objContext = Nothing
        End If

    Exit Function

    errHandle:
```

```
      If Not objContext Is Nothing Then
        objContext.SetAbort
        Set objContext = Nothing
      End If
      Err.Clear

  End Function
```

The Get_ID Function

```
    Public Function Get_ID(strTable As String, strValue) As String

      Set objContext = GetObjectContext()

      On Error GoTo errHandle

    cnNorthwind.Open
    cnNorthwind.CursorLocation = adUseClient

    Select Case strTable

      Case "Customers"
        strSQL = "SELECT * FROM Customers WHERE CompanyName = '" & strValue & "'"
        Set rsGeneric = cnNorthwind.Execute(strSQL)
        Get_ID = rsGeneric("CustomerID")

      Case "Employees"
        strSQL = "SELECT * FROM Employees WHERE " _
              & "LastName = '" & Left(strValue, InStr(strValue, ",") - 1) _
              & "' AND FirstName = '" & _
                Right(strValue, Len(strValue) - InStr(strValue, ",") - 1) & "'"
        Set rsGeneric = cnNorthwind.Execute(strSQL)
        Get_ID = rsGeneric("EmployeeID")

      Case "Shippers"
        strSQL = "SELECT * FROM Shippers WHERE CompanyName = '" & strValue & "'"
        Set rsGeneric = cnNorthwind.Execute(strSQL)
        Get_ID = rsGeneric("ShipperID")

    End Select

    rsGeneric.ActiveConnection = Nothing
    cnNorthwind.Close

      If Not objContext Is Nothing Then
        objContext.SetComplete
        Set objContext = Nothing
      End If

    Exit Function

    errHandle:

      If Not objContext Is Nothing Then
        objContext.SetAbort
        Set objContext = Nothing
      End If
      Err.Clear

    End Function
```

The Send_Order Function

```
Public Function Send_Order(rsNewOrder As ADODB.Recordset, rsNewOrderDetail As _
                           ADODB.Recordset) As String

    On Error GoTo BadSend

    Set objContext = GetObjectContext()

    cnNorthwind.Open
    cnNorthwind.CursorLocation = adUseServer

    strSQL = "SELECT * FROM Orders WHERE 1=2"
    rsOrder.LockType = adLockOptimistic
    rsOrder.CursorType = adOpenKeyset
    rsOrder.Open strSQL, cnNorthwind, , , adCmdText

    strSQL = "SELECT * FROM [Order Details] WHERE 1 =2"
    rsOrderDetails.LockType = adLockOptimistic
    rsOrderDetails.CursorType = adOpenKeyset
    rsOrderDetails.Open strSQL, cnNorthwind, , , adCmdText

    rsStock.LockType = adLockOptimistic
    rsStock.CursorType = adOpenKeyset

    With rsOrder
      .AddNew
      !CustomerID = rsNewOrder!CustomerID
      !EmployeeID = rsNewOrder!EmployeeID
      !OrderDate = rsNewOrder!OrderDate
      !RequiredDate = rsNewOrder!RequiredDate
      !ShipVia = rsNewOrder!ShipVia
      !Freight = rsNewOrder!Freight
      !ShipName = rsNewOrder!ShipName
      !ShipAddress = rsNewOrder!ShipAddress
      !ShipCity = rsNewOrder!ShipCity
      If Trim(rsNewOrder!ShipRegion) <> "" Then
         !ShipRegion = rsNewOrder!ShipRegion
      End If
      !ShipCountry = rsNewOrder!ShipCountry
      !ShipPostalCode = rsNewOrder!ShipPostalCode
      .Update
      Send_Order = !OrderID
    End With

    If rsNewOrderDetail.RecordCount > 0 Then
      rsNewOrderDetail.MoveFirst
      Do Until rsNewOrderDetail.EOF
        With rsOrderDetails
          .AddNew
          !OrderID = rsOrder!OrderID
          !ProductID = rsNewOrderDetail!ProductID
          !UnitPrice = rsNewOrderDetail!UnitPrice
          !Quantity = rsNewOrderDetail!Quantity
          !Discount = rsNewOrderDetail!Discount
          .Update

          rsNewOrderDetail.MoveNext
```

```
        strSQL = "SELECT * FROM Products WHERE ProductID = " & !ProductID
        rsStock.Open strSQL, cnNorthwind, , , adCmdText
        rsStock!UnitsInStock = rsStock!UnitsInStock - !Quantity
        rsStock.Update
        rsStock.Close
    End With
  Loop
End If

    cnNorthwind.Close

    If Not objContext Is Nothing Then
      objContext.SetComplete
      Set objContext = Nothing
    End If

Exit Function

BadSend:

    Debug.Print Err.Number & Err.Description
    Err.Clear
    cnNorthwind.Close
    Send_Order = "Error Entering Order"
    If Not objContext Is Nothing Then
      objContext.SetAbort
      Set objContext = Nothing
    End If

End Function
```

Using the ObjectControl

There is a final change we need to make to our component, the object being hosted by MTS is created, activated, deactivated and destroyed transparently from the client. However, we must add some additional code to our components so that MTS can do this.

All good components running under MTS should implement something known as the ObjectControl interface. This interface informs an object when it has been activated and deactivated. We can implement the ObjectControl interface by adding the following line to the General Declarations section:

```
Implements ObjectControl
```

The ObjectControl interface has three methods, all of which must be exposed.

The Activate Method

The Activate method is called the first time that a client invokes a method in the server component. All initialization code that was previously placed into Class_Initialize should be placed in the ObjectControl_Activate. Delete the code from the Class_Initialize event procedure. Place the code that had been present in the Class_Initialize event into ObjectControl_Activate:

```
Private Sub ObjectControl_Activate()

    Set cnNorthwind = New ADODB.Connection
    cnNorthwind.ConnectionString = "DSN=NorthWind;uid=sa;pwd="

End Sub
```

The Deactivate Method

This method is called when the real object, not the `ObjectContext` object, is destroyed. Even though we don't intend to place any code in `ObjectControl_Deactivate` we still need to place the "shell", otherwise we'll get an error when we try to compile:

```
Private Sub ObjectControl_Deactivate()

End Sub
```

The CanBePooled Method

This method is called just after the `Deactivate` method is called by MTS. The purpose of this method is to allow components to be pooled in the future. MTS does not currently support object pooling so we won't add any code here either. However, as with the `Deactivate` method, we still need to add the "shell":

```
Private Function ObjectControl_CanBePooled() As Boolean

End Function
```

With these changes made, recompile the DLL.

Adding the DLL to MTS

Create a new package by right-clicking on the Packages Installed folder and selecting New | Package. In the Package Wizard dialog select Create an empty package. Name the new package, New Order Form. Finally, in the Set Package Identity dialog, keep the default settings and click on Finish.

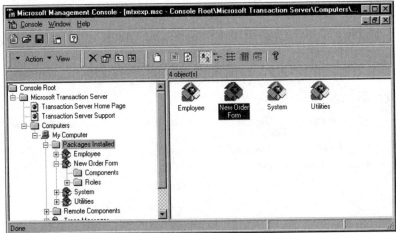

Now add `ServerApp.clsServer` as a component to the package, by right-clicking on the **Components** folder beneath **New Order Form** and selecting **New | Component**. Select **I**mport component(s) that are already registered. In the **Import** window, select **ServerApp.clsServer** and click on the **Finish** button:

Indicate that the component will always require a transaction, by right-clicking on the component and selecting **Properties**. Click on the **Transaction** tab, and then select **R**equires a transaction.

Following the same test criteria as earlier in this chapter, retest the client and server applications.

Summary

This chapter followed many of the concepts we covered in Chapters 11 and 12. In this chapter, we not only created a 3-tier solution that we rolled out to MTS, we used a more efficient method of passing data between tiers than we first saw in Chapter 12: that of using disconnected recordsets. The example produced in this chapter demonstrates some of the challenges associated with passing recordsets between the client and middle tier, then on to the database, as discussed in Chapter 12. We also looked at the `ObjectControl` interface and moved all the code from our `Class_Initialize` event into the `Activate` method of `ObjectControl`.

In Chapter 14, we will take a look at yet another 3-tier solution involving an object that is a **black-box**. A black-box object is one that exposes properties, methods and events to other developers that are using our object. However, unlike the examples we have looked at before, a black-box should be as simple to use as possible, so that a developer does not need to how our object works before he or she can access it from a client application.

Suppliers

- SupplierID
- CompanyName
- ContactName
- ContactTitle
- Address
- City
- Region
- PostalCode
- Country
- Phone
- Fax
- HomePage

Products

- ProductID
- ProductName
- SupplierID
- CategoryID
- QuantityPerUnit
- UnitPrice
- UnitsInStock
- UnitsOnOrder
- ReorderLevel
- Discontinued

Categories

- CategoryID
- CategoryName
- Description
- Picture

6

The Three Class Concept

The most important thing when building an ActiveX DLL or EXE that will be responsible for manipulating and maintaining data in a database is to build this object like a **black box**. A black box is an object in which everything done on the object occurs inside of the object and external objects should not be aware of what and how the things are done. In the object-oriented world, this is called **encapsulation**.

In this chapter, we will build a *Customer* object that will use the `Northwind` database that ships with SQL Server 7.0. This *Customer* object will feed us the customer data from `Northwind`. This could be from one table or from many tables, but in this example, we'll just use the `Customers` table.

Customers Example			_ □ ×

CustomerID:	ALFKI	Company Name:	Alfreds Futterkiste
Contact Name:	Maria Anders	Contact Title:	Sales Representative
Address:	Obere Str. 57	City:	Berlin
Region:		Postal Code:	12209
Phone:	030-0074321	Fax:	030-0076545
Country:	Germany		

Record 1 of 91

This looks very similar to the kind of application we've been producing up until now - maybe even simpler. So what's new?

The Customer Data Object

The *Customer* object is an example of a **data object**. Data objects do not contain any business rules; they only manage data. The objects that we have been looking at previously contained business logic, for this reason they are called **business objects**.

One of the most important features of data objects is that they are completely reusable. We can take our *Customer* object and use it in fifty different applications, all with different purposes and different business rules. Better still, most data objects are very similar in construction, you should find it relatively simple to change the *Customer* object into an *Order* object, simply by replacing every instance of the word Customer with Order and changing the field names used in the *Customer* object for ones more relevant to the *Order* object.

Our *Customer* object will be made of three separate classes, clsCustomerSrvr, colCustomers and clsCustomer:

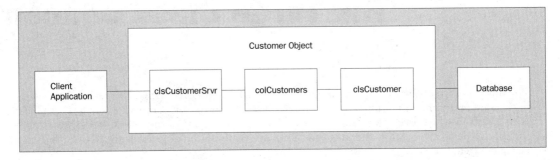

Any developers using our *Customer* object, perhaps to create a user interface similar to the one we'll produce at the end of this chapter, will access it only via the clsCustomerSrvr class - they will not be allowed to access either colCustomers or clsCustomer directly.

Building the Customer Object

Start a new ActiveX DLL project called dataCustomer and add three class modules called clsCustomerSrvr, colCustomers and clsCustomer. Save the project in a new Chapter14 folder in the ProVB6DB folder.

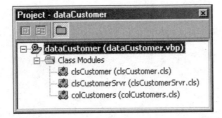

Add a reference to the Microsoft ActiveX Data Objects 2.x Library.

Now set the `Instancing` property of both `clsCustomer` and `colCustomers` to 2 - `PublicNotCreatable`. Leave the `Instancing` property of `clsCustomerSrvr` as the default, 5 - `MultiUse`.

Setting a class' `Instancing` property to `MultiUse` allows clients to create objects from it. In addition, one component can be used to create multiple objects. This means that multiple clients can access the object.

With `PublicNotCreatable`, a class is public, but clients cannot make calls to it until another class in the same component has created an instance of it first. By setting `clsCustomer` and `colCustomers` to `PublicNotCreatable` we force users of our *Customer* object to access `clsCustomerSrvr` first.

Adding Code to clsCustomerSrvr

The `clsCustomerSrvr` class offers us the interface into the data object that we are exposing to other developers. We've achieved this by setting its `Instancing` property to `MultiUse`. Had we set the `Instancing` property of the `clsCustomer` object to `MultiUse` also, the developer would have been able to instantiate it directly, without using the `clsCustomerSrvr` object.

The General Declarations Section

The first declaration is for the `colCustomers` collection object:

```
'Internal Customers collection
Private m_colCustomers As colCustomers
```

The following constants are used throughout `clsCustomerSrvr`. They represent actual stored procedures that we will add to `Northwind` later in this chapter. This way if we need to use a different stored procedure we just need to update the declaration with the correct name. For example, if we decide to use `sp_CustomerDetails` instead of `sps_Customer`, we do not have to search through the entire code for any references to `sps_Customer`, we just replace this declaration:

```
Const SPS = "sps_Customer"
Const SPI = "spi_Customer"
Const SPD = "spd_Customer"
Const SPU = "spu_Customer"
```

We will create an internal *Customers* collection by calling the `Load` method of `clsCustomerSrvr` and passing in a `LoadType` argument. There are two possible values for the `LoadTypes` argument, 0 and 1. We will set `LoadType` equal to 0 if we want all the records from the `Customers` table to be returned as objects. If we only wish to retrieve a single record from the `Customers` table as an object, we will set `LoadType` equal to 1. By creating an enumeration, we can provide any user of our *Customer* object with a list of possible values instead of the less descriptive 0 and 1:

```
Customer_Tester - frmCustomer (Code)                    _ □ ×
Form                              ▼   Load                         ▼
    'Get a reference to a new Customer Server object          ▲
        Set m_objCustomerSrvr = New clsCustomerSrvr
    'Load all of the Customer objects
        m_objCustomerSrvr.Load
    'Get a reference to the  ┌──────────────┐ lection
        Set m_colCustomers = │ ⊞ All         │ rvr.Customers
        m_iCustomerIndicator │ ⊠ Customer    │
    'Load the First Customer └──────────────┘
        LoadCustomerRecord
    End Sub
                                                            ▼
≡▐ ◄ ▐                                                   ►
```

Enter the following code into the General Declarations section:

```
Public Enum Types
    All = 0
    Customer = 1
End Enum
```

We use the keyword New to indicate a new *Customer* object that has not been saved yet to the database. We create a constant called CNEW, just in case we decide to change the keyword in the future:

```
Private Const CNEW = "New"
```

The Class_Initialize Event

The Class_Initialize event procedure speaks for itself, we just instantiate an m_colCustomers object from our colCustomers class:

```
Private Sub Class_Initialize()

    Set m_colCustomers = New colCustomers

End Sub
```

Delete Method

The Delete method gives us away to mark a customer to be removed from the database. We specify which customer should be deleted by calling the Item property of the m_colCustomers collection and providing the Key value, which identifies the customer we want to delete.

Note that I said, "marked to be removed". Nothing is done to the database until a call is made to the Save method of m_colCustomers:

```
Public Sub Delete(varKey As Variant)

    On Error GoTo ErrorHandler

    m_colCustomers.Item(varKey).IsDeleted = True
```

```
    Exit Sub

    ErrorHandler:

        ' Raise an error back to the calling application/object that something
        ' went wrong when trying to mark the item to be deleted when saved

        Err.Raise 1002, , "Unable to mark customer as deleted!"

    End Sub
```

As you can see here we are updating the `IsDeleted` property for the *Customer* object that the user requested to be marked as deleted.

IsDirty Method

The `IsDirty` method checks each of the `objCustomer` objects to see if any have been changed since they were loaded:

```
    Public Function IsDirty() As Boolean

        On Error GoTo ErrorHandler

        Dim objCustomer As clsCustomer

        IsDirty = False
        For Each objCustomer In m_colCustomers
            If objCustomer.IsDirty Then
                IsDirty = True
                Exit For
            End If
        Next
        Set objCustomer = Nothing

    Exit Function

    ErrorHandler:

        If Not objCustomer Is Nothing Then
            Set objCustomer = Nothing
        End If

        ' Raise the error back to the calling application/object
        Err.Raise 1004, , _
            "Unable to check to see if the customer objects have changed!"

    End Function
```

As you can see in the code above, we are going to loop through the `m_colCustomers` collection and see if any of the `objCustomer` objects have been changed. To determine if they have changed since they have been loaded we will look at the `IsDirty` property for each of the `objCustomer` objects. If we find one that has changed, we will set the return value of the `IsDirty` method equal to `True` and then exit the function. Otherwise, we return a `False`.

This method is normally called before the calling object, for example a client application using the *Customer* object, closes down. Before the client application is closed down, we need to check if the user has made any changes. To find this out we call the clsCustomerSrvr's IsDirty method. Now if we get a True back, we know that we must prompt the user to save the changes.

Load Method

The Load method has the job of building our *Customers* collection. To do this it will take two parameters: LoadType and Key. LoadType is just one of our Types enumeration values. The Key parameter holds the CustomerID. The Key parameter is optional and is only set if the LoadType parameter is set to Customer.

If the LoadType parameter is set to All, then all the records in the database will be returned as objCustomer objects. If the LoadType parameter is set to Customer, then a single, specified record will be returned as an objCustomer object.

Enter the following code:

```
Public Sub Load(LoadType As Types, Optional Key As Long)

    On Error GoTo ErrorHandler
    Dim objConnect As ADODB.Connection
    Dim objRecordset As ADODB.Recordset
    Dim objCustomer As Customer
    Dim strSQL As String

    Set objConnect = New ADODB.Connection
    Set objRecordset = New ADODB.Recordset

    'Set the ConnectionString
    objConnect.ConnectionString = "driver={SQL Server};" & _
            "server=gifforddr;uid=sa;pwd=;database=Northwind"

    'Open a connection to the database
    objConnect.Open

    strSQL = SPS

    'Set the LoadType parameter
    strSQL = strSQL & " " & LoadType

    'Set the CustomerID, if LoadType is 0 then set CustomerID = Null.
    'Otherwise set the CustomerID parameter = to the Key value.
    If LoadType = All Then
        strSQL = strSQL & ", " & "Null"
    Else
        strSQL = strSQL & ", '" & Key & "'"
    End If

    'Open the Recordset
    objRecordset.Open strSQL, objConnect, adOpenForwardOnly

    'Now load the customers returned by the database into their objects
    Do While Not objRecordset.EOF
        Set objCustomer = m_colCustomers.Add(objRecordset("CustomerID"))
        With objCustomer
            .IsLoading = True
```

```
        .CustomerID = objRecordset("CustomerID")
        .CompanyName = objRecordset("CompanyName")

        'All of the following properties can be Null, to handle this
        'we do a check to see before updating the property

        If Not IsNull(objRecordset("Address")) Then
           .Address = objRecordset("Address")
        End If

        If Not IsNull(objRecordset("City")) Then
           .City = objRecordset("City")
        End If

        If Not IsNull(objRecordset("ContactName")) Then
           .ContactName = objRecordset("ContactName")
        End If

        If Not IsNull(objRecordset("ContactTitle")) Then
           .ContactTitle = objRecordset("ContactTitle")
        End If

        If Not IsNull(objRecordset("Country")) Then
           .Country = objRecordset("Country")
        End If

        If Not IsNull(objRecordset("Fax")) Then
           .Fax = objRecordset("Fax")
        End If

        If Not IsNull(objRecordset("Phone")) Then
           .Phone = objRecordset("Phone")
        End If

        If Not IsNull(objRecordset("PostalCode")) Then
           .PostalCode = objRecordset("PostalCode")
        End If

        If Not IsNull(objRecordset("Region")) Then
           .Region = objRecordset("Region")
        End If

        .IsLoading = False
      End With
      objRecordset.MoveNext

   Loop

   Set objCustomer = Nothing
   Set objRecordset = Nothing
   Set objConnect = Nothing

Exit Sub

ErrorHandler:

   Err.Raise 1003, , "Load Customer object failure!"

End Sub
```

Starting at the top of the method above you will see that we first setup the connection to the Northwind database. Once we have this, we build the stored procedure call that we will use for this load. The constant SPS represents a stored procedure called sps_Customer, which we will add to the Northwind database later in this chapter. If we are loading all of the customer records into objects then we set the last parameter of strSQL equal to Null. Otherwise, we set the last parameter equal to the CustomerID value being passed into the Load method, in other words Key:

```
strSQL = SPS

'Set the LoadType parameter
strSQL = strSQL & " " & LoadType

'Set the CustomerID, if LoadType is 0 then set CustomerID = Null.
'Otherwise set the CustomerID parameter = to the Key value.
If LoadType = All Then
    strSQL = strSQL & ", " & "Null"
Else
    strSQL = strSQL & ", '" & Key & "'"
End If
```

Once we have the stored procedure ready, we open a recordset that holds the records that we just asked to be loaded:

```
objRecordset.Open strSQL, objConnect, adOpenForwardOnly
```

Now we could pass all of the fields for each record into the Add method, but if we did this we would have a large parameter list and it would become very difficult to maintain. Instead, what we have done is pass in the Key for the objCustomer object (CustomerID). The Add method in turn hands us back the objCustomer object for us to work with, so that we can load all of the other properties for the objCustomer object:

```
Set objCustomer = m_colCustomers.Add(objRecordset("CustomerID"))
```

Then we set the value of the IsLoading property of objCustomer equal to True. We'll look at the IsLoading property in more detail when we come to add code to the clsCustomer class. The IsLoading property just lets the objCustomer object know that it is in a "Loading" state and that its IsDirty property should not be set:

```
With objCustomer
    .IsLoading = True
```

Before we just load each property, we first check to see if it is Null or not. If it is not then we load the property. If it is we leave the property alone:

```
If Not IsNull(objRecordset("Address")) Then
    .Address = objRecordset("Address")
End If
```

When all the properties for a particular objCustomer object have been set, we set its IsLoading property to False so that the object is in a "Not Loading" state:

```
    .IsLoading = False
```

Once we have finished loading all the objCustomer objects requested, we close all of our object references:

```
Set objCustomer = Nothing
Set objRecordset = Nothing
Set objConnect = Nothing
```

NewCustomer Method

The NewCustomer method will create a new objCustomer object and add it to the m_colCustomers collection. This routine will return a string (strKey) that represents the Key used in clsCustomerSrvr's Load and Save methods. Before we return the strKey variable, we also mark the new objCustomer object as being dirty:

```
Public Function NewCustomer() As String

    Dim strKey As String
    Static intNewCount As Integer

    strKey = CNEW & " - " & intNewCount

    Call m_colCustomers.Add(strKey)

    m_colCustomers.Item(strKey).IsDirty = True

    intNewCount = intNewCount + 1
    NewCustomer = strKey

Exit Function

ErrorHandler:

    Err.Raise 2004, , "New Customer Failure"

End Function
```

Again, nothing fancy here! We set the CNEW constant appended to a hyphen and the value of the intNewCount integer equal to a string called strKey:

```
strKey = CNEW & " - " & intNewCount
```

We then add a new objCustomer object to the m_colCustomers collection and set the new object's IsDirty property equal to True:

```
Call m_colCustomers.Add(strKey)

m_colCustomers.Item(strKey).IsDirty = True
```

We then increment the value of intNewCount by one. intNewCount has been declared as Static, so it will retain its value as long as the instance of m_colCustomers exists. If we had declared intNewCount with Dim, the value which we had assigned to it in this procedure would be lost the next time NewCustomer was called. This could result in two objects having the same Key and an error would be raised.

Save Method

The Save method is really the heart and soul of the clsCustomerSrvr class as it handles the saving of new records, the updating of old records and the deleting of records marked for deletion.

The Save method works by looping through all the objects in the m_colCustomers collection. If it finds an objCustomer object marked as dirty it will save it to the database. If it finds any that have an IsDeleted property of True it will delete the associated record from the database:

```
Public Sub Save()

  On Error GoTo ErrorHandler

    Dim objConnect As ADODB.Connection
    Dim objCommand As ADODB.Command
    Dim objParam As ADODB.Parameter
    Dim objCustomer As clsCustomer
    Dim objHoldCustomer As clsCustomer
    Dim strSQL As String
    Dim intFor As Integer

    Set objConnect = New ADODB.Connection

    'Set the ConnectionString
    objConnect.ConnectionString = "driver={SQL Server};" & _
             "server=gifforddr;uid=sa;pwd=;database=Northwind"

    'Open a connection to the database
     objConnect.Open

    For intFor = m_colCustomers.Count To 1 Step -1
       Set objCustomer = m_colCustomers.Item(intFor)

       If objCustomer.IsDirty Then
          With objCustomer
             Set objCommand = New ADODB.Command
             Set objCommand.ActiveConnection = objConnect

             'If the customer is a new customer and is also deleted then
             'just remove it from the collection as we have not added the
             'customer to the database yet
             If InStr(.Key, "New") And .IsDeleted Then
                m_colCustomers.Remove objCustomer.Key

             'Otherwise, add the customer to the database
             ElseIf InStr(.Key, "New") > 0 Then
                'Load the parameters for the Customer object
                LoadParameters objCommand, objCustomer
                'Set which stored procedure to use
                objCommand.CommandText = SPI
                objCommand.CommandType = adCmdStoredProc
                'Execute the stored procedure
                objCommand.Execute
                'Update the new customer to use the CustomerID instead
                'of the New indicator
                UpdateCustomer objCustomer
                'Remove the old customer from the Customers collection
                m_colCustomers.Remove .Key
                Set objHoldCustomer = Nothing
```

```
                    'Remove the object from the database and the Customers
                    'collection
                    ElseIf .IsDeleted = True Then
                        'Load the parameters for the Customer object
                        Set objParam = objCommand.CreateParameter _
                            ("CustomerID", adVarChar, adParamInput, 5, .CustomerID)
                        objCommand.Parameters.Append objParam
                        'Set the stored procedure to be used
                        objCommand.CommandText = SPD
                        objCommand.CommandType = adCmdStoredProc
                        'Execute the stored procedure
                        objCommand.Execute
                        'Remove the object from the collection
                        m_colCustomers.Remove objCustomer.Key

                    'Default for a Save is an Update
                    Else
                        'Load the parameters for the Customer object
                        LoadParameters objCommand, objCustomer
                        'Set the stored procedure to use
                        objCommand.CommandText = SPU
                        objCommand.CommandType = adCmdStoredProc
                        'Execute the Stored Procedured
                        objCommand.Execute
                        .IsDirty = False
                    End If
                End With
            End If
            Set objParam = Nothing
            Set objCommand = Nothing
        Next intFor

        Set objCustomer = Nothing
        Set objConnect = Nothing

    Exit Sub

    ErrorHandler:

        Err.Raise 2001, , "Customer Save Failure"

    End Sub
```

The above routine has four key parts to it. First, we check to see if we have a new objCustomer
object that has also been marked as deleted - this can happen when we add a new customer and
decide to undo the addition before saving it to the database. If this is the case, then we just remove
the objCustomer object from the m_colCustomers collection.

```
                    'If the customer is a new customer and is also deleted then
                    'just remove it from the collection as we have not added the
                    'customer to the database yet
                    If InStr(.Key, "New") And .IsDeleted Then
                        m_colCustomers.Remove objCustomer.Key
```

Next, we check to see if the objCustomer object is new. If it is, we call LoadParameters method of clsCustomerSrvr to build the parameters for the spi_Customer stored procedure, which is represented by the constant SPI. Then we execute the stored procedure to insert the new customer record into the database by calling objCommand.Execute. If this works then we add the new objCustomer object to the collection using the UpdateCustomer method. We then remove the old objCustomer object by calling the Remove method of the m_colCustomers collection, passing in the Key property the objCustomer object that we want to remove:

```
'Otherwise, add the customer to the database
ElseIf InStr(.Key, "New") > 0 Then
    'Load the parameters for the Customer object
    LoadParameters objCommand, objCustomer
    'Set which stored procedure to use
    objCommand.CommandText = SPI
    objCommand.CommandType = adCmdStoredProc
    'Execute the stored procedure
    objCommand.Execute
    'Update the new customer to use the CustomerID instead
    'of the New indicator
    UpdateCustomer objCustomer
    'Remove the old customer from the Customers collection
    m_colCustomers.Remove .Key
    Set objHoldCustomer = Nothing
```

Thirdly, we check to see if the objCustomer object's IsDeleted property has been set to True, marking this object for deletion. If this is the case, we add the CustomerID as a parameter and then we execute the stored procedure responsible for deletion, which is held in the SPD constant. If all of this was successful, we remove the objCustomer object from our m_colCustomers collection:

```
'Remove the object from the database and the Customers
'collection
ElseIf .IsDeleted = True Then
    'Load the parameters for the Customer object
    Set objParam = objCommand.CreateParameter _
        ("CustomerID", adVarChar, adParamInput, 5, .CustomerID)
    objCommand.Parameters.Append objParam
    'Set the stored procedure to be used
    objCommand.CommandText = SPD
    objCommand.CommandType = adCmdStoredProc
    'Execute the stored procedure
    objCommand.Execute
    'Remove the object from the collection
    m_colCustomers.Remove objCustomer.Key
```

Lastly, we assume that the object has been marked as dirty, since we would not be in these If statements if the objCustomer object did not have an IsDirty property of True. The first step for updating the object is to build the parameters for the spu_Customer stored procedure represented by the SPU constant. We do this by calling LoadParameters. Once we have the parameters set then we execute the spu_Customer stored procedure:

```
'Default for a Save is an Update
Else
    'Load the parameters for the Customer object
    LoadParameters objCommand, objCustomer
    'Set the stored procedure to use
```

```
              objCommand.CommandText = SPU
              objCommand.CommandType = adCmdStoredProc
              'Execute the Stored Procedured
              objCommand.Execute
              .IsDirty = False
```

Once we have looped through each `objCustomer` object loaded in the `m_colCustomers` collection, we set our objects equal to `Nothing` and exit the method.

The LoadParameters Method

The `LoadParameters` method adds the required parameters for the update and insert stored procedures called by the `Save` method:

```
Private Sub LoadParameters(objCommand As ADODB.Command, _
                       objCustomer As clsCustomer)

    Dim objParam As ADODB.Parameter

    With objCustomer
        'Load the parameters for the Customer object
        Set objParam = objCommand.CreateParameter _
            ("CustomerID", adVarChar, adParamInput, 5, .CustomerID)
        objCommand.Parameters.Append objParam
        Set objParam = objCommand.CreateParameter _
            ("CompanyName", adVarChar, adParamInput, 40, .CompanyName)
        objCommand.Parameters.Append objParam
        Set objParam = objCommand.CreateParameter _
            ("ContactName", adVarChar, adParamInput, 30, .ContactName)
        objCommand.Parameters.Append objParam
        Set objParam = objCommand.CreateParameter _
            ("ContactTitle", adVarChar, adParamInput, 30, .ContactTitle)
        objCommand.Parameters.Append objParam
        Set objParam = objCommand.CreateParameter _
            ("Address", adVarChar, adParamInput, 60, .Address)
        objCommand.Parameters.Append objParam
        Set objParam = objCommand.CreateParameter _
            ("City", adVarChar, adParamInput, 15, .City)
        objCommand.Parameters.Append objParam
        Set objParam = objCommand.CreateParameter _
            ("Region", adVarChar, adParamInput, 15, .Region)
        objCommand.Parameters.Append objParam
        Set objParam = objCommand.CreateParameter _
            ("PostalCode", adVarChar, adParamInput, 10, .PostalCode)
        objCommand.Parameters.Append objParam
        Set objParam = objCommand.CreateParameter _
            ("Country", adVarChar, adParamInput, 15, .Country)
        objCommand.Parameters.Append objParam
        Set objParam = objCommand.CreateParameter _
            ("Phone", adVarChar, adParamInput, 24, .Phone)
        objCommand.Parameters.Append objParam
        Set objParam = objCommand.CreateParameter _
            ("Fax", adVarChar, adParamInput, 24, .Fax)
        objCommand.Parameters.Append objParam
    End With

End Sub
```

The `LoadParameters` method is designed to add the required parameters for the update and insert stored procedures, which we will create later in the chapter. There are three reasons why this is better in its own routine:

> ➢ It's easier to maintain
> ➢ It's easier to read
> ➢ Both the insert and update stored procedures need the same parameters

This routine takes two arguments, the first is the `Command` object that we want the parameters to be added to and the other is the `objCustomer` object that holds the values for the parameters.

The UpdateCustomer Method

The `UpdateCustomer` method adds a new customer object called `objHoldCustomer` using the `CustomerID` as the Key. We can the remove the old `objCustomer` object marked with the word New from the `m_colCustomers` collection.

```
Private Sub UpdateCustomer(objCustomer As clsCustomer)

    Dim objHoldCustomer As clsCustomer

    With objCustomer
        Set objHoldCustomer = m_colCustomers.Add(.CustomerID)
        objHoldCustomer.Key = .CustomerID
        objHoldCustomer.CustomerID = .CustomerID
        objHoldCustomer.Address = .Address
        objHoldCustomer.City = .City
        objHoldCustomer.CompanyName = .CompanyName
        objHoldCustomer.ContactName = .ContactName
        objHoldCustomer.ContactTitle = .ContactTitle
        objHoldCustomer.Country = .Country
        objHoldCustomer.Fax = .Fax
        objHoldCustomer.Phone = .Phone
        objHoldCustomer.PostalCode = .PostalCode
        objHoldCustomer.Region = .Region
        objHoldCustomer.IsDirty = False
    End With

End Sub
```

Think back to the `Save` method; if the Key was `"New"` and we wanted to save a new customer record to the database we called `UpdateCustomer` and passed `objCustomer` as an argument. This routine will move all the information for the `objCustomer` object with a Key of New into the `objHoldCustomer` object.

If you remember, we create new `objCustomer` objects with the word New as their Key, however we hold the existing `objCustomer` objects by their `CustomerID`. Once we have used this routine to add a new `objCustomer` object with the `CustomerID` as a Key instead of New, we can return to the `Save` method and delete the old `objCustomer` object.

Customers Property

The `Customers` property returns the `m_colCustomers` collection of loaded customers:

```
Public Property Get Customers() As colCustomers
    Set Customers = m_colCustomers
End Property
```

Stored Procedures

Before we add code to our `clsCustomer` and `colCustomers` class modules, let's take a look at the stored procedures that are used by `clsCustomerSrvr`.

We shall create four stored procedures:

> `sps_Customer`: This is responsible for selecting records from the `Customers` table in `Northwind`. This stored procedure was called by the `Load` method.

> `spi_Customer`: This is responsible for inserting a new record into the `Customers` table. This stored procedure is called in the `Save` method when an `objCustomer` object is new and has not been marked for deletion.

> `spd_Customer`: This is responsible for removing a record from the `Customers` table. This stored procedure is called in the `Save` method when an `objCustomer` object has been marked for deletion but is not new. New objects do not exist in the database, so if they need to be deleted they can just be removed from the collection.

> `spu_Customer`: This is responsible for removing and updating a record in the `Customers` table. This stored procedure is called in the `Save` method when an `objCustomer` object has not met any of the `If` conditions (an update is the default action in `Save`).

Add the following stored procedures to the `Northwind` database in SQL Server by right-clicking on the **Stored Procedures** folder under **Northwind** and selecting **New Stored Procedure**. When you have entered a stored procedure, check its syntax by clicking on the **Check Syntax** button and then press **OK**.

Select

The `sps_Customer` stored procedure is pretty simple to write as it will only need to return two different recordsets. The first is all of the records from `Customers` and the second type returns a specific customer. To determine which to return we pass in a parameter called `Type`:

```
CREATE PROCEDURE sps_Customer
    @Type    Int,
    @CustomerID    nChar(5) = NULL
AS

SET NOCOUNT ON
DECLARE @errNo        Int,
        @ErrMsg       varchar(255)

/* Validate that we have the correct information being
supplied by the calling routine */
    IF    @Type = 1 AND @CustomerID IS NULL
```

```
      BEGIN
         SELECT @ErrNo = 15000,
                @ErrMsg = "When requesting a single customer you must supply
                           a CustomerID."
            GOTO Err
      END

/* If Type is a 0 then return all the customers */
   IF @Type = 0
      SELECT  CustomerID,
              CompanyName,
              ContactName,
              ContactTitle,
              Address,
              City,
              Region,
              PostalCode,
              Country,
              Phone,
              Fax
       FROM    Customers
   ELSE IF @Type = 1
      SELECT  CustomerID,
              CompanyName,
              ContactName,
              ContactTitle,
              Address,
              City,
              Region,
              PostalCode,
              Country,
              Phone,
              Fax
       FROM    Customers
       WHERE   CustomerID = @CustomerID

   RETURN 0

   Err:
      RAISERROR @ErrNo @ErrMsg
      RETURN -1
```

The first interesting line here is this:

```
SET NOCOUNT ON
```

This statement disables the default of returning the number of returned rows. If this line is not included, we will increase the network traffic.

The first step of the stored procedure is to make sure that the parameters are set correctly. If they are not, we will call the Err routine at the bottom of the stored procedure to raise back an error explaining to the user of our *Customer* object what is wrong:

```
    IF  @Type = 1 AND @CustomerID IS NULL
    BEGIN
        SELECT @ErrNo = 15000,
               @ErrMsg = "When requesting a single customer you must supply
                          a CustomerID."
        GOTO Err
    END
```

Once this check is done, the procedure determines whether to return all the records in the
Customers table or just the specific customer requested. If @Type is 0, we return all the records,
however if @Type is 1, we return a single record. As you can see the SELECT statements are almost
identical except for the WHERE clause at the end of the SELECT statement which returns a single
record.

Note that in the case where @Type = 0, *the* @CustomerID *parameter is ignored and takes
the default value of* NULL.

Insert

The spi_Customer stored procedure will take in an entire Customers record as parameters and
then insert the new record into the database using the INSERT SQL statement:

```
CREATE PROCEDURE spi_Customer
    @CustomerID    nchar(5),
    @CompanyName   nvarchar(40),
    @ContactName   nvarchar(30),
    @ContactTitle  nvarchar(30),
    @Address       nvarchar(60),
    @City          nvarchar(15),
    @Region        nvarchar(15),
    @PostalCode    nvarchar(10),
    @Country       nvarchar(15),
    @Phone         nvarchar(24),
    @Fax           nvarchar(24)

AS

    INSERT INTO Customers (CustomerID, CompanyName, ContactName, ContactTitle,
                           Address, City, Region, PostalCode, Country,
                           Phone, Fax)
    VALUES (@CustomerID, @CompanyName, @ContactName, @ContactTitle, @Address,
            @City, @Region, @PostalCode, @Country, @Phone, @Fax)

    IF @@Error <> 0
        RETURN -1
    ELSE
        RETURN 0
```

There's nothing fancy in this stored procedure, we just call the INSERT statement. In the event of an
error we return a -1, in the event of success we return a 0.

One thing to note here is that the CustomerID *field has been defined as the primary key. We
could have added a check to see if the* CustomerID *value is unique. However, SQL Server will
do this for us, so in this instance there is no need for us to do this.*

Delete

The `spd_Customer` stored procedure will remove a `Customers` record from the database. To do this it takes in a `CustomerID` as a parameter and then executes a `DELETE` statement on the record where the `CustomerID` field equals the value passed in:

```
CREATE PROCEDURE spd_Customer
    @CustomerID    nvarchar(5)
AS

    DELETE Customers
    WHERE CustomerID = @CustomerID

    IF @@Error = 0
        RETURN 0
    ELSE
        RETURN -1
```

Update

The `spu_Customer` stored procedure will take in all of the fields for the `Customers` record that needs to be updated and then update the record based on the `CustomerID` parameter:

```
CREATE PROCEDURE spu_Customer
    @CustomerID     nchar(5),
    @CompanyName    nvarchar(40),
    @ContactName    nvarchar(30),
    @ContactTitle   nvarchar(30),
    @Address        nvarchar(60),
    @City           nvarchar(15),
    @Region         nvarchar(15),
    @PostalCode     nvarchar(10),
    @Country        nvarchar(15),
    @Phone          nvarchar(24),
    @Fax            nvarchar(24)
AS

    UPDATE Customers
    SET     CompanyName  = @CompanyName,
            ContactName  = @ContactName,
            ContactTitle = @ContactTitle,
            Address      = @Address,
            City         = @City,
            Region       = @Region,
            PostalCode   = @PostalCode,
            Country      = @Country,
            Phone        = @Phone,
            Fax          = @Fax
    WHERE   CustomerID   = @CustomerID

    IF @@Error <> 0
        RETURN -1
    ELSE
        RETURN 0
```

This is another very simple stored procedure. We have taken in all of the fields as parameters of the stored procedure. Then we update the `Customers` record in using an `UPDATE` SQL statement making sure that the correct customer is updated by using the `WHERE` clause.

Adding Code to colCustomers

The colCustomers class works in a similar manner to the Collection object that comes with Visual Basic except that we will add a couple of extra methods to our version of Collection - Exists and Clear.

Add the following code to the colCustomers class.

Module-Level Variables

We have only one module-level variable exposed in the colCustomers class. m_custCollection is a Collection object that holds the objCustomer objects for us:

```
Private m_custCollection As New Collection
```

Add Method

The Add method will create a new objCustomer object and add it to the m_custCollection collection:

```
Public Function Add(strKey As String) As clsCustomer

    'Create a new Customer object
    Dim objCustomer As New clsCustomer

    'Now add the new member to the private collection
    m_custCollection.Add objCustomer, strKey

    objCustomer.Key = strKey

    objCustomer.IsDirty = False
    Set Add = objCustomer
    Set objCustomer = Nothing

End Function
```

Notice that the method first creates a new objCustomer object and then adds it to the m_custCollection collection, using the strKey value that was passed in as the Key to the object in the collection:

```
    'Create a new Customer object
    Dim objCustomer As New clsCustomer

    'Now add the new member to the private collection
    m_custCollection.Add objCustomer, strKey
```

Then we update the Key property of the objCustomer object to the strKey value:

```
    objCustomer.Key = strKey
```

We then ensure that the object is not marked as dirty:

```
    objCustomer.IsDirty = False
```

Finally, we set the return value of the Add method equal to the newly created objCustomer object:

```
Set Add = objCustomer
```

Clear Method

The Clear method is designed to remove all of the objCustomer objects from the m_custCollection collection.

There are two ways we could do this. The first method removes our reference to the m_custCollection collection from memory and creates a new empty collection for us:

```
Public Sub Clear()

    Set m_custCollection = Nothing
    Set m_custCollection = New Collection

End Sub
```

The second method will call the Remove method and actually take the object away from the collection. This way we never de-reference the collection and recreate the collection again. Both methods work so it really is up to you on which one you use. Personally, I prefer second method:

```
Public Sub Clear()

    Dim intI As Integer

    For intI = 1 To m_custCollection.Count
        Remove 1
    Next intI

End Sub
```

Note the line Remove 1. This 1 is correct because Visual Basic will reorder the collection after the removal of an element.

Count Property

The Count property is a very easy property to implement but a very important one. The Count property returns the number of objects that we have loaded into m_custCollection at any one time:

```
Public Property Get Count() As Long
    Count = m_custCollection.Count
End Property
```

Exists Method

The Exists method has the job of telling the calling routine whether or not an objCustomer object already exists in the m_custCollection collection.

```
Public Function Exists(varKey As Variant) As Boolean

    On Error GoTo ErrorHandler
```

```
        If Not (m_custCollection.Item(varKey) Is Nothing) Then Exists = True

    Exit Function

    ErrorHandler:

        Exists = False

    End Function
```

So how does this method work? We do an `Is Nothing` check on the `m_custCollection` collection using the `Key`, which was passed in as `varKey`. If the object is `Not Nothing` then it must be there and we set the return value of `Exists` equal to `True`.

If the object does not exist, an error will be raised and the code in `ErrorHandler` runs. `Errorhandler` sets the return value of `Exists` equal to `False`, so telling the calling routine that the object does not exist.

Item Property

The `Item` property will return an `objCustomer` object to the calling routine, based on the `varKey` parameter. This `varKey` parameter can either be the `Key` for the object or the `Index` value of the object in the `m_custCollection` collection. Hence, we have declared the `varKey` parameter as a `Variant`:

```
    Public Property Get Item(varKey As Variant) As clsCustomer

        'Return the Item referenced by the Key
        Set Item = m_custCollection.Item(varKey)

    End Property
```

NewEnum Property

The `NewEnum` Property gives us the ability to do `For...Each` calls on the `colCustomers` class:

```
    Public Property Get NewEnum() As IUnknown
        Set NewEnum = m_custCollection.[_NewEnum]
    End Property
```

Notice again that we are making use of the `Collection` object that is exposed by Visual Basic. The `[]` and `_` are required as `NewEnum` is a hidden property of the `Collection` object.

There's one last thing that needs to be done if we want to be able to do a `For..Each` on the class. Select **Tools | Procedure Attributes** from the menu and the **Procedure Attributes** dialog will appear. Select **NewEnum** from the **Name** drop-down. Click on **Advanced>>** and set the Procedure **ID** to –4:

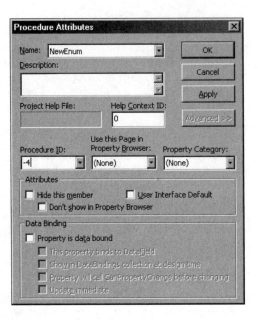

Then click on OK.

Remove Method

The `Remove` method will give us the ability to remove an `objCustomer` object from the collection. Do not confuse this with performing a delete on the database. To delete a record from the `Customers` table in the database, we must mark the object as deleted and then call the `Save` method.

```
Public Sub Remove(varKey As Variant)
    m_custCollection.Remove varKey
End Sub
```

Again, we are using the `Remove` method that is exposed to us by the Visual Basic `Collection` object.

Adding Code to clsCustomer Class

The `clsCustomer` class is the one we'll use to instantiate the object that we are going to feed out to the users of our *Customer* object. All of the properties internal to the object (that is `Address`, `City`, `CompanyName`, `ContactName`, `ContactTitle`, `Country`, `CustomerID`, `Fax`, `Phone`, `PostalCode` and `Region`) will follow the same format. They will have a private variable and then a `Let` and `Get Property` method exposed.

There a few extra properties that we need to add though as they help us keep track of the object. These are `Key`, `IsLoading`, `IsDeleted` and `IsDirty`.

Add the following code to the `clsCustomer` class.

Key Property

The Key property is the value that we use to create a *Customer* object in the collection. In this way they user of our *Customer* object can look at this property and know how the object was created.

Add the following declaration to the **General Declarations** section:

```
Private m_strKey As String
```

Now add the following to the **General** section of the clsCustomer class module:

```
Public Property Get Key() As String
    Key = m_strKey
End Property
```

```
Friend Property Let Key(strValue As String)
    m_strKey = strValue
End Property
```

The Property Get returns the Key property and the Property Let updates the Key property.

Before we create the Property Let and Get, we declare a private variable (m_strKey) that will hold the value of the Key property.

Note that we have not declared the Property Let as Public but as Friend. A procedure that has been declared as Friend can be called anywhere inside the dataCustomer project, but it cannot be called from outside the project. This means that only procedures within dataCustomer will be able to update the Key property. As far as any user of our *Customer* object is concerned, Key is read-only.

IsLoading Property

The Isloading property lets the object know that it is in a "Loading" state and that it should not set its IsDirty property.

Add the following declaration to the **General Declarations** section:

```
Private m_blnIsLoading As Boolean   ' = False
```

Now add the following code to the **General** section of clsCustomer:

```
Public Property Get IsLoading() As Boolean
    IsLoading = m_blnIsLoading
End Property
```

```
Friend Property Let IsLoading(blnValue As Boolean)
    m_blnIsLoading = blnValue
End Property
```

Once again like the Key property, we have the Let set to Friend, making sure that no routines outside the dataCustomer project can set this property.

IsDeleted Property

The `IsDeleted` property is used to identify that the object is to be removed from the database.

Add the following declaration to the **General Declarations** section:

```
Private m_blnIsDeleted As Boolean
```

Now add the following to the **General** section of the `clsCustomer` class module:

```
Public Property Get IsDeleted() As Boolean
   IsDeleted = m_blnIsDeleted
End Property
```

```
Friend Property Let IsDeleted(blnValue As Boolean)
   If blnValue <> m_blnIsDeleted Then
      m_blnIsDeleted = blnValue
      IsDirty = True
   End If
End Property
```

The `Property Get` is similar to the previous `Property Get`s that we have looked at.

The `Property Let` is a little different. We first check to see if this object has actually changed (the `blnValue` variable passed into this `Property Let` will not match the value of `m_blnIsDeleted` if this is the case). It is important that we make this check to ensure that `IsDirty` does not get changed unless something has actually changed.

IsDirty Property

The `IsDirty` property tells the collection that the *Customer* object has changed since it was loaded. This property works very closely with the `IsLoading` property; we do not want to change the `IsDirty` property if we are just loading the object.

Add the following declaration to the **General Declarations** section:

```
Private m_blnIsDirty As Boolean ' = False
```

Now add the following to the **General** section of the `clsCustomer` class module:

```
Public Property Get IsDirty() As Boolean
   IsDirty = m_blnIsDirty
End Property
```

```
Friend Property Let IsDirty(blnValue As Boolean)
   If Not IsLoading Then
      m_blnIsDirty = blnValue
   End If
End Property
```

In the `Property Let`, we check the `IsLoading` property to see if we are in a "Loading" state. If we are then we do not change the `IsDirty` property.

The Other Properties

The following properties of the *Customer* object all represent the fields of the associated recordset in the database:

Add the following variable declarations to the General Declarations section:

```
Private m_strCustomerID As String * 5
Private m_strCompanyName As String
Private m_strContactName As String
Private m_strContactTitle As String
Private m_strAddress As String
Private m_strCity As String
Private m_strRegion As String
Private m_strPostalCode As String
Private m_strCountry As String
Private m_strPhone As String
Private m_strFax As String
```

Now add the following Property Lets and Gets:

```
Public Property Get CustomerID() As String
    CustomerID = m_strCustomerID
End Property

Public Property Let CustomerID(strValue As String)
    If strValue <> m_strCustomerID Then
        m_strCustomerID = strValue
        IsDirty = True
    End If
End Property

Public Property Get CompanyName() As String
    CompanyName = m_strCompanyName
End Property

Public Property Let CompanyName(strValue As String)
    If strValue <> m_strCompanyName Then
        m_strCompanyName = strValue
        IsDirty = True
    End If
End Property

Public Property Get ContactName() As String
    ContactName = m_strContactName
End Property

Public Property Let ContactName(strValue As String)
    If strValue <> m_strContactName Then
        m_strContactName = strValue
        IsDirty = True
    End If
End Property

Public Property Get ContactTitle() As String
    ContactTitle = m_strContactTitle
End Property
```

```
Public Property Let ContactTitle(strValue As String)
    If strValue <> m_strContactTitle Then
        m_strContactTitle = strValue
        IsDirty = True
    End If
End Property

Public Property Get Address() As String
    Address = m_strAddress
End Property

Public Property Let Address(strValue As String)
    If strValue <> m_strAddress Then
        m_strAddress = strValue
        IsDirty = True
    End If
End Property

Public Property Get City() As String
    City = m_strCity
End Property

Public Property Let City(strValue As String)
    If strValue <> m_strCity Then
        m_strCity = strValue
        IsDirty = True
    End If
End Property

Public Property Get Region() As String
    Region = m_strRegion
End Property

Public Property Let Region(strValue As String)
    If strValue <> m_strRegion Then
        m_strRegion = strValue
        IsDirty = True
    End If
End Property

Public Property Get PostalCode() As String
    PostalCode = m_strPostalCode
End Property

Public Property Let PostalCode(strValue As String)
    If strValue <> m_strPostalCode Then
        m_strPostalCode = strValue
        IsDirty = True
    End If
End Property

Public Property Get Country() As String
    Country = m_strCountry
End Property

Public Property Let Country(strValue As String)
    If strValue <> m_strCountry Then
        m_strCountry = strValue
        IsDirty = True
    End If
End Property
```

```
Public Property Get Phone() As String
    Phone = m_strPhone
End Property

Public Property Let Phone(strValue As String)
    If strValue <> m_strPhone Then
        m_strPhone = strValue
        IsDirty = True
    End If
End Property

Public Property Get Fax() As String
    Fax = m_strFax
End Property

Public Property Let Fax(strValue As String)
    If strValue <> m_strFax Then
        m_strFax = strValue
        IsDirty = True
    End If
End Property
```

Now all these `Property Lets` and `Gets` act in a very similar fashion so let's just examine one, `CustomerID`. The `Get` is very simple, we just send back the value stored in the private variable for the property. The `Let` on the other hand is a little different, we first check to see if the property has actually changed. If it has, then we update the internal variable `m_strCustomerID` and set `IsDirty` to `True`. Note that even though we have set `IsDirty`, it does not mean that the object is now "dirty". Remember that we do not change the value of `IsDirty` unless we are *not* in a loading state. However, no property has to worry about this as `IsDirty` takes care of this for us.

We have now added all the code for our `dataCustomer` project, so save it.

The Tester Application

We can't do much with our three class *Customer* object at the moment. So let's build a simple application to test out all of the functionality that we have built into the *Customer* object. In this case, we need to test the ability save, add new, delete and load customer objects.

With the `dataCustomer` project still open, select **File | Add Project** and select the **Standard EXE** project type from the **Add Project** dialog.

Name the new project `Customer_Tester` and the new form `frmCustomer`, also give the form a `Caption` of **Customers Example**. Finally, right-click on the **Customer_Tester** project in the Project Explorer window and select **Set as Start Up**:

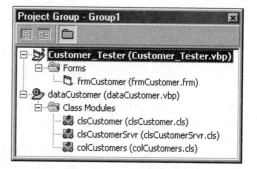

455

Building the User Interface

Bring up the Components dialog for the Customer_Tester project and add the Microsoft Windows Common Controls 6.0.

The Toolbar Control

Place a Toolbar control on your form and name it tbMain. Notice that it doesn't matter where you place it, it will always align itself to the top. Right-click on the Toolbar control and select Properties. The Property Pages dialog will appear, select the Buttons tab:

To add a new button to out Toolbar, click on the Insert Button button. Enter the word New in the Key textbox and New Customer in the ToolTipText textbox:

Then click on Insert Button again to add another button to the Toolbar. This time set the Key to Save and the ToolTipText to Save Customers.

Repeat the process again to add another button with a Key property of Delete and a ToolTipText property of Delete Current Customer.

When you've added these three buttons click on the OK button to save the buttons and close the dialog.

The ImageList Control

To actually get the buttons to display pictures rather than being solid gray, we need to add an ImageList control to our form. Place this control anywhere you like, as it will be invisible at run-time. Name the ImageList control, `imlMain`.

Right-click on `imlMain` and select Properties, another Property Pages dialog will open. Click on the Images tab:

To add a picture, click on the Insert Picture button and browse to bitmap that could be used to represent a deletion (there should be plenty to choose from in the `Graphics` folder that was installed with Visual Basic). Set the Key property of this picture to Delete.

Click on Insert Picture again to add another picture, this time add a bitmap that could be used to represent adding a new object. Set the Key property to New.

Add a third picture to represent saving and set its Key property to Save.

When you've added all three pictures click on OK.

The StatusBar

Add a StatusBar control to `frmCustomer` and name it `sbMain`. Right-click on `sbMain` and select Properties. From the Property Pages dialog that appears, select the Panels tab:

To add panels to the StatusBar, click on the Insert Panel button. Add panels to the StatusBar according to the following table:

Panel Index Number	Property	Value
1	Text	l<
	ToolTipText	Move First
	Key	MoveFirst
	Minimum Width	250.01
	Alignment	1 - sbrCenter
	Style	0 - sbrText
	Bevel	2 - sbrRaised
	AutoSize	2 - sbrContents
2	Text	<
	ToolTipText	Move Previous
	Key	MovePrevious
	Minimum Width	250.01
	Alignment	1 - sbrCenter
	Style	0 - sbrText

Panel Index Number	Property	Value
3	Bevel	2 - sbrRaised
	AutoSize	2 - sbrContents
	Text	Record 1 of ?
	ToolTipText	Current Record of Total Loaded Records
	Key	RecordIndicator
	Minimum Width	1440.00
	Alignment	1 - sbrCenter
	Style	0 - sbrText
	Bevel	0 - sbrNoBevel
	AutoSize	1 - sbrSpring
4	Text	>
	ToolTipText	Move Next
	Key	MoveNext
	Minimum Width	250.01
	Alignment	1 - sbrCenter
	Style	0 - sbrText
	Bevel	2 - sbrRaised
	AutoSize	2 - sbrContents
5	Text	>|
	ToolTipText	Move Last
	Key	MoveLast
	Minimum Width	250.01
	Alignment	1 - sbrCenter
	Style	0 - sbrText
	Bevel	2 - sbrRaised
	AutoSize	2 - sbrContents

The Textboxes and Labels

Add eleven textboxes and labels and arrange them according to the following screenshot:

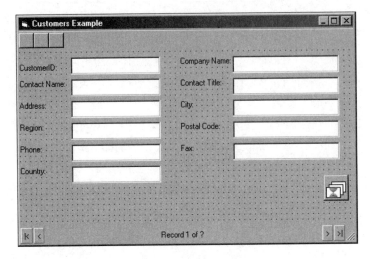

Clear the Text properties of the textboxes and name them as follows:

```
txtCustomerID      txtCompanyName
txtContactName     txtContactTitle
txtAddress         txtCity
txtRegion          txtPostalCode
txtPhone           txtFax
txtCountry
```

Our form is now complete, so let's add the code behind it!

The Code

We can split our test application into four parts or functions, which are:

> The form needs to get a reference to clsCustomerSrvr when it first loads, so that it can load the first record in the Customers table of the database onto the screen.

> We need to allow the user of the Customer_Tester application to navigate through our *Customer* objects with buttons at the bottom of frmCustomer.

> We need to allow the user to delete, save and create new *Customer* objects.

> We need to ensure that the properties are updated as the user changes them.

The Module-Level Variables

Add the following variables to the **General Declarations** section of frmCustomer:

```
Private m_objCustomerSrvr As clsCustomerSrvr
Private m_colCustomers As colCustomers
Private m_intCustomerIndicator As Integer
```

The Form_Load Event Procedure

Add the following code to the `Form_Load` event procedure:

```
Private Sub Form_Load()

    tbMain.ImageList = imlMain
    tbMain.Buttons("New").Image = "New"
    tbMain.Buttons("Save").Image = "Save"
    tbMain.Buttons("Delete").Image = "Delete"

    Set m_objCustomerSrvr = New clsCustomerSrvr
    m_objCustomerSrvr.Load All
    Set m_colCustomers = m_objCustomerSrvr.Customers
    m_intCustomerIndicator = 1
    LoadCustomerRecord

End Sub
```

The first four lines of the `Load` procedure set up the images for the toolbar. Next we instantiate a `m_objCustomerSrvr` object from the `clsCustomerSrvr` class. Once we have done that, we call the `Load` method of `m_objCustomerSrvr`, passing in the parameter `All`, which will load all of the `Customers` records in the database as objects. Next, we get a reference to our own `m_colCustomers` collection by calling the `Customers` property exposed by the `m_objCustomerSrvr` object. The last step is to set our internal record index (held in `m_intCustomerIndicator`) to 1 and call the `LoadCustomerRecord` method.

The LoadCustomerRecord Method

Add the following code to `frmCustomer`'s code module:

```
Private Sub LoadCustomerRecord()

    Dim objCustomer As clsCustomer

    If m_intCustomerIndicator >= m_colCustomers.Count Then
        m_intCustomerIndicator = m_colCustomers.Count
    ElseIf m_intCustomerIndicator <= 1 Then
        m_intCustomerIndicator = 1
    End If

    Set objCustomer = m_colCustomers.Item(m_intCustomerIndicator)
    With objCustomer
        txtCustomerID = .CustomerID
        txtAddress = .Address
        txtCity = .City
        txtCompanyName = .CompanyName
        txtContactName = .ContactName
        txtContactTitle = .ContactTitle
        txtCountry = .Country
        txtFax = .Fax
        txtPhone = .Phone
        txtPostalCode = .PostalCode
        txtRegion = .region
    End With
```

```
        sbMain.Panels("RecordIndicator").Text = "Record " _
            & m_intCustomerIndicator & " of " & m_colCustomers.Count

    Set objCustomer = Nothing

End Sub
```

The `LoadCustomerRecord` method begins by checking to see if we are past the last object in the collection or before the first. If we are, we set the record index to be the last or first. If we are at neither point in the collection then we do nothing to the indicator:

```
    If m_intCustomerIndicator >= m_colCustomers.Count Then
        m_intCustomerIndicator = m_colCustomers.Count
    ElseIf m_intCustomerIndicator <= 1 Then
        m_intCustomerIndicator = 1
    End If
```

We then load the correct record (indicated by `m_intCustomerIndicator`) to the form:

```
    Set objCustomer = m_colCustomers.Item(m_intCustomerIndicator)
        With objCustomer
            txtCustomerID = .CustomerID
            txtAddress = .Address
            txtCity = .City
            txtCompanyName = .CompanyName
            txtContactName = .ContactName
            txtContactTitle = .ContactTitle
            txtCountry = .Country
            txtFax = .Fax
            txtPhone = .Phone
            txtPostalCode = .PostalCode
            txtRegion = .region
        End With
```

We then display the number of the current record and the number of total records in the `RecordIndicator` panel of the `sbMain` StatusBar:

```
        sbMain.Panels("RecordIndicator").Text = "Record " _
            & m_intCustomerIndicator & " of " & m_colCustomers.Count
```

The PanelClick Event of the StatusBar Control

Add the following code to the `sbMain_PanelClick` event procedure:

```
    Private Sub sbMain_PanelClick(ByVal Panel As MSComctlLib.Panel)

        Select Case Panel.Key
            Case "MoveNext"
                m_intCustomerIndicator = m_intCustomerIndicator + 1
            Case "MoveFirst"
                m_intCustomerIndicator = 1
            Case "MoveLast"
                m_intCustomerIndicator = m_colCustomers.Count
            Case "MovePrevious"
```

```
            m_intCustomerIndicator = m_intCustomerIndicator - 1
      End Select

      LoadCustomerRecord

End Sub
```

The code here is simple. If the user clicks the MoveNext button then we increment the record indicator by one. If the user clicks the MoveFirst button then we set the record indicator to 1. If the user clicks on the MoveLast button we set the record indicator equal to the total number of objects in the m_colCustomers collection. If the user clicks the MovePrevious button then we decrement the record indicator by 1.

Then we call the LoadCustomerRecord method, which refreshes the user interface with the object in the collection specified by the new value of m_intCustomerIndicator.

The ButtonClick of the Toolbar Control

Add the following code to the tbMain_ButtonClick event procedure:

```
Private Sub tbMain_ButtonClick(ByVal Button As MSComctlLib.Button)

   Select Case Button.Key
      Case "Delete"
         m_objCustomerSrvr.Delete m_intCustomerIndicator
         m_objCustomerSrvr.Save
         m_intCustomerIndicator = 1
         LoadCustomerRecord
      Case "Save"
         m_objCustomerSrvr.Save
         m_intCustomerIndicator = 1
         LoadCustomerRecord
      Case "New"
         Call m_objCustomerSrvr.NewCustomer
         m_intCustomerIndicator = m_colCustomers.Count
         LoadCustomerRecord
   End Select

End Sub
```

If the user clicks on the Delete button then we call the Delete method of the m_objCustomerSrvr object and pass in the record indicator value, m_intCustomerIndicator. Don't forget that we have merely marked the object for deletion, we haven't actually deleted it so we need to call the Save method of the m_objCustomerSrvr object. Finally, we direct the user back to the first record:

```
      Case "Delete"
         m_objCustomerSrvr.Delete m_intCustomerIndicator
         m_objCustomerSrvr.Save
         m_intCustomerIndicator = 1
         LoadCustomerRecord
```

If the user clicks on the Save button then we call the Save method of the m_objCustomerSrvr object and then return to the first record in the collection:

```
Case "Save"
    m_objCustomerSrvr.Save
    m_intCustomerIndicator = 1
    LoadCustomerRecord
```

Now if the user clicks the New button we call the NewCustomer method of the m_objCustomerSrvr object to create a new Customer object. Once we have done this we set the record indicator to the last record in the collection and reload the user interface:

```
Case "New"
    Call m_objCustomerSrvr.NewCustomer
    m_intCustomerIndicator = m_colCustomers.Count
    LoadCustomerRecord
```

The LostFocus Events of the Textboxes

Add the following code to the LostFocus event procedures of the textboxes:

```
Private Sub txtAddress_LostFocus()
    m_colCustomers.Item(m_intCustomerIndicator).Address = txtAddress.Text
End Sub
```

```
Private Sub txtCity_lostfocus()
    m_colCustomers.Item(m_intCustomerIndicator).City = txtCity.Text
End Sub
```

```
Private Sub txtCompanyName_LostFocus()
    m_colCustomers.Item(m_intCustomerIndicator).CompanyName = _
                txtCompanyName.Text
End Sub
```

```
Private Sub txtContactName_LostFocus()
    m_colCustomers.Item(m_intCustomerIndicator).ContactName = _
                txtContactName.Text
End Sub
```

```
Private Sub txtContactTitle_LostFocus()
    m_colCustomers.Item(m_intCustomerIndicator).ContactTitle = _
                txtContactTitle.Text
End Sub
```

```
Private Sub txtCountry_LostFocus()
    m_colCustomers.Item(m_intCustomerIndicator).Country = txtCountry.Text
End Sub
```

```
Private Sub txtCustomerID_LostFocus()
    m_colCustomers.Item(m_intCustomerIndicator).CustomerID = txtCustomerID.Text
End Sub
```

```
Private Sub txtFax_LostFocus()
    m_colCustomers.Item(m_intCustomerIndicator).Fax = txtFax.Text
End Sub
```

```
Private Sub txtPhone_LostFocus()
    m_colCustomers.Item(m_intCustomerIndicator).Phone = txtPhone.Text
End Sub

Private Sub txtPostalCode_LostFocus()
    m_colCustomers.Item(m_intCustomerIndicator).PostalCode = txtPostalCode.Text
End Sub

Private Sub txtRegion_LostFocus()
    m_colCustomers.Item(m_intCustomerIndicator).Region = txtRegion.Text
End Sub
```

Now remember that we do not care if the user has made any changes or not. The reason for this is that the property itself will check to see if there has been a change or not. All we need to worry about is updating the property.

Testing the Customer Object

Now run the `Customer_Tester` project, the `frmCustomer` form will appear:

Check that the navigation bar, New, Save and Delete buttons work as you would expect.

Summary

In this chapter, we have seen the benefits of using three classes to create a single *Customer* object. We can therefore force any user of our object to access and use it the way that we want. There is no danger of a user of our object accidentally using it incorrectly. This three class *Customer* object is one example of how we can encapsulate the data in our object and protect it. Obviously, there are other ways to do this, but personally, I find this to be one of the best.

We rounded up the chapter by creating a tester application. This application looks very similar to others that we have created earlier in this book; however, we know that under the hood this data object is very different.

Suppliers
- SupplierID
- CompanyName
- ContactName
- ContactTitle
- Address
- City
- Region
- PostalCode
- Country
- Phone
- Fax
- HomePage

Products
- ProductID
- ProductName
- SupplierID
- CategoryID
- QuantityPerUnit
- UnitPrice
- UnitsInStock
- UnitsOnOrder
- ReorderLevel
- Discontinued

Categories
- CategoryID
- CategoryName
- Description
- Picture

The Microsoft Distributed Transaction Coordinator

In this chapter we'll take a look at a tool supplied with SQL Server called Microsoft Distributed Transaction Coordinator (MS DTC). MS DTC's greatest strength is its ability to allow developers to create transactions that involve more than one database, which may not even be of the same type. Using MS DTC, we can create a transaction involving a SQL Server database, an Oracle database and a DB2 database.

We'll begin this chapter by looking at the T-SQL commands BEGIN TRANSACTION, COMMIT TRANSACTION and ROLLBACK TRANSACTION. Then we'll discuss what a distributed transaction is and the role that MS DTC plays in supporting them. Finally, we'll see how we use MS DTC.

Database Transactions

In Chapter 10 we looked at transactions and at the BeginTrans, CommitTrans and RollBackTrans methods of the ADO Connection object. We can also use transactions in our stored procedures. In T-SQL, we use the command, BEGIN TRANSACTION to mark the beginning of the transaction. If the transaction completes successfully, the COMMIT TRANSACTION command makes all the actions in the transaction permanent. In the event that the transaction fails, ROLLBACK TRANSACTION is used to return everything back to the original state.

Let's look at an example. Fred has two accounts in XYZ Bank, called Checking and Savings. He wants to move $500 from Checking to Savings. Therefore, the transaction consists of deducting $500 from the Checking account, waiting until the action has completed successfully and then crediting $500 to his Savings account.

Our transaction would look like this in SQL code:

```
BEGIN TRANSACTION

    INSERT CheckingTransaction (TransactionNo, CustName, Date, Amount)
        VALUES (01, 'Fred', '01/05/99', -500)

    IF @@error <> 0
    BEGIN
        ROLLBACK TRANSACTION
        RETURN
    END

    UPDATE Checking
        SET BalanceChecking = BalanceChecking - 500
        WHERE TransactionNo = 01

    IF @@error <> 0
    BEGIN
        ROLLBACK TRANSACTION
        RETURN
    END

    INSERT SavingsTransaction (TransactionNo, CustName, Date, Quantity)
        VALUES (01, 'Fred', '01/05/99', 500)

    IF @@error <> 0
    BEGIN
        ROLLBACK TRANSACTION
        RETURN
    END

    UPDATE Savings
        SET BalanceSavings = BalanceSavings + 500
        WHERE TransactionNo = 01

    IF @@error <> 0
    BEGIN
        ROLLBACK TRANSACTION
        RETURN
    END

COMMIT TRANSACTION
```

The Architecture of Distributed Transactions

As business requirements increase and applications become more complex, it is becoming increasingly common to access multiple databases, often at different locations. Suppose we have a transaction that requires data changes to occur in two separate databases and still require that all the properties of the ACID test be met. Basic transaction management using SQL Server will not suffice anymore. There is no way to ensure that if one database server fails, the other has not already committed and become permanent. In other words, there is no way to guarantee atomicity without a way to coordinate multiple transaction processes occurring at multiple locations.

A **distributed transaction** is one that spans two or more data sources, such as database servers. To ensure proper commit or rollback of the transaction, it must be coordinated by a transaction manager. **Microsoft Distributed Transaction Coordinator** acts as that transaction manager.

Two-Phase Commit with MS DTC

Take another look at the SQL code for Fred's transaction. Note that two parts of this transaction must complete for a commit to occur – an INSERT and UPDATE is required for changes to Fred's Checking account and another INSERT and UPDATE is required for Fred's Savings account. Suppose Fred uses MS SQL Server to record changes to his Checking account and Oracle to record changes to his Savings account. What if the server where Oracle resides goes down? How can we guarantee atomicity? The solution comes from a protocol called **two-phase commit** and is coordinated by the Microsoft Distributed Transaction Coordinator (MS DTC).

> **MS DTC is integrated into both SQL Server and MTS. By adding another factor into the transaction process, MS DTC verifies all processes are ready and able to commit.**

In order for the two-phase commit protocol to be coordinated, each data source in the transaction must have MS DTC installed. From these installations, the main coordinator is always going to be where the transaction originates. This main coordinator is referred to as the **commit coordinator** and it is responsible for ensuring that the transaction either commits or aborts on all servers that are involved in the transaction. It is also the responsibility of the commit coordinator to report back to the client application whether the transaction has successfully committed or rolled back.

Fred's transaction requires changing data in one database to reflect his Checking account and changing data in another database to reflect his Savings account:

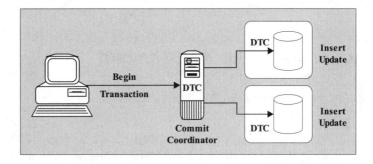

The commit coordinator is then notified about the transaction's status:

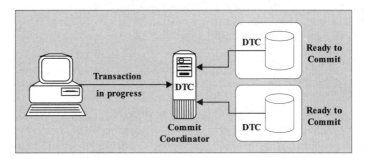

If the commit coordinator receives a "ready to commit" message from each data source, the transaction is committed:

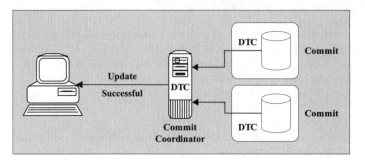

However, if one "failure" message is received from any data source that is to be effected, the commit coordinator will issue a roll back and notify the client application:

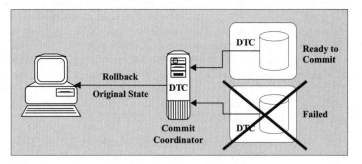

OLE Transactions and the XA Standard

OLE Transactions is a Microsoft protocol that allows applications to communicate with MS DTC. OLE Transactions is object-oriented and (like Microsoft's other object-oriented technologies) is based on COM.

XA is a different protocol that is common in the Unix database world. Similar to OLE Transactions, the XA standard allows applications and data sources to communicate with a transaction manager. However, XA is not object-oriented or COM-based.

Fortunately, MS DTC supports both OLE Transactions and XA protocols. This means that XA-compliant resource managers, such as the ones found in Oracle, Sybase, Informix and DB2, can participate in MTS transactions.

MTS and MS DTC

Microsoft Transaction Server provides a transaction model that eliminates the complex transaction-processing code required for distributed transactions coordinated by MS DTC. This transactional model can *transparently* merge distributed transactions with our middle-tier components.

All we have to do is configure our component's transaction support using the MTS Explorer as we discussed in Chapters 11 and 13, and modify the components to behave according to the transaction outcome.

MTS automatically handles the rest of the complex and redundant details of beginning and committing or aborting transactions by interacting with the MS DTC on the behalf of a component, based on the component's transaction support. Any operations a component performs against databases will automatically be performed within a distributed transaction.

Since MTS relies on MS DTC to coordinate transactions, a single component can perform operations against several different types of databases within a *single* MTS transaction. For example, an MTS object could perform one operation against a SQL Server database and another against an Oracle database within the same MTS transaction.

The MS DTC in Action

Enough talking, let's actually see how MS DTC works. We're going to write a Transact-SQL statement and run it though MS DTC. As you may not have multiple database servers to experiment with, we will simulate a distributed transaction by using MS DTC, but we'll only write to one database, pubs.

Start the **SQL Server Enterprise Manager** from the **Start** menu and navigate to the **pubs** folder. We need to create two new tables in the pubs database: DatabaseBooks and DatabaseOutOfPrint.

Right-click on **Tables** and select **New Table**. In the **Choose Name** dialog, enter **DatabaseBooks** and click on **OK**. Then add the following fields:

Column Name	Datatype	Length	Allow Nulls
Author	char	20	No
Title	char	50	No
Available	char	2	No

The **New Table** window should now look like this:

Click on the **Save** button and close the **New Table** window. Now create the `DatabaseOutOfPrint` table with the following fields:

Column Name	Datatype	Length	Allow Nulls
BookID	char	5	No
InStock	char	2	No
OutOfPrint	char	2	No

Our two tables will now appear in the Enterprise Manager:

Now that we've created both tables, we need to create the transasction.

Select <u>T</u>ools | SQL Server <u>Q</u>uery Analyzer from the menu and select **pubs** from the DB drop-down box. Type the following T-SQL statement in the **Query Analyzer**:

```
BEGIN DISTRIBUTED TRANSACTION

INSERT DatabaseBooks (Author, Title, Available)
VALUES ("Charles Williams","Professional VB6 Database Programming","Y")

IF @@error <> 0
BEGIN
    ROLLBACK TRANSACTION
    RETURN
END

INSERT DatabaseOutOfPrint (BookID, InStock, OutOfPrint)
VALUES ("ac12","N","Y")

IF @@error <> 0
BEGIN
    ROLLBACK TRANSACTION
    RETURN
END

COMMIT TRANSACTION
```

Notice that this transaction starts with BEGIN DISTRIBUTED TRANSACTION. Our previous SQL statement started with BEGIN TRANSACTION. By using the keyword DISTRIBUTED, we are invoking MS DTC.

Remember it's not a true distributed transaction. Even though multiple tables are modified and we're using MS DTC, it is only effecting one database on one server.

Before we can execute the transaction, we need to make sure that MS DTC is actually running. Select the MSDTC **Administrative Console** option from the **Microsoft SQL Server 7.0** program group on your **Start** menu. A dialog called **MS DTC Admin Console** will appear:

Make sure the **Service Control Status** frame says **Status: Started**. Now swap back to the **Query Analyzer** and execute the transaction by clicking on the green arrow.

Go back to the **MS DTC Admin Console** dialog and click on the **Statistics** tab. Although items were updated in two different tables, both are treated as one transaction. Either both successfully completed and committed, or both transactions are rolled back and aborted:

Summary

This chapter has provided an introduction to the MS DTC. Despite the brevity of this chapter, I'm sure that you can understand its importance.

The MS DTC's support for XA-compliant database servers such as Oracle, means that the MTS transactions we have created in previous chapters are not restricted to SQL Server. Furthermore, MS DTC's support of distributed transactions means that our transactions can include actions on many databases, all of differing types.

All that is required to invoke MS DTC, is to replace `BEGIN TRANSACTION` in our T-SQL statements with `BEGIN DISTRIBUTED TRANSACTION`.

Suppliers

- SupplierID
- CompanyName
- ContactName
- ContactTitle
- Address
- City
- Region
- PostalCode
- Country
- Phone
- Fax
- HomePage

Products

- ProductID
- ProductName
- SupplierID
- CategoryID
- QuantityPerUnit
- UnitPrice
- UnitsInStock
- UnitsOnOrder
- ReorderLevel
- Discontinued

Categories

- CategoryID
- CategoryName
- Description
- Picture

6

Securing Client-Server Applications

The greater the number of users for any given client server application, the greater the need for security. Curious minds are typically the cause of corrupt data. While it may be unintentional, it's important to restrict users from accessing data that they have no need to view or update. It's not only the possibility of corrupt data that calls for security. Privacy is a greater concern with most organizations today. Any organization that transports or handles personal information can be held responsible if they are negligent in securing this data. The need for security is uncontested; the question is how to implement it. We have covered many client-server models in the past chapters, including 2-tier, 3-tier and n-tier rolled out using Microsoft Transaction Server. To implement our projects, we have used SQL Server as our primary database server. Of course, there are a number of other database servers available; mixing and matching the possible databases available to the combinations of client server architectures, we are left with a vast array of possible security implementations. This chapter will focus on outlining some of the possible solutions and providing examples of how each is rolled out.

Security Models for Client-Server

Before looking in detail at how to implement security in our applications, we must first consider *where* we want our validation to take place: on the client, on the server or (in a multi-tier application) in the middle-tier objects. Naturally, the optimal solution depends on the application's architecture. We will look first at possible security setups in a two-tier solution, then consider security in an n-tier application.

Two-Tier Solutions

For a two-tier client-server application, you can implement security validation at two points: at the client and/or at the server. Because database servers typically provide this functionality, it's usual to implement security on the server side. To implement this in a SQL Server database, the database server is configured with **users** and **roles**.

> ➤ A user is a defined login profile which can be used to access the various objects of a database, including tables, views and stored procedures.

> ➤ Roles are used to define the access rights of one or more users with common functions. If multiple users are to have similar rights with respect to the database objects, they can be assigned the same role; these roles carry privileges to execute specific tasks, which are transferred to the users with that role. These users therefore have the same access privileges (although a user may have more than one role). The benefit of using roles is that a lot of time can be saved by not having to assign security rights to each user individually.

The objects in a database, such as a table or stored procedure, are then configured to grant access to users and/or roles with authority to execute specific functionality, such as SELECT, UPDATE, DELETE, or INSERT statements, or to perform basic database administration. A user, therefore, may have authority to view records or to insert a new record into table ABC, but not the authority to delete or update existing records. The same holds true for roles: users with specific roles can have authority to select records from a table, with no rights to delete, insert or update records.

The client application will be configured to accept a user name and password. This information is then passed to the server in the connection string, and the login is either rejected or accepted. If the login is accepted, the application is opened for the user. If the login is rejected, the client closes down, or allows the user a second attempt.

N-Tier Solutions

N-tier client server applications allow greater flexibility with regard to where security is implemented: security checks can take place either on the server itself, or inside our middle-tier components.

Security on the Middle Tier

A convenient solution is to pass this functionality off to the middle-tier component. When implementing security in the middle tier, Microsoft Transaction Server provides an easy-to-build (and even easier to maintain) solution. This is because MTS extends the security features of Windows NT to the objects it encapsulates. This means that we can use re-use the user IDs of Windows NT, so we don't have to deal with managing them.

If we plan to pool our components, or just want extra peace of mind, MTS allows us to implement a security model where requests can be authorized or rejected for each individual component that is created. Our components can query MTS to ensure that each function called is properly authorized. The benefit of this method over traditional server-side security is that server-side security is limited to authorizing access to each table, while MTS can authorize access to a table according to the function which requested the access.

The setup of MTS security is similar to the setup of most database servers. The first step is to configure the users and roles. Secondly, we assign permissions to the specific classes in each package. The middle-tier application is then coded to validate that the user has access to perform a specific function. If the user does not, then the function is aborted, and an error is returned to the user.

Security on the Server

If you should decide to push the responsibility of security to the server, your middle tier would then be designed to receive the user name and password, and validate the user upon request. This can be implemented in a number of ways. Here's an example of how it might work:

When a user logs in to the client application, a method in the middle-tier object is called to validate the user name and password. If the validation is successful, the user will then be able to access the primary forms of the application. This ensures that any future calls to the database won't be rejected due to authorization failure. Later, when the user requires a method from the middle tier object to be executed, the user ID and password will be sent along with any other parameters required by the method. The user ID and password are used to make the connection, and the method is then executed.

Implementing Server-Side Security

In order to understand the process of programming security in a client-server model, we first need to understand how users are created and assigned permissions on the server. To demonstrate this, we'll walk through the process of creating users and assigning permissions in a SQL Server database. We'll then build an application to test the permissions we assign.

Managing Security in a SQL Server Database

If security is a serious consideration for your application, then you *must* use an enterprise-class relational database such as SQL Server, Oracle or Sybase. SQL Server 7.0 combines great flexibility with ease of implementing, maintaining, and monitoring security. Although there are a number of ways to secure a database, I find it quite easy to implement security with SQL Server. In this section, we'll explore the requirements for implementing security with SQL Server. It is important to distinguish between the two aspects of security: **authentication** and **authorization**. Authentication is the process of identifying a user. Authorization is the process of checking that an identified user has the necessary permissions to perform the operations requested.

SQL Server provides two ways to authenticate a user: through Windows NT Authentication and through SQL Server Authentication.

> **Windows NT Authentication**. This type of authentication tightly knits SQL Server with the security manager of Windows NT. All accounts are created in Windows NT, then users can be granted permissions to connect to SQL Server. The advantage of this system is that the user ID and password for connecting to SQL Server are identical to those of the NT account. Because the user has already entered his or her user name and password when connecting to NT, the user does not have to re-enter them when connecting to SQL Server. This is known as a **trusted connection**. SQL Server places the responsibility of ensuring proper authentication on Windows NT.

> **SQL Server Authentication**. If you would prefer not to have SQL Server security associated with NT Security, you can use SQL Server's built-in security features. Here, each user must be defined before they are permitted to connect to the server. In this case, the user ID and password will have to be entered each time the user connects, and SQL Server will take on the responsibility for validating the user. This is also known as a **nontrusted connection** because SQL Server delegates no responsibility to, and hence places no trust in, Windows NT.

Let's open SQL Server and see how this applies: open the SQL Server Enterprise Manager by selecting Start | Programs | Microsoft SQL Server 7.0 | Enterprise Manager and expand the server group, so that all servers are showing. Now right-click on your server (in my case, this is CHARLESW) and select Properties:

This will open a dialog with a number of pages; to view security settings, click on the Security tab:

The Security tab presents two options. We can declare that Windows NT security will always be used, or we can specify that a mixture of NT and SQL Server security will be used for authentication. If we want to use just SQL Server security, we must choose the SQL Server and Windows NT option button. Remember that the existence of an account in Windows NT does not automatically permit a user to connect to a database. The NT user still has to be declared as a user of the database.

The Audit level options allow us to specify on what occasions SQL Server will log attempted logins. If we click Success, only successful login attempts will be logged, whereas selecting Failure will cause SQL Server only to log failed login attempts; choosing None disables auditing and choosing All logs both successful and unsuccessful login attempts. Auditing applies to both modes of authentication (Windows NT and SQL Server), and records login attempts from both trusted and nontrusted connections.

The bottom frame on this page gives us the opportunity to set the Startup service account. This account is used by SQL Server Agent, the service SQL Server uses to perform automated administrative tasks. This can be set either to the default SQL Server system account or to a Windows NT account. The second option must be selected if jobs require access to network resources.

We're going to be looking chiefly at SQL Server authentication, so ensure that the SQL Server and Windows NT option button is checked, and click on the OK button.

Adding a New User to SQL Server

The next step in implementing security on SQL Server is to add the user name to the server. The user may be created in SQL Server, or may be pulled from a Windows NT domain. Once the user's login profile has been added, it may be used to apply for permissions across the entire server.

Expand the Security folder underneath the folder representing your server, and inside that there is an item titled Logins. Right-click on this, and then select New Login. This will bring up a dialog box where new users can be added with access rights to your database server:

The above dialog can be used to add a new user, regardless of whether you are implementing security through Windows NT or creating a new login using SQL Server. If you are using Windows NT authentication, select the appropriate Domain from the drop-down box and enter the name of a user or group in the top text box. If you are using SQL Server Authentication, you will still need to enter a password and a user name in the top text box; however, this will not be associated with any Windows NT user name. In both scenarios, you must choose a default database to which the user will be assigned. For illustrative purposes, we'll select SQL Server Authentication with the user name "SNOOPY", the password "Woodstock", and pubs as the default database.

Assigning Server Roles

Click on the Server Roles tab when you've finished entering these details, and the following page will be displayed:

This page allows us to assign administrative roles to the new login and give it security permissions that apply at the server level. These permissions are usually granted only to database administrators and programmers. For the most part, the end users of the database would not have such privileges. Here's a breakdown of the available privilege roles:

> **System Administrators**. These have full permissions and can perform any operation in SQL Server.

> **Security Administrators**. These have the authority to manage users.

> **Server Administrators**. These may configure settings at the server level.

> **Setup Administrators**. These have authority to manage extended stored procedures.

> **Process Administrators**. These can manage the process running in SQL Server.

> **Disk Administrators**. These have permissions to manage SQL Server's disk files.

> **Database Creators**. These have the authority to create and alter databases.

Assigning Access Rights

We don't want our new user messing about with system settings, so leave all the checkboxes blank and click on the Database Access tab:

Here we may specify which databases the user will be permitted to access. We can check off all the databases that the user needs access to, and then provide security roles of which the user should be a member. Roles are used to provide many SQL Server users with the same access permissions. We'll cover database roles in more detail when we get to the next section.

Check the pubs database, and you should see the user name SNOOPY appear in the user box next to the database. When we check the pubs database, the user will by default become a member of the public role. All registered users are members of this role, and we may not remove them.

Select the public role by clicking on the word public in the Database roles section. The Properties button to the right should now become enabled. Note that if we attempt to uncheck the public role, we will receive an error message. Clicking on the Properties button will display a list of users in the public role:

From this dialog, we can add additional users to the role and view the access rights granted to the role as it pertains to the selected database (in this case the `pubs` database). To see these permissions, click on the Permissions button:

This dialog allows you to view and set the permissions available to users with the `public` role for every object in the database, such as views, tables and stored procedures. To set a permission, check the box for the type of operation which will be available to the user (such as `SELECT`, `UPDATE` or `EXECUTE`). Notice that some tables are not available to the users of the `public` role; however, views which access these tables are available. This allows the user limited access to these tables. Each view is designed to return specific columns of the table(s), so that restricted information is not available to all users.

Click on the **OK** button to close the **Permissions** dialog, and then click on **OK** again in the **Database Role Properties** dialog. We now have set up the user `"SNOOPY"` with limited access to the `pubs` database. Now click on the **OK** button of the **New Login** dialog to finish building the login ID.

We are prompted again to confirm the new password. Enter `"Woodstock"` once more and click on the **OK** button.

The user name has now been built and it should appear in the list of logins in the **Security** folder:

Permission Precedence

At the database level, we can extend the available permission of any user assigned to that database. This is an important concept to understand because permission can be assigned at many levels. When we first created the `"SNOOPY"` user name, we had the option of assigning server permissions and then database permissions. When we assigned database permissions, they were at the role level (specifically, we assigned permissions to the `public` role). However, we can also assign permissions to an individual user.

We are now in a position where permissions could conflict. For example, a user could be granted access to one resource, but belong to a role to which that resource is denied. So the question now arises: which permissions take precedence over others? The answer to this is that they all work together - users accumulate all the permissions assigned to them individually and as members of roles. So, when we define access permissions, we only need to declare the permission for a user at one level, not at all of levels. If a user is assigned permissions at the user level for an object, he or she doesn't also need to be assigned permission at the role level.

However, there is one exception to this. We can explicitly deny a user or role permission to a database object. A DENY permission prevents the user from accessing a database object, regardless of whether other permissions exist. For example, if a DENY permission is assigned to the employee table at the user level, the user will not be able to access the table regardless of any permissions granted to roles that user belongs to. Conversely, when you assign permissions, you should remember that a user will be unable to access an object if he or she belongs to role which has been assigned a DENY permission on that object, even if the user has been assigned a SELECT permission at the user level.

Assigning User-Level Permissions

Now that we've seen some of the theory behind permissions, let's put it to work. Expand the Databases folder for your server, and then expand the pubs folder. Now click on the Users item to view all users with access to the database:

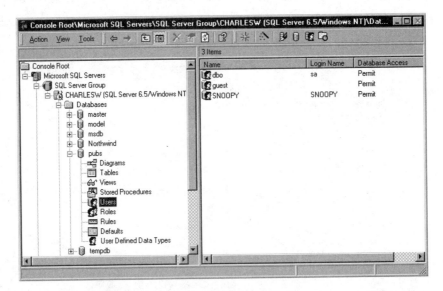

Let's see how we can assign and deny access rights to our new user. Double-click on SNOOPY to view the roles he is a member of, and then click on the Permissions button.

By default, members of the public role do not have access to the tables of the pubs database. We can change that for SNOOPY by assigning permissions at the user level. Click on the check box below the SELECT option of the employee table, and a check will appear. This means that SNOOPY now has permission to SELECT data from the employee table, even though the other members of the public role do not. Click on the check box again, and a red cross will appear in the box. This indicates a DENY permission. If the public role were now to be given access to the employee table, SNOOPY would still not be able to view the table because the DENY permission takes precedence:

Click on the SELECT checkbox for both the employee and jobs tables so that each has a black check mark next to them. We'll use these tables later in this chapter.

Now a client application can connect into SQL Server with the user ID "SNOOPY" and query the employee and jobs tables. Next, as promised, we'll explore in more detail the world of roles.

The World of Roles

Roles serve a similar function as groups in NT authentication. Groups are specific to Windows NT security. Each group consists of a number of users which require the same security permissions. A group in the NT world can then be assigned permissions to a database in SQL Server, so that we don't need to add all of the users individually.

A role works in a similar way, except that it is designed specifically to manage SQL Server user names. Before being assigned a role, the users must already have been added to SQL Server. Once a role has been created, permissions are assigned to it. Then, when a user is added to the role, those permissions are automatically rolled down to the user.

Fixed Roles

There are also a number of built in roles for each database. These roles will be automatically added for each database you create. Their names and details are as follows:

> **db_accessadmin.** Has permission to allow and disallow access to the Windows NT groups and users or SQL Server authentication users in the database.

> **db_backupoperator.** Has permission to access all objects required to back up and restore the tables of a specific database.

> **db_datareader.** Has permission to view all data in all tables of the database.

> ➤ **db_datawriter**. Has permission to modify all data in all tables of the database, including inserting data, updating data, and deleting data.

> ➤ **db_ddladmin**. Has permission to create, alter or delete all object of the database.

> ➤ **db_denydatareader**. Specifically does *not* have permission to read the data of the database tables.

> ➤ **db_denydatawriter**. Specifically does *not* have permission to alter data in the database tables.

> ➤ **db_owner**. Also referred to as dbo, has permission to perform *all* activities, using all objects of the database.

> ➤ **db_securityadmin**. Has permission to administer object permissions in the database.

Creating Roles

Let's look at an example of how to create a role. With the pubs database folder expanded, right-click on the Roles item and select New Database Role from the pop-up menu. You may also notice that the fixed roles for the database are listed in the right pane:

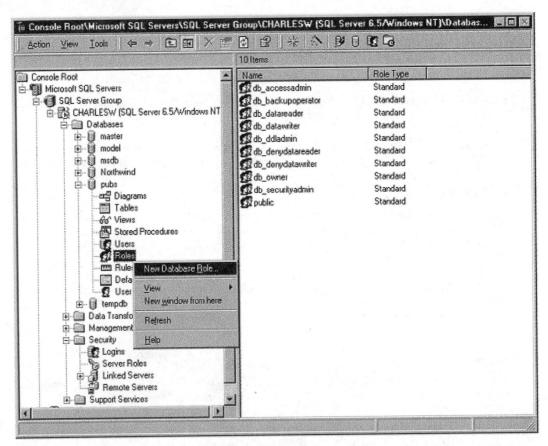

The New Role dialog allows us to create a new role and to add users to it. To demonstrate this, we'll create a new role titled "pubs_users", then add our SNOOPY user to this role:

Enter `pubs_users` in the **Name** text box, then click on the **Add** button. A list of the available users will be displayed:

To add SNOOPY to the role, click on **SNOOPY** to select him and then click on the **OK** button. The name **SNOOPY** should now appear in the user list box of the **New Role** dialog. Click on the **OK** button, and the role will be added. You should now be able to view the role in the right pane of Enterprise Manager.

Now that we've created the role, let's define some permissions for it. Double-click on the `pubs_users` role to open its **Properties** dialog and click on the **Permissions** button to view the permissions that have already been assigned to it:

Add permissions for this role, allowing the user to apply a SELECT command against the sales and stores tables. Then click on the OK button, and then on the OK button of the role's Properties dialog to accept the changes.

Your permissions are now effective, and the user SNOOPY can use the tables just as though the permissions had been assigned directly to the user ID. As you can see, there are a number of ways to implement security against your database. The goal when implementing security on an enterprise-wide basis is to minimize the amount of maintenance that will be required. For example, if you have 100 users to configure with similar permission needs, create a role that addresses the permissions required by all users, then address the specific needs on a "as needed" basis by assigning permissions to each user ID.

Implementing Security in a Two-Tier Solution

Now that we have implemented security on a SQL Server database, the next step is to demonstrate how to communicate with a secure database by passing a user ID and password during login. In this section, we'll create a project that connects to the pubs database, and then attempts to retrieve the data from some of its tables. In doing this, we'll first retrieve data from the employee and jobs tables where permission was assigned at the user level, then we'll attempt to retrieve results from the sales and stores tables where permissions were assigned at the role level. Finally, we'll attempt to retrieve results from a table for which our user has not yet been assigned permissions.

We'll create a new project in this chapter, so create a new folder called Chapter16 off the ProVB6DB directory. Next, create a folder titled Lab1 off the new Chapter16 folder. This is where we'll save our project.

The Data Form

Open Visual Basic and create a new **Standard EXE** project. Rename the form `frmDataView`, and the project as `Security1`. Save the form and project in the `Lab1` directory as `DataView.frm` and `Security1.vbp` respectively. Next, add a new module to the project by selecting **Project | Add Module** from the menu. Rename this `Globals`, and save the module in the `Chapter16` folder as `Globals.bas`. We will use this module to declare our `Connection` and `Recordset` objects as `Public` variables, allowing us to create a login form (to establish the connection), then retrieve the results with another form. Finally, add the **Microsoft ActiveX Data Objects 2.x Library** reference and the **Microsoft Hierarchical FlexGrid Control** to your project.

In the `Globals` module, declare two variables (one as a `Connection` object, and one as a `Recordset` object):

```
Option Explicit
Public cnPubs As ADODB.Connection
Public rsSelect_Results As ADODB.Recordset
```

Add the Hierarchical FlexGrid control, a text box and three command buttons to the project. Set their properties as follows:

Object	Property	Setting
Hierarchical FlexGrid	Name	MSHFlexGrid1
Command Button	Name	cmdExecute
	Caption	Execute Query
Text Box	Name	txtTable
	Text	{BLANK}
Command Button	Name	cmdExit
	Caption	Exit

Your form should look similar to the following when complete:

The Login Form

Add a new form to the project by selecting Project I Add Form. This new form will act as a login dialog box where the user can enter a user name and password, which we'll add dynamically to our connection string when we open the connection. Conveniently, a pre-designed form for this purpose is provided with Visual Basic, and we will use this. Select the Log in Dialog form and click on Open. This will add a form called `frmLogin` to your project with a few pre-configured controls on it - text boxes to enter a user name (`txtUserName`) and password (`txtPassword`), and OK and Cancel command buttons (`cmdOK` and `cmdCancel`):

Code for handling the login is automatically added to the form, and you are free to use this code. However, my preference has always been to create code in my own style, so we'll delete all of the code attached to the form (except for the `Option Explicit` statement).

We'll also modify the form a little to tailor it to our purposes. Shift the OK and Cancel buttons down, then add one text box and one label. Name these `txtServer` and `lblServer` respectively. Change the caption of the label to `&Server:` and clear the `Text` property of the text box, and the form should look like this:

This server text box will be used to allow access to the various servers enterprise-wide. We'll use all three text box values as part of our connection string.

Now add the following code to the `cmdCancel_Click` event. This will signify that the user wishes to abort the login and end the application:

```
Private Sub cmdCancel_Click()
    Unload Me
End Sub
```

The Code Behind the Forms

We'll put the code for making the connection in the `cmdOK_Click` event. Pay close attention to the specifics of how the connection string is built. The values of the text boxes are embedded in the string, together with some hard-coded information. In this case, we are going to connect to the `pubs` database of SQL Server:

```
Private Sub cmdOK_Click()
    Set cnPubs = New ADODB.Connection

    On Error GoTo BadAccount

    If Trim(txtPassword) <> "" And Trim(txtUserName) <> "" And _
        Trim(txtServer) <> "" Then
        cnPubs.ConnectionString = "Provider=SQLOLEDB.1;Password=" & _
                                  txtPassword & ";Persist Security Info=" & _
                                  "True;User ID=" & txtUserName & _
                                  ";Initial Catalog=pubs;Data Source=" & _
                                  txtServer
        cnPubs.Open

        Unload Me
        frmDataView.Show

    End If
    Exit Sub

BadAccount:
    MsgBox "Invalid Password, try again!", , "Login"
    txtPassword.SetFocus
    SendKeys "{Home}+{End}"
End Sub
```

App Reactivated

Because the cnPubs Connection object has been declared as a Public variable, both forms can share it. In this scenario, the login form creates the Connection object, then attempts to login. If the login is successful, control is shifted to the frmDataView form and the login form is unloaded from memory. If the login is a failure, focus is shifted back to the login form (specifically the password textbox).

> **The line** SendKeys "{Home}+{End}" **is used to highlight the current text in the password text box. The user can then type in a different password, and the old text will be deleted. If you are not familiar with the** SendKeys **statement, it passes keystrokes to the active application, in this case, the Visual Basic application you're programming.**

Now, let's add some code for the frmDataView form. In the cmdExit_Click event, add code to close the application:

```
Private Sub cmdExit_Click()
    Set cnPubs = Nothing
    Set rsSelect_Results = Nothing

    Unload Me
    Unload frmLogin        ' Just in case it's open
End Sub
```

If the user clicks on the cmdExecute button, we need to populate the recordset with the results of a SELECT statement that calls for all records from the table specified in the txtTable text box. The results are then posted to the FlexGrid control. If an error should occur, we'll show the user a message box with the details:

```
Private Sub cmdExecute_Click()
   On Error GoTo errHandle

   Set rsSelect_Results = cnPubs.Execute("SELECT * FROM " & txtTable)
   Set MSHFlexGrid1.Recordset = rsSelect_Results

   Exit Sub

errHandle:
   MsgBox Err.Number & Err.Description
End Sub
```

The final step before we test this project is to change the startup form to the login form. To do this, select Project | Security1 Properties from the menu. Locate and change the startup form to frmLogin.

The `frmDataView` form should open when we click OK, verifying that our user has been authenticated and the connection has succeeded. We can now test the permissions we assigned to the user. Enter the name of the jobs table in the text box, then click on the Execute Query button. The results should appear in the FlexGrid control, because permission was assigned to the user at the user level:

Testing the Permissions

Now let's test our application. Run the project and enter the user information built in SQL Server earlier: the user name "SNOOPY" and the password "Woodstock". Finally, enter the name of the server that the database resides on:

494

Try querying the `employee` table. Again, the FlexGrid should be populated. Similarly, if we attempt to execute a query against the `stores` and `sales` tables, the results should appear in the FlexGrid control because permissions were assigned through the use of a role.

Finally, let's attempt to query a table that has had no permissions assigned to it. Attempt to retrieve results from the `discounts` table, and an error should appear as below:

As you can see, there's nothing very difficult about implementing security in your client applications. The previous example could use a great deal more error handling, but it gives you a solid understanding of the requirements for securing your applications. In the next section we'll discover techniques for securing a three-tier client server system.

Implementing Security in a Three-Tier Solution

In this section, we'll take an existing three-tier application (the `Employee` project) that we built in a previous chapter, and add security to it. To do this we'll need to modify two applications. The client application will need to receive the login information and pass it to the middle-tier application. This will therefore need to be coded to receive the login information and log in using it, rather than the trusted connection, which has been used to this point.

Firstly, create a new folder in the `ProVB6DB\Chapter16` directory called `Lab2`, and copy into this the contents of the folder `C:\ProVB6DB\Chapter11\Lab1`. As you recall, this is the generic three-tier application that we built where we call the four SQL statements `Insert`, `Update`, `Delete` and `Select` against the `employee` table.

Open the `Employee.vbp` project, and create a new `Public Function` in the `Employee.cls` class, and name it `Login`. This function will receive two arguments as strings, and return one Boolean argument to indicate whether or not the login attempt was successful:

```
Public Function Login(username As String, password As String) As Boolean

End Function
```

Cut the contents of the `Class_Initialize` event to the clipboard, then paste it in the new function (`Login`). We'll modify this code slightly, as follows:

```
Public Function Login(username As String, password As String) As Boolean

On Error GoTo BadLogin

    Set cnEmployee = New ADODB.Connection
    cnEmployee.ConnectionString = "Provider=SQLOLEDB.1;" & _
                                  "Persist Security Info=False;" & _
                                  "Initial Catalog=PUBS;User ID=" & username & _
                                  ";Password=" & password

    cnEmployee.Open
    Login = True
    Exit Function

BadLogin:
    Login = False
End Function
```

This converts our login routine into a function and allows us to return a Boolean value to the calling client application, indicating whether or not the login attempt succeeded. The client will call this function when the object is created. Once the login is established, the middle-tier object (`Employee.dll`) will hold the connection information so that it's connected when the other functions are needed. As with the previous project, we modified the connection string to populate it dynamically with the contents of the password and username, which are passed to the function from the client. Error handling is used to identify whether an error occurred during login. If an error occurs, we know the login was unsuccessful, and we return a `False` value to the client.

Modify the `Class_Terminate` event as shown below. This will handle the possibility that the user may click on the Cancel button without establishing an error. If we don't handle this possibility, an error will be generated:

```
Private Sub Class_Terminate()
    If cnEmployee.State = adStateOpen Then
        cnEmployee.Close
    End If
    Set cnEmployee = Nothing
End Sub
```

Save and re-compile the project. The middle-tier component is now capable of handling the login.

We still need to modify the client application so that it can pass the user's details to the middle tier, so add `ClientApp.vbp` to the group. Add a new module by selecting Project | Add Module from the menu. This module will be used to create a public instance of the `Employee` object. Change its Name property to `modGlobals`, and save it as `Globals.bas`.

In this module, add the following declaration:

```
Public objEmployee As Employee.clsEmployee
```

Locate where objEmployee was declared in our form (in the General Declarations section) and remove or comment out that line of code. (Now that it's been declared publicly, we don't need to declare it again.)

Also, in the Form_Load event of the client form, comment out the code that creates a new instance of our Employee object. Rather than instantiate the object in Form_Load, we'll do this from a new login form that we'll add next.

```
Private Sub Form_Load()
    'Set objEmployee = New Employee.clsEmployee
    Select_Data
End Sub
```

Select Project | Add Form to add the new form. Again, we'll use Visual Basic's pre-built login form, so select the Log in Dialog form here, then click on the OK button. Remove all code from the form (with the exception of the Option Explicit statement). As in the previous application, we'll write our own code.

In the General Declarations section of this form, declare one Boolean variable. We will use this to indicate whether the attempt to login was successful:

```
Option Explicit
Dim blnLoginSuccess As Boolean
```

In the Form_Load event of the frmLogin form, create an instance of the Employee object:

```
Private Sub Form_Load()
    Set objEmployee = New Employee.clsEmployee
End Sub
```

In the cmdCancel_Click event, we'll destroy the object and unload the form.

```
Private Sub cmdCancel_Click()
    Set objEmployee = Nothing
    Unload Me
End Sub
```

Finally, in the cmdOK_Click event, we'll add the code to attempt to connect to the database:

```
Private Sub cmdOK_Click()

    If Trim(txtPassword) = "" or Trim(txtUserName) = "" Then
        MsgBox "User Name and Password cannot be blank!"
        Exit Sub
    Else
        blnLoginSuccess = objEmployee.Login(txtUserName, txtPassword)
        If blnLoginSuccess = True Then
            Unload Me
            frmClient.Show
```

```
        Else
            MsgBox "Invalid UserName or Password, try again!", , "Login"
            txtPassword.SetFocus
            SendKeys "{Home}+{End}"
        End If
    End If
End Sub
```

In this procedure, we call the `Login` function of our `Employee` object, passing it a password and user name. We then examine the returned Boolean value indicating if the attempt was successful. If so, we unload the login form and load `frmClient`; otherwise, we send the user back to try again.

Change the startup form to `frmLogin` on the Project I Client Properties dialog, and we're ready to test the changes. To do this, run the application, log in and update some records.

This solution should work fine; however, you should keep in mind that it might not be the most scalable solution. Should you move to an architecture where you want to pool components, this may cause problems if you expect to be able to monitor the activities made by the user. Specifically, we hold the connection to the database open during processing, so many components could not use it until the client releases it.

The next step is to look at implementing security on the middle tier using Microsoft Transaction Server, which would be more suitable for such a scenario.

Implementing Security with MTS

Now that we have seen how security is implemented on the server side, it's a good time to explore how we can use Microsoft Transaction Server to roll out security. Conceptually, implementing security using MTS is not very different to what we have already explored. Users are created and permissions are assigned to them, and these permissions are enforced by the middle-tier object. This will run a check against MTS to validate whether the user has been assigned the requisite permissions.

Let's take a look at the Microsoft Management Console for MTS. As you recall, each package is broken down into two sections. The first section comprises the components, and the second its roles (each of these sections has its own folder). Roles are similar to those in SQL Server; each role contains a number of users with similar security access.

The `Employee` object was originally added to MTS in Chapter 11. Because the component has been recompiled, it should be refreshed in the Management Console to prevent its Registry settings from being overridden. Click on the **Components** folder under **Employee**, then select **Action | Refresh**.

To create a new role, right click on the **Roles** folder and select **New | Role**. The following dialog will appear:

Enter the name of your new role; for this example, we'll use the name `Users`. Then click on the **OK** button.

The Users role will be added to the Roles folder, and a new folder is added to the new role. This new folder will contain all users who are members of the role. We'll add a new user to this role, so right-click on the Users folder, then select New | User.

The Add Users and Groups to Role dialog will appear. This dialog allows you to specify any users on the NT Server (or local domain) that should be added to the role. Remember that these users are NT users, not SQL Server users: MTS authentication is closely tied in to NT authentication (this feature does not exist in the cut-down version of MTS supplied with PWS).

Select the server from the top combo box, and click on the Show Users command button. This will cause a list of all available users to appear in the Names list box. Select the names of any users you want to add to the role and click on the Add button. When finished, click on OK, and the user should be added to the role:

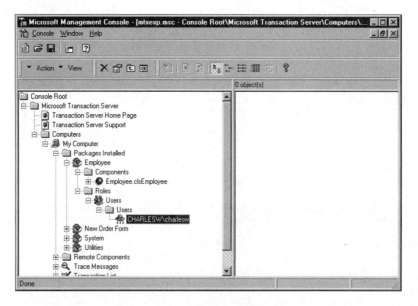

We'll now assign roles to your components. Expand Employee.clsEmployee in the Components folder until you get to the Role Membership folder, as shown below:

To add a new role to our `Employee` component, right-click on this folder and select New | Role. The Select Roles dialog will now appear. This lists all the available roles that can be added to the component's role membership listing. Currently, there is only one role available:

Select the `Users` role from the list, then click on the OK button. If there were more than one user in the `Users` role, they would all have been inherently added to the component's role membership.

We now have just one more step to take: actually to enable the security. To do this, right-click on the `Employee` package and select **Properties** from the pop-up menu. This will open the property pages for the component. Click on the **Security** tab.

Select the **Enable authorization checking** box to turn MTS authorization on, then select **Packet** from the **Authentication level for calls** combo box. This gives us a fair degree of security: the caller ID will be encrypted to protect the user ID from being impersonated by an external attacker. MTS supports a number of authentication levels:

> ➤ **None**: No checking or verification is performed.
>
> ➤ **Connect**: Checking is performed only once (when the package is first called).
>
> ➤ **Call**: Checking occurs during every time the package is called.
>
> ➤ **Packet**: Provides encryption of the caller's ID.
>
> ➤ **Packet Integrity**: Provides encryption and checks for tampering.
>
> ➤ **Packet Privacy**: The highest level, encrypting all communication over the network.

We're now ready to code the component so that it checks whether a user has the required permission to use the component. To do this, review the following code:

We must first declare and instantiate the `ObjectContext` object, as we did when we rolled out existing projects to MTS in Chapters 11 and 13:

```
Dim objContext As ObjectContext
Set objContext = GetObjectContext()
```

The next step is to validate the user against the role. We do this in three steps. If all tests are passed, the user is verified as a valid user.

The first step is to check that MTS is running. If MTS isn't active, there's no sense in checking security, so we'll bypass the check:

```
If Not objContext Is Nothing Then   ' MTS is active
```

If security isn't enabled, then once again, there is no need to continue:

```
If objContext.IsSecurityEnabled Then
```

Next we check the caller's user ID against the role. If it's not in the Role Membership, we abort the execution, and exit the function:

```
If Not objContext.IsCallerInRole("Users") Then
    GetObjectContext.SetAbort
    Exit Sub

End If
End If
End If
```

If we make it through the above validation, then we're OK to execute our SQL code and commit the transaction:

```
' *** ADD YOUR SQL CODE HERE TO EXECUTE THE PROCEDURE ***
GetObjectContext.SetComplete
```

Of course, we'll also have to implement error handling just as we did before. As an example, this is how our `Delete_Employee` function might look when we've implemented MTS security. This assumes that an MTS role called `Supervisor` has been set up, to which any NT user must belong if he or she is to call the function successfully:

```
Public Function Delete_Employee(emp_id As String) As Boolean

    Dim strSQL As String

    Dim objContext As ObjectContext
    Set objContext = GetObjectContext()

    On Error GoTo BadDelete

    If Not objContext Is Nothing Then
        If objContext.IsSecurityEnabled Then
            If Not objContext.IsCallerInRole("Supervisor") Then
                GetObjectContext.SetAbort
                Exit Sub
            End If
        End If
    End If

    strSQL = "DELETE FROM employee"
    strSQL = strSQL & " WHERE emp_id = '"
    strSQL = strSQL & emp_id & "'"

    cnConnection.Execute strSQL
```

```
                    Delete_Employee = True

                    If objContext Is Nothing Then
                        GetObjectContext().SetComplete
                    End If

                    Exit Function

                BadDelete:

                    MsgBox Err.Number & Err.Description
                    Delete_Employee = False

                    If objContext Is Nothing Then
                        GetObjectContext().SetAbort
                    End If

                End Function
```

That's all there is to it! Try implementing security in the remaining three functions.

Using SQL to Implement Security

If we need to administer security in your database server through code, there are a few SQL statements that can help us achieve this. These are:

➢ GRANT. Allows us to provide access rights to objects in a database.

➢ REVOKE. Allows us to remove access rights to objects in a database.

➢ DENY. Allows us to prevent users from accessing objects in a database, overriding all previously set permissions.

The GRANT Command

The GRANT command is used to assign permission to objects in a database. A GRANT command consists of the following parts:

➢ The keyword GRANT with the operations that are to be authorized

➢ The objects to which access is to be granted

➢ The user or role to which the permission is to be assigned

A sample GRANT statement might look like this:

```
GRANT SELECT, UPDATE
ON myTable
TO SNOOPY
```

In this statement, the user SNOOPY is assigned permissions to SELECT and UPDATE the myTable table.

If we want to provide permissions to all commands on a specific object, we can use the ALL keyword, as in the following statement:

```
GRANT ALL
ON myTable
TO SNOOPY
```

Further, if we want to allow the user to grant the same privileges to other users, we can append the WITH GRANT OPTION keyword to our statement:

```
GRANT SELECT, UPDATE
ON myTable
TO SNOOPY
WITH GRANT OPTION
```

The REVOKE Command

The REVOKE statement has a similar syntax to the GRANT statement. The primary difference is that we are removing privileges that were previously assigned:

```
REVOKE SELECT, UPDATE
ON myTable
TO SNOOPY
```

Again, we can use the ALL keyword to specify that the statement will affect all operations:

```
REVOKE ALL
ON myTable
TO SNOOPY
```

If we wish to revoke the right to grant or revoke privileges for other users, we can use the clause GRANT OPTION FOR. We must also append the CASCADE keyword, which specifies that the command will cascade down, and grant options will also be revoked for users to whom the (former) grantor assigned rights:

```
REVOKE GRANT OPTION FOR SELECT
ON myTable
TO SNOOPY
CASCADE
```

The DENY Command

Just like the REVOKE statement, DENY has the same syntax as the GRANT statement. Here, the difference is that you are denying privileges that were previously assigned. As with denying permissions through Enterprise manager, the DENY command is a bit more powerful because it overrides all privileges at any level. In contrast, revoking privileges does not deal with privileges assigned at other levels:

```
DENY SELECT, UPDATE
ON myTable
TO SNOOPY
```

We cannot use DENY to revoke grant option privileges, but we can use ALL as with REVOKE:

```
DENY ALL
ON myTable
TO SNOOPY
```

Summary

In this chapter, we explored implementing security at many levels. We discovered how security could be implemented with SQL Server or with Microsoft Transaction Server. We built applications that validate security on the middle tier and on the server. While we covered many of the common techniques for securing a client-server application, there are no limitations to the number of security checkpoints you can implement, or how you can implement them. We have just scratched the surface of implementing security on your client-server systems. This chapter demonstrates just a few of the most common techniques for securing your systems. For more information on this subject, you should consult documentation that pertains to your specific database server.

Suppliers

- SupplierID
- CompanyName
- ContactName
- ContactTitle
- Address
- City
- Region
- PostalCode
- Country
- Phone
- Fax
- HomePage

Products

- ProductID
- ProductName
- SupplierID
- CategoryID
- QuantityPerUnit
- UnitPrice
- UnitsInStock
- UnitsOnOrder
- ReorderLevel
- Discontinued

Categories

- CategoryID
- CategoryName
- Description
- Picture

6

17

Deploying Client-Server Applications

Up to this point we have been looking at how to build client-server applications. However, the application is not complete until it has successfully been deployed to all of the required workstations. This chapter will focus on distributing our client-server applications using the wizard that is available through Visual Basic. The examples in this chapter require you to have completed the examples in Chapter 13, so if you have not, do so now, or download the code from the web. In this chapter we will focus on three major areas:

1. Deploying a Data Source Name

2. Three-tier deployment techniques

3. Deploying the client application

The first of these sections relates chiefly to the deployment of two-tier client-server applications, while the second concerns only three-tier applications.

Why Do We Need to Package Our Application?

Now that you have built and tested your client application, you're ready to deploy it to the users. To accomplish this you first must consider all aspects of the deployment process. You've compiled the application into an executable; however, if you simply pass the executable around to the users, and tell them to copy it onto their machine, the odds of getting any one of them to work are non-existent. In addition to the executable, there are a number of files that must be distributed along with the executable. They include:

> ➤ **Any ActiveX controls used in the application**. Many computers will already have a copy of the controls; however, if any of them are missing, the application will generate an error. These controls will need to be registered during the setup process.

> ➤ **The Visual Basic Runtime library**. For Visual Basic 6.0, the file is MSVBM60.DLL.

> ➤ **Any supporting files**: If the application is to have it's own version of a database, such as Access, you'll need to distribute a copy of it. Don't forget any text files, data files, report files or registry files.

> ➤ **Other Dependency Files**. These include DLLs which are called by the application.

> ➤ **Documentation and Help Files**. Many products are available to assist you in creating help files. One of the most popular and easy-to-use is RoboHelp.

Of course, even allowing for all the necessary files, we can't just hand them around. Some files will have to be placed in specific directories, and we can't expect users to install the application correctly on their own. So we'll create a setup utility that will install all the files itself, so we won't have to help out hundreds of users who haven't read the installation instructions. Fortunately, Visual Basic provides yet another handy tool to help us in this task - the **Package and Deployment Wizard**.

For this chapter example, we'll distribute the Northwind Order Application that we built in Chapter 13. This is a three-tier application, but the concepts are largely identical for two-tier applications, until the final section on distributing MTS components.

The connection to the Northwind application is made using the ODBC driver, and the Data Source Name (DSN) "NorthWind". Because the connection is made by our middle-tier object, we don't need to worry about the database connection in the client application (we only to communicate with our middle tier), but we will need to set up a DSN on any machine to which we wish to deploy our middle-tier object. Moreover, if we wish to deploy a two-tier application, we'll have to connect directly to the database from our client, so we'll have to create a setup program that will not only install all required files, but also create the DSN on every computer that we wish to deploy the application to. The Package and Deployment Wizard is quite resourceful when it comes to acknowledging the required files; however, it does not have a built-in capability to create ODBC DSNs. For this reason, we'll need to handle this ourselves.

Deploying Data Source Names

To export a DSN to another machine, we have to start by looking at the registry. This is where system settings are stored and where COM objects are registered. If you're not familiar with the Windows registry, it's important that you're careful what you do to it. The registry is used for the configuration of your entire windows system, and should it become corrupt, you may find yourself re-installing Windows.

Using the Registry Editor

To open the registry, select Run from the Start menu, and enter regedit in the Open text box:

This opens the Registry Editor, which allows us to view, modify and backup registry entries. This program looks and works a bit like Windows Explorer. We can navigate through folders (called **keys**) in the tree just as you do with Windows Explorer. Each of these keys can contain either subkeys or **values**, and each value consists of a name and an item of data. Locate the following key:

```
HKEY_LOCAL_MACHINE\SOFTWARE\ODBC\ODBC.INI\ODBC Data Sources
```

When we configure a DSN, it is automatically registered here. This registry key identifies all DSNs currently configured on your computer; we'll need to add an entry in the registry of each computer that we deploy our application to: this will allow our client application to use the DSN, without having to configure a DSN on the local machine.

In the following screenshot of the Registry Editor, you can see that a DSN NorthWind of type SQL Server has already been added to the list. Your Registry Editor will look similar to this, but may have more or fewer settings depending on the number of DSN entries that have previously been created on your computer:

This NorthWind value indicates that a DSN named NorthWind, and that it connects to a SQL Server database, but contains no more information than that. However, there is also a NorthWind key in the registry (in the ODBC.INI key); locate this and double-click on it to display the values that it contains. You'll see that the registry holds information about the DSN which ODBC needs to make the connection, such as the name of the server and database to connect to and the path and filename of the ODBC driver to use:

Exporting Registry Files

We'll export this key to a file so that we can build a registry merge file. This is a configuration file that contains registry settings, which can easily be merged to any computer's registry, updating any new values or keys. In this case, we'll merge the NorthWind registry information with the client computer's. With the NorthWind registry still showing, select Registry | Export Registry File from the menu. This will open the dialog box shown below:

Save the file as `NorthWind.reg` in the C:\ProVB6DB\Chapter17 folder. We also need to export the information from the `ODBC Data Source` key. If we add the `NorthWind` DSN with no pointer to it, it will be of no use to us (or any other application that needs it).

Repeat the same steps for the `ODBC Data Sources` registry key. Export this to `DSNNames.reg` (in the `ProVB6DB/Chapter17` folder).

> **Be aware that when these two files** (`NORTHWIND.reg` **and** `DSNNames.reg`) **are merged with the client registry, the keys and values may overwrite the existing values of that machine (if a name conflict exists).**

Now close the Registry Editor, and open the ODBC Data Source Administrator from Control Panel:

Locate the `NorthWind` DSN under the **System DSN** tab and click on the **R**emove button. By removing the DSN, then merging the extracted file with our registry, we can confirm that our process is working successfully.

Creating the New Registry File

When you've closed the ODBC Data Source Administrator, open both of the registry files that you created using a simple text editor such as Notepad. We want to bring the keys of these two files together into one single file.

> **Do not double click on registry files. This will cause them to run, merging the file with the registry.**

The first part of our file is the header. The header identifies the type of script; for registry files, the header will be REGEDIT4.

The next step is to add the DSN to the registry. The first line identifies the location of the key in the registry, and the second line identifies the name and data content of the value.

> *If the key already exists containing different values, the new value will be appended to the key. If another value with the same name already exists, the new value will overwrite it.*

Remove any values in the ODBC Data Sources key that don't relate to the NorthWind DSN. Your file should now look similar to this one:

```
REGEDIT4

[HKEY_LOCAL_MACHINE\SOFTWARE\ODBC\ODBC.INI\ODBC Data Sources]
"NorthWind"="SQL Server"
```

Once you've added a key for the NorthWind DSN to your file, we'll need to identify the setting associated with the DSN. Copy the contents of NorthWind.reg, and paste them to your new registry file.

> **Note that, for deployment, you may need to modify the security and the "Server" values. If you are not comfortable with this, move to one of the remote machines and export the registry entries after you have created a DSN with the ODBC Data Source Administrator. You will then have the required values created for you. Also note that the "Driver" value varies between Windows NT and Windows 95 or 98. It may be desirable to create a setup procedure for each operating system.**

```
[HKEY_LOCAL_MACHINE\SOFTWARE\ODBC\ODBC.INI\NorthWind]
"Driver"="C:\\WINNT\\System32\\sqlsrv32.dll"
"Server"="(local)"
"Database"="Northwind"
"LastUser"=""
"Trusted_Connection"="Yes"
```

> Note that the double back-slashes in the above example are part of the
> registry value. Do not modify them.

When you have completed building the file, it should look similar to the one in the screenshot. Save the file as `Registry.reg`, and make a copy of it in the `C:\ProVB6DB\Chapter17` folder. We'll see later how to include this file in our setup program.

```
DSNNames.reg - Notepad
File  Edit  Search  Help
REGEDIT4

[HKEY_LOCAL_MACHINE\SOFTWARE\ODBC\ODBC.INI\ODBC Data Sources]
"NorthWind"="SQL Server"

[HKEY_LOCAL_MACHINE\SOFTWARE\ODBC\ODBC.INI\NorthWind]
"Driver"="C:\\WINNT\\System32\\sqlsrv32.dll"
"Server"="(local)"
"Database"="Northwind"
"LastUser"=""
"Trusted_Connection"="Yes"
```

Deploying an N-Tier Application

In the last section of this chapter, we will see how to create a setup utility for the `Northwind` application. When we deploy this n-tier solution, we will need to tell the client applications where to instantiate the `ServerApp` DLL. Remember that this is the DLL that connects to the database and processes the client requests. The following section will demonstrate how to configure and deploy the client application in an n-tier solution. In addition, we'll touch upon the configuration of the server and all middle-tier objects.

> The database server may reside on a different machine to MTS (and the
> middle-tier components). If the database is moved to a new machine,
> remember that the DSN name must be modified on the machine with the
> middle-tier objects.

There are three extra steps that are necessary for configuring the client machine for an n-tier application; we'll cover each of these in turn:

> ➤ Install DCOM on the client (if necessary)
> ➤ Export the remote registry information from the server
> ➤ Install the remote registry information on the client

What is DCOM?

Before we install DCOM, it's probably a good idea to understand what it is. DCOM stands for Distributed COM (Component Object Model), but what does this actually mean? Let's start with COM. We've already met COM once or twice in this book: it's the binary standard for objects that identifies how an object should present itself to the system. What this means is that if any object conforms to COM, that object will be able to communicate with other COM-compliant objects, regardless of what language they were created in. For example, an object created in VB could communicate with an object created in Visual C++ if they are both COM-compliant. COM objects are language-neutral, allowing you to use objects created in Visual C++ in your VB applications (or vice versa).

When a three-tier solution is implemented, COM is the means by which Visual Basic communicates with the middle tier object. The middle tier object exposes a number of methods and properties for the client application to work with. The client application calls these methods, and results are returned on demand:

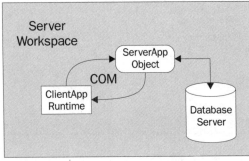

When the middle tier objects reside on a different machine, COM by itself cannot bridge the network gap. This is where DCOM comes into play. DCOM allows the client (on one machine) to instantiate an object on another machine. When the client application attempts to instantiate an object on another machine, COM is first called to identify where the object is listed in its registry. If the object is to be executed on a remote system, the request is passed to DCOM. DCOM communicates with the server machine, and the object is instantiated. Note that the component runs on the server machine, not the client machine:

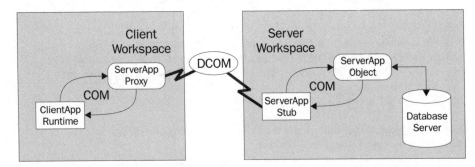

To handle the communications between the client application and the middle tier object, DCOM will create a proxy on the client machine, and a stub on the server machine. The function of these is:

> ➤ **Proxy**: this component packages all requests from the client, and passes them over the network to the stub. When the stub returns the results, it then packages them for presentation to the client. The proxy presents a duplicate set of the object's methods; however, it contains no logic. The requests are simply packaged and passed to the stub.

> ➤ **Stub**: this component runs on the machine as the object itself, and works in a very similar way to the proxy. The difference is that the stub actually calls the methods of the object, and packages the results, passing them to the proxy.

The instantiation and query-response model of DCOM is invisible to the user. When a component is instantiated using DCOM, the stub and proxy act as the glue that binds together the client application and the middle tier object. To the user, there is nothing to indicate that the components are not just using COM to communicate.

Installing DCOM

To use DCOM, both the client and server machines must have DCOM installed. It may therefore be necessary to install DCOM on the client, particularly if this is a Windows 95 machine. DCOM is freely available for download on Microsoft's web page at:

http://www.microsoft.com/com/dcom/dcom98/download.asp for Windows 98 and
http://www.microsoft.com/com/dcom/dcom95/download.asp for Windows 95.

Of course, we aren't entitled to distribute Microsoft software, so we can't add this file to our package, but we can add a `Readme.txt` text file containing installation instructions which inform users that they must download DCOM, and point the user to Microsoft's site.

Exporting the Client Configuration From MTS

The registry of each client computer needs to be configured to instantiate the component using DCOM on a specific machine (where the object resides). This is much easier than it might sound. Microsoft Transaction Server has a built-in utility that creates an executable that can be run on the client machines. When run, the executable will modify the client computer's registry, making all required changes to the keys and values.

Open the Microsoft Management Console for Transaction Server from the **Start** menu and navigate to the `New Order Form` package that we installed in Chapter 13. Right-click on this package and select **E**xport, and the following dialog will appear:

Enter `"C:\ProVB6DB\Chapter17\Export\ServerApp"` in the path for the package to be created in. We have not created the `Export` folder yet, but MTS will create it for us. This utility also allows us to export security information. This would be used if you were planning to import the package to another MTS machine. To create the file, click on the Export button.

MTS will now create some files and a folder:

> ➤ `ServerApp.pak`. A file that can be used to import the package into another MTS session.
> ➤ `ServerApp.dll`. A copy of the original `ServerApp.dll` for distribution.

MTS will also create a `Clients` folder, which contains our configuration executable:

> ➤ `ServerApp.exe`. The executable file that will automatically configure the registry on the client machines.

Because this file must be run on all client computers, we will include it as part of our setup utility.

> **Note that you should not run this executable on the same machine that created the client configuration executable. DCOM is not necessary because any client application running on the same machine as MTS is local.**

When this executable is run, it will automatically unpack itself and execute against the registry. This requires no user interaction. The client machine does not require MTS to be installed, and even if MTS is installed, the new package will not appear in MTS Explorer after the MTS `.exe` file has run.

The version of MTS supplied with PWS for Windows 95 and 98 does not create this `.exe` file. It does, however, create the `.PAK` file, which can be imported into the client's version of MTS. The Component Services Manager which replaces MTS Explorer in Windows 2000 does not create a `.PAK` or an `.exe` file, but an `.MSI` file which will automatically be executed and register the package when our setup application runs.

Creating the Setup Utility

Now we can move on to creating the setup utility for our `NorthWind` application. If you have not yet compiled the `NorthWind` application, do this now. The Visual Basic Package and Deployment Wizard will do this for you, but I have come across errors when allowing the wizard to compile the project.

Open the Package and Deployment Wizard from the Visual Basic folder (or the Visual Studio 6.0 Tools folder if you have Visual Studio) from the Programs menu.

The Package and Deployment Wizard will open and prompt you to select the project you want to deploy. Locate the `ClientApp.vbp` file from the `Chapter13` folder:

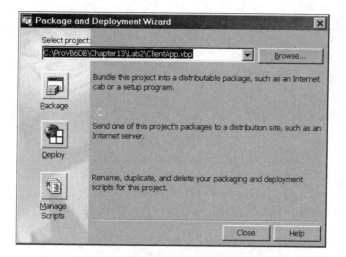

This dialog give us a number of options for creating, deploy and maintaining application setup files. The <u>D</u>eploy option allows us to create a distribution site on the Internet, and the <u>M</u>anage Scripts option allows us to view and modify any setup scripts that we have previously saved with the Visual Basic Setup wizard. We're interested here in the <u>P</u>ackage function that allows us to build a setup utility, so click on the <u>P</u>ackage icon:

Here we can specify the type of the package we wish to create by indicating whether the application is to be deployed as a dependency file or as a standard package. A dependency file is a file which our application, or components within our application, require to run. It might consist of a DLL, for example, that is used by many clients. If we made revisions to our dependency file, we would want to re-distribute it to all users. This utility would allow us to do this. Here we want to distribute an executable file, so select Standard Setup Package and click on the <u>N</u>ext > button:

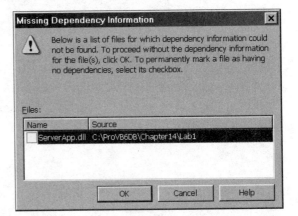

The **Package Folder** dialog allows us to specify where we would like to save the setup files after they have been generated. You may elect to place these files where you like; however, for deployment purposes, you may find it most convenient to save them on the network. For this example, select the `ProVB6DB/Chapter17` folder, and then click on the **Next >** button.

At this point, you may encounter a warning that the wizard cannot find the dependencies of the `ServerApp.dll` file:

We could compile a list of the dependency files that this DLL needs by running through the Package and Deployment Wizard for this project, but choosing **Dependency File** at the **Package Type** dialog. However, this component will be running on the middle-tier, and not on the client, so the client machine does not need to have its dependencies installed. Therefore we can just click on **OK**.

The Included Files dialog presents us with a list of files that Visual Basic will automatically include in the package. This is compiled from the references and components we added to the project. We can uncheck any files if we're absolutely certain that they are not needed, and we can also add any files that we may want to deploy with our application. This is where we would want to include any text files, supporting databases, registry files or other DLLs not listed. As you can see, Visual Basic has done a good job of identifying the OCX and DLL files required.

At this point, we must add the `ServerApp.exe` file we exported from MTS earlier in the chapter. In addition, if we're deploying a two-tier application which uses a DSN, this is where we have to include our new registry file; it's worth seeing how to do this, even though we don't need it for this example. So click on the Add button:

Locate the `ServerApp.exe` file we saved earlier in the `Chapter17/` folder. Once you have selected the file, click on the Open button. If we wanted to export a DSN, we would have to repeat this for `Registry.reg`, and then click on Next > on the Included Files screen.

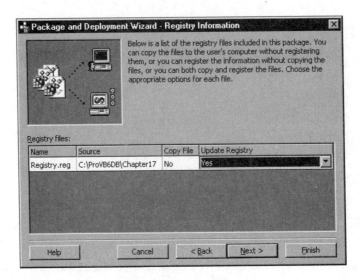

If we added a `.reg` file in the previous dialog, we will now see the Registry Information dialog. This allows us to specify how the registry file should be handled. There are two configurable choices here: the first is to merge the file with the registry; the second is to save a copy of the file to the hard drive. In most cases, we would probably use the default settings - automatically to update the registry, but not to make a copy of the registry file on the hard drive. This saves users from having to register the DSNs themselves. Clicking on the Next > button takes us to the Cab Options dialog:

This dialog allows us to specify whether we wish to distribute our application in a single file or in several smaller files. The application will be distributed in Cabinet (Cab) files. These are compressed files which work similarly to Zip files; each Cab file can contain a number of files which must be extracted before they can be used. In this dialog, we can specify the number of Cab files we want to create and the size of each file. If we plan to distribute this application on floppy disks, then we will want to select the Multiple Cabs option and limit the size of each Cab to 1.44 megabytes. Do this and click on the Next > button.

We are then given the option of displaying the name of our company or the application name during the setup process. For this example, enter `"NorthWind Application"`, and click on the **N**ext > button.

The Start Menu Items dialog allows us to place files in the startup folder, or in the folder which will be created specifically for your application, so that they will be accessible from the Start button. This is a great place to put other executables or help files that are part of your application. Click on the **N**ext > button to accept the default values (in this case to put our `ClientApp` program in its own group off the Programs folder). This takes us to the Install Locations dialog, where we can specify the folders where our individual files will be saved:

For the most part, Visual Basic knows where the associated files need to be placed, but the Install Locations dialog gives us the option of changing the defaults and placing files in a specific directory. If, for example, we want to place a specific DLL in the application path rather than the Windows Directory, we can change this here. Click on the Next > button to accept the defaults.

We now have just one final decision to make before the package is created. Visual Basic will identify any applications or DLLs that might be candidates to be shared by other applications. In this case, VB has identified only the ClientApp.exe file. If you want to share the file, click in the box next to the filename. In this case, just click on the Next > button, since we don't want any other applications using our program!

The last dialog is the Finished dialog. Here we can save the script by name so that we can re-use it if we want to make any modifications later. It is quite common to want to modify the setup utility later, so always choose a name that is logical to the project. Finally, click on the Finish button.

It may take a few minutes to build and copy the files to your drive. When this process has been completed, the dialog shown above will appear, giving us detailed information about the package. This information will change from application to application. Be sure to read the comments closely; then click on the Close button.

You will be brought back to the original dialog. Click on the Close button unless you want to build another setup utility.

Testing the Setup Utility

There should now be a number of setup files in the Chapter17 directory, including Setup.exe. This is the file our users will run to install the application. We'll run through the setup process to ensure the process runs properly.

> **You may want to consider installing the application on another machine other than the development machine. Running the setup on the development machine will not ensure that it will work everywhere because all the components needed are already registered and installed correctly on the development computer.**

When this Setup.exe file is run (either from the Run command or through Windows Explorer), the setup wizard will copy some preliminary files that it needs to install our application:

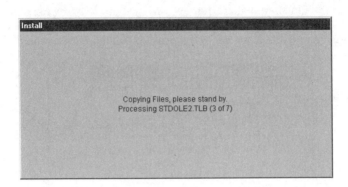

Then the setup wizard itself will start; this wizard will guide the user through the process of installing our application on their machine. Notice the professional look of the setup application the Deployment and Package Wizard created for us:

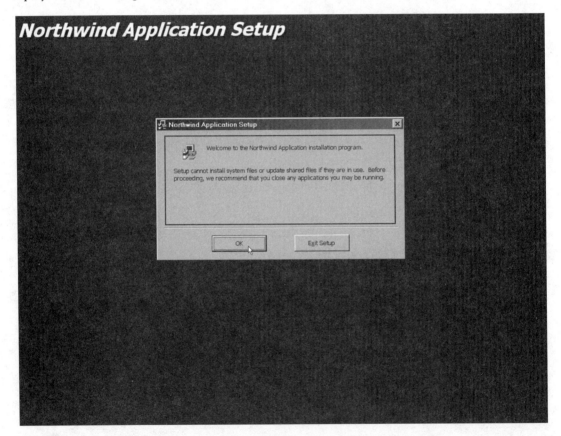

The setup utility will warn the user to close all applications before continuing. It's important that this advice is followed. Any shared files cannot be overwritten if they are being used.

After clicking on the OK button, the Setup dialog appears. This allows the user to change the setup location. For this test, accept the default location and click on the setup button.

Select the Program Group in which your program will reside. The default is for the utility to create a group specially for the application. This is fine, so click on Continue.

After all of the files have been moved to their proper directories and registered, the user will be notified that the installation is complete. The ServerApp.exe file must still be run to ensure that the proxy component is registered with MTS. At this point, you should reboot your PC, even if no prompt asks you to. This will allow Windows to overwrite any files that were being used during installation. Also, if we were using a DSN, the registry would not be updated until the machine has been rebooted.

And that's it. The program should exist in the Start | Programs menu. Run the application to test it has been installed correctly.

Summary

Deploying your application, as you have seen in this chapter, is not a difficult task. However, it should not be taken for granted. Spend time testing the setup utility on various machines with different operating systems and different CPUs. You'll be surprised by some of the issues you will come across while testing. Also, you may want to think about any upgrade process that may be forecasted. If you can save time later, make the extra effort now. Visual Basic's Package and Deployment Wizard is great at deploying your applications; however, don't disregard the option of using third party setup tools, such as Install Shield. These tools provide even greater flexibility with their own built-in language. This chapter examined the final step in building a three-tier database application. You have now been introduced to all the tools you need to create a powerful client-server system, exploiting the power of, amongst other technologies, Visual Basic, ADO and SQL Server.

Data Warehousing

This chapter presents an overview of data warehousing, a subject that has quickly excited considerable commercial interest. In the previous chapters, we spent a lot of time understanding how we can effectively enter, modify, and retrieve data from relational databases. Now we'll look at how we can move historical database data into a warehouse and use advanced tools to analyze this data in order to make informed business decisions. We'll discuss some of the advantages of a data warehouse, and a few of the many design models available, concentrating mainly on multidimensional data structure. Once we've covered all the basic concepts, we'll implement one of the data analysis solutions (Online Analytical Processing) available for use with warehoused data.

What is Data Warehousing?

Just about everyone seems to have a different opinion as to what exactly is involved in Data Warehousing. In a nutshell, a data warehouse is "a repository for historical data, used to make decisions." Of course there's much more to it than that. The concepts of a data warehouse are quite simple. Actually implementing an effective data warehouse that allows you to retrieve all the information you need quickly and easily…that is a rather more difficult task.

Data warehouses are used to store useful information. Later, the stored information is retrieved and organized in a manner that allows us to make decisions. The key word here is 'useful'. Having invested in data warehousing technology there is, understandably, some anxiety to ensure that all the data that may ever be needed for business analysis is stored there. This can lead to the misconception that a data warehouse is simply a place to dump old data, just in case it's needed at some later date. This does not make for an effective implementation - the more the warehouse becomes cluttered with junk, the harder it will be to retrieve useful information. It is far better to have an efficient, focused warehouse (just focusing on a specific area of sales activity, for example) from which relevant and useful data can be quickly retrieved. The lesson to take home is: carefully analyze your business needs before creating your warehouse.

Once you've decided on a focus for your warehouse, then the fun starts:

> What will be the structure of the data in your warehouse? Will the tables follow the traditional relational structure? Or will you need to implement a complex "multidimensional" structure?

> From what sources will you pull your data? Just one internal source or several sources, including some external to your company (in which case you will probably have to deal with several different data structures)?

> How will you transform, validate and transfer this data so that it can all be stored in one place?

One of the keys to implementing a successful data warehouse is deciding on the data structure that will best suit your data analysis requirements. We'll discuss data table layouts a bit later on but for now I just want to stress that the ideal solution is to build the data tables around the type and range of information that you will need to get out of the warehouse. In other words, you should spend some time evaluating the "Who, What, When, Where and Why" of your needs. Cast your mind back to our discussion on the design of an effective relational database, back in Chapter 2. Remember that it is important to evaluate the fields you need to report on first, and then construct the database tables. The fields that you might use for analysis and reporting will probably not encompass all of the fields available in the production database tables, so the best solution may not be to simply use table structures identical to the production database.

OK, what can a data warehouse do for your business? At this stage, let's just take a look at a practical implementation of a data warehouse with which we are all familiar: The president of a grocery store chain asks the CIO of his company to retrieve information about the buying habits of his customers. To do this, the CIO needs to know specific information about each customer, such as address, sex and, possibly, profession. To retrieve this information, each store issues 'Discount Cards' to their customers. In order to receive these cards, the customer is required to fill in a short application form, giving the store the above relevant information. When making a purchase, the discount card (which has a bar-code) is swiped across the bar code scanner, thus linking a customer identity to the specific purchases made, along with other relevant information such as store location and date and time of purchase etc. All of this information is stored in a data warehouse. This information can then be analyzed to determine summary information about customer shopping habits. The store can look for trends or tendencies in the shopping habits of certain "groups" of people. For example:

> Frequency of shopping.
> Specific product preferences, such as Nescafé vs. store brand coffee.
> Bargain hunting, use of coupons, purchase of economy size goods etc.

When this data is grouped together with thousands of other consumers, this aggregated data can allow the store to:

> Quickly weed out products that don't sell in specific stores, or in all stores.
> Find out which products are most commonly purchased, so that they can be placed on the 'end caps' to promote impulse purchasing.
> Make accurate sales projections for each store, allowing adequate ordering of stock.
> Market specific products directly to those who use them.

In this instance, the data warehouse proves successful in helping service the consumer while maintaining profitability. The scope of each data warehouse will vary depending on the industry and the size of the corporation. The first step in developing a data warehouse should be to consider all the benefits that one could bring to your particular organization and to weigh them against the cost of implementation and the various difficulties that may be associated with it. Essentially, what can a data warehouse do for you and is it worth it? Let's take a more general look at some of the possible uses for a data warehouse.

What is Data Warehousing Used for?

Data warehouses are typically used for the following four different tasks (we'll cover each of them in more detail later):

> **Reporting**: General queries applied to the data warehouse with the intent of finding answers to specific questions. This is the basic "who, what, when, where and how many" of the data. For example: How many widgets did the company sell in quarter three? Who bought them? Are sales up on quarter two? If not, why not?

> **OnLine Analytical Processing** (**OLAP**): Used in business analysis to investigate market trends and their underlying cause. For example, the last question listed above may lead a company to branch into OLAP. It is a very powerful tool for complex data analysis.

> **Data Mining**: Searching for patterns and correlations in data, with the intention of making business decisions. Here, software is designed to search for statistical patterns in your data in order to find trends that nobody knew existed before.

> **Executive Informational Processing**: Finding key summary information, for the purpose of making business decisions, without having to wade through reams of data. The "tell me precisely what I need to know" philosophy.

> One of the best and most comprehensive products to handle data warehousing, OLAP, reporting and data mining is Business Objects. For more information, go to www.BusinessObjects.com on the Internet.

OK, let's discuss these areas, and in particular OLAP, in more detail.

Reporting

Reporting is one of the most common uses of a data warehouse. These are simple ad hoc reports that are produced in response to a basic question. Working with the pubs database, for example, the question may arise: "How many books have Wrox Press sold in the past five years?" A query can then be executed against the archived data to produce a report breaking the information out by year, by quarter, or even by month. Much of this processing will occur on a scheduled basis: possibly monthly, or even weekly.

The bulk of basic reporting information comes from Online Transaction Processing (OLTP) - order and invoice processing etc. Due to the frequent access and updates that occur during OLTP, the data is stored in relational databases (which, as we know, have powerful functionality in place to prevent the occurrence of update anomalies). Once the historical data is transferred to a warehouse then, although it will still be regularly queried, it will not be subject to individual updating. Instead, this task is generally performed by a bulk "reloading" operation. Thus, the structure of this data is often modified, prior to storage in a data warehouse, in order to give it a more "report-friendly" structure. One option is to de-normalize the data (as we discussed in Chapter 6) so that relevant data spread over multiple tables is pulled together and stored on a single table. The data warehouse can then be queried and data retrieved using basic SQL commands. A reporting package - such as the Visual Basic 6.0 (Enterprise edition) Data Report Designer, which we will discuss in the next chapter, or Seagate's Crystal Reports - can then be used to package the data in a professional report.

If your company's business requirements extend beyond basic querying and reporting then you may adopt a complex multidimensional data structure, amenable to more complex analytical techniques, such as OLAP.

Online Analytical Processing (OLAP)

In Chapter 6 we briefly looked at SQL's ability to generate a "time-dimensional" view of specific data, whereby a basic analysis could be performed of, say, sales of a particular product over a period of months. With SQL, we can create very complex statements to retrieve just about any type of information. However, the problem here is that each view of the data requires execution of a new SQL statement. OLAP takes this whole process a step (well, a giant step, actually) forward and facilitates true multidimensional analysis. With OLAP we can look beyond the summary data for details of what may have caused the trend demonstrated by the summary! While there are tools available to assist us in finding trends and the reason for trends, and the reasons for the reasons etc. - a human component is still required. Someone has to make sense of the data and this can take hours of close observation.

The foundation of OLAP is the ability to "drill down" into the data, as far into its minute detail as is necessary to get the answers you need. We will discuss this process in more detail when we look at the different flavors of OLAP, and again when we walk through an OLAP implementation. But for now, consider the following scenario:

We need to review the results of a straw poll taken before a national election, in order to evaluate the possible outcome. Analysis of the results of this poll on a countrywide level could tell us, essentially, who was likely to win the election. We could then drill-down to state level and identify those states where the result was likely to be marginal. We could then go down to county level and find out whether it was a close call between the contesting parties all over the state, or if support for a certain party was strong in some areas and poor in others. If data was available from other years we could look for strong swings in voting habits and try to assess the reasons for this.

Having described a process ripe for OLAP-style analysis in the previous paragraph, you may still be thinking that we could have got at the information using SQL and a reporting tool. The major convenience of OLAP tools is their ability to dynamically represent the data without re-querying the database. Let's say, for example, that the data is summarized by year. If a particular year's summary looks peculiar, then the details for that specific year can be viewed with a click of a button, while the remaining years remain in summary view. With traditional reporting tools, we must initially specify if we would like to display the data by detail or by summary view. If we want to re-display the data then we must re-query the data source.

Three Flavors of OLAP

There are three types of OLAP. These classifications are based on the degree of normalization in the database tables. Any one of these formats may be applied to implement a successful solution. Many vendors, including Microsoft, boast that they support all three.

> **MOLAP (MultiDimensional OLAP)**: This format of data storage and analysis has become de-facto in the data warehousing industry. Here, the data tables are designed in multidimensional structures, rather than the traditional relational structure. One primary table, called the fact table, stores the bulk of the data then corresponding (dimensional) tables store information that relate to the fields in the fact table. The structure is highly de-normalized. In one possible schema (the star schema), the central fact table is surrounded by dimensional tables, which define the points of a star. There may, for example, be a Time field in the fact table and a Time dimension table that identifies fields for year, quarter, month, week or even day. We can then identify very quickly the time (in any format) of any record in the fact table.

> **ROLAP (Relational OLAP)**: This format of data storage and analysis calls for the traditional relational storage of data for analysis. The one downside of ROLAP is that relationships between the tables can become quite complex, requiring the DBMS to perform cross-table joining. The more tables involved, and the deeper they are embedded in the relationship structure, the slower the data will be returned.

> **HOLAP (Hybrid OLAP)**: HOLAP is an attempt to bring the benefits of MOLAP and ROLAP together. This is being implemented in a number of ways. In this scenario, fact tables may be derived from a ROLAP system, but aggregated data stored as in the MOLAP format. The efficiency of this model is in question, as the amount of processing between the two models can be cumbersome.

Taking a Closer Look at MOLAP

As I mentioned, MOLAP requires the data to be stored in a multidimensional format. It involves the creation of multidimensional blocks of data called data cubes. The cube may have three axes (dimensions), or it may have more. Each axis (dimension) represents a logical category of data. One axis may for example represent the geographic location of the data, while others may indicate a state of time or a specific product sold. Each of the categories can be broken down into successive levels as follows, and it is possible to drill up or down between the levels:

Geographical Dimension

If a company sells domestically in the US, this dimension may have the following levels:

United States, which can be broken down into:
Regions, which can be broken down into:
States, which can be broken down into:
Cities

Products Dimension

If the company is a book and record dealer, this dimension may contain:

Products, which can be broken down into:
Categories, which can be broken down into:
Titles

Time Dimension

If the company follows a fiscal year, we have the following levels:

Fiscal year, which can be broken down into:
Quarters, which can be broken down into:
Months, which can be broken down into:
Weeks

This concept is demonstrated in the following figure:

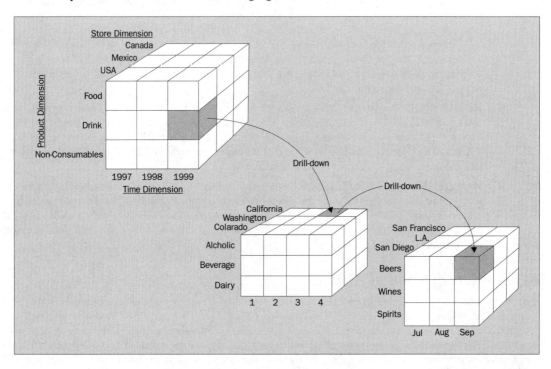

As we move from one data cube to the next we are drilling down a level in each dimension. Thus, in the first cube, we are concerned with the sale of drinks by a particular retailer, in the USA, in 1999. In the final cube we are investigating sales of beer at chain outlets in San Diego in the month of September. Of course, from here we could drill-down even further and investigate sale of specific brands of beer at one specific store. It is important to bear in mind that the fact table will contain measures - numeric values such as unit sales and dollar sales and marketing costs. Thus the **sales measure** arising from the middle cube would be the revenue generated from the sale of alcoholic drinks in the state of California in the third quarter of 1999. Of course, we may then wish to "drill sideways" and compare this measure to the analogous one obtained for Washington State. As you can see, this provides the basis for powerful and in-depth analysis. Bear in mind, though, that the available data may not always permit drilling down to the bottom level and also, that sideways drilling may not always be possible - e.g. a comparable sales measure might not actually exist for a different state.

As OLAP data processing becomes more common, third party vendor products are emerging into the marketplace to handle the process of transforming data into a cube. Microsoft's OLAP Server, for example, can convert data into a cube, and then allows viewing of the data in a two-dimensional pivot table. When displaying the data in an OLAP format, it allows the modification of the types of measures used and specification of the levels of data to be included in the cube.

Once our data is stored in the multidimensional format, we need to access it. This is where OLE DB comes into play. We can download the Microsoft Data Access 2.0 SDK to obtain a copy of the OLE DB provider for OLAP. This is a set of COM-based interface objects that utilize OLE DB to provide access to multidimensional data sources, such as the one described previously. In a nutshell, by using OLE DB for OLAP, you can access multidimensional data using Visual Basic 6.0, or another tool supported by ADO.

> **To download the Microsoft Data Access 2.0 SDK,** locate
> **www.microsoft.com/data/mdac2.htm on the Internet.**

Data Mining

Data mining is a technique that can utilize the power of multidimensional databases to help the user extract meaningful information from vast amounts of data. Again, you may be thinking that we can do the same thing with SQL. Well, yes, we can - but only if we know what information we are looking for and, therefore, know how to ask for it. What's unique about data mining is that we don't need to ask any questions. The tools assume that we don't know exactly what information we're looking for. The tool will evaluate our data for statistical patterns and return any patterns it locates. Almost everyone in the data industry has heard of the correlation between diapers and beer. When a male purchaser buys diapers, there is a high probability that he will also buy beer. This correlation wasn't found on a hunch; it was found by data mining. Data mining tools typically search for two types of patterns:

> ➤ **Associations**: Association searching looks for the existence of one element while another element exists. For example, data mining may provide us with the following association: "If a customer purchases a new computer from XYZ Computer Store, there's a 40% chance that they will return to that store to purchase software within two weeks." The question for the store is then how to up this percentage. They may decide to send any customer who purchases a computer a sales flyer (or a discount card), in order to increase the possibility that the customer will return.

> ➤ **Classifications:** Classifications identify how two or more elements relate. When discussing associations, we identified that if a customer purchased a computer, a specific behavioral pattern would follow (the customer also purchased software). If sales of computers increased, then it would follow that sales of software would also increase. The question then becomes: How does the store sell more computers? Data mining classifications facilitate the identification of two or more related data elements. Consider this: if it was possible to decipher the relationship between, say, customer demographics and computer sales, then that information might be used in the development of a new marketing campaign - aimed directly at the people most likely to buy computers. For example, data mining might indicate that a high percentage of computer sales are to people who have two children, and also have a family income of $50,000 or greater.

It's common practice to classify data by geographic region. Here, the aim is to identify specific market segments that tend to purchase a particular product most frequently or in the greatest quantity. If you have ever supplied your Zip Code while making a purchase, you may have voluntarily contributed to the company's geographic database.

Executive Information Systems (EIS)

Executive Information Systems are designed to give key information (indicators) to decision makers, without the decision maker having to work too hard to come to his or her decision. EIS is for executives who don't have time to use the above tools or evaluate the results of the tool's output. EIS gives the user only key information (or indicators) or provides access to specific reports and documents in, say, an easy-to-use touch-screen environment. To summarize, the key benefits of these tools for decision-making are:

> The indicators are returned in the form of a summary, rather than a full-scale report. This removes the need for the user to spend time reading lengthy reports, and even more time evaluating the results. The summary may be returned in the form of a chart, report, document, or a single value.

> The tools are typically pre-programmed for the user. This allows the user to work with a simple 'point and click' environment.

When shopping around for an EIS tool, it is worth evaluating reporting and OLAP tools. Many o these also contain a component of an Executive Information System.

Data Warehouse Models

OK, we have many questions to answer here and we're only going to scratch the surface of some of them. How can we pull data from a range of sources then translate it into a format compatible with the data structure implemented in our warehouse? How do we ensure that it is free from errors? How do we get the data into the warehouse? How and when do we update it?

The data warehouse architecture accommodates many different models with various levels of scalability. To make the model easier to understand, the data flow can be broken out into two basic functions: 1. Populating the data warehouse with useful information. 2. Retrieving information from the data warehouse via queries, or one of the data aggregation and summarization tools discussed previously. The following diagram depicts a generic data warehouse model:

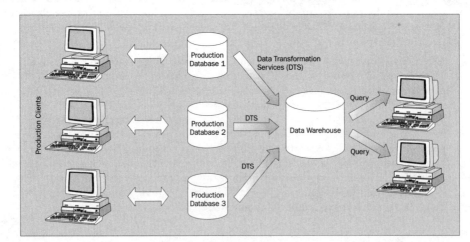

Populating the Data Warehouse

Typically, a data warehouse is populated with historical information from within a particular organization. This need not be followed strictly and, in many circumstances, a company's warehouse tables may be populated from a wide variety of data sources, often including data providing information concerning a competitor business. Collecting all of this different data and storing it in one place is an extremely challenging process, a full description of which is beyond the scope of this book. Data Transformation Services (DTS) assist in the import and export of data between heterogeneous data sources, using OLE DB-based architecture. Thus, transformation is used to populate a warehouse and to update the data in the warehouse.

However, remember that there is no lower restriction on the size of the data warehouse. When the technology hit the headlines, a misconception grew that they had to be BIG. Some companies operate relatively small warehouses that generally take their data from one source and which, therefore, avoid much of the complexity involved in data transformation.

In the previous illustration, the warehouse was populated with data from three production databases. These databases may be broken out by geographical locations, by product, or by some other criteria. When new records are added or existing records are modified, the results are posted to the production database. This data is then forwarded to the data warehouse. During the stage where data is moved from the production database to the data warehouse, the data is typically cleaned and validated. Records that are no longer required can be filtered out at this stage.

Retrieving Data from the Data Warehouse

The process of retrieving data from the warehouse can vary greatly depending on the desired results. We have already covered many of the possible uses for a data warehouse. It's this flexibility that will drive how this architecture works. If your plan is simple query and reporting, you may find yourself building SQL statements and using Crystal Reports, VB Report Generator, or some other third party tool. As your need expands to OLAP, Data Mining and EIS, the structure will include many more third party tools, pushing your data warehouse server to the max.

There are many inherent problems associated with data warehousing. These include the limited amount of portability, and the often-vast amount of data that must be sifted through for each query. We'll next take a look at data marts and see how they play a role in alleviating these problems.

Data Marts

Data marts are used to transform the data warehouse records into logical groups of databases. The benefit of this is that the data warehouse doesn't become overloaded with query tasks. Only relevant data exists in the data mart, so when queries are run against a data mart it takes less time to execute than when run against the warehouse. The server is required to search through a fraction of the data. Another advantage of the data mart is its portability. Data marts can be loaded onto laptop computers and used by people who require access to the information while they travel.

The following example demonstrates the use of two data marts. It may be that the first data mart is used for specific querying and reporting while the second data mart is used for OLAP, data mining, EIS or even another instance of reporting. When designing your data warehouse model, you may have unlimited data marts, and each data mart may have repeated data, if necessary.

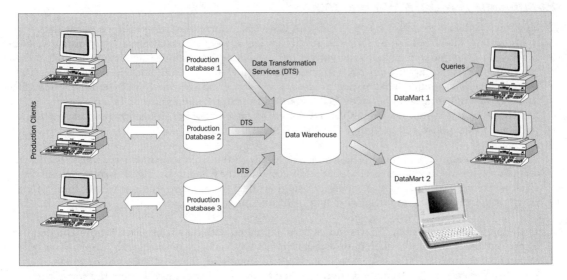

This example also demonstrates use of a laptop computer with a data mart. Because computers are constantly becoming more flexible (with more hard drive and CPU processing speed) it's not uncommon to replicate a data mart on a laptop. This becomes especially useful when traveling salespeople need 'availability' or 'product' information at the customer's site. The laptop computer may be transformed monthly, weekly, or even daily if necessary.

When transforming data from a production database to a data mart, you should always design your system to replicate through the data warehouse. When replicating directly from production databases to the data marts, the production database may slow down. This is especially true when production database records are transformed over several data marts.

Defining the Data Structure

In all of the previous chapters of this book, we have relied on having a well-normalized database. As I mentioned earlier, storing data in warehouses often involves breaking those rules you worked so hard to understand. Take warning, this topic may become the focus of controversy in your organization.

The decision to normalize the data warehouse, or de-normalize it can be one of the most difficult decisions to make. Certainly, most database administrators will argue the benefits of normalization. However, there are also many advantages of a de-normalized database when it comes to warehousing data. Here are a few key points to consider:

> *Speed of data retrieval*: When retrieving data, the need to perform complex table-joining operations, to pull data from multiple tables, can slow down the response time considerably. When the query is very complex, numerous look-ups may be required. Denormalising and aggregating data can, potentially, speed up such queries considerably. The key to successful denormalisation is to pinpoint the fields that are of interest, and discard any unnecessary fields. We can then index the really important fields, which will probably be used for grouping and in the WHERE clause. The gain in speed is attributed to the numerous indexes that can be used, and to the elimination of time-consuming joins.

> ➤ *Updating of data*: Most data warehouses are not built with the intention of giving users the ability to update data. We can therefore discount one of the primary reasons that we normalize databases: to avoid update anomalies. However, there is one other consideration to bear in mind if we de-normalize our data, we lose the ability to cascade updates and deletes. If, for example, a customer changes their business name then, in a de-normalized system, all records that are associated with the business must also be changed. These cascade changes could be performed automatically in a normalized database.

> ➤ *Hard drive space*: When it comes to hard drive space, the decision to normalize or de-normalize depends on the number of fields in each table, and the amount of data to be populated. Storing data in one table rather than two will typically require more hard drive space. This is because we will inevitably store duplicated data. We discussed the importance of avoiding this, when normalizing our relational databases, back in Chapter 2. Hard drive space may not be a primary concern if sufficient hardware resources are available to accommodate de-normalization of th database. This is especially true as prices of hardware continue to fall.

To clarify the de-normalization process, let's look at a basic example. In the `pubs` database three tables "revolve" around the `employee` table. Each employee has a `job_id`, which identifies a job description and a minimum and maximum employment level for that job, in the `jobs` table. In addition the `employee` table is linked to two other tables via the `pub_id` field. Each employee works for a publishing organization or company. The publisher, in turn, has attributes available such as name, country and even a logo:

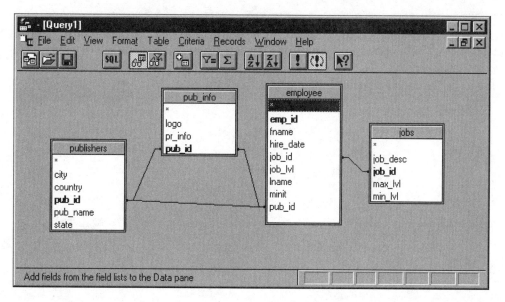

Keeping the three previously listed considerations in mind, let's assume we want to warehouse all employee records:

The first step is to consider all fields on which we may want to report or generate summaries. For now, let's assume the following list meets our needs. There are three tables, which contain 10 fields we will eventually want to report on:

Table	Field	Data Type
employee	emp_id	char(9)
	fname	varchar(20)
	lname	varchar(30)
	minit	char(1)
	hire_date	datetime
jobs	job_desc	varchar(50)
publishers	pub_name	varchar(40) varchar(20)
	city	char(2)
	state	varchar(30)
	country	
pub_info	pr_info	text(16)

Now, let's de-normalize the tables. This is a lot easier than applying the three normalization rules! Simply take all of the tables, and grind them into one table that contains all of the required fields:

Table	Field	Data Type
Employee_info	emp_id	char(9)
	fname	varchar(20)
	lname	varchar(30)
	minit	char(1)
	hire_date	datetime
	job_desc	varchar(50)
	pub_name	varchar(40) varchar(20)
	city	char(2)
	state	varchar(30)
	country	text(16)
	pr_info	

If we had wanted to use the 'logo' field from the pub_info table then we might have chosen to break this structure out into two tables. The reason for this is that the logo is a BLOB (Binary Large Object). Each image takes up large amounts of hard drive space, and to duplicate the logo for every employee would be a massive abuse of our available storage space. Also bear this in mind for fields that contains large volumes of data, such as memos or large text fields.

In our example we do compromise some storage space (e.g. many employees will work for the same publisher so publisher details will be duplicated), but it's nothing too drastic. From here, all that needs to be done is to create the table. If you want some practice, build a SQL statement for the above table definition, and execute it against the `pubs` database.

All that remains is the periodic population of records from the production database. This layer of functionality is called the Data Transformation Services (DTS). DTS allows us to pull data from our production databases periodically (or real-time), and place it in the data warehouse. This process may include de-normalizing the data, or even translation of the data. While products are available to handle this, you can certainly be creative in building your own DTS. You may find it more economical to create the DTS using triggers, stored procedures, Visual Basic, and good old reliable SQL: it may even turn out to be more flexible than software out of the box! Having said this, if you're using Microsoft SQL Server 7.0, it's well worth checking out DTS Services, which ships with SQL Server. These Services are new to SQL Server, and are actually quite powerful.

Let's assume that we want to move our data on a timed basis. Given this, we can build a Visual Basic project that selects records from one database, say `pubs`, and pushes the records to a second database of our choosing. We need to:

1. Connect to both databases

2. Extract new or modified data from the first database, and put it in a `Recordset`

3. Push the data to the data warehouse

> When building production databases, it's wise to include a data and time stamp to identify when a record has been added. This allows you to query for all new records when it comes time to move the records to a data warehouse. Additionally, if you need to move modified data, you should use a Boolean field to identify a change to the record.

Data Extraction

Before running off and building your own DTS, you need to consider a few options. The first consideration is whether your data will be copied real-time or batch. Your business needs will drive this decision. If the data warehouse is to be used for reporting, you may elect to copy your data just before running the report. This may be at any interval of your liking (taking into account the time required to copy the data, of course). If the need for the data is more immediate, you may prefer to copy the data real-time. When copying data real-time, consider the amount of processing that is taking place. If the process will cause a slow-down in your system, you may need to allocate a specific timeframe for the process (typically slow or down times).

The following illustration demonstrates data being transformed real-time. When a new record is entered into the production database, the data is immediately transformed to the data warehouse. DTS then evaluates if any of the data marts are to receive the data. If a data mart does require a copy of the data, it's copied once more. Again, the process may be performed using triggers, or by a DTS software package.

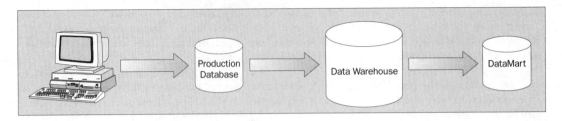

The next illustration demonstrates data being copied in a batch process. These processes are typically performed at specific time intervals, probably after everyone has gone home for the day. In general, batch processes require less network traffic, take less time to execute and don't slow down the use of the production databases during normal business hours. As data is entered into the production database, the new records are stored normally. When it's time to copy the new records to the data warehouse, all of the records are collected by your preferred DTS mechanism and passed to the data warehouse. If you opt to use MS SQL Server's DTS, then OLE DB and ADO are used to create the batches of data. The data warehouse then determines which data marts will receive which records and copies only those records to the data mart.

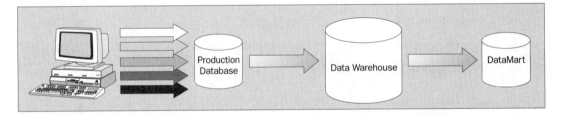

There are a number of methods for copying data. If the data warehouse and production databases are networked, the task may be relatively simple. If, on the other hand, they have no means of communication, it may be necessary to manually back the data up to a tape device, and then load it onto the data warehouse. Whatever the means, the key is to get the data to one central location. User interaction is not always avoidable.

Implementing an OLAP Solution

For the remainder of this chapter, we'll explore a solution for implementing OLAP analysis. The project includes:

> Installing Microsoft OLAP Server

> Creating a multidimensional Cube

> Securing the multidimensional Cube

> Storing our data in the MOLAP format

> Building a Visual Basic application to browse the Cube

There's a lot to learn about OLAP, and this chapter won't cover it all. However, this exercise should help clarify some of the concepts we've dealt with in the earlier sections.

The Mission

In this example, we'll be working with a database that is already full of data and is installed with Microsoft OLAP Server. This database (FoodMart.mdb) contains information regarding the sales, inventory, and warehousing of a national food chain. Our goal is to provide the management with a tool that allows them to analyze sales in each of their stores in considerable detail. It should allow them to drill-down into geographical, time and product dimensions in order that they may look for sales patterns and thereby improve their advertising and marketing strategies.

We are faced with two choices:

1. We could create an ad-hoc reporting tool that gives the managers the ability to create reports on the fly, as they want to break out the data. In this situation, each request would require the manager (who may have little programming knowledge) to enter a new query.

2. We could create an OLAP analysis tool that allows the users to view the data, aggregated or broken down, with the click of a mouse. It would be easy to use and the results would be available nearly instantly.

After giving it some thought, we'd all probably go for option two (OK, I know I stacked the deck in this one!). The bottom line, however, is to choose the solution that best suits the requirements of your business.

Installing Microsoft OLAP Server

Microsoft SQL Server 7.0 OLAP Server is not installed by default when installing SQL Server 7.0. It is a component that snaps into the Microsoft Management Console.

If you do not have this component, you will need to run through the installation process. When you insert the CD, select Install SQL Server 7.0 Components, then, from the next dialog SQL Server 7.0 OLAP Services. I won't walk you through the install process because there are no tricks to it. Select the defaults as you run through the dialogs. When you're prompted to decide which type of install you would like, select Complete. This will ensure that all sample files are copied to your local machine.

The FoodMart Database

The database we'll be working with in this chapter should have been installed automatically when you installed the OLAP Server. The database is called FoodMart.mdb. If you accepted the default location during installation, this database will be located at C:\Program Files\OLAP Services\Samples.

The installation should have also created a Data Source Name to the database. Verify this by opening the ODBC Data Source Administrator from the Control Panel (just as we have done in previous chapters).

The DSN should appear as an Access database (FoodMart.mdb), with a System level DSN of FoodMart. If it is not yet created, do this now:

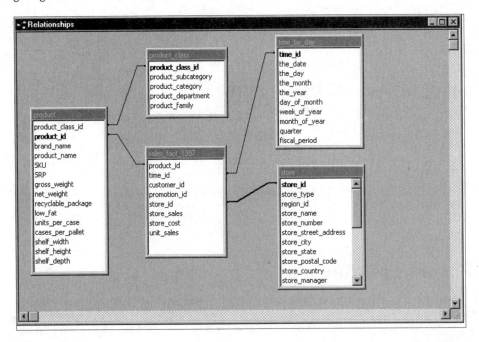

Now that we have our DSN properly configured, let's take a look at the tables we're interested in. The following diagram outlines the structure of our database:

The Fact Table

The bulk of the data is stored in a single table, known as the fact table. The fact table contains key pieces of data that can then be used in conjunction with the dimensional tables to drill down to any level of detail. In this case, the sales_fact_1997 table contains key fields (product_id, store_id, and time_id) that relate to the dimensional tables in the database. For example, the store_id field provides the link to records in the store table. The fact table also contains our measure data: store_sales, store_cost, and unit_sales.

Measures are the numeric (or currency) fields that are used for analysis. For example, `store_sales` *identifies, in currency, how much revenue exists for any given store. Measures can include any type of numeric data, such as sales, census figures and time expenditures.*

The Dimensional Tables

The composite primary key fields in the fact table point to foreign key fields in each of the dimension tables. Data in these tables is hierarchical (year-month-week-day etc.) and is thus highly de-normalized. This arrangement allows quick access to data at any level in the hierarchy. As an example, we may have a `Location` primary key in the fact table, then a `Location` table (our dimensional table) that has a corresponding foreign key value. By locating that value in the dimension table, we can identify and return data relating to region, state or city, for the record in the fact table.

The dimension tables in the `Foodmart` database are:

> `time_by_day`: Each key will represent specific elements of the date and time of the indicated record. In this example, there are three fields that will collectively be used to build our dimension. Our dimension will specify year, quarter and then month.

> `store`: This table will be used to identify the location of each store. In this scenario, we need to evaluate the data by country, region, and then state.

> `product` and `product_class`: It's not uncommon that the data we need for any given dimension is located in more that one table. When a dimension is located in this structure, it's known as a **snowflake** schema. Here, the `product` and `product_class` tables are used to create a dimension that provides product categories, sub-categories, brand names and product names.

Creating the Fact and Dimension Tables

In this example, our data has already been provided for us in a convenient multidimensional format. This is not likely to happen in your own organization. However, if you get any volunteers for the task, take them up on it. It's truly not that difficult, but you need to be very organized in order to bring the all the pieces together and carefully consider the following points:

> In what format is the data delivered? The data will probably be extracted from a production database. It's common that the data, especially for the fact table, will come from multiple tables. You will probably need to use Data Transformation Services to handle the task of extracting this data.

> Before you can map the data from a production system to the multidimensional format, you need to understand your goal. Identify the fields that will be used for your measures and your dimension tables. Keep in mind that some of your data in the dimension tables will be acquired through a detailed algorithm. The region for example is acquired by evaluating the state where the store is located.

> ➤ What is the precise format of your multidimensional data? Just when you finally become used to the concepts of a relational database, you must often break those rules. The best way to understand how to build a multidimensional structure is to study an existing structure. The time_by_day table for example provides an outstanding example of the creation of a dimensional table based on time.

Don't sweat it too much. Just as with relational databases, the creation of multidimensional databases takes time and experience to perfect. After building a database, push test data into it, and build a test cube. This will help identify any potential problems with the structure.

Building the MultiDimensional (MD) Cube

We're now ready to build our multidimensional cube. To do this, we'll use the OLAP Manager that comes packaged as part of the OLAP Server.

To open the OLAP Manager, select Start | Programs | Microsoft SQL Server 7.0 | OLAP Services | OLAP Manager:

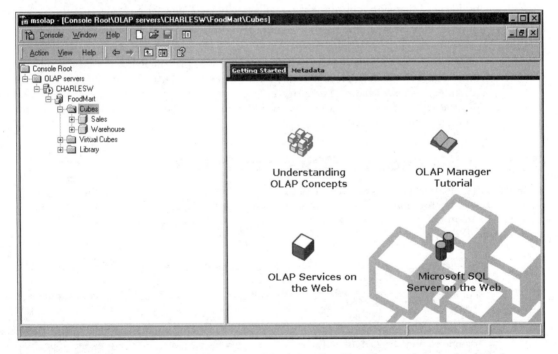

The console that appears has two major panes. The left pane allows us to navigate through the server to different databases and cubes that are installed. The right pane allows us to view Metadata (details of the object selected in the left pane) or the Getting Started page (as displayed), which provides links to tutorials and some basic OLAP concepts.

If we expand the server icon (CHARLESW in my case), we will see all of the databases installed. If we select the FoodMart icon, then expand the Cubes folder we will see that two data cubes already exist: Sales and Warehouse.

Two other folders are available:

> Virtual Cubes are hooks into existing cubes that allow us to provide access to aggregate data or limited data. We might for example show all US sales instead of worldwide sales.

> The Library folder contains information regarding security as well as shared and virtual dimensions. When you connect to a database, all connection information is stored in this folder for other cubes to use. This folder is also where any Roles and security information is stored to enable users to log into the server.

OK, let's build a new data cube. We'll use the built in Cube Wizard.

> Right click on the Cubes folder, and select New Cube I Wizard...:

> Click on the Next button:

➤ The first piece of information the wizard needs to know is the fact table that we'll be using. In this case, our fact table will be `sales_fact_1997`. When we click on this table, the columns in the table will be displayed in the right hand side of the dialog. If you want to browse the data in the table, click on the **Browse Data** button. When you're ready to proceed, click on the **Next** button:

➤ This dialog allows us to specify the fields in the fact table that will be used as measures. Remember that measures must be numeric. We have identified `store_sales`, `store_cost`, and `unit_sales` as our measure fields. Add them to the list by double-clicking on them (or clicking on the > button for each dimension). Click on the **Next** button:

We're now ready to add dimensions to our cube. If a dimension already exists in the database, and it is capable of being shared between cubes, it will appear in the left-hand pane. These are stored in the Library folder of the server pane. The above image shows a number of dimensions that already exist in the `Sales` and `Warehouse` cubes. Note that each dimension must have a unique name for that specific database.

➤ We'll create our own dimensions, so click on the New Dimension button:

The dimension wizard opens. Here, we can indicate whether the dimensions will be pulled from a single table, or multiple tables. As you may recall, schemas such as Snowflake allow a dimension to be pulled from multiple tables.

➤ Ensure that A single dimension table is selected, and then click on the Next button:

> Just as we chose the fact table, so we must select the dimension tables. Our first dimension table is the `time_by_day` table (our dimension of time). Select this table, then click on the **Next** button:

> Since the dimension relates to time, we must choose a single column that identifies each of the component parts. Select `the_date` field, and click on the **Next** button:

> The above dialog allows us to specify the levels of time we want to use in our dimension. Select **Year, Quarter, Month** from the **Select time levels** Combo box. The dimension structure appears below our selection. Also notice that we can specify a specific date for the start of the fiscal year. It is through this that the server knows how to break out the quarters. When you're done, click on the **Next** button:

> Name the dimension `DATE_DIMENSION`. Here, we may also preview the structure of the dimension. We can also elect to share the dimension with other cubes (this is a great idea if you plan to build numerous cubes). Click on the **Finish** button. `DATE_DIMENSION` should appear in the dialog at this point. We need to build two more dimensions, so click on the **New Dimension** button again. First we will build our product dimension. For this, we need to pull fields from two tables (`product` and `product_class`), so at the following dialog, select **Multiple dimension tables** and click on **Next**:

➢ Select the `product` table and then the `product_class` table so that they both appear in the right hand pane (as shown above). Click on the **Next** button:

➢ This dialog allows us to specify the field through which our tables are related. The wizard will attempt to locate this automatically but, however; if the fields do not have the same name, we would have to identify them ourselves. In this example, the field is `product_class_id` for each table. Click on the **Next** button:

➢ All the fields available from each table appear in the preceding dialog. Here, again, we may specify the component fields for our dimension. Choose the following fields: `product_category`, `product_subcategory`, `brand_name`, and `product_name`.

We must select our fields in a logical hierarchical order. For example: country, state and then city. To validate this requirement we count the number of records for each level. There should, for example, be an equal or greater amount of cities than states. If this is unbalanced, the concept of drilling down is destroyed. To enforce this rule, ensure that the Count level members automatically check box is checked. For large cubes, the processing time is quite long. If you are confident that you can choose your levels correctly, you may un-check the box for faster processing.

> Click on the Next button:

> Name this new dimension PRODUCT_DIMENSION, and click on the Finish button. We've now finished building the second dimension.

> Let's add our third dimension. Click on the New Dimension button.

> This dimension will be a single table dimension, so select A single dimension table and click on the Next button.

> This dimension will be built from the store table, so select it, and click on the Next button.

> ➤   When the dimension type dialog opens, select Standard dimension and click on the Next button.

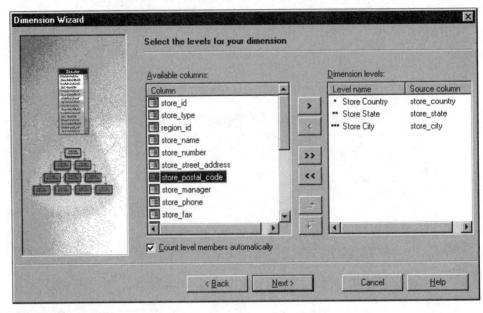

> ➤   The dimension levels will be: store_country, store_state, and store_city. Select them in that order and click on the Next button:

➤ Name this dimension STORE_DIMENSION and click on the Finish button.

All three dimensions should appear in the right hand pane of the Select the dimensions dialog. Remember, a cube isn't limited to three axes. We could add more now if we chose to.

➤ Click on the Next button.

This dialog allows us to name our cube. We can use numbers and letters, but we *cannot* use spaces or underscores. While the documentation may say this is allowed, I ran into some problems connecting to it from a client application when the name included an underscore. This dialog also allows us to preview our measures and dimensions. Expand each of the dimensions to preview their structure.

Name the cube `SalesCube`, and then click on the Finish button:

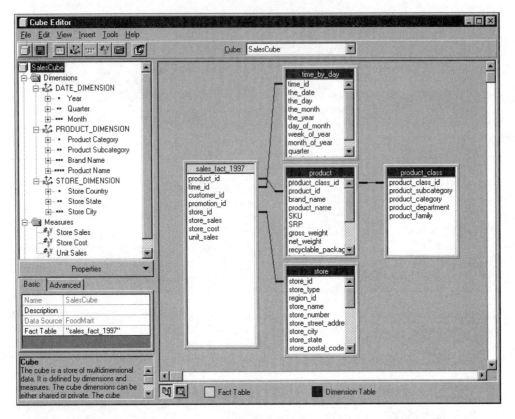

After some grinding of the hard drive, the Cube Editor will open. We'll need this window to declare the structure of our data, and then process the data into a cube that is usable.

Designing the Cube Storage Type

The next step in the project is to design the storage type of our data, then compile the database into a usable data store.

> From the Cube Editor, select Tools | Design Storage.
> At the introduction screen, click on the Next button.

> At the Data Storage Type dialog, select MOLAP and click on the Next button:

When the Storage Design Wizard opens, we are prompted to choose an aggregation option. This allows us to pre-compact of our data by summarizing the multiple records. This is not critical for smaller databases but for larger databases it may be essential. The three options are:

1. Choose a storage limit, such as 64 MB. This says that the database should be compacted enough to restrict the size to 64 MB or less.

2. Apply a performance scheme. This allows us to indicate how much of a performance increase we would like to see.

3. Allow the database to create aggregates until you click on stop. I wouldn't recommend this, as there is no science to clicking on a button randomly.

> Click on the Start button. The graph display shows the relationship between size and query performance.

> After it finishes processing, click on the Next button.

> The final dialog allows us to process (compile) the data. Before we can view the data, we *must* process it. Choose this option then click on the Finish button:

> Processing the data may take several minutes so unless you truly enjoy watching the status bar slowly fill; go get yourself a cup of coffee.

> When the data has been processed, close the cube editor by selecting File | Exit.

Setting Up Security for the New Cube

Before the cube can be viewed from an external client, security roles *must* be in place. This is tightly integrated with your NT server (NT workstation for local domains), so it's a simple task.

The first step is to create a role. A role is a user (or a group of users) who has specific rights to objects of a particular database. In this case, we will allow access to our SalesCube object.

> Look in the Library folder under the FoodMart database; you will see a Roles folder. A new role is already configured, so we don't need to add one but let's walk through the steps anyhow.

> ➢ Right click on the Roles folder and select New Role:

> ➢ Here, we can create a new role and add as many users as we wish to have access to the objects in our database. The All Users option may already be configured, in which case just click on cancel. Otherwise, add the new role and click on OK.

> *If you want to locate a user or group on a network, click on the Groups and Users button. Because this is tightly integrated with Windows NT Security, you can view a list of all available Groups and Users in a domain, and then select each as desired.*

The last step is to apply the new role to our SalesCube. If we don't apply a role to the Cube, we will not be able to extract the cube's data.

> ➢ Locate the Roles folder under SalesCube and right click on it. Select Manage Roles:

> ➢ Add the All Users group to the Cube access window by double-clicking on it, then click on OK

Browsing the Cube

Now that we have our cube built, lets see what it looks like. The OLAP Manager has a built in utility for viewing the data in our cubes. This is the best place to ensure that the structure of our data is valid, and that we can access the data we need.

➤ To view the data, right click on `SalesCube` in the OLAP Manager, and select **Browse Data**. The following dialog will appear:

This dialog allows us to drill down to the data we want. Drilling down can be carried out in two ways:

➤ We can drill down to the **DATE_DIMENSION** from the grid that is displayed. Notice that the left-hand side of the grid lists all years (Year being the top level of the dimension), and a total for all of the years (**All DATE_DIMENSION**). To drill down into any year, simply double-click on the year. The year will expand, representing quarters. We can then drill down beyond quarters if necessary.

➤ The second method is to select the required level from the combo-boxes in the top pane. Select the dimension you wish to explore, choose the level, and the results are displayed instantly:

The manager can now see, for example, how much bread was sold in the United States in 1997. Then he can find out in which quarter they sell the most bread, which stores sell the widest range etc.

Using OLE DB for OLAP to Build a Client Application

Now that we know that the structure of our data is correct, and the data we want is readily available, we may want to build a custom client application for viewing these Cubes. Why not just use the OLAP Manager? Well, this may need to be distributed to multiple managers. By creating a client application, all Managers can share the data.

In this section, we'll walk through building such an application using Visual Basic. The complexity involved in building these applications can vary wildly. First, we'll do it the quick and dirty way, then later in the chapter we'll discuss how to provide further flexibility and functionality through more sophisticated code.

Open Visual Basic and open a new **Standard EXE** project. Call the project `prjCube`, and the form `frmCube` and save it in the appropriate directory.

In this example, we'll use a Cube Browser control that looks identical to the grid used in the previous Cube Browser. To add the ActiveX Control to your toolbox, right-click in the toolbox, select **Components** and locate **OLAP Manager Cube Browser**. The control should appear in the toolbox.

Add the Cube Browser, a Combo box, and two command buttons to your form. Use the following table to modify the properties of the objects in your project:

Object	Property	Value
Form	Name	frmCube
	Caption	Cube Viewer
Cube Browser	Name	cbSalesOLAP
ComboBox	Name	cboCube
	Text	{BLANK}
Command Button	Name	cmdExecute
	Caption	View Cube
Command Button	Name	cmdExit
	Caption	Exit

Arrange the controls so that your form looks something like this:

We're now ready to code. There's not a lot to do here. We just need to open a connection to the Server, apply the connection to Cube Browser, and then open the desired cube.

> Add a Reference to the Microsoft ActiveX Data Objects 2.x Library by selecting it from the Project | References from the menu.

> In the General Declarations section of your form, declare a new ADODB connection.

```
Option Explicit
Dim cnOLAP_Sales As New ADODB.Connection
```

When the form loads, we want to establish a connection to the OLAP Server, and display the names of our cubes in the Combo box. The following code handles this process:

```
Private Sub Form_Load()
' Establish Connection
"cnOLAP_Sales.ConnectionString = "Provider=MSOLAP.1;Persist Security" & _
"Info=False;Data Source=CHARLESW;Location=FoodMart;Connect Timeout=60;" & _
"Client Cache Size=25;Auto Synch Period=10000"
cnOLAP_Sales.Open

' Fill the Combo Box
cboCube.AddItem "Sales"
cboCube.AddItem "SalesCube"
cboCube.AddItem "Warehouse"
cboCube.ListIndex = 0
End Sub
```

The connection string may look a little different to the ones you've seen previously. I built this connection string using the ADO Wizard. To do this, I added an ADO Data Control to the form, built my connection string using the property pages, and then copied it to my code. Note that the provider used is "Microsoft OLE DB Provider for OLAP Services" (MSOLAP.1). When you move to the Connection Tab, the DataSource should consist of your server name (CHARLESW in my case), and a location (FoodMart).

Some of the properties in the above connection string are optional. However; I would avoid leaving any of them out. They all play a critical role in establishing and maintaining a connection to the server.

When a user selects a cube from the Combo box, and clicks on the Execute command button, the Cube Browser's (cbSalesOLAP) Connect method should be called. This connect method should indicate the active connection and the name of the cube to be opened (located in the cboCube text box). We wrap this statement within code that changes the mouse pointer. The initial connection may take a few seconds, so the user should be aware that the process is running.

```
Private Sub cmdExecute_Click()

    'Show a new Mouse Pointer while the user waits
    Me.MousePointer = vbHourglass

    ' Open the Cube Browser with specified Cube
    cbSalesOLAP.Connect cnOLAP_Sales, cboCube.Text

    Me.MousePointer = vbDefault
End Sub
```

When the user wants to exit, the Cube Browser should be disconnected, and then the Connection object should be closed and set to Nothing. It's never a bad idea to set an object to do this before terminating the application.

```
Private Sub cmdExit_Click()
    ' Disconnect the Cube Browser and Exit
    cbSalesOLAP.Disconnect

    ' Close the Connection
    cnOLAP_Sales.Close
    Set cnOLAP_Sales = Nothing

    Unload Me
End Sub
```

That's all the code there we need to build our own Cube Browser. Run the project, select a Cube, and then click on the View Cube button. Again, you may have to wait a few seconds the first time you open a Cube.

If you encounter an error to the effect that "Cannot connect to the Cube", ensure your Security Roles are properly configured, and that your connection string is correct.

The results should be identical to those seen previously.

MultiDimensional Expressions (MDX)

Multidimensional expressions are SQL-like statements used to return cube data sets. OLAP Manager's Cube Browser passes these expressions to the MSOLAP data provider. Here are some benefits of the MDX language:

> MDX are essentially an extension of ANSI-92 SQL, so you should have a good idea how to implement them.

> A larger number of aggregate functions are made available, providing great flexibility with regards to summary data.

> Like SQL, MDX can be embedded in you code.

> MDX can be dynamically generated.

Here's an MDX statement to return a data set from our SalesCube:

```
SELECT [STORE_DIMENSION].MEMBERS ON ROWS,
NEST ([PRODUCT_DIMENSION].[Product Category].MEMBERS,
[DATE_DIMENSION].[Month].MEMBERS) ON COLUMNS
FROM SalesCube
```

The general syntax should look rather familiar. Many statements and clauses are common to MDX and SQL (such as SELECT and FROM), but MDX adds many additional clauses (such as NEST). Following are a few of the commonly used keywords that are specific to the MDX syntax:

<Dimension Name>.MEMBERS ON ROWS

Indicates that all levels of the dimension should be returned to the grid.

MEMBERS: Returns the levels identified in the list.

```
NEST (<Dimension 1>.MEMBERS,<Dimension 2>.MEMEBERS) ON COLUMNS
```

Stacks the dimensions or dimension levels for display, in this case in the columns of the grid.

If you want to explore other statements and functions, have a look in the OLAP Server Documentation help file.

The MDX Sample Application

When the sample files of OLAP Server are installed, a sample OLAP browser application is installed along with it. This application allows us to view cubes and apply MDX statements against them. This is a great tool for building MDX statements because it allows us to drag the dimensions, measures and functions to the statement window. This provides accuracy and ease of use.

The MDX Sample Application comes as an Executable, and as a Visual Basic project. This is a great place to learn more about what can be done with the OLAP controls and references. The Visual Basic project can be found in the Samples folder of your installed location (most likely C:\Program Files\OLAP Services\Samples).

> Locate the MDX Sample Application in the OLAP Services folder, start it up, connect to your Server and specify the Provider. The following dialog should appear:

> ➤ Type in the MDX statement to retrieve a data set from the SalesCube. Apply the MDX statement by clicking on the green process arrow, your application should look like the below illustration. You may need to scroll down, as there is no data for Canadian or Mexican offices.

Summary

This chapter has just scratched the surface of data warehousing. Entire books are available on this subject, as well as magazines. We covered:

> ➤ Data Warehouses. What they are and what they can do for you. We discussed some of the possible structures that can be used and had a brief look at the processes involved in populating the warehouse with data (retrieving data from various sources, transforming it into a compatible format etc.). We also briefly discussed Data marts, and how they could reduce query times.

> ➤ Data analysis techniques. We looked at some of the powerful analytical techniques that could be implemented with warehoused data, namely, OLAP, data mining and EIS. We concentrated our discussion on mutli-dimensional OLAP and had a look at data cubes, fact tables, dimension tables, measures and how the multidimensional structure allowed "drilling-down" into the data to perform detailed analysis.

We then implemented a practical OLAP solution to analyze data in the Foodmart database. We constructed a 3-dimensional data cube then built a client application to access and display the data. We briefly covered the use of multidimensional expressions, syntactical extensions SQL used to retrieve data sets from data cubes.

If this is to be you are thinking about implementing your first data warehouse, I'm sure you still have plenty of questions, such as: "Do we need a third-party tool?" and "Do we need a consultant?" If your needs revolve around basic reporting, you can get by with SQL and the reporting tools available with Visual Basic and your database vendor. If you're heading into the OLAP, data mining, or EIS world, you probably *will* need a tool to assist you. This is not to say that you must have a third party tool; rather, if the tools are available, don't waste too much time trying to re-invent one. Remember that this is the whole idea of component programming.

We demonstrated in this chapter how easy it is to roll out an OLAP project using Visual Basic, and the OLAP Server. This example covered a lot of pages in this chapter, but most of them were illustrations. If you have further questions about OLAP, I would highly recommend browsing through the Help files of the OLAP Server, and run through the Tutorial in the OLAP Manager.

Suppliers
- SupplierID
- CompanyName
- ContactName
- ContactTitle
- Address
- City
- Region
- PostalCode
- Country
- Phone
- Fax
- HomePage

Products
- ProductID
- ProductName
- SupplierID
- CategoryID
- QuantityPerUnit
- UnitPrice
- UnitsInStock
- UnitsOnOrder
- ReorderLevel
- Discontinued

Categories
- CategoryID
- CategoryName
- Description
- Picture

6

Generating Reports

The release of Visual Basic 6 has seen the advent of the Data Environment Designer (DED) and the Data Report Designer(DRD).

The DED has many uses. It minimizes the amount of code required to establish a connection to OLE DB compliant databases. It returns `Recordset` objects bound to ADO data-bound controls (such as the MSHFlexGrid). In particular, the DED provides an impressive and easy-to-use drag-and-drop environment for the creation of hierarchical `Recordsets`.

The DRD supplies reporting capabilities. It is powerful enough to build fairly complex reports but, however, it does lack some of the functionality of Crystal Reports (which is still available as an add-in through Visual Basic). It makes some difficult tasks very trivial, while the functionality to execute some simple tasks seem to be non-existent (for example, I encountered problems when trying to multiply two report text boxes together to provide a single value in a third text box!). Of course, there are plenty of plus points too. When a project is compiled, for example, the report becomes an embedded part of the project executable making it very easy to distribute the report to multiple users. The DRD was designed specifically to work with Visual Basic and many of the wrinkles will doubtless be ironed out with subsequent releases.

In this chapter we'll demonstrate the capabilities of these two tools by building two projects. The first project will demonstrate how the DED can be used to establish database connections and recordsets in a drag-and-drop environment. For the second project we will be build a sales invoice report. When the user enters an OrderID, all Order Details will be retrieved and the Invoice will be generated.

The Data Environment Designer

The DED is, essentially, a container for `Connection`, `Command`, and `Recordset` objects that allows quick access to data in your database tables from a drag-and-drop environment. The visual component provided by the DED is very helpful in demonstrating the hierarchy of these objects

The drag-and-drop environment of the DED makes it particularly effective at creating hierarchical `Recordsets`. `Command` objects can be dragged onto a form and all the available fields, along with appropriate data-bound controls are automatically added. The DED is also effective for generating parameters for stored procedures, although we do not discuss this aspect in the chapter.

The data environment can be used in a number of situations. I have found it quite useful in creating both forms and reports. It is especially useful when you want to create a detailed report without a lot of work. First, let's get to grips with the basics of `DataEnvironment`.

Using the DED to create a hierarchical recordset

Lets create a simple project with the Data Environment to see what it can do.

1. Open Visual Basic and then double click on **Data Project** in the **New Project** dialog.

2. When the project is created, a `DataEnvironment` object, a `DataReport` object, and a standard form are automatically included. We'll work with the `DataReport` object later. For now, open the **DataEnvironment** window by double clicking on the `DataEnvironment1` object from **DataProject** window:

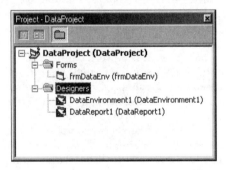

3. When the Data Environment window opens, a default connection will be listed (`Connection1`). Right click on `Connection1`, and select **Rename** from the pop-up menu. Change the name of the connection to `cnPubs`.

4. Right click on `cnPubs` and select **Properties**. The **Data Link Properties** window will open. Choose the "Microsoft OLE DB Provider for SQL Server Provider", and then click on the **Next** button. Configure a connection to the `pubs` database just as we have done in previous chapters by setting the server, the security information, and then specifying the database.

> If you wish to use Access, then build your connection string to the Northwind
> database using the Jet 3.51 OLE DB Provider, as we did in Chapter 4.

5. The next step is to add a new Command object. Simply right click on cnPubs and then select
Add Command from the menu. Change the name of the new Command object to cmJobs.

6. Right click on cmJobs, and select **Properties**. The **Properties** dialog provides information
about the parent connection, relationships to child commands, and groupings of data. We want
to use the **General** tab of this dialog to specify the data source. We will use the Command
object to apply a SQL statement against the Connection object. We will then be able to work
with any fields detailed in the SQL statement. We want to pull data from the jobs table, so
enter SELECT * FROM Jobs in the text box:

7. Click on the **OK** button. The fields of the jobs table are now available for use on a form:

8. We now want to establish the hierarchical relationship between the `jobs` table and the `employee` table. The relationship is one-to-many (several employees will have the same job title). Right-click on the `cmJobs Command` and select **Add Child Command**. Rename the new `Command cmEmployee`.

9. Pull up the **Properties** window for `cmEmployee` and enter `SELECT * FROM Employee` in the SQL text box to make available all the fields in the `employee` table.

10. In order to define the relationship between the Child (`employee` table) and Parent (`jobs` table) fields, click on the **Relation** tab. In this example, the `job_id` field provides the link between the tables. Select these fields (although it will probably have been done for you!), then click on the **Add** button:

11. Click on the **OK** button, and `cmEmployee` will display the fields of the `employee` table:

12. Not, strictly speaking, a step in the development of our project: more of a quick look at what's going on under the hood to see exactly what the DED is doing for us. Right-click on `cmJobs` and select **Hierarchical Info...** from the context menu. You will see that DED is actually creating a `SHAPE` construct for us. This is great to know, even if you prefer not to use the DED for your projects. This tool can be used to build complex `SHAPE` constructs (with as many levels as you desire), which can then be pasted into Visual Basic code:

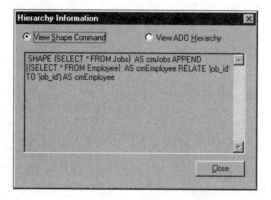

13. Now that we have the `DataEnvironment` configured, we are ready to build the form that will display the records from our tables. Open the project form and add an instance of the Microsoft Hierarchical FlexGrid control (it should already exist in the component toolbox). Make the form and the new control large enough to view multiple records simultaneously.

14. Change the `DataSource` property of the MSHFlexGrid to `DataEnvironment1`. Change the `DataMember` property to `cmJobs`. Run the project to view the results:

	job_id	job_desc	min_lvl	max_lvl	emp_id	fname	minit	lname
	1	New Hire - J	10	10				
⊟	2	Chief Execu	200	250	PTC11962M	Philip	T	Cramer
⊟	3	Business Or	175	225	AMD15433F	Anne	M	Devon
⊟	4	Chief Financ	175	250	F-C16315M	Francisco		Chang
⊟					PXH22250M	Paul	X	Henriot
					CFH28514M	Carlos	F	Hernadez
					JYL26161F	Janine	Y	Labrune
	5	Publisher	150	250	LAL21447M	Laurence	A	Lebihan
					RBM23061F	Rita	B	Muller
					SKO22412M	Sven	K	Ottlieb
					MJP25939M	Maria	J	Pontes
⊟					VPA30890F	Victoria	P	Ashworth
	6	Managing E	140	225	MGK44605M	Matti	G	Karttunen
					DWR65030	Diego	W	Roel
					A-R89858F	Annette		Roulet
⊟					L-B31947F	Lesley		Brown
	7	Marketing M	120	200	PDI47470M	Palle	D	Ibsen
					M-L67958F	Maria		Larsson
					HAN90777M	Helvetius	A	Nagy
⊟					ARD36773F	Anabela	R	Domingue:
	8	Public Relat	100	175	PSP68661F	Paula	S	Parente
					M-P91209M	Manuel		Pereira

As you can see, the MSHFlexGrid control does a pretty good job of displaying the data without any tweaking. There are a few things we can do to clean up the appearance, through the MSHFlexGrid properties:

> In the General tab of the Properties window, change the Fixed Col property to 0. This will get rid of the leading gray column on the left side of your grid.

> In the Bands tab, we can restrict specific fields from appearing in the grid. The job_id field, for example, appears twice because it exists in both commands. There are two Bands in this project (cmJobs and cmEmployee). Simply uncheck the box next to any field in either Band in order to prevent it appearing in the grid. Uncheck the job_id field in both Bands.

There is different and slightly nicer way to view our data. If you want to try it, I suggest you add a new form to your project. From the Project | DataProject Propereties menu, select this new form as the start-up form.

> Instead of manually adding the MSHFlexGrid to the form, as we did in step 13, left-click on cmJobs and drag it onto the form. Text boxes will automatically be added to deal with the data from the Parent table (jobs) and the MSHFlexGrid to deal with the employee fields (right-click and drag will allow you to add an instance of, e.g., the MSHFlexgrid, as previously).

> Arrange the controls on the from, then add our old friend the ADODC.

> Now we need to code the Activate event of the form in order to bind the data control to the rscmJobs Recordset. The code should go something like this:

```
Private Sub Form_Activate()
Set Adodc1.Recordset = DataEnvironment1.rscmJobs
End Sub
```

Run your project and you should see something like this (the DED isn't perfect - you may have to resize some of the text boxes to view the data properly):

As you can see, you can get some pretty fancy results in minimal time using the DED and the Hierarchical FlexGrid. You're not restricted to the MSHFlexGrid control though. Use your imagination and you'll be surprised at what you can produce.

Report Generation

We'll now use the DED and the Data Report Designer to create a project with reporting capabilities. The goal of this project is to produce two reports. The first report will produce a products listing from the `Products` table on the `Northwind` database, then the second will produce a complete sales invoice report for products sold. First we'll use the `DataEnvironment` to connect to our database and make available all the data we require for our report:

> Create a new folder in the `ProVB6DB` directory called `Chapter19`. Open a new Visual Basic project of the **Data Project** type.

> Change the `Name` property of the project to `prjReport` and the `Name` property of the form to `frmReport`.

> Change the `Name` property of the `DataEnvironment` object to `deReports`. Change the `Name` property of the `Connection` (in the `DataEnvironment` window) to `cnReports`.

> Change the `Name` Property of the `DataReport` to `rptProducts`.

> Save the project. Save `frmReport` as `Report.frm`, `deReports` as `Reports.Dsr`, `rptProducts` as `Products.Dsr` and `prjReport` as `Report.vbp`.

> Establish a database connection as we did earlier in the chapter, but this time we want to connect to the `Northwind` database on SQL Server:

> ➢ Add a `Command` object to your `DataEnvironment`: **Right** click on the `cnReports` `Connection`, and select **Add Command**. Change the `Name` property of the new `Command` to `cmProducts`.

> ➢ The **Properties** window of `cmProducts` allows us to specify the class of database object we wish to select as our data source (Table, Stored Procedure, View or Synonym for Oracle). In this case, we wish to select the `Products` table:

Click on **OK**, then expand `CmProducts` inside the `DataEnvironment` by clicking on the '+':

As you can see, this exposes all available fields for display in the report. We're now ready to use the Data Report Designer.

The Data Report Designer

Prior to Visual Basic 6.0; the embedded Seagate Crystal Report designer (that came packaged in the Professional and Enterprise editions of Visual Basic) was most often used to create project data reports. With the release of Visual Basic 6.0 comes the Data Report Designer (DRD). The DRD is easy to use, and reports can be generated quickly. However, it currently lacks functionality compared to Crystal Reports. We'll encounter some of the limitations of the DRD as we progress through these projects. If you need to prepare highly complex reports, you may wish to consider using a third party tool.

Designing a Simple Products Report

Locate `rptProducts` in the Project window. Double-click on it and the `DataReport` will open in design mode:

The report consist of the following sections:

Report Header:
Any information in this section will appear in the entire report once, at the beginning of the report, before the Page Header of the first page.

Page Header:
Information in this section will appear at the beginning of every page in the report.

Group Header/Footer:
This section allows you to group the information found in the Detail section. For example, if we want our products listed by category, we could specify the `CategoryID` field as the grouping field. Note that it is possible to have multiple groups per report and multiple fields per group.

Chapter 19

Detail:
The **Detail** section will present the repeating content of our report (i.e. every row for a specific field included in the `DataReport`).

Page Footer:
This section allows us to place information at the bottom of every report page.

Report Footer:
Information in this section appears at the end of the last page of the report. This is typically used to summarize any detailed information, such as counts or totals.

Each section can be reduced in size, closed off or excluded. To restrict the size of each section, drag up the section definition bar for the section below the one to be closed up. For example, to restrict the size of the **Report Header** section, position the mouse cursor at the top of the **Page Header** bar such that the cursor icon changes to two arrows pointing up and down, then click and drag the bar up. You may elect not to view, or to remove, certain sections by right-clicking on the report and choosing the appropriate options. In the following shot, the **Group Header /Footer** sections have been excluded:

When preparing to build the report, it's best to arrange the **DataEnvironment** window and the **DataReport** window so that both can be easily accessed. If there is room, place them side-by-side. This will make it much easier to drag a field form the **DataEnvironment** window and drop it on to the report.

Our next task is to associate the `DataReport` object with the `DataEnvironment` object. Open the **Properties** window for the report object (`rptProducts`) and set the following properties:

```
DataSource = deReports
DataMember = cmProducts
```

We are now ready to add some data. To add field to the report, simply drag it from the **DataEnvironment** window and drop it in the **Detail** section of the `DataReport`. Start with `ProductID`:

Two boxes are added to our report. Whenever a new text box is added, a corresponding label is automatically added as well. The label (RptLabel) is for column names and appears to the left of the text box (RptTextBox), which will hold row values. Have a look at the Properties window for the RptTextBox and notice that the DataMember and DataField properties are automatically assigned to indicate where the box is bound:

You will also notice that TextBox objects, along with every other type of object placed on the report, can be resized via their Width, Height, Left, and Top properties (of course, the alternative is to grab and drag one of the six block handlebars). A width of around 1200 twips should be about right.

Drag the label into the Page Header section and arrange as follows:

Add the following fields to the report and arrange them from left to right:

ProductID: If you have not added it already.
ProductName
QuantityPerUnit
UnitPrice
UnitsInStock
UnitsOnOrder

> **If you have problems moving your controls exactly where you want them, right click on the report and uncheck the Snap to Grid option.**

When all fields are added, and arranged neatly, bring the Page Footer section up to the bottom of the fields in the Detail section:

Displaying the Report

You can now preview the report. Open
`frmReport`, and add a command button.
Rename the button `cmdProducts` and change
the caption to **Products Report**.

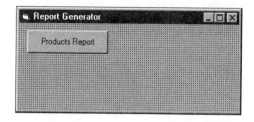

Add the following code:

```
Private Sub cmdProducts_Click()
    rptProducts.Show
End Sub
```

When previewing reports, treat them just like any other form. The `DataReport` object has the same
`Show` property and can be used in the same manner.

Run the project, and click on the **Products Report** button. After a short delay, the report should
appear (note that it will be several pages long):

ProductID:	ProductName	QuantityPerUnit:	UnitPrice:	UnitsInStock:	UnitsOnOrde
1	Chai	10 boxes x 20	18	39	0
2	Chang	24 - 12 oz bottles	19	17	40
3	Aniseed Syrup	12 - 550 ml	10	13	70
4	Chef Anton's Cajun	48 - 6 oz jars	22	53	0
5	Chef Anton's Gumbo	36 boxes	21.35	0	0
6	Grandma's Boysenberry	12 - 8 oz jars	25	120	0
7	Uncle Bob's Organic	12 - 1 lb pkgs.	30	15	0
8	Northwoods Cranberry	12 - 12 oz jars	40	6	0
9	Mishi Kobe Niku	18 - 500 g pkgs.	97	29	0
10	Ikura	12 - 200 ml jars	31	31	0
11	Queso Cabrales	1 kg pkg.	21	22	30

The report comes nicely packaged with toolbar buttons that allow printing, exporting and changing
the zoom factor. The export feature can be very beneficial – it allows data to be exported as HTML
or as text. To add even more flexibility to the project, I would recommend coding the various report
views into the project. These views include:

<u>Preview</u>: The report is previewed on screen.

<u>Print</u>: Sends the report to the default printer.

<u>Export as HTML</u>: Creates an HTML file of the report.

<u>Export as Text</u>: Creates a text file of the report.

Add a Frame control to the form and change its caption to Print Options. Add four option buttons within the Frame control and set the following properties:

Object	Property	Value
Option Button	Name	optPreview
	Caption	Preview Report
	Value	True
Option Button	Name	optPrint
	Caption	Print Report
Option Button	Name	optHTML
	Caption	Export as HTML
Option Button	Name	optText
	Caption	Export as Text

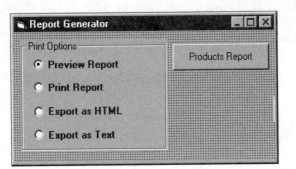

Change the cmdProducts code as follows:

```
Private Sub cmdProducts_Click()
    If optPreview Then rptProducts.Show
    If optPrint Then rptProducts.PrintReport False, rptRangeAllPages
    If optHTML Then rptProducts.ExportReport rptKeyHTML, "C:\test.html", True
    If optText Then rptProducts.ExportReport rptKeyText, "C:\test.txt", True
End Sub
```

The above code handles the four most common report previews. We used two constants to identify the export types as HTML or Text. These were rptKeyHTML and rptKeyText, respectively. In order to export Unicode, there are two other constants that can be used: rptKeyUnicodeHTML_UTF8 and rptKeyUnicodeText. The export methods also allow declaration of the number of pages to export and whether or not to export the file if it already exists.

When printing reports, there are several optional arguments that can be passed. The first argument indicates whether the print dialog should be displayed. The second indicates if all pages should be printed, or if a range of pages should be printed. If you choose to print a range, the following two arguments should indicate the start and end pages to print.

Adding Splash to Your Report

The Report Generator provides a DataReport toolbox that contains a number of controls designed for use with the report. These controls do not work with any other objects (such as a form). From this toolbox, you may add an unbound control and then apply a function to the box, or define its `DataMember`, and `DataField` manually. Notice that in addition to the text box, there are also controls for labels, functions, shapes, lines, and pictures:

Each of these controls has many properties that can be changed to provide a more colorful and professional layout. To fully understand the potential of each control it's best to learn by trial and error. For example, try changing the `BorderColor` property, and then view the results. I added horizontal lines and then changed their `BorderColor` and `BorderStyle` properties. In addition, I added an image control to my report, then imported an image as a bitmap file:

Adding Calculations

The report generator comes with a control that is specifically designed to calculate values. If the Report Footer is still closed up, re-open it and add a function control from the DataReports toolbox. The control is temporarily assigned to be of the Sum type, and is unbound to any field:

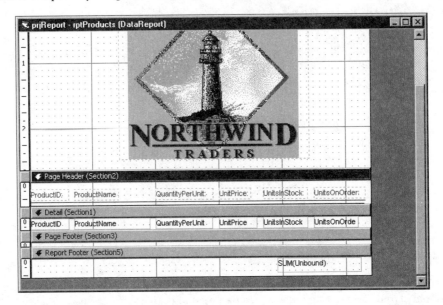

Our goal is to calculate the total number of UnitsInStock. To do this, change the following properties of the new control:

```
DataMember: cmProducts
DataField: UnitsInStock
FunctionType: 0 - rptFuncSum
```

Run the project and view the results. The calculated total will be displayed at the very end of the report.

Other functions available in this control include:

Function	Description
rptFuncAve	Returns the Mean Average of all Records for a given field.
rptFuncMin	Returns the Minimum value of all records for a given field
rptFuncMax	Returns the Maximum value of all records for a given field
rptFuncRCnt	Counts the rows of all records in a specific section
rptFuncVCnt	Counts the rows that don't have a NULL value in a specific field
rptFuncSDEV	Calculates the standard deviation for all records in a specific section
rptFuncSERR	Calculates the standard error for all records in a specific section

The next section of this book will extend the current project. Save your project now and we'll continue.

Building an Invoice Report

In this next section we will add functionality to allow the user to prepare an invoice, displaying all information relevant to a placed order. It will build and expand on the skills we learned in the previous section, to produce a truly professional report. A Group Header section will contain customer and shipping information. Order details will be placed in the Detail section and the total cost of the order, along with any other relevant information (e.g. employeeID, Orderdate etc.), will be placed in the Group Footer.

Creating a SQL Command Using the Drag and Drop Method

For this report we need to pull information from a number of tables. Thus, we will create a new command object and specify the source of our data through a rather lengthy SQL command. Don't worry though: you won't have to do much typing!

Add a new Command to cnReports, and rename it cmInvoice:

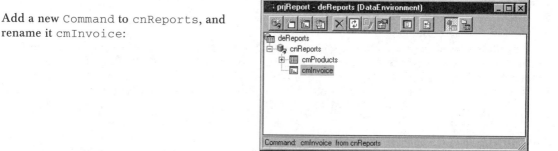

Right-click on cmInvoice and open up its Properties window. Select the SQL statement option button and click on the SQL Builder... command button. Two dialogs should open - the SQL Design dialog:

And the Data View dialog:

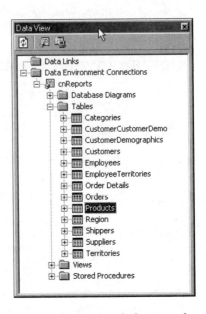

Specific tables or views can be dragged from the Data View dialog to the Design dialog in order to dynamically construct a SQL statement. We'll be working with 3 tables for now, so drag the following tables from the Data View dialog to top tier of the SQL Design dialog: Orders, Order Details and Products. The Design window should now show all three tables and all fields available from each. The DED will automatically identify the relationship keys between the tables. The SQL statement is continuously built and modified as fields are added and selections changed.

To select a field to be included in the Invoice report, simply check the box to the left of the field. To select all available fields from a table, check the *(All Columns) box. Following is a list of the fields to select from each table:

Orders	Order Details	Products
CustomerID	Discount	Product Name
EmployeeID	OrderID	
Freight	ProductID	
OrderDate	Quantity	
ShipAddress	UnitPrice	
ShipCity		
ShipCountry		
ShipName		
ShipPostalCode		
ShipVia		

Once all fields are added, enter '=10373' into the criteria box of the OrderID field. This will allow us to view only the details of this OrderID and provides the basis for creating the dynamic SQL builder in Visual Basic. We'll modify this criterion later. However, right now we need to work with a limited recordset.

The SQL statement is now complete. Test the statement by right clicking on the Design window, and selecting Run. In effect, we have just designed a **view** and when we execute this view the virtual table is displayed in the bottom tier of the design window:

Close the design window (click on **X**) and, when prompted, save the changes. The results will be posted to the CommandText property of cmInvoice automatically. Open the cmInvoice Properties window to view the changes.

Grouping Fields

During the grouping step, we will identify a number of fields to be displayed in the Group Header. The Group Header is used to display a set of information that relates to multiple fields in a recordset. It is a good idea, for example, to summarize customer information pertaining to an order (Name, Address, CustomerID etc.) in this section. The OrderDetails information can then be placed in the Details section of the report. This conserves space on our report, and allows the user to read the data easily.

The first step is to identify what grouping should take place to produce the summary fields. In our example, grouping should be applied to the CustomerID, but also to any repeating Shipping information such as ShipName and Address.

From within the DataEnvironment window, open the cmInvoice Properties window and select the Grouping tab:

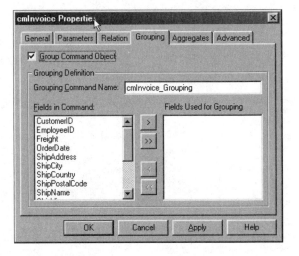

Activate the Group Command Object check box. This will allow us to select new fields for grouping. Allow the default name for the new group (cmInvoice_Grouping), and then add the following fields to the Fields Used for Grouping list box (we're adding these fields because we want them to appear in the Group Header portion of the DataReport. If they are not declared as being part of a group, you will not be able to drag them into this section):

CustomerID, EmployeeID, OrderDate, ShipAddress, ShipCity, ShipCountry, ShipName, ShipPostalCode, ShipVia, Freight

Click on the OK button and the fields of the `cmInvoice` command will be broken out into two "folders": Summary fields (for the Group Header section) and Detail fields (for the Detail section):

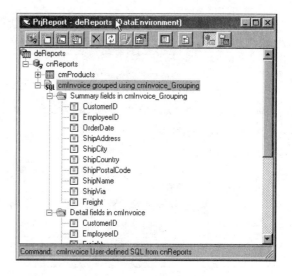

Designing the Invoice Report

From the project menu bar, select Project | Add Data Report. Call it `rptInvoice` and save it in the Chapter19 folder as `Invoice.Dsr`.

Change the `DataSource` property `rptInvoice` to `deReports`.
Change the `DataMember` property of `rptInvoice` to `cmInvoice_Grouping`.

We'll need to add a grouping section to the report so right-click on the report and select Insert Group Header/Footer. A Group Header section will be added, which we'll use to display the CustomerID and shipping information.

From the folder Detail Fields in cmInvoice, drag and drop the following fields to the Detail section of your report:

```
ProductID
ProductName
Quantity
UnitPrice
Discount
```

To conserve space, place each `RptLabel` at the bottom of the Group Header. The result should look like this:

Adding an Extended Price Field

In order to present an extended price, modify the SQL statement to include a new field with an alias of Extended.

An extended price equates to the value of Quantity *field multiplied by* UnitPrice, *minus any* Discount *applied. It's a subtotal for the sales order.*

The addition to the SQL statement might look like this:

```
SELECT Orders.CustomerID, Orders.EmployeeID, Orders.Freight, Orders.OrderDate,
    Order_Details.Discount, Order_Details.OrderID, Order_Details.ProductID,
    Order_Details.Quantity, Products.ProductName, Order_Details.UnitPrice,
    Orders.ShipAddress, Orders.ShipCity, Orders.ShipCountry, Orders.ShipName,
    Orders.ShipPostalCode, Orders.ShipVia,
    (Order_Details.Quantity * Order_Details.UnitPrice * (1-Order_Details.Discount)) AS
    Extended
    FROM Order_Details, Products, Orders
    WHERE Order_Details.ProductID = Products.ProductID AND Order_Details.OrderID =
    Orders.OrderID AND (Order_Details.OrderID = 10373)
```

When the new SQL statement is applied, ensure that the grouping remains intact, and then add the Extended field to the **Detail** section of the report. Finally, change the DataFormat properties of the UnitPrice, and Extended text boxes to Currency. This will enhance the professional format of your report.

Add a new command button to frmReport, and name it cmdInvoice. Change the Caption to **Invoice**. Add the following code to display the Invoice report:

```
Private Sub cmdInvoice_Click()
   rptInvoice.Show
End Sub
```

Run the project, and view the report. When generating complex reports I would recommend that you test your report frequently. You may occasionally make a mistake, so frequent testing will make it easier to backtrack and locate the problem. Another way to assist in this process is to use a product such as SourceSafe, where code is marked with a revision identifier to make it easier to return the project to its original state.

The next step is to add the shipping details. From Summary fields in cmInvoice_Grouping, in the DataEnvironment window, add the following fields to the Group Header and Footer:

Header	Footer
CustomerID	EmployeeID
ShipName	OrderDate
ShipAddress	ShipVia
ShipCity	
ShipCountry	
ShipPostalCode	

Arrange the labels and textboxes so that the information is easy to read. Add line and shape controls to emphasize grouping. You might end up with something that looks like this:

Again, after placing the controls on the report, run the project. Align the labels and text boxes for maximum visual appeal.

Displaying the Cost of an Order

We know how much each item costs, how many were ordered and any discount that might have applied, so we can display a subtotal for the customer order. We then need to add on freight costs and display the total cost of the order. All this information will be placed in the **Group Footer**.

> ➤ The `Freight` field (label included) can simply be dragged from the **DataEnvironment** window to the **Group Footer** section of the **DataReport** window.

> ➤ Add a new label to the report, and change the caption to **SubTotal:**. Then, add a new function control to the report. We will use this to display the order subtotal. Change the `DataMember` property of the function control to `cmInvoice` and the `DataField` to `Extended`. The `FunctionType` should be `rptFuncSum`.

The last step is to calculate the grand total for the order. I must admit, I found this to be the most challenging aspect of the report. You might think that you could add a text box, and set its value equal to the value of the **Subtotal** text box plus the **Freight** text box, but this is not the case. To handle this problem, you must use a formula in your SQL statement to pre-process the value. That value can then be pulled as a field and then displayed.

The formula for the total is as follows:

```
Freight + (Quantity * UnitPrice * (1-Discount))
```

There are a number of ways in which you can embed the function in a SQL statement. Here's how I did it:

```
SELECT Orders.Freight+Sum(Quantity*UnitPrice*(1-Discount))
FROM Order_Details
INNER JOIN Orders ON Order_Details.OrderID = Orders.OrderID
GROUP BY Orders.Freight, Orders.OrderID
HAVING ((Orders.OrderID)=10373
```

Add this sub-query to the SQL statement in the `cmInvoice` command:

```
SELECT Orders.CustomerID, Orders.EmployeeID, Orders.Freight, Orders.OrderDate,
Order_Details.Discount, Order_Details.OrderID, Order_Details.ProductID,
Order_Details.Quantity, Products.ProductName, Order_Details.UnitPrice,
Orders.ShipAddress, Orders.ShipCity, Orders.ShipCountry, Orders.ShipName,
Orders.ShipPostalCode, Orders.ShipVia, (Order_Details.Quantity *
Order_Details.UnitPrice * (1-Order_Details.Discount)) AS Extended,
(SELECT Orders.Freight+Sum(Quantity*UnitPrice*(1-Discount))
FROM Order_Details
INNER JOIN Orders ON Order_Details.OrderID = Orders.OrderID
GROUP BY Orders.Freight, Orders.OrderID
HAVING ((Orders.OrderID)=10373)) as Total
FROM Order_Details, Products, Orders WHERE Order_Details.ProductID =
Products.ProductID AND Order_Details.OrderID = Orders.OrderID
AND (Order_Details.OrderID = 10373)
```

The new sub-query returns a value that is held by an alias. In this case, the alias will be called Total, which can be pulled as a field from the DataEnvironment.

After modifying the SQL statement, click on the **Grouping** tab in the cmInvoice **Properties** dialog and add the Total field to the grouping.

Click on the **OK** button, and save the project. We can now drag the Total field from the DataEnvironment to rptInvoice.

Modify the properties of all three of the new text boxes in order to present the data in the most logical manner. For example, change the Alignment property of each to rptJustifyRight and the DataFormat property to Currency.

Your report should now look something like this (add titles, lines, and shading as desired):

Dynamic Modification of the SQL Command

Now that we have a well-designed report, we can think about applying specific SQL code during runtime, in order to create an invoice report for a specific OrderID. Currently, we have the OrderID '10373' hard-coded into our SQL statement.

Add a new label and a new text box to frmReport. Change the Name property of the text box to txtOrderID, and set its Text property to a default value of 10373. Add a label above the textbox, and change the caption to OrderID.

We can now "dynamically" change the SQL statement in order to display details for any specified OrderID - and we don't have to re-invent the wheel to do it! Open the **Properties** window of cmInvoice and simply replace both instances of the hard-coded 10373 with a "?":

When you click on the **Apply** button, you *may* be prompted to move to the **Parameters** tab and configure parameters to fill in the missing question marks. What we're doing here is creating an unknown value in our statement. Each question mark in the SQL statement identifies a missing value. The missing value will be posted to an argument that is configured in the **Parameters** tab, then passed by the Visual Basic program when the report is opened.

Click on the **OK** button if the above dialog appears, then click on the **Parameters** tab. Two default parameters will be created for you. Here, you should ensure that both parameters are being passed as integers (**adInteger**), and that the direction is **Input** (as in the following illustration):

Now, all that remains is to write some code. We need to pass the parameters that we just configured to the report just before opening it. In the `cmdInvoice` command button's click event, modify the code as follows:

```
Private Sub cmdInvoice_Click()

    If deReports.rscmInvoice_Grouping.State = adStateOpen Then
        deReports.rscmInvoice_Grouping.Close
    End If

    deReports.cmInvoice_Grouping txtOrderID, txtOrderID

    If optPreview Then rptInvoice.Show

    If optPrint Then rptProducts.PrintReport False, rptRangeAllPages
    If optHTML Then rptInvoice.ExportReport rptKeyHTML, "C:\Invoice.html", True
    If optText Then rptInvoice.ExportReport rptKeyText, "C:\Invoice.txt", True

End Sub
```

The first section evaluates whether or not the recordset is already open. If it is, it must be closed before applying a new parameter otherwise an error will be generated.

The second section applies the parameters that were configured to populate the '?' in the SQL statement. We send the value of the `txtOrderID` twice because the `OrderID` is used as the parameter in both circumstances. It doesn't get much easier than this. As an alternative, we could have rebuilt the SQL statement, but I have found it much easier to configure a parameter, and pass it from a text box.

After the parameter is assigned, the `Show`, `Print`, or `Export` method is assigned as previously.

Run the project, and enter a new `OrderID`. View the report and then close it. Enter another `OrderID`, and view the results again. This process ensures that the recordset is being closed properly each time and that the new SQL statement is being re-assigned.

Summary

In this chapter, we explored Microsoft's Data Environment Designer and used it to create a hierarchical recordset. Using the `DataEnvironment` object, a `Connection` object comes ready made and it is quick and easy to add a `Command` object and make available fields from tables in a database.

We used the Data Report Designer to create a professional sales invoice report. We explored the SQL building tool and how to view our reports in a number of different formats, including: preview, printer, and exporting as text or HTML. The DED and the DRD provide very useful drag-and-drop environment and are more than capable of handling fairly complex reporting tasks, as we demonstrated. However, while the Data Report Designer is quite a useful tool for creating and deploying reports, it does suffer from a certain lack of functionality. For more complex tasks it might, for the time being, be worth sticking with Seagate's Crystal Reports or checking out some other tools.

Suppliers

- SupplierID
- CompanyName
- ContactName
- ContactTitle
- Address
- City
- Region
- PostalCode
- Country
- Phone
- Fax
- HomePage

Products

- ProductID
- ProductName
- SupplierID
- CategoryID
- QuantityPerUnit
- UnitPrice
- UnitsInStock
- UnitsOnOrder
- ReorderLevel
- Discontinued

Categories

- CategoryID
- CategoryName
- Description
- Picture

6

CASE STUDY

An Example 3-Tier Distributed Application using Microsoft Transaction Server

Building our Example

Now that we've seen some of the many different technologies that you can employ to build a Visual Basic database application, we're going to look at building a distributed database application. In fact, we're going to build an e-commerce site!

We'll use as an example an entrepreneur called Darren Clarke, who for the past six years has operated a retail outlet for car audio and security products. He's watched the growth of e-commerce and thinks it'd be a good direction for his business to move in.

What we're going to do is build a very basic e-commerce site – a site where visitors can browse Darren's product catalog and add items they'd like to buy to a cart. To keep this example short and sweet, we're not going to worry about any of the other aspects of building an e-commerce site, such as credit card verification, capturing private information over secure sockets, inventory, etc. All we're going to do is build a simple front-end, and give an example of a good way of building business objects.

This site will mostly be built using technologies you've already learned about. We're going to build the business objects in Visual Basic, presentation code for the site in Active Server Pages and hold the data for the site in Microsoft SQL Server 7 – a classic 3-tier approach. Later in the chapter, we'll use Microsoft Transaction Server to help make this architecture a viable reality in a production environment

Active Server Pages (ASP) is a technology developed by Microsoft which provides a server-side scripting environment. This is in contrast to the client-side scripting environment provided by Dynamic HTML (DHTML), where scripts are executed on the browser. ASP provides state - allowing the use of variables with session scope (that is, variables which retain their values for the entire session). The ASP scripting engine is provided with both Internet Information Server and Personal Web Server. Typically, an Active Server Page will consist of a mixture of sections of ASP script (placed between special <% ... %> delimiters) and sections of plain HTML – contained in a file with the extension .asp. When the page is requested, its contents are sent to the ASP script engine, which generates an HTML stream 'on the fly'. The resulting stream is then sent on to the browser. Thus, the browser does not need to support ASP in order to view the page. For more information on ASP, see Appendix K.

Building the Database

Obviously, Darren needs a place to store his product catalog. We're going to use Microsoft SQL Server 7, because this particular database has excellent support for transactions, which will be essential later on when we look at how to run Darren's business objects inside MTS transactions.

We'll create a new database to hold this information. This database will contain Darren's basic product catalog, which comprises four tables: `Products`, `Categories`, `Suppliers` and `Manufacturers`.

To create the database in SQL Server, load Enterprise Manager, right-click on the **Databases** folder under the appropriate server and select **New Database**:

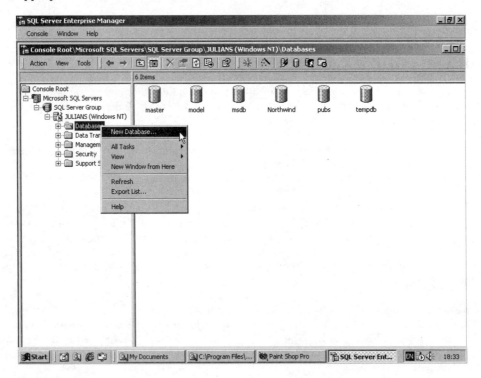

When prompted for the name of the
database, enter Darren. This dialog also
allows us to set properties for the
database: the physical location and name
of the file which will contain the data and
options for the initial size and the file
growth of the database:

Since we're only building a sample database here, we'll leave the default settings. Press OK, and SQL
Server will build the database. Now we're ready to start adding the tables.

The Categories Table

First of all, let's build the Categories table. We'll use this table to group the products in our catalog
into categories, such as: "Receivers", "Amplifiers" and "Speakers". When we build our
storefront, these categories will be the main way for users to navigate through the catalog. On e-
commerce sites, customers are typically either looking for a specific product, or want to browse
products in a major category. This table will facilitate that.

To build the table, open up the Darren database in Enterprise Manager, right-click on Tables and
select New Table. When prompted, enter the name of the table as Categories, and the Design
Table form will be displayed. This form allows us to enter the columns and set their properties. This
table will have two columns, CategoryID and Name. Both of these will contain text data, so set their
data types to varchar. The CategoryID will always consist of a four-letter identifier, so set its
Length to 4. It will be used to identify the category in our Products table, so it will be the primary
key for this table. To set this column as the PK, right-click anywhere on the row for the column and
select Set Primary Key. Name will be a more user-friendly description which is presented to visitors
to the web site; we will leave its Length as 50 characters. Finally, neither column will contain empty
values, so uncheck Allows Nulls for both columns.

When you've set these properties, save the table. We can now enter the actual data for the table. While still in **Design Table** mode, right-click on the form and select <u>T</u>ask I <u>O</u>pen Table. This will open the table for adding and editing data. Add some entries such as those in the screenshot below (remembering that the `CategoryID` column must contain only four letters):

Manufacturers Table

The next table we're going to build is the `Manufacturers` table. This table will not only let us give the user extra information about the manufacturer, but will give us the option of letting the user view all products by a given manufacturer. Like category listings, viewing all products by manufacturer is another common e-commerce method for letting visitors navigate your site.

Again, we'll have as the primary key a four-character ID column, this time called `MfrID`, and a 50-character `Name` column. For this table, we'll also add a `URL` column, giving the address of the manufacturer's web site. We may not have this information for all manufacturers, so we'll leave the **Allow Nulls** box checked for this column.

Save the table design and open the table to add data. Add some entries for your favorite electronics companies, such as:

Suppliers Table

Our next table will hold information about Darren's suppliers. For the sake of brevity, we're not going to go into this table in too much detail. In a real-life application we would store all of the contact information for the supplier and all sorts of other useful information. Here we're just going to store the email address of our sales contact.

So for this table, we'll have three columns: our familiar four-character primary key field `SupplierID` and 50-character `Name` column, and also the `SalesEmail` column to contain our contact's email address. We may not have an email contact at every supplier, so we have left **Allow Nulls** checked for this column.

Column Name	Datatype	Length	Precision	Scale	Allow Nulls	Default Value	Identity	Identity Seed	Identity Increment	Is RowGuid
SupplierID	varchar	4	0	0						
Name	varchar	50	0	0						
SalesEmail	varchar	50	0	0	✓					

Save the table and enter some data. This won't appear in the application's front-end, so it doesn't really matter what we enter here, so long as the data conforms to the data type and restrictions imposed when we designed the table.

SupplierID	Name	SalesEmail
TEDS	Ted's Electronics	ted@eted.com

When we've built and populated this table, we've only got one more to build!

Products Table

This is the table where we pull everything together. One row here represents one product that Darren sells. We're going to store information about cost, price and inventory in here. These items will be used both in the storefront presentation and in the final order processing.

The primary key for this table will be an auto-incrementing `int` column, so we will set an `IDENTITY` constraint on this column. To do this, check the **Identity** box. Selecting this also causes the **Identity Seed** and **Identity Increment** properties to be set. The first of these specifies the value for the first entry, from which the auto-increment will begin; the second is the number by which the value will be increased for each new entry. These can be left at their default values.

We also need references in this table to the primary keys of the other tables. We'll use the same names for these foreign keys as in the other tables: `CategoryID`, `MfrID` and `SupplierID`. We can use different names, but it is important that the other properties have exactly the same values as the corresponding columns in the other tables.

We'll also add a `Name` column, `Cost` and `Price` columns with a data type of `money`, and a `StockLevel` column with a data type of `int`. Leave the default **Length** settings for these coulmns, but since we will require values for all rows, uncheck the **Allow Nulls** box. Finally, we'll also add a `Description` column of data type `varchar` and a **Length** of 255 characters.

```
SQL Server Enterprise Manager - [2:New Table in 'Darren' on 'JULIANS']
    Console   Window   Help
```

Column Name	Datatype	Length	Precision	Scale	Allow Nulls	Default Value	Identity	Identity Seed	Identity Increment	Is RowGuid
ProductID	int	4	10	0			✓	1	1	
Name	varchar	50	0	0						
CategoryID	varchar	4	0	0						
MfrID	varchar	4	0	0						
SupplierID	varchar	4	0	0						
Cost	money	8	19	4						
Price	money	8	19	4						
StockLevel	int	4	10	0						
Description	varchar	255	0	0	✓					

Save the table and populate it with some sample data, and we've almost finished building the database! Remember that the entries in the `CategoryID`, `MfrID` and `SupplierID` columns should correspond to entries in the corresponding columns in the referenced tables.

```
SQL Server Enterprise Manager - [2:Data in Table 'Products']
    Console   Window   Help
```

ProductID	Name	CategoryID	MfrID	SupplierID	Cost	Price	StockLevel	Description
1	CDX-2250	RECS	SONY	TEDS	180	230	5	Single CD receiver, active :
2	CDX-C5750	RECS	SONY	TEDS	250	300	7	Single CD receiver, active :

Building a Database Diagram

There's just one more task before we've finished building the database: we must specify the relationships between the tables. We can do this by building a database diagram, including all the tables and then specifying the relationships between them. SQL Server provides a wizard to create the diagram; to run this, right-click on **Diagrams** in the `Darren` database and select **New Diagram**. After the splash screen, you will be invited to choose the tables you want to include:

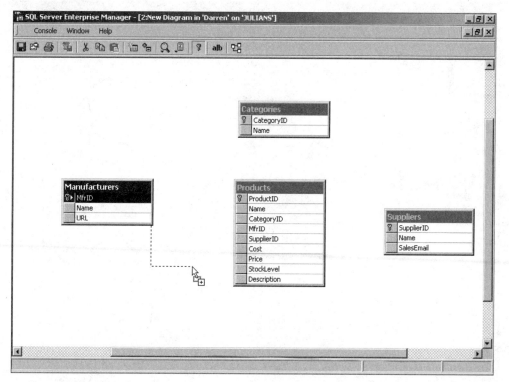

Select all the tables and click on the **Add >** button. When you click **Next >**, the final screen of the wizard is displayed; this lists the tables selected. Click on **Finish**, and SQL Server will add the tables to the diagram. However, we have not yet defined any foreign keys, so at the moment, no relationships exist between the tables. To define the relationship, click on the gray area next to the primary key in the `Categories`, `Manufacturers` or `Suppliers` table, and drag the mouse pointer to the `Products` table:

SQL Server will now display a dialog box allowing you to specify the foreign key in the `Products` table. Ensure that the column in the Foreign key table matches that in the Primary key table (i.e. that the two columns have the same name), click on OK, and repeat the process for the other two tables.

You have now defined all the relationships for the table, and should see a diagram similar to the one below:

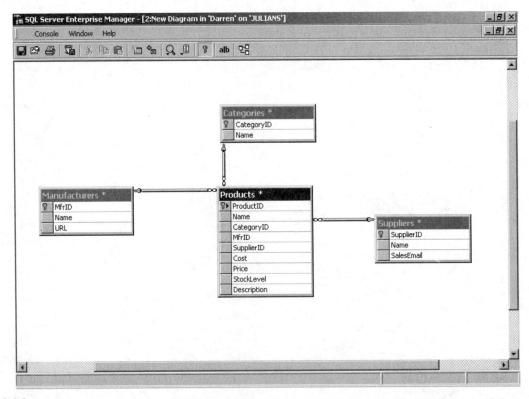

We have now completed our database design. If we anticipated a very large number of records, we would of course also need to add indexes. However, in our small sample database, these would entail no performance advantage.

Creating the View

Before you close Enterprise Manager, there's still one more task we have to complete. When we access the database from our middle-tier objects, we'll execute queries against a pre-defined view which executes an INNER JOIN on our database tables. To set this up, create a new view by right-clicking on Views in the Darren database and selecting New View. Then enter this code into the SQL pane and save the view as vProducts:

```
SELECT Products.ProductID, Products.Name AS ProductName,
    Products.CategoryID, Categories.Name AS CatName,
    Products.MfrID, Manufacturers.Name AS MfrName, Manufacturers.URL,
    Products.SupplierID, Suppliers.Name AS SupplierName, Suppliers.SalesEmail,
    Products.Cost, Products.Price, Products.StockLevel, Products.Description
FROM Products INNER JOIN
    Suppliers ON
    Products.SupplierID = Suppliers.SupplierID INNER JOIN
    Manufacturers ON
    Products.MfrID = Manufacturers.MfrID INNER JOIN
    Categories ON Products.CategoryID = Categories.CategoryID
```

This view helps us to avoid having to write very complicated SQL statements whenever we want to query the database. It simply performs an INNER JOIN statement on our tables and selects all the columns from our Products table and the Name columns from the Categories, Manufacturers and Suppliers tables. Since each table has a Name column, we give each of these columns an alias to distinguish it from the others.

> *If you don't want to type all of the code in, create a new view, add all four tables and then add all of the columns in each table to the query. You'll need to enter the aliases for the* Products.Name, Categories.Name, Manufacturers.Name *and* Suppliers.Name *columns.*

Building the Storefront

Now that we've got our database in place, we can go ahead and start building the ASP pages that will make up our storefront. To *present* our storefront to our visitors, we need to build some **presentation logic**. Presentation logic is the name given to code that manipulates data from the database so it can be presented to the user in a nicely formatted manner. This is distinct from business logic which, as we've already seen, is the encapsulation of business processes into objects that can be deployed into our distributed system.

We have two distinct options when we design how our presentation logic is to work. Our first option is to build all of the presentation logic into Visual Basic components and call them from ASP. Our second is to put all of the presentation logic directly into the ASP pages themselves. There are advantages and disadvantages to both, but they boil down to that fact that putting presentation logic into VB objects is very fast, yet can't be developed and maintained very easily, whereas presentation logic in ASP isn't as fast, but it is much easier to develop and maintain.

In this example, we're going to build our presentation logic using Active Server Pages, because for this site, performance is not the issue – rapid development is.

Before we get into building the logic, however, we have one more decision to make. Imagine a situation where we need to get a list of all the categories from the database. We can get this list by executing a query against the database, with the result returned as a recordset. The question is whether we want to execute the query directly from within our ASP page, or place the ADO code for executing the query inside a business object, and calling that from our ASP page. To put it another way, we can call either:

```
' The "presentation code" developer calls into the database directly...
Set objRecCategories = objConn.Execute("SELECT * FROM Categories")
```

Or:

```
' The developer uses functions which abstract him or her away from the
' implementation of the underlying database...
Set objRecCategories = darrenStore.GetCategories()
```

In this example, we're going to use the latter method and attempt to remove the ASP developer from the database as much as possible. All the presentation logic will remain inside ASP, but we will try to keep all of the business logic in our middle-tier objects.

Let's extend that example to show how we could render the categories:

```
Set objRecCategories = darrenStore.GetCategories()
Do While Not objRecCategories.EOF
    Response.Write objRecCategories("Name")
    objRecCategories.MoveNext
Loop
```

Notice that all the code that communicates directly with the database is abstracted away from the ASP developer, but the presentation logic is still in the ASP realm. This approach ensures the ASP developer can make the site look exactly how he or she wants, but won't have to deal with any database logic.

Creating an ASP Component

Let's get started by designing this middle-tier component to access the database. Create a new Visual Basic **ActiveX DLL** project. Save the project as `"DarrenStore.vbp"` and set the name of the project to `DarrenStore`.

When you create an **ActiveX DLL** project, VB automatically creates a new class module. Rename this class to `Store` and your project should look like the one illustrated below:

Connecting to the Database

When we build our application, we're going to make sure that all the business objects we build and the ASP code will use `DarrenStore.Store` as a central "management" object. One of the tasks this object will undertake is to provide "environmental" information to the other objects in the system, i.e. other objects will be able to ask it for database connections and other system resources.

Let's get started by creating a method that we can use to connect to the database. We'll create a global variable that will hold an ADO `Connection` object and a property called `DB` that will return that object back to the caller. We'll put some logic in the property so that the connection is created "on-demand", i.e. not created until it is requested.

```
' Define a global variable that'll hold the connection
Private g_objConn As Variant

' Our read-only property that'll return the database connection
Public Property Get propConn()

    ' have we already established a connection?
    If TypeName(g_objConn) = "Empty" Then

        ' Create the object and connect...
        ' Remember to change "username" and "password" to
        ' values appropriate to your setup
        Set g_objConn = CreateObject("adodb.connection")
        g_objConn.Open "DarrenStore", "username", "password"

    End If

    ' return the connection we have...
    Set propConn = g_objConn

End Property

' Called when the object is destroyed
Private Sub Class_Terminate()
```

```
    ' do we need to close the connection?
    If TypeName(g_objConn) = "Connection" Then
        g_objConn.Close
        g_objConn = Empty
    End If

End Sub
```

For that code to work, you'll obviously need to configure an ODBC Data Source Name to connect to your SQL Server database. In our example, we've called that data source `DarrenStore`.

See Chapter 3 for a reminder of how to set up an ODBC DSN.

Testing the Connection

To see this in action, we need to create a test ASP page. You can use Microsoft Visual Interdev to write and debug ASP, but any other text editor, such as Windows Notepad, is fine too. Type in the following code and save the file as `default.asp` in the `inetpub/wwwroot` directory or another directory which may be accessed from the Web.

```html
<html>
    <body>
        <%
            Set Darren = Server.CreateObject("darrenstore.store")
            response.write typename(Darren.propConn)
            Set Darren = Nothing
        %>
    </body>
</html>
```

ASP code is usually written in VBScript, a scripting language based on Visual Basic, so it should be fairly easy to follow. As we saw earlier, ASP code is embedded within an HTML page. The outer tags in this page are simply HTML tags which define the start and end of the HTML page, and the start and end of the body of the page. The ASP code itself is contained within the <%...%> delimiters. The first line of the ASP creates an instance of our `Store` class. We then write to the browser (using ASP's `Response.Write` method) the object type of our `propConn` property. To run this test, make sure your VB project and IIS (or PWS) is running and point your browser at the `default.asp` page on your server (e.g. http://my_server/default.asp). You should see the word **Connection** displayed on the page:

Querying the Database

Next, let's create a few database methods so we can get started building our ASP storefront. We need to be able to return lists of the categories, lists of all products in a given category and to return information on a single product. We'll build this functionality into three methods of our Store class, GetCategories, GetProductsInCategory and GetProductInfo, so add this code to the class:

```
' Return all the categories in the database
Public Function GetCategories() As Variant

    ' run a simple query...
    Set GetCategories = propConn.Execute("select * from categories" & _
                                    " order by name")

End Function
```

This first method simply executes a SQL query against the ADO Connection object exposed by our propConn propety. This returns a recordset containing all rows (ordered by the Name column) and columns in the Categories table.

```
' Return all the products in a given category
Public Function GetProductsInCategory(strCategoryID) As Variant

    ' make a SQL statement...
    Dim strSQL
    strSQL = "select * from vproducts"
    strSQL = strSQL & " where categoryid='" & strCategoryID & "'"
    strSQL = strSQL & " order by productname"

    ' run the query...
    Set GetProductsInCategory = propConn.Execute(strSQL)

End Function
```

This method is similar in structure, but this time the query is executed against the vProducts view which we created after we had built the database. This query returns a recordset containing all the columns in the view for those rows where the CategoryID has the same value as the string parameter passed into the function. In other words, it provides the details of all products belonging to the specified category.

```
' Return details on a specific product
Public Function GetProductInfo(ProductID) As Variant

    ' make a SQL statement...
    Dim strSQL
    strSQL = "select * from vproducts"
    strSQL = strSQL & " where productid=" & ProductID

    ' run the query
    Set GetProductInfo = propConn.Execute(sql)

End Function
```

Our final method also executes a query against the vProducts view. This function takes a string parameter, and the query selects all columns of the Products table for the entry with a ProductID the same as that parameter. So we feed the ProductID into the method, and it returns all the details of that product.

Testing our Page

Now that we've got some real code to test, we can change our `default.asp` code to see if we can bring back a list of the categories from the database. To do this, we create an instance of the `Store` and call `GetCategories`. We then iterate through the recordset returned and display each one. Notice that, as well as sending unformatted text to the browser with `Response.Write`, we can send HTML tags too, so we've added a `<BR>` tag after each category to ensure that the next appears on a new line:

```
<%
    ' connect to the store
    Set Darren = Server.CreateObject("darrenstore.store")

    ' get the categories and loop each one...
    Set objRecCats - Darren.GctCategories
    Do While Not objRecCats.EOF

        ' draw each one
        response.write objRecCats("name") & "<br>"
        objRecCats.MoveNext

    loop

    ' close the store
    Set Darren = Nothing

%>
```

If you run this page, you'll see each of the categories in the database rendered onto the page:

The power of this approach of abstracting database functionality comes into play when you realize that the ASP developer doesn't have to worry about the underlying database. You could, if you wanted, port the SQL Server database to an Oracle database running on a Linux box. All the ASP developer needs to know is which columns are available, and which methods and properties are exposed by the objects.

The Storefront Layout

We're at a point now where we can wrap up the storefront presentation code. What we're going to do is build a page that will present the categories to the visitor and then show all the products in a selected category. Change `default.asp` as follows:

```
<html>
    <%
        ' connect to the store
        Set Darren = Server.CreateObject("darrenstore.store")
    %>

<body>

    <font size=5>Darren's Store</font>
    <br>

    <b>Categories:</b>
    <%

        ' get the categories and loop each one...
        Set objRecCats = Darren.GetCategories
        num = 0
        Do While Not objRecCats.eof

            ' spacer?
            if num <> 0 then response.write " . "

            ' draw each one and make a link that'll call back into
            ' the page with the selected category
            response.write "<a href=""" & request("script_name")
            response.write "?catid=" & objRecCats("categoryid") & """>"
            response.write objRecCats("name")
            response.write "</a>"

            ' next
            objRecCats.MoveNext
            num = num + 1

        loop

    %>

    <hr>

    <!-- have we selected a category? -->
    <% if request("catid") = "" then %>

    Select a category from the list above to see the products.

    <% else %>

    <!-- start a product list -->
    <table border=1>
    <%

        ' get the products in the category...
        dim objRecProducts
        set objRecProducts = Darren.getproductsincategory(request("catid"))
        if not objRecProducts.eof then
```

Continued on Following Page

617

```
                ' loop the products
            do while not objRecProducts.eof

                ' draw the item name...
                response.write "<tr><td>"
                response.write "<b>"
                response.write objRecProducts("mfrname")
                response.write " "
                response.write objRecProducts("productname")
                response.write "</b>"

                ' draw the item price
                response.write "</td><td align=right>"
                response.write formatcurrency(objRecProducts("price"), 2)

                ' add the stock level
                response.write "</td><td align=center>"
                if objRecProducts("stocklevel") > 0 then
                    response.write "In stock"
                else
                    response.write "Out of stock"
                end if

                ' add a "Buy" button - we'll implement this later
                response.write "</td><td align=center>"
                response.write "Buy"

                ' finish the item row
                response.write "</td></tr>"

                ' draw the description on a separate row
                response.write "<tr><td colspan=4><small>"
                response.write objRecProducts("description")
                response.write "</small></td></tr>"

                ' spacer...
                response.write "<tr><td height=10></td></tr>"

                ' next
                objRecProducts.movenext

            loop

        else
            response.write "There are no products in this category."
        end if
        objRecProducts.close
        set objRecProducts = nothing

    %>
    </table>

    <% end if %>

</body>

<%
    ' close the store
    Set darren = Nothing
%>

</html>
```

We can't go into this ASP and HTML code in too much detail, but you should be able to follow the basic outline. The page lists the categories available as in the previous version of the page, but in this case, each category name becomes a hyperlink. When the user clicks on one of these links, this same `default.asp` page is re-loaded with the corresponding `CategoryID` added as a request at the end of the URL. When the page is loaded with a category chosen, our `GetProductsInCategory` method is called, and the details of all the products in the specified category are displayed in an HTML table. We also provide a Buy button, for the user to press to order a product. However, we will not implement this until a bit later.

This screenshot shows the result when you point your browser at this new `default.asp` and select Receivers:

Capturing the Order

We're at a stage now where Darren can present his product catalog to the world, but none of his customers will be able to buy anything!

The order processing operation can be split into two halves: we must first capture the order, and then process it. In this section, we're going to deal with how we create a "shopping cart" that the customer can add items to. Our approach will be to build an object that holds a list of the products the visitor has selected. When the user clicks "Checkout", we can pass that populated object over to another object that will perform the actual order processing segment of the operation.

The Cart Class

Our first job is to create a new object to represent the shopping cart; we will call this `Cart`. We'll use this object to keep track of the items our visitor has added to his or her cart. We need to be careful that we keep the cart around for the life of the application. The `DarrenStore.Store` objects we've used so far have only existed for the life of the page, mainly because we don't want to tie up database resources while the user isn't actively using the application. ASP provides a `Session` object which persists for the life of an entire session, and we can store variables in this object. So, we're going to want to keep the `Cart` object around in a `Session` variable so it will persist between pages.

You can consider the `Cart` object to be a general use object. The example you're about to see holds just a product ID and a quantity – it's not specifically tied into the `DarrenStore` database. Code re-use is another very powerful feature of building distributed applications using this methodology. Once you have built and debugged the `Cart` object, you can give it to other developers, or re-use it in other projects with minimum hassle.

So let's create a new Visual Basic class module in our `DarrenStore` project and call it `Cart`. VB provides its own `Collection` class to contain a group of objects, so let's use this to manage the items in our cart. We'll create a new read-only property that will return this collection to the user:

```
Private m_colItems As New Collection

' Create a property to return the cart to the user
Public Property Get Items() As Variant
   Set Items = m_colItems
End Property
```

Notice that we use `Private g_colItems as New Collection` to create a new `Collection` object as soon as our `Cart` object is created. Recall how the `propConn` property on our store object didn't create the connection resource until it was first requested. Well, in this case it's inexpensive to generate a collection when it's instantiated, so we'll save cycles in the `Get` routine.

Now that we have our `Cart` object with our collection in place, we need a way of passing one of these back to our ASP developer. Let's create a method on our original `Store` object:

```
' Return a new Cart object to the ASP developer
Public Function NewCart() As Variant
   Set NewCart = New Cart
End Function
```

Again, our approach with these objects is to abstract the ASP developer away from the particulars of how we've designed the underlying system. By providing a method that can be used to create a `Cart` object, the ASP doesn't have to remember the ProgID (the programmable name by which the object is registered) of the object (in this case `DarrenStore.Cart`). It also means we can perform large-scale changes to the cart implementation without having to re-engineer the ASP code.

Now, let's change our `default.asp` page so that the **Buy** button actually does something. It will open a new ASP page (called `cart.asp`) and pass in the `ProductID` of the item that was clicked. So we'll get rid of the lines where we defined the button:

```
' add a "Buy" button - we'll implement this later
response.write "</td><td align=center>"
response.write "Buy"
```

And replace them with the following code:

```
' now we'll create our buy button
response.write "</td><td align=center>"
response.write "<a href=""cart.asp?add=" & objRecProducts("productid") & """>"
response.write "Buy"
response.write "</a>"
```

The CartItem Class

Once we have a cart, we need to be able to add items. For this example, we want to hold just the IDs of the items in it, and the quantities that we've added. Add a new class module called `CartItem` to our VB project; this will hold an individual item, so we will have one instance of this class for each product in the cart. We'll add to this two read-write properties: one for the ID, and one for the quantity. These will be held in two internal long variables, `m_lngProductID` and `m_lngQuantity`:

```
Private m_lngProductID As Long
Private m_lngQuantity As Long
```

When the class is initialized, we define the quantity as one and the product ID as minus one:

```
' Set the default values
Private Sub Class_Initialize()
    m_lngQuantity = 1
    m_lngProductID = -1
End Sub
```

```
' Handle the product ID
Public Property Let ProductID(value)
    m_lngProductID = value
End Property
Public Property Get ProductID()
    ProductID = m_lngProductID
End Property
```

```
' Handle the quantity
Public Property Get Quantity()
    Quantity = m_lngQuantity
End Property
Public Property Let Quantity(value)
    m_lngQuantity = value
End Property
```

In the code for setting the values of these properties, we merely make the internal variable equal to the value passed in. Conversely, when we return values from the properties, we just return the value in the variable.

Adding an Item to the Cart

Now that we have a way of storing the individual items in the cart, we need to create a method on the `Cart` object that we can use to add new items or to increase the quantity of an item in the cart (in case the user wants more than one of any product).

```
Public Sub Add(ProductID)

    ' Make sure we know for certain what type the ID is
    ProductID = CLng(ProductID)

    ' Loop the existing items in the collection
    Dim blnOK As Boolean
    blnOK = False
    Dim objItem As CartItem
```

Continued on Following Page

```
    For Each objItem In Items

        ' Is this item already in the cart?
        If objItem.ProductID = ProductID Then

            ' Incremement the quantity, flag as "found" and quit the loop
            objItem.Quantity = objItem.Quantity + 1
            blnOK = True
            Exit For

        End If

    Next

    ' Did we manage to find it?
    If blnOK = False Then

        ' Create and configure the new item
        Dim objNewItem As CartItem
        Set objNewItem = New CartItem
        objNewItem.ProductID = ProductID

        ' Add the item to the collection
        Items.Add objNewItem

    End If
End Sub
```

This code iterates through our `Items` collection, to see whether we already have the product with the supplied ID in it. If so, we add one to the `CartItem`'s `Quantity` property. If not, we add a new item with the specified `ProductID` to the `Cart`'s `Items` collection.

The Shopping Cart Page

Now that we've got all that in place, we can start to build our `cart.asp` page, which will represent the customer's shopping cart.

Checking for an Existing Cart

Firstly, let's see how we can check to see whether a cart's already been created for the visitor, and if not, how we are to create one:

```
<html>
<title>Darren's Store</title>
<%

    ' Connect to the store
    Set Darren = Server.CreateObject("DarrenStore.Store")

    ' Do we have a cart already?
    if isempty(session("cart")) then
        set session("cart") = Darren.NewCart
    end if
```

We instantiate our `Store` object; then we check to see whether the `cart` session variable has already been assigned a value. All variables in VBScript are of type `Variant`, and any to which no value has yet been assigned are said to be `Empty`. VBScript provides an `IsEmpty` function which returns `True` if the variable is `Empty` and `False` if it has been populated. So we can use this function to see whether we already have a `Cart` object instantiated; if not, we call our `NewCart` method to set the `cart` variable to equal a new instance of the `Cart` object.

Adding a Product to the Cart

Before we finish this first section of ASP code, we will add the new item to the cart. To do this, we call our `Cart` object's `Add` method:

```
    session("cart").add Request.QueryString("add")
%>
```

When the user clicked on **Buy**, `cart.asp` was requested with a query appended to the URL with a question mark. This query consisted of the variable `"add"` and the item's `ProductID`:

```
response.write "<a href=""cart.asp?add=" & products("productid") & """">"
```

This line writes a hyperlink to the browser, which when followed will produce a request for a page in this format:

cart.asp?add=1

The query following the URL can be accessed in an Active Server Page through the `Request.QueryString` collection. This collection contains all the variables passed into the query and their values. In our case, we only have the variable `add`, with (in the example above) the value 1. We can access this value by calling `Request.QueryString` with the name of the variable passed in, and we can in turn pass this value to our `Add` method.

The Table for the Cart Items

Now we can start building the framework for the page. The items in the cart will be displayed in an HTML table, together with the price of each item, the quantity ordered and the total cost.

```
<!-- header, and a link back to the catalog -->
<font size=5>Your Cart</font>
<br>
<a href="default.asp">Back to catalog</a>
<br><br>

<!-- table for cart items -->
<table border=1>

<!--Table heading -->
<tr><td>Name</td><td>Quantity</td><td>Each</td><td>Total</td></tr>
```

Once the framework for this table is in place, we can retrieve the items from the `Cart` object and add each one to the table. The `CartItem` object holds only the ID of the product, so in order to display the name, price etc., we must use the `Store` object to get that information from the database.

```
<%
    ' Hold the total somewhere...
    total = 0

    ' Loop all of the items in the cart
    for each item in session("cart").items

        ' Each cart item only holds the ID of the product.
        ' We have to use the DarrenStore.Store object to get the
        ' item details back from the database
        set objRecProduct = Darren.GetProductInfo(item.productid)
        if not objRecProduct.eof then

            ' Draw in the name of the item
            response.write "<tr><td>"
            response.write objRecProduct("mfrname") & " " & _
                        objRecProduct("productname")

            ' Draw in the quantity that we've chosen
            response.write "</td><td>"
            response.write item.quantity

            ' Draw in the line price
            response.write "</td><td align=right>"
            response.write FormatCurrency(objRecProduct("price"), 2)

            ' Draw in the total for the line and increase the total
            response.write "</td><td align=right>"
            response.write FormatCurrency(objRecProduct("price") _
                        * item.quantity, 2)
            total = total + (objRecProduct("price") * item.quantity)
            response.write "</td></tr>"

        end if
        objRecProduct.close
        set objRecProduct = nothing

    next

    ' Draw the total
    response.write "<tr><td colspan=4 align=right><b>Total: "
    response.write formatcurrency(total, 2)
    response.write "</b></td></tr>"
%>

</table>
</body>
```

Iterating through all the objects in the `Items` collection, we call the `GetProductInfo` method for each one, and add the details to our HTML table representing the shopping cart.

Finally, we have to close the resources that we've used on the page:

```
<%
    ' Close the store
    Set Darren = Nothing
%>
</html>
```

The screenshot shows our cart when it's been populated with a couple of items:

Processing the Order

We've got our storefront set up now, and visitors to the web site can fill their carts with all sorts of goodies, but there's still no way for the customer to send in their order. This is where we're going to have to start looking at how we can bring transactions into the picture. Up until now, we haven't been doing anything that needs transactions. Now money will be changing hands, and we need to follow specific business procedures, so we will have to use transactions.

Building the Business Object

To isolate our business object, let's start another VB project. Call this one `DarrenBusiness`. Rename our starter class to `OrderProcessor`.

Now we have to set up our project to create objects suitable for running inside MTS. As we've seen, the first step in is to set the `MTSTransactionMode` property of our class to `RequiresNewTransaction`. This tells MTS that when the object is created, a new transaction should be started:

When our component is running inside MTS, MTS can provide us with some environmental information as well as a few methods that we have to use in order to tell MTS about the state of *our* transaction's execution. It's critical that we inform MTS whether our transaction succeeded or failed.

To tie our component in with MTS, we need to include a reference to the MTS type library. Select Project | References and select the Microsoft Transaction Server Type Library checkbox.

The ObjectControl Interface

When an application (in this case, our Active Server Page) creates an instance of our component, COM will manage the connection to MTS for us. Immediately after our component has been created, MTS will look for an implementation of an `ObjectControl` interface; it uses this to tell our object when a client has started to use it, and when it has finished using it. We can use the `ObjectControl`'s `Activate` event (fired when a client starts to use the object) to instantiate an `ObjectContext` object, which we can use to report back to MTS the state of our transaction as it executes. We met this object earlier in the applications we developed in Chapters 11 and 13. Similarly, we can release the `ObjectContext` object in the `ObjectControl`'s `Deactivate` event, fired when a client releases the object.

The following code is designed both to manage the `ObjectContext` object that MTS gives us and to tell MTS that we support the `ObjectControl` interface:

```
' Create somewhere to put the ObjectContext object
' that MTS will give us...
Private m_objCtx As ObjectContext

' Tell MTS that we support the ObjectControl interface...
Implements ObjectControl
```

```
' MTS will call this when our object is instantiated...
Private Sub ObjectControl_Activate()
    Set m_objCtx = GetObjectContext
End Sub
```

```
' and MTS will call this when our object is deleted...
Private Sub ObjectControl_Deactivate()
    Set m_objCtx = Nothing
End Sub
```

The ProcessOrder Method

Remember that we've created this object in order to process an order from the Web site. For a complete order, we're going to need a list of the items the customer wants to purchase, and his or her address and payment information. To keep this example as compact as possible, we're not going to worry about creating forms and validation code to capture the customer's information. Instead, before making the call we're going to manually construct a `Scripting.Dictionary` object and populate this with dummy data. This object acts a bit like a two-dimensional array and holds key/item pairs, each of which contains a name (or key) for the item, and its value. We're going to cover all this in a little while, but we do need to make a reference to it in the `ProcessOrder` method we're about to start building.

Add the following `ProcessOrder` method to the object. We'll come back to it in a later section and make it do something!

```
Public Function ProcessOrder(cart, address)
    ProcessOrder = True
End Function
```

Setting Binary Compatibility

Unlike IIS, MTS requires a binary copy of the VB DLL to exist. To do this, we need to save the project and make the DLL by selecting File | Make DarrenBusiness.dll from the toolbar.

IIS does not require a binary copy of the VB DLL. Visual Basic can, in effect, trick IIS into believing the object exists by using a small stub DLL that marshals calls from ASP into your Visual Basic debugging environment.

Once we've compiled the DLL, we need to configure the project to use binary compatibility to protect the project from changes that would affect the objects running in other processes. Simply put, VB will throw an error if you try and take anything *out* of the project, so you can't remove any properties or methods once they've been imported into the MTS environment.

Version compatibility can be set on the Component tab of the Project Properties dialog box:

For more information about version compatibility, see Chapter 11.

Creating the MTS Package

That's all we need to do in VB; now we have to set up MTS. This process is essentially the same as that followed for the applications developed in Chapters 11 and 13, so we'll run through it quite quickly. Open MTS Explorer and navigate to the Packages Installed branch of the management tree, under My Computer. Right-click on Packages Installed and select New | Package.

The Package Wizard will appear and ask us if we want to install a pre-built package, or create a new one. We're going to create a new one now, but later in this chapter we'll see how to export a package so we can transfer it to another computer.

On the next screen, select Create an Empty Package to proceed, and when prompted for a package name, enter DarrenBusiness.

For system security, MTS needs to know which user we'll be impersonating when we use this object. It does this to make sure that the component can only access the resources that the system administrator deems suitable. For this example, we'll use the Administrator account, so set up the identity as shown in this screenshot:

After this step, the new package will be created. Now let's add our new business object component.

Installing the Component

Expand the DarrenBusiness package, right-click on Components and select New | Component. The Component Wizard will now appear. The opening screen of this wizard presents two options: to Install new component(s) or to Import component(s) that are already registered. We'll install a new component here, so click on the first button.

Although our VB component was registered on the computer when it was compiled, it's easier to install new components. The dialog displayed if you choose to import existing components will display a massive list of every ActiveX object on your computer. It's quicker and simpler to point to a DLL on your disk.

After this, we'll be prompted to supply the file names of the DLLs we want to add to the package. Click Add Files and select the Visual Basic DLL that we compiled earlier (DarrenBusiness.dll). When you add the component, MTS will give us a list of the objects that it found inside this object:

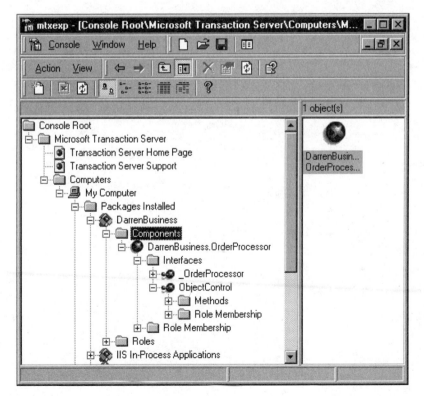

You should now be able to see the new package and its OrderProcessor component inside MTS Explorer:

The Checkout Page

So now we're ready to implement the functionality to complete the order. We'll put this in a new Active Server Page, so that when the user navigates to this page, the order will automatically be finalized. Create this new ASP file and call it `Checkout.asp`:

```
<html>

<title>Darren's Store</title>

<%
    ' connect to the store
    Set darren = Server.CreateObject("darrenstore.store")
%>

    <body>

        <font size=5>Checkout</font>
        <br><br>

        <%

            ' Create the order processor object...
            Set processor = Server.CreateObject("darrenbusiness.orderprocessor")

            ' Create some dummy address and credit card info...
            ' (usually, we'd capture this in a form, but we want this
            ' example to be brief)
            Dim address
            Set address = Server.CreateObject("scripting.dictionary")
            address.Add "FirstName", "Alex"
            address.Add "LastName", "Drew"
            address.Add "Address 1", "1234 Nowhere St."
            address.Add "Address 2", "#1115"
            address.Add "City", "Tempe"
            address.Add "State", "AZ"
            address.Add "ZIP", "85044"
            address.Add "Country", "USA"
            address.Add "Email", "alexd@nocompany.com"
            address.Add "Card", "4929 1234 1234 1234"
            address.Add "CartExpires", "04/2001"

            ' now, pass the cart and the address to the processor...
            result = processor.ProcessOrder(session("cart"), address)
            if result = true then
                response.write "Your order was processed!"
            else
                response.write "Your order was not processed..."
            end if

            ' cleanup
            set address = nothing
            set processor = nothing

        %>

    </body>

    <%
```

```
        ' Close the store
        Set Darren = Nothing
    %>

</html>
```

As mentioned earlier, we're going to cheat a bit and just use dummy details for a fictitious customer, rather than create a form for the user to input details. So after creating instances of our `Store` and `OrderProcessor` objects, we instantiate the ASP `Scripting.Dictionary` object and populate it with some key/item pairs containing details about our customer, such as name, address and credit card number. We then call the `ProcessOrder` method; this returns a Boolean value indicating whether or not the order was successfully completed (although at the moment, remember, it always returns `True`). When we've got this value, we just inform the customer what the result is and release all our objects.

Before we test the code, we need to add a link to the checkout page, so go quickly back to `cart.asp` and add this line after the table that renders the cart:

```
<a href="checkout.asp">Checkout!</a>
```

Now test the page by filling your cart with goodies and clicking on Checkout! You should see a screen like this:

Exploring the ObjectContext Object

To test the code further, switch to the VB project and put a breakpoint on the beginning of the `ObjectControl_Activate` method. Now start the project again, open the site, browse the product catalog, add a few things to the cart and then click the checkout link.

Visual Basic will break on the `ObjectControl_Activate` line. The `GetObjectContext` method is a global method that stays around for as long as your component is executing. Its function is to provide access to the MTS `ObjectContext` object. Open the Immediate Window and try exploring this object a little. Print the values of some of its properties such as those below, and see what results you get.

```
' Ask if we're running inside of a transaction...
?GetObjectContext.IsInTransaction
True

' Ask if security is enabled...
?GetObjectContext.IsSecurityEnabled
True

' Ask for the name of the user making the call...
' (in this case, because we're inside IIS, we'll get IIS's
' anonymous user)
?GetObjectContext.Security.GetDirectCallerName
MARS\IUSR_MYWEBANON
```

Managing the Transaction

We're now at a point where we have all our presentation and business objects in place. Now we can start writing some code that will manage our transaction. Again, to keep this brief we won't go into detail about how you actually process an e-commerce transaction – we'll just demonstrate one method of returning error information and show how you can commit or abort the transaction.

In a production environment, our ProcessOrder method would create a customer, check stock levels, produce pick lists, produce delivery notes and process credit cards. Each of those operations would be broken down into one or more "primitive" private functions; we'll just define a CreateCustomer method to create the customer. It's a good idea to design these objects so that they use a common method of returning success or error codes. Here, we're using a Boolean variable called blnResult. Each primitive function will return a simple True or False value to indicate its success. (We'll cover methods later that will let the primitive functions themselves deal with sending an error report to the appropriate persons.) Then, when we've finished processing the order, we check the value of blnResult and tell MTS whether to commit (SetComplete) or roll back (SetAbort) the transaction. Enter this ProcessOrder method to replace the dummy method we created earlier:

```
' Process the order...
Public Function ProcessOrder(cart, address) As Boolean

    ' Somewhere to put the result...
    Dim blnResult As Boolean
    blnResult = False

    ' Firstly, create a new customer...
    ' (we'll implement this function in the next section)
    blnResult = CreateCustomer(address)

    ' Only do the rest if that succeeded...
    If blnResult = True Then
        ' This is where we would mess about with the
        ' products and create the actual order...
    End If

    ' Did we manage it?
    If blnResult = True Then

        ' Tell MTS we did it!
        m_objCtx.SetComplete

    Else
```

```
            ' Tell MTS it all went wrong!
            m_objCtx.SetAbort

      End If

      ' Return the result back to the caller...
      ProcessOrder = blnResult

End Function
```

Creating a New Customer

This calls a private `CreateCustomer` function to create the new customer, so create one of those too:

```
' Insert a new customer into the database based on the information
' contained in the "address" collection...
Private Function CreateCustomer(address)

    ' pretend we succeeded...
    CreateCustomer = True

End Function
```

If you try refreshing the checkout page now, you should get a "success" message. Return a `False` value from `CreateCustomer` and you'll get a "failure" message.

Better Error Reporting

The message "Your order was not processed..." is unlikely to help either your customer or your system administrator, but we can return better error messages to both.

As you know, ASP is running inside the MTS environment, just like our own objects. ASP makes our lives easier by making its five intrinsic objects (`Response`, `Request`, `Session`, `Server` and `Application`) available to us inside our VB component. (If you're unfamiliar with the ASP object model, have a look at Appendix K). This means that we can write HTML directly to the client from anywhere in our component. It also means we can log the error somewhere, or even send an email to a system administrator.

To illustrate this, let's change the `CreateCustomer` function so that it raises an error:

```
Private Function CreateCustomer(address)

    ' report an error
    ReportError "I don't like the name " & address("FirstName") & _
                address("LastName") & "!"

    ' tell it we failed...
    CreateCustomer = False

End Function
```

This function now calls a `ReportError` subroutine, which we'll see in just a bit, passing in an error message as a parameter, and returns the value `False`.

We can access the ASP intrinsic objects through the `Item` property of the `ObjectContext` object. However, we have to allow for the fact that the object may not be running inside ASP (our object should be portable to different environments), so we need to check to make sure the object is available before we call it. We can do this by calling the `TypeName` function on the object. This function returns a string indicating the data type of a variable; for an object of a defined type, it returns the specific type name for that object.

This `ReportError` method writes the supplied error message to the ASP `Response` object if it's there, and emails the system administrator even if it's not. If we do actually have a `Response` object, it will have a type name of `"IResponse"`, and if so, we can use this to send our error message to the browser. The second part of this code illustrates how we might send an email to the system administrator for the site.

```
Private Function ReportError(message)

    ' Do we have the ASP Response intrinsic object?
    If TypeName(m_objCtx.Item("Response")) = "IResponse" Then
        m_objCtx.Item("Response").Write "<font color=#800e000f>"
        m_objCtx.Item("Response").Write message
        m_objCtx.Item("Response").Write "</font><br><br>"
    End If

    ' Either way, send an e-mail to the sysadmin...
    Dim email
    Set email = CreateObject("SomeEmailComponent")
    email.AddRecipient "sysadmin@darrenstore.com"
    email.AddText "An error has occurred: " & message
    email.Send
    Set email = Nothing

End Function
```

> The `SomeEmailComponent` object in the example, obviously, won't exist on your system. If you want this functionality in your objects, you should replace these lines with the lines suited to your favorite e-mail component.

The screenshot shows our new Checkout page, complete with error message:

You can access each of the ASP intrinsic objects using the same approach, for example using `m_objCtx.Item("Request")` or `m_objCtx.Item("Server")`. A word of warning, however: keys on dictionaries like `Item` are case sensitive, so none of these will work:

```
m_objCtx.Item("RESPONSE")
m_objCtx.Item("resPONSE")
m_objCtx.Item("response")   ' careful of this one!
```

> **Be particularly careful of the last one. I spent ages trying to get this to work, but VB refused to give me access to the ASP objects, even though I strongly suspected they were there! Like a lot of people, I tend to write Visual Basic code all in lower-case. I forgot that dictionaries are case-sensitive, so my calls to `Item("response")` would yield no results!**

How Does MTS Handle Database Changes?

When I first started to investigate MTS, this was one of the things that most confused me. I couldn't understand how to tell SQL Server to behave differently when it's running inside a transaction.

The reason for my misunderstanding is that you don't have to tell SQL Server *anything* about that fact you're running inside of a transaction. When you ask for a database connection inside a transaction, the actual connection comes from something called an "ODBC Resource Dispenser".

The Dispenser keeps a "pool" of connections available, so that objects that need database connections don't have to go through the relatively expensive operation of actually connecting to the database. It will keep a few connection objects available and simply return handles to them when the objects need them. Secondly, the Dispenser tells SQL Server that it's running inside a transaction *automatically*, so you don't have to worry about it. But it will only do this if a new transaction has been started. By setting the `RequiresNewTransaction` property on our object, we're telling MTS to start a new transaction so, by association, the ODBC Resource Dispenser will tell SQL Server we are running inside a transaction.

The Customers Table

Let's try this out quickly so you can get a feel for how it works. In SQL Server Enterprise Manager, add a table called `Customers` to the `Darren` database and enter fields as in the screenshot:

Column Name	Datatype	Length	Precision	Scale	Allow Nulls	Default Value	Identity	Identity Seed	Identity Increment	Is RowGuid
CustomerID	int	4	10	0			✓	1	1	
First	nvarchar	50	0	0	✓					
Last	nvarchar	50	0	0	✓					
Email	nvarchar	50	0	0	✓					

Now let's change our `CreateCustomer` function so that it populates this table from our `Dictionary` object:

```
Private Function CreateCustomer(address)

    ' get a connection to the store...
    Dim store
    Set store = CreateObject("darrenstore.store")

    ' make a SQL string based on the address Dictionary...
    Dim strSQL
    strSQL = "insert into customers (first, last, email) values ("
    strSQL = strSQL & "'" & address("FirstName") & "', "
    strSQL = strSQL & "'" & address("LastName") & "', "
    strSQL = strSQL & "'" & address("Email") & "')"
    store.propConn.Execute strSQL

    ' cleanup...
    Set store = Nothing

    ' tell it we succeeded...
    CreateCustomer = True

End Function
```

> **Remember, watch the case on the "address" dictionary items!**

Now put a breakpoint on the `store.propConn.Execute strSQL` line and run the project and then refresh your Browser. Visual Basic should stop on the appropriate line.

Viewing Tables Used by Transactions

With VB still stopped, switch to SQL Server Enterprise Manager, right-click on the `Customers` table and select **Open Table | Return all Rows**. Enterprise Manager will return an empty table.

Now, switch back to VB and step over the `Execute` line. Switch to Enterprise Manager and click the Run toolbar button. What happens now is strange, and I wanted to bring it to your attention. Basically, when a table is being used in a transaction, Enterprise Manager is unable to open it properly. You will either get a message stating that the operation has been canceled, or the table will just remain empty, displaying no rows. What's important is that Enterprise Manager will not return the row you have just inserted, because the transaction has neither been committed nor aborted and so the row is in an unknown state.

If you run your VB project, your object will finish its work. When it returns to the `ProcessOrder` method, the `True` value you returned from `CreateCustomer` will instruct `ProcessOrder` to go ahead and commit the transaction by calling `m_objCtx.SetComplete`. When the ASP code releases the reference to the `DarrenBusiness.OrderProcessor` object the transaction will be deemed finished and the rows will then and only then be visible to Enterprise Manager and to any other objects which are also using the database.

If any of the objects inside the transaction called `GetObjectContext.SetAbort`, then none of the changes by any of the objects running inside that transaction would be committed to the database.

Exporting Packages

When you start building your applications, you'll find that your packages will end up containing quite a few separate components. If you then want to get the same application running inside MTS on another computer, you'll have to recreate the package on that new computer.

MTS tries to make this a little easier by allowing you to export the configuration of the package to a .PAK file. To make a .PAK file, right-click on the DarrenBusiness package and select Export. The Export Package dialog will appear:

With your package saved to a .PAK file, you can now recreate the package on another computer by selecting Install pre-built packages in the MTS Package Wizard. A word of warning, however - the package does *not* contain the actual components themselves. You'll still need to transfer the objects over to the new computer; we looked at the topic of deploying components in Chapter 17.

Summary

Most of the material in this case study has been met before, but it should have provided you with more experience of building n-tier database applications. We also added a new element by showing you how to incorporate ASP into your applications, so that they can be run across the Internet. So now you should:

> Know how to build a database in SQL Server.

> Know how to separate your business objects from your presentation code.

> Understand the concepts behind abstracting database connectivity away from the presentation code developers.

> Know how to create new MTS packages and import your components into them.

> Know how to split your component's methods into a number of primitive functions, each of which are responsible for a specific task inside the transaction.

> Know how to listen to MTS and communicate back to it the state of your objects.

> Know how to return informative errors back to customers and system administrators.

> Understand what happens to database rows when transactions are committed or aborted.

> Know how to export your MTS packages for deployment onto other computers.

Suppliers

- SupplierID
- CompanyName
- ContactName
- ContactTitle
- Address
- City
- Region
- PostalCode
- Country
- Phone
- Fax
- HomePage

Products

- ProductID
- ProductName
- SupplierID
- CategoryID
- QuantityPerUnit
- UnitPrice
- UnitsInStock
- UnitsOnOrder
- ReorderLevel
- Discontinued

Categories

- CategoryID
- CategoryName
- Description
- Picture

6

SQL: Overview and the ANSI SQL-92 Standard

Overview

SQL (Structured Query Language) is a language used to manipulate and retrieve data from a relational database. Using SQL, you can update information in database tables, create or change the structure of the database and query the database to retrieve information. ANSI SQL-92 is the most recent formal release of the industry standard that defines the core elements of SQL. Although it has established a comprehensive baseline for the implementation of many contemporary database features, not all vendors implement the standard perfectly.

Three levels of ANSI SQL-92 conformance have been established. They are:

> **Entry SQL** – representing essentially a full implementation of the previous ANSI SQL standard, SQL-89.

> **Intermediate SQL** – indicates Entry SQL conformance, plus implementation of a specific subset of the new capabilities of ANSI SQL-92

> **Full SQL** – indicates Intermediate SQL conformance, plus nearly a dozen additional features.

A full discussion of the complete SQL standard is not one for the programming "faint of heart". Such a complete discussion would take up an entire book and, as such, is beyond the scope of this appendix. Instead it will provide an overview of the most commonly used ANSI SQL commands and is intended as a basic command reference rather than a detailed technical treatise.

The three appendices following this one will address specific areas in which various major vendors' products depart from or enhance behavior defined by ANSI SQL-92. Specifically, it will deal with the different flavors of SQL provided by MS SQL Server, Oracle and MS Access (Jet)

Notation

As with any programming language, knowledge of the language syntax is necessary to understand its definitions. This appendix uses a standard format for the presentation of SQL command syntax. Adherence to certain conventions, in this manner, aids in the identification of the various elements of each command. Such conventions (or similar) are used consistently in the presentation of SQL command syntax across the industry:

> < > Element names in the SQL syntax will be enclosed in angle brackets, e.g. <table name>. The angle brackets are not to be included in the SQL command.

> {} Required portions of the SQL syntax are enclosed in braces. The entire portion contained in the braces must be entered. The braces are not to be included in the SQL command.

> [ ] Optional portions of the SQL syntax will be enclosed in square brackets. The square brackets are not to be included in the SQL command.

> | When a choice of parameters or elements is offered, the pipe character will separate the choices. The pipe is not to be included in the SQL command.

> ::= Certain important commands (e.g. CREATE TABLE, SELECT) are investigated in some detail. When defining a portion of the syntax separate from the command, the definition operator will be used.

> … When a particular portion of the SQL syntax can be repeated, this will be indicated by the ellipsis.

> KEYWORD SQL keywords are displayed in uppercase. Keywords in the syntax must be typed exactly as they are displayed. Interpretation of keywords is not case sensitive, so they can be entered in either upper or lower case (although upper case is recommended).

SQL Data Types

Each column of a table essentially represents an allocated space for storage of data. In order for the database to know how to represent and use this data, it must know what type of data it is. SQL provides a series of data types that can be used to define columns in the database.

Data types in SQL fall into three categories: **character**, **numeric**, and **date/time**.

Character Data Types

Character data types can be defined as either fixed length or variable length strings.

CHAR(n) (or CHARACTER(n)) represents a fixed length string of (n) characters. The value of (n) must be greater than zero.

VARCHAR(n) (or CHARACTER VARYING(n)) represents a string which can vary in length from one to n characters. Again, n must be greater than zero.

The primary reason for the existence of these different data types is resource usage. Implementation of variable length strings allows use of data types with large lengths (e.g. VARCHAR(255)), without having to pay the disk resource usage penalty of allocating 255 characters for each instance of the column. However, there is a processing overhead penalty to be paid for using variable length rather than fixed length strings. If the column value will always contain code that is n characters in length and the column will always (almost always) be populated, then use fixed length strings (CHAR). If the column will contain varying lengths of strings (like a description field, for example) or may often be empty, use variable strings (VARCHAR).

Here is an example of a table creation command using these character types:

```
CREATE TABLE MyTable
(MyFixedString CHAR(10),
MyVariableString VARCHAR(10) )
```

Numeric Types

There is a wide range of numeric data types available in SQL. An important goal in database development is the storage and manipulation of data in as efficient a manner as possible. This goal has led to the definition of several different numeric types that allow exact modeling of the type of numbers to be used.

In a similar vein to the definition of fixed and variable length strings, numeric data types can be defined as either **exact** or **approximate** numbers.

Exact Numerics

INTEGER: No fractional component. Precision (maximum allowed number of digits) depends on specific implementation (e.g. 16-bit or 32-bit).
SMALLINT: As INTEGER. Precision cannot be greater than INTEGER, for a specific implementation.
NUMERIC(precision, scale): Can have fractional and integer components. Precision and scale(number of digits in fractional component) exactly as specified.
DECIMAL(precision, scale): As NUMERIC except that precision may be equal to or greater than that specified.

Approximate Numerics

REAL: A single-precision floating-point value (precision depends on implementation).
DOUBLE PRECISION: double-precision floating point number (precision depends on implementation).
FLOAT [(precision)]: A floating point number for which the precision may be specified.

For example:

```
CREATE TABLE MyNumericTable
(MyInteger INTEGER,
MyNumeric NUMERIC(8,2),
MyFloat FLOAT )
```

Date/Time Data Types

The ANSI-92 standard defines DATE, TIME and TIMESTAMP data types. Although all SQL implementations offer DATE data types and most also have TIME and TIMESTAMP (combination of date and time) data types, it is very important that to check your specific vendor type list.

Now that we have discussed our syntax conventions and understand what types of data we can deal with, we are ready to begin reviewing the actual SQL commands. Before we do that, however, let's discuss how SQL commands can be arranged by their function. This will provide us a logical sequence for discussing the specific commands.

SQL Sublanguages

SQL can be divided into three sublanguages, each providing a specific set of functions. These sublanguages serve to categorize the available functions in a similar manner to the way in which we may categorize the creation, loading and maintenance of the database itself. The three SQL sublanguages are: Data Definition Language (DDL), Data Manipulation Language (DML) and Data Control Language (DCL).

Data Definition Language (DDL)

Data Definition Language allows the creation, modification and deletion of objects in the database structure. DDL represents the starting point for database creation and maintenance processes. DDL does not enable the addition or retrieval of data in the database - it's strictly for building and maintaining the structure.

Sample commands: CREATE, ALTER, DELETE

Data Manipulation Language (DML)

Data Manipulation Language enables retrieval as well as addition, deletion and updating of information in the database. The vast majority of the average developer's time is spent using the data retrieval capabilities of DML. Note that DML cannot be used to change the structure of the underlying database.

Sample commands: SELECT, INSERT, UPDATE, DELETE

Data Control Language (DCL)

Data Control Language enables control over the security of objects in the database. Each user can be granted rights to specific objects in the database such as tables, views and procedures. DCL can also be used to control database level rights, such as who has permission to assign access rights to other users.

Sample commands: `GRANT, REVOKE`

ANSI SQL-92

This section covers some of the most common ANSI-92 SQL commands and functions. The most commonly used commands are covered in considerable detail, while for others only the general syntax is given. Occasionally, examples are given to elucidate the manner in which the syntax works.

Explicit Transaction Commands

ANSI-92 supports certain commands dealing with transactions (it does not specify any command for starting a transaction):

COMMIT (or COMMIT WORK)

Writes the changes from the transaction to the database and marks the transaction as completed.

ROLLBACK (or ROLLBACK WORK)

Any changes made are undone and database restored to original state.

ANSI SQL-92 Commands

The following commands are all part of the ANSI SQL-92 specification and are dealt with in alphabetical order. Occasionally, specific examples are given to illustrate use of the general syntax.

ALTER DOMAIN

The domain of a table column defines the finite range of values that can be stored in that column.

```
ALTER DOMAIN <domain name>
ADD <domain constraint definition> |
DROP CONSTRAINT <constraint name> |
SET DEFAULT <default value> |
DROP DEFAULT
```

ALTER TABLE

```
ALTER TABLE <table name> <action>
```

<action> ::= <add table constraint> | <drop table constraint> | <add column> |
<alter column> | <drop column>

> <add table constraint> ::= ADD <table constraint definition>

> <drop table constraint> ::= DROP CONSTRAINT <constraint name> [RESTRICT |
>   CASCADE].

The RESTRICT and CASCADE qualifiers are referred to as drop behaviors. They control the manner in which a drop is executed if table relationships are being used. Technically they are required elements, however most database vendors either do not have them implemented or have them implemented as optional elements. Check your vendor's SQL implementation to find out if and how these qualifiers are implemented.

> <add column> ::= ADD [COLUMN] <column definition>. The new column will be added after the last column in the table. The new column must obey all rules defined in the table.

> <alter column> ::= ALTER [COLUMN] <column name> { SET<default specifier> |
>   DROP DEFAULT }

The SET<default specifier> command will change the existing default condition applied to a column (see CREATE TABLE). The DROP DEFAULT command will remove an existing default condition on a column.

You cannot change the data type of a column using ALTER TABLE. Each vendor uses their own methods of storing database columns based on the data type, the hardware implementation, and their own experience of what works best. Combine this with the complexities of trying to decide whether or not existing data can be changed from one data type to another and you have quite a mess on your hands. In order to change a column's data type, the table must be recreated from scratch (preserving the existing data for reloading if applicable).

> <drop column> ::= DROP [COLUMN] <column name> [RESTRICT | CASCADE]

For example:
```
ALTER TABLE Customers DROP COLUMN Region
```

CLOSE

```
CLOSE <cursor name>
```

CONNECT

Connects to a database.

CREATE ASSERTION

Creates an assertion (a constraint not associated with a specific table).

CREATE CHARACTER SET

CREATE DOMAIN

```
CREATE DOMAIN <domain name> [AS] < data type>[DEFAULT <default value>]
CHECK <check predicate>[INITIALLY DEFERRED | INITIALLY IMMEDIATE |DEFERRABLE | NOT
DEFERRABLE]
```

CREATE SCHEMA

A schema is a complete description of the structure of the entire database, including the database data, rules governing the structure of this data, operators and any other defined rules.

```
CREATE SCHEMA <schema name> | AUTHORIZATION <authorization ID> | <schema name>
AUTHORIZATION <authorization ID>
```

CREATE TABLE

```
CREATE TABLE [[GLOBAL|LOCAL] TEMPORARY]<table name>
                ({ <column definition> [ <column constraint> ] } [,…])
                [ON COMMIT DELETE|PRESERVE ROWS]
```

<column definition> ::= <column name> (<data type>| <domain name>) [<default specifier>]

You cannot define a column without also specifying the type of data it will hold (the designation of a domain - an expression of permissible values for the column- is also supported):

```
CREATE TABLE MyTable
            (Column1 INTEGER,
            Column2 CHARACTER(3),
            Column4 REAL)
```

<default specifier> ::= DEFAULT <value> | <system value> | NULL

The optional <default specifier> is used to assign standard, or default, values to particular columns. Three options are available for the <default specifier>:

> ➤ <value> : literal value, such as "99.99" or "USA".

> ➤ <system value> : such as the current date and time, server name, or other system provided value.

> ➤ NULL : a null value is assigned (this is the default if <default specifier> is not included in the statement.

```
<column constraint> ::= NOT NULL | <uniqueness> | <references> | <check
constraint>
```

A constraint is applied to a column and represents a rule that will be applied to values entered into that column. There are four types of constraints that can be applied to a column. One or more can be can be used together with NOT NULL:

> ➤ NOT NULL: This constraint prevents a row from being added if no value is provided for that specific field. Note that if a default is specified for the field, that value will be used automatically and the NOT NULL constraint will be satisfied even if you don't provide a value.

> ➤ <uniqueness> ::= UNIQUE | PRIMARY KEY. Each of these keywords instructs the database server not to allow duplicate values in a specified column. The PRIMARY KEY keyword indicates that the column should be used as the primary key for that table. Only one primary key column per table is allowed whereas several columns may have the UNIQUE constraint applied. The primary key determines in what default order records are to be retrieved. When declaring a primary key, the NOT NULL constraint is applied automatically. The UNIQUE constraint does not automatically invoke the NOT NULL condition. One or more null-valued rows for a column are allowed with the UNIQUE constraint, unless NOT NULL is also specified.

> ➤ <references> ::= REFERENCES <referenced table name> [(referenced table column name)]. This constraint does not specifically control the value to be inserted in a column, but rather establishes a relationship between the column and another column of a referenced table. This means that a value inserted into a column in one table must also exist in a particular column of the referenced table:

```
CREATE TABLE Orders
     (...(other columns),
      CustomerID INTEGER NOT NULL REFERENCES Customers(CustomerID))
```

> ➤ <check constraint> ::= CHECK (<logical expression>). This allows the application of a test (or condition), based on a logical expression, to each row that inserted. If the expression evaluates to FALSE or UNKNOWN, then the insert will fail. The <logical expression> can be any condition that is a valid SQL logical expression (e.g. ordervalue > 500). Powerful rules can be established linking various columns (from multiple tables) using this constraint.

CREATE TRANSLATION

CREATE VIEW

```
CREATE VIEW <virtual table name> [ (<column list>) ]
AS <query expression> [WITH [CASCADED | LOCAL]CHECK OPTION]
```

<column list> is optional and allows you to control the name of the columns referenced through the view.

<query expression> can be any valid SELECT statement.

```
CREATE VIEW MyOrderView AS
     (SELECT C.Name, CO.Quantity, E.Name
      FROM Customers AS C, CustomerOrders AS CO, Employees AS E
      WHERE C.CustomerID = CO.CustomerID
      AND E.EmployeeID = CO.EmployeeID)
```

DECLARE CURSOR

Cursors convert result sets from SQL queries into records whereby the application program can access each row individually. DECLARE CURSOR defines the name of the cursor and its scope.

```
DECLARE <cursor name> [INSENSITIVE] [SCROLL]
CURSOR FOR <cursor specification>
```

>   <cursor specification> ::= <query expression> [ORDER BY <sort specification list>] [<updatability clause>]

>   <updatability clause> ::= FOR {READ ONLY | UPDATE [OF <column name list>]}

>   <sort specification list> ::= <sort specification> [(<comma><sort specification>)...]

>   <sort specification> ::= <sort key> [<collate clause>] [ASC | DESC]

>   <sort key> ::= <column name> | <unsigned integer>

DECLARE LOCAL TEMPORARY TABLE

DELETE

```
DELETE FROM <table name> [ WHERE <search condition> ]
```

The following statement would remove every row from the Orders table:

```
DELETE FROM Orders
```

DISCONNECT

DROP ASSERTION

Removes an assertion from a schema.

DROP CHARACTER SET

DROP COLLATION

DROP DOMAIN

```
DROP DOMAIN <domain name> [RESTRICT | CASCADE]
```

DROP SCHEMA

```
DROP SCHEMA <schema name> [RESTRICT | CASCADE]
```

DROP TABLE

This statement deletes the table definition and all the data from the table. Thus, unless there exists script for the table creation and/or a backup of the data, the table would need to be rebuilt from scratch, should it be needed again.

```
DROP TABLE <table name> [RESTRICT | CASCADE]
```

DROP TRANSLATION

DROP VIEW

```
DROP VIEW <table name> [RESTRICT | CASCADE]
```

FETCH

The FETCH statement retrieves data using a cursor.

```
FETCH [<fetch orientation>]
FROM <cursor name>
INTO <fetch target list>
```

>   `<fetch orientation>` ::= NEXT |PRIOR | FIRST | LAST | {ABSOLUTE | RELATIVE} `<ROW NUMBER>`

>   `<fetch target list>` ::= `<target specification>` [(`<comma><target specification>`...]

Variables in the `<fetch target list>` are host variables, so values from the SQL database must be converted into their data types. The ANSI-92 standard defines rules for matching SQL and host language data types

GET DIAGNOSTICS

GRANT

The GRANT statement will assign privileges to users on particular objects in the database.

```
GRANT <access rights>
ON <object name>
TO {PUBLIC | <user identifier>}
[WITH GRANT OPTION]
```

<access rights> ::= ALL PRIVILEGES | SELECT | DELETE | INSERT |UPDATE | |REFERENCES | USAGE

The use of the GRANT statement assumes that a <user identifier> record exists in the database. Consult your vendor's manuals for details regarding how to maintain user records.

INSERT

```
INSERT INTO <table name> [(<column list>)] <data source>
```

<column list>. This optional item tells the database what columns will have data inserted, and in what order they will be populated. If <column list> is not specified, then columns will be populated in the order they were created in the table. It is not necessary to provide values for all columns when inserting a row, providing the columns for which you do not wish to insert data have been assigned a valid default value. All existing column constraints will be applied to the inserted data.

<data source> ::= VALUES (<value list>) | DEFAULT VALUES | <query expression>

> VALUES(<value list>) : An explicit list of values that will be inserted a single row at a time. Values in the <value list> must be listed in the same order as the columns they will populate (the order of which can be implicitly or explicitly implied, as described above). Also the data type must match that specified for a particular column. Consult your specific vendor manual for details about specifying data types.

> DEFAULT VALUES: Fills each column with its specified default value. Bear in mind that certain columns (e.g. primary key columns) do not have default values (since each entry must be unique).

> <query expression>: A complete SELECT statement that retrieves (multiple) rows and columns from one table for insertion into another table. All rules concerning column constraints, column order, data types etc. apply here also. An example of use of the <query expression> is given below.

```
INSERT INTO CustomerOrders (CustomerID, OrderID, Terms, Comments)
SELECT CustomerID, OrderID, Terms, AgentComments + CustomerComments
FROM ImportTable
```

Beware that if, for example, the length of the character strings in the two comment fields in the ImportTable, when combined, exceeds the length of the CustomerOrders Comments field in the CustomerOrders table, then an error will result.

OPEN

The OPEN statement collects the table rows selected by the DECLARE CURSOR expression.

```
OPEN <cursor name>
```

REVOKE

The REVOKE statement will remove privileges to users on particular objects in the database. See the GRANT command for details of component parts.

```
REVOKE [GRANT OPTION FOR] <access rights> ON <object name> FROM {PUBLIC | <user
identifier>,…} {RESTRICT | CASCADE}
```

SELECT

The SELECT statement can contain numerous clauses and predicates. Only the most commonly used ones will be covered in any detail. For the sake of clarity, the explanation has been divided into several sections. Each section deals with the SELECT statement with regard to single table queries. Only the final section covers multiple table queries.

```
SELECT [DISTINCT | ALL] {<column expression> | *}
FROM {<table name> [AS <correlation name>]} | {<table name> [<complete join table
statement>]}
[WHERE <search condition>]
[GROUP BY <column list>]
     [HAVING <group selection predicate>]
[{UNION | INTERSECT | EXCEPT} [CORRESPONDING BY <column list>] <complete SELECT
statement>]
[ORDER BY <sort expression>]
```

<column expression>. Essentially a list of column names, but which can also include literal values, and logical expressions:

Example 1 - column names only:

```
SELECT CustomerID, OrderID FROM CustomerOrders
```

Example 2 - column names and literal values (with examples of use of correlation names):

```
SELECT CustomerID, OrderID, 12 AS Quantity,
'These are comments.' AS Comments
FROM CustomerOrders
```

Example 3 - column names and logical expressions:

```
Select CustomerID, OrderID, Comments + Terms, Quantity * UnitPrice
From CustomerOrders
```

<complete join table statement> ::= {<join statement> <table name>[<join
specification>]}

> ➤   <join statement> :**For example,** INNER JOIN, LEFT OUTER JOIN, RIGHT OUTER JOIN
> ➤   <join specification> ::= ON< join condition>.

<search condition> ::= {<logical expression> [{<Boolean operator> <logical expression>}...] | <complete comparison predicate> | <complete SELECT statement>}

If the result of this search expression is TRUE, the row is displayed in the result set. If the result is FALSE or UNKNOWN, the row is dropped from the result set.

< logical expression>: **e.g.** Quantity>10.

<complete comparison predicate:

> ➤   <IN predicate> ::= {<expression> [**NOT**] IN (<value1>,...)}
> ➤   <LIKE predicate>::= {<expression> [NOT] LIKE <pattern>}

Two wildcard characters are used to specify the <pattern> *string. The* '%' *character represents multiple characters and the* '_' *represents a single character*

> ➤   <BETWEEN predicate>::= <expression> [NOT] BETWEEN <low value expression> AND <high value expression>

<sort expression> ::= {{<column name> [ASC | DESC]} , ...}

SET CATALOG

    SET CATALOG <catalog name>

SET CONNECTION

SET CONSTRAINTS MODE

    SET CONSTRAINTS MODE {<constraint name>, … | ALL}
    DEFERRED | INTERMADIATE

SET SCHEMA

    SET SCHEMA <schema name>

SET SESSION AUTHORISATION

SET TIME ZONE

SET TRANSACTION

Specify the characteristics of a transaction.

UPDATE

The UPDATE statement enables changes to be made to the data after the rows have been inserted into the table.

```
UPDATE <table name> SET <set list> [WHERE <search condition> ]
```

<set list> ::= {<column name> = {<value expression> | NULL | DEFAULT}}, ...}

ANSI SQL-92 Aggregate Functions

The following functions provide aggregate calculations in ANSI SQL-92. These aggregate functions cannot be nested and the <value expression> cannot be a subquery.

Count

```
COUNT (* | [ALL | DISTINCT] <value expression>)
```

COUNT (*) will return a count of all the rows in a table including those with null values. The use of COUNT with a <value expression> will return the count of the members in the <value expression>.

SUM

```
SUM([ALL | DISTINCT] <value expression> )
```

The SUM function will return the total of all values in the <value expression>.

AVG

```
AVG( [ALL | DISTINCT] <value expression> )
```

The AVG function returns the average of all members of the <value expression>.

MAX

```
MAX( [ALL | DISTINCT] <value expression> )
```

The MAX function returns the largest value from the <value expression>.

MIN

```
MIN( [ALL | DISTINCT] <value expression> )
```

The MIN function returns the smallest value from the <value expression>.

Suppliers

- SupplierID
- CompanyName
- ContactName
- ContactTitle
- Address
- City
- Region
- PostalCode
- Country
- Phone
- Fax
- HomePage

Products

- ProductID
- ProductName
- SupplierID
- CategoryID
- QuantityPerUnit
- UnitPrice
- UnitsInStock
- UnitsOnOrder
- ReorderLevel
- Discontinued

Categories

- CategoryID
- CategoryName
- Description
- Picture

6

Transact-SQL

Microsoft SQL Server 7.0

This appendix deals with enhancements to and departures from the ANSI SQL-92 standard for TRANSACT-SQL of Microsoft SQL Server version 7.0. This product has *Entry SQL* conformance.

This appendix, and the two that follow on PL/SQL and Jet SQL, do not attempt to cover every possible nuance of the particular product's departure from, or enhancement of, SQL-92. Such a tome would likely weigh more than your kitchen refrigerator, and possibly compromise the structural integrity of your bookshelf. Some vendor's features represent a decidedly non-SQL enhancement, and are thus not explored with great detail. Additionally, these appendices focus on syntactic differences. For specific details regarding the implementation of particular extensions, consult your DBMS documentation.

General ANSI SQL-92 Compatibility

SQL Server compliance with SQL-92 can be established for the duration of a running trigger or stored procedure by setting the ANSI_DEFAULTS option ON via the SET statement:

```
SET ANSI_DEFAULTS ON
SET ANSI_NULLS
SET ANSI_NULL_DFLT_ON
SET ANSI_PADDING
SET ANSI_WARNINGS
SET CONCURRENCY LOCKCC
SET CURSORTYPE CUR_STANDARD
SET CURSOR_CLOSE_ON_COMMIT ON
SET FETCHBUFFER 1
SET IMPLICIT_TRANSACTIONS
SET QUOTED_IDENTIFIER
SET SCROLLOPTION FORWARD
```

It should be noted that SET ANSI_DEFAULTS OFF is not supported. Reverting to normal SQL Server behavior requires individual reset of affected options to their original value.

Special Information

Distributed Queries

ANSI SQL-92 distributed query behavior is supported. However, any connection which must execute distributed queries must first set the ANSI_NULLS and ANSI_WARNINGS options for the connection via the SET statement:

```
SET ANSI_NULLS ON
SET ANSI_WARNINGS ON
```

Entity Naming Scheme

The SQL-92 standard specifies a three-part naming convention regarding entities that contain system metadata. The actual names of these entities within SQL Server does not match those called out in the standard. However, a view exists for each table that maps the SQL Server entity name with the correct corresponding SQL-92 name. The mapping is as follows:

SQL Server	SQL 92
DATABASE	CATALOG
OWNER	SCHEMA
OBJECT	OBJECT
User-defined data type	DOMAIN

Explicit Transaction Commands

SQL Server 7.0 supports commands to explicitly define the start and end points of a transaction:

BEGIN TRAN[SACTION] [name]

Indicates the beginning of a transaction.

COMMIT TRAN[SACTION]

Writes the changes from the transaction to the database and marks the transaction as completed.

ROLLBACK TRAN[SACTION] [name | savept_name]

When an abnormal condition is encountered, requiring an in-process transaction to be aborted, this command rolls back all pending changes to affected database tables and restores them to their pre-transaction state. If savept_name is supplied, only those elements of the transaction up to the declaration of the savepoint are rolled back.

SAVE TRAN[SACTION] savept_name

This statement establishes a `savepoint` to which a transaction may be partially rolled back. To accomplish a partial rollback, issue the `ROLLBACK TRAN` command, supplying the name of the `savepoint` established in this statement.

ANSI SQL-92 Commands in Transact-SQL

The following commands are all part of the ANSI SQL-92 specification. This section indicates the degree to which the database supports the command along with special syntax enhancements that may be implemented.

ALTER DOMAIN

Not implemented.

ALTER TABLE

The basic SQL-92 syntax is implemented, with the following exceptions or enhancements:

> ➤   When adding columns a `ROWGUIDCOL` can be added or dropped.

> ➤   When altering columns, defaults cannot be dropped.

> ➤   Constraints can be added with the optional `WITH CHECK` / `WITH NOCHECK` clause. This allows checking against a foreign key or check constraint.

> ➤   The `NOT FOR REPLICATION` clause is used to inhibit column replication.

CLOSE

The `CLOSE` command supports the `GLOBAL` qualifier to determine the namespace to be searched to find the target cursor.

COMMIT [WORK]

Identical to `COMMIT TRANSACTION`, except that it does not accept a user-defined transaction name.

CONNECT

Not supported.

CREATE ASSERTION

Not supported.

CREATE CHARACTER SET

Not supported.

CREATE COLLATION

Not supported.

CREATE DOMAIN

Not supported.

CREATE SCHEMA

This statement is supported, with the following differences:

> Schemas cannot be named.

> The AUTHORIZATION clause is mandatory, and must represent a valid security account.

> The CREATE ASSERTION, CREATE CHARACTER SET, CREATE COLLATION, CREATE DOMAIN, CREATE TRANSLATION, and DEFAULT CHARACTER SET clauses are not supported.

CREATE TABLE

This statement is supported, with the following differences:

> The ANSI-optional [{GLOBAL|LOCAL} TEMPORARY] qualifier is not supported.

> The ON COMMIT {DELETE|PRESERVE ROWS} clause is not supported.

> For column names, the COLLATION clause is not supported.

> For table creation, the ON {filegroup | DEFAULT} clause allows specification of the storage location of the table.

> For column definitions with the table, the [ROWGUIDCOL] qualifier is allowed to define a column as a holder of a globally unique identifier.

> The {CLUSTERED | NONCLUSTERED} qualifier is supported for PRIMARY KEY and UNIQUE constraints.

> ANSI SQL-92 supports the designation of a domain for column; this is not supported.

CREATE TRANSLATION

Not supported.

CREATE VIEW

This statement is supported, with the following differences:

> The ANSI-optional [CASCADED | LOCAL] qualifier of the WITH CHECK OPTION clause is not supported.

> An optional WITH ENCRYPTION clause is supported that causes the text of the view within the <syscomments> table to be encrypted.

DECLARE CURSOR

Two distinct forms of this command are supported; one is the exact SQL-92 syntax, the other is specific to TRANSACT-SQL. The two forms cannot be intermixed. The extended TRANSACT-SQL syntax is as follows:

```
DECLARE <cursor_name> CURSOR
[LOCAL | GLOBAL]
[FORWARD_ONLY | SCROLL]
[STATIC | KEYSET | DYNAMIC | FAST_FORWARD]
[READ_ONLY | SCROLL_LOCKS | OPTIMISTIC]
[TYPE_WARNING]
FOR <select statement>
[FOR UPDATE [OF <column name> [,...n]]]
```

[LOCAL | GLOBAL] defines the scope of the cursor: whether local to the entity in which the cursor was created, or global to the connection.

[FORWARD_ONLY] specifies that the cursor can only be scrolled from the first record to the last, and not back.

[SCROLL] specifies the cursor can be scrolled in any direction.

[STATIC | KEYSET | DYNAMIC | FAST_FORWARD] defines how storage of records is handled within the cursor. STATIC causes a temporary copy of the actual data to be used. KEYSET causes the keys of the underlying data to be copied, thus causing cursor membership to be fixed upon creation. DYNAMIC causes the cursor to reflect the current status of the underlying data; records may be added or removed between each fetch. FAST_FORWARD is a FORWARD_ONLY, READ_ONLY cursor with performance optimizations.

[READ_ONLY] disallows updates through the cursor.

[SCROLL_LOCKS] guarantees successful cursor updates by locking rows in underlying tables.

[OPTIMISTIC] does not guarantee successful cursor updates; underlying table rows are not locked.

[TYPE_WARNING] causes a message to be sent to the client if an implicit data type conversion has taken place.

[FOR UPDATE] causes the cursor to allow updates on all columns unless the [OF <column name>] clause is also specified.

DECLARE LOCAL TEMPORARY TABLE

Not supported.

DELETE

The full SQL-92 syntax is supported, with the following extensions:

> The FROM clause can specify a <rowset_function_limited> qualifier that maps either to the OPENQUERY or OPENROWSET function. This is specific to OLEDB data providers.

> WITH (<table_hint_limited>) allows certain locking characteristics to be defined.

> An optional OPTION (<query_hint>) qualifier can be specified.

DISCONNECT

Not supported.

DROP ASSERTION

Not supported.

DROP CHARACTER SET

Not supported.

DROP COLLATION

Not supported.

DROP DOMAIN

Not supported.

DROP SCHEMA

Not supported.

DROP TABLE

The [CASCADE | RESTRICT] clauses are not supported.

DROP TRANSLATION

Not supported.

DROP VIEW

The statement is supported, with the following exceptions:

> The [CASCADE | RESTRICT] clauses are not supported.
> Multiple views can be dropped in the same statement via comma-delimited list of view names.

FETCH

The statement is supported, with the following exceptions:

> The [GLOBAL] qualifier is allowed to specify the namespace to be searched for the specified cursor.
> With the ABSOLUTE and RELATIVE qualifiers, an integer literal or TRANSACT-SQL variable name can be specified.

GET DIAGNOSTICS

Not supported.

GRANT

The statement is supported, with the following differences:

> TRANSACT-SQL allows assignment of privileges to specific TRANSACT-SQL statements via the following syntax:

```
GRANT {ALL | <statement_list>} TO <security_account_list>
```

> The DOMAIN, COLLATION, CHARACTER SET and TRANSLATION qualifiers are not supported.
> The USAGE qualifier is not supported.
> An additional [WITH GRANT OPTION] clause is supported to give individual users the ability to grant a particular privilege.
> An additional [AS {group | role}] is supported to indicate the identity of the grantor.
> SQL-92 specifies an optional column list with the permission to be granted; however, TRANSACT-SQL places the column list after the target table or view:

SQL-92 sample: GRANT INSERT (<column list>) ON TABLE

TRANSACT-SQL sample: GRANT INSERT ON TABLE (<column list>)

> TRANSACT-SQL also allows assignment of permissions to stored procedures and extended stored procedures.

INSERT

This statement is supported with the following differences:

> The WITH (<table_hint_limited>) clause specifies locking characteristics of the insert.
> The target can be a <rowset_function>, which is specific to OLEDB data providers.
> The source data can be derived from an EXECUTE statement that returns data with a SELECT.
> Single-record inserts can be performed via the VALUES (<value list>) clause.

OPEN

This statement is supported, with the following exception:

> The optional [USING <values source>] clause is not supported.

REVOKE

This statement is supported, with the following differences:

> Permissions can be granted to specific statements.
> The target of the revoke can be a stored procedure or extended stored procedure.
> The target of the revoke can be restricted to a specific column within a table or view.
> The RESTRICT clause is not supported.
> An additional [AS {group | role}] clause is provided to specify the security context of the REVOKE.

ROLLBACK [WORK]

Fully supported. The WORK keyword is optional.

SELECT

This statement is supported, with the following differences and extensions:

> An additional [{TOP INTEGER} | {TOP INTEGER PERCENT} [WITH TIES]] clause is allowed, to specify only those records that fall into the first INTEGER records of the entire result set, or that percentage of all records in the record. SET [WITH TIES] specifies whether duplicate records are included in the criteria.

- ➤ The INTERSECT and EXCEPT qualifiers are not supported.
- ➤ The CORRESPONDING clause is not supported.
- ➤ An optional [INTO] clause allows for record insertion into a separate table.
- ➤ An optional [WITH {CUBE | ROLLUP}] clause is supported in conjunction with GROUP BY for summary statistical information.
- ➤ An optional COMPUTE BY clause allows for breaks and subtotals based on various aggregate functions.
- ➤ An optional FOR BROWSE clause is used for applications communicating with SQL Sever via DB-Library.
- ➤ An optional OPTION clause specifies a query hint that should be used for the query.
- ➤ JOINS across a named list of columns is not supported.
- ➤ An optional [join_hint] can be specified for optimization purposes.
- ➤ The source of a table can be a table, a view, or a rowset function, or a table derived from a nested SELECT statement. A rowset function is specific to OLEDB data providers.
- ➤ Aliases can be provided for source tables and columns.
- ➤ All ANSI SQL-92 standard JOIN types are supported.
- ➤ Search conditions using LIKE may include an [ESCAPE <esc_char>] clause.
- ➤ The UNIQUE clause, and the MATCH and OVERLAPS predicates are not supported.

Because the SELECT statement is fundamental to the operation of SQL and by its nature can be extremely complex, you are is strongly encouraged to study the vendor-specific documentation to become conversant in the subtleties of the SELECT statement for your particular product and application.

SET CATALOG

Not supported.

SET CONNECTION

Not supported.

SET CONSTRAINTS MODE

Not supported.

SET SESSION AUTHORIZATION

Not supported.

SET TIME ZONE

Not supported.

SET TRANSACTION

Supported with the following exception:

> ➤ The {READ ONLY | READ WRITE} qualifier is not supported.
> ➤ The {DIAGNOSTICS SIZE} qualifier is not supported.

UPDATE

This statement is supported with the following extensions:

> ➤ When used in stored procedures, the SET qualifier can include a variable name.
> ➤ The source for update can be a table, view, rowset function, or derived table (table derived from a SELECT statement). Rowset functions are specific to OLEDB data providers.
> ➤ An optional [OPTION <query_hint>] qualifier is supported.
> ➤ An optional [WITH <table_hint>] is supported as a qualifier against the <table name> parameter.

ANSI SQL-92 Functions in Transact-SQL

The following describes various implementation specifics of SQL-92 standard functions in TRANSACT-SQL.

Aggregate Functions

For all aggregate functions, the DISTINCT | ALL qualifier is supported.

AVG

Supported.

COUNT

Supported.

MAX

Supported.

MIN

Supported.

SUM

Supported.

Non ANSI SQL-92 Mathematical Functions

Function	Description
ABS	Absolute value
ACOS	Arccosine
ASIN	Arcsine
ATAN	Arctangent – one argument
ATN2	Arctangent – two arguments
CEILING	Ceiling function for numerics
COS	Cosine
COT	Cotangent
DEGREES	Converts radian angle measurement
EXP	Exponential
FLOOR	Floor
LOG	Natural Logarithm
LOG10	Logarithm (base 10)
PI	Constant value of PI
POWER	Carries x to y power
RADIANS	Converts degree angle measurement
RAND	Generates random number
ROUND	Performs rounding to n decimal places
SIGN	Returns sign of number
SIN	Sine
SQUARE	Returns square of argument
SQRT	Returns square root of argument
TAN	Tangent

String-Related Functions

Function	Description
ASCII	Returns integer representing numeric value of character
CHAR	Returns character corresponding to integer value
CHARINDEX	Returns location of substring within string
DIFFERENCE	Returns difference between SOUNDEX values of strings
LEFT	Returns left *n* characters of string
LEN	Returns length of string
LOWER	Converts all characters to lower case
LTRIM	Removes leading blanks
NCHAR	Returns Unicode character of given integer code
PATINDEX	Returns starting position of pattern in an expression
REPLACE	Replace substring with new string
QUOTENAME	Adds quotes to Unicode string to create valid SQL Server identifier
REPLICATE	Repeat a character *n* times
REVERSE	Reverse the order of characters in a string
RIGHT	Return rightmost *n* characters of string
RTRIM	Strip trailing blanks
SOUNDEX	Return value corresponding to phonetic equivalent of string
SPACE	Return *n* spaces
STR	Convert argument to string
STUFF	Deletes a number of characters and inserts another set of characters
SUBSTRING	Returns a substring of a string
UNICODE	Returns value corresponding to first character of a Unicode string
UPPER	Converts all characters to uppercase

Date and Time Functions

Function	Description
DATEADD	Adds a unit of time to a date
DATEDIFF	Returns the number of date units (i.e. days) between two dates
DATENAME	Returns name corresponding to portion of date variable
DATEPART	Returns a portion of a date value
DAY	Returns integer portion of date value, representing day of month
GETDATE	Returns current system date
MONTH	Returns month of specified date
YEAR	Returns year of specified date

Conversion Functions

Function	Description
CAST*	Explicitly converts expression of one type to another
CONVERT	Explicitly converts expression of one type to another

ANSI SQL-92 compliant

Other Unlisted Functions

Transact-SQL supports numerous other functions to interrogate SQL Server about system status, system configuration, system table information, security, users, and file systems related to a particular database. However, these functions arise from the implementation specifics of SQL Server, and as such are beyond the scope of this document.

Commands not Part of ANSI SQL-92

SQL Server's implementation of ANSI SQL-92 includes non ANSI-standard extensions, or alternative formats to existing commands. A brief description of many commands is provided; however, if the command is specific to features significantly departed from ANSI SQL-92 or is obvious by its name, a description may be omitted. Statements marked with an asterisk are not part of ANSI SQL-92. Those without indicate a command that may be defined in ANSI SQL-92, but only with a specialized syntax or in a context that is not consistent with ANSI SQL-92.

ALTER DATABASE*

Modify structure of a database.

ALTER PROCEDURE*

Updates a stored procedure.

ALTER TRIGGER*

Updates a table trigger.

ALTER VIEW*

Updates a view.

BEGIN DISTRIBUTED TRANSACTION*

Establishes the starting point of a transaction. The transaction may be distributed to multiple remote systems.

BEGIN TRANSACTION*

Establishes the starting point of a transaction.

COMMIT TRANSACTION*

Establishes the end point of a transaction.

CREATE DATABASE*

Creates a new database.

CREATE DEFAULT*

Creates a named default.

CREATE INDEX*

Creates an index on one or more columns of a table.

CREATE PROCEDURE*

Defines a new stored procedure.

CREATE STATISTICS*

Creates histogram for specified columns.

CREATE TRIGGER*

Defines a new table trigger.

DROP DATABASE*

Removes a database and its tables.

DROP DEFAULT*

Removes a named default.

DROP INDEX*

Removes a table index.

DROP PROCEDURE*

Removes a stored procedure.

DROP RULE*

Removes a rule.

DROP STATISTICS*

Removes statistical information generated by CREATE STATISTICS.

DROP TRIGGER*

Removes a table trigger.

ROLLBACK TRANSACTION*

Rolls a transaction back, optionally to a named savepoint.

Data Types

Some SQL Server data type names differ from those established in SQL-92 for the same physical data. The correspondences are as follows:

SQL Server	SQL 92
varbinary	binary varying
char	character
varchar	char varying or character varying

Other SQL Server Data Types

Data Type	Description
Bit	32-bit integer with a value of 1 or 0
Int	32-bit signed integer
Smallint	16-bit signed integer
Tinyint	8-bit unsigned integer
Decimal	Fixed precision and scale numeric data from $-10^38\text{-}1$ to $10^38\text{-}1$
Numeric	Synonym for decimal
Money	64-bit signed value
Smallmoney	Monetary values from −214,748.3648 to 214,748.3647
float	Floating precision value from −1.79E+308 to 1.79E+308
real	Floating precision value from −3.40E+38 to 3.40E+38
datetime	Date and time data from Jan 1, 1753 to Dec 31, 9999, accurate to 3.33 milliseconds
smalldatetime	Date and time data from Jan 1, 1900 to June 6, 2079, accuracy of one minute
Cursor	Reference to a cursor
TimeStamp	Database-wide unique number
Uniqueidentifier	Globally unique identifier (GUID)
char	Fixed-length non-Unicode data <=8,000 characters
Varchar	Variable-length non-Unicode data <=8,000 characters
Text	Variable-length non-Unicode data <= $2^31\text{-}1$ characters
Nchar	Fixed length Unicode data <=4,000 characters
Nvarchar	Variable-length Unicode data <=4,000 characters
Ntext	Variable-length Unicode data <=$2^30\text{-}1$ characters
Binary	Fixed-length binary data <=8,000 bytes
Varbinary	Variable-length binary data <=8,000 bytes
Image	Variable-length binary data <=$2^31\text{-}1$ bytes

Suppliers

- SupplierID
- CompanyName
- ContactName
- ContactTitle
- Address
- City
- Region
- PostalCode
- Country
- Phone
- Fax
- HomePage

Products

- ProductID
- ProductName
- SupplierID
- CategoryID
- QuantityPerUnit
- UnitPrice
- UnitsInStock
- UnitsOnOrder
- ReorderLevel
- Discontinued

Categories

- CategoryID
- CategoryName
- Description
- Picture

PL/SQL

Oracle Corporation Oracle8

This appendix deals with enhancements to and departures from ANSI SQL-92 for PL/SQL of Oracle8. Oracle8 has *Entry SQL* conformance.

General ANSI SQL-92 Compatibility

The following is a general discussion of the more significant departures of PL/SQL from ANSI SQL-92.

OUTER JOINS

Oracle8 does not support the ANSI SQL-92 syntax for outer joins (LEFT OUTER JOIN, RIGHT OUTER JOIN, FULL JOIN). A modification to the SELECT statement's WHERE clause using the "+" symbol indicates the direction of the join.

LEFT OUTER JOIN

An example of the syntax is as follows:

```
SELECT <column list>
FROM{<Table list>}
WHERE TABLE1.FIELD = + TABLE2.FIELD;
```

RIGHT OUTER JOIN

```
SELECT <column list>
FROM{<Table list>}
WHERE TABLE1.FIELD (+) = TABLE2.FIELD;
```

FULL JOIN

```
SELECT <column list>
FROM{<Table list>}
WHERE TABLE1.FIELD (+) = + TABLE2.FIELD;
```

INNER JOINS

Oracle8 does not support the ANSI SQL-92 syntax for inner joins. The correct syntax for an inner join under Oracle8 is as follows:

```
SELECT * FROM <table name> WHERE {<table name>.field1= <table alias>.field2}
```

Null Values in Group Column of GROUP BY Clause

When a GROUP BY clause includes two or more rows with null values in the same column, and all other columns contain identical values, the ANSI SQL-92 standard specifies that the rows should be grouped together. However, Oracle8 does not implement this standard. The query rows that include null values are treated as a separate grouping.

Object Enhancements

Oracle8 supports a full object database paradigm within the context of a traditional relational database model. Many SQL-92 statements include alternate syntax to take advantage of these features; many additional statements, not part of SQL-92, are provided for this purpose. Although these and other extended commands are listed, they are not explored in detail as a particular vendor's implementation of an object database is beyond the scope of this appendix.

ANSI SQL-92 Commands

The following commands are all part of the ANSI SQL-92 specification. This section indicates the degree to which the database supports the command, along with special syntax enhancements that may be implemented.

ALTER DOMAIN

Not implemented.

CLOSE

Implemented only within embedded SQL.

COMMIT [WORK]

Supported.

CONNECT

Implemented only within embedded SQL.

CREATE ASSERTION

Not supported.

CREATE CHARACTER SET

Not supported.

CREATE COLLATION

Not supported.

CREATE DOMAIN

Not supported.

CREATE SCHEMA

This statement is supported, with the following differences:

> The AUTHORIZATION clause is mandatory, and must represent a valid security account.
> The CREATE ASSERTION, CREATE CHARACTER SET, CREATE COLLATION, CREATE DOMAIN, CREATE TRANSLATION, and DEFAULT CHARACTER SET clauses are not supported.

CREATE TABLE

The Oracle8 version of CREATE TABLE supports two distinct syntax formats. One is the SQL-92 implementation and the other is Oracle8's implementation in support of object-oriented databases. This discussion is limited to the SQL-92 implementation version as Oracle8's object implementation is beyond the scope of this text.

CREATE TABLE is supported with the following differences:

> The ANSI-optional [{GLOBAL|LOCAL} TEMPORARY] qualifier is not supported.
> The [ON COMMIT {DELETE|PRESERVE} ROWS] clause is not supported.
> The COLLATE clause for column definitions is not supported.
> The name of the table may be prepended with the name of a schema followed by a dot.
> ANSI SQL-92 supports the designation of a domain for column; this is not supported.

The standard CREATE TABLE clause contains numerous extensions for allocation of space, arrangement of indices, table partitioning, parallel clauses, and caching.

CREATE TRANSLATION

Not supported.

CREATE VIEW

This statement is supported, with the following differences:

> - The ANSI-optional [CASCADED | LOCAL] qualifier of the WITH CHECK OPTION clause is not supported.

Oracle8 enhanced syntax supports the following qualifiers and clauses:

> - WITH READ ONLY in addition to WITH CHECK OPTION.
> - CONSTRAINT clause.
> - OF syntax for Oracle8 object extensions.

DECLARE CURSOR

Supported only for Embedded SQL.

DECLARE LOCAL TEMPORARY TABLE

Not supported.

DELETE

The statement is supported, with the following differences:

> - The FROM clause, mandatory in SQL-92, is optional..
> - The WHERE CURENT OF <cursor name> is not supported.

The Oracle8 syntax provides extensions that support the following:

> - Deletes drawn from a designated table partition or linked table.
> - Extended syntax for support of Oracle8 object features.
> - A RETURNING clause that directs output into a designated destination.

DISCONNECT

Not supported.

DROP ASSERTION

Not supported.

DROP COLLATION

Not supported.

DROP DOMAIN

Not supported.

DROP SCHEMA

Not supported.

DROP TABLE

The statement is supported, with the following exceptions:

> The RESTRICT clause is not supported.
> The CASCADE clause requires the CONSTRAINT keyword.

DROP VIEW

The statement is supported, with the following exception:

> The CASCADE | RESTRICT clause is not supported.

FETCH

Supported only in Embedded SQL.

GET DIAGNOSTICS

Not supported.

GRANT

The statement is supported, with the following differences:

> The DOMAIN, COLLATION, CHARACTER SET and TRANSLATION qualifiers are not supported.
> The USAGE qualifier is not supported.
> The PRIVILEGES portion of the ALL PRIVILEGES qualifier, required in ANSI SQL-92, is optional.
> The ON clause supports an additional DIRECTORY qualifier to grant permissions to a DIRECTORY object.

INSERT

The statement is supported, with the following differences:

> The DEFAULT VALUES qualifier is not supported.

Oracle8 PL/SQL supports syntax to implement the following:

> Inserts directed to linked tables.
> Inserts to partitions of tables.
> Inserts into Oracle8 object tables.
> RETURNING clause directing specific output to a destination.

OPEN

Supported only for Embedded SQL.

REVOKE

The statement is supported, with the following differences:

> ➤ The GRANT OPTION FOR clause is not supported.
> ➤ The PUBLIC keyword of the FROM clause is not supported for the revocation of object privileges; the keyword ALL is used in its place.
> ➤ The RESTRICT clause is not supported.
> ➤ The CASCADE keyword requires the additional CONSTRAINTS keyword.
> ➤ For system privileges, the ON <object name> clause is not used.
> ➤ Oracle8 supports enhanced syntax such that the ON <object name> clause can refer to a DIRECTORY <directory name> qualifier.
> ➤ The PRIVILEGES keyword of the ALL PRIVILEGES qualifier is mandatory under ANSI SQL-92; in Oracle8, it is optional.
> ➤ The object name in the ON clause can be qualified by prepending a schema name and a period.

ROLLBACK [WORK]

The statement is supported. Oracle8 supports an extended syntax that allows the specification of a savepoint destination with the TO SAVEPOINT <savepoint> clause. When multiple SQL statements are executed, a savepoint basically marks a transaction out into "steps". It is a label that marks a subset of the changes made by the transaction.

SELECT

The statement is supported, with the following exceptions:

> ➤ The ANSI SQL-92 Join syntax is not supported. Oracle8 supports outer joins only with the + operator, as noted earlier. This includes CROSS JOIN, NATURAL, UNION JOIN, JOIN <table name> ON <predicate>, JOINT <table name> USING <column list>, INNER, LEFT, RIGHT, and FULL OUTER.
> ➤ The EXCEPT query correlation qualifier is not supported.
> ➤ The optional <column list> in the FROM clause is not supported.

The Oracle8 syntax provides extended functionality for the following:

> ➤ FOR UPDATE clause.
> ➤ Query correlation qualifiers of MINUS and UNION ALL.
> ➤ FROM clauses specifying linked tables or a table PARTITION.
> ➤ CONNECT BY qualifier with optional START WITH clause within the WHERE clause.

The SELECT statement is fundamental to the operation of SQL and by its nature can be extremely complex. The reader is strongly encouraged to study the vendor-specific documentation to become conversant in the subtleties of the SELECT statement for their particular product and application.

SET CATALOG

Not supported.

SET CONNECTION

Not supported.

SET CONSTRAINTS MODE

Not supported.

SET SESSION AUTHORIZATION

Not supported.

SET TIME ZONE

Not supported.

SET TRANSACTION

The statement is supported with the following differences:

> The READ UNCOMMITTED and REPEATABLE READ qualifiers of the ISOLATION LEVEL clause are not supported.
> The DIAGNOSTICS SIZE clause is not supported.
> Oracle8 supports the USE ROLLBACK SEGMENT to direct the use of a designated rollback segment name.

UPDATE

The statement is supported with the following differences:

> The WHERE CURRENT OF <cursor name> clause is not supported.

Oracle8 supports extended syntax for the following:

> Updates against linked tables and table partitions
> RETURNING clause to specify return values to a specific destination

ANSI SQL-92 Functions in Oracle8 PL/SQL

The following describes various implementation specifics of SQL-92 standard functions in PL/SQL.

Aggregate Functions

For all aggregate functions, the DISTINCT | ALL qualifier is supported.

AVG

Supported.

COUNT

Supported.

MAX

Supported.

MIN

Supported

SUM

Supported.

Non ANSI SQL-92 Mathematical Functions

Function	Description
ABS	Absolute value
ACOS	Arccosine
ASIN	Arcsine
ATAN	Arctangent – single argument
ATAN2	Arctangent - two arguments
CEIL	Ceiling
COS	Cosine
COSH	Hyberbolic Cosine
EXP*	Exponential
FLOOR	Floor
LN	Natural Logarithm
LOG	Logarithm (base 10)
MOD	Modulo division
POWER	Carries x to y power
ROUND	Rounds value to specified precision
SIGN	Returns sign of argument (+, 0, -)
SIN	Sine

Function	Description
SINH	Hyperbolic sine
SQRT	Square root
TAN	Tangent
TANH	Hyperbolic tangent
TRUNC	Truncation of numeric value to *n* decimal places

"E" and "e" can be used for exponential notation representation of numeric data

String-Related Functions

Function	Description
ASCII	Returns ASCII value of character
CHR	Returns character corresponding to numerical argument
CONCAT	Concatenates two strings
INITCAP	Capitalizes first letter of each word in argument
INSTR	Returns location of substring within string
INSTRB	Same as INSTR with binary (byte) arguments
LENGTH	Length of string in characters
LENGTHB	Length of string in bytes
LOWER	Changes case of all letters in argument to lower case
LPAD	Left-pad argument to specified length with space or other character
LTRIM	Trims leading left-blanks
NLS_INITCAP	Language version of INITCAP
NLS_LOWER	National Language version of LOWER
NLSSORT	Returns string of characters that performed sort
NLS_UPPER	National Language version of UPPER
REPLACE	Replace one string with another
RPAD	Right-pad argument to specified length with space or other character
RTRIM	Trims right trailing blanks
SOUNDEX	Returns value corresponding to phonetic representation of word
SUBSTR	Returns subset of string
SUBSTRB	Returns subset of string with binary arguments
TRANSLATE	Exchanges letters from standard alphabet to those of specified alphabet
UPPER	Forces all characters in string to uppercase

Date and Time Functions

Function	Description
ADD_MONTHS	Returns date plus *n* months
LAST_DAY	Returns last day of given month
MONTHS_BETWEEN	Returns number of months between two dates
NEW_TIME	Adjusts time for time zone
NEXT_DAY	Returns next day following given date
ROUND	Round function relating to date expressions
SYSDATE	Current date
TRUNC	Returns date truncated as specified.

Conversion Functions

Function	Description
CHARTOROWID	Converts char representation of rowid to rowid type
CONVERT	Converts string from one character set to another
HEXTORAW	Converts hexadecimal string to raw bytes
RAWTOHEX	Converts raw bytes to hexadecimal string
ROWIDTOCHAR	Converts rowid type to char
TO_CHAR	Converts numbers and dates to character representations
TO_DATE	Converts character representations of date to date type
TO_MULTI_BYTE	Converts character expressions to multi-byte character set
TO_NUMBER	Converts character representations of numbers to numeric type
TO_SINGLE_BYTE	Converts multi-byte character string to single-byte character string
TRANSLATE USING	Translates string according to language character set.

Statistical Functions

Function	Description
STDDEV	Returns standard deviation of a set of numbers
VARIANCE	Returns variance of a set of numbers

Miscellaneous Functions

Function	Description
DUMP	Returns data about internal representation of expression
EMPTY_BLOB	Returns empty BLOB locator
EMPTY_CLOB	Returns empty CLOB locator
BFILENAME	Returns filename associated with LOB
GREATEST	Returns largest in sequence of expressions
LEAST	Returns smallest in sequence of expressions
NLS_CHARSET_DECL_LEN	Returns declaration length of character column
NLS_CHARSET_ID	Returns NLS character set ID associated with text argument
NLS_CHARSET_NAME	Returns character set name associated with numerical argument
NVL	Null-dependent value function
UID	Integer representing current user.
USER	Character representation of user
USERENV	Returns attributes of user environment
VSIZE	Returns size of internal representation of expression

Other Unlisted Functions

Oracle8 features a complete object database superimposed within the structure of a conventional relational database system. Numerous additional functions have been incorporated into PL/SQL to take advantage of this object hierarchy; however, they are beyond the scope of this text.

Commands Not Part of ANSI SQL-92

Oracle8's implementation of ANSI SQL-92 includes non ANSI-standard extensions, or alternative formats to existing commands. A brief description of many commands is provided; however, if the command is specific to features significantly departed from ANSI SQL-92 or is obvious by its name, a description may be omitted. Statements marked with an asterisk are not part of ANSI SQL-92. Those without indicate a command that may be defined in ANSI SQL-92, but only with a specialized syntax or in a context that is not consistent with ANSI SQL-92.

ALTER CLUSTER*

Redefines storage characteristics for a cluster.

ALTER DATABASE*

Supports various Oracle8-specific features.

ALTER FUNCTION*

Changes the definition of a function.

ALTER INDEX*

Changes allocation for an index.

ALTER PACKAGE*

Recompiles a stored package (or package body). Object extension.

ALTER PROCEDURE*

Recompiles stand-alone procedure.

ALTER PROFILE*

Changes a resource limit for a profile.

ALTER RESOURCE COST*

Specifies a formula to determine cost of a resource.

ALTER ROLE*

Changes authorization to enable a role.

ALTER ROLLBACK SEGMENT*

Changes a rollback segment by either bringing it online, or taking it offline.

ALTER SEQUENCE*

Changes a numerical sequence.

ALTER SESSION*

Changes parameters for current session, including such elements as SQL tracing, name resolution, and rollback inhibition.

ALTER SNAPSHOT*

Updates a snapshot's storage parameters, or its AUTOMATIC REFRESH criteria.

ALTER SNAPSHOT LOG*

Changes characteristics of the snapshot log.

ALTER SYSTEM*

Changes system parameters.

ALTER TABLE

Changes the definition of a table, or changes its storage parameters. This function has significant additional syntax and functional capability than that required by ANSI SQL-92; most of these extensions are in place to support various Oracle8 system features for database location and storage allocation.

ALTER TABLESPACE*

Performs one of several possible operations to a defined `tablespace`.

ALTER TRIGGER*

Enables, disables, or recompiles a trigger on a database.

ALTER TYPE*

Modifies the definition of an object.

ALTER USER*

Updates characteristics of a database user.

ALTER VIEW*

Updates an existing view.

ANALYZE*

Maintenance function to validate tables, perform statistical computations, etc.

AUDIT*

Selects statements or objects for auditing.

COMMENT*

Inserts comment into data dictionary.

CREATE CLUSTER*

Creates a cluster for tables that share at least one column.

CREATE CONTROLFILE*

Rebuilds a control file for a database.

CREATE DATABASE*

Supports extensions specific to Oracle8.

CREATE DATABASE LINK*

Establishes a reference to a database contained on a remote database.

CREATE DIRECTORY*

Creates a directory on host computer's file system.

CREATE FUNCTION*

Defines a procedure that returns a value to the caller.

CREATE INDEX*

Defines an index on one or more columns in a table.

CREATE LIBRARY*

Establishes schema entry representing a shared object code library for external procedures.

CREATE PACKAGE*

Defines a container for database objects.

CREATE PACKAGE BODY*

Defines the body of a package.

CREATE PROCEDURE*

Defines stand alone procedure.

CREATE PROFILE*

Establishes user identity.

CREATE ROLE*

Defines a class of permissions that can be granted to users.

CREATE ROLLBACK SEGMENT*

Define an area used to contain information used for a rollback.

CREATE SEQUENCE*

Defines a way to generate unique integers.

CREATE SNAPSHOT*

Captures a particular result set into a table.

CREATE SNAPSHOT LOG*

Creates a log corresponding to the master table of a snapshot.

CREATE SYNONYM*

Creates an alternate name for a database entity.

CREATE TABLE

When used with a CREATE TYPE <object name> AS OBJECT statement, this form of the CREATE TABLE statement allows for the creation of tables that hold object references.

CREATE TABLESPACE*

Defines a block of space in the database in which objects are stored.

CREATE TRIGGER*

Defines a procedure that fires in response to specific table and/or database events.

CREATE TYPE object AS OBJECT*

This allows for the creation of a user-defined type.

CREATE TYPE BODY name AS OBJECT*

This allows for the definition of the body of an object defined with a previous CREATE TYPE statement.

CREATE USER*

Defines a database user.

CREATE VIEW

Defines a virtual table consisting of a query with specific columns.

DROP CLUSTER*

Removes a cluster from an Oracle8 database.

DROP DATABASE LINK*

Removes a link to a remote database.

DROP DIRECTORY dirname*

Removes directory object.

DROP INDEX*

Removes index from table.

DROP LIBRARY*

Removes external library from schema.

DROP PACKAGE*

Removes a package from the database.

DROP PROCEURE*

Removes a stand-alone procedure.

DROP PROFILE*

Removes a named set of privileges.

DROP ROLE*

Removes a class of permissions that can be granted to users.

DROP ROLLBACK SEGMENT*

Removes a segment of data reserved to contain information for a rollback.

DROP SEQUENCE*

Removes a named mechanism for producing unique integers.

DROP SNAPSHOT*

Removes table containing result of a particular query.

DROP SNAPSHOT LOG*

Removes log associated with master table of snapshot.

DROP SYNONYM*

Removes alternative database object name.

DROP TABLE

Removes table from database.

DROP TABLESPACE*

Releases allocated space within a database.

DROP TYPE object*

Removes specified type from database.

DROP TYPE BODY object*

Removes specified object definition from database.

EXPLAIN PLAN*

Constructs execution plan for query.

NOAUDIT*

Discontinues auditing initiated by the AUDIT command.

RENAME*

Renames a database entity.

REVOKE

Removes specific privileges from roles or users.

SAVEPOINT*

Establishes point to which a transaction can be rolled back.

SET CONSTRAINT*

SET TRANSACTION

Establishes characteristics of system transactions.

TRUNCATE*

Deletes all rows from a table.

Oracle8 Additions to Standard Commands

The following represent special additions or contexts supported under Oracle8.

COMMIT

This statement accepts two additional clauses; either COMMENT or FORCE.

The SQL-92 specification requires Entry-level compliant SQL grammars to require a WORK keyword immediately after the COMMIT command. Oracle8 does not enforce this requirement.

CREATE TABLE

The CREATE TABLE supports several additional clauses:

> AS, ENABLE, DISABLE, CLUSTER, ORGANIZATION, STORAGE

And parameters:

> INITRANS, MAXTRANS, PCTFREE, PCTTHRESHOLD, PCTUSED, TABLESPACE

Within the CREATE TABLE statement, the CONSTRAINT clause also supports the following options:

> ON DELETE CASCADE
> ENABLE
> DISABLE
> CONSTRAINT

Within the CREATE TABLE statement, column definitions support these clauses:

> WITH ROWID
> SCOPE

Any Oracle8 pre-defined data type can be used for the definition of a column.

CREATE VIEW

This command supports the following additional options:

> OR REPLACE.
> FORCE and NOFORCE.
> CONSTRAINT identifier with WITH CHECK OPTION.

Unless expressly defined, column names for the view are inherited from those used in the composing query.

DELETE

Oracle8 provides modified syntax that supports the following:

> Links to external tables and views.
> Aliases to tables in correlated queries.
> PARTITION clause.
> RETURNING clause.

The SQL-92 specification requires the FROM keyword to follow the DELETE statement. Oracle8 does not enforce this requirement.

SQL-92 does not permit a DELETE operation against a join view; however, Oracle8 will allow such a command against a modifiable join view provided exactly one key-preserved table in the join.

GRANT

As it applies within Oracle8 to system privileges and roles, the GRANT command is an extension to standard SQL. The GRANT command, as it applies to object privileges, supports these following privileges in addition to those supported by Entry SQL-92:

> ALTER
> EXECUTE
> INDEX
> READ

INSERT

Oracle8 is capable of performing inserts into remote databases via database links. A variant of the INSERT statement implements this capability.

ROLLBACK

The ROLLBACK statement under Oracle8 supports two additional clauses:

> ➤ TO
> ➤ FORCE

SQL-92 requires the keyword WORK to follow the ROLLBACK statement. Oracle8 does not enforce this requirement.

SELECT

Oracle8's SELECT statement supports the following additional clauses and non-standard syntax:

Clauses:

> ➤ START WITH
> ➤ CONNECT BY
> ➤ FOR UPDATE

Non-standard syntax:

> ➤ SELECT statements are possible against remote databases via database links.
> ➤ Outer joins are supported only via use of (+) operator; ANSI SQL-92 standard of INNER JOIN, OUTER JOIN, and FULL JOIN are not supported.
> ➤ Column aliases and NULL can be specified in the SELECT list.

GROUP BY Clause

A SELECT statement drawn from a view defined by group functions or a GROUP BY clause can, itself, contain GROUP BY, HAVING, and WHERE clauses.

Additionally, a SELECT statement can join against a view defined with the GROUP BY clause.

ORDER BY Clause

This clause can use any expression that contains columns referenced in the FROM clause, and is not limited to expressions within the select list or select list expression positions.

A column name can be qualified via the use of the following syntax:

{<table name>.column} or {<view name>.column }.

QUERIES (Nested Forms of SELECT Statements)

The GROUP BY clause may be used. Queries can select from views defined with the GROUP BY clause.

UPDATE

Oracle8's UPDATE statement supports the following additional clauses and non-standard syntax:

Clauses:

- ➢ PARTITION
- ➢ RETURNING

Non-standard syntax:

- ➢ Through the linked database syntax, data on remote database can be updated.
- ➢ Table aliases can be used with correlated queries.
- ➢ Parenthesized lists of columns are allowed on the left side of the SET clause, instead of merely single columns.
- ➢ Queries are allowed on the right side of the SET clause.

Additional functionality:

- ➢ An UPDATE statement against a view can, itself, contain a query.
- ➢ A subquery within the WHERE or SET clauses of an UPDATE statement can be self-referencing; that is, it may reference the affected table.
- ➢ An UPDATE can be performed on a modifiable join view if the columns to be updated in the same key-preserved table of the join. If the WITH CHECK OPTION is used in the view, the joined columns cannot be modified.
- ➢ A view with columns defined as complex expressions can be updated.
- ➢ UPDATE can be used in conjunction with a subquery.

Additional Functionality for SQL-92 Operators

- ➢ The left member of an expression containing the IN operator can be a parenthesized list of expressions, not only a single expression.
- ➢ The operators IS NULL and IS NOT NULL can be used against any expression.
- ➢ The LIKE operator matching pattern can be used against any expression of type CHAR or VARCHAR2.

Data Types

DATE (also dissimilar to the DATE type defined in Intermediate SQL-92)
NUMBER
VARCHAR2
LONG
RAW
LONG RAW
ROWID
BLOB
CLOB
BFILE
NCLOB
Object
REF
COLLECTION

Other Information

> ➤ Oracle supports maximum name lengths of 30 bytes.
> ➤ Names can contain # and $ characters, as well as repeated underscores.

Suppliers

- SupplierID
- CompanyName
- ContactName
- ContactTitle
- Address
- City
- Region
- PostalCode
- Country
- Phone
- Fax
- HomePage

Products

- ProductID
- ProductName
- SupplierID
- CategoryID
- QuantityPerUnit
- UnitPrice
- UnitsInStock
- UnitsOnOrder
- ReorderLevel
- Discontinued

Categories

- CategoryID
- CategoryName
- Description
- Picture

6

D

Jet SQL

Microsoft Access Database Engine (Jet)

Microsoft Access was originally designed as a single-user database system. As the PC became pervasive in business environments, more and more "part-time" developers began to leverage the Access environment for increasingly complex tasks. Unfortunately, as the demands upon Access grew, so did the cracks in its proverbial armor. In its defense, Access was never designed or intended to handle large-scale multi-user applications; that it leveraged at all could be viewed as surprising. Yet ask any Access veteran a naïve question about writing a multi-user Access database application, resolving Access locking disputes, or Access "you name it" problems, and you're likely to get a bruise on the head from the Access manual, thrown at you for your trouble.

This "personal database" heritage of Access makes it fundamentally different from its larger cousins, SQL Server and Oracle8. Where the latter strive to meet or exceed the goals of ANSI SQL-92, offer client-server performance (in whatever way that might be defined this week) and provide differentiation in the marketplace with vendor-specific extensions and scalability, the former sought to serve as an increasingly competent relational database. Moreover, Access sought to hide the technical complexities of queries and databases through a graphical user interface; most Access users have little or no formal SQL training or exposure. This is in sharp contrast to the Enterprise Manager (SQL Server) or SQL*Plus (Oracle) applications that provide a direct, interactive query interface to the database itself.

Mixed with this offering was tight integration into the Office suite of productivity applications. Most of that integration is achieved through Visual Basic for Applications, the common programming language among all Office products. Less important in the Access world is rigid adherence to conventional SQL; in fact, a significant portion of ANSI SQL-92, such as cursors GRANT-type database security, isn't even remotely supported.

Access by itself is really the name of a front end to the actual database "engine" itself, known as the "Jet Database Engine." Its legacy dates back to the oft-treacherous days of Windows 3.x, when the letters "ODBC" looked like a typographical error and Bill Gates wasn't worth more than the gross national product of most third world countries. With this brief bit of Jet history behind us, let's dive into its SQL-92 compatibility issues.

One important note: This section covers the Jet engine as implemented for Access97. Documentation for Access2000, as a part of the Office 2000 suite of productivity applications, was not available at the time of writing. Further, this version of the Jet engine was compared with ANSI SQL-89; however, most of the relevant information carries forward to this document.

General SQL-92 Compatibility Issues

> The BETWEEN condition has the following form:

\<expression\> [NOT] BETWEEN \<value1\>and \<value2\>

In Jet SQL, \<value1\> can be greater than \<value2\>. This is a departure from the ANSI standard.

> Grouping on expressions is allowed
> '?' and '*' are used for wildcard character and string matching instead of the ANSI '_' and '%'.

ANSI SQL-92 Commands

The following commands are all part of the ANSI SQL-92 specification. This section indicates the degree to which the database supports the command along with special syntax enhancements that may be implemented.

ALTER DOMAIN

Not supported.

ALTER TABLE

This command is supported, with the following differences:

> The ALTER COLUMN clause is not supported
> The RESTRICT | CASCADE clause of the DROP clause is not supported
> Column constraints can be added via the ADD CONSTRAINT clause
> Constraints can be dropped via the DROP CONSTRAINT clause

CLOSE

Not supported.

COMMIT [WORK]

Not supported.

CREATE ASSERTION

Not supported.

CREATE CHARACTER SET

Not supported.

CREATE COLLATION

Not supported.

CREATE DOMAIN

Not supported.

CREATE SCHEMA

Not supported.

CREATE TABLE

This statement is supported, with the following differences:

> The ANSI-optional [{GLOBAL|LOCAL} TEMPORARY] qualifier is not supported.
> The ON COMMIT {DELETE|PRESERVE ROWS} clause is not supported.
> For column names, the COLLATION clause is not supported.
> A multi-column index can be defined using the CONSTRAINT clause.

CREATE VIEW

Not supported.

DECLARE CURSOR

Not supported.

DECLARE LOCAL TEMPORARY TABLE

Not supported.

DELETE

The statement is supported, with the following difference:

> The WHERE CURRENT OF <cursor name> clause is not supported.

DROP ASSERTION

Not supported.

DROP CHARACTER SET

Not supported.

DROP COLLATION

Not supported.

DROP DOMAIN

Not supported.

DROP SCHEMA

Not supported.

DROP TABLE

The statement is supported, with the following differences:

> ➢ The [CASCADE | RESTRICT] clauses are not supported.

DROP TRANSLATION

Not supported.

DROP VIEW

Not supported.

FETCH

Not supported.

GET DIAGNOSTICS

Not supported.

GRANT

Not supported.

INSERT

The statement is supported, with the following differences:

> ➢ The DEFAULT VALUES clause is not supported.
> ➢ Inserts can be performed into an external database via the IN <externaldb> clause.
> ➢ Single-record inserts can be performed via the VALUES <(value list)> clause.

OPEN

Not supported.

REVOKE

Not supported.

ROLLBACK [WORK]

Not supported.

SELECT

The statement is supported, with the following differences:

> The UNION, INTERSECT, and EXCEPT qualifiers are not supported.

> The CORRESPONDING BY <column list> is not supported.

> An additional DISTINCTROW and TOP predicates restrict the number of records returned.

> The records forming the FROM source of the query can be an external database via the IN <external database name> clause.

> The WITH OWNERACCESS OPTION allows a query to be executed by someone other than its owner.

SET CATALOG

Not supported.

SET CONNECTION

Not supported.

SET CONSTRAINTS MODE

Not supported.

SET SESSION AUTHORIZATION

Not supported.

SET TIME ZONE

Not supported.

SET TRANSACTION

Not supported.

UPDATE

The statement is supported, with the following differences:

> The WHERE CURRENT OF <cursor name> clause is not supported.

ANSI SQL-92 Functions in Microsoft Access

Aggregate Functions

Note that for all aggregate functions, the DISTINCT qualifier is not supported.

AVG

Supported.

COUNT

Supported.

MAX

Supported.

MIN

Supported.

SUM

Supported.

Non ANSI SQL-92 Mathematical Functions

Most extended functions, such as those seen in Oracle8 and SQL Server, are provided by the Visual Basic for Applications environment within Access, or within Visual Basic itself.

FIRST (field)

Returns value of *field* in the first row of a query.

LAST (field)

Returns value of *field* in the last row of a query.

STDEV(expr)

Returns standard deviation of a population sample.

STDEVP(expr)

Returns standard deviation of a population.

VAR(expr)

Returns variance of a population sample.

VARP(expr)

Returns variance of a population.

String-Related Functions

Most extended functions, such as those seen in Oracle8 and SQL Server, are provided by the Visual Basic for Applications environment within Access, or within Visual Basic itself.

Date and Time Functions

Most extended functions, such as those seen in Oracle8 and SQL Server, are provided by the Visual Basic for Applications environment within Access, or within Visual Basic itself.

Conversion Functions

Most extended functions, such as those seen in Oracle8 and SQL Server, are provided by the Visual Basic for Applications environment within Access, or within Visual Basic itself.

Commands Not Part of ANSI SQL-92

The Jet Database Engine supports several specialized commands that are not part of SQL-92. A brief summary of these commands is provided here.

PARAMETERS

Defines one or more parameters to a parameterized query.

PROCEDURE

Declares a stored query.

TRANSFORM

Creates a crosstab query to display summary data. For example:

```
TRANSFORM Count([OrderID]) AS [The Value]
SELECT CustomerID, Count([OrderID]) AS [TotalCount]
FROM Orders
GROUP BY [CustomerID]
PIVOT Format([OrderDate], "yyyy")
```

Data Types

Jet	SQL-92
BINARY	BIT, BIT VARYING
TEXT	CHARACTER, CHARACTER VARYING
DOUBLE	DOUBLE PRECISION, FLOAT
SINGLE	REAL

Other Jet Data Types

Data Type	Description
BIT	8 bit unsigned integer
BYTE	8 bit unsigned integer
COUNTER	32 bit unsigned integer
CURRENCY	Scaled integer between - 922,337,203,685,477.5808 and 922,337,203,685,477.5807
GUID	128-bit Globally Unique Identifier
LONGBINARY	As needed
LONGTEXT VALUE	Byte per character

Suppliers

- SupplierID
- CompanyName
- ContactName
- ContactTitle
- Address
- City
- Region
- PostalCode
- Country
- Phone
- Fax
- HomePage

Products

- ProductID
- ProductName
- SupplierID
- CategoryID
- QuantityPerUnit
- UnitPrice
- UnitsInStock
- UnitsOnOrder
- ReorderLevel
- Discontinued

Categories

- CategoryID
- CategoryName
- Description
- Picture

E

ADO Object Summary

Microsoft ActiveX Data Objects 2.1 Library Reference

Properties and methods that are new to version 2.1 are indicated in the first column.

> **All properties are read/write unless otherwise stated.**

The Objects

The Main Objects

Object	Description
Command	A Command object is a definition of a specific command that is to be executed against a data source.
Connection	A Connection object represents a connection to a data store.
Recordset	A Recordset object represents the entire set of records from a base table or the results of an executed command. At any given time, the 'current record' of a Recordset object refers to a single record within the recordset.

The Other Objects

Object	Description
Error	An Error object contains the details of data access errors pertaining to a single operation involving the provider.
Field	A Field object represents a column of data within a common data type.
Parameter	A Parameter object represents a parameter or argument associated with a Command object based on a parameterized query or stored procedure.
Property	A Property object represents a dynamic characteristic of an ADO object that is defined by the provider.

The Collections

Collection	Description
Errors	The Errors collection contains all of the Error objects created in response to a single failure involving the provider.
Fields	A Fields collection contains all of the Field objects of a Recordset object.
Parameters	A Parameters collection contains all the Parameter objects of a Command object.
Properties	A Properties collection contains all the Property objects for a specific instance of an object.

The Command Object

Methods

Method	Return Type	Description
Cancel		Cancels execution of a pending Execute or Open call.
CreateParameter	Parameter object	Creates a new Parameter object.
Execute	Recordset object	Executes the query, SQL statement, or stored procedure specified in the CommandText property.

Properties

Property	Return Type	Description
ActiveConnection	Variant	Indicates to which Connection object the command currently belongs.
CommandText	String	Contains the text of a command to be issued against a data provider.
CommandTimeout	Long	Indicates how long to wait, in seconds, while executing a command before terminating the command and generating an error. Default is 30.
CommandType	CommandType Enum	Indicates the type of command specified by the Command object.
Name	String	Indicates the name of the Command object.
Prepared	Boolean	Indicates whether or not to save a compiled version of a command before execution.
State	Long	Describes whether the Command object is open or closed. Read only.

Collections

Collection	Return Type	Description
Parameters	Parameters collection	Contains all of the Parameter objects for a Command object.
Properties	Properties collection	Contains all of the Property objects for a Command object.

The Connection Object

Methods

Method	Return Type	Description
BeginTrans	Integer	Begins a new transaction.
Cancel		Cancels the execution of a pending, asynchronous Execute or Open operation.
Close		Closes an open connection and any dependent objects.
CommitTrans		Saves any changes and ends the current transaction.

Table Continued on Following Page

Method	Return Type	Description
Execute	Recordset object	Executes the query, SQL statement, stored procedure, or provider-specific text.
Open		Opens a connection to a data source, so that commands can be executed against it.
OpenSchema	Recordset object	Obtains database schema information from the provider.
RollbackTrans		Cancels any changes made during the current transaction and ends the transaction.

Properties

Property	Return Type	Description
Attributes	Long	Indicates one or more characteristics of a Connection object. Default is 0.
CommandTimeout	Long	Indicates how long, in seconds, to wait while executing a command before terminating the command and generating an error. The default is 30.
ConnectionString	String	Contains the information used to establish a connection to a data source.
ConnectionTimeout	Long	Indicates how long, in seconds, to wait while establishing a connection before terminating the attempt and generating an error. Default is 15.
CursorLocation	Cursor LocationEnum	Sets or returns the location of the cursor engine.
DefaultDatabase	String	Indicates the default database for a Connection object.
IsolationLevel	Isolation LevelEnum	Indicates the level of transaction isolation for a Connection object. Write only.
Mode	ConnectMode Enum	Indicates the available permissions for modifying data in a Connection.
Provider	String	Indicates the name of the provider for a Connection object.
State	Long	Describes whether the Connection object is open or closed. Read only.
Version	String	Indicates the ADO version number. Read only.

Collections

Collection	Return Type	Description
Errors	Errors collection	Contains all of the Error objects created in response to a single failure involving the provider.
Properties	Properties collection	Contains all of the Property objects for a Connection object.

Events

Event	Description
BeginTransComplete	Fired after a BeginTrans operation finishes executing.
CommitTransComplete	Fired after a CommitTrans operation finishes executing.
ConnectComplete	Fired after a connection starts.
Disconnect	Fired after a connection ends.
ExecuteComplete	Fired after a command has finished executing.
InfoMessage	Fired whenever a ConnectionEvent operation completes successfully and additional information is returned by the provider.
RollbackTransComplete	Fired after a RollbackTrans operation finished executing.
WillConnect	Fired before a connection starts.
WillExecute	Fired before a pending command executes on the connection.

The Error Object

Properties of the Error Object	Return Type	Description
Description	String	A description string associated with the error. Read only.
HelpContext	Integer	Indicates the ContextID in the help file for the associated error. Read only.
HelpFile	String	Indicates the name of the help file. Read only.
NativeError	Long	Indicates the provider-specific error code for the associated error. Read only.

Table Continued on Following Page

Properties of the Error Object	Return Type	Description
Number	Long	Indicates the number that uniquely identifies an Error object. Read only.
Source	String	Indicates the name of the object or application that originally generated the error. Read only.
SQLState	String	Indicates the SQL state for a given Error object. It is a five-character string that follows the ANSI SQL standard. Read only.

The Errors Collection

Methods

Method	Return Type	Description
Clear		Removes all of the Error objects from the Errors collection.
Refresh		Updates the Error objects with information from the provider.

Properties

Property	Return Type	Description
Count	Long	Indicates the number of Error objects in the Errors collection. Read only.
Item	Error	Allows indexing into the Errors collection to reference a specific Error object. Read only.

The Field Object

Methods

Method	Return Type	Description
AppendChunk		Appends data to a large or binary Field object.
GetChunk	Variant	Returns all or a portion of the contents of a large or binary Field object.

Properties

Property	Return Type	Description
ActualSize	Long	Indicates the actual length of a field's value. Read only.
Attributes	Long	Indicates one or more characteristics of a Field object.
DataFormat	Variant	Identifies the format in which data should be displayed.
DefinedSize	Long	Indicates the defined size of the Field object. Write only.
Name	String	Indicates the name of the Field object.
NumericScale	Byte	Indicates the scale of numeric values for the Field object. Write only.
OriginalValue	Variant	Indicates the value of a Field object that existed in the record before any changes were made. Read only.
Precision	Byte	Indicates the degree of precision for numeric values in the Field object. Read only.
Type	DataTypeEnum	Indicates the data type of the Field object.
UnderlyingValue	Variant	Indicates a Field object's current value in the database. Read only.
Value	Variant	Indicates the value assigned to the Field object.

Collections

Collection	Return Type	Description
Properties	Properties collection	Contains all of the Property objects for a Field object.

The Fields Collection

Methods

Method	Return Type	Description
Append		Appends a Field object to the Fields collection.
Delete		Deletes a Field object from the Fields collection.
Refresh		Updates the Field objects in the Fields collection.

Properties

Property	Return Type	Description
Count	Long	Indicates the number of Field objects in the Fields collection. Read only.
Item	Field object	Allows indexing into the Fields collection to reference a specific Field object. Read only.

The Parameter Object

Methods

Method	Return Type	Description
AppendChunk		Appends data to a large or binary Parameter object.

Properties

Property	Return Type	Description
Attributes	Long	Indicates one or more characteristics of a Parameter object.
Direction	Parameter DirectionEnum	Indicates whether the Parameter object represents an input parameter, an output parameter, an input/output parameter, or if the parameter is a return value from a stored procedure.
Name	String	Indicates the name of the Parameter object.
NumericScale	Byte	Indicates the scale of numeric values for the Parameter object.
Precision	Byte	Indicates the degree of precision for numeric values in the Parameter object.
Size	Long	Indicates the maximum size (in bytes or characters) of a Parameter object.
Type	DataTypeEnum	Indicates the data type of the Parameter object.
Value	Variant	Indicates the value assigned to the Parameter object.

Collections

Collection	Return Type	Description
Properties	Properties collection	Contains all of the Property objects for a Parameter object.

The Parameters Collection

Methods

Method	Return Type	Description
Append		Appends a Parameter object to the Parameters collection.
Delete		Deletes a Parameter object from the Parameters collection.
Refresh		Updates the Parameter objects in the Parameters collection.

Properties

Property	Return Type	Description
Count	Long	Indicates the number of Parameter objects in the Parameters collection. Read only.
Item	Parameter object	Allows indexing into the Parameters collection to reference a specific Parameter object. Read only.

The Properties Collection

Methods

Method	Return Type	Description
Refresh		Updates the Property objects in the Properties collection with the details from the provider.

Properties

Property	Return Type	Description
Count	Long	Indicates the number of Property objects in the Properties collection. Read only.
Item	Property	Allows indexing into the Properties collection to reference a specific Property object. Read only.

The Property Object

Properties

Property	Return Type	Description
Attributes	Long	Indicates one or more characteristics of a Property object.
Name	String	Indicates the name of the Property object. Read only.
Type	DataTypeEnum	Indicates the data type of the Property object.
Value	Variant	Indicates the value assigned to the Property object.

The Recordset Object

Methods

Method	Return Type	Description
AddNew		Creates a new record for an updateable Recordset object.
Cancel		Cancels execution of a pending asynchronous Open operation.
CancelBatch		Cancels a pending batch update.
CancelUpdate		Cancels any changes made to the current record, or to a new record prior to calling the Update method.
Clone	Recordset object	Creates a duplicate Recordset object from an existing Recordset object.

Method	Return Type	Description
Close		Closes the Recordset object and any dependent objects.
CompareBookmarks	CompareEnum	Compares two bookmarks and returns an indication of the relative values.
Delete		Deletes the current record or group of records.
Find		Searches the Recordset for a record that matches the specified criteria.
GetRows	Variant	Retrieves multiple records of a Recordset object into an array.
GetString	String	Returns a Recordset as a string.
Move		Moves the position of the current record in a Recordset.
MoveFirst		Moves the position of the current record to the first record in the Recordset.
MoveLast		Moves the position of the current record to the last record in the Recordset.
MoveNext		Moves the position of the current record to the next record in the Recordset.
MovePrevious		Moves the position of the current record to the previous record in the Recordset.
NextRecordset	Recordset object	Clears the current Recordset object and returns the next Recordset by advancing to the next in a series of commands.
Open		Opens a Recordset.
Requery		Updates the data in a Recordset object by re-executing the query on which the object is based.
Resync		Refreshes the data in the current Recordset object from the underlying database.
Save		Saves the Recordset to a file.
Seek (new in ADO 2.1)		Searches the recordset index to locate a value
Supports	Boolean	Determines whether a specified Recordset object supports particular functionality.
Update		Saves any changes made to the current Recordset object.
UpdateBatch		Writes all pending batch updates to disk.

Properties

Property	Return Type	Description
AbsolutePage	PositionEnum	Specifies in which page the current record resides.
AbsolutePosition	PositionEnum	Specifies the ordinal position of the Recordset object's current record.
ActiveCommand	Object	Indicates the Command object that created the associated Recordset object. Read only.
ActiveConnection	Variant	Indicates to which Connection object the Recordset object currently belongs.
BOF	Boolean	Indicates whether the record pointer is pointing before the first record in the Recordset object. Read only.
Bookmark	Variant	Returns a bookmark that uniquely identifies the current record in the Recordset object, or sets the record pointer to point to the record identified by a valid bookmark.
CacheSize	Long	Indicates the number of records from the Recordset object that are cached locally in memory.
CursorLocation	CursorLocation Enum	Sets or returns the location of the cursor engine.
CursorType	CursorTypeEnum	Indicates the type of cursor used in the Recordset object.
DataMember	String	Specifies the name of the data member to be retrieved from the object referenced by the DataSource property. Write only.
DataSource	Object	Specifies an object containing data, to be represented by the Recordset object. Write only.
EditMode	EditModeEnum	Indicates the editing status of the current record. Read only.
EOF	Boolean	Indicates whether the record pointer is pointing beyond the last record in the Recordset object. Read only.
Filter	Variant	Indicates a filter for data in the Recordset.

Property	Return Type	Description
Index (new in ADO 2.1)	String	Identifies the name of the index currently being used.
LockType	LockTypeEnum	Indicates the type of locks placed on records during editing.
MarshalOptions	MarshalOptionsEnum	Indicates which records are to be marshaled back to the server.
MaxRecords	Long	Indicates the maximum number of records that can be returned to the Recordset object from a query. Default is zero (no limit).
PageCount	Long	Indicates how many pages of data are contained in the Recordset object (and is thus dependent on the values of PageSize and RecordCount). Read only.
PageSize	Long	Indicates how many records constitute one page in the Recordset.
RecordCount	Long	Indicates the current number of records in the Recordset object. Read only.
Sort	String	Specifies one or more field names the Recordset is sorted on, and the direction of the sort.
Source	String	Indicates the source for the data in the Recordset object.
State	Long	Indicates whether the recordset is open, closed, or whether it is executing an asynchronous operation. Read only.
Status	Integer	Indicates the status of the current record with respect to match updates or other bulk operations. Read only.
StayInSync	Boolean	Indicates, in a hierarchical Recordset object, whether the parent row should change when the set of underlying child records changes. Read only.

Collections

Collection	Return Type	Description
Fields	Fields collection	Contains all of the Field objects for the Recordset object.
Properties	Properties collection	Contains all of the Property objects for the current Recordset object.

Events

Event	Description
EndOfRecordset	Fired when there is an attempt to move to a row past the end of the Recordset.
FetchComplete	Fired after all the records in an asynchronous operation have been retrieved into the Recordset.
FetchProgress	Fired periodically during a lengthy asynchronous operation, to report how many rows have currently been retrieved.
FieldChangeComplete	Fired after the value of one or more Field objects has been changed.
MoveComplete	Fired after the current position in the Recordset changes.
RecordChangeComplete	Fired after one or more records change.
RecordsetChangeComplete	Fired after the Recordset has changed.
WillChangeField	Fired before a pending operation changes the value of one or more Field objects.
WillChangeRecord	Fired before one or more rows in the Recordset change.
WillChangeRecordset	Fired before a pending operation changes the Recordset.
WillMove	Fired before a pending operation changes the current position in the Recordset.

ADO Method Calls – Quick Reference

Command Object Methods

Command.Cancel
Parameter = Command.CreateParameter(*Name As String, Type As DataTypeEnum,_
    Direction As ParameterDirectionEnum, Size As Integer, [Value As Variant]*)
Recordset = Command.Execute(*RecordsAffected As Variant, Parameters As Variant, _
    Options As Integer*)

Connection Object Methods

Integer = Connection.BeginTrans
Connection.Cancel
Connection.Close
Connection.CommitTrans
Recordset = Connection.Execute(*CommandText As String, RecordsAffected As Variant, _*
    Options As Integer)
Connection.Open(*ConnectionString As String, UserID As String, Password As String, _*
    Options As Integer)
Recordset = Connection.OpenSchema(*Schema As SchemaEnum, [Restrictions As Variant], _*
    [*SchemaID As Variant*])
Connection.RollbackTrans

Errors Collection Methods

Errors.Clear
Errors.Refresh

Field Object Methods

Field.AppendChunk(*Data As Variant*)
Variant = Field.GetChunk(*Length As Integer*)

Fields Collection Methods

Fields.Append(*Name As String, Type As DataTypeEnum, DefinedSize As Integer, _*
    Attrib As FieldAttributeEnum)
Fields.Delete(*Index As Variant*)
Fields.Refresh

Parameter Object Methods

Parameter.AppendChunk(*Val As Variant*)

Parameters Collection Methods

Parameters.Append(*Object As Object*)
Parameters.Delete(*Index As Variant*)
Parameters.Refresh

Properties Collection Methods

Properties.Refresh

Recordset Object Methods

Recordset.AddNew([*FieldList As Variant*], [*Values As Variant*])
Recordset.Cancel
Recordset.CancelBatch(*AffectRecords As AffectEnum*)
Recordset.CancelUpdate
Recordset = Recordset.Clone(*LockType As LockTypeEnum*)
Recordset.Close

CompareEnum = *Recordset*.CompareBookmarks(*Bookmark1 As Variant, Bookmark2 As Variant*)
Recordset.Delete(*AffectRecords As AffectEnum*)
Recordset.Find(*Criteria As String, SkipRecords As Integer, _*
    SearchDirection As SearchDirectionEnum, [Start As Variant])
Variant = *Recordset*.GetRows(*Rows As Integer, [Start As Variant], [Fields As Variant]*)
String = *Recordset*.GetString(*StringFormat As StringFormatEnum, _*
    NumRows As Integer, ColumnDelimeter As String, RowDelimeter As String, _
    NullExpr As String)
Recordset.Move(*NumRecords As Integer, [Start As Variant]*)
Recordset.MoveFirst
Recordset.MoveLast
Recordset.MoveNext
Recordset.MovePrevious
Recordset = *Recordset*.NextRecordset([*RecordsAffected As Variant*])
Recordset.Open(*Source As Variant, ActiveConnection As Variant, _*
    CursorType As CursorTypeEnum, LockType As LockTypeEnum, _
    Options As Integer)
Recordset.Requery(*Options As Integer*)
Recordset.Resync(*AffectRecords As AffectEnum, ResyncValues As ResyncEnum*)
Recordset.Save(*FileName As String, PersistFormat As PersistFormatEnum*)
Recordset.Seek(*KeyValues As Variant, SeekOption As SeekEnum*)
Boolean = *Recordset*.Supports(*CursorOptions As CursorOptionEnum*)
Recordset.Update([*Fields As Variant], [Values As Variant]*)
Recordset.UpdateBatch(*AffectRecords As AffectEnum*)

Suppliers

- SupplierID
- CompanyName
- ContactName
- ContactTitle
- Address
- City
- Region
- PostalCode
- Country
- Phone
- Fax
- HomePage

Products

- ProductID
- ProductName
- SupplierID
- CategoryID
- QuantityPerUnit
- UnitPrice
- UnitsInStock
- UnitsOnOrder
- ReorderLevel
- Discontinued

Categories

- CategoryID
- CategoryName
- Description
- Picture

6

ADO Constants

Standard Constants

The following constants are predefined by ADO. For scripting languages these are included in `adovbs.inc` or `adojava.inc`, which can be found in the `Program Files\Common Files\System\ado` directory. In Visual Basic, these constants are included automatically when you reference the ADO library.

AffectEnum

Name	Value	Description
adAffectAll	3	Operation affects all records in the recordset.
adAffectAllChapters	4	Operation affects all child (chapter) records.
adAffectCurrent	1	Operation affects only the current record.
adAffectGroup	2	Operation affects records that satisfy the current `Filter` property.

BookmarkEnum

Name	Value	Description
adBookmarkCurrent	0	Default. Start at the current record.
adBookmarkFirst	1	Start at the first record.
adBookmarkLast	2	Start at the last record.

CEResyncEnum

Name	Value	Description
adResyncAll	15	Resynchronizes the data for each pending row.
adResyncAutoIncrement	1	Resynchronizes the auto-increment values for all successfully inserted rows. This is the default.
adResyncConflicts	2	Resynchronizes all rows for which an update or delete operation failed due to concurrency conflicts.
adResyncInserts	8	Resynchronizes all successfully inserted rows, including the values of their identity columns.
adResyncNone	0	No resynchronization is performed.
adResyncUpdates	4	Resynchronizes all successfully updated rows.

CommandTypeEnum

Name	Value	Description
adCmdFile	256	Indicates that the provider should evaluate CommandText as a previously persisted file.
adCmdStoredProc	4	Indicates that the provider should evaluate CommandText as a stored procedure.
adCmdTable	2	Indicates that the provider should generate a SQL query to return all rows from the table named in CommandText.
adCmdTableDirect	512	Indicates that the provider should return all rows from the table named in CommandText.

Name	Value	Description
adCmdText	1	Indicates that the provider should evaluate CommandText as textual definition of a command, such as a SQL statement.
adCmdUnknown	8	Indicates that the type of command in CommandText unknown.
adCmdUnspecified	-1	The command type is unspecified.

CompareEnum

Name	Value	Description
adCompareEqual	1	The bookmarks are equal.
adCompareGreaterThan	2	The first bookmark is after the second.
adCompareLessThan	0	The first bookmark is before the second.
adCompareNotComparable	4	The bookmarks cannot be compared.
adCompareNotEqual	3	The bookmarks are not equal and not ordered.

ConnectModeEnum

Name	Value	Description
adModeRead	1	Indicates read-only permissions.
adModeReadWrite	3	Indicates read/write permissions.
adModeShareDenyNone	16	Prevents others from opening connection with any permissions.
adModeShareDenyRead	4	Prevents others from opening connection with read permissions.
adModeShareDenyWrite	8	Prevents others from opening connection with write permissions.
adModeShareExclusive	12	Prevents others from opening connection.
adModeUnknown	0	Default. Indicates that the permissions have not yet been set or cannot be determined.
adModeWrite	2	Indicates write-only permissions.

ConnectOptionEnum

Name	Value	Description
adAsyncConnect	16	Open the connection asynchronously
adConnectUnspecified	-1	The connection mode is unspecified.

ConnectPromptEnum

Name	Value	Description
adPromptAlways	1	Always prompt for connection information.
adPromptComplete	2	Only prompt if not enough information was supplied.
adPromptCompleteRequired	3	Only prompt if not enough information was supplied, but disable any options not directly applicable to the connection.
adPromptNever	4	Default. Never prompt for connection information.

CursorLocationEnum

Name	Value	Description
adUseClient	3	Use client-side cursors supplied by the local cursor library.
adUseClientBatch	3	Use client-side cursors supplied by the local cursor library.
adUseNone	1	No cursor services are used.
adUseServer	2	Default. Uses data provider driver supplied cursors.

CursorOptionEnum

Name	Value	Description
adAddNew	16778240	You can use the AddNew method to add new records.
adApproxPosition	16384	You can read and set the AbsolutePosition and AbsolutePage properties.
adBookmark	8192	You can use the Bookmark property to access specific records.
adDelete	16779264	You can use the Delete method to delete records.
adFind	524288	You can use the Find method to find records.
adHoldRecords	256	You can retrieve more records or change the next retrieve position without committing all pending changes.
adIndex	8388608	You can use the Index property to set the current index.
adMovePrevious	512	You can use the MoveFirst, MovePrevious, Move and GetRows methods.
adNotify	262144	The recordset supports notifications.
adResync	131072	You can update the cursor with the data visible in the underlying database with the Resync method.
adSeek	4194304	You can use the Seek method to find records by an index.
adUpdate	16809984	You can use the Update method to modify existing records.
adUpdateBatch	65536	You can use the UpdateBatch or CancelBatch methods to transfer changes to the provider in groups.

CursorTypeEnum

Name	Value	Description
adOpenDynamic	2	Opens a dynamic type cursor.
adOpenForwardOnly	0	Default. Opens a forward-only type cursor.
adOpenKeyset	1	Opens a keyset type cursor.
adOpenStatic	3	Opens a static type cursor.
adOpenUnspecified	-1	Indicates as unspecified value for cursor type.

DataTypeEnum

Name	Value	Description
adBigInt	20	An 8-byte signed integer.
adBinary	128	A binary value.
adBoolean	11	A Boolean value.
adBSTR	8	A null-terminated character string.
adChapter	136	A chapter type, indicating a child recordset.
adChar	129	A string value.
adCurrency	6	A currency value. An 8-byte signed integer scaled by 10,000, with 4 digits to the right of the decimal point.
adDate	7	A date value. A Double where the whole part is the number of days since December 30 1899, and the fractional part is a fraction of the day.
adDBDate	133	A date value (yyyymmdd).
adDBFileTime	137	A database file time.
adDBTime	134	A time value (hhmmss).
adDBTimeStamp	135	A date-time stamp (yyyymmddhhmmss plus a fraction in billionths).
adDecimal	14	An exact numeric value with fixed precision and scale.
adDouble	5	A double-precision floating point value.
adEmpty	0	No value was specified.
adError	10	A 32-bit error code.

Name	Value	Description
adFileTime	64	A DOS/Win32 file time. The number of 100-nanosecond intervals since Jan 1 1601.
adGUID	72	A globally unique identifier.
adIDispatch	9	A pointer to an IDispatch interface on an OLE object.
adInteger	3	A 4-byte signed integer.
adIUnknown	13	A pointer to an IUnknown interface on an OLE object.
adLongVarBinary	205	A long binary value.
adLongVarChar	201	A long string value.
adLongVarWChar	203	A long null-terminated string value.
adNumeric	131	An exact numeric value with a fixed precision and scale.
adPropVariant	138	A variant that is not equivalent to an Automation variant.
adSingle	4	A single-precision floating point value.
adSmallInt	2	A 2-byte signed integer.
adTinyInt	16	A 1-byte signed integer.
adUnsignedBigInt	21	An 8-byte unsigned integer.
adUnsignedInt	19	An 4-byte unsigned integer.
adUnsignedSmallInt	18	An 2-byte unsigned integer.
adUnsignedTinyInt	17	A 1-byte unsigned integer.
adUserDefined	132	A user-defined variable.
adVarBinary	204	A binary value.
adVarChar	200	A string value.
adVariant	12	An Automation variant.
adVarNumeric	139	A variable width exact numeric, with a signed scale value.
adVarWChar	202	A null-terminated Unicode character string.
adWChar	130	A null-terminated Unicode character string.

EditModeEnum

Name	Value	Description
adEditAdd	2	Indicates that the AddNew method has been invoked and the current record in the buffer is a new record that hasn't been saved to the database.
adEditDelete	4	Indicates that the Delete method has been invoked.
adEditInProgress	1	Indicates that data in the current record has been modified but not saved.
adEditNone	0	Indicates that no editing is in progress.

ErrorValueEnum

Name	Value	Description
adErrBoundToCommand	3707	The application cannot change the ActiveConnection property of a Recordset object with a Command object as its source.
adErrDataConversion	3421	The application is using a value of the wrong type for the current application.
adErrFeatureNotAvailable	3251	The operation requested by the application is not supported by the provider.
adErrIllegalOperation	3219	The operation requested by the application is not allowed in this context.
adErrInTransaction	3246	The application cannot explicitly close a Connection object while in the middle of a transaction.
adErrInvalidArgument	3001	The application is using arguments that are the wrong type, are out of the acceptable range, or are in conflict with one another.
adErrInvalidConnection	3709	The application requested an operation on an object with a reference to a closed or invalid Connection object.

Name	Value	Description
adErrInvalidParamInfo	3708	The application has improperly defined a Parameter object.
adErrItemNotFound	3265	ADO could not find the object in the collection.
adErrNoCurrentRecord	3021	Either BOF or EOF is True, or the current record has been deleted. The operation requested by the application requires a current record.
adErrNotExecuting	3715	The operation is not executing.
adErrNotReentrant	3710	The operation is not reentrant.
adErrObjectClosed	3704	The operation requested by the application is not allowed if the object is closed.
adErrObjectInCollection	3367	Can't append. Object already in collection.
adErrObjectNotSet	3420	The object referenced by the application no longer points to a valid object.
adErrObjectOpen	3705	The operation requested by the application is not allowed if the object is open.
adErrOperationCancelled	3712	The operation was cancelled.
adErrProviderNotFound	3706	ADO could not find the specified provider.
adErrStillConnecting	3713	The operation is still connecting.
adErrStillExecuting	3711	The operation is still executing.
adErrUnsafeOperation	3716	The operation is unsafe under these circumstances.

EventReasonEnum

Name	Value	Description
adRsnAddNew	1	A new record is to be added.
adRsnClose	9	The object is being closed.
adRsnDelete	2	The record is being deleted.
adRsnFirstChange	11	The record has been changed for the first time.

Table Continued on Following Page

Name	Value	Description
adRsnMove	10	A Move has been invoked and the current record pointer is being moved.
adRsnMoveFirst	12	A MoveFirst has been invoked and the current record pointer is being moved.
adRsnMoveLast	15	A MoveLast has been invoked and the current record pointer is being moved.
adRsnMoveNext	13	A MoveNext has been invoked and the current record pointer is being moved.
adRsnMovePrevious	14	A MovePrevious has been invoked and the current record pointer is being moved.
adRsnRequery	7	The recordset was requeried.
adRsnResynch	8	The recordset was resynchronized.
adRsnUndoAddNew	5	The addition of a new record has been cancelled.
adRsnUndoDelete	6	The deletion of a record has been cancelled.
adRsnUndoUpdate	4	The update of a record has been cancelled.
adRsnUpdate	3	The record is being updated.

EventStatusEnum

Name	Value	Description
adStatusCancel	4	Request cancellation of the operation that is about to occur.
adStatusCantDeny	3	A Will event cannot request cancellation of the operation about to occur.
adStatusErrorsOccurred	2	The operation completed unsuccessfully, or a Will... event cancelled the operation.
adStatusOK	1	The operation completed successfully.
adStatusUnwantedEvent	5	Events for this operation are no longer required.

ExecuteOptionEnum

Name	Value	Description
adAsyncExecute	16	The operation is executed asynchronously.
adAsyncFetch	32	The records are fetched asynchronously.
adAsyncFetchNonBlocking	64	The records are fetched asynchronously without blocking subsequent operations.
adExecuteNoRecords	128	Indicates CommandText is a command or stored procedure that does not return rows. Always combined with adCmdText or adCmdStoreProc.

FieldAttributeEnum

Name	Value	Description
adFldCacheDeferred	4096	Indicates that the provider caches field values and that subsequent reads are done from the cache.
adFldFixed	16	Indicates that the field contains fixed-length data.
adFldIsNullable	32	Indicates that the field accepts Null values.
adFldKeyColumn	32768	The field is part of a key column.
adFldLong	128	Indicates that the field is a long binary field, and that the AppendChunk and GetChunk methods can be used.
adFldMayBeNull	64	Indicates that you can read Null values from the field.
adFldMayDefer	2	Indicates that the field is deferred, that is, the field values are not retrieved from the data source with the whole record, but only when you access them.
adFldNegativeScale	16384	The field has a negative scale.
adFldRowID	256	Indicates that the field some kind of record ID.
adFldRowVersion	512	Indicates that the field time or date stamp used to track updates.
adFldUnknownUpdatable	8	Indicates that the provider cannot determine if you can write to the field.
adFldUnspecified	-1	Attributes of the field are unspecified.
adFldUpdatable	4	Indicates that you can write to the field.

FilterGroupEnum

Name	Value	Description
adFilterAffectedRecords	2	Allows you to view only records affected by the last `Delete`, `Resync`, `UpdateBatch` or `CancelBatch` method.
adFilterConflictingRecords	5	Allows you to view the records that failed the last batch update attempt.
adFilterFetchedRecords	3	Allows you to view records in the current cache.
adFilterNone	0	Removes the current filter and restores all records to view.
adFilterPendingRecords	1	Allows you to view only the records that have changed but have not been sent to the server. Only applicable for batch update mode.
adFilterPredicate	4	Allows you to view records that failed the last batch update attempt.

GetRowsOptionEnum

Name	Value	Description
adGetRowsRest	-1	Retrieves the remainder of the rows in the recordset.

IsolationLevelEnum

Name	Value	Description
adXactBrowse	256	Indicates that from one transaction you can view uncommitted changes in other transactions.
adXactChaos	16	Default. Indicates that you cannot overwrite pending changes from more highly isolated transactions.

Name	Value	Description
adXactCursorStability	4096	Default. Indicates that from one transaction you can view changes in other transactions only after they have been committed.
adXactIsolated	1048576	Indicates that transactions are conducted in isolation of other transactions.
adXactReadCommitted	4096	Same as adXactCursorStability.
adXactReadUncommitted	256	Same as adXactBrowse.
adXactRepeatableRead	65536	Indicates that from one transaction you cannot see changes made in other transactions, but that requerying can bring new recordsets.
adXactSerializable	1048576	Same as adXactIsolated.
adXactUnspecified	-1	Indicates that the provider is using a different IsolationLevel than specified, but that the level cannot be identified.

LockTypeEnum

Name	Value	Description
adLockBatchOptimistic	4	Optimistic batch updates.
adLockOptimistic	3	Optimistic locking, record by record. The provider locks records when Update is called.
adLockPessimistic	2	Pessimistic locking, record by record. The provider locks the record immediately upon editing.
adLockReadOnly	1	Default. Read only, data cannot be modified.
adLockUnspecified	-1	The clone is created with the same lock type as the original.

MarshalOptionsEnum

Name	Value	Description
adMarshalAll	0	Default. Indicates that all rows are returned to the server.
adMarshalModifiedOnly	1	Indicates that only modified rows are returned to the server.

ObjectStateEnum

Name	Value	Description
adStateClosed	0	Default. Indicates that the object is closed.
adStateConnecting	2	Indicates that the object is connecting.
adStateExecuting	4	Indicates that the object is executing a command.
adStateFetching	8	Indicates that the rows of the recordset are being fetched.
adStateOpen	1	Indicates that the object is open.

ParameterAttributesEnum

Name	Value	Description
adParamLong	128	Indicates that the parameter accepts long binary data.
adParamNullable	64	Indicates that the parameter accepts Null values.
adParamSigned	16	Default. Indicates that the parameter accepts signed values.

ParameterDirectionEnum

Name	Value	Description
adParamInput	1	Default. Indicates an input parameter.
adParamInputOutput	3	Indicates both an input and output parameter.
adParamOutput	2	Indicates an output parameter.
adParamReturnValue	4	Indicates a return value.
adParamUnknown	0	Indicates parameter direction is unknown.

PersistFormatEnum

Name	Value	Description
adPersistADTG	0	Default. Persist data in Advanced Data TableGram format.
adPersistXML	1	Persist data in XML format.

PositionEnum

Name	Value	Description
adPosBOF	-2	The current record pointer is at BOF.
adPosEOF	-3	The current record pointer is at EOF.
adPosUnknown	-1	The Recordset is empty, or the current position is unknown, or the provider does not support the AbsolutePage property.

PropertyAttributesEnum

Name	Value	Description
adPropNotSupported	0	Indicates that the property is not supported by the provider.
adPropOptional	2	Indicates that the user does not need to specify a value for this property before the data source is initialized.
adPropRead	512	Indicates that the user can read the property.
adPropRequired	1	Indicates that the user must specify a value for this property before the data source is initialized.
adPropWrite	1024	Indicates that the user can set the property.

RecordStatusEnum

Name	Value	Description
adRecCanceled	256	The record was not saved because the operation was cancelled.
adRecCantRelease	1024	The new record was not saved because of existing record locks.
adRecConcurrencyViolation	2048	The record was not saved because optimistic concurrency was in use.
adRecDBDeleted	262144	The record has already been deleted from the data source.
adRecDeleted	4	The record was deleted.

Table Continued on Following Page

Name	Value	Description
adRecIntegrityViolation	4096	The record was not saved because the user violated integrity constraints.
adRecInvalid	16	The record was not saved because its bookmark is invalid.
adRecMaxChangesExceeded	8192	The record was not saved because there were too many pending changes.
adRecModified	2	The record was modified.
adRecMultipleChanges	64	The record was not saved because it would have affected multiple records.
adRecNew	1	The record is new.
adRecObjectOpen	16384	The record was not saved because of a conflict with an open storage object.
adRecOK	0	The record was successfully updated.
adRecOutOfMemory	32768	The record was not saved because the computer has run out of memory.
adRecPendingChanges	128	The record was not saved because it refers to a pending insert.
adRecPermissionDenied	65536	The record was not saved because the user has insufficient permissions.
adRecSchemaViolation	131072	The record was not saved because it violates the structure of the underlying database.
adRecUnmodified	8	The record was not modified.

ResyncEnum

Name	Value	Description
adResyncAllValues	2	Default. Data is overwritten and pending updates are cancelled.
adResyncUnderlyingValues	1	Data is not overwritten and pending updates are not cancelled.

SchemaEnum

Name	Value	Description
adSchemaAsserts	0	Request assert information.
adSchemaCatalogs	1	Request catalog information.
adSchemaCharacterSets	2	Request character set information.
adSchemaCheckConstraints	5	Request check constraint information.
adSchemaCollations	3	Request collation information.
adSchemaColumnPrivileges	13	Request column privilege information.
adSchemaColumns	4	Request column information.
adSchemaColumnsDomainUsage	11	Request column domain usage information.
adSchemaConstraintColumnUsage	6	Request column constraint usage information.
adSchemaConstraintTableUsage	7	Request table constraint usage information.
adSchemaCubes	32	For multi-dimensional data, view the Cubes schema.
adSchemaDBInfoKeywords	30	Request the keywords from the provider.
adSchemaDBInfoLiterals	31	Request the literals from the provider.
adSchemaDimensions	33	For multi-dimensional data, view the Dimensions schema.
adSchemaForeignKeys	27	Request foreign key information.
adSchemaHierarchies	34	For multi-dimensional data, view the Hierarchies schema.
adSchemaIndexes	12	Request index information.
adSchemaKeyColumnUsage	8	Request key column usage information.
adSchemaLevels	35	For multi-dimensional data, view the Levels schema.
adSchemaMeasures	36	For multi-dimensional data, view the Measures schema.

Table Continued on Following Page

Name	Value	Description
adSchemaMembers	38	For multi-dimensional data, view the Members schema.
adSchemaPrimaryKeys	28	Request primary key information.
adSchemaProcedureColumns	29	Request stored procedure column information.
adSchemaProcedureParameters	26	Request stored procedure parameter information.
adSchemaProcedures	16	Request stored procedure information.
adSchemaProperties	37	For multi-dimensional data, view the Properties schema.
adSchemaProviderSpecific	-1	Request provider specific information.
adSchemaProviderTypes	22	Request provider type information.
adSchemaReferentialContraints	9	Request referential constraint information.
adSchemaReferentialConstraints	9	Request referential constraint information.
adSchemaSchemata	17	Request schema information.
adSchemaSQLLanguages	18	Request SQL language support information.
adSchemaStatistics	19	Request statistics information.
adSchemaTableConstraints	10	Request table constraint information.
adSchemaTablePrivileges	14	Request table privilege information.
adSchemaTables	20	Request information about the tables.
adSchemaTranslations	21	Request character set translation information.
adSchemaTrustees	39	Request trustee information.
adSchemaUsagePrivileges	15	Request user privilege information.
adSchemaViewColumnUsage	24	Request column usage in views information.
adSchemaViews	23	Request view information.
adSchemaViewTableUsage	25	Request table usage in views information.

Due to a misspelling in the type library, `adSchemaReferentialConstraints` is included twice – once for the original spelling and once for the corrected spelling.

SearchDirectionEnum

Name	Value	Description
adSearchBackward	-1	Search backward from the current record.
adSearchForward	1	Search forward from the current record.

SeekEnum

Name	Value	Description
adSeekAfter	8	Seek the key just after the match.
adSeekAfterEQ	4	Seek the key equal to or just after the match.
adSeekBefore	32	See the key just before the match.
adSeekBeforeEQ	16	Seek the key equal to or just before the match.
adSeekFirstEQ	1	Seek the first key equal to the match.
adSeekLastEQ	2	Seek the last key equal to the match.

StringFormatEnum

Name	Value	Description
adClipString	2	Rows are delimited by user defined values.

XactAttributeEnum

Name	Value	Description
adXactAbortRetaining	262144	The provider will automatically start a new transaction after a `RollbackTrans` method call.
adXactAsyncPhaseOne	524288	Perform an asynchronous commit.
adXactCommitRetaining	131072	The provider will automatically start a new transaction after a `CommitTrans` method call.
adXactSyncPhaseOne	1048576	Performs an synchronous commit.

Miscellaneous Constants

These values are not included in the standard adovbs.inc include file (and are not automatically supplied when using Visual Basic), but can be found in adocon.inc (for ASP) and adocon.bas (for Visual Basic). These can be downloaded from the web page for ADO 2.1 Programmer's Reference, also from Wrox, at http://webdev.wrox.co.uk/books/2688.

Many of these may not be necessary to you as an ADO programmer, but they are included here for completeness, and are only really useful as bitmask values for entries in the Properties collection.

DBBINDURLFLAG

Name	Value	Description
DBBINDURLFLAG_DELAYFETCHCOLUMNS	32768	This value is not supported by this version of ADO.
DBBINDURLFLAG_DELAYFETCHSTREAM	16384	This value is not supported by this version of ADO.
DBBINDURLFLAG_OUTPUT	8388608	Bind to the executed output, rather than the resource source.
DBBINDURLFLAG_RECURSIVE	4191304	This value is not supported by this version of ADO.

DB_COLLATION

Name	Value	Description
DB_COLLATION_ASC	1	The sort sequence for the column is ascending.
DB_COLLATION_DESC	2	The sort sequence for the column is descending.

DB_IMP_LEVEL

Name	Value	Description
DB_IMP_LEVEL_ANONYMOUS	0	The client is anonymous to the server, and the server process cannot obtain identification information about the client and cannot impersonate the client.
DB_IMP_LEVEL_DELEGATE	3	The process can impersonate the client's security context while acting on behalf of the client. The server process can also make outgoing calls to other servers while acting on behalf of the client.

Name	Value	Description
DB_IMP_LEVEL_IDENTIFY	1	The server can obtain the client's identity, and can impersonate the client for ACL checking, but cannot access system objects as the client.
DB_IMP_LEVEL_IMPERSONATE	2	The server process can impersonate the client's security context whilst acting on behalf of the client. This information is obtained upon connection and not on every call.

DB_MODE

Name	Value	Description
DB_MODE_READ	1	Read only.
DB_MODE_READWRITE	3	Read/Write (equal to DB_MODE_READ + DB_MODE_WRITE).
DB_MODE_SHARE_DENY_NONE	16	Neither read nor write access can be denied to others.
DB_MODE_SHARE_DENY_READ	4	Prevents others from opening in read mode.
DB_MODE_SHARE_DENY_WRITE	8	Prevents others from opening in write mode.
DB_MODE_SHARE_EXCLUSIVE	12	Prevents others from opening in read/write mode (equal to DB_MODE_SHARE_DENY_WRITE + DB_MODE_SHARE_DENY_WRITE).
DB_MODE_WRITE	2	Write only.

DB_PROT_LEVEL

Name	Value	Description
DB_PROT_LEVEL_CALL	2	Authenticates the source of the data at the beginning of each request from the client to the server.
DB_PROT_LEVEL_CONNECT	1	Authenticates only when the client establishes the connection with the server.

Table Continued on Following Page

Name	Value	Description
DB_PROT_LEVEL_NONE	0	Performs no authentication of data sent to the server.
DB_PROT_LEVEL_PKT	3	Authenticates that all data received is from the client.
DB_PROT_LEVEL_PKT_INTEGRITY	4	Authenticates that all data received is from the client and that it has not been changed in transit.
DB_PROT_LEVEL_PKT_PRIVACY	5	Authenticates that all data received is from the client, that it has not been changed in transit, and protects the privacy of the data by encrypting it.

DB_PT

Name	Value	Description
DB_PT_FUNCTION	3	Function; there is a returned value.
DB_PT_PROCEDURE	2	Procedure; there is no returned value.
DB_PT_UNKNOWN	1	It is not known whether there is a returned value.

DB_SEARCHABLE

Name	Value	Description
DB_ALL_EXCEPT_LIKE	3	The data type can be used in a WHERE clause with all comparison operators except LIKE.
DB LIKE_ONLY	2	The data type can be used in a WHERE clause only with the LIKE predicate.
DB_SEARCHABLE	4	The data type can be used in a WHERE clause with any comparison operator.
DB_UNSEARCHABLE	1	The data type cannot be used in a WHERE clause.

DBCOLUMNDESCFLAG

Name	Value	Description
DBCOLUMNDESCFLAG _CLSID	8	The CLSID portion of the column description can be changed when altering the column.
DBCOLUMNDESCFLAG _COLSIZE	16	The column size portion of the column description can be changed when altering the column.
DBCOLUMNDESCFLAG _DBCID	32	The DBCID portion of the column description can be changed when altering the column.
DBCOLUMNDESCFLAG _ITYPEINFO	2	The type information portion of the column description can be changed when altering the column.
DBCOLUMNDESCFLAG _PRECISION	128	The precision portion of the column description can be changed when altering the column.
DBCOLUMNDESCFLAG _PROPERTIES	4	The property sets portion of the column description can be changed when altering the column.
DBCOLUMNDESCFLAG _SCALE	256	The numeric scale portion of the column description can be changed when altering the column.
DBCOLUMNDESCFLAG _TYPENAME	1	The type name portion of the column description can be changed when altering the column.
DBCOLUMNDESCFLAG _WTYPE	64	The data type portion of the column description can be changed when altering the column.

DBCOLUMNFLAGS

Name	Value	Description
DBCOLUMNFLAGS_CACHEDEFERRED	4096	Indicates that the value of a deferred column is cached when it is first read.
DBCOLUMNFLAGS_ISCHAPTER	8192	The column contains a chapter value.
DBCOLUMNFLAGS_ISFIXEDLENGTH	16	All of the data in the column is of a fixed length.
DBCOLUMNFLAGS_ISLONG	128	The column contains a BLOB value that contains long data.

Table Continued on Following Page

Name	Value	Description
DBCOLUMNFLAGS_ISNULLABLE	32	The column can be set to NULL, or the provider cannot determine whether the column can be set to NULL.
DBCOLUMNFLAGS_ISROWID	256	The column contains a persistent row identifier.
DBCOLUMNFLAGS_ISROWVER	512	The column contains a timestamp or other row versioning data type.
DBCOLUMNFLAGS_MAYBENULL	64	NULLs can be retrieved from the column.
DBCOLUMNFLAGS_MAYDEFER	2	The column is deferred.
DBCOLUMNFLAGS_WRITE	4	The column may be updated.
DBCOLUMNFLAGS_WRITEUNKNOWN	8	It is not know if the column can be updated.

DBLITERAL

Name	Value	Description
DBLITERAL_INVALID		An invalid value.
DBLITERAL_BINARY_LITERAL		A binary literal in a text command.
DBLITERAL_CATALOG_NAME		A catalog name in a text command.
DBLITERAL_CATALOG_SEPARATOR		The character that separates the catalog name from the rest of the identifier in a text command.
DBLITERAL_CHAR_LITERAL		A character literal in a text command.
DBLITERAL_COLUMN_ALIAS		A column alias in a text command.
DBLITERAL_COLUMN_NAME		A column name used in a text command or in a data-definition interface.
DBLITERAL_CORRELATION_NAME		A correlation name (table alias) in a text command.

Name	Value	Description
DBLITERAL_CURSOR_NAME		A cursor name in a text command.
DBLITERAL_ESCAPE_PERCENT_PREFIX		The character used in a LIKE clause to escape the character returned for the DBLITERAL_LIKE_PERCENT literal.
DBLITERAL_ESCAPE_PERCENT_SUFFIX		The escape character, if any, used to suffix the character returned for the DBLITERAL_LIKE_PERCENT literal.
DBLITERAL_ESCAPE_UNDERSCORE_PREFIX		The character used in a LIKE clause to escape the character returned for the DBLITERAL_LIKE_UNDERSCORE literal.
DBLITERAL_ESCAPE_UNDERSCORE_SUFFIX		The escape character, if any, used to suffix the character returned for the DBLITERAL_LIKE_UNDERSCORE literal.
DBLITERAL_INDEX_NAME		An index name used in a text command or in a data-definition interface.
DBLITERAL_LIKE_PERCENT		The character used in a LIKE clause to match zero or more characters.
DBLITERAL_LIKE_UNDERSCORE		The character used in a LIKE clause to match exactly one character.
DBLITERAL_PROCEDURE_NAME		A procedure name in a text command.
DBLITERAL_SCHEMA_NAME		A schema name in a text command.
DBLITERAL_SCHEMA_SEPARATOR		The character that separates the schema name from the rest of the identifier in a text command.

Table Continued on Following Page

Name	Value	Description
DBLITERAL_TABLE_NAME		A table name used in a text command or in a data-definition interface.
DBLITERAL_TEXT_COMMAND		A text command, such as an SQL statement.
DBLITERAL_USER_NAME		A user name in a text command.
DBLITERAL_VIEW_NAME		A view name in a text command.
DBLITERAL_QUOTE_PREFIX		The character used in a text command as the opening quote for quoting identifiers that contain special characters.
DBLITERAL_QUOTE_SUFFIX		The character used in a text command as the closing quote for quoting identifiers that contain special characters.

DBPARAMTYPE

Name	Value	Description
DBPARAMTYPE_INPUT	1	The parameter is an input parameter.
DBPARAMTYPE_INPUTOUTPUT	2	The parameter is both an input and an output parameter.
DBPARAMTYPE_OUTPUT	3	The parameter is an output parameter.
DBPARAMTYPE_RETURNVALUE	4	The parameter is a return value.

DBPROMPT

Name	Value	Description
DBPROMPT_COMPLETE	2	Prompt the user only if more information is needed.
DBPROMPT_COMPLETEREQUIRED	3	Prompt the user only if more information is required. Do not allow the user to enter optional information.
DBPROMPT_NOPROMPT	4	Do not prompt the user.
DBPROMPT_PROMPT	1	Always prompt the user for initialization information.

DBPROPVAL_AO

Name	Value	Description
DBPROPVAL_AO_RANDOM	2	Columns can be accessed in any order.
DBPROPVAL_AO_SEQUENTIAL	0	All columns must be accessed in sequential order determined by the column ordinal.
DBPROPVAL_AO _SEQUENTIALSTORAGEOBJECTS	1	Columns bound as storage objects can only be accessed in sequential order as determined by the column ordinal.

DBPROPVAL_ASYNCH

Name	Value	Description
DBPROPVAL_ASYNCH _BACKGROUNDPOPULATION	8	The rowset is populated asynchronously in the background.
DBPROPVAL_ASYNCH _INITIALIZE	1	Initialization is performed asynchronously.
DBPROPVAL_ASYNCH _POPULATIONDEMAND	32	The consumer prefers to optimize for getting each individual request for data returned as quickly as possible.
DBPROPVAL_ASYNCH_ PREPOPULATE	16	The consumer prefers to optimize for retrieving all data when the row set is materialized.
DBPROPVAL_ASYNCH _RANDOMPOPULATION	4	Rowset population is performed asynchronously in a random manner.
DBPROPVAL_ASYNCH _SEQUENTIALPOPULATION	2	Rowset population is performed asynchronously in a sequential manner.

DBPROPVAL_BG

Name	Value	Description
DBPROPVAL_GB_COLLATE	16	A COLLATE clause can be specified at the end of each grouping column.

Table Continued on Following Page

Name	Value	Description
DBPROPVAL_GB_CONTAINS_SELECT	4	The GROUP BY clause must contain all non-aggregated columns in the select list. It can contain columns that are not in the select list.
DBPROPVAL_GB_EQUALS_SELECT	2	The GROUP BY clause must contain all non-aggregated columns in the select list. It cannot contain any other columns.
DBPROPVAL_GB_NO_RELATION	8	The columns in the GROUP BY clause and the select list are not related. The meaning on non-grouped, non-aggregated columns in the select list is data source dependent.
DBPROPVAL_GB_NOT_SUPPORTED	1	GROUP BY clauses are not supported.

DBPROPVAL_BI

Name	Value	Description
DBPROPVAL_BI_CROSSROWSET	1	Bookmark values are valid across all rowsets generated on this table.

DBPROPVAL_BMK

Name	Value	Description
DBPROPVAL_BMK_KEY	2	The bookmark type is key.
DBPROPVAL_BMK_NUMERIC	1	The bookmark type is numeric.

DBPROPVAL_BO

Name	Value	Description
DBPROPVAL_BO_NOINDEXUPDATE	1	The provider is not required to update indexes based on inserts or changes to the rowset. Any indexes need to be re-created following changes made through the rowset.

Name	Value	Description
DBPROPVAL_BO_NOLOG	0	The provider is not required to log inserts or changes to the rowset.
DBPROPVAL_BO_REFINTEGRITY	2	Referential integrity constraints do not need to be checked or enforced for changes made through the rowset.

DBPROPVAL_BP

Name	Value	Description
DBPROPVAL_BP_NOPARTIAL	2	Fail the bulk operation if there is a single error.
DBPROPVAL_BP_PARTIAL	1	Allow the bulk operation to partially complete, possibly resulting in inconsistent data.

DBPROPVAL_BT

Name	Value	Description
DBPROPVAL_BT_DEFAULT	0	Use the value defined in the dynamic property Jet OLEDB:Global Bulk Transactions
DBPROPVAL_BT_NOBULKTRANSACTIONS	1	Bulk operations are not transacted.
DBPROPVAL_BT_BULKTRANSACTION	2	Bulk operations are transacted.

DBPROPVAL_CB

Name	Value	Description
DBPROPVAL_CB_NON_NULL	2	The result is the concatenation of the non-NULL valued column or columns.
DBPROPVAL_CB_NULL	1	The result is NULL-valued.

DBPROPVAL_CB

Name	Value	Description
DBPROPVAL_CB_DELETE	1	Aborting a transaction deletes prepared commands.
DBPROPVAL_CB_PRESERVE	2	Aborting a transaction preserves prepared commands.

DBPROPVAL_CD

Name	Value	Description
DBPROPVAL_CD_NOTNULL	1	Columns can be created non-nullable.

DBPROPVAL_CL

Name	Value	Description
DBPROPVAL_CL_END	2	The catalog name appears at the end of the fully qualified name.
DBPROPVAL_CL_START	1	The catalog name appears at the start of the fully qualified name.

DBPROPVAL_CO

Name	Value	Description
DBPROPVAL_CO_BEGINSWITH	32	Provider supports the BEGINSWITH and NOTBEGINSWITH operators.
DBPROPVAL_CO_CASEINSENSITIVE	8	Provider supports the CASEINSENSITIVE operator.
DBPROPVAL_CO_CASESENSITIVE	4	Provider supports the CASESENSITIVE operator.
DBPROPVAL_CO_CONTAINS	16	Provider supports the CONTAINS and NOTCONTAINS operators.
DBPROPVAL_CO_EQUALITY	1	Provider supports the following operators: LT, LE, EQ, GE, GT, NE.
DBPROPVAL_CO_STRING	2	Provider supports the BEGINSWITH operator.

DBPROPVAL_CS

Name	Value	Description
DBPROPVAL_CS_COMMUNICATIONFAILURE	2	The DSO is unable to communicate wit the data store.
DBPROPVAL_CS_INITIALIZED	1	The DSO is in an initialized state and able to communicate with the data store.
DBPROPVAL_CS_UNINITIALIZED	0	The DSO is in an uninitialized state.

DBPROPVAL_CU

Name	Value	Description
DBPROPVAL_CU_DML_STATEMENTS	1	Catalog names are supported in all Data Manipulation Language statements.
DBPROPVAL_CU_INDEX_DEFINITION	4	Catalog names are supported in all index definition statements.
DBPROPVAL_CU_PRIVILEGE_DEFINITION	8	Catalog names are supported in all privilege definition statements.
DBPROPVAL_CU_TABLE_DEFINITION	2	Catalog names are supported in all table definition statements.

DBPROPVAL_DF

Name	Value	Description
DBPROPVAL_DF_INITIALLY_DEFERRED	1	The foreign key is initially deferred.
DBPROPVAL_DF_INITIALLY_IMMEDIATE	2	The foreign key is initially immediate.
DBPROPVAL_DF_NOT_DEFERRABLE	3	The foreign key is not deferrable.

DBPROPVAL_DL

Name	Value	Description
DBPROPVAL_DL_OLDMODE	0	Mode used in previous versions of the Jet database.
DBPROPVAL_DL_ALCATRAZ	1	Use new method, allowing row level locking.

DBPROPVAL_DST

Name	Value	Description
DBPROPVAL_DST_MDP	2	The provider is a multidimensional provider (MD).
DBPROPVAL_DST_TDP	1	The provider is a tabular data provider (TDP).
DBPROPVAL_DST_TDPANDMDP	3	The provider is both a TDP and a MD provider.
DBPROPVAL_DST_DOCSOURCE	4	The provider is a document source (Internet Publishing Provider).

DBPROPVAL_GU

Name	Value	Description
DBPROPVAL_GU_NOTSUPPORTED	1	URL suffixes are not supported. This is the only option supported by the Internet Publishing Provider in this version of ADO.
DBPROPVAL_GU_SUFFIX	2	URL suffixes are generated by the Internet Publishing Provider.

DBPROPVAL_HT

Name	Value	Description
DBPROPVAL_HT_DIFFERENT_CATALOGS	1	The provider supports heterogeneous joins between catalogs.
DBPROPVAL_HT_DIFFERENT_PROVIDERS	2	The provider supports heterogeneous joins between providers.

DBPROPVAL_IC

Name	Value	Description
DBPROPVAL_IC_LOWER	2	Identifiers in SQL are case insensitive and are stored in lower case in system catalog.
DBPROPVAL_IC_MIXED	8	Identifiers in SQL are case insensitive and are stored in mixed case in system catalog.
DBPROPVAL_IC_SENSITIVE	4	Identifiers in SQL are case sensitive and are stored in mixed case in system catalog.
DBPROPVAL_IC_UPPER	1	Identifiers in SQL are case insensitive and are stored in upper case in system catalog.

DBPROPVAL_IN

Name	Value	Description
DBPROPVAL_IN_ALLOWNULL	0	The index allows NULL values to be inserted.
DBPROPVAL_IN_DISALLOWNULL	1	The index does not allow entries where the key columns are NULL. An error will be generated if the consumer attempts to insert a NULL value into a key column.
DBPROPVAL_IN_IGNOREANYNULL	4	The index does not insert entries containing NULL keys.
DBPROPVAL_IN_IGNORENULL	2	The index does not insert entries where some column key has a NULL value.

DBPROPVAL_IT

Name	Value	Description
DBPROPVAL_IT_BTREE	1	The index is a B+ tree.
DBPROPVAL_IT_CONTENT	3	The index is a content index.
DBPROPVAL_IT_HASH	2	The index is a hash file using linear or extensible hashing.
DBPROPVAL_IT_OTHER	4	The index is some other type of index.

DBPROPVAL_JCC

Name	Value	Description
DBPROPVAL_JCC_PASSIVESHUTDOWN	1	New connections to the database are disallowed.
DBPROPVAL_JCC_NORMAL	2	Users are allowed to connect to the database.

DBPROPVAL_LG

Name	Value	Description
DBPROPVAL_LG_PAGE	1	Use page locking.
DBPROPVAL_LG_ALCATRAZ	2	Use row-level locking.

DBPROPVAL_LM

Name	Value	Description
DBPROPVAL_LM_INTENT	4	The provider uses the maximum level of locking to ensure that changes will not fail due to a concurrency violation.
DBPROPVAL_LM_NONE	1	The provider is not required to lock rows at any time to ensure successful updates.
DBPROPVAL_LM_READ	2	The provider uses the minimum level of locking to ensure that changes will not fail due to a concurrency violation.
DBPROPVAL_LM_SINGLEROW	2	The provider uses the minimum level of locking to ensure that changes will not fail due to a concurrency violation.
DBPROPVAL_LM_WRITE	8	This constant is not documented.

DBPROPVAL_MR

Name	Value	Description
DBPROPVAL_MR_CONCURRENT	2	More than one rowset create by the same multiple results object can exist concurrently.
DBPROPVAL_MR_NOTSUPPORTED	0	Multiple results objects are not supported.
DBPROPVAL_MR_SUPPORTED	1	The provider supports multiple results objects.

DBPROPVAL_NC

Name	Value	Description
DBPROPVAL_NC_END	1	NULLs are sorted at the end of the list, regardless of the sort order.
DBPROPVAL_NC_HIGH	2	NULLs are sorted at the high end of the list.
DBPROPVAL_NC_LOW	4	NULLs are sorted at the low end of the list.
DBPROPVAL_NC_START	8	NULLs are sorted at the start of the list, regardless of the sort order.

DBPROPVAL_NP

Name	Value	Description
DBPROPVAL_NP_ABOUTTODO	2	The consumer will be notified before an action (ie the Will event).
DBPROPVAL_NP_DIDEVENT	16	The consumer will be notified after an action (ie the Complete event).
DBPROPVAL_NP_FAILEDTODO	8	The consumer will be notified if an action failed (ie a Will or Complete event).
DBPROPVAL_NP_OKTODO	1	The consumer will be notified of events.
DBPROPVAL_NP_SYNCHAFTER	4	The consumer will be notified when the rowset is resynchronized.

DBPROPVAL_NT

Name	Value	Description
DBPROPVAL_NT_MULTIPLEROWS	2	For methods that operate on multiple rows, and generate multiphased notifications (events), then the provider calls OnRowChange once for all rows that succeed and once for all rows that fail.
DBPROPVAL_NT_SINGLEROW	1	For methods that operate on multiple rows, and generate multiphased notifications (events), then the provider calls OnRowChange separately for each phase for each row.

DBPROPVAL_OA

Name	Value	Description
DBPROPVAL_OA_ATEXECUTE	2	Output parameter data is available immediately after the Command.Execute returns.
DBPROPVAL_OA_ATROWRELEASE	4	Output parameter data is available when the rowset is release. For a single rowset operation this is when the rowset is completely released (closed) and for a multiple rowset operation this is when the next rowset if fetched. The consumer's bound memory is in an indeterminate state before the parameter data becomes available.
DBPROPVAL_OA_NOTSUPPORTED	1	Output parameters are not supported.

DBPROPVAL_OO

Name	Value	Description
DBPROPVAL_OO_BLOB	1	The provider supports access to BLOBs as structured storage objects.
DBPROPVAL_OO_DIRECTBIND	16	The provider supports direct binding to BLOBs.

Name	Value	Description
DBPROPVAL_OO_IPERSIST	2	The provider supports access to OLE objects through OLE.
DBPROPVAL_OO_SCOPED	8	The provider supports scoped operations.

DBPROPVAL_ORS

Name	Value	Description
DBPROPVAL_ORS_TABLE		The provider supports opening tables.
DBPROPVAL_ORS_INDEX		The provider supports opening indexes.
DBPROPVAL_ORS_INTEGRATEDINDEX		The provider supports both the table and index in the same open method.
DBPROPVAL_ORS_STOREDPROPC		The provider supports opening rowsets over stored procedures.

DBPROPVAL_OS

Name	Value	Description
DBPROPVAL_OS_ENABLEALL	-1	All services should be invoked. This is the default.
DBPROPVAL_OS_RESOURCEPOOLING	1	Resources should be pooled.
DBPROPVAL_OS_TXNENLISTMENT	2	Sessions in an MTS environment should automatically be enlisted in a global transaction where required.
DBPROPVAL_OS_DISABLEALL	0	All services should be disabled.

DBPROPVAL_PT

Name	Value	Description
DBPROPVAL_PT_GUID	8	The GUID is used as the persistent ID type.
DBPROPVAL_PT_GUID_NAME	1	The GUID Name is used as the persistent ID type.

Table Continued on Following Page

Name	Value	Description
DBPROPVAL_PT_GUID_PROPID	2	The GUID Property ID is used as the persistent ID type.
DBPROPVAL_PT_NAME	4	The Name is used as the persistent ID type.
DBPROPVAL_PT_PGUID_NAME	32	The Property GUID Name is used as the persistent ID type.
DBPROPVAL_PT_PGUID_PROPID	64	The Property GUID Property ID is used as the persistent ID type.
DBPROPVAL_PT_PROPID	16	The Property ID is used as the persistent ID type.

DBPROPVAL_RD

Name	Value	Description
DBPROPVAL_RD_RESETALL	-1	The provider should reset all state associated with the data source, with the exception that any open object is not released.

DBPROPVAL_RT

Name	Value	Description
DBPROPVAL_RT_APTMTTHREAD	2	The DSO is apartment threaded.
DBPROPVAL_RT_FREETHREAD	1	The DSO is free threaded.
DBPROPVAL_RT_SINGLETHREAD	4	The DSO is single threaded.

DBPROPVAL_SQ

Name	Value	Description
DBPROPVAL_SQ_COMPARISON	2	All predicates that support subqueries support comparison subqueries.
DBPROPVAL_SQ_CORRELATEDSUBQUERIES	1	All predicates that support subqueries support correlated subqueries.

Name	Value	Description
DBPROPVAL_SQ_EXISTS	4	All predicates that support subqueries support EXISTS subqueries.
DBPROPVAL_SQ_IN	8	All predicates that support subqueries support IN subqueries.
DBPROPVAL_SQ_QUANTIFIED	16	All predicates that support subqueries support quantified subqueries.

DBPROPVAL_SQL

Name	Value	Description
DBPROPVAL_SQL_ANSI89_IEF	8	The provider supports the ANSI SQL-89 IEF level.
DBPROPVAL_SQL_ANSI92_ENTRY	16	The provider supports the ANSI SQL-92 Entry level.
DBPROPVAL_SQL_ANSI92_FULL	128	The provider supports the ANSI SQL-92 Full level.
DBPROPVAL_SQL_ANSI92_INTERMEDIATE	64	The provider supports the ANSI SQL-92 Intermediate level.
DBPROPVAL_SQL_CORE	2	The provider supports the ODBC 2.5 Core SQL level.
DBPROPVAL_SQL_ESCAPECLAUSES	256	The provider supports the ODBC escape clauses syntax.
DBPROPVAL_SQL_EXTENDED	4	The provider supports the ODBC 2.5 EXTENDED SQL level.
DBPROPVAL_SQL_FIPS_TRANSITIONAL	32	The provider supports the ANSI SQL-92 Transitional level.
DBPROPVAL_SQL_MINIMUM	1	The provider supports the ODBC 2.5 EXTENDED SQL level.
DBPROPVAL_SQL_NONE	0	SQL is not supported.
DBPROPVAL_SQL_ODBC_CORE	2	The provider supports the ODBC 2.5 Core SQL level.

Table Continued on Following Page

Name	Value	Description
DBPROPVAL_SQL_ODBC_EXTENDED	4	The provider supports the ODBC 2.5 EXTENDED SQL level.
DBPROPVAL_SQL_ODBC_MINIMUM	1	The provider supports the ODBC 2.5 EXTENDED SQL level.
DBPROPVAL_SQL_SUBMINIMUM	512	The provider supports the DBGUID_SQL dialect and parses the command text according to SQL rules, but does not support either the minimum ODBC level nor the ANSI SQL-92 Entry level.

DBPROPVAL_SS

Name	Value	Description
DBPROPVAL_SS_ILOCKBYTES	8	The provider supports IlockBytes.
DBPROPVAL_SS_ISEQUENTIALSTREAM	1	The provider supports ISequentialStream.
DBPROPVAL_SS_ISTORAGE	4	The provider supports IStorage.
DBPROPVAL_SS_ISTREAM	2	The provider supports IStream.

DBPROPVAL_SU

Name	Value	Description
DBPROPVAL_SU_DML_STATEMENTS	1	Schema names are supported in all Data Manipulation Language statements.
DBPROPVAL_SU_INDEX_DEFINITION	4	Schema names are supported in all index definition statements.
DBPROPVAL_SU_PRIIVILEGE_DEFINITION	8	Schema names are supported in all privilege definition statements.
DBPROPVAL_SU_TABLE_DEFINITION	2	Schema names are supported in all table definition statements.

DBPROPVAL_TC

Name	Value	Description
DBPROPVAL_TC_ALL	8	Transactions can contain DDL and DML statements in any order.
DBPROPVAL_TC_DDL_COMMIT	2	Transactions can contain DML statements. DDL statements within a transaction cause the transaction to be committed.
DBPROPVAL_TC_DDL_IGNORE	4	Transactions can only contain DML statements. DDL statements within a transaction are ignored.
DBPROPVAL_TC_DDL_LOCK	16	Transactions can contain both DDL and DML statements, but DDL statements within a transaction lock the database object until the transaction completes.
DBPROPVAL_TC_DML	1	Transactions can only contain Data Manipulation (DML) statements. DDL statements within a transaction cause an error.
DBPROPVAL_TC_NONE	0	Transactions are not supported.

DBPROPVAL_TI

Name	Value	Description
DBPROPVAL_TI_BROWSE	256	Changes made by other transactions are visible before they are committed.
DBPROPVAL_TI_CHAOS	16	Transactions cannot overwrite pending changes from more highly isolated transactions. This is the default.
DBPROPVAL_TI_CURSORSTABILITY	4096	Changes made by other transactions are not visible until those transactions are committed.
DBPROPVAL_TI_ISOLATED	1048576	All concurrent transactions will interact only in ways that produce the same effect as if each transaction were entirely executed one after the other.
DBPROPVAL_TI_READCOMMITTED	4096	Changes made by other transactions are not visible until those transactions are committed.

Table Continued on Following Page

Name	Value	Description
DBPROPVAL_TI_READUNCOMMITTED	256	Changes made by other transactions are visible before they are committed.
DBPROPVAL_TI_REPEATABLEREAD	65536	Changes made by other transactions are not visible.
DBPROPVAL_TI_SERIALIZABLE	1048576	All concurrent transactions will interact only in ways that produce the same effect as if each transaction were entirely executed one after the other.

DBPROPVAL_TR

Name	Value	Description
DBPROPVAL_TR_ABORT	16	The transaction preserves its isolation context (i.e., it preserves its locks if that is how isolation is implemented) across the retaining abort.
DBPROPVAL_TR_ABORT_DC	8	The transaction may either preserve or dispose of isolation context across a retaining abort.
DBPROPVAL_TR_ABORT_NO	32	The transaction is explicitly not to preserve its isolation across a retaining abort.
DBPROPVAL_TR_BOTH	128	Isolation is preserved across both a retaining commit and a retaining abort.
DBPROPVAL_TR_COMMIT	2	The transaction preserves its isolation context (i.e., it preserves its locks if that is how isolation is implemented) across the retaining commit.
DBPROPVAL_TR_COMMIT_DC	1	The transaction may either preserve or dispose of isolation context across a retaining commit.
DBPROPVAL_TR_COMMIT_NO	4	The transaction is explicitly not to preserve its isolation across a retaining commit.

Name	Value	Description
DBPROPVAL_TR_DONTCARE	64	The transaction may either preserve or dispose of isolation context across a retaining commit or abort. This is the default.
DBPROPVAL_TR_NONE	256	Isolation is explicitly not to be retained across either a retaining commit or abort.
DBPROPVAL_TR_OPTIMISTIC	512	Optimistic concurrency control is to be used.

DBPROPVAL_UP

Name	Value	Description
DBPROPVAL_UP_CHANGE	1	Indicates that SetData is supported.
DBPROPVAL_UP_DELETE	2	Indicates that DeleteRows is supported.
DBPROPVAL_UP_INSERT	4	Indicates that InsertRow is supported.

JET_ENGINETYPE

Name	Value	Description
JET_ENGINETYPE_UNKNOWN	0	The database type is unknown.
JET_ENGINETYPE_JET10	1	Jet 1.0
JET_ENGINETYPE_JET11	2	Jet 1.1
JET_ENGINETYPE_JET2X	3	Jet 2.x
JET_ENGINETYPE_JET3X	4	Jet 3.x
JET_ENGINETYPE_JET4X	5	Jet 4.x
JET_ENGINETYPE_DBASE3	10	DBase III
JET_ENGINETYPE_DBASE4	11	DBase IV
JET_ENGINETYPE_DBASE5	12	DBase V
JET_ENGINETYPE_EXCEL30	20	Excel 3
JET_ENGINETYPE_EXCEL40	21	Excel 4
JET_ENGINETYPE_EXCEL50	22	Excel 5 (Excel 95)

Table Continued on Following Page

Name	Value	Description
JET_ENGINETYPE_EXCEL80	23	Excel 8 (Excel 97)
JET_ENGINETYPE_EXCEL90	24	Excel 9 (Excel 2000)
JET_ENGINETYPE_EXCHANGE4	30	Exchange Server
JET_ENGINETYPE_LOTUSWK1	40	Lotus 1
JET_ENGINETYPE_LOTUSWK3	41	Lotus 3
JET_ENGINETYPE_LOTUSWK4	42	Lotus 4
JET_ENGINETYPE_PARADOX3X	50	Paradox 3.x
JET_ENGINETYPE_PARADOX4X	51	Paradox 4.5
JET_ENGINETYPE_PARADOX5X	52	Paradox 5.x
JET_ENGINETYPE_PARADOX7X	53	Paradox 7.x
JET_ENGINETYPE_TEXT1X	60	Text
JET_ENGINETYPE_HTML1X	70	HTML

MD_DIMTYPE

Name	Value	Description
MD_DIMTYPE_MEASURE	2	A measure dimension.
MD_DIMTYPE_OTHER	3	The dimension is neither a time nor a measure dimension.
MD_DIMTYPE_TIME	1	A time dimension.
MD_DIMTYPE_UNKNOWN	0	The provider is unable to classify the dimension.

SQL_FN_NUM

Name	Value	Description
SQL_FN_NUM_ABS	1	The ABS function is supported by the data source.
SQL_FN_NUM_ACOS	2	The ACOS function is supported by the data source.
SQL_FN_NUM_ASIN	4	The ASIN function is supported by the data source.

Name	Value	Description
SQL_FN_NUM_ATAN	8	The ATAN function is supported by the data source.
SQL_FN_NUM_ATAN2	16	The ATAN2 function is supported by the data source.
SQL_FN_NUM_CEILING	32	The CEILING function is supported by the data source.
SQL_FN_NUM_COS	64	The COS function is supported by the data source.
SQL_FN_NUM_COT	128	The COT function is supported by the data source.
SQL_FN_NUM_DEGREES	262144	The DEGREES function is supported by the data source.
SQL_FN_NUM_EXP	256	The EXP function is supported by the data source.
SQL_FN_NUM_FLOOR	512	The FLOOR function is supported by the data source.
SQL_FN_NUM_LOG	1024	The LOG function is supported by the data source.
SQL_FN_NUM_LOG10	524288	The LOG10 function is supported by the data source.
SQL_FN_NUM_MOD	2048	The MOD function is supported by the data source.
SQL_FN_NUM_PI	65536	The PI function is supported by the data source.
SQL_FN_NUM_POWER	1048576	The POWER function is supported by the data source.
SQL_FN_NUM_RADIANS	2097152	The RADIANS function is supported by the data source.
SQL_FN_NUM_RAND	131072	The RAND function is supported by the data source.
SQL_FN_NUM_ROUND	4194304	The ROUND function is supported by the data source.
SQL_FN_NUM_SIGN	4096	The SIGN function is supported by the data source.

Table Continued on Following Page

Name	Value	Description
SQL_FN_NUM_SIN	8192	The SIN function is supported by the data source.
SQL_FN_NUM_SQRT	10384	The SQRT function is supported by the data source.
SQL_FN_NUM_TAN	32768	The TAN function is supported by the data source.
SQL_FN_NUM_TRUNCATE	8388608	The TRUNCATE function is supported by the data source.

SQL_FN_STR

Name	Value	Description
SQL_FN_STR_ASCII	8192	The ASCII function is supported by the data source.
SQL_FN_STR_BIT_LENGTH	524288	The BIT_LENGTH function is supported by the data source.
SQL_FN_STR_CHAR	16384	The CHAR function is supported by the data source.
SQL_FN_STR_CHAR_LENGTH	1048576	The CHAR_LENGTH function is supported by the data source.
SQL_FN_STR_CHARACTER_LENGTH	2097152	The CHARACTER_LENGTH function is supported by the data source.
SQL_FN_STR_CONCAT	1	The CONCAT function is supported by the data source.
SQL_FN_STR_DIFFERENCE	32768	The DIFFERENCE function is supported by the data source.
SQL_FN_STR_INSERT	2	The INSERT function is supported by the data source.
SQL_FN_STR_LCASE	64	The LCASE function is supported by the data source.
SQL_FN_STR_LEFT	4	The LEFT function is supported by the data source.
SQL_FN_STR_LENGTH	16	The LENGTH function is supported by the data source.
SQL_FN_STR_LOCATE	32	The LOCATE function is supported by the data source.

Name	Value	Description
SQL_FN_STR_LOCATE_2	65536	The LOCATE_2 function is supported by the data source.
SQL_FN_STR_LTRIM	8	The LTRIM function is supported by the data source.
SQL_FN_STR_OCTET_LENGTH	4194304	The OCTET_LENGTH function is supported by the data source.
SQL_FN_STR_POSITION	8388608	The POSITION function is supported by the data source.
SQL_FN_STR_REPEAT	128	The REPEAT function is supported by the data source.
SQL_FN_STR_REPLACE	256	The REPLACE function is supported by the data source.
SQL_FN_STR_RIGHT	512	The RIGHT function is supported by the data source.
SQL_FN_STR_RTRIM	1024	The RTRIM function is supported by the data source.
SQL_FN_STR_SOUNDEX	131072	The SOUNDEX function is supported by the data source.
SQL_FN_STR_SPACE	262144	The SPACE function is supported by the data source.
SQL_FN_STR_SUBSTRING	2048	The SUBSTRING function is supported by the data source.
SQL_FN_STR_UCASE	4096	The UCASE function is supported by the data source.

SQL_FN_SYS

Name	Value	Description
SQL_FN_SYS_DBNAME	2	The DBNAME system function is supported.
SQL_FN_SYS_IFNULL	4	The IFNULL system function is supported.
SQL_FN_SYS_USERNAME	1	The USERNAME system function is supported.

SQL_OJ

Name	Value	Description
SQL_OJ_ALL_COMPARISON_OPS	64	The comparison operator in the ON clause can be any of the ODBC comparison operators. If this is not set, only the equals (=) comparison operator can be used in an outer join.
SQL_OJ_FULL	4	Full outer joins are supported.
SQL_OJ_INNER	32	The inner table (the right table in a left outer join or the left table in a right outer join) can also be used in an inner join. This does not apply to full out joins, which do not have an inner table.
SQL_OJ_LEFT	1	Left outer joins are supported.
SQL_OJ_NESTED	8	Nested outer joins are supported.
SQL_OJ_NOT_ORDERED	16	The column names in the ON clause of the outer join do not have to be in the same order as their respective table names in the OUTER JOIN clause.
SQL_OJ_RIGHT	2	Right outer joins are supported.

SQL_SDF_CURRENT

Name	Value	Description
SQL_SDF_CURRENT_DATE	1	The CURRENT_DATE system function is supported.
SQL_SDF_CURRENT_TIME	2	The CURRENT_TIME system function is supported.
SQL_SDF_CURRENT_TIMESTAMP	4	The CURRENT_TIMESTAMP system function is supported.

SSPROP_CONCUR

Name	Value	Description
SSPROP_CONCUR_LOCK	4	Use row locking to prevent concurrent access.
SSPROP_CONCUR_READ_ONLY	8	The rowset is read-only. Full concurrency is supported.
SSPROP_CONCUR_ROWVER	1	Use row versioning to determining concurrent access violations. The SQL Table or tables must contain a timestamp column.
SSPROP_CONCUR_VALUES	2	Use the values of columns in the rowset row.

SSPROPVAL_USEPROCFORPREP

Name	Value	Description
SSPROPVAL_USEPROCFORPREP_OFF	0	A temporary stored procedure is not created when a command is prepared.
SSPROPVAL_USEPROCFORPREP_ON	1	A temporary stored procedure is created when a command is prepared. Temporary stored procedures are dropped when the session is released.
SSPROPVAL_USEPROCFORPREP_ON_DROP	2	A temporary stored procedure is created when a command is prepared. The procedure is dropped when the command is unprepared, or a new command text is set, or when all application references to the command are released.

Suppliers

- SupplierID
- CompanyName
- ContactName
- ContactTitle
- Address
- City
- Region
- PostalCode
- Country
- Phone
- Fax
- HomePage

Products

- ProductID
- ProductName
- SupplierID
- CategoryID
- QuantityPerUnit
- UnitPrice
- UnitsInStock
- UnitsOnOrder
- ReorderLevel
- Discontinued

Categories

- CategoryID
- CategoryName
- Description
- Picture

6

ADO Properties Collection

We've seen that each ADO object has its own fixed set of properties (things like `Name` and `Value`). Since ADO is designed for use with different providers, we *also* need a way to allow providers to specify their *own* properties. Therefore, ADO gives us the `Properties` collection, which deals with dynamic properties that are specific to the provider. This appendix deals with which providers support which properties, and what these properties actually do.

Some of the properties refer to **rowsets**. This is just the OLE DB term for recordsets.

Property Usage

As you can see from the tables in this appendix, there are very many properties – however, using them is actually quite simple. You simply index into the `Properties` collection by using the property name itself. For example, to find out the name the provider gives to procedures you could do this:

```
MsgBox objConn.Properties("Procedure Term")
```

For SQL Server, this returns `stored procedure` and for Access this returns `STORED QUERY`.

You can iterate through the entire set of properties very simply:

```
For Each objProp In objConn.Properties
    MsgBox objProp.Name & ": " & objProp.Value
Next
```

This will display the property name and value.

For those properties that return custom types, you need to identify whether these return a bitmask or a simple value – the property description identifies this, as it says 'one of' or 'one or more of'. In its simplest forms, these properties will just return a single value. For example, to find out whether your provider supports output parameters on stored procedures you can query the Output Parameter Availability property. This is defined as returning values of type DBPROPVAL_OA, which are as follows:

Constant	Value
DBPROPVAL_OA_ATEXECUTE	2
DBPROPVAL_OA_ATROWRELEASE	4
DBPROPVAL_OA_NOTSUPPORTED	1

Examining this property when connected to SQL Server gives you a value of 4, indicating that output parameters are available when the recordset is closed. Access, on the other hand, returns a value of 1, indicating that output parameters are not supported.

For those properties that return bitmask, you'll need to use Boolean logic to identify which values are set. For example, to query the provider and examine what features of SQL are supported, you can use the SQL Support property. For Access this returns 512, which corresponds to DBPROPVAL_SQL_SUBMINIMUM, indicating that not even the ANSI SQL92 Entry-level SQL facilities are provided. On the other hand, SQL Server returns 283, but there isn't a single value for this, so it must be a combination of values. In fact, it corresponds to the sum of the following:

Constant	Value
DBPROPVAL_SQL_ESCAPECLAUSES	256
DBPROPVAL_SQL_ANSI92_ENTRY	16
DBPROPVAL_SQL_ANSI89_IEF	8
DBPROPVAL_SQL_CORE	2
DBPROPVAL_SQL_MINIMUM	1

In order to see whether a specific value is set, use the Boolean AND operator. For example:

```
lngSQLSupport = objConn.Properties("SQL Support")
If (lngSQLSupport AND DBPROPVAL_SQL_CORE) = DBPROPVAL_SQL_CORE Then
    'Core facilities are supported
End If
```

A full description of the constants is given in Appendix F.

Property Support

The following table shows a list of all OLEDB properties, and indicates which of them are supported by three widely-used drivers: the Microsoft OLEDB driver for Jet, the Microsoft OLEDB driver for ODBC, and the Microsoft OLEDB driver for SQL Server. Since this list contains dynamic properties, not every property may show up under all circumstances. Other providers may also implement properties not listed in this table.

A tick (✓) indicates that the property is supported, and a blank space indicates it is not supported. Note that support for recordset properties may depend upon the locking type, cursor type and cursor location.

> *Note. This list doesn't include the* `Iproperty` *(such as* `IRowset`*, etc) properties. Although these are part of the collection they are not particularly useful for the ADO programmer.*

For the *Object Type* column, the following abbreviations are used:

> ➤ R = Recordset
> ➤ C = Connection
> ➤ F = Field

Property Name	Object Type (R/F/C)	ODBC	Jet	SQL	Internet Publishing	MSDataShape	Persist	Remote	Index Server
Access Order	R	✓	✓	✓	✓	✓	✓	✓	
Access Permission	C				✓				
Accessible Procedures	C	✓							
Accessible Tables	C	✓							
Active Sessions	C	✓	✓	✓	✓				✓
Active Statements	C	✓							
Alter Column Support	C		✓						
Always use content index	R								✓

Table Continued on Following Page

Property Name	Object Type (R/F/C)	ODBC	Jet	SQL	Internet Publishing	MSDataShape	Persist	Remote	Index Server
Append-Only Rowset	R	✓	✓	✓	✓	✓	✓	✓	
Application Name	C			✓					
Asynchable Abort	C	✓	✓	✓					
Asynchable Commit	C	✓	✓	✓					
Asynchronous Processing	C					✓			
Asynchronous Rowset Processing	R	✓	✓	✓	✓	✓	✓	✓	
Auto Recalc	R	✓	✓	✓	✓	✓	✓	✓	
Auto Translate	C			✓					
Autocommit Isolation Levels	C	✓	✓	✓		✓	✓	✓	✓
Background Fetch Size	R	✓	✓	✓	✓	✓	✓	✓	
Background thread Priority	R	✓	✓	✓	✓	✓	✓	✓	
BASECATALOGNAME	F	✓	✓	✓	✓	✓	✓	✓	
BASECOLUMNNAME	F	✓	✓	✓	✓	✓	✓	✓	
BASESCHEMANAME	F	✓	✓	✓	✓	✓	✓	✓	
BASETABLENAME	F	✓	✓	✓	✓	✓	✓	✓	
Batch Size	R	✓	✓	✓	✓	✓	✓	✓	
Bind Flags	C				✓				
BLOB accessibility on Forward-Only cursor	R	✓							

Property Name	Object Type (R/F/C)	ODBC	Jet	SQL	Internet Publishing	MSDataShape	Persist	Remote	Index Server
Blocking Storage Objects	R	✓	✓	✓	✓	✓	✓	✓	✓
Bookmark Information	R	✓		✓					
Bookmark Type	R	✓	✓	✓	✓	✓	✓	✓	✓
Bookmarkable	R	✓	✓	✓	✓	✓	✓	✓	✓
Bookmarks Ordered	R	✓	✓	✓	✓	✓	✓	✓	✓
Cache Aggressively	C				✓				
Cache Authentication	C		✓			✓		✓	
Cache Child Rows	R	✓	✓	✓	✓	✓	✓	✓	
Cache Deferred Columns	R	✓	✓	✓	✓	✓	✓	✓	
CALCULATIONINFO	F	✓	✓	✓	✓	✓	✓	✓	
Catalog Location	C	✓	✓	✓					
Catalog Term	C	✓	✓	✓					
Catalog Usage	C	✓		✓					
Change Inserted Rows	R	✓	✓	✓	✓	✓	✓	✓	
Chapter	C						✓		
CLSID	F	✓							
COLLATINGSEQUENCE	F	✓	✓						
Column Definition	C	✓	✓	✓					✓
Column Privileges	R	✓	✓	✓	✓	✓	✓	✓	✓

Table Continued on Following Page

Property Name	Object Type (R/F/C)	ODBC	Jet	SQL	Internet Publishing	MSDataShape	Persist	Remote	Index Server
Column Set Notification	R	✓	✓	✓	✓	✓	✓	✓	
Column Writable	R	✓	✓	✓	✓	✓	✓	✓	
Command Properties	C							✓	
Command Time Out	R	✓	✓	✓	✓	✓	✓	✓	✓
COMPUTEMODE	F	✓							
Connect Timeout	C	✓		✓	✓	✓	✓	✓	
Connection Status	C	✓		✓					
Current Catalog	C	✓	✓	✓					✓
Current DFMode	C							✓	
Current Language	C			✓					
Cursor Engine Version	R	✓	✓	✓	✓	✓	✓	✓	
Data Provider	C					✓			
Data Source	C	✓	✓	✓	✓	✓		✓	✓
Data Source Name	C	✓	✓	✓					
Data Source Object Threading Model	C	✓	✓	✓		✓		✓	✓
Datasource Type	C				✓				
DATETIMEPRECISION	F	✓		✓					
DBMS Name	C	✓	✓	✓					✓
DBMS Version	C	✓	✓	✓					✓
DEFAULTVALUE	F	✓							

Property Name	Object Type (R/F/C)	ODBC	Jet	SQL	Internet Publishing	MSDataShape	Persist	Remote	Index Server
Defer Column	R	✓	✓	✓	✓	✓	✓	✓	
Defer scope and security testing	R								✓
Delay Storage Object Updates	R	✓	✓	✓	✓	✓	✓	✓	
DFMode	C							✓	
DOMAINCATALOG	F	✓							
DOMAINNAME	F	✓							
DOMAINSCHEMA	F	✓							
Driver Name	C	✓							
Driver ODBC Version	C	✓							
Driver Version	C	✓							
Enable Fastload	C			✓					
Encrypt Password	C		✓			✓		✓	
Extended Properties	C	✓	✓	✓		✓		✓	
Fastload Options	R			✓					
Fetch Backwards	R	✓	✓	✓	✓	✓	✓	✓	✓
File Usage	C	✓							
Filter Operations	R	✓	✓	✓	✓	✓	✓	✓	
Find Operations	R	✓	✓	✓	✓	✓	✓	✓	

Table Continued on Following Page

Property Name	Object Type (R/F/C)	ODBC	Jet	SQL	Internet Publishing	MSDataShape	Persist	Remote	Index Server
Force no command preparation when executing a parameterized command	R	✓							
Force no command reexecution when failure to satisfy all required properties	R	✓							
Force no parameter rebinding when executing a command	R	✓							
Force SQL Server Firehose Mode cursor	R	✓							
Generate a Rowset that can be marshalled	R	✓							
Generate URL	C				✓				
GROUP BY Support	C	✓	✓	✓					✓
Handler	C							✓	
HASDEFAULT	F	✓							
Heterogeneous Table Support	C	✓	✓	✓					✓
Hidden Columns	R	✓	✓	✓	✓	✓	✓	✓	
Hold Rows	R	✓	✓	✓	✓	✓	✓	✓	✓
Identifier Case Sensitivity	C	✓	✓	✓					

Property Name	Object Type (R/F/C)	ODBC	Jet	SQL	Internet Publishing	MSDataShape	Persist	Remote	Index Server
Ignore Cached Data	C				✓				
Immobile Rows	R	✓	✓	✓	✓	✓	✓	✓	
Impersonation Level	C					✓		✓	
Include SQL_FLOAT, SQL_DOUBLE, and SQL_REAL in QBU where clauses	R	✓							
Initial Catalog	C	✓		✓		✓		✓	
Initial Fetch Size	R	✓	✓	✓	✓	✓	✓	✓	
Initial File Name	C			✓					
Integrated Security	C			✓		✓		✓	
Integrity Enhancement Facility	C	✓							
Internet Timeout	C							✓	
ISAUTOINCREMENT	F	✓	✓	✓	✓	✓	✓	✓	
ISCASESENSITIVE	F	✓	✓	✓					
Isolation Levels	C	✓	✓	✓					✓
Isolation Retention	C	✓	✓	✓					✓
ISSEARCHABLE	F	✓		✓					
ISUNIQUE	F	✓							
Jet OLEDB:Bulk Transactions	R		✓						

Table Continued on Following Page

Property Name	Object Type (R/F/C)	ODBC	Jet	SQL	Internet Publishing	MSDataShape	Persist	Remote	Index Server
Jet OLEDB:Compact Reclaimed Space Amount	C		✓						
Jet OLEDB:Compact Without Replica Repair	C		✓						
Jet OLEDB:Connection Control	C		✓						
Jet OLEDB:Create System Database	C		✓						
Jet OLEDB:Database Locking Mode	C		✓						
Jet OLEDB:Database Password	C		✓						
Jet OLEDB:Don't Copy Locale on Compact	C		✓						
Jet OLEDB:Enable Fat Cursors	R		✓						
Jet OLEDB:Encrypt Database	C		✓						
Jet OLEDB:Engine Type	C		✓						
Jet OLEDB:Exclusive Async Delay	C		✓						
Jet OLEDB:Fat Cursor Cache Size	R		✓						

Property Name	Object Type (R/F/C)	ODBC	Jet	SQL	Internet Publishing	MSDataShape	Persist	Remote	Index Server
Jet OLEDB:Flush Transaction Timeout	C		✓						
Jet OLEDB:Global Bulk Transactions	C		✓						
Jet OLEDB:Global Partial Bulk Ops	C		✓						
Jet OLEDB:Grbit Value	R		✓						
Jet OLEDB:Implicit Commit Sync	C		✓						
Jet OLEDB:Inconsistent	R		✓						
Jet OLEDB:Lock Delay	C		✓						
Jet OLEDB:Lock Retry	C		✓						
Jet OLEDB:Locking Granularity	R		✓						
Jet OLEDB:Max Buffer Size	C		✓						
Jet OLEDB:Max Locks Per File	C		✓						
Jet OLEDB:New Database Password	C		✓						
Jet OLEDB:ODBC Command Time Out	C		✓						
Jet OLEDB:ODBC Parsing	C		✓						

Table Continued on Following Page

Property Name	Object Type (R/F/C)	ODBC	Jet	SQL	Internet Publishing	MSDataShape	Persist	Remote	Index Server
Jet OLEDB:ODBC Pass-Through Statement	R		✓						
Jet OLEDB:Page Locks to Table Lock	C		✓						
Jet OLEDB:Page Timeout	C		✓						
Jet OLEDB:Partial Bulk Ops	R		✓						
Jet OLEDB:Pass Through Query Bulk-Op	R		✓						
Jet OLEDB:Pass Through Query Connect String	R		✓						
Jet OLEDB:Recycle Long-Valued Pages	C		✓						
Jet OLEDB:Registry Path	C		✓						
Jet OLEDB:Reset ISAM Stats	C		✓						
Jet OLEDB:Sandbox Mode	C		✓						
Jet OLEDB:SFP	C		✓						
Jet OLEDB:Shared Async Delay	C		✓						
Jet OLEDB:Stored Query	R		✓						

Property Name	Object Type (R/F/C)	ODBC	Jet	SQL	Internet Publishing	MSDataShape	Persist	Remote	Index Server
Jet OLEDB:System database	C		✓						
Jet OLEDB:Transaction Commit Mode	C		✓						
Jet OLEDB:Use Grbit	R		✓						
Jet OLEDB:User Commit Sync	C		✓						
Jet OLEDB:Validate Rules On Set	R		✓						
Keep Identity	R			✓					
Keep Nulls	R			✓					
KEYCOLUMN	F	✓	✓	✓	✓	✓	✓	✓	
Like Escape Clause	C	✓							
Literal Bookmarks	R	✓	✓	✓	✓	✓	✓	✓	✓
Literal Row Identity	R	✓	✓	✓	✓	✓	✓	✓	✓
Locale Identifier	C	✓	✓	✓	✓	✓		✓	✓
Location	C	✓				✓		✓	✓
Lock Mode	R		✓	✓					
Lock Owner	C				✓				
Maintain Change Status	R	✓	✓	✓	✓	✓	✓	✓	
Maintain Property Values	C						✓		

Table Continued on Following Page

Property Name	Object Type (R/F/C)	ODBC	Jet	SQL	Internet Publishing	MSDataShape	Persist	Remote	Index Server
Mark For Offline	C				✓				
Mask Password	C		✓			✓		✓	
Max Columns in Group By	C	✓							
Max Columns in Index	C	✓							
Max Columns in Order By	C	✓							
Max Columns in Select	C	✓							
Max Columns in Table	C	✓							
Maximum BLOB Length	R			✓					
Maximum Index Size	C	✓	✓	✓					
Maximum Open Chapters	C			✓					✓
Maximum Open Rows	R	✓	✓	✓	✓	✓	✓	✓	✓
Maximum Pending Rows	R	✓	✓	✓	✓	✓	✓	✓	
Maximum Row Size	C	✓	✓	✓					✓
Maximum Row Size Includes BLOB	C	✓	✓	✓					
Maximum Rows	R	✓	✓	✓	✓	✓	✓	✓	✓
Maximum Tables in SELECT	C	✓	✓	✓					✓
Memory Usage	R	✓	✓	✓	✓	✓	✓	✓	✓

Property Name	Object Type (R/F/C)	ODBC	Jet	SQL	Internet Publishing	MSDataShape	Persist	Remote	Index Server
Mode	C	✓	✓		✓	✓		✓	
Multi-Table Update	C	✓	✓	✓					
Multiple Connections	C			✓					
Multiple Parameter Sets	C	✓	✓	✓				✓	✓
Multiple Results	C	✓	✓	✓		✓		✓	✓
Multiple Storage Objects	C	✓	✓	✓					✓
Network Address	C			✓					
Network Library	C			✓					
Notification Granularity	R	✓	✓	✓	✓	✓	✓	✓	
Notification Phases	R	✓	✓	✓	✓	✓	✓	✓	
NULL Collation Order	C	✓	✓	✓					✓
NULL Concatenation Behavior	C	✓	✓	✓					
Numeric Functions	C	✓							
Objects Transacted	R	✓	✓	✓	✓	✓	✓	✓	
OCTETLENGTH	F	✓		✓					
ODBC Concurrency Type	R	✓							
ODBC Cursor Type	R	✓							
OLE DB Services	C	✓							

Table Continued on Following Page

Property Name	Object Type (R/F/C)	ODBC	Jet	SQL	Internet Publishing	MSDataShape	Persist	Remote	Index Server
OLE DB Version	C	✓	✓	✓	✓			✓	✓
OLE Object Support	C	✓	✓	✓					✓
OLE Objects	C				✓				
Open Rowset Support	C	✓	✓	✓					
OPTIMIZE	F	✓	✓	✓	✓	✓	✓	✓	
ORDER BY Columns in Select List	C	✓	✓	✓					✓
Others' Changes Visible	R	✓	✓	✓	✓	✓	✓	✓	✓
Others' Inserts Visible	R	✓	✓	✓	✓	✓	✓	✓	✓
Outer Join Capabilities	C	✓							
Outer Joins	C	✓							
Output Parameter Availability	C	✓	✓	✓				✓	✓
Own Changes Visible	R	✓	✓	✓	✓	✓	✓	✓	
Own Inserts Visible	R	✓	✓	✓	✓	✓	✓	✓	
Packet Size	C			✓					
Pass By Ref Accessors	C	✓	✓	✓					✓
Password	C	✓	✓	✓	✓	✓		✓	
Persist Encrypted	C					✓			

Property Name	Object Type (R/F/C)	ODBC	Jet	SQL	Internet Publishing	MSDataShape	Persist	Remote	Index Server
Persist Format	C						✓		
Persist Schema	C						✓		
Persist Security Info	C	✓		✓		✓		✓	
Persistent ID Type	C	✓	✓	✓					✓
Position on the last row after insert	R	✓							
Prepare Abort Behavior	C	✓	✓	✓					
Prepare Commit Behavior	C	✓	✓	✓					
Preserve on Abort	R	✓	✓	✓	✓	✓	✓	✓	
Preserve on Commit	R	✓	✓	✓	✓	✓	✓	✓	
Procedure Term	C	✓	✓	✓					
Prompt	C	✓	✓	✓	✓	✓		✓	✓
Protection Level	C					✓		✓	
Protocol Provider	C				✓				
Provider Friendly Name	C	✓	✓	✓				✓	
Provider Name	C	✓	✓	✓	✓			✓	✓
Provider Version	C	✓	✓	✓	✓			✓	✓
Query Based Updates/Deletes/Inserts	R	✓							
Query Restriction	R								✓

Table Continued on Following Page

Property Name	Object Type (R/F/C)	ODBC	Jet	SQL	Internet Publishing	MSDataShape	Persist	Remote	Index Server
Quick Restart	R	✓	✓	✓	✓	✓	✓	✓	✓
Quoted Catalog Names	C			✓					
Quoted Identifier Sensitivity	C	✓		✓					
Read-Only Data Source	C	✓	✓	✓					✓
Reentrant Events	R	✓	✓	✓	✓	✓	✓	✓	✓
RELATIONCONDITIONS	F	✓	✓	✓	✓	✓	✓	✓	
Remote Provider	C							✓	
Remote Server	C							✓	
Remove Deleted Rows	R	✓	✓	✓	✓	✓	✓	✓	✓
Report Multiple Changes	R	✓	✓	✓	✓	✓	✓	✓	
Reshape Name	R	✓	✓	✓	✓	✓	✓	✓	
Resync Command	R	✓	✓	✓	✓	✓	✓	✓	
Return PROPVARIANTs in variant binding	R								✓
Return Pending Inserts	R	✓	✓	✓	✓	✓	✓	✓	
Row Delete Notification	R	✓	✓	✓	✓	✓	✓	✓	
Row First Change Notification	R	✓	✓	✓	✓	✓	✓	✓	

Property Name	Object Type (R/F/C)	ODBC	Jet	SQL	Internet Publishing	MSDataShape	Persist	Remote	Index Server
Row Insert Notification	R	✓	✓	✓	✓	✓	✓	✓	
Row Privileges	R	✓	✓	✓	✓	✓	✓	✓	✓
Row Resynchronization Notification	R	✓	✓	✓	✓	✓	✓	✓	
Row Threading Model	R	✓	✓	✓	✓	✓	✓	✓	✓
Row Undo Change Notification	R	✓	✓	✓	✓	✓	✓	✓	
Row Undo Delete Notification	R	✓	✓	✓	✓	✓	✓	✓	
Row Undo Insert Notification	R	✓	✓	✓	✓	✓	✓	✓	
Row Update Notification	R	✓	✓	✓	✓	✓	✓	✓	
Rowset Conversions on Command	C	✓	✓	✓					✓
Rowset Fetch Position Change Notification	R	✓	✓	✓	✓	✓	✓	✓	
Rowset Query Status	R								✓
Rowset Release Notification	R	✓	✓	✓	✓	✓	✓	✓	
Schema Term	C	✓	✓	✓					
Schema Usage	C	✓	✓	✓					
Scroll Backwards	R	✓	✓	✓	✓	✓	✓	✓	✓

Table Continued on Following Page

Property Name	Object Type (R/F/C)	ODBC	Jet	SQL	Internet Publishing	MSDataShape	Persist	Remote	Index Server
Server Cursor	R	✓	✓	✓	✓	✓	✓	✓	✓
Server Data on Insert	R		✓	✓					
Server Name	C	✓		✓					
Skip Deleted Bookmarks	R	✓	✓	✓	✓	✓	✓	✓	✓
Special Characters	C	✓							
SQL Content Query Locale String	R								✓
SQL Grammar Support	C	✓							
SQL Support	C	✓	✓	✓					✓
Stored Procedures	C	✓							
String Functions	C	✓							
Strong Row Identity	R	✓	✓	✓	✓	✓	✓	✓	✓
Structured Storage	C	✓	✓	✓					✓
Subquery Support	C	✓	✓	✓					✓
System Functions	C	✓							
Table Term	C	✓	✓	✓					
Time/Date Functions	C	✓							
Transact Updates	C							✓	
Transaction DDL	C	✓	✓	✓					✓
Treat As Offline	C				✓				

Property Name	Object Type (R/F/C)	ODBC	Jet	SQL	Internet Publishing	MSDataShape	Persist	Remote	Index Server
Unicode Comparison Style	C			✓					
Unicode Locale Id	C			✓					
Unique Catalog	R	✓	✓	✓	✓	✓	✓	✓	
Unique Reshape Names	C					✓			
Unique Rows	R	✓	✓	✓	✓	✓	✓	✓	
Unique Schema	R	✓	✓	✓	✓	✓	✓	✓	
Unique Table	R	✓	✓	✓	✓	✓	✓	✓	
Updatability	R	✓	✓	✓	✓	✓	✓	✓	✓
Update Criteria	R	✓	✓	✓	✓	✓	✓	✓	
Update Resync	R	✓	✓	✓	✓	✓	✓	✓	
Use Bookmarks	R	✓	✓	✓	✓	✓	✓	✓	✓
Use Procedure for Prepare	C			✓					
User ID	C	✓	✓	✓	✓	✓		✓	
User Name	C	✓	✓	✓					
Window Handle	C	✓	✓	✓	✓	✓		✓	✓
Workstation ID	C			✓					

Object Properties

This section details the properties by object type, including the enumerated values that they support. These values are not included in the standard adovbs.inc include file (and are not automatically supplied when using Visual Basic), but can be found in adoconvb.inc and adoconjs.inc (for ASP, in VBScript and JScript format) and adocon.bas (for Visual Basic). These can be downloaded from the web site for ADO 2.1 Programmer's Reference, also from Wrox, at http://webdev.wrox.co.uk/books/2688.

Some properties in this list are undocumented, and we've had to make an educated guess as to their purpose. We've marked these properties with a * *symbol in their description field.*

The Connection Object's Properties

Property Name	Description	DataType
Access Permissions	Identifies the permissions used to access the data source. Read/Write.	ConnectModeEnum
Accessible Procedures	Identifies accessible procedures. Read-only.	Boolean
Accessible Tables	Identifies accessible tables. Read-only.	Boolean
Active Sessions	The maximum number of sessions that can exist at the same time. A value of 0 indicates no limit. Read-only.	Long
Active Statements	The maximum number of statements that can exist at the same time. Read-only.	Long
Alter Column Support	Identifies which portions of the column can be altered.	DBCOLUMNDESCFLAG
Application Name	Identifies the client application name. Read/Write.	String
Asynchable Abort	Whether transactions can be aborted asynchronously. Read-only.	Boolean
Asynchable Commit	Whether transactions can be committed asynchronously. Read-only.	Boolean

Property Name	Description	DataType
Asynchronous Processing	Specifies the asynchronous processing performed on the rowset. Read/Write.	DBPROPVAL_ASYNCH
Auto Translate	Indicates whether OEM/ANSI character conversion is used. Read/Write.	Boolean
Autocommit Isolation Level	Identifies the transaction isolation level while in auto-commit mode. Read/Write.	DBPROPVAL_OS
Bind Flags	Identifies the binding behaviour for resources. Allows binding to the results of a resource rather than the resource itself.	DBBINDURLFLAG
Cache Aggressively	Identifies whether or not the provider will download and cache all properties of the resource, and its stream.	Boolean
Cache Authentication	Whether or not the data source object can cache sensitive authentication information, such as passwords, in an internal cache. Read/Write.	Boolean
Catalog Location	The position of the catalog name in a table name in a text command. Returns 1 (DBPROPVAL_CL_START) if the catalog is at the start of the name (such as Access with \Temp\Database.mdb), and 2 (DBPROPVAL_CL_END) if the catalog is at the end of name (such as Oracle with ADMIN.EMP@EMPDATA). Read/Write.	DBPROPVAL_CL
Catalog Term	The name the data source uses for a catalog, e.g. 'catalog' or 'database'. Read/Write.	String

Table Continued on Following Page

Property Name	Description	DataType
Catalog Usage	Specifies how catalog names can be used in text commands. A combination of zero or more of DBPROPVAL_CU constants. Read/Write.	DBPROPVAL_CU
Column Definition	Defines the valid clauses for the definition of a column. Read/Write.	DBPROPVAL_CD
Command Properties	The dynamic properties of the Command.*	String
Connect Timeout	The amount of time, in seconds, to wait for the initialization to complete. Read/Write.	Long
Connection Status	The status of the current connection. Read-only.	DBPROPVAL_CS
Current Catalog	The name of the current catalog. Read/Write.	String
Current DFMode	Identifies the actual version of the Data Factory on the server. Can be: "21" (the default) for version 2.1 "20" for version 2.0 "15" for version 1.5	String
Current Language	Identifies the language used for system messages selection and formatting. The language must be installed on the SQL Server or initialization of the data source fails. Read/Write.	Boolean
Data Provider	For a shaped (hierarchical) recordset, this identifies the provider who supplies the data.	String
Data Source	The name of the data source to connect to. Read/Write.	String
Data Source Name	The name of the data source. Read-only.	String

Property Name	Description	DataType
Data Source Object Threading Model	Specifies the threading models supported by the data source object. Read-only.	DBPROPVAL_RT
Datasource Type	The type of data source.	DBPROPVAL_DST
DBMS Name	The name of the product accessed by the provider. Read-only.	String
DBMS Version	The version of the product accessed by the provider. Read-only.	String
DFMode	Identifies the Data Factory mode. Can be: "21" (the default) for version 2.1 "20" for version 2.0 "15" for version 1.5	String
Driver Name	Identifies the ODBC Driver name. Read-only.	String
Driver ODBC Version	Identifies the ODBC Driver version. Read-only.	String
Driver Version	Identifies the Driver ODBC version. Read-only.	String
Enable Fastload	Indicates whether bulk-copy operations can be used between the SQL Server and the consumer.	Boolean
Encrypt Password	Whether the consumer required that the password be sent to the data source in an encrypted form. Read/Write.	Boolean
Extended Properties	Contains provider specific, extended connection information. Read/Write.	String
File Usage	Identifies the usage count of the ODBC driver. Read-only.	Long

Table Continued on Following Page

Property Name	Description	DataType
Generate URL	Identifies the level of support of the Internet Server for generating URL suffixes.	DBPROPVAL_GU
GROUP BY Support	The relationship between the columns in a GROUP BY clause and the non-aggregated columns in the select list. Read-only.	DBPROPVAL_BG
Handler	The name of the server-side customization program, and any parameters the program uses.	String
Heterogeneous Table Support	Specifies whether the provider can join tables from different catalogs or providers. Read-only.	DBPROPVAL_HT
Identifier Case Sensitivity	How identifiers treat case. Read-only.	DBPROPVAL_IC
Ignore Cached Data	Identifies whether the provider should ignore any cached data for this resource.	Boolean
Impersonation Level	Identifies the level of client impersonation the server can take whilst performing actions on behalf of the client.	DB_IMP_LEVEL
Initial Catalog	The name of the initial, or default, catalog to use when connecting to the data source. If the provider supports changing the catalog for an initialized data source, a different catalog name can be specified in the Current Catalog property. Read/Write.	String
Initial File Name	The primary file name of an attachable database. *	String
Integrated Security	Contains the name of the authentication service used by the server to identify the user. Read/Write.	String
Integrity Enhancement Facility	Indicates whether the data source supports the optional Integrity Enhancement Facility. Read-only.	Boolean

Property Name	Description	DataType
Internet Timeout	The maximum number of milliseconds to wait before generating an error.	Long
Isolation Levels	Identifies the supported transaction isolation levels. Read-only.	DBPROPVAL_TI
Isolation Retention	Identifies the supported transaction isolation retention levels. Read-only.	DBPROPVAL_TR
Jet OLEDB:Compact Reclaimed Space Amount	The amount of space reclaimed during a compaction.*	Long
Jet OLEDB:Compact Without Replica Repair	Indicates whether or not to find and repair damaged replicas.	Boolean
Jet OLEDB:Compact Without Relationships	Indicates whether or not to copy relationships to the new database.	Boolean
Jet OLEDB:Connection Control	Identifies the state of the connection, indicating whether other users are allowed to connect to the database or not.	DBPROPVAL_JCC
Jet OLEDB:Create System Database	Indicates whether or not a system database is generated when creating a new data source.	Boolean
Jet OLEDB:Database Locking Mode	Identifies the mode to use when locking the database. The first person to open a database identifies the mode.	DBPROPVAL_DL
Jet OLEDB:Database Password	The database password. Read/Write.	String
Jet OLEDB:Don't Copy Locale on Compact	Indicates that the database sort order should be used when compacting, rather than the locale.	Boolean
Jet OLEDB:Encrypt Database	Indicates whether or not to encrypt the new database.	Boolean

Table Continued on Following Page

Property Name	Description	DataType
Jet OLEDB:Engine Type	Identifies the version of the database to open, or the version of the database to create.	JET_ENGINETYPE
Jet OLEDB:Exclusive Async Delay	The maximum time (in milliseconds) that Jet will delay asynchronous writes to disk, when the database is open in exclusive mode.	Long
Jet OLEDB:Flush Transaction Timeout	Amount of time of inactivity before the asynchronous write cache is written to the disk.	Long
Jet OLEDB:Global Bulk Transactions	Identifies whether bulk operations are transacted.	DBPROPVAL_BT
Jet OLEDB:Global Partial Bulk Ops	Identifies whether bulk operations are allowed with partial values. Read/Write.	DBPROPVAL_BP
Jet OLEDB:Implicit Commit Sync	Indicates whether or not implicit transactions are written synchronously.	Boolean
Jet OLEDB:Lock Delay	The number of times to repeat attempts to access a locked page.	Long
Jet OLEDB:Lock Retry	The number of attempts made to access a locked page.	Long
Jet OLEDB:Max Buffer Size	The largest amount of memory (in Kb) that can be used before it starts flushing changes to disk.	Long
Jet OLEDB:Max Locks Per File	The maximum number of locks that can be placed on a database. This defaults to 9500.	Long
Jet OLEDB:New Database Password	Sets the database password.	String
Jet OLEDB:ODBC Command Time Out	The number of seconds before remote ODBC queries timeout.	Long
Jet OLEDB:ODBC Parsing	Indicates whether or not Jet performs parsing of SQL statements on ODBC connections. *	Boolean

Property Name	Description	DataType
Jet OLEDB:Page Locks to Table Lock	The percentage of page locks to apply to a table before escalating the lock to a table lock. *	Long
Jet OLEDB:Page Timeout	The amount of time (in milliseconds) that are waited before Jet checks to see if the cache is out of date with the database.	Long
Jet OLEDB:Recycle Long-Valued Pages	Indicates whether or not Jet aggressively tries to reclaim BLOB pages when they are freed.	Boolean
Jet OLEDB:Registry Path	The registry key that contains values for the Jet database engine. Read/Write.	String
Jet OLEDB:Reset ISAM Stats	Determines whether or not the ISAM statistics should be reset after the information has been returned.	Boolean
Jet OLEDB:Sandbox Mode	Indicates whether the database is in Sandbox mode. *	Boolean
Jet OLEDB:Shared Async Delay	The maximum time (in milliseconds) to delay asynchronous writes when in multi-user mode.	Long
Jet OLEDB:System database	The path and file name for the workgroup file. Read/Write.	String
Jet OLEDB:Transaction Commit Mode	A value of 1 indicates that the database commits updates immediately, rather than caching them.	Long
Jet OLEDB:User Commit Sync	Indicates whether or not explicit user transactions are written synchronously.	Boolean
Like Escape Clause	Identifies the LIKE escape clause. Read-only.	String
Locale Identifier	The locale ID of preference for the consumer. Read/Write.	Long
Location	The location of the data source to connect to. Typically this will be the server name. Read/Write.	String

Table Continued on Following Page

Property Name	Description	DataType
Lock Owner	The string to show when you lock a resource and other users attempt to access that resource. Ignored for the WEC protocol, used with FrontPage Server Extensions. Read/Write.	String
Log text and image writes	Identifies whether writes to text and images fields are logged in the transaction log. Read/Write.	Boolean
Maintain Property Values	Indicates whether or not the property values are persisted along with the data when saving a recordset. Defaults to True. [*]	Boolean
Mark For Offline	Indicates that the URL can be marked for offline use. [*]	Integer
Mask Password	The consumer requires that the password be sent to the data source in masked form. Read/Write.	Boolean
Max Columns in Group By	Identifies the maximum number of columns in a GROUP BY clause. Read-only.	Long
Max Columns in Index	Identifies the maximum number of columns in an index. Read-only.	Long
Max Columns in Order By	Identifies the maximum number of columns in an ORDER BY clause. Read-only.	Long
Max Columns in Select	Identifies the maximum number of columns in a SELECT statement. Read-only.	Long
Max Columns in Table	Identifies the maximum number of columns in a table. Read-only.	Long
Maximum Index Size	The maximum number of bytes allowed in the combined columns of an index. This is 0 if there is no specified limit or the limit is unknown. Read-only.	Long
Maximum Open Chapters	The maximum number of chapters that can be open at any one time. If a chapter must be released before a new chapter can be opened, the value is 1. If the provider does not support chapters, the value is 0. Read-only.	Long

Property Name	Description	DataType
Maximum OR Conditions	The maximum number of disjunct conditions that can be supported in a view filter. Multiple conditions of a view filter are joined in a logical OR. Providers that do not support joining multiple conditions return a value of 1, and providers that do not support view filters return a value of 0. Read-only.	Long
Maximum Row Size	The maximum length of a single row in a table. This is 0 if there is no specified limit or the limit is unknown. Read-only.	Long
Maximum Row Size Includes BLOB	Identifies whether Maximum Row Size includes the length for BLOB data. Read-only.	Boolean
Maximum Sort Columns	The maximum number of columns that can be supported in a View Sort. This is 0 if there is no specified limit or the limit is unknown. Read-only.	Long
Maximum Tables in SELECT	The maximum number of tables allowed in the FROM clause of a SELECT statement. This is 0 if there is no specified limit or the limit is unknown. Read-only.	Long
Mode	Specifies the access permissions. Read/Write.	DB_MODE
Multi-Table Update	Identifies whether the provider can update rowsets derived from multiple tables. Read-only.	Boolean
Multiple Connections	Identifies whether the provider silently creates additional connections to support concurrent Command, Connection or Recordset objects. This only applies to providers that have to spawn multiple connections, and not to providers that support multiple connections natively. Read/Write.	Boolean
Multiple Parameter Sets	Identifies whether the provider supports multiple parameter sets. Read-only.	Boolean

Table Continued on Following Page

Property Name	Description	DataType
Multiple Results	Identifies whether the provider supports multiple results objects and what restrictions it places on those objects. Read-only.	DBPROPVAL_MR
Multiple Storage Objects	Identifies whether the provider supports multiple, open storage objects at the same time. Read-only.	Boolean
Network Address	Identifies the network address of the SQL Server. Read/Write.	String
Network Library	Identifies the name of the Net-Library (DLL) used to communicate with SQL Server. Read/Write.	String
NULL Collation Order	Identifies where NULLs are sorted in a list. Read-only.	DBPROPVAL_NC
NULL Concatenation Behavior	How the data source handles concatenation of NULL-valued character data type columns with non-NULL valued character data type columns. Read-only.	DBPROPVAL_CB
Numeric Functions	Identifies the numeric functions supported by the ODBC driver and data source. Read-only.	SQL_FN_NUM
OLE DB Services	Specifies the OLEDB services to enable. Read/Write.	DBPROPVAL_OS
OLE DB Version	Specifies the version of OLEDB supported by the provider. Read-only.	String
OLE Object Support	Specifies the way on which the provider supports access to BLOBs and OLE objects stored in columns. Read-only.	DBPROPVAL_OO
OLE Objects	Indicates the level of binding support for OLE Objects.	DBPROPVAL_OO
Open Rowset Support	Indicates the level of support for opening rowsets.	DBPROPVAL_ORS
ORDER BY Columns in Select List	Identifies whether columns in an ORDER BY clause must be in the SELECT list. Read-only.	Boolean

Property Name	Description	DataType
Outer Join Capabilities	Identifies the outer join capabilities of the ODBC data source. Read-only.	SQL_OJ
Outer Joins	Identifies whether outer joins are supported or not. Read-only.	Boolean
Output Parameter Availability	Identifies the time at which output parameter values become available. Read-only.	DBPROPVAL_OA
Packet Size	Specifies the network packet size in bytes. It must be between 512 and 32767. The default is 4096. Read/Write.	Long
Pass By Ref Accessors	Whether the provider supports the DBACCESSOR_PASSBYREF flag. Read-only.	Boolean
Password	The password to be used to connect to the data source. Read/Write.	String
Persist Encrypted	Whether or not the consumer requires that the data source object persist sensitive authentication information, such as a password, in encrypted form. Read/Write.	Boolean
Persist Format	Indicates the format for persisting data.	PersistFormatEnum
Persist Schema	Indicates whether or not the schema is persisted along with the data.	Boolean

Table Continued on Following Page

Property Name	Description	DataType
Persist Security Info	Whether or not the data source object is allowed to persist sensitive authentication information, such as a password, along with other authentication information. Read/Write.	Boolean
Persistent ID Type	Specifies the type of DBID that the provider uses when persisting DBIDs for tables, indexes and columns. Read-only.	DBPROPVAL_PT
Prepare Abort Behavior	Identifies how aborting a transaction affects prepared commands. Read-only.	DBPROPVAL_CB
Prepare Commit Behavior	Identifies how committing a transaction affects prepared commands. Read-only.	DBPROPVAL_CB
Procedure Term	Specifies the data source providers name for a procedure, e.g. 'database procedure' or 'stored procedure'. Read-only.	String
Prompt	Specifies whether to prompt the user during initialization. Read/Write.	DBPROMPT
Protection Level	The level of protection of data sent between client and server. This property applies only to network connections other than RPC. Read/Write.	DB_PROT_LEVEL
Protocol Provider	The protocol to use when using the IPP to connect to a resource. This should be WEC to use the FrontPage Web Extender Client protocol, and DAV to use the Web Distributed Authoring and Versioning (WebDAV) protocol.	String
Provider Friendly Name	The friendly name of the provider. Read-only.	String
Provider Name	The filename of the provider. Read-only.	String
Provider Version	The version of the provider. Read-only.	String

Property Name	Description	DataType
Quoted Catalog Names	Indicates whether or not quoted identifiers are allowed for catalog names.	Boolean
Quoted Identifier Sensitivity	Identifies how quoted identifiers treat case. Read-only.	DBPROPVAL_IC
Read-Only Data Source	Whether or not the data source is read-only. Read-only.	Boolean
Remote Provider	The data provide used to supply the data from a remote connection.	String
Remote Server	The name of the server supplying data from a remote connection.	String
Reset Datasource	Specifies the data source state to reset. Write only.	DBPROPVAL_RD
Rowset Conversions on Command	Identifies whether callers can enquire on a command and about conversions supported by the command. Read-only.	Boolean
Schema Term	The name the data source uses for a schema, e.g. "schema" or "owner". Read-only.	String
Schema Usage	Identifies how schema names can be used in commands. Read-only.	DBPROPVAL_SU
Server Name	The name of the server. Read-only.	String
Sort on Index	Specifies whether the provider supports setting a sort order only for columns contained in an index. Read-only.	Boolean
Special Characters	Identifies the data store's special characters. Read-only.	String
SQL Grammar Support	Identifies the SQL grammar level supported by the ODBC driver. 0 represents no conformance, 1 indicates Level 1 conformance, and 2 represents Level 2 conformance. Read-only.	Long
SQL Support	Identifies the level of support for SQL. Read-only.	DBPROPVAL_SQL

Table Continued on Following Page

Property Name	Description	DataType
SQLOLE execute a SET TEXTLENGTH	Identifies whether SQLOLE executes a SET TEXTLENGTH before accessing BLOB fields. Read-only. *	Boolean
Stored Procedures	Indicates whether stored procedures are available. Read-only.	Boolean
String Functions	Identifies the string functions supported by the ODBC driver and data source. Read-only.	SQL_FN_STR
Structured Storage	Identifies what interfaces the rowset supports on storage objects. Read-only.	DBPROPVAL_SS
Subquery Support	Identifies the predicates in text commands that support sub-queries. Read-only.	DBPROPVAL_SQ
System Functions	Identifies the system functions supported by the ODBC driver and data source. Read-only.	SQL_FN_SYS
Table Term	The name the data source uses for a table, e.g. 'table' or 'file'. Read-only.	String
Time/Date Functions	Identifies the time/date functions supported by the ODBC driver and data source. Read-only.	SQL_SDF_CURRENT
Transact Updates	Indicates whether or not updates on the remote server are transacted. *	Boolean
Transaction DDL	Indicates whether Data Definition Language (DDL) statements are supported in transactions. Read-only.	DBPROPVAL_TC
Treat As Offline	Indicates whether or not the resource should be treated as an offline resource.	Boolean
Unicode Comparison Style	Determines the sorting options used for Unicode data.	Long
Unicode Locale Id	The locale ID to use for Unicode sorting.	Long

Property Name	Description	DataType
Unique Reshape Names	Indicates whether or not the value of the Name property of a recordset would conflict with an existing name, resulting in a unique name being generated.	Boolean
Use Procedure for Prepare	Indicates whether SQL Server is to use temporary stored procedures for prepared statements. Read/Write.	SSPROPVAL_ USEPROCFORPREP
User Authentication mode	Indicates whether Windows NT Authentication is used to access SQL Server. Read/Write.	Boolean
User ID	The User ID to be used when connecting to the data source. Read/Write.	String
User Name	The User Name used in a particular database. Read-only.	String
Window Handle	The window handle to be used if the data source object needs to prompt for additional information. Read/Write.	Long
Workstation ID	Identifies the workstation. Read/Write.	String

The Recordset Object's Properties

Property Name	Description	DataType
Access Order	Indicates the order in which columns must be accessed on the rowset. Read/Write.	DBPROPVAL_AO
Always use content index	Indicates whether or not to use the content index to resolve queries, even if the index is out of date.	Boolean
Append-Only Rowset	A rowset opened with this property will initially contain no rows. Read/Write.	Boolean
Asynchronous Rowset Processing	Identifies the asynchronous processing performed on the rowset. Read/Write.	DBPROPVAL_ASYNCH
Auto Recalc	For chaptered recordsets using COMPUTE, automatically recalculate the summary if the detail lines change. Read/Write. [*]	Integer

Table Continued on Following Page

Property Name	Description	DataType
Background Fetch Size	The number of rows to fetch in each batch, during asynchronous reads.	Long
Background thread Priority	The priority of the background thread for asynchronous actions. Read/Write.	Integer
Batch Size	The number of rows in a batch. Read/Write.	Integer
BLOB accessibility on Forward-Only cursor	Indicates whether or not BLOB columns can be accessed irrespective of their position in the column list. If True then the BLOB column can be accessed even if it is not the last column. If False then the BLOB column can only be accessed if it the last BLOB column, and any non-BLOB columns after this column will not be accessible. Read/Write.	Boolean
Blocking Storage Objects	Indicates whether storage objects might prevent use of other methods on the rowset. Read/Write.	Boolean
Bookmark Information	Identifies additional information about bookmarks over the rowset. Read-only.	DBPROPVAL_BI
Bookmark Type	Identifies the bookmark type supported by the rowset. Read/Write.	DBPROPVAL_BMK
Bookmarkable	Indicates whether bookmarks are supported. Read-only.	Boolean
Bookmarks Ordered	Indicates whether boomarks can be compared to determine the relative position of their rows in the rowset. Read/Write.	Boolean
Bulk Operations	Identifies optimizations that a provider may take for updates to the rowset. Read-only.	DBPROPVAL_BO
Cache Child Rows	Indicates whether child rows in a chaptered recordset are cached. Read/Write. *	Boolean
Cache Deferred Columns	Indicates whether the provider caches the value of a deferred column when the consumer first gets a value from that column. Read/Write.	Boolean

Property Name	Description	DataType
Change Inserted Rows	Indicates whether the consumer can delete or update newly inserted rows. An inserted row is assumed to be one that has been transmitted to the data source, as opposed to a pending insert row. Read/Write.	Boolean
Column Privileges	Indicates whether access rights are restricted on a column-by-column basis. Read-only.	Boolean
Column Set Notification	Indicates whether changing a column set can be canceled. Read-only.	DBPROPVAL_NP
Column Writable	Indicates whether a particular column can be written to. Read/Write.	Boolean
Command Time Out	The number of seconds to wait before a command times out. A value of 0 indicates an infinite timeout. Read/Write.	Long
Concurrency control method	Identifies the method used for concurrency control when using server based cursors. Read/Write.	SSPROPVAL_CONCUR
Cursor Engine Version	Identifies the version of the cursor engine. Read-only.	String
Defer Column	Indicates whether the data in a column is not fetched until specifically requested. Read/Write.	Boolean
Defer scope and security testing	Indicates whether or not the search will defer scope and security testing.	Boolean
Delay Storage Object Updates	Indicates whether, when in delayed update mode, if storage objects are also used in delayed update mode. Read/Write.	Boolean
Fastload Options	Indicates the options to use when in Fastload mode.	String
Fetch Backward	Indicates whether a rowset can fetch backwards. Read/Write.	Boolean

Table Continued on Following Page

Property Name	Description	DataType
Filter Operations	Identifies which comparison operations are supported when using Filter on a particular column. Read-only.	DBPROPVAL_CO
Find Operations	Identifies which comparison operations are supported when using Find on a particular column. Read-only.	DBPROPVAL_CO
FOR BROWSE versioning columns	Indicates the rowset contains the primary key or a timestamp column. Only applicable with rowsets created with the SQL FOR BROWSE statement. Read/Write.	Boolean
Force no command preparation when executing a parameterized command	Identifies whether or not a temporary statement is created for parameterized commands. Read/Write. *	Boolean
Force no command reexecution when failure to satisfy all required properties	Identifies whether or not the command is re-executed if the command properties are invalid. Read/Write. *	Boolean
Force no parameter rebinding when executing a command	Identifies whether or not the command parameters are rebound every time the command is executed. Read/Write. *	Boolean
Force SQL Server Firehose Mode cursor	Identifies whether or not a forward-only, read-only cursor is always created. Read/Write. *	Boolean
Generate a Rowset that can be marshalled	Identifies whether or not the rowset that is to be created can be marshalled across process boundaries. Read/Write. *	Boolean
Hidden Columns	Indicates the number of hidden columns in the rowset added by the provider to uniquely identify rows.	Long
Hold Rows	Indicates whether the rowset allows the consumer to retrieve more rows or change the next fetch position whilst holding previously fetched rows with pending changes. Read/Write.	Boolean

Property Name	Description	DataType
Immobile Rows	Indicates whether the rowset will reorder insert or updated rows. Read/Write.	Boolean
Include SQL_FLOAT, SQL_DOUBLE, and SQL_REAL in QBU where clauses	When using a query-based update, setting this to True will include REAL, FLOAT and DOUBLE numeric types in the WHERE clause, otherwise they will be omitted. Read/Write.	Boolean
Initial Fetch Size	Identifies the initial size of the cache into which records are fetched. Read/Write. [*]	Long
Jet OLEDB:Bulk Transaction	Determines whether bulk operations are transacted.	DBPROPVAL_BT
Jet OLEDB:Enable Fat Cursors	Indicates whether or not Jet caches multiple rows for remote row sources.	Boolean
Jet OLEDB:Fat Cursor Cache Size	The number of rows that should be cached if the dynamic property Jet OLEDB:Enable Fat Cursors is set to True.	Long
Jet OLEDB:Inconsistent	Indicates whether or not inconsistent updates are allowed on queries.	Boolean
Jet OLEDB:Locking Granularity	Identifies the lock mode used to open a table. This only applies if Jet OLEDB:Database Locking Mode is set to DBPROPVAL_DL_ALCATRAZ.	DBPROPVAL_LG
Jet OLEDB:ODBC Pass-Through Statement	Identifies the statement used for a SQL pass-through statement. Read/Write.	String
Jet OLEDB:Partial Bulk Ops	Indicates whether on not bulk operations will complete if some of the values fail.	
Jet OLEDB:Pass Through Query Bulk-Op	Indicates whether or not pass-through queries allow bulk operations. [*]	Boolean
Jet OLEDB:Pass Through Query Connect String	Identifies the connection string for an ODBC pass through query. Read/Write.	String
Jet OLEDB:Stored Query	Indicates whether or not the command should be interpreted as a stored query.	Boolean
Jet OLEDB:Validate Rules On Set	Indicates whether Jet validation rules are applied when the value in a column is set (True) or when the changes are committed (False).	Boolean

Table Continued on Following Page

Property Name	Description	DataType
Keep Identity	Indicates whether or not IDENTITY columns should keep the values if supplied by the client during an INSERT.	Boolean
Keep Nulls	Indicates whether or not NULL values supplied by the client should be kept if DEFAULT values exist on the columns. *	Boolean
Literal Bookmarks	Indicates whether bookmarks can be compared literally, i.e. as a series of bytes. Read/Write.	Boolean
Literal Row Identity	Indicates whether the consumer can perform a binary comparison of two row handles to determine whether they point to the same row. Read-only.	Boolean
Lock Mode	Identifies the level of locking performed by the rowset. Read/Write.	DBPROPVAL_LM
Maintain Change Status	Indicates whether or not to maintain the status of a row if a conflict happens during row updates. *	Boolean
Maximum BLOB Length	Identifies the maximum length of a BLOB field. Read-only.	Long
Maximum Open Rows	Specifies the maximum number of rows that can be active at the same time. Read/Write.	Long
Maximum Pending Rows	Specifies the maximum number of rows that can have pending changes at the same time. Read/Write.	Long
Maximum Rows	Specifies the maximum number of rows that can be returned in the rowset. This is 0 if there is no limit. Read/Write.	Long
Memory Usage	Estimates the amount of memory that can be used by the rowset. If set to 0 the amount is unlimited. If between 1 and 99 it specifies a percentage of the available virtual memory. If 100 or greater it specifies the number of kilobytes. Read/Write.	Long
Notification Granularity	Identifies when the consumer is notified for methods that operate on multiple rows. Read/Write.	DBPROPVAL_NT

Property Name	Description	DataType
Notification Phases	Identifies the notification phases supported by the provider. Read-only.	DBPROPVAL_NP
Objects Transacted	Indicates whether any object created on the specified column is transacted. Read/Write.	Boolean
ODBC Concurrency Type	Identifies the ODBC concurrency type. Read-only.	Integer
ODBC Cursor Type	Identifies the ODBC cursor type. Read-only.	Integer
Others' Changes Visible	Indicates whether the rowset can see updates and deletes made by someone other that the consumer of the rowset. Read/Write.	Boolean
Others' Inserts Visible	Indicates whether the rowset can see rows inserted by someone other than the consumer of the rowset. Read/Write.	Boolean
Own Changes Visible	Indicates whether the rowset can see its own updates and deletes. Read/Write.	Boolean
Own Inserts Visible	Indicates whether the rowset can see its own inserts. Read/Write.	Boolean
Position on the last row after insert	Identifies whether or not the cursor is placed on the last row after an insert. Read-only. *	Boolean
Preserve on Abort	Indicates whether, after aborting a transaction, the rowset remains active. Read/Write.	Boolean
Preserve on Commit	Indicates whether after committing a transaction the rowset remains active. Read/Write.	Boolean
Query Based Updates/Deletes/Inserts	Identifies whether or not queries can be used for updates, deletes, and inserts. Read/Write. *	Boolean
Quick Restart	Indicates whether RestartPosition is relatively quick to execute. Read/Write.	Boolean
Query Restriction	Indicates the restriction to use for a query.	String
Reentrant Events	Indicates whether the provider supports re-entrancy during callbacks. Read-only.	Boolean

Table Continued on Following Page

Property Name	Description	DataType
Remove Deleted Rows	Indicates whether the provider removes rows it detects as having been deleted from the rowset. Read/Write.	Boolean
Report Multiple Changes	Indicates whether an update or delete can affect multiple rows and the provider can detect that multiple rows have been updated or deleted. Read-only.	Boolean
Reshape Name	Indicates the name of the recordset that can be used in reshaping commands.	String
Resync Command	The command string that the Resync method will use to refresh data in the Unique Table.	String
Return PROPVARIANTs in variant binding	Indicates whether or not to return PROPVARIANTS when binding to variant columns.	Boolean
Return Pending Inserts	Indicates whether methods that fetch rows can return pending insert rows. Read-only.	Boolean
Row Delete Notification	Indicates whether deleting a row can be canceled. Read-only.	DBPROPVAL_NP
Row First Change Notification	Indicates whether changing the first row can be canceled. Read-only.	DBPROPVAL_NP
Row Insert Notification	Indicates whether inserting a new row can be canceled. Read-only.	DBPROPVAL_NP
Row Privileges	Indicates whether access rights are restricted on a row-by-row basis. Read-only.	Boolean
Row Resynchronization Notification	Indicates whether resynchronizing a row can be canceled. Read-only.	DBPROPVAL_NP
Row Threading Model	Identifies the threading models supported by the rowset. Read/Write.	DBPROPVAL_RT
Row Undo Change Notification	Indicates whether undoing a change can be canceled. Read-only.	DBPROPVAL_NP
Row Undo Delete Notification	Indicates whether undoing a delete can be canceled. Read-only.	DBPROPVAL_NP
Row Undo Insert Notification	Indicates whether undoing an insert can be canceled. Read-only.	DBPROPVAL_NP

Property Name	Description	DataType
Row Update Notification	Indicates whether updating a row can be canceled. Read-only.	DBPROPVAL_NP
Rowset Fetch Position Change Notification	Indicates whether changing the fetch position can be canceled. Read-only.	DBPROPVAL_NP
Rowset Release Notification	Indicates whether releasing a rowset can be canceled. Read-only.	DBPROPVAL_NP
Scroll Backward	Indicates whether the rowset can scroll backward. Read/Write.	Boolean
Server Cursor	Indicates whether the cursor underlying the rowset (if any) must be materialized on the server. Read/Write.	Boolean
Server Data on Insert	Indicates whether, at the time an insert is transmitted to the server, the provider retrieves data from the server to update to update the local row cache. Read/Write.	Boolean
Skip Deleted Bookmarks	Indicates whether the rowset allows positioning to continue if a bookmark row was deleted. Read/Write.	Boolean
SQL Content Query Locale String	The locale string to use for queries.	String
Strong Row Identity	Indicates whether the handles of newly inserted rows can be compared. Read-only.	Boolean
Unique Catalog	Specifies the catalog, or database name containing the table named in the Unique Table property.	String
Unique Rows	Indicates whether each row is uniquely identified by its column values. Read/Write.	Boolean
Unique Schema	Specifies the schema, or owner of the table named in the Unique Table property.	String
Unique Table	Specifies the name of the base table upon which edits are allowed. This is required when updateable recordsets are created from one-to-many JOIN statements.	String
Updatability	Identifies the supported methods for updating a rowset. Read/Write.	DBPROPVAL_UP

Table Continued on Following Page

Property Name	Description	DataType
Update Criteria	For chaptered recordsets, identifies the criteria used when performing a `Requery`. Read/Write. [*]	String
Update Operation	For chaptered recordsets, identifies the operation to be performed with a `Requery`. Read/Write.	String
Update Resync	Specifies whether an implicit `Resync` method is called directly after an `UpdateBatch` method	CEResyncEnum
Use Bookmarks	Indicates whether the rowset supports bookmarks. Read/Write.	Boolean

The Field Object's Properties

The field properties' names differ from the other properties in that they are less readable and appear more like the schema column names.

Property Name	Description	DataType
BASECATALOGNAME	The name of the catalog. Read-only.	String
BASECOLUMNNAME	The name of the column. Read-only.	String
BASESCHEMANAME	The name of the schema. Read-only.	String
BASETABLENAME	The table name. Read-only.	String
CALCULATIONINFO	This is only available of client cursors.	Binary
CLSID	The class id of the field.	GUID
COLLATINGSEQUENCE	The locale ID of the sort sequence.	Long
COMPUTEMODE	Indicates the mode of recalculation for computed fields.	DBCOMPUTEMODE
DATETIMEPRECISION	The number of digits in the fraction seconds portion of a date/time column. Read-only.	Long
DEFAULTVALUE	The default value of the field.	Variant
DOMAINCATALOG	The name of the catalog containing this column's domain.	String

Property Name	Description	DataType
DOMAINNAME	The name of the domain of which this column is a member.	String
DOMAINSCHEMA	The name of the schema containing this column's domain.	String
HASDEFAULT	Indicates whether or not the field has a default value.	Boolean
ISAUTOINCREMENT	Identifies whether the column is an auto increment column, such as an Access AutoNumber or a SQL Server IDENTITY column. Read-only.	Boolean
ISCASESENSITIVE	Identifies whether the contents of the column are case sensitive. Useful when searching. Read-only.	Boolean
ISSEARCHABLE	Identifies to what extent the column can be searched. Read-only.	DB_SEARCHABLE
ISUNIQUE	Indicates whether or not the field uniquely identifies the row.	Boolean
KEYCOLUMN	Identifies whether or not the column is a key column, used to uniquely identify the row. Read-only.	Boolean
OCTETLENGTH	The maximum column length in bytes, for character or binary data columns. Read-only.	Long
OPTIMIZE	Identifies whether the column is indexed locally. This is only available of client cursors. Read/Write.	Boolean
RELATIONCONDITIONS	Identifies the relationship between fields. This is only available on client cursors.	Binary

Suppliers

- SupplierID
- CompanyName
- ContactName
- ContactTitle
- Address
- City
- Region
- PostalCode
- Country
- Phone
- Fax
- HomePage

Products

- ProductID
- ProductName
- SupplierID
- CategoryID
- QuantityPerUnit
- UnitPrice
- UnitsInStock
- UnitsOnOrder
- ReorderLevel
- Discontinued

Categories

- CategoryID
- CategoryName
- Description
- Picture

6

ADO Error Codes

The following table lists the standard errors than might get returned from ADO operations:

Constant name	Number	Description
adErrInvalidArgument	3001	The application is using arguments that are of the wrong type, are out of acceptable range, or are in conflict with one another.
adErrNoCurrentRecord	3021	Either BOF or EOF is True, or the current record has been deleted; the operation requested by the application requires a current record.
adErrIllegalOperation	3219	The operation requested by the application is not allowed in this context.
adErrInTransaction	3246	The application cannot explicitly close a Connection object while in the middle of a transaction.
adErrFeatureNotAvailable	3251	The operation requested by the application is not supported by the provider.
adErrItemNotFound	3265	ADO could not find the object in the collection corresponding to the name or ordinal reference requested by the application.

Table Continued on Following Page

Constant name	Number	Description
adErrObjectInCollection	3367	Can't append. The object is already in the collection.
adErrObjectNotSet	3420	The object referenced by the application no longer points to a valid object.
adErrDataConversion	3421	The application is using a value of the wrong type for the current operation.
adErrObjectClosed	3704	The operation requested by the application is not allowed if the object is closed.
adErrObjectOpen	3705	The operation requested by the application is not allowed if the object is open.
adErrProviderNotFound	3706	ADO could not find the specified provider.
adErrBoundToCommand	3707	The application cannot change the ActiveConnection property of a Recordset object with a Command object as its source.
adErrInvalidParamInfo	3708	The application has improperly defined a Parameter object.
adErrInvalidConnection	3709	The application requested an operation on an object with a reference to a closed or invalid Connection object.

The following lists the extended ADO errors and their descriptions:

Error Number	Description
-2147483647	Not implemented.
-2147483646	Ran out of memory.
-2147483645	One or more arguments are invalid.
-2147483644	No such interface supported.
-2147483643	Invalid pointer.
-2147483642	Invalid handle.
-2147483641	Operation aborted.

Error Number	Description
-2147483640	Unspecified error.
-2147483639	General access denied error.
-2147483638	The data necessary to complete this operation is not yet available.
-2147467263	Not implemented.
-2147467262	No such interface supported.
-2147467261	Invalid pointer.
-2147467260	Operation aborted.
-2147467259	Unspecified error.
-2147467258	Thread local storage failure.
-2147467257	Get shared memory allocator failure.
-2147467256	Get memory allocator failure.
-2147467255	Unable to initialize class cache.
-2147467254	Unable to initialize RPC services.
-2147467253	Cannot set thread local storage channel control.
-2147467252	Could not allocate thread local storage channel control.
-2147467251	The user supplied memory allocator is unacceptable.
-2147467250	The OLE service mutex already exists.
-2147467249	The OLE service file mapping already exists.
-2147467248	Unable to map view of file for OLE service.
-2147467247	Failure attempting to launch OLE service.
-2147467246	There was an attempt to call `CoInitialize` a second time while single threaded.
-2147467245	A remote activation was necessary but was not allowed.
-2147467244	A remote activation was necessary but the server name provided was invalid.
-2147467243	The class is configured to run as a security ID different to the caller.
-2147467242	Use of OLE1 services requiring DDE windows is disabled.
-2147467241	A `RunAs` specification must be `<domain name>\<user name>` or simply `<user name>`.
-2147467240	The server process could not be started. The pathname may be incorrect.

Error Number	Description
-2147467239	The server process could not be started as the configured identity. The pathname may be incorrect or unavailable.
-2147467238	The server process could not be started because the configured identity is incorrect. Check the username and password.
-2147467237	The client is not allowed to launch this server.
-2147467236	The service providing this server could not be started.
-2147467235	This computer was unable to communicate with the computer providing the server.
-2147467234	The server did not respond after being launched.
-2147467233	The registration information for this server is inconsistent or incomplete.
-2147467232	The registration information for this interface is inconsistent or incomplete.
-2147467231	The operation attempted is not supported.
-2147418113	Catastrophic failure.
-2147024891	General access denied error.
-2147024890	Invalid handle.
-2147024882	Ran out of memory.
-2147024809	One or more arguments are invalid.

Listed below are the OLEDB errors, and whilst they might not be relevant for some ADO work, they are included for completeness:

Error Number	Description
-2147217920	Invalid accessor.
-2147217919	Creating another row would have exceeded the total number of active rows supported by the rowset.
-2147217918	Unable to write with a read-only accessor.
-2147217917	Given values violate the database schema.
-2147217916	Invalid row handle.
-2147217915	An object was open.
-2147217914	Invalid chapter.

Error Number	Description
-2147217913	A literal value in the command could not be converted to the correct type due to a reason other than data overflow.
-2147217912	Invalid binding info.
-2147217911	Permission denied.
-2147217910	Specified column does not contain bookmarks or chapters.
-2147217909	Some cost limits were rejected.
-2147217908	No command has been set for the command object.
-2147217907	Unable to find a query plan within the given cost limit.
-2147217906	Invalid bookmark.
-2147217905	Invalid lock mode.
-2147217904	No value given for one or more required parameters.
-2147217903	Invalid column ID.
-2147217902	Invalid ratio.
-2147217901	Invalid value.
-2147217900	The command contained one or more errors.
-2147217899	The executing command cannot be cancelled.
-2147217898	The provider does not support the specified dialect.
-2147217897	A data source with the specified name already exists.
-2147217896	The rowset was built over a live data feed and cannot be restarted.
-2147217895	No key matching the described characteristics could be found within the current range.
-2147217894	Ownership of this tree has been given to the provider.
-2147217893	The provider is unable to determine identity for newly inserted rows.
-2147217892	No non-zero weights specified for any goals supported, so goal was rejected; current goal was not changed.
-2147217891	Requested conversion is not supported.
-2147217890	`lRowsOffset` would position you past either end of the rowset, regardless of the `cRows` value specified; `cRowsObtained` is 0.
-2147217889	Information was requested for a query, and the query was not set.

Table Continued on Following Page

Error Number	Description
-2147217888	Provider called a method from `IRowsetNotify` in the consumer and the method has not yet returned.
-2147217887	Errors occurred.
-2147217886	A non-`NULL` controlling `IUnknown` was specified and the object being created does not support aggregation.
-2147217885	A given `HROW` referred to a hard- or soft-deleted row.
-2147217884	The rowset does not support fetching backwards.
-2147217883	All `HROW`s must be released before new ones can be obtained.
-2147217882	One of the specified storage flags was not supported.
-2147217881	Invalid comparison operator.
-2147217880	The specified status flag was neither `DBCOLUMNSTATUS_OK` nor `DBCOLUMNSTATUS_ISNULL`.
-2147217879	The rowset cannot scroll backwards.
-2147217878	Invalid region handle.
-2147217877	The specified set of rows was not contiguous to or overlapping the rows in the specified watch region.
-2147217876	A transition from `ALL*` to `MOVE*` or `EXTEND*` was specified.
-2147217875	The specified region is not a proper subregion of the region identified by the given watch region handle.
-2147217874	The provider does not support multi-statement commands.
-2147217873	A specified value violated the integrity constraints for a column or table.
-2147217872	The given type name was unrecognized.
-2147217871	Execution aborted because a resource limit has been reached; no results have been returned.
-2147217870	Cannot clone a command object whose command tree contains a rowset or rowsets.
-2147217869	Cannot represent the current tree as text.
-2147217868	The specified index already exists.
-2147217867	The specified index does not exist.
-2147217866	The specified index was in use.
-2147217865	The specified table does not exist.

Error Number	Description
-2147217864	The rowset was using optimistic concurrency and the value of a column has been changed since it was last read.
-2147217863	Errors were detected during the copy.
-2147217862	A specified precision was invalid.
-2147217861	A specified scale was invalid.
-2147217860	Invalid table ID.
-2147217859	A specified type was invalid.
-2147217858	A column ID occurred more than once in the specification.
-2147217857	The specified table already exists.
-2147217856	The specified table was in use.
-2147217855	The specified locale ID was not supported.
-2147217854	The specified record number is invalid.
-2147217853	Although the bookmark was validly formed, no row could be found to match it.
-2147217852	The value of a property was invalid.
-2147217851	The rowset was not chaptered.
-2147217850	Invalid accessor.
-2147217849	Invalid storage flags.
-2147217848	By-ref accessors are not supported by this provider.
-2147217847	Null accessors are not supported by this provider.
-2147217846	The command was not prepared.
-2147217845	The specified accessor was not a parameter accessor.
-2147217844	The given accessor was write-only.
-2147217843	Authentication failed.
-2147217842	The change was canceled during notification; no columns are changed.
-2147217841	The rowset was single-chaptered and the chapter was not released.
-2147217840	Invalid source handle.
-2147217839	The provider cannot derive parameter info and `SetParameterInfo` has not been called.

Error Number	Description
-2147217838	The data source object is already initialized.
-2147217837	The provider does not support this method.
-2147217836	The number of rows with pending changes has exceeded the set limit.
-2147217835	The specified column did not exist.
-2147217834	There are pending changes on a row with a reference count of zero.
-2147217833	A literal value in the command overflowed the range of the type of the associated column.
-2147217832	The supplied HRESULT was invalid.
-2147217831	The supplied LookupID was invalid.
-2147217830	The supplied DynamicErrorID was invalid.
-2147217829	Unable to get visible data for a newly inserted row that has not yet been updated.
-2147217828	Invalid conversion flag.
-2147217827	The given parameter name was unrecognized.
-2147217826	Multiple storage objects cannot be opened simultaneously.
-2147217825	Cannot open requested filter.
-2147217824	Cannot open requested order.
-2147217823	Invalid tuple.
-2147217822	Invalid coordinate.
-2147217821	Invalid axis for this dataset.
-2147217820	One or more cell ordinals is invalid.
-2147217819	Invalid ColumnID.
-2147217817	Command does not have a DBID.
-2147217816	DBID already exists.
-2147217815	Maximum number of sessions supported by the provider already created. Consumer must release one or more currently held sessions before obtaining a new session object.
-2147217814	Invalid trustee value.
-2147217813	Trustee is not for the current data source.
-2147217812	Trustee does not support memberships/collections.

Error Number	Description
-2147217811	Object is invalid or unknown to the provider.
-2147217810	No owner exists for the object.
-2147217809	Invalid access entry list.
-2147217808	Trustee supplied as owner is invalid or unknown to the provider.
-2147217807	Invalid permission in the access entry list.
-2147217806	Invalid index ID.
-2147217805	Initialization string does not conform to specification.
-2147217804	OLE DB root enumerator did not return any providers that matched any requested `SOURCES_TYPE`.
-2147217803	Initialization string specifies a provider that does not match the currently active provider.
-2147217802	Invalid `DBID`.
-2147217801	`ConstraintType` is invalid or not supported by the provider.
-2147217800	`ConstraintType` is not `DBCONSTRAINTTYPE_FOREIGNKEY` and `cForeignKeyColumns` is not zero.
-2147217799	Deferrability is invalid or the value is not supported by the provider.
-2147217798	`MatchType` is invalid or the value is not supported by the provider.
-2147217782	`UpdateRule` or `DeleteRule` is invalid or the value is not supported by the provider.
-2147217781	`pConstraintID` does not exist in the data source.
-2147217780	Invalid `dwFlags`.
-2147217779	`rguidColumnType` points to a GUID that does not match the object type of this column, or this column was not set.
-2147217778	URL is out of scope.
-2147217776	Provider cannot drop the object.
-2147217775	No source row.
-2147217774	OLE DB object represented by this URL is locked by one or more other processes.
-2147217773	Client requested an object type that is valid only for a collection.
-2147217772	Caller requested write access to a read-only object.
-2147217771	Provider does not support asynchronous binding.

Table Continued on Following Page

Error Number	Description
-2147217770	Provider cannot connect to server for this object.
-2147217769	Attempt to bind to the object timed out.
-2147217768	Provider cannot create an object at this URL because an object named by this URL already exists.
-2147217767	Constraint already exists.
-2147217766	Provider cannot create an object at this URL because the server is out of physical storage.
-2147217765	Unsafe operation was attempted in safe mode. Provider denied this operation.
265920	Fetching requested number of rows would have exceeded total number of active rows supported by the rowset.
265921	One or more column types are incompatible; conversion errors will occur during copying.
265922	Parameter type information has been overridden by caller.
265923	Skipped bookmark for deleted or non-member row.
265924	Errors found in validating tree.
265925	There are no more rowsets.
265926	Reached start or end of rowset or chapter.
265927	The provider re-executed the command.
265928	Variable data buffer full.
265929	There are no more results.
265930	Server cannot release or downgrade a lock until the end of the transaction.
265931	Specified weight was not supported or exceeded the supported limit and was set to 0 or the supported limit.
265932	Consumer is uninterested in receiving further notification calls for this operation.
265933	Input dialect was ignored and text was returned in different dialect.
265934	Consumer is uninterested in receiving further notification calls for this phase.
265935	Consumer is uninterested in receiving further notification calls for this reason.
265936	Operation is being processed asynchronously.

Error Number	Description
265937	In order to reposition to the start of the rowset, the provider had to re-execute the query; either the order of the columns changed or columns were added to or removed from the rowset.
265938	The method had some errors; errors have been returned in the error array.
265939	Invalid row handle.
265940	A given HROW referred to a hard-deleted row.
265941	The provider was unable to keep track of all the changes; the client must re-fetch the data associated with the watch region using another method.
265942	Execution stopped because a resource limit has been reached; results obtained so far have been returned but execution cannot be resumed.
265943	Method requested a singleton result but multiple rows are selected by the command or rowset. First row is returned.
265944	A lock was upgraded from the value specified.
265945	One or more properties were changed as allowed by provider.
265946	Errors occurred.
265947	A specified parameter was invalid.
265948	Updating this row caused more than one row to be updated in the data source.
265948	Row has no row-specific columns.

Suppliers

- SupplierID
- CompanyName
- ContactName
- ContactTitle
- Address
- City
- Region
- PostalCode
- Country
- Phone
- Fax
- HomePage

Products

- ProductID
- ProductName
- SupplierID
- CategoryID
- QuantityPerUnit
- UnitPrice
- UnitsInStock
- UnitsOnOrder
- ReorderLevel
- Discontinued

Categories

- CategoryID
- CategoryName
- Description
- Picture

6

Database Data Types

Relational databases define each field to be a certain data type. RDBMS vendors differ somewhat in what they call those types.

The databases that are used in this book have already been built for you, but, it's important to know the specifics of each data type. You'll be entering and extracting data from these tables using Visual Basic and SQL statements. To build these SQL statements, it's commonly required that you understand how the database server expects data to be passed.

You'll notice immediately that there are more data types available in SQL Server than in Access. SQL Server has been built to optimize data storage. In order to do this, we should use the minimum amount of physical space.

As an example, there are three types of integers in SQL Server. If your requirements are to store a value that may be anywhere between 1 and 10, there is no need to specify the field as a `Smallint` or `Int` because these data types use more storage space than required. The appropriate data type would then be `TinyInt`.

> **If you plan to use Oracle, Sybase or another RDBMS, and need documentation on data types, you may find that your best source is the Internet.**

MS Access Data Types

Data Type	Description
Text	Any combination of text characters, numbers or symbols, up to 255 characters long.
Memo	Contains the same type of data as a text field, but may be used for strings up to 64,000 characters long.
Number	Contains numbers of the types: Byte, Integer, Long Integer, Single, Double or Replication ID (GUID).
Date/Time	Contains a date or time for the years 100 to 9999 AD.
Currency	Used for mathematical calculations with 1 to 4 decimal places. Accurate to 15 digits to the left of the decimal point.
AutoNumber	There are three types of automatically generated numbers for new records: 1. Increment by one (generates a unique number to that specific table). 2. Randomly generated numbers. 3. Replication ID (also known as a GUID).
Yes/No	Used as a Boolean switch (Yes/No, On/Off, True/False).
OLE Object	Used to link or embed any object in a table. These could be pictures, documents, spreadsheets or sounds.

MS SQL Server Data Types

Data Type	Description
TinyInt	Whole numbers between 0 and 255 (1 byte)
SmallInt	Whole numbers between -32767 and +32767
Int[eger]	Whole numbers between -2,147,483,647 and +2,147,483,647 (4 bytes)
Float	4 bytes for precision <16 8 bytes for precision =>16 (precision is identified by the number of digits stored to the right of the decimal place)
Real	Number (4 bytes)

Data Type	Description
Money	-922,337,203,685,477.5808 to +922,337,203,685,477.5807 (8 bytes)
SmallMoney	-214,748.3648 to +214,748.3647 (4 bytes)
DateTime	Jan 1, 1753 to Dec 31, 9999 + Time (8 bytes)
SmallDateTime	Jan 1, 1900 to June 6, 2079 + Time (4 bytes)
Char	Fixed length data
varChar	Variable length data
Binary	Fixed length binary data (up to 255 bytes)
varBinary	Variable length binary data (up to 255 bytes)
bit	Either 0 or 1 (1 byte)
Text	Variable length data up to 2,147,483,647 bytes
Image	BLOB (Binary Large Object) of data up to 2,147,483,647 bytes

Support for Unicode

Until SQL Server 7, a limitation existed on the standard character set supported by the Char, varChar and Text data types. The cause of this is the fact that each could only support a single character set that consisted of 256 (2^8) characters, numbers or symbols. If you had decided that you needed to change the character set, you would be required to re-compile the database tables and reload the data.

Unicode is a standard that is very similar to the standard character set, however; it is made up of the 65,536 (2^{16}) possible values. Of course, the limitation of using the Unicode standard is its increased storage space.

Microsoft SQL Server 7 supports Unicode by adding three new data types from which you can build your fields. They are nChar, nvarChar and nText. The structure of each of these is identical to their base data types with the exception that they can contain up to 65,536 different values and more storage space is required. Following is a table showing where each of the new data types originated:

Character Set	Unicode
Char	nChar
varChar	nvarChar
Text	nText

Suppliers

- SupplierID
- CompanyName
- ContactName
- ContactTitle
- Address
- City
- Region
- PostalCode
- Country
- Phone
- Fax
- HomePage

Products

- ProductID
- ProductName
- SupplierID
- CategoryID
- QuantityPerUnit
- UnitPrice
- UnitsInStock
- UnitsOnOrder
- ReorderLevel
- Discontinued

Categories

- CategoryID
- CategoryName
- Description
- Picture

Installing Microsoft Transaction Server

Before attempting to install Microsoft Transaction Server, you should ensure that your PC meets the minimum requirements as follows:

> Either Windows NT Workstation 4.0 or Server 4.0 with Service Pack 3 (if you don't install Service Pack 3, don't be surprised if you encounter problems). If you have Service Pack 4 or greater, you may receive an error message indication that MTS has not been tested in this environment. However, I have run MTS on Service Pack 4 with no problems.

If you are using Windows 95/98, you can install MTS from the installation CD for Windows 95/95. MTS is supplied with Personal Web Server (PWS), however; it is a limited version with restricted functionality. Security Roles for example do not exist. My recommendation is that you only use Windows 95/98 for learning purposes. Both Windows NT and 2000 provide a more stable environment within which to work. Also, if you are using Windows 9x, you cannot run programs in Visual Basic that use MTS. You must compile the program first. This complicates the process of writing applications that use MTS since they are very difficult to debug.

> Internet Explorer 4.01 is required (you will be prompted to install it if it's not located on your system).
> Pentium 90 MHz (recommended).
> 32 MB of memory (RAM) with 64 MB recommended.
> 100 MB of available hard-disk space.

MTS is available for installation by a variety of methods:

> It is currently available with Visual Studio Enterprise Edition. The setup option will appear on the main menu screen when you insert Visual Studio CD-ROM #1.

> A free diskette can be obtained by request from the following address on Microsoft's web site: http://www.microsoft.com/ntserver/nts/downloads/recommended/NT4OptPk/.

> For those of you who have not purchased the Enterprise Edition of Visual Studio, and don't want to wait for Microsoft to mail a copy, you can download a trial version from the web. While this is a good way of trying out the most recently released product, I wouldn't recommend it to those of you with slow modems (approx. 37MB download)

We will now run through the installation of MTS from the Windows NT 4.0 Option Pack CD. Don't worry if you want to use a different method, the installation options should be very similar and the outcome will be the same.

When Windows 2000 hits the market, you will find that MTS has been replaced with the **Component Services Manager**. *CSM is more closely integrated with COM+ and packages are now called COM+ applications.*

> Locate and run the Setup.exe file and the following screen should appear:

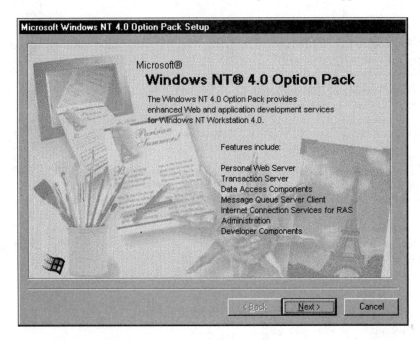

> Click on Next:

Microsoft Windows NT 4.0 Option Pack Setup

Microsoft
Windows NT 4.0 Option Pack

End User License Agreement

MICROSOFT WINDOWS NT 4.0 OPTION PACK

ADDENDUM TO END-USER LICENSE AGREEMENT FOR MICROSOFT SOFTWARE

IMPORTANT: READ CAREFULLY The Microsoft software components which are collectively identified above, including any online or electronic documentation (collectively referred to as Software Components), are subject to the terms and conditions of the End-User License Agreement for Microsoft Software (each such license referred to individually as a EULA), for the applicable Microsoft software product which you licensed previously from Microsoft, and the terms and conditions of this Addendum. By installing, copying or otherwise using the Software Components, you agree to be bound by the

[Accept]   [Decline]

[< Back]   [Next >]   [Cancel]

> Accept the license agreement by clicking on the Accept button:

Microsoft Windows NT 4.0 Option Pack Setup

Microsoft
Windows NT 4.0 Option Pack

Minimum — Requires the least amount of disk space. Provides the basic functionality to deploy Web sites.

Typical — The recommended configuration. Includes all of the Minimum components, along with basic documentation and additional components to allow you to build and deploy Web applications.

Custom — For advanced Web site developers. Provides the option to choose and customize all components. All options included in the Typical installation are pre-selected.

[< Back]   [Next >]   [Cancel]

> Option pack includes a number of tools that deal specifically with the web. We only need a few items of the option pack, so select the Custom button in order to choose which applications to install:

> To deselect any option, simply uncheck it from the list. In order to work through the projects in this book you should opt to install: Microsoft Management Console, NT Option Pack Common Files, and Transaction Server. Click on Next when you're ready:

> The setup process may take several minutes. Progress can be monitored on the Overall progress bar.

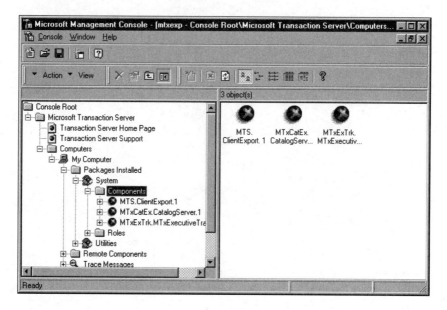

> ➤ When complete, click on the Finish button, and reboot your machine. The installation process is now complete.

> ➤ After rebooting, select Start | Programs | Windows NT Option Pack | Microsoft Transaction Server | Transaction Server Explorer. In the left hand pane, you should see a tree view with multiple folders and the installed components.

Suppliers

- SupplierID
- CompanyName
- ContactName
- ContactTitle
- Address
- City
- Region
- PostalCode
- Country
- Phone
- Fax
- HomePage

Products

- ProductID
- ProductName
- SupplierID
- CategoryID
- QuantityPerUnit
- UnitPrice
- UnitsInStock
- UnitsOnOrder
- ReorderLevel
- Discontinued

Categories

- CategoryID
- CategoryName
- Description
- Picture

Active Server Pages

The Internet is a huge client-server architecture. The web browsers are clients; they request data from another server computer, which can exist anywhere in the world. These servers provide information to web browsers in the form of **HTML** (**HyperText Markup Language**). HTML is static, once it has been sent from the client to the server it does not change - the purpose being that the web page should be understood by as many different web browsers as possible.

You can think of an **Active Server Page** (**ASP**) as an HTML file with extended features. An ASP file (which always has a file ending of .asp) contains normal HTML tags, but also some **server-side scripting**, which is contained within <% %> tags. A server computer interprets and executes any server-side script before it sends the file to the client, with the result that the client receives a plain HTML page. What this means is that we can create sophisticated web applications - but the client web browsers can be any version and do not need to be from a particular vendor. There's no need for our users to install special plug-ins.

An Introduction to HTML

An important part of most Active Server Pages is HTML code. So let's begin by discussing the basics of HTML.

An HTML document is saved with a file ending of .htm or .html. If you open up an HTML file in a text editor such as Notepad.exe or Visual Interdev, you'll see that the entire file is contained within the following tags:

```
<HTML>

</HTML>
```

Beneath the <HTML> tag there are often title tags:

```
<HTML>
<TITLE>An Overview of HTML</TITLE>
</HTML>
```

The title tags tell the web browser what should appear at the top of the browser. This should be as descriptive as possible as the title is often used as a reference to visited sites.

Beneath the <HEAD> and <TITLE> tags is the body of the HTML file which is placed between <BODY> and </BODY>. The <BODY> tags contain everything that will be displayed within the browser. This is where we'll place our ASP script.

Note that HTML tags are often written in uppercase to distinguish them from the surrounding text. However, HTML is actually case insensitive.

Formatting Text

There are a number of tags we use to format text that will be presented in a web page. One of the most important is the <FONT> tag. By setting an attribute of the <FONT> tag, such as SIZE or COLOR, we can change the way that text is displayed. For example, the following code will display "Darren's Store" in blue, size 5 letters:

```
<FONT SIZE=5 COLOR=blue>Darren's Store</FONT>
```

SIZE can be any number between 1 and 7, where 7 is large and 1 is small.

If we want to bold any text, we just place it between the <B> tags:

```
Single CD receiver, active servo control, repeat play, <B>35Wx4 output</B>.
```

Text in an HTML file will continue on the same line unless we use <BR>.
 is known as a Line Break and acts just like a carriage return. So by writing the following HTML code:

```
The first line<BR>
The second line
```

Will result in the "The second line" appearing directly beneath "The first line". If we left out <BR>, we would end up with both expressions appearing on the same line in the web browser.

If you want to add a horizontal line across your page at any point use the <HR> tag.

Note that both the <BR> and <HR> do not have closing tags of </BR> and </HR>.

Adding Tables

To create a table in HTML we use the `<TABLE>` tag:

```
<TABLE ALIGN=center BORDER=0 CELLPADDING=5 WIDTH=200>...</TABLE>
```

The `ALIGN` attribute tells the browser how we want the entire table aligned. The possible values are `left`, `right` and `center`. The default value is `left`.

The `BORDER` attribute tells the browser how thick we want the border around the table in pixels.

The `CELLPADDING` attribute tells the browser how much space to leave between the frame of the table and the cells in the table. The value is given in pixels.

The `WIDTH` attribute tells the browser how wide to make the browser. Here the table has been set to 200 pixels wide. If we wanted to set the width as a percentage of the window size, we would append `%` to the end of the value.

Then we must set the table rows and their data:

```
<TABLE BORDER=1>

<!-- Begin our column header row -->
<TR>
<TD HEIGHT=50>Name</TD>

<TD HEIGHT=50>Age</TD>

</TR>

<!-- Add our data entry -->
<TR><TD ALIGN=right>Fred</TD>
        <TD>38</TD></TR>

<TR><TD ALIGN=right>Bernard</TD>
        <TD>10</TD></TR>

</TABLE>
```

The table row tag `<TR>` defines the start of a new row in the table, `</TR>` defines the end of a new row in a table. Note that the closing tag `</TR>` is optional.

Once we have started a new row, we must add data to it. We do this using the table data tag `<TD>`. Just as with the `<TABLE>` tag we can assign attributes to the `<TD>` tag. Here we have the `ALIGN` attribute to right (so that the contents of the cell in the table will be aligned to the right) and the `HEIGHT` attribute to 50 pixels.

There are other attributes available, including `COLSPAN`, which specifies the number of table columns that the cell spans. Using `COLSPAN` we can join cells, just like in a spreadsheet program.

Note that we can add comments to our HTML files by placing them within the `<!-- -->` tags.

Adding Hypertext Links

Hypertext links, that allow you to jump to another page in the web site or another web site altogether are created by using the anchor tag <A>. Anything that is placed between the start anchor tag <A> and the closing anchor tag </A>, will become activated by the browser, allowing the user to click on that part of the document to jump to somewhere else. A very simple anchor tag looks as follows:

```
<BODY>
Click <A HREF="<index.html"here</A> to open the index.html page
</BODY>
```

This will highlight the word here in the browser and allow the user to jump to Index.html on the same web site. If you want to allow the user to jump to another web site altogether you will need to include the http://servername/ part at the front as well.

Active Server Pages

To run Active Server Pages on your local machine you will need to have:

- ➢ Microsoft Internet Explorer 3 or higher
- ➢ Microsoft's Internet Information Server (IIS) or Personal Web Server (PWS), which can be downloaded for free from Microsoft's web site (http://www.microsoft.com). PWS is also available on the Windows NT4 Option Pack CD, and is supplied on the CD for Windows 95 and 98.

Hello World from an Active Server Page

Believe it or not, the following code is an ASP page. It doesn't do anything more than we could do with standard HTML, but it is an Active Server Page because it has the extension .asp.

That means that IIS will "read" this file and perform any tasks the server-side code on the page directs it to perform before it delivers the page to the user.

Write the code exactly as shown using Notepad, save it using HelloWorld.asp as the filename, and place it in the root directory for your web server (usually wwwroot):

```
<HTML>
    <HEAD>
    </HEAD>

        <BODY>
         Hello World from ASP
        </BODY>

</HTML>
```

You can "execute" this page by using your browser and typing in http://YourServerName/HelloWorld.asp as the address. Of course, you will have to replace YourServerName with the name of your IIS server:

Server-Side Code

OK let's add a few lines of server-side code and put the server to work. Modify your
`HelloWorld.asp` file as follows and save it again without changing the name or location of the file.
Execute the changed page the same way you did earlier.

```
<%@ Language=VBScript %>
<HTML>
<%
    strUserName = "Steven"
    strMessage="Hello " & strUserName
%>

<HEAD>
</HEAD>
    <BODY>
        <% = strMessage %>
    </BODY>
</HTML>
```

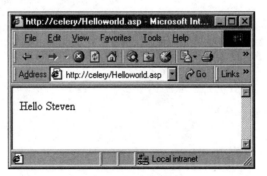

When you execute the page, your browser should display a page something like the one above. We
will go over the syntax we used to make this happen in a minute. First, I would like you to view the
source code the browser used to display this page. We really need to compare it with the
`HelloWorld.asp` file from above. In order to view the source code, place your cursor somewhere
on the page, right-click the mouse and select the View Source option from the menu:

Your browser will open up Notepad and you will see something like the following:

```
<HTML>

<HEAD>
</HEAD>
    <BODY>
        Hello Steven
    </BODY>

</HTML>
```

What Notepad is displaying is the file that the server delivered to the browser (client). Notice that it is quite different than the file that we just saved and asked the server to deliver. In the original file we had two variables and we performed a concatenation. None of this shows up on the client. That is because the server executed the code that we enclosed between the <% and %> characters before it delivered the page. As far as the browser was concerned, it just displayed the file exactly as it received it from the server. IIS actively read and executed the instructions in the page before it served the page to the client – hence the name Active Server Pages. This is a simple example of HTML that was dynamically created by the server.

The code is really quite simple. Notice that we didn't declare the variables before we used them. As far as we are concerned, in ASP all variables are treated as variants. We don't need to use the Dim statement unless we are creating an array. Other than the missing Dim statements and the curious <% and %> characters, this code looks just like regular VB. That is because this code is really just another flavor of VB – VBScript.

Notice that in the only line of code between the <BODY> tags, there appears to be an ill-placed equal sign. The equal sign directs the server to write the results of the statement on the page. In this case, the server wrote the words "Hello Steven" in place of the original line in the file:

```
<BODY>
    <% = strMessage %>.
</BODY>
```

Although this example was incredibly simple, it illustrates the primary purpose of ASP. Active Server Pages write HTML code. We use a server-side scripting language, in this case VBScript, to instruct the server exactly how to create each line of HTML code.

Let's take a look at another simple example. Change the HelloWorld.asp file to look like the following:

```
<%@ Language=VBScript %>
<HTML>
    <HEAD>
    </HEAD>

        <BODY>
            <% For i = 1 to 10 %>
                The Value of i = <% = i %><BR>
            <% Next %>
        </BODY>
</HTML>
```

It should come as no surprise that when you request this file, your browser displays something like the following image:

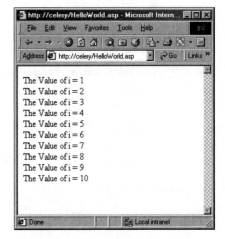

Notice that this time we instructed the server to write a line of code in a `For...Next` loop. The `<% Next %>` line disturbs a lot of VB programmers. It is a common, but unnecessary, practice in VB to write something more akin to `Next i` where we identify the control variable `i`. You may be surprised to learn that this practice is optional in standard VB, and that the code actually executes a little faster if we omit the reference to the control variable in the `Next` line. Anyway, with VBScript, we *cannot* use the name of the control variable in the `Next` line. Sadly, this practice causes an error in VBScript. Let's take a look at the source code for this page.

```
<HTML>
<HEAD>
</HEAD>
<BODY>
        The Value of i = 1<BR>
        The Value of i = 2<BR>
        The Value of i = 3<BR>
        The Value of i = 4<BR>
        The Value of i = 5<BR>
        The Value of i = 6<BR>
        The Value of i = 7<BR>
        The Value of i = 8<BR>
        The Value of i = 9<BR>
        The Value of i = 10<BR>
</BODY>
</HTML>
```

Notice that the server did exactly what we told it to do. It wrote a line for each iteration in the `For...Next` loop, and placed the value of the control variable `i` in each line.

The ASP Object Model

ASP supplies five main objects to every script:

> ➤   `Application`
> ➤   `Request`
> ➤   `Response`

➤ Server

➤ Session

For a full treatment of these objects and their properties and methods, please refer to the ASP 2.0 Programmer's Reference (1-861002-45-9) from Wrox Press.

The Request Object

We can use the `Request` object's methods to easily get at any information supplied by the user or provided as arguments on the URL.

QueryString

`QueryString` allows our ASP script to retrieve the values of **query strings**, which are parameters tagged onto the end of a requested URL. For example, we could call the following page:

```
PageTwo.asp?Parameter1=Hello&Parameter2=World&Parameter3=9
```

We could extract the values out of the query string using `Request.QueryString` as follows:

```
<%
    vntParameter1 = Request.QueryString("Parameter1")
    vntParameter2 = Request.QueryString("Parameter2")
    vntParameter3 = Request.QueryString("Parameter3")
%>
```

As you can see, `QueryString` requires that you indicate the name of the parameter for which you are looking. You can also use a numeric value to indicate the parameter by position, to retrieve the value of the second parameter you would use `Request.QueryString(2)`.

The Response Object

The `Response` object is the opposite of the `Request` object. Instead of collecting information from the user, the `Response` object is what we use to send information back to the browser.

Write

The `Write` method is used to send a specified string to the client. Let's rewrite our `HelloWorld.asp` file so that it contains no HTML, only server-side code:

```
<%
Response.Write "<HTML>"
Response.Write "<HEAD>"
Response.Write "</HEAD>"
Response.Write "<BODY>"
For i = 1 to 10
    Response.Write "The Value of i = " & i & "<BR>"
Next
Response.Write "</BODY>"
Response.Write "</HTML>"
%>
```

Rather than mixing HTML and code, this new script is all code. By using `Response.Write`, we are sending exactly the same HTML code to the client. From the browser's perspective, this is no different from the previous page.

The Server Object

The `Server` object is used to instantiate all of the objects that we want our ASP code to interact with.

CreateObject

The `CreateObject` method does pretty much what you'd expect. Just like the `CreateObject` method that's available in Visual Basic, you provide it with an ActiveX server name and a class name and it will return a reference to the object:

```
<%
Set objCustomer = Server.CreateObject("CustomerApp.clsCustomer")
%>
```

The Session Object

The `Session` object is the most powerful object for creating applications using Active Server Pages. It has solved a problem that has existed in creating web-based applications, which is that the connection between the client and the server is **stateless**. This means that when a client requests a page, the server has no mechanism for tying this request back to any previous made by the same client. Each request that a client makes of the web server is treated independently of the rest. While this allows for a very efficient and fast web server, it makes writing applications nearly impossible.

The `Session` object allows you to:

> ➢ Be notified when a user session begins. You can then take appropriate actions for a new client.
> ➢ Be notified when a client has ended his or her session.
> ➢ Store information that can be accessed by the client throughout the session.

This is why the `Session` object is an invaluable tool in a web application!

Contents

The `Contents` collection stores all the variables established for a session through script commands.

For example, we could store a value into a session-level variable called `VisitorID` in the following manner:

```
Session.Contents("VisitorID") = Request("VisitorID")
```

Because `Contents` is the default property for the `Session` object, we can also write:

```
Session("VisitorID") = Request("VisitorID")
```

Suppliers

- SupplierID
- CompanyName
- ContactName
- ContactTitle
- Address
- City
- Region
- PostalCode
- Country
- Phone
- Fax
- HomePage

Products

- ProductID
- ProductName
- SupplierID
- CategoryID
- QuantityPerUnit
- UnitPrice
- UnitsInStock
- UnitsOnOrder
- ReorderLevel
- Discontinued

Categories

- CategoryID
- CategoryName
- Description
- Picture

6

Index

A

Access
compared to SQL Server
benchmarks, 128
Backup, 129
TPC, 129
budget, 128
database connections, number required, 130
functionality, 129
batch requests, 129
recovery mechanism, 129
security, 129
storage capacity, 127
indexes
viewing, 49
ActiveX Data Objects (ADO)
see ADO
ADO, 66
see also Recordsets
ADODB
compared to ADOR, 201
ADOR
compared to ADODB, 201
Command object, 67
compared to ADO Data Control, 202
compared to DAO, 72
compared to RDO, 72
Connection object, 67
database, connecting to, 203
Connection object, 203, 204
connection string
Connection object, assigning to, 205
setting, 204
OLE DB providers, 204-207
connection, closing, 208
connection, opening, 207
OpenOptions, 208
connection, re-opening, 208
database, querying, 208
Command object, creating, 209
declarations, 209

Command object, referencing, 209
command text, building, 209
CommandType property, 209
returning no records, 210
command, executing
Command object, without, 212
Connection object, 212
connection, specifying, 210
Execute method, 210
Recordset object, 213
Parameter collection, 217
Append method, 217
Count property, 217
Delete method, 217
Item method, 217
Parameter objects, 217
Refresh method, 217
stored procedure, passing to, 218
Parameter object, creating, 214
Direction property, 216
Name property, 215
properties, optional, 214
Size property, 216
Type property, 215
Value property, 217
parameters, 214
downloading, 202
error handling, 242
Error object, 243
Description property, 243
NativeError property, 244
Number property, 243
Errors collection, 242
clearing, 243
Count property, 242
Item property, 242
referencing, 242
Refresh method, 243
Error object, 67
error trapping, 324
ErrorLog, 325, 327
displaying, 328
For Append keyword, 328
FreeFile function, 328
Resume statement, 327

events, 236
  accessing, 237
  classes, 237
  Connection object, 237
    ConnectComplete event, 239
    Disconnect event, 240
    WillConnect event, 237
  Recordset object, 240
    MoveComplete event, 240
    RecordChangeComplete event, 241
Field object
  Value property, 219
Fields object, 67
Object Model, 200
  Command object
    defined, 200
  Connection object
    defined, 200
  object hierarchy, 200
    Command object, 201
    Connection object, 201
    Error object, 201
    Field object, 201
    Parameter object, 201
    Property object, 201
    Recordset object, 201
  objects, main, 200
  objects, subsidiary, 200
  Recordset object
    defined, 200
Parameters object, 67
records
  field values, retrieving, 219
referencing, 202, 285
relation to OLE DB, 66, 67
SHAPE construct, 296
  APPEND keyword, 297
  DataGrid control
    applying to, 297
    fields, adding, 298
    fields, removing, 297
  parts, 297
  RELATE keyword, 297
  SHAPE keyword, 297
transactions
  Connection object
    creating, 319
  methods, 319
    BeginTrans, 320, 322
    CommitTrans, 320, 322
    RollBackTrans, 320, 322
  uses
    records, stepping through, 322

VB controls, binding, 244
  DataField property, 244
  DataSource property, 244
  objects, uninstatiating, 245
ADO Data Control, 95
compared to ADO, 202
compared to DAO Data Control, 96
compared to RDO Data Control, 96
connection string, building, 97
  database location, selecting, 98
  database properties, displaying, 99
  database properties, modifying, 99
  database provider, selecting, 98
  security, implementing, 98
  testing, 98
  time-out setting, 98
connection string, setting, 293
grids, binding, 294
hiding, 301
Masked Edit Control, binding, 107
overview, 107
properties, setting, 101
  BOFAction, 101
  EOFAction, 101
RecordCount, displaying, 294
records
  adding, 115
    protecting, 115
  deleting, 116
  finding, 117
    form, adding, 117
    InStr function, 119
    Len keyword, 119
    MoveNext method, 120
    SelLength property, 119
    SelStart property, 119
    SetFocus method, 119
    testing, 120
  refreshing, 116
  updating, 116
    Requery method, 116
Recordset object, 107
RecordSource property, setting, 100
  connection types, 101
Toolbox, adding to, 95
Application Wizard
see VB Application Wizard
applications
see client-server applications
see three-tier applications
see two-tier applications

ASP, 609
  component, creating, 610
  database, connecting to, 611
    testing, 612
  database, querying, 613
    GetCategories method, 613
    GetProductInfo method, 613
    GetProductsInCategory method, 613
  page, testing, 614
  presentation page, 615
  query, executing
    options, 610

B

benchmarks
  Backup, 129
  defined, 128
  TPC, 129
black box
  defined, 429
business objects, 617
  order, capturing, 617
    Cart class, 617
      ASP, 618
      Collection class, 618
      Items, adding, 619
    cart.asp page, 620
      cart table, 621
        GetProductInfo method, 622
      cart table, Store object, 621
      cart, adding product, 621
      cart, checking for, 620
    CartItem class, 619
      initialization, 619
  order, processing, 623
    Checkout.asp page, 628
      customer, creating, 631
      error reporting, improved, 631
      ObjectContext object, 629
      transaction, managing, 630
    MTS
      database changes, handling, 633
    object building, 623
      binary compatability, setting, 625
      component, installing, 626
        Component Wizard, 626
      MTS library, referencing, 624
      MTS package, creating, 625
        Package Wizard, 626
      MTSTransactionMode property, 623
      ObjectControl interface, 624
      ProcessOrder method, 624

C

Check constraints
  adding, 313
    Constraint clause, 313
child forms
  creating, 293
  modifying, 295
class
  instance, 332
client, 340, 403
  cboCompany_Click event procedure, 412
  cmdClear_Click event procedure, 347
  cmdDelete_Click event procedure, 345
  cmdExit_Click event procedure, 347
  cmdInsert_Click event procedure, 346
  cmdNew_Click event procedure, 417
  cmdRefresh_Click event procedure, 345
  cmdSend_Click event procedure, 418
    business rules, 418
    Hierarchical FlexGrid control, refreshing, 418
    recordset, populating, 418
  cmdUpdate_Click event procedure, 346
  coding, 343
  components, adding, 404
  Create_New_Order method, 412
  Create_New_Order_Detail method, 413
  creating, 340
  data validation, 315
    key press, upon, 317
      DataField property, 317
      KeyPress event, 317
    methods, 315
    updating, upon, 315
      current record, navigating from, 316
      Update button, 316
  declarations, 343
  drag-and-drop functionality, 414
    DataGrid's DragDrop event, 415
      duplicates, checking for, 415
      products, adding, 415
    DataGrid's DragOver event, 414
    Hierarchical FlexGrid's MouseDown event, 414
      Drag method, 414
    icons, 414
  fat, 21
    advantages of, 22
    compared to fat server, 20, 22
    disadvantages of, 22

Form_Load event procedure, 344, 409
  functions, calling, 409
  Hierarchical FlexGrid control, populating, 410
  Hierarchical FlexGrid control, properties, 410
  middle-tier object, instantiation, 409
  recordset structure, assigning, 410
GUI design, 341
  ListView control
    adding, 341
    columns, adding, 342
    configuring, 342
    properties, viewing, 342
  references, adding, 343
ListView1_Click event procedure, 346
references, adding, 404
Select_Data event procedure, 344
  ListItem object, 345
    Add method, 345
startup project, setting as, 348
Total_All function, 416
  DatGrid's AfterColUpdate function, 417
user interface
  building, 404
  DataGrid control, properties, 408
  Hierarchical FlexiGrid control, properties, 407
variables, module-level, 408
  declaring, 408
  fields, declaring, 409
  recordsets, declaring, 408
client-server
compiling, 349
  DLLs, registering, 349
testing, 348, 368
client-server applications, deploying
see also three-tier applications
see also two-tier application
DSN, 510
  Registry Editor, 510
    DSN key, 511, 512
    opening, 511
  registry files, creating, 514
    DSN, adding to registry, 514
    DSN, setting, 514
    header, 514
  registry files, exporting, 512
    ODBC Data Source Administrator, 513
N-tier, 515
  client configuration, exporting from MTS, 517
  Microsoft Management Console for Transaction Server, 517
  Microsoft Management Console for Transaction Server, exporting packages, 518

DCOM
  COM, benefits over, 516
  download site, 517
  installing, 517
  overview, 516
  proxy, 517
  stub, 517
  uses, 516
  extra steps, 515
packaging, reasons for
  overview, 509
setup utility,
  creating, 518
    Package and Deployment Wizard, 518
    Cab options, 522
    dependency files, 520
    included files, 521
    included files, adding, 521
    Install Locations dialog, 524
    options, initial, 519
    package, location, 520
    package, specifications, 519
    Packaging Report, 525
    Registry Infromation dialog, 522
    shared files, 524
    Start Menu Items dialog, 523
  testing, 525
    setup wizard, 525
    closing applications, importance of, 526
    program group, selecting, 527
    rebooting, 527
    setup location, changing, 527
    Setup.exe file, 525
client-server applications
OLAP multidimensional cubes, viewing, 563
  connection string, creating, 564
  Cube Browser control, 563
    Connect method, 565
    disconnecting, 565
security models, 477
  MTS, using, 498
    components, adding roles, 501
    components, coding, 503
    components, properties, 503
    components, refreshing, 499
    Microsoft Management Console, 498
    role, creating, 499
  N-tier solutions, 478
    middle tier, 478
    server, 479
  server-side, 479
    SQL Server database, 479
  SQL, using, 505
    DENY command, 506
    GRANT command, 505
    REVOKE command, 506

three-tier solutions, 495
  client, 496
  middle-tier, 496
two-tier solutions, 478, 490
  application, closing, 493
  connection string, building, 492
  data form, 491
  forms, coding, 492
  login form, 492
  recordset, populating, 493
  roles, 478
  startup form, setting, 494
  testing, 494
  users, 478
client-server architecture
client, fat, 21
  advantages of, 22
  compared to fat server, 20, 22
  disadvantages of, 22
considerations, 34
database servers
  functionality, 30
  stored procedures, 31
    advantages of, 31
  triggers, 30
    uses, 30
  views, 32
    advantages of, 32
    information, retrieving, 33
defined, 20
estimating, 35
examples, 33
extended, 33
middle tier
  components, 27
  roles, 27
N-tier, 27
  compared to two-tier, 34
  data, passing, 371
overview, 20
planning, 34
replication
  advantages of, 24
  considerations, 26
  defined, 24
  example, 24
  uses, 24, 25
    when not to, 25
scalability, 23
scheduling, 35
server, fat, 21
  advantages of, 22
  compared to fat client, 20, 22
  disadvantages of, 22

TCP/IP connections, 33
three-tier, 27, 28
  advantages of, 28
  disadvantages of, 29
  middle tier
    components, 27
    roles, 27
  TP monitor
    choosing, 34
    roles, 30
  TP monitor, 29
two-tier, 26
  compared to N-tier, 34
universality, 23
usage, 23
World Wide Web, 33
COM
defined, 63
Command object
ActiveConnection property, 210
Cancel method, 212
CommandText property, 209
  CommandType property, 209
CommandTimeout property, 211
CreateParameter method, 214
  arguments, optional, 214
  Direction argument, 216
  Name argument, 215
  Size argument, 216
    required, 216
  syntax, 214
  Type argument, 215
  Value argument, 217
creating, 209
  declarations, 209
defined, 200
Execute method, 210
  arguments, optional, 210
    example, 211
parameters
  passing to stored arguments, 218
    command object, instantiating, 218
    Parameter object, creating, 218
    recordset, instantiating, 218
records, returning none, 210
referencing, 209
commit coordinator
distributed transactions, 469
MS DTC, 469
Component Object Model (COM)
see COM

components
  building, 334
    ActiveX DLL, creating, 334
    ADO, referencing, 335
    database calling functions, 336
      Add_Employee, 336, 337, 361
      Delete_Employee, 336, 338, 362
      Select_Employee, 337, 339
      Update_Employee, 337, 338, 362
    SQL Server, connecting to, 335
      Connection object, 336
      Initialize event, 336
      Terminate event, 336
    testing, 340
      debugging, preliminary, 340
      Instancing property, 340
  defined, 28
  designing, 333
    considerations, 334
  in process server
    defined, 28
  instance of
    defined, 28
  middle tier, 332
  MTS
    properties
      General tab, 353
      modifying, 353
      Security tab, 355
      Transaction tab, 354
    transaction control, 351
  MTS, modifying for, 357
    installing, 364
    MTSTransactionMode property, 358
    ObjectContext object, 360
      errors, 360
      instantiation, 360
      methods, 361, 363
    packages, 364
      adding to, 367
      creating, 364
    project properties, setting, 358
      Pessimistic Tear Down, avoiding, 359
    recompiling, 363
    version compatibility, 359
      Binary Compatibility, 360
      No Compatibility, 360
      options, 360
      Project Compatibility, 360
  objects, 332
  out of process server
    defined, 28
Connection object
  Close method, 208

command, executing, 212
  Cancel method, 212
  Execute method, 212
    arguments, 212
    CommandTimeout property, 212
connection string, assigning, 205
connection string, setting, 204
  OLE DB providers, 204, 207
    database server, 205, 206, 207
    default, 205
    desktop database, 206, 207
    Driver, specifying, 205
    examples, 206, 207
    Microsoft Jet, 207
    ODBC, 205
    SQL Server database, 207
  creating, 203
  declaring, 203
  defined, 200
  destroying, 208
  error handling, 242
  Errors collection, 242
    clearing, 243
    Count property, 242
    Error object, 243
    Item property, 242
    referencing, 242
    Refresh method, 243
  events, 237
    Disconnect event, 240
      arguments, 240
      uses, 240
    WillConnect event, 237
      arguments, 237
      uses, 238
    WillConnectComplete event, 239
      arguments, 239
      uses, 239
  implicit, 204
  Open method, 207
    OpenOptions, 208
  referencing, 204
  re-opening, 208
constraints
  SQL Server, 307, 311
    Check, 307
      adding, 313
      Constraint clause, 313
    creating, 307
      scripts, 307
    Default, 307
    Foreign Key, 307
    Primary Key, 307
    testing, 311

types, 307
Unique, 307
viewing with Access, 312
  properties, 313
controls
  ADO Data, 95
  check box, 121
  Cube Browser, 563
  Data Repeater, 125
  DataCombo, 123, 299
    filter, adding, 300
    LIKE keyword, 300
  DataGrid, 122
    ADO Data Control, binding to, 294
    data format, changing, 299
    fields, adding, 298
    fields, removing, 297
    layout, modifying, 298
    SHAPE construct, applying, 297
  DataList, 123
  Hierarchical FlexGrid, 122
  image, 122
  ImageList, 457
    properties, 457
      picture, adding, 457
  label, 121
  ListView
    adding, 341
    columns, adding, 342
    configuring, 342
    properties, viewing, 342
  Masked Edit, 107
  MS Chart, 124
  OLE Container, 124
  picture, 122
  rich text box, 124
  StatusBar, 458
    PanelClick event procedure, 462
    properties, 458
      panels, adding, 458
  textboxes
    LostFocus event procedures, 464
  Toolbar, 456
    ButtonClick event procedure, 463
      Delete method, calling, 463
      NewCustomer method, calling, 464
      Save method, calling, 464
    properties, 456
      buttons, adding, 456
conventions used, 11

D

DAO, 70
  compared to ADO, 72
  compared to ODBCDirect, 71
  compared to RDO, 72
  JET workspaces, 70
  ODBCDirect, 70
    compared to DAO, 70
    upgrading to, 71
  workspaces, 70
DAO Data Control
  compared to ADO Data Control, 96
data
  see also data access
  Currency format, 299
  defined, 59
  passing
    N-tier application
      methods, 373
      methods not to use, 371
  type, converting
    Microsoft Data Formatting Object Library, 299
data access
  see also data
  ADO, 66
    compared to DAO, 72
    compared to RDO, 72
  ASCII file
    disadvantages of, 60
  DAO, 70
    compared to ADO, 72
    compared to ODBCDirect, 71
    compared to RDO, 72
    JET workspaces, 70
    ODBCDirect, 70
      compared to DAO, 70
      upgrading to, 71
    workspaces, 70
  data sources, 61
  MDAC, 73
    contents, 73
    installing, 73
    web page, 73
  ODBC, 68
    Application Programming Interface (API), 68
    architecture, 69
    compared to OLE DB, 72
    compliance levels, 68
    components, 68
    data source, 69

Data Source Name (DSN)
  authentication, choosing, 77
  configuration options, default settings, 77
  connecting to, 80
  connection characteristics, 76
  Connection Pooling, 75
  Drivers, 75
  File, 75
  icon, 74
  language settings, 79
  ODBC Data Source Administrator, 75
  setting up, 74
  set-up screen, 76
  statistics, recording, 79
  System, 75
  testing, 80
  Tracing, 75
  User, 75
  driver, 69
  Driver Manager, 69
ODBCDirect, 70
  compared to DAO, 70
  upgrading to, 71
OLE Automation
  advantages of, 60
  disadvantages of, 60
OLE DB, 63
  compared to ODBC, 72
  consumers, 65
  providers, 64
options, 60
RDO, 70
  compared to ADO, 72
  compared to DAO, 72
technologies
  choosing, 71
  considerations, 71
  installing, 73
  locating, 73
UDA, 61
  ADO, 66
    Command object, 67
    Connection object, 67
    Error object, 67
    Fields object, 67
    Parameters object, 67
    Recordset object, 67
    relation to OLE DB, 66, 67
  benefits of, 62
  defined, 61
  DNA
    defined, 62
  importance of, 61
  OLE DB, 63
    advantages of, 63

COM, 63, 64
  consumers, 65
  defined, 63, 64
  providers, 64
  relation to ADO, 66, 67
two-tier structure
  architecture, 62
  importance of, 61
Data Access Objects (DAO)
  see DAO
Data Environment Designer (DED)
  see DED
Data Formatting Object Library
  see Microsoft Data Formatting Object
  Library
data objects
  ADO, referencing, 430
  building, 430
  classes
    instancing property, 431
  clsCustomers class
    coding, 450
    IsDeleted property, 452
      declaring, 452
    IsDirty property, 452
      declaring, 452
    IsLoading property, 451
      declaring, 451
    Key property, 451
      declaring, 451
      read-only, setting as, 451
    properties, 453
      declaring, 453
      Property Gets, 453, 455
      Property Lets, 453, 455
    use, 450
  clsCustomerSrv classr
    IsDirty method, 433
  clsCustomerSrvr class
    Class_Intialize event, 432
    coding, 431
    Customers property, 443
    Delete method, 432
    general declarations, 431
      Collection, creating, 431
    Load method, 434
      IsLoading property, 436
      parameters, 434
      recordset, opening, 436
    LoadParameters method, 441
      arguments, 442
    New Customer method, 437
    Save method, 438
      objects, adding, 440

objects, saving, 440
stored procedures, 443
 delete, 446
 insert, 445
 select, 443
 update, 446
 UpdateCustomer method, 442
 use, 431
colCustomers class
 Add method, 447
 Clear method, 448
 collection reference, removing, 448
 Remove method, 448
 coding, 447
 Count property, 448
 Exists method, 448
 ErrorHandler, 449
 Is Nothing check, 449
 Item property, 449
 VarKey parameter, 449
 NewEnum property, 449
 Procedure Attributes dialog, 449
 Remove method, 450
 use, 447
 variables, module-level, 447
defined, 430
importance of, 430
test application, 455
 ButtonClick event procedure, 463
 Delete method, calling, 463
 NewCustomer method, calling, 464
 Save method, calling, 464
 code, 460
 Form_Load event procedure, 461
 LoadCustomerRecord method, 461
 record index, 462
 LostFocus event procedures, 464
 PanelClick event procedure, 462
 setting up, 455
 testing, 465
 user interface, 456
 ImageList control, 457
 labels, 460
 Microsoft Common Controls, adding, 456
 StatusBar, 458
 textboxes, 460
 Toolbar control, 456
 variables, module-level, 460
 declaring, 460
data passing
 N-tier application, 371
 ADO recordset, 382
 batch mode updating, 382
 connectionless, creating, 384
 database, creating from, 383
 value, passing by, 385

arguments, passing to a method, 372
 problems with, 373
data serialization, 373
 techniques, 373
PropertyBag object, 386
 deserializing data, 387
 serializing data, 386
single properties, calling, 372
 problems with, 372
UDTs, 373
 GetData function, 375
 problems with, 377
UDTs/LSet command, 377
 background, 378
 filler space, 382
 implementation, 379
 LenB function, 381
 longword alignment, 381, 382
 memory alignment, 381
 word alignment, 381
Variant arrays, 375
 advantages of, 376
 considerations, 376
 disadvantages of, 376
 GetRows method, 377
Data Report Designer (DRD)
see DRD
data validation
 client, 315
 key press, upon, 317
 DataField property, 317
 KeyPress event, 317
 methods, 315
 updating, upon, 315
 current record, navigating from, 316
 Update button, 316
 constraints
 SQL Server
 Check, 307, 313
 criteria, common, 305
 defined, 305
 placing, 306
 server, 306
 constraints
 creating, 307
 defined, 306
 SQL Server, 307, 311
 testing, 311
 viewing with Access, 312
 problems with, 307
Data Warehousing
 architecture, 538
 data extraction, 543
 batch process, 544
 considerations, 543

real-time transformation, 543
data marts, 539
  advantages of, 539
  uses, 539
data structure, defining, 540
  considerations, 540
  data retrieval, speed of, 540
  Data Transformation Services (DTS), 543
  data, updating, 541
  example, 541
  hard drive space, 541
data warehouse
  populating, 539
  retrieving data from, 539
considerations, 532
data mining, 537
  associations, 537
  classifications, 537
  defined, 533
defined, 531
Executive Information Systems (EIS), 538
  advantages of, 538
  defined, 533
models, 538
  data extraction, 543
    batch process, 544
    considerations, 543
    real-time transformation, 543
  data marts, 539
    advantages of, 539
    uses, 539
  data structure, defining, 540
    considerations, 540
    data retrieval, speed of, 540
    Data Transformation Services (DTS), 543
    data, updating, 541
    example, 541
    hard drive space, 541
  data warehouse
    retrieving data from, 539
    populating, 539
OLAP
  advantages of, 534
  defined, 533
  dimension tables, 547
    creating, 547
  example database, 545
    dimension tables, 547
    fact table, 546
  fact table, 546
    creating, 547
  foundation, 534
  HOLAP, 535
  implementing, 544

MDX, 566
  benefits of, 566
  MEMBERS keyword, 567
  MEMBERS ON ROWS keyword, 567
  NEST keyword, 567
  sample application, 567
Microsoft OLAP Server, installing, 545
MOLAP, 535
  data cubes, 535
  geographic dimension, 535
  OLAP Server, 537
  OLE DB, 537
  products dimension, 535
  time dimension, 536
multidimensional cube, browsing, 562
  drilling down, 562
multidimensional cube, building, 548
  Cube Editor, 558
  Cube Wizard, 549
  OLAP Manager, opening, 548
  security, setting up, 560
  storage type, designing, 558
multidimensional cube, viewing
  client application, 563
overview, 534
ROLAP, 535
types, 535
  Hybrid, 535
  MultiDimensional, 535
  Relational, 535
overview, 531
reporting
  defined, 533
  OnLine Transaction Processing (OLTP), 534
  overview, 533
  packages, 534
uses, 532, 533
database design, 39
see also databases
brainstorming, 52
  data types, selecting, 53
  missing fields, avoiding, 52
fields, grouping, 53
  primary key, allocating, 54
indexes, 43
  advantages of, 45
  B-Tree, 46
    clustered indexes, 47
    intermediary levels, 46
    leaf, 47
    page size, 46
    pages, 46
    parts, 46
    root, 46

clustered, 47
  advantages of, 47
  considerations, 48
  uses, 48
creating, 49
  undesirable, 52
defined, 43
editing
  SQL Server, 51
example, 44
multiple references, 44
  problems with, 45
non-clustered, 48
  considerations, 49
  uses, 49
non-unique, 43
query logic, 45
restrictions, 45
unique
  advantages of, 43
uses, 44
viewing
  Access, 49
  SQL Server, 50
normalization, 39, 56
  considerations, 43
  first normal form, 40
  non-key fields
    dependency on primary key, 41
    no fields depend on, 42
  problems with, 43
  repeating groups
    problems with, 40
    removing, 40
  second normal form, 41
  tables, 56
    storage space, saving, 56
  third normal form, 42
relationships, building, 54
  Database Documenter
    options, 55
    selecting, 54
  documentation, 54
  software packages, 54
stages, 52
structure, testing, 57
database servers, 18
advantages of, 18, 19
choosing, 19
considerations, 19
functionality, 30
security, advanced, 18
stored procedures, 31
  advantages of, 31

triggers, 30
  uses, 30
views, 32
  advantages of, 32
  information, retrieving, 33
database transactions, 467
BEGIN TRANSACTION
  defined, 467
COMMIT TRANSACTION
  defined, 467
ROLLBACK TRANSACTION
  defined, 467
databases
see also database design
see also desktop databases
building
  VisData, 86
    data, adding, 94
    Database Window pane, 88, 93
    first record, entering, 93
    functionality, 86
    opening, 86
    quirks, 93
    SQL Statement pane, 88
    table, creating, 88, 92
defined, 4, 60
indexes, 10
pubs
  overview, 8
  rules, 8
  structure, 8
  tables
    described, 9
recordset
  defined, 17
referential integrity, 9
  cascade delete related fields, 10
  cascade update related fields, 10
  importance of, 9
  problems without, 9
relational
  defined, 4
  fields, 4
  records, 4
  relationships, 4
    considerations, 8
    defining, 5
    foreign key, 6
    many-to-many, 7
    one-to-many, 5, 7
    one-to-one, 7
    primary key, 5
    types, 7

DCOM
COM, benefits over, 516
download site, 517
installing, 73, 517
overview, 516
proxy
  function, 517
stub
  function, 517
uses, 516

DED
hierarchical recordset, creating, 572
  Command object, adding, 573
  Data Link Properties, 572
  data, viewing, 576
  DataEnvironment window, opening, 572
  Hierarchical FlexGrid properties, 576
    fields, restricting, 576
  hierarchy information, 575
  one-to-many relationship, establishing, 574
introduction, 572
overview, 571
report generation, 577
  example, 587

DELETE statement, 174
WHERE clause, 174

deployment of applications
see client-server applications, deploying

deserialization
PropertyBag object
  Contents property, 387
  ReadProperty method, 388

desktop databases
flexibility, 16
introduction, 16
portability, 16
see also databases, 16
structure, 16

Distributed Component Object Model (DCOM)
see DCOM

Distributed interNet Applications (DNA)
see DNA

distributed transactions
architecture, 468
commit coordinator, 469
defined, 468
MS DTC, 468, 469

DNA
defined, 62

DRD
introduction, 579
overview, 571
report generation, 579
  calculations, adding, 586
    functions available, 586
  data, adding, 580
    properties, 581
  DataEnvironment object, associating with, 580
  DataReport, opening, 579
  displaying, 583
    views, 583
  example, 587
  report sections, 579
    excluding, 580
    reducing, 580
  splash screen, adding, 585
    DataReport toolbox, 585

DSN
deploying, 510
  Registry Editor, 510
    DSN key, 511, 512
    opening, 511
  registry files, creating, 514
    DSN, adding to registry, 514
    DSN, setting, 514
    header, 514
  registry files, exporting, 512, 513

E

encapsulation
defined, 429

error handling
ADO, 242
  Error object, 243
    Description property, 243
    NativeError property, 244
    Number property, 243
  Errors collection, 242
    clearing, 243
    Count property, 242
    Item property, 242
    referencing, 242
    Refresh method, 243

Error Object, 243
Description property, 243
NativeError property, 244
Number property, 243

error trapping, 324
ADO, 324
defined, 305

ErrorLog, 325, 327
  displaying, 328
  For Append keyword, 328
  FreeFile function, 328
OLE DB Provider, 324
Resume statement, 327

F

Field object, 233, 235
ActualSize property, 235
Attributes property, 235
Fields collection
  Append method, 234
  Count property, 234
  default property, 234
  Delete method, 235
  Item property, 233
  Refresh method, 234
Fields collection, referencing, 233
Name property, 235
Type property, 235
Value property, 219
forms
child
  creating, 293
  modifying, 295
control, passing, 295
counter
  implementing, 288
    Static keyword, 288
creating, 282, 283
DataGrid layout
  modifying, 298
focus, giving, 287
loading, 287
Master/Detail
  defined, 283
modifying, 287, 291, 294
  fields layout, 292
  fields, removing, 292
  fields, searching, 299
    filter, applying, 300
    LIKE keyword, 300
  MouseDown event, 294
  tooltip, adding, 295
navigation bar
  adding, 289
removing, 286
unloading, 295

Front-End application, building, 94
ADO Data Control, 95
  connection string, building, 97
    database location, selecting, 98
    database properties, displaying, 99
    database properties, modifying, 99
    database provider, selecting, 98
    security, implementing, 98
    testing, 98
    time-out setting, 98
  Masked Edit Control, binding, 107
  overview, 107
  properties, setting, 101
    BOFAction, 101
    EOFAction, 101
  Recordset object, 107
  RecordSource property, setting, 100
    connection types, 101
  Toolbox, adding to, 95
controls, databound
  check box, 121
  Data Repeater, 125
  DataCombo, 123
    data-binding properties, 123
  DataGrid, 122
  DataList, 123
    data-binding properties, 123
  Hierarchical FlexGrid, 122
  image, 122
  label, 121
  MS Chart, 124
  OLE Container, 124
  picture, 122
  rich text box, 124
enhancements, 113
Masked Edit Control, 107
  ADO Data Control, binding to, 107
  Format property, 108
  Mask property, 108
    placeholders, 108
  PromptChar property, 108
  PromptInclude check box, 108
  TabIndex, 109
  Toolbox, adding to, 107
navigation bar, creating, 109
  advantages, 109
  recordset navigation, 111
    BOF, avoiding, 111
    current position, 112
    EOF marker, avoiding, 111
    error handling, 111
    MoveComplete event, 112
    total number of records, 112
  testing, 113
overview, 107

records, adding, 115
   protecting, 115
records, deleting, 116
records, finding, 117
   form, adding, 117
   InStr function, 119
   Len keyword, 119
   MoveNext method, 120
   SelLength property, 119
   SelStart property, 119
   SetFocus method, 119
   testing, 120
records, refreshing, 116
records, updating, 116
   Requery method, 116
testing, 106
user interface, 102
   control array, creating, 102
      advantages of, 103
      alternatives, 103
   text boxes
      data field, specifying, 105
      MultiLine property, 104
      TabIndex property, setting, 106

G

Globally Unique Identifier (GUID)
   see GUID
Graphical User Interface (GUI)
   see GUI
GUI
   designing, 341
      ListView control
         adding, 341
         columns, adding, 342
         configuring, 342
         properties, viewing, 342
   references, adding, 343
GUIDs
   defined, 359

H

hierarchical recordset, creating
   DED, 572
      Command object, adding, 573
      Data LinkProperties, 572
      data, viewing, 576
      DataEnvironment window, opening, 572
      Hierarchical FlexGrid properties, 576
      fields, restricting, 576
      hierarchy information, 575
      one-to-many relationship, establishing, 574

I

Indexed Sequential Access Method (ISAM)
   see ISAM
indexes, 10, 43
   advantages of, 45
   B-Tree, 46
      clustered indexes, 47
         advantages of, 47
         considerations, 48
         uses, 48
      intermediary levels, 46
      leaf, 47
      page size, 46
      pages, 46
      parts, 46
      root, 46
   clustered, 47
      advantages of, 47
      considerations, 48
      uses, 48
   creating, 49
      undesirable, 52
   defined, 43
   editing
      SQL Server, 51
         features, 51
   example, 44
   Manage Indexes dialog
      SQL Server, 50
         editing indexes, 50
   multiple references, 44
      problems with, 45
   non-clustered, 48
      considerations, 49
      uses, 49
   non-unique, 43
   query logic, 45
   restrictions, 45
   unique
      advantages of, 43
   uses, 44
   viewing
      Access, 49
      SQL Server, 50
INSERT INTO statement, 172
   VALUES keyword, 172
      NULL, 173
      null fields, 173
INSERT statement, 172, 175
   subqueries, 175
      uses, 175

interfaces
building, 281
VB Application Wizard, 281
Data Access Forms, creating, 282, 283
ISAM
defined, 70

L

ListItem object, 345
Add method, 345
parameters, 345
ListView control
adding, 341
columns, adding, 342
configuring, 342
properties, viewing, 342

M

Masked Edit Control, 107
ADO Data Control, binding to, 107
Format property, 108
Mask property, 108
placeholders, 108
PromptChar property, 108
PromptInclude check box, 108
TabIndex, 109
Toolbox, adding to, 107
MDAC, 73
contents, 73
installing, 73
web page, 73
MDI forms
defined, 280
MDX, 566
benefits of, 566
MEMBERS keyword, 567
MEMBERS ON ROWS keyword, 567
NEST keyword, 567
sample application, 567
Microsoft Data Access Components (MDAC)
see MDAC
Microsoft Data Formatting Object Library
referencing, 299
Microsoft Distributed Transaction Coordinator
see MS DTC

Microsoft Transaction Server (MTS)
see MTS
middle tier, 394
ADO reference, 395
Class_Initialize event, 396
Open method, 396
components, 27, 332
in process server, 28
MTS packages, 364
adding to, 367
creating, 364
MTS, installing in, 364
MTS, modifying for, 357
MTSTransactionMode property, 358
ObjectContext object, 360
errors, 360
instantiation, 360
methods, 361, 363
objects, 332
out of process server, 28
project properties, setting, 358
Pessimistic TearDown, avoiding, 359
recompiling, 363
version compatibility, 359
Binary Compatibility, 360
No Compatibility, 360
options, 360
Project Compatibility, 360
components, building, 334
ActiveX DLL, creating, 334
ADO, referencing, 335
database calling functions, 336
Add_Employee, 336, 337, 361
Delete_Employee, 336, 338, 362
Select_Employee, 337, 339
Update_Employee, 337, 338, 362
SQL Server, connecting to, 335
Connection object, 336
Initialize event, 336
Terminate event, 336
testing, 340
debugging, preliminary, 340
Instancing property, 340
components, designing, 333
considerations, 334
Get_Customer_Details function, 397
MTS, rolling out to, 422
Get_ID function, 398
MTS, rolling out to, 423
Get_Products function, 397
MTS, rolling out to, 421
Get_Table_Recordset function, 396
CursorLocation property, 396
MTS, rolling out to, 421

records, retrieving, 396
recordset, assigning, 396
roles, 27
Send_Order function, 399
arguments, 400
CursorType property, 400
LockType property, 400
MTS, rolling out to, 424
quantity, maintaining, 402
recordset, opening, 400
recordset, transferring contents, 401
varaiables, module-level, 395
declaring, 395
models
Data Warehousing, 538
data extraction, 543
batch process, 544
considerations, 543
real-time transformation, 543
data marts, 539
advantages of, 539
uses, 539
data structure, defining, 540
considerations, 540
data retrieval, speed of, 540
Data Transformation Services (DTS), 543
data, updating, 541
example, 541
hard drive space, 541
populating, 539
retrieving data from, 539
MS DTC
advantages of, 467
commit coordinator, 469
distributed transactions, 468, 469
introduction, 469
invoking, 473
MTS transaction model, 471
running, checking for, 473
Transaction Statistics, 473
two-phase commit, 469
using, 471
MTS, 351, 470
administration, 353
benefits of, 351
component
transaction control, 351
component modification, 357
component properties
General tab, 353
modifying, 353
Security tab, 355
Transaction tab, 354

components, installing, 364
database changes, handling, 633
customers table, 633
ODBC Resource Dispenser, 633
transactions
tables used, viewing, 634
defined, 351
monitoring, 352
Transaction Statistics
information available, 352
viewing, 352
MTSTransactionMode property, 358
object brokering, 355
advantages of, 355
object pooling, 356
ObjectContext object, 360
errors, 360
instantiation, 360
methods, 361, 363
overview, 351
packages, 364
component, adding, 367
importing, 367
installing, 367
transaction required, indicating, 368
creating, 364
Components folder, 366
empty package, 364
information, specifying, 366
Roles folder, 366
exporting, 635
project properties, setting, 358
Pessimistic Tear Down, avoiding, 359
referencing, 357
security, 352
roles, 353
security, rolling out, 498
components
roles, adding, 501
components, coding, 503
error handling, 504
ObjectContext object, instantiating, 503
user, validating, 503
components, properties, 503
authentication levels, 503
security, 503
components, refreshing, 499
Microsoft Management Console, 498
role, creating, 499
user, adding, 500
security, using for, 505
DENY command, 506
ALL keyword, 507
defined, 505

GRANT command, 505
  ALL keyword, 506
  defined, 505
  WITH GRANT OPTION keyword, 506
  REVOKE command, 506
  ALL keyword, 506
  CASCADE keyword, 506
  defined, 505
  GRANT OPTION FOR clause, 506
version compatibility, 359
  Binary Compatibility, 360
  No Compatibility, 360
  options, 360
  Project Compatibility, 360
MTS transaction model
  description, 470
  MS DTC, 471
  MTS Explorer, 471
MultiDimensional Expressions (MDX)
  see MDX
Multiple Document Interface (MDI) forms
  see MDI forms

N

navigation bar
  adding, 289
  creating, 109
    advantages, 109
    recordset navigation, 111
      BOF, avoiding, 111
      current position, 112
      EOF marker, avoiding, 111
      error handling, 111
      MoveComplete event, 112
      total number of records, 112
    testing, 113
normalization, 39, 56
  considerations, 43
  first normal form, 40
  non-key fields
    dependency on primary key, 41
    no fields depend on, 42
  problems with, 43
  repeating groups
    problems with, 40
    removing, 40
  second normal form, 41
  tables, 56
    storage space, saving, 56
  third normal form, 42

N-tier applications
  security models, 478
    middle tier, 478
    benefits of, 478
    MTS, 478
    server, 479
N-tier architecture, 27
  compared to two-tier, 34
  data, passing, 371
    ADO recordset, 382
      batch mode updating, 382
      connectionless, creating, 384
      database, creating from, 383
      value, passing by, 385
    arguments, passing to a method, 372
      problems with, 373
    data serialization, 373
      techniques, 373
    methods, 373
    methods not to use, 371
    PropertyBag object, 386
      deserializing data, 387
      serializing data, 386
    single properties, calling, 372
      problems with, 372
    UDTs, 373
      GetData function, 375
      problems with, 377
    UDTs/LSet command, 377
      background, 378
      filler space, 382
      implementation, 379
      LenB function, 381
      longword alignment, 381, 382
      memory alignment, 381
      word alignment, 381
    Variant arrays, 375
      advantages of, 376
      considerations, 376
      disadvantages of, 376
      GetRows method, 377

O

Object Linking and Embedding for Databases (OLE DB)
  see OLE DB
ObjectContext object, 360
objects
  brokering
    MTS, 355
    advantages of, 355
  class, 332

data
  see data objects
  defined, 28, 332
  pooling
    MTS, 356
ODBC, 68
  Application Programming Interface (API),
  68
  architecture, 69
  compared to OLE DB, 72
  compliance levels, 68
  components, 68
  data source, 69
  Data Source Name (DSN)
    connecting to, 80
      Data Form Designer, 81
      Data Form Designer, opening, 81
      VisData, 80
      VisData, opening, 80
    ODBC Data Source Administrator, 75
      authentication, choosing, 77
      configuration options, default settings, 77
      connection characteristics, 76
      Connection Pooling, 75
      Drivers, 75
      File, 75
      language settings, 79
      set-up screen, 76
      statistics, recording, 79
      System, 75
      testing, 80
      Tracing, 75
      User, 75
    setting up, 74
      icon, 74
  driver, 69
  Driver Manager, 69
ODBCDirect, 70
  compared to DAO, 70
  updating to, 71
OLAP
  advantages of, 534
  defined, 533
  dimension tables, 547
    creating, 547
      considerations, 547
  example database, 545
    dimension tables, 547
    fact table, 546
  fact table, 546
    creating, 547
      considerations, 547

foundation, 534
HOLAP, 535
implementing, 544
MDX, 566
  benefits of, 566
  MEMBERS keyword, 567
  MEMBERS ON ROWS keyword, 567
  NEST keyword, 567
  sample application, 567
Microsoft OLAP Server, installing, 545
MOLAP, 535
  data cubes, 535
  geographic dimension, 535
  OLAP Server, 537
  OLE DB, 537
  products dimension, 535
  time dimension, 536
multidimensional cube, browsing, 562
  drilling down, 562
multidimensional cube, building, 548
  Cube Editor, 558
  Cube Wizard, 549
    Count level members automatically, 555
    cube, naming, 557
    dimension tables, choosing, 552
    dimension tables, components, 552
    dimensions, previewing, 553
    dimensions, sharing, 553
    dimensions, adding, 551
    dimensions, creating, 551
    dimensions, displaying, 557
    fact table, choosing, 550
    fact table, fields, 550
    tables, setting related field, 554
  OLAP Manager
    opening, 548
    Virtual Cubes, 549
  security, setting up, 560
    role, applying, 561
    role, creating, 560
  storage type, designing, 558
    aggregation options, 559
    data, processing, 559
    Storage Design Wizard, 559
multidimensional cube, viewing
  client application, 563
    connection string, creating, 564
    Cube Browser control, 563
overview, 534
ROLAP, 535
types, 535
  Hybrid, 535
  MultiDimensional, 535
    data cubes, 535

geograhical dimension, 535
OLAP Server, 537
OLE DB, 537
products dimension, 535
time dimension, 536
Relational, 535
OLE DB, 63
  advantages of, 63
  COM, 63, 64
  compared to ODBC, 72
  consumers, 65
    defined, 65
    interfaces required, 66
  defined, 63, 64
  providers, 64
    minimum requirements, 65
    objects exposed, 64
      Command, 65
      DataSource, 65
      Enumerator, 64
      Error, 65
      Rowset, 65
      Session, 65
      Transaction, 65
  relation to ADO, 66, 67
OLE DB Provider
  error trapping, 324
    ErrorLog, 325, 327
      displaying, 328
      For Append keyword, 328
      FreeFile function, 328
    Resume statement, 327
OLE Transactions, 470
OnLine Analytical Processing (OLAP)
  see OLAP
Open DataBase Connectivity (ODBC)
  see ODBC
order processing, 617, 623
  business object, building, 623
    binary compatability, setting, 625
    component, installing, 626
      Component Wizard, 626
    MTS library, referencing, 624
    MTS package, creating, 625
      Package Wizard, 626
    MTSTransactionMode property, 623
    ObjectControl interface, 624
    ProcessOrder method, 624
  Checkout.asp page, 628
    customer, creating, 631
    error reporting, improved, 631
      ReportError method, 631
    ObjectContext object, 629

transaction, managing, 630
  error handling, 630
MTS
  database changes, handling, 633
    Customers table, 633
    ODBC Resource Dispenser, 633
    transaction tables, viewing, 634
  order, capturing, 617
    Cart class, 617
      ASP, 618
      Collection class, 618
      Items, adding, 619
    cart.asp page, 620
      cart table, 621
      cart table, GetProductInfo method, 622
      cart table, Store object, 621
      cart, adding product, 621
      cart, checking for, 620
    CartItem class, 619
      initialization, 619

P

Parameter object
  creating, 214
    Direction property, 216
    Name property, 215
    properties, optional, 214
    Size property, 216
      required, 216
    Type property, 215
    Value property, 217
  Parameters collection, 217
    Append method, 217
    Count property, 217
    Delete method, 217
    Item method, 217
    Parameter objects, 217
    Refresh method, 217
    stored procedure, passing to, 218
      Command object, instantiating, 218
      Parameter object, creating, 218
      recordset, instantiating, 218
pubs database
  overview, 8
  rules, 8
  structure, 8
  tables
    described, 9

R

RDBMS
see database servers
RDO, 70
compared to ADO, 72
compared to DAO, 72
RDO Data Control
compared to ADO Data Control, 96
Recordsets, 235
cursor
location, 232
Client-side cursors, 232
CursorLocation property, 232
default, 232
none, 232
Server-side cursors, 232
types, 231
considerations, 231
CursorType property, 232
default, 231
data, modifying, 226
lock type property, 226
database, updating, 230
cancelling, 230
CancelBatch method, 231
CancelUpdate method, 230
Update method, 230
UpdateBatch method, 230
parameter, 230
defined, 17
disconnected
defined, 236
updating, 236
Field object, 233, 235
ActualSize property, 235
Attributes property, 235
Name property, 235
Type property, 235
Fields collection
Append method, 234
Count property, 234
default property, 234
Delete method, 235
Item property, 233
Refresh method, 234
referencing, 233
filtering, 224
Filter property, 224
AND keyword, 224
bookmarks, using, 224
OR keyword, 224
rest, 224

hierarchical
creating, 296
lock
types, 232
batch optimistic locking, 233
LockType property, 232
optimistic locking, 233
pessimistic locking, 233
navigating, 220
AbsolutePosition property, 220
bookmarks, 221
assigning, 221
MoveFirst method, 220
MoveLast method, 220
MoveNext method
considerations, 220
MovePrevious method
considerations, 220
multiple records, by, 221
Move method, 221
specifications, 221
RecordCount property, 220
pages, 222
AbsolutePage property, 222
PageCount property, 222
PageSize property, 222
persisted, 236
opening, 236
Save method, 236
XML format, saving as, 236
records
field values, retrieving, 219
adding, 227
AddNew method, 227
INSERT statement, 228
deleting, 228
current record, 228
Delete method, 228
group of records, 228
editing, 219, 226
UPDATE statement, 227
locating, 223
retrieving into array, 225
GetRows method, 225
viewing, 219
refreshing, 229
Requery method, 229
Options argument, 229
Resync method, 229
AffectRecords argument, 229
ResyncValues argument, 229
sorting
Sort property, 226

specific records, locating, 223
  Find method, 223
    Criteria argument, 223
    SearchDirection parameter, 223
    SkipRecords argument, 223
    Start argument, 223
Recordset object
  command, executing, 213
    Cancel method, 214
    Open method, 213
      arguments, 213
  defined, 200
  events, 240
    MoveComplete event, 240
      arguments, 240
      uses, 241
    RecordChangeComplete event, 241
      arguments, 241
      uses, 241
referential integrity, 9
  cascade delete related fields, 10
  cascade update related fields, 10
  importance of, 9
  problems without, 9
registry
  files, creating, 514
    DSN, adding to registry, 514
    DSN, setting, 514
    header, 514
  files, exporting, 512
    ODBC Data Source Administrator, 513
Registry Editor, 510
  DSN key, 511, 512
  opening, 511
Relational Database Management Systems (RDBMS)
  see database servers
relational databases
  defined, 4
  fields, 4
  indexes, 10
  records, 4
  relationships, 4
    considerations, 8
    defining, 5
    foreign key, 6
    many-to-many, 7
    one-to-many, 5, 7
    one-to-one, 7
    primary key, 5
    types, 7

relationships, 4
  considerations, 8
  defining, 5
    foreign key, 6
    primary key, 5
    types, 7
  many-to-many, 7
  one-to-many, 5, 7
  one-to-one, 7
Remote Data Objects (RDO)
  see RDO
replication
  advantages of, 24
  considerations, 26
  defined, 24
  example, 24
  uses, 24, 25
    when not to, 25
report generation
  DED, 577
  designing, 591
    grouping section, adding, 591
  DRD, 579
    calculations, adding, 586
      functions available, 586
    data, adding, 580
      properties, 581
    DataEnvironment object, associating with, 580
    DataReport, opening, 579
    report sections, 579
      excluding, 580
      reducing, 580
    report, displaying, 583
      views, 583
    splash screen, adding, 585
      DataReport toolbox, 585
  Extended Price Field, adding, 592
  fields, grouping, 590
    Grouping tab, 590
  order cost, displaying, 594
    function, embedding in SQL statement, 594
  SQL command
    creating, 587
      Data View dialog, 588
      drag and drop, 587
      SQL Design dialog, 588
      testing, 589
    dynamic modification, 596
      parameters, 597
      parameters, applying, 597

S

security models
client-server applications, 477
MTS, using, 498
  components
    roles, adding, 501
  components, coding, 503
    error handling, 504
    ObjectContext object, instantiating, 503
    user, validating, 503
  components, properties, 503
    authentication levels, 503
    security, 503
  components, refreshing, 499
  Microsoft Management Console, 498
  role, creating, 499
    user, adding, 500
N-tier applications, 478
  middle tier, 478
    benefits of, 478
    MTS, 478
  server, 479
server-side, 479
  SQL Server database, 479
    Audit level options, 481
    authentication, 479
    authorization, 479
    nontrusted connection, 479
    NT/SQL Server security, mixed, 481
    permission precedence, 485
    properties, security, 480
    roles, 487
    SQL Enterprise Manager, 480
    SQL Server authentication, 479
    trusted connection, 479
    user, adding, 481
    user-level permissions, 486
    user-level permissions, assigning, 486
    user-level permissions, denying, 486
    Windows NT authentication, 479
    Windows NT security, 481
SQL, using, 505
  DENY command, 506
    ALL keyword, 507
    defined, 505
  GRANT command, 505
    ALL keyword, 506
    defined, 505
    WITH GRANT OPTION keyword, 506
  REVOKE command, 506
    ALL keyword, 506
    CASCADE keyword, 506
    defined, 505
    GRANT OPTION FOR clause, 506

three-tier applications, 495
  client, 496
    Form_Load event procedure, 497
    login form, 497
    login form, cmdCancel_Click event procedure, 497
    login form, cmdOK_Click event procedure, 497
    login form, declarations, 497
    login form, Form_Load evnt procedure, 497
    startup form, setting, 498
  middle-tier
    Class_Terminate event procedure, 496
    login function, 496
two-tier applications, 478, 490
  application, closing, 493
  connection string, building, 492
  data form, 491
  forms, coding, 492
  login form, 492
    login, aborting, 492
    selecting, 492
  recordset, populating, 493
    error handling, 493
  roles
    defined, 478
  startup form, setting, 494
  testing, 494
  users
    defined, 478
SELECT statement, 146
aliases, creating, 149
  AS keyword, 149
clauses, 148
data manipulation, simple, 149
DISTINCT clause, 148
fields, selecting, 146
  advantages of, 147
FROM clause, 146, 148
GROUP BY clause, 148, 164
  aggregate functions, 165, 168, 183
    AVG, 167
    COUNT, 166
    MAX, 167
    MIN, 167
    SUM, 165
  considerations, 165
  HAVING clause, 169
  problems, 165
HAVING clause, 148, 169
multiple fields, concatenating, 152
ORDER BY clause, 148, 162
  descending order, 164
  fields, multiple, 163
specific data, retrieving, 153

subqueries, 169
  considerations, 170
tables, joining, 176
  equi-join, 177
  INNER JOIN, 178
    nested, 178
    ON clause, 178
  OUTER JOIN, 180
    LEFT, 180
    RIGHT, 180
  UNION, 181
    CONVERT function, 182
text, concatenating, 151
  CONVERT function, 151
value expressions, joining, 150
  arithmetic operators, 150
  hard-coded values, 150
WHERE clause, 148, 153
  operators, using, 154
    AND, 154
    AND and OR, 156
    NOT, 157
    OR, 155
  predicates, using, 154, 158
    BETWEEN, 160, 161
    dates, 161
    IN, 158
    LIKE, 159
    NULL, 161
  subqueries, 169
  considerations, 170

serialization
ADO recordset, 382
  batch mode updating
    defined, 382
  connectionless, creating, 384
    example, 384
    steps, 384
  database, creating from, 383
    CursorLocation property, 383, 384
    CursorType property, 383
    LockType property, 383, 384
  value, passing by, 385
PropertyBag object, 386
  Contents property, 387
  deserializing
    Contents property, 387
    ReadProperty method, 388
  WriteProperty method, 387
techniques, 373
UDTs, passing, 373
  GetData function, 375
  problems with, 377

UDTs/LSet command, 377
  background, 378
  filler space, 382
  implementation, 379
    PrintValues subroutine, 380
  LenB function, 381
  longword alignment, 381, 382
  memory alignment, 381
  word alignment, 381
Variant arrays, 375
  advantages of, 376
  considerations, 376
  disadvantages of, 376
  GetRows method, 377

servers
database, 18
  advantages of, 18, 19
  choosing, 19
  considerations, 19
  functionality, 30
  security, advanced, 18
  stored procedures, 31
    advantages of, 31
  triggers, 30
    uses, 30
  views, 32
    advantages of, 32
    information, retrieving, 33
data validation, 306
  constraints
    defined, 306
    SQL Server, 307, 311
    testing, 311
    viewing with Access, 312
  problems with, 307
fat, 21
  advantages of, 22
  compared to fat client, 20, 22
  disadvantages of, 22
SHAPE construct, 296
APPEND keyword, 297
DataGrid control
  applying to, 297
  fields, adding, 298
  fields, removing, 297
parts, 297
RELATE keyword, 297
SHAPE keyword, 297
SQL
see also SQL Server
see also stored procedures
advanced, 176

aggregate functions, 165, 183
  AVG, 167
  COUNT, 166
  GROUP BY clause, 168
  MAX, 167
  MIN, 167
  SUM, 165
clauses, 148
constraints, 307
  creating, 307
    scripts, 307
  types, 307
Data Control Language (DCL), 145
Data Definition Language (DDL), 145
Data Manipulation Language (DML), 145
data, modifying
  cautions, 170
  overview, 170
database queries, generating, 145
  Data Manipulation Language (DML), 146
    DELETE statement, 174
    INSERT statement, 172, 175
    SELECT statement, 146
    UPDATE statement, 171
  Data Manipulation Language (DML)
    INSERT INTO statement, 172
DELETE statement, 174
  WHERE clause, 174
editors, 141
  MS Access, 141
  MS Query, 141
  VisData, 141
indexes
  creating, 190
    CREATE statement, 190
  removing, 190
    DROP statement, 190
INSERT INTO statement, 172
  VALUES keyword, 172
    NULL, 173
    null fields, 173
INSERT statement, 172, 175
  subqueries, 175
  uses, 175
introduction, 140
MDX, 566
  benefits of, 566
  MEMBERS keyword, 567
  MEMBERS ON ROWS keyword, 567
  NEST keyword, 567
  sample application, 567
overview, 140
search conditions, 145
  null values, 145

SELECT statement, 146
  aliases, creating, 149
    AS keyword, 149
  clauses, 148
  data manipulation, simple, 149
  DISTINCT clause, 148
  fields, selecting, 146
    advantages of, 147
    SQL clauses, 148
  FROM clause, 146, 148
  GROUP BY clause, 148, 164
    aggregate functions, 165, 168, 183
    considerations, 165
    HAVING clause, 169
    problems, 165
  HAVING clause, 148, 169
  multiple fields, concatenating, 152
  ORDER BY clause, 148, 162
    descending order, 164
    fields, multiple, 163
  refining, 146
    SQL clauses, 148
  specific data, retrieving, 153
  subqueries, 169
    considerations, 170
  tables, joining, 176
    equi-join, 177
    INNER JOIN, 178
    OUTER JOIN, 180
    UNION, 181
  text, concatenating, 151
    CONVERT function, 151
  value expressions, joining, 150
    arithmetic operators, 150
  WHERE clause, 148, 153
    operators, using, 154
    predicates, using, 154, 158
    subqueries, 169
Server Enterprise Manager
  scripts
    generating, 308
    loading, 311
    viewing, 310
statements, 30
  data, modifying
    considerations, 172
    errors, 172
  DELETE, 174
  INSERT, 172, 175
  SELECT, 146
    using, 322
  UPDATE, 171
subqueries, 169, 175
  considerations, 170
  uses, 175

tables
 unmatched records, finding, 193
   EXISTS predicate, 195
   NOT EXISTS predicate, 195
 backup
   CREATE TABLE command, 191
   making, 191
   SELECT INTO statement, 193
 changing, 189
   ALTER TABLE statement, 189
 creating, 184
   check constraints, 187
   IN keyword, 187
   INSERT statement, 188
   lookups, 189
   maximum values, 188
   minimum values, 188
   NULL values, disallowing, 189
   search conditions, 189
   validating ranges, 189
   CONSTRAINT clause, 185
   Primary Key, 185
   CREATE statement, 184
   default values, 187
   Foreign Key, 186
   UNIQUE constraint, 185
   viewing, 186
 destroying, 190
   DROP TABLE statement, 190
 joining, 176
   equi-join, 177
   INNER JOIN, 178
   nested, 178
   ON clause, 178
   OUTER JOIN, 180
   LEFT, 180
   RIGHT, 180
   UNION, 181
   CONVERT function, 182
tester program, building, 141
 DataGrid control, 143
 MoveComplete event, 144
 property pages
   Command Text, 142
 RecordSource property, 144
 Refresh method, 144
UPDATE statement, 171
 SET keyword, 171
views
 calling, 256
 complex SQL statements, hiding, 255
 creating, 254
   benefits of, 256
   considerations, 256
   errors, 254

 INSERT statement, 256
 ORDER BY clause, viewing, 255
 seeing, 254
 SELECT statement, 254
 UPDATE statement, 256
 uses, 256
 WITH CHECK OPTION parameter, 256
SQL Server
 see also SQL
 case study, 602
   Categories table, 603
     creating, 603
     data manipulation, 604
     primary key, 603
   database diagram, 606
     foreign keys, defining, 608
     relationships, defining, 607
     wizard, 606
   database, creating, 602
   Manufacturers table, 604
     primary key, 604
   Products table, 605
     primary key, 605
     references, 606
   relationships, specifying, 606
   Suppliers table, 605
     creating, 605
   view, creating, 609
 compared to Access
   benchmarks, 128
     Backup, 129
     TPC, 129
   budget, 128
   database connections, number required, 130
   functionality, 129
     batch requests, 129
     recovery mechanism, 129
     security, 129
   storage capacity, 127
 connection, building, 250
 constraints, 311
   testing, 311
   viewing with Access, 312
     properties, 313
 Enterprise Manager
   opening, 135, 252
   scripts
     constraints, 311
   stored procedures, 258
     creating, 259
   views, 252
     AS keyword, 253
     creating, 253
     properties, 252

indexes
editing, 51
features, 51
Manage Indexes dialog, 50
editing indexes, 50
viewing, 50
MS DTC
advantages of, 467
commit coordinator, 469
distributed transactions, 469
invoking, 473
MTS transaction model, 471
running, checking for, 473
Transaction Statistics, 473
two-phase commitment, 469
using, 471
security models, 479
Audit level options, 481
authentication, 479
authorization, 479
nontrusted connection, 479
NT/SQL Server security, mixed, 481
permission precedence, 485
DENY permission, 486
properties, security, 480
roles, 487
roles, creating, 488
permissions, defining, 489
users, adding, 489
roles, fixed, 487
SQL Enterprise Manager, 480
SQL Server authentication, 479
trusted connection, 479
user, adding, 481
Access Rights, assigning, 483
Database Access, 483
Database Role Properties, public, 483
New Login dialog, 481
Server Roles, assigning, 482
Server Roles, options, 482
user-level permissions, 486
assigning, 486
denying, 486
Windows NT authentication, 479
advantages of, 479
Windows NT security, 481
transactions, 467
upsizing to
benchmarks, 128
Backup, 129
TPC, 129
connection string, converting, 135
considerations, 127
benchmarks, 128
budget, 128

database connections, number required, 130
functionality, 129
storage capacity, 127
databases, 131
options, 130
precautions, 131
Upsizing Wizard, 131
application changes, 134
opening, 131
report produced, 134
table attributes, 132
tables, specifying, 132
timestamp fields, 133
views, 251
benefits of, 251
information, modifying, 252
relevant information, extracting, 251
security, 251
defined, 251
Enterprise Manager, 252
AS keyword, 253
view properties, 252
views, creating, 253
stored procedures
executing, 261, 264
Command object, 261
ActiveConnection property, 261
CommandText property, 262
CommandType property, 261
destroying, 262
Execute method, 262
database, conmnecting to, 264
declarations, 263
DELETE select procedure, 266
Form_Load event, 264
INSERT select procedure, 266
SELECT stored procedure, 266
UPDATE select procedure, 266
variant array, 261
output parameters, 267
Parameter object, 267
SQL, 257
benefits of, 257
error handling, 258
network traffic, reducing, 257
security improved, 257
server-side advantages, 257
speed, 258
creating, 259
DELETE stored procedures, 261
INSERT stored procedures, 260
SELECT stored procedures, 259
UPDATE stored procedures, 260
testing
SQL Server Query analyser, 259

SQL Server
  Enterprise Manager, 258
    creating, 259
system level, 268
  prefix, 268
  sp_addgroup procedure, 269
  sp_addlogin procedure, 268
  sp_addUser procedure, 270
  sp_droplogin procedure, 270
  sp_dropuser procedure, 270
  sp_help procedure, 270
  sp_helptext procedure, 270
  sp_helpuser procedure, 270
  sp_password procedure, 269
triggers, 270
  advantages of, 271
  constraints, 271
  creating, 273
    fields, populating, 274
    specifications, 274
    table, creating, 273
    variables, declaring, 274
  existing, 272
    creation, 272
    validation rules, 273
    values, retrieving, 272
    viewing, 272
  implementing, 275
    rollback of changes, 275
    testing, 275
  mode of operation, 271
  uses, 271
    business rules, enforcing, 271
    data integrity, maintaining, 271
    transactions, logging, 271
Structured Query Language (SQL)
  see SQL

T

three-tier applications
  see also client-server applications
  see also client-server applications,
    deploying
  see also three-tier applications (case study)
  see also three-tier architecture
  client, 340, 403
    cboCompany_Click event procedure, 412
    cmdClear_Click event procedure, 347
    cmdDelete_Click event procedure, 345
    cmdExit_Click event procedure, 347
    cmdInsert_Click event procedure, 346
    cmdNew_Click event procedure, 417
    cmdRefresh_Click event procedure, 345

cmdSend_Click event procedure, 418
  business rules, 418
  Hierarchical FlexGrid control, refreshing, 418
  recordset, populating, 418
cmdUpdate_Click event procedure, 346
coding, 343
components, adding, 404
Create_New_Order method, 412
Create_New_Order_Detail method, 413
creating, 340
declarations, 343
drag-and-drop functionality, 414
  DataGrid's DragDrop event, 415
  DataGrid's DragOver event, 414
  Hierarchical FlexGrid's MouseDown event, 414
  icons, 414
Form_Load event procedure, 344, 409
  functions, calling, 409
  Hierarchical FlexGrid control, 410
  middle-tier object, instantiation, 409
  recordset structure, assigning, 410
GUI design, 341
  ListView control, adding, 341, 342
  references, adding, 343
ListView1_Click event procedure, 346
references, adding, 404
Select_Data event procedure, 344
  ListItem object, 345
startup project, setting as, 348
Total_All function, 416
  DataGrid's AfterColUpdate event, 417
user interface
  building, 404
  DataGrid control, properties, 408
  Hierarchical FlexGrid control, properties, 407
variables, module-level, 408
  declaring, 408
  fields, declaring, 409
  recordsets, declaring, 408
client-server
  compiling, 349
  DLLs, registering, 349
  testing, 348, 368
components, 332
  MTS packages, 364
    adding to, 367
    creating, 364
  MTS
    installing in, 364
    modifying for, 357
  MTSTransactionMode property, 358
  ObjectContext object, 360
    errors, 360
    instantiation, 360
    methods, 361, 363
  objects, 332

project properties, setting, 358
  Pessimistic Tear Down, avoiding, 359
recompiling, 363
version compatibility, 359
  Binary Compatibility, 360
  No Compatibility, 360
  options, 360
  Project Compatibility, 360
components, building, 334
  ActiveX DLL, creating, 334
  ADO, referencing, 335
  database calling functions, 336
    Add_Employee, 336, 337, 361
    Delete_Employee, 336, 338, 362
    Select_Employee, 337, 339
    Update_Employee, 337, 338, 362
  SQL Server, connecting to, 335
    Connection object, 336
    Initialize event, 336
    Terminate event, 336
  testing, 340
    debugging, preliminary, 340
    Instancing property, 340
components, designing, 333
  considerations, 334
deploying, 509
middle tier, 394
  ADO reference, 395
  Class_Initialize event, 396
    Open method, 396
  components, 332
  Get_Customer_Details function, 397
    MTS, rolling out to, 422
  Get_ID function, 398
    MTS, rolling out to, 423
  Get_Products function, 397
    rolling out to, 421
  Get_Table_Recordset function, 396
    CursorLocation property, 396
    MTS, rolling out to, 421
    records, retrieving, 396
    recordset, assigning, 396
  Send_Order function, 399
    arguments, 400
    CursorType property, 400
    LockType property, 400
    MTS, rolling out to, 424
    quantity, maintaining, 402
    recordset, opening, 400
    recordset, transferring contents, 401
  variables, module-level, 395
    declaring, 395
MTS, 351
  administration, 353
  benefits of, 351

component
  transaction control, 351
component modification, 357
  installing, 364
  MTS packages, 364
  MTSTransactionMode property, 358
  ObjectContext object, 360
  project properties, setting, 358
  recompiling, 363
  version compatibility, 359
component properties
  General tab, 353
  modifying, 353
  Security tab, 355
  Transaction tab, 354
defined, 351
monitoring, 352
  Transaction Statistics, viewing, 352
object brokering, 355
  advantages of, 355
object pooling, 356
overview, 351
referencing, 357
security, 352
  roles, 353
MTS, rolling out to, 420
  DLL, adding, 426
  Get_Customer_Details function, 422
  Get_ID function, 423
  Get_Products function, 421
  Get_Table_Recordset function, 421
  MTS Type Library, referencing, 420
  ObjectControl, using, 425
    Activate method, 425
    CanBePooled method, 426
    Deactivate method, 426
  properties, changing, 420
  Send_Order function, 424
project overview
  event order, 393
  form, 392
  functionality, 392
security models, 495
  client, 496
    Form_Load event procedure, 497
    login form, 497
    login form, cmdCancel_Click event procedure, 497
    login form, cmdOK_Click event procedure, 497
    login form, declarations, 497
    login form, Form_Load event procedure, 497
    startup form, setting, 498
  middle-tier
    Class_Terminate event procedure, 496
    login function, 496

testing, 419
transactions, 350
  ACID properties, 350
  atomicity, 350
  consistency, 350
  durability, 350
  isolation, 350
three-tier applications (case study), 601
  see also three-tier applications
  ASP, using, 609
    component, 610
    database, connecting to, 611
      testing, 612
    database, querying, 613
      GetCategories method, 613
      GetProductInfo method, 613
      GetProductsInCategory method, 613
    page, testing, 614
    presentation page, 615
    query, executing
      options, 610
  business objects, 617
    order, capturing, 617
      Cart class, 617
      Cart class, adding items, 619
      cart.asp page, 620
      CartItem class, 619
    order, processing, 623
      Checkout.asp page, 628
    object building, 623
  database, building, 602
    Categories table, 603
      creating, 603
      data manipulation, 604
      primary key, 603
    diagram, 606
      foreign keys, defining, 608
      realtionships, defining, 607
      wizard, 606
    Manufacturers table, 604
      primary key, 604
    Products table, 605
      primary key, 605
      references, 606
    relationships, specifying, 606
    Suppliers table, 605
      creating, 605
    view, creating, 609
  introduction, 601
  middle-tier component, building, 609, 610
    database, connecting to, 611
      testing, 612
    database, querying, 613
      GetCategories method, 613
      GetProductInfo method, 613
      GetProductsInCategory method, 613

    page, testing, 614
    presentation page, 615
MTS packages
  exporting, 635
order processing, 617, 623
  business object, building, 623
    binary compatability, setting, 625
    component, installing, 626
    MTS library, referencing, 624
    MTS package, creating, 625
    MTSTransactionMode property, 623
    ObjectControl interface, 624
    ProcessOrder method, 624
  Checkout.asp page, 628
    customer, creating, 631
    error reporting, improved, 631
    ObjectContext object, 629
    transaction, managing, 630
  MTS
    database changes, handling, 633
  order, capturing, 617
    Cart class, 617
    Cart class, adding items, 619
    cart.asp page, 620
    CartItem class, 619
SQL Server, 602
  Categories table, 603
    creating, 603
    data manipulation, 604
    primary key, 603
  database diagram, 606
    foreign keys, defining, 608
    relationships, defining, 607
    wizard, 606
  database, creating, 602
  Manufacturers table, 604
    primary key, 604
  Products table, 605
    primary key, 605
    references, 606
  relationships, specifying, 606
  Suppliers table, 605
    creating, 605
  view, creating, 609
storefront, building, 609
  ASP component, creating, 610
  database, connecting to, 611
    testing, 612
  database, querying, 613
    GetCategories method, 613
    GetProductInfo method, 613
    GetProductsInCategory method, 613
  layout, 615
  page, testing, 614
  presentation logic
    options, 609

query, executing
    options, 610
three-tier architecture, 27, 28
  advantages of, 28
  benefits of, 332
  database servers
    functionality, 30
  disadvantages of, 29
  middle tier
    components, 27
    roles, 27
  TP monitor, 29
    choosing, 34
    roles, 30
tooltip
  adding, 295
TP monitor, 29
  choosing, 34
  roles, 30
Transaction Processing monitor (TP monitor)
  see TP monitor
transactions, 350
  ACID properties, 350
    atomicity, 350
    consistency, 350
    durability, 350
    isolation, 350
  committed, 318
  Connection object
    creating, 319
      Microsoft ActiveX Data Objects 2.0 Library,
        referencing, 319
  databases, 467
  defined, 305, 317
  importance of, 317
  methods, 319
    BeginTrans, 320, 322
    CommitTrans, 320, 322
    RollBackTrans, 320, 322
  rolled back, 318
  SQL Server, 467
  uses, 317
    records, stepping through, 322
      BeginTrans method, 322
      CommitTrans method, 322
      MoveFirst method, 322
      RollBackTrans method, 322
triggers, 270
  advantages of, 271
  constraints, 271

creating, 273
  fields, populating, 274
  specifications, 274
  table, creating, 273
  variables, declaring, 274
existing, 272
  creation, 272
  validation rules, 273
  values, retrieving, 272
  viewing, 272
implementing, 275
  rollback of changes, 275
  testing, 275
mode of operation, 271
uses, 271
  business rules, enforcing, 271
  data integrity, maintaining, 271
  transactions, logging, 271
two-phase commit
  MS DTC, 469
two-tier applications
  see also client-server applications
  see also client-server applications, deploying
  ADO, referencing, 285
  architecture, 26
    compared to N-tier, 34
  building, 279
  child forms
    creating, 293
    modifying, 295
  Customers form
    counter
      implementing, 288
    modifying, 287
    navigation bar
      adding, 289
  deploying, 302, 509
  Details form
    creating, 293
    modifying, 295
  forms
    focus, giving, 287
    loading, 287
    removing, 286
  interface, building, 281
    VB Application Wizard, 281
      Data Access Forms, creating, 282, 283
  MDI forms
    defined, 280
  Orders form code
    DataGrid layout
      modifying, 298

modifying, 291, 294
  fields layout, 292
  fields, removing, 292
  fields, searching, 299
overview, 279
security models, 478, 490
  application, closing, 493
  connection string, building, 492
  data form, 491
  forms, coding, 492
  login form, 492
    login, aborting, 492
    selecting, 492
  recordset, populating, 493
    error handling, 493
  roles
    defined, 478
  startup form, setting, 494
  testing, 494
  users
    defined, 478
shell, building, 281

U

UDA, 61
  ADO, 66
    Command object, 67
    Connection object, 67
    Error object, 67
    Fields object, 67
    Parameters object, 67
    Recordset object, 67
    relation to OLE DB, 66, 67
  benefits of, 62
  defined, 61
  DNA
    defined, 62
  importance of, 61
  OLE DB, 63
    advantages of, 63
    COM, 63, 64
    consumers, 65
      defined, 65
      interfaces required, 66
    defined, 63, 64
    providers, 64
      Command, 65
      DataSource, 65
      Enumerator, 64
      Error, 65
      minimum requirements, 65
      objects exposed, 64
      Rowset, 65
      Session, 65

Transaction, 65
  relation to ADO, 66, 67
two-tier structure
  architecture, 62
  importance of, 61
Universal Data Access (UDA)
  see UDA
Unix
  XA standard, 470
UPDATE statement, 171
  SET keyword, 171
user interface, building, 102
  control array, creating, 102
    advantages of, 103
    alternatives, 103
  text boxes
    data field, specifying, 105
    DataFormat property, 105
    MultiLine property, 104
    TabIndex property, setting, 106

V

validation constraints
  see Check constraints
VB Application Wizard, 281
  Data Access Forms, creating, 282
    Master/Detail form, 283
views
  SQL
    calling, 256
    complex SQL statements, hiding, 255
    creating, 254
      benefits of, 256
      considerations, 256
      errors, 254
      INSERT statement, 256
      ORDER BY clause, applying, 255
      seeing, 254
      SELECT statement, 254
      UPDATE statement, 256
      uses, 256
      WITH CHECK OPTION parameter, 256
  SQL Server, 251
    benefits of, 251
      information, modifying, 252
      relevant information, extracting, 251
      security, 251
    defined, 251
    Enterprise Manager, 252
      AS keyword, 253
      view properties, 252
      views, creating, 253

VisData
data, adding, 94
Database Window pane, 88, 93
properties, modifying, 93
databases
building, 86
first record, entering, 93
SQL statement, using, 93
functionality, 86
ODBC DSN, connecting to, 80
Data Form Designer, 81
fields, adding, 82
opening, 81
opening, 86
quirks, 93
SQL Statement pane, 88
table, creating, 88, 92
fields, adding, 89
AllowZeroLength, 89
DefaultValue, 89
FixedField/VariableField, 89
increment automatically, 89
options, 89
OrdinalPosition, 89
Size, 89
ValidationRule, 89
ValidationText, 89
indexes, adding, 91

properties, modifying, 93
properties, viewing, 92
Table Structure dialog, 89, 91, 92
Visual Data Manager
see VisData

W

Wizards
Application VB, 281
Component, 626
Create Database Diagram, 606
Cube, 549
Data Form Designer, 81
Package, 626
Package and Deployment, 518
setup, 525
Storage Design, 559
Upsizing, 131

X

XA standard, 470

Suppliers

- SupplierID
- CompanyName
- ContactName
- ContactTitle
- Address
- City
- Region
- PostalCode
- Country
- Phone
- Fax
- HomePage

Products

- ProductID
- ProductName
- SupplierID
- CategoryID
- QuantityPerUnit
- UnitPrice
- UnitsInStock
- UnitsOnOrder
- ReorderLevel
- Discontinued

Categories

- CategoryID
- CategoryName
- Description
- Picture

6

Wrox writes books for you. Any suggestions, or ideas about how you want information given in your ideal book will be studied by our team. Your comments are always valued at Wrox.

Free phone in USA 800-USE-WROX
Fax (312) 397 8990

UK Tel. (0121) 687 4100   Fax (0121) 687 4101

Professional Visual Basic 6 Databases - Registration Card

Name _____

Address _____

_____

_____

City _____ State/Region _____

Country _____ Postcode/Zip _____

E-mail _____

Occupation _____

How did you hear about this book? _____

☐ Book review (name) _____

☐ Advertisement (name) _____

☐ Recommendation _____

☐ Catalog _____

☐ Other _____

Where did you buy this book? _____

☐ Bookstore (name) _____ City _____

☐ Computer Store (name) _____

☐ Mail Order _____

☐ Other _____

What influenced you in the purchase of this book?

☐ Cover Design
☐ Contents
☐ Other (please specify) _____

How did you rate the overall contents of this book?

☐ Excellent   ☐ Good
☐ Average   ☐ Poor

What did you find most useful about this book? _____

What did you find least useful about this book? _____

Please add any additional comments. _____

What other subjects will you buy a computer book on soon? _____

What is the best computer book you have used this year? _____

Note: This information will only be used to keep you updated about new Wrox Press titles and will not be used for any other purpose or passed to any other third party.

Check here if you DO NOT want to receive support for this book ☐

wrox
PROGRAMMER TO PROGRAMMER™

NB. If you post the bounce back card below in the UK, please send it to:

Wrox Press Ltd., Arden House, 1102 Warwick Road,
Acocks Green, Birmingham B27 6BH. UK.

——— *Computer Book Publishers* ———